MULTICULTURAL EDUCATION 97/98
Fourth Edition

Editor

Fred Schultz
University of Akron

Fred Schultz, professor of education at the University of Akron, attended Indiana University to earn a B.S. in social science education in 1962, an M.S. in the history and philosophy of education in 1966, and a Ph.D. in the history and philosophy of education and American studies in 1969. His B.A. in Spanish was conferred from the University of Akron in May 1985. He is actively involved in researching the development and history of American education with a primary focus on the history of ideas and social philosophy of education. He also likes to study languages.

A Library of Information from the Public Press
Dushkin/McGraw·Hill
Sluice Dock, Guilford, Connecticut 06437

Visit us on the Internet—http://www.dushkin.com

The Annual Editions Series

ANNUAL EDITIONS is a series of over 65 volumes designed to provide the reader with convenient, low-cost access to a wide range of current, carefully selected articles from some of the most important magazines, newspapers, and journals published today. ANNUAL EDITIONS are updated on an annual basis through a continuous monitoring of over 300 periodical sources. All ANNUAL EDITIONS have a number of features that are designed to make them particularly useful, including topic guides, annotated tables of contents, unit overviews, and indexes. For the teacher using ANNUAL EDITIONS in the classroom, an Instructor's Resource Guide with test questions is available for each volume.

VOLUMES AVAILABLE

Abnormal Psychology
Adolescent Psychology
Africa
Aging
American Foreign Policy
American Government
American History, Pre-Civil War
American History, Post-Civil War
American Public Policy
Anthropology
Archaeology
Biopsychology
Business Ethics
Child Growth and Development
China
Comparative Politics
Computers in Education
Computers in Society
Criminal Justice
Criminology
Developing World
Deviant Behavior
Drugs, Society, and Behavior
Dying, Death, and Bereavement

Early Childhood Education
Economics
Educating Exceptional Children
Education
Educational Psychology
Environment
Geography
Global Issues
Health
Human Development
Human Resources
Human Sexuality
India and South Asia
International Business
Japan and the Pacific Rim
Latin America
Life Management
Macroeconomics
Management
Marketing
Marriage and Family
Mass Media
Microeconomics

Middle East and the
   Islamic World
Multicultural Education
Nutrition
Personal Growth and Behavior
Physical Anthropology
Psychology
Public Administration
Race and Ethnic Relations
Russia, the Eurasian Republics,
   and Central/Eastern Europe
Social Problems
Social Psychology
Sociology
State and Local Government
Urban Society
Western Civilization,
   Pre-Reformation
Western Civilization,
   Post-Reformation
Western Europe
World History, Pre-Modern
World History, Modern
World Politics

Cataloging in Publication Data
Main entry under title: Annual editions: Multicultural Education. 1997/98.
    1. Intercultural education—Periodicals. I. Schultz, Fred, *comp.* II. Title: Multicultural education.
ISBN 0–697–37326–6   370.19'341'05

© 1997 by Dushkin/McGraw-Hill, Guilford, CT 06437, A Division of The McGraw-Hill Companies.

Copyright law prohibits the reproduction, storage, or transmission in any form by any means of any portion of this publication without the express written permission of Dushkin/McGraw-Hill, and of the copyright holder (if different) of the part of the publication to be reproduced. The Guidelines for Classroom Copying endorsed by Congress explicitly state that unauthorized copying may not be used to create, to replace, or to substitute for anthologies, compilations, or collective works.

Annual Editions® is a Registered Trademark of Dushkin/McGraw-Hill,
A Division of The McGraw-Hill Companies.

Fourth Edition

Cover image © 1996 PhotoDisc, Inc.

Printed in the United States of America   Printed on Recycled Paper

Editors/Advisory Board

Members of the Advisory Board are instrumental in the final selection of articles for each edition of ANNUAL EDITIONS. Their review of articles for content, level, currentness, and appropriateness provides critical direction to the editor and staff. We think that you will find their careful consideration well reflected in this volume.

EDITOR

Fred Schultz
University of Akron

ADVISORY BOARD

Martha Allexsaht-Snider
University of Georgia

Julie Bao
Shippensburg University

Ruth Benns-Suter
Millersville University

Timothy J. Bergen
University of South Carolina, Columbia

Anna Lou Blevins
University of Pittsburgh

Janice White Clemmer
Brigham Young University

Michael L. Fischler
Plymouth State College

Mary Ann Flowers
Cleveland State University

Mary G. Harris
Bloomsburg University

Inez A. Heath
Valdosta State University

Gwendolyn W. Henderson
University of North Carolina, Asheville

Jacqueline J. Irvine
Emory University

E. Joseph Kaplan
Florida International University

Edith W. King
University of Denver

Rebecca Oxford
University of Alabama

Patricia T. Rooke
University of Alberta

Quirico S. Samonte Jr.
Eastern Michigan University

David Strom
San Diego State University

Mary R. Sudzina
University of Dayton

Joan Thrower Timm
University of Wisconsin, Oshkosh

Staff

Ian A. Nielsen, Publisher

EDITORIAL STAFF

Roberta Monaco, Developmental Editor
Addie Raucci, Administrative Editor
Cheryl Greenleaf, Permissions Editor
Deanna Herrschaft, Permissions Assistant
Diane Barker, Proofreader
Lisa Holmes-Doebrick, Program Coordinator
Joseph Offredi, Photo Coordinator

PRODUCTION STAFF

Brenda S. Filley, Production Manager
Charles Vitelli, Designer
Shawn Callahan, Graphics
Lara M. Johnson, Graphics
Laura Levine, Graphics
Mike Campbell, Graphics
Juliana Arbo, Typesetting Supervisor
Jane Jaegersen, Typesetter
Marie Lazauskas, Word Processor
Kathleen D'Amico, Word Processor
Larry Killian, Copier Coordinator

To the Reader

In publishing ANNUAL EDITIONS we recognize the enormous role played by the magazines, newspapers, and journals of the *public press* in providing current, first-rate educational information in a broad spectrum of interest areas. Many of these articles are appropriate for students, researchers, and professionals seeking accurate, current material to help bridge the gap between principles and theories and the real world. These articles, however, become more useful for study when those of lasting value are carefully *collected, organized, indexed,* and *reproduced* in a *low-cost format*, which provides easy and permanent access when the material is needed. That is the role played by ANNUAL EDITIONS. Under the direction of each volume's *academic editor*, who is an expert in the subject area, and with the guidance of an *Advisory Board*, each year we seek to provide in each ANNUAL EDITION a current, well-balanced, carefully selected collection of the best of the public press for your study and enjoyment. We think that you will find this volume useful, and we hope that you will take a moment to let us know what you think.

There probably has not been a time of greater need for serious consideration of intercultural relations and multicultural realities in the field of education. We share much in common as human beings and as the heirs of great civilizations, yet we must also cherish and value those cultural values and heritages that make us unique and diverse. An education for transformative intellectual and social development should focus on those concepts that emancipate us from cultural stereotypes. No voices should be excluded from the dialogue regarding how to achieve such educational goals; all should be included. How we help our students to best develop their voices and to be heard is a major question for concerned teachers.

The concept of multicultural education evolved and took shape in the United States out of the social travail that wrenched the nation in the late 1960s, through the 1970s and 1980s, and into the present decade. Accordingly, there has been enthusiastic support for the idea of a volume in this series exclusively devoted to multicultural education. Having been teaching and studying multicultural education for 28 years, it is a pleasure for me to serve as editor of *Annual Editions: Multicultural Education 97/98*.

The critical literature on gender, race, and culture in educational studies increases our knowledge regarding the multicultural mosaic that so richly adorns North American cultures. When the first courses in multicultural education were developed in the 1960s, the United States was in the midst of urban and other social crises, and there were no textbooks available. Educators who taught this subject had to draw heavily from academic literature in anthropology, sociology, social psychology, social history, sociolinguistics, and psychiatry. Today, there are textbooks available in the field, but there is also a need for a regular, annually published volume that offers samples from the recent journal literature in which the knowledge bases for multicultural education are developed. This volume is intended to address that need.

The National Council for the Accreditation of Teacher Education (NCATE) in the United States has national accreditation standards requiring that accredited teacher education programs offer course content in multicultural education. A global conception of the subject is usually recommended, in which prospective teachers are encouraged to develop empathetic cultural sensitivity to the demographic changes and cultural diversity that continue to develop in the public schools as a result of dramatic demographic shifts in the population.

In this volume we first explore the national and global social contexts for the development of multicultural education. Its role in teacher education is then briefly defined in the essays in unit 2. In unit 3 the nature of multicultural education as an academic discipline is discussed, and several issues related to this topic are explored. The readings in unit 4 look at multicultural education from the perspective of how people develop their own unique identities in the context of their interactions with their own as well as others' cultural heritages and personal life experiences. The readings in unit 5 focus on curriculum and instruction in multicultural perspective. Unit 6 addresses topics relevant to development of multicultural insight, and the essays in unit 7 explore the need for a conscious quest for emancipatory educational futures for people of all cultural heritages.

This year I would like to acknowledge the very helpful contributions of the members of the advisory board for this volume in finding useful sources. I would also like to acknowledge Dr. Stephen H. Aby, research librarian at the University of Akron, whose assistance is greatly valued.

This volume will be useful in courses in multicultural education at the undergraduate and graduate levels. It will add considerable substance to the sociocultural foundations of education, educational policy studies, and leadership, as well as to course work in other areas of preservice and inservice teacher education programs. We hope you enjoy this volume, and we would like you to help us improve future editions. Please complete and return the form at the back of the book. We look forward to hearing from you.

Fred Schultz
Editor

Contents

UNIT 1

The Social Contexts of Multicultural Education

Eight articles discuss the importance of a multicultural curriculum in sensitizing students to an integrated world society.

To the Reader	iv
Topic Guide	2
Overview	4

1. **A New Vision for City Schools,** Diane Ravitch and Joseph Viteritti, *Public Interest,* Winter 1996. — 6
   Diane Ravitch and Joseph Viteritti offer a bold new proposal for rethinking our vision of *urban schools.* They critically review the *history of urban schools* in the United States and the steady expansion of urban public school systems' bureaucracies. They review alternative approaches to urban schooling and state an *agenda for change.*

2. **Ethnicity and Adolescent Achievement,** Laurence Steinberg with B. Bradford Brown, and Sanford M. Dornbusch, *American Educator,* Summer 1996. — 12
   The authors report on the effects of *ethnic identity* on *adolescent development,* based on their research concerning the academic achievement of an ethnically heterogeneous population. The study dispelled, they point out, certain widely held beliefs about student *academic achievement.*

3. **A Developmental Strategy to Prevent Lifelong Damage,** David A. Hamburg, *Carnegie Corporation of New York,* December 1995. — 24
   David Hamburg reviews efforts of the Carnegie Corporation in recent years to learn about *child and adolescent development.* He reports on research findings as to the best ways to adopt *preventive strategies* to ensure *healthy child and adolescent development.*

4. **The End of Integration,** James S. Kunen, *Time,* April 29, 1996. — 32
   James Kunen argues that the United States is becoming more and more racially separated and that efforts to achieve *racial integration in American schools* have not been successful. In the course of his argument, Kunen reviews the *history of efforts to desegregate American schools.*

5. **Putting Tongues in Check,** Margot Hornblower, *Time,* October 9, 1995. — 38
   Margot Hornblower reviews the criticisms of bilingual education programs in the public schools and describes studies that point to the importance and value of *bilingual education.* Hornblower reports on public views as well as recent research on this topic.

6. **One Nation, One Language?** *U.S. News & World Report,* September 25, 1995. — 41
   Several journalists cover the current debate over whether or not *English* ought to be declared the *official language* of the United States. The debate centers around the question of whether this would unite or divide the nation. Of the students in American schools in the fall of 1995, more than a third speak a "first" language other than English.

The concepts in bold italics are developed in the article. For further expansion please refer to the Topic Guide and the Index.

UNIT 2

Teacher Education in Multicultural Perspective

Six selections examine some of the major issues being debated on how to effectively integrate the multicultural dynamic into teacher education programs.

7. **Tongue-Tied in the Schools,** U.S. News & World Report, September 25, 1995. — 44
   Susan Headden describes the debate occurring over *bilingual education* across the United States. The author discusses some of the reasons behind the debate over whether or not bilingual educational programming is appropriate for all "limited English proficient" (LEP) students.

8. **Go North, Young Man,** Richard Rodriguez, Mother Jones, July/August 1995. — 46
   Richard Rodriguez discusses the new trends in *immigration into the United States* from south *(Latin America)* to north. He notes that the old movement from east to west has given way to the new mass migrations of Latin Americans to the United States.

Overview — 50

9. **Accommodating Cultural Differences and Commonalities in Educational Practice,** Ronald Gallimore and Claude Goldenberg, Multicultural Education, Fall 1996. — 52
   Ronald Gallimore and Claude Goldenberg deal with the question of how educators can be responsive to different cultures and avoid *cultural stereotypes* that prevent us from seeing *our common human heritage* as persons. In the process of doing this, they engage in a clarifying discussion of the meanings of *culture* and *ethnicity*.

10. **Of Pigs and Wolves at the OK Corral: Or the Emerging Alternative Paradigm and the Construction of Knowledge,** Tonya Huber, Multicultural Education, Summer 1996. — 56
    Tonya Huber raises some very important issues regarding cultural stereotyping and perceiving events from differing *cultural perspectives*. She discusses how to explore different *cultural paradigms* for seeing the world through literature and other means of communication. She relates these themes well to *teacher education* programs and the knowledge construction process in courses in *multicultural education*.

11. **Recognizing Diversity within a Common Historical Narrative,** John Wills and Hugh Mehan, Multicultural Education, Fall 1996. — 60
    John Wills and Hugh Mehan explore issues in social studies education concerning the formation of course content for *preservice teachers*. They discuss the *social construction of knowledge* from individual as well as cultural perspectives and how school knowledge emerges in the interactions among teachers, students, and texts.

12. **South Carolina Unrevised: Portrayals of Race in Current South Carolina History Textbooks,** Alan Wieder, Multicultural Education, Spring 1996. — 68
    Alan Wieder discusses issues relevant to *teacher education* in his analysis of the content of *textbooks* on the history of the state of South Carolina. In this case study of how texts can influence students' knowledge of the past, Wieder gives examples of how *cultural bias and prejudice* can be embedded in texts used in schools.

The concepts in bold italics are developed in the article. For further expansion please refer to the Topic Guide and the Index.

UNIT 3

Multicultural Education as an Academic Discipline

Four selections examine the dynamics of integrating multicultural education into the discipline of education.

13. **Correspondence in Cooperating Teachers' and Student Teachers' Interpretations of Classroom Events,** Luz E. Gonzalez and Kathy Carter, *Teaching & Teacher Education,* Volume 12, Number 1, 1996. — 74

    Luz Gonzalez and Kathy Carter examine how student teachers and their cooperating teachers developed their respective perceptions of classroom life. The authors' discussion sheds some light on a most important experience in any *teacher education* program, the *student teaching experience.*

14. **Why Do We Need This Class? Multicultural Education for Teachers,** Valerie Ooka Pang, *Phi Delta Kappan,* December 1994. — 80

    The author discusses her beliefs about how multicultural education ought to be conducted in *teacher education programs.* She cites Paulo Freire's ideas and relates her own views about the practice of teacher education to *critical theoretical perspectives.*

Overview — 84

15. **Multiculturalism and Multicultural Education in an International Perspective,** Lotty Eldering, *Anthropology & Education Quarterly,* September 1996. — 86

    Lotty Eldering compares differing approaches to *multiculturalism* and *multicultural education* in use in Europe, North America, and Australia. Using these comparisons as a conceptual framework, the author then turns her attention to the Netherlands, where she teaches, to analyze that nation's *objective reality, ideology, official policy, and practices.*

16. **Multicultural Education and Curriculum Transformation,** James A. Banks, *The Journal of Negro Education,* Fall 1995. — 93

    Focusing on the *knowledge construction process,* professor James Banks describes five dimensions of multicultural education. This process, according to Banks, assists students in becoming effective citizens in a pluralistic, democratic society.

17. **Multicultural Education: A Movement in Search of Meaning and Positive Connections,** Leonard Davidman, *Multicultural Education,* Spring 1995. — 104

    Leonard Davidman identifies key questions that need to be addressed in developing a meaningful and constructive approach to *multicultural curriculum development.* He addresses important values and concepts that should drive the development of multicultural studies, stressing that *ethnic and cultural self-disclosure* is vital to the process.

18. **Bridging Multicultural Theory and Practice,** Geneva Gay, *Multicultural Education,* Fall 1995. — 109

    The author discusses several issues that make it difficult for teachers to bridge the gap between *theory and practice in multicultural education,* such as how suggested activities can be integrated with traditional academic subjects. Geneva Gay advocates continuing research and evaluation and an inclusive approach to this crucial educational task.

UNIT 4

Identity and Personal Development: A Multicultural Focus

Six articles consider the interconnections between gender, social class, racial or ethnic heritage, and primary cultural values.

Overview   114

19. **Families and Schools: Building Multicultural Values Together,** Kevin J. Swick, Gloria Boutte, and Irma Van Scoy, *Childhood Education,* Winter 1995/96.   116

    The authors of this essay discuss the importance of developing *proactive multicultural learning frameworks* in schools among teachers, parents, and students as a means of contributing to *positive personal identity development* among students.

20. **Self-Identification, Pan-Ethnicity, and the Boundaries of Group Identity,** Dag McLeod, *Multicultural Education,* Winter 1995.   121

    Dag McLeod surveys how people define themselves and the boundaries between personal and ethnic group identity formation. He discusses the *multiple levels* of considerations in personal identity development and certain *equity issues* related to this process.

21. **Counseling for Dropout Prevention: Applications from Multicultural Counseling,** Jerry Trusty, *Journal of Multicultural Counseling and Development,* April 1996.   125

    Jerry Trusty argues for the development of a model of individual counseling with high school students that will help to reduce the dropout rate among those *at risk*. Drawing on the literature in *multicultural counseling,* he argues that students can be counseled in ways that lead to *positive personal identities*.

22. **Problems Caused for Mental Health Professionals Worldwide by Increasing Multicultural Populations and Proposed Solutions,** Thomas L. Chiu, *Journal of Multicultural Counseling and Development,* April 1996.   132

    Thomas Chiu argues for a greater *awareness of cross-cultural factors* among psychiatric patients. The author, a New York psychiatrist, explains that mental health professionals may have difficulty diagnosing and treating clients with unfamiliar cultural backgrounds and recommends continuing *education and field experience* to overcome the difficulty.

23. **The Inside Story,** David Aronson, *Teaching Tolerance,* Spring 1995.   138

    David Aronson points out that people can be *taught tolerance* and helped to unlearn or to avoid acceptance of *prejudice,* something the psychiatric community has known since the 1940s. Aronson argues that counseling children to be *tolerant, accepting persons* in their early years is extremely important.

24. **Respect, Cultural Sensitivity, and Communication,** Jinhee K. Hyun and Susan A. Fowler, *Teaching Exceptional Children,* Fall 1995.   144

    The authors present insightful suggestions for ways to help the *parents and children of different cultures* to feel welcome and supported at school. They discuss *culturally acceptable family outcomes* and several other useful concepts.

The concepts in bold italics are developed in the article. For further expansion please refer to the Topic Guide and the Index.

UNIT 5

Curriculum and Instruction in Multicultural Perspective

Five articles review how curriculum and instruction must be formulated to sensitize young people to the multicultural reality of a national civilization.

Overview 148

25. **Proposal: An Anti-Bias and Ecological Model for Multicultural Education,** Francis Wardle, *Childhood Education,* Spring 1996. 150

    Francis Wardle proposes a new model for enhancing the *personal identity development* of all students that affirms the uniqueness of *cultural heritages.* The author critiques the assumptions underlying traditional concepts of multicultural education in the United States in an essay that is relevant to the education of *biracial or bicultural students.*

26. **Beyond Socialization and Multiculturalism: Rethinking the Task of Citizenship Education in a Pluralistic Society,** Bruce Grelle and Devon Metzger, *Social Education,* March 1996. 155

    Bruce Grelle and Devon Metzger present a reconceptualization of *citizenship education* that incorporates scholarship in the field of *multicultural education.* They critique traditional approaches to citizenship and socialization in American schools and recommend new models of *social studies education.*

27. **Multiculturalism: Practical Considerations for Curricular Change,** Tony R. Sanchez, *The Clearing House,* January/February 1996. 161

    Tony Sanchez provides a useful, practice-oriented discussion of how to *implement multicultural content* in the teaching-learning process in schools. He offers guidelines for *curriculum development* and proposes recommended goals and objectives for learning.

28. **Who Needs Multicultural Education? White Students, U.S. History, and the Construction of a Usable Past,** John S. Wills, *Anthropology & Education Quarterly,* September 1996. 164

    John Wills discusses issues involved in developing *multicultural school curricula* in U.S. history courses, focusing on students' failure to make desired connections between historical slavery and current racism. His in-depth analysis of classroom activities in a San Diego school illuminates the difficulty of drawing relevant and appropriate *parallels between America's past and its present.*

29. **Teaching: The Challenge of Change; Reclaiming Democracy through Schooling,** Sudia Paloma McCaleb, *Multicultural Education,* Spring 1995. 175

    The author describes her efforts to use *critical theoretical perspectives* designed to create democratic school and classroom environments that liberate and *empower students and teachers* to take control of their own visions for their lives. She tells about this new emphasis in the *teacher education* program at New College in San Francisco.

The concepts in bold italics are developed in the article. For further expansion please refer to the Topic Guide and the Index.

UNIT 6

Special Topics in Multicultural Education

Six articles explore some of the ways students succeed or fail in culturally pluralistic school settings.

Overview   182

30. **Resurgence of Ethnic Nationalism in California and Germany: The Impact on Recent Progress in Education,** José Macias, *Anthropology & Education Quarterly,* June 1996.   184
    José Macias presents a telling explanation of the origins and development of anti-Chicano bias on the part of Anglo nationalists in the nineteenth and twentieth centuries. He also discusses the resurgence of *anti-immigrant bias* in both the United States and Germany in the 1990s, and he skillfully explains the development of Anglo support for *Proposition 187* in California in 1994.

31. **Telling Stories: On Ethnicity, Exclusion, and Education in Upstate New York,** Ellen Bigler, *Anthropology & Education Quarterly,* June 1996.   193
    Ellen Bigler analyzes stories related by participants in a heated community debate over multicultural and bilingual education. Their discussion revealed sharp disparities between *Anglo and Latino views* of *equality of opportunity in America.* The author follows five themes that characterized Euro-Americans' continuing arguments over the issue and presents the opposing views of minority-group members.

32. **Teaching Homeless Children: Exemplary Field Experience for Teacher Education Candidates,** John P. Gustafson and Stacy M. Cichy, *The Educational Forum,* Fall 1996.   201
    Stacy Cichy movingly recounts her preservice internship teaching homeless children in Chicago—their learning difficulties, general fear of white people, chaotic lives, and cycle of welfare dependency. Professor John Gustafson contributes an overview and commentary on the *value* of such *internships in teacher education.*

33. **The Road to Auschwitz: What's So Funny about Schindler's List?** Bernard Beck, *Multicultural Education,* Spring 1995.   206
    Bernard Beck offers a reflective analysis of the Jewish experience in the post-Holocaust years and the use of *mass media,* in this case the popular film *Schindler's List,* in portraying Jewish culture. Beck offers an insightful, sensitive, and much-needed appraisal of Jewish concerns regarding how they are portrayed in films and other mass media.

34. **New Colors,** Melissa Steel, *Teaching Tolerance,* Spring 1995.   210
    Melissa Steel reports on the increase of *interracial marriages* in the United States as well as the continuing challenges and social resistance that children of these interracial marriages still confront, especially in their early school years. Steel urges teachers to avoid racial stereotyping and offers an encouraging outlook for biracial young people who come to terms with their unique heritages.

35. **Another School's Reality,** Jeffrey Raison, Lee Anna Hanson, Cheryl Hall, and Maynard C. Reynolds, *Phi Delta Kappan,* February 1995.   214
    The authors focus on a positive outcome of mainstreaming under very challenging conditions at one Minneapolis magnet school. They help to clarify the educational issues relating to the inclusion of *the physically and mentally handicapped in the multicultural educational effort.*

The concepts in bold italics are developed in the article. For further expansion please refer to the Topic Guide and the Index.

UNIT 7

For Vision and Voice: A Call to Conscience

Five selections address the concerns that must be kept in mind for the future improvement of our educational system.

Overview   216

36. **Multicultural Education and Technology: Promise and Pitfalls,** Jim Cummins and Dennis Sayers, *Multicultural Education,* Spring 1996.   218

    Jim Cummins and Dennis Sayers discuss the promises and potential limitations of *technology in teaching with a multicultural focus.* The authors discuss how computer technology can be used to promote *critical literacy* and multicultural awareness through *global learning networks.*

37. **Invisibility: The Language Bias of Political Control and Power,** Marta I. Cruz-Janzen, *National Coalition for Sex Equity in Education (NCSEE),* Winter 1996.   225

    Marta Cruz-Janzen discusses the *importance of voice* and the fact that many women and persons of color still feel excluded from the mainstream of social life. They experience social *invisibility* and a sense that their voices go unheard as a result, the author asserts, of the ways in which official language is used to maintain existing power structures.

38. **Home Was a Horse Stall,** Jim Carnes, *Teaching Tolerance,* Spring 1995.   229

    The author describes the ordeal of a *Japanese American* family in California from the time of their arrival in America in 1905 through their experiences in World War II-era *internment camps.* The *racial bias* he and his friends and family encountered from the beginning grew ever harsher, culminating in imprisonment and loss of their homes.

39. **Turning the Tide: A Call for Radical Voices of Affirmation,** Bakari Chavanu, *Multicultural Education,* Fall 1995.   233

    Bakari Chavanu gives eloquent voice to his experience as an African American who was *bused into a predominantly white secondary school* in the 1970s. He speaks of the *"cultural silence"* that exists in most American classrooms today, calling for teachers to help students confront racism, poverty, and sexism.

40. **Knocking on Heaven's Door,** Jonathan Kozol, *Teacher,* October 1995.   235

    Jonathan Kozol interviews *children and youth of the South Bronx* in New York City and eloquently records *their voices* as they express their feelings regarding the conditions of their lives. This article is from Kozol's *Amazing Grace: The Lives of Children and the Conscience of a Nation,* published in October 1995 by Crown Publishers.

Index   241
Article Review Form   244
Article Rating Form   245

The concepts in bold italics are developed in the article. For further expansion please refer to the Topic Guide and the Index.

Topic Guide

This topic guide suggests how the selections in this book relate to topics of traditional concern to students and professional educators involved with the study of education. It is useful for locating articles that relate to each other for reading and research. The guide is arranged alphabetically according to topic. Articles may, of course, treat topics that do not appear in the topic guide. In turn, entries in the topic guide do not necessarily constitute a comprehensive listing of all the contents of each selection.

TOPIC AREA	TREATED IN	TOPIC AREA	TREATED IN
Anthropology and Education	15. Multiculturalism and Multicultural Education in an International Perspective 28. Who Needs Multicultural Education? 30. Resurgence of Ethnic Nationalism in California and Germany 31. Telling Stories	Democracy and Education Ecological Model English Language	29. Teaching: The Challenge of Change 25. Proposal: An Anti-Bias and Ecological Model 5. Putting Tongues in Check 6. One Nation, One Language? 7. Tongue-Tied in the Schools
Anti-Semitism	33. Road to Auschwitz: What's So Funny about *Schindler's List*?	Ethnicity	2. Ethnicity and Adolescent Achievement 20. Self-Identification, Pan-Ethnicity and the Boundaries of Group Identity 30. Resurgence of Ethnic Nationalism in California and Germany 31. Telling Stories
Asian Americans	38. Home Was a Horse Stall		
Bilingual Education	5. Putting Tongues in Check 6. One Nation, One Language? 7. Tongue-Tied in the Schools		
Biracial/Bicultural Students	34. New Colors 37. Invisibility	Families and Schools	19. Families and Schools 20. Self-Identification, Pan-Ethnicity, and the Boundaries of Group Identity
Child and Adolescent Development	2. Ethnicity and Adolescent Achievement 3. Developmental Strategy to Prevent Lifelong Damage 21. Counseling for Dropout Prevention	Identity	19. Families and Schools 20. Self-Identification, Pan-Ethnicity, and the Boundaries of Group Identity 21. Counseling for Dropout Prevention 22. Problems Caused for Mental Health Professionals Worldwide by Increasing Multicultural Populations and Proposed Solutions 23. Inside Story 24. Respect, Cultural Sensitivity, and Communication 37. Invisibility
Counseling	21. Counseling for Dropout Prevention 22. Problems Caused for Mental Health Professionals		
Cultural Diversity	9. Accommodating Cultural Differences and Commonalities 10. Of Pigs and Wolves at the OK Corral 11. Recognizing Diversity within a Common Historical Narrative 12. South Carolina Unrevised 15. Multiculturalism and Multicultural Education in an International Perspective 16. Multicultural Education and Curriculum Transformation 24. Respect, Cultural Sensitivity, and Communication	Immigration International Perspectives	8. Go North, Young Man 30. Resurgence of Ethnic Nationalism in California and Germany 15. Multiculturalism and Multicultural Education in an International Perspective 30. Resurgence of Ethnic Nationalism in California and Germany
Cultural Stereotypes	9. Accommodating Cultural Differences and Commonalities in Educational Practice 28. Who Needs Multicultural Education? 30. Resurgence of Ethnic Nationalism in California and Germany 31. Telling Stories	Multicultural Education as an Academic Discipline	15. Multiculturalism and Multicultural Education in an International Perspective 16. Multicultural Education and Curriculum Transformation 17. Multicultural Education 18. Bridging Multicultural Theory and Practice
Curriculum and Instruction	16. Multicultural Education and Curriculum Transformation 25. Proposal: An Anti-Bias and Ecological Model 26. Beyond Socialization and Multiculturalism 27. Multiculturalism 28. Who Needs Multicultural Education? 29. Teaching: The Challenge of Change	Novice Teachers	13. Correspondence in Cooperating Teachers' and Student Teachers' Interpretations of Classroom Events

TOPIC AREA	TREATED IN	TOPIC AREA	TREATED IN
Parents	24. Respect, Cultural Sensitivity, and Communication	Special Topics	30. Resurgence of Ethnic Nationalism in California and Germany 31. Telling Stories 32. Teaching Homeless Children 33. Road to Auschwitz: What's So Funny about *Schindler's List*? 34. New Colors 35. Another School's Reality
Proposition 187 (California)	30. Resurgence of Ethnic Nationalism in California and Germany		
Race	34. New Colors 37. Invisibility		
Racial Integration of Schools	4. End of Integration	Teacher Education	9. Accommodating Cultural Differences and Commonalities in Educational Practice 10. Of Pigs and Wolves at the OK Corral 11. Recognizing Diversity within a Common Historical Narrative 12. South Carolina Unrevised 13. Correspondence in Cooperating Teachers' and Student Teachers' Interpretations of Classroom Events 14. Why Do We Need This Class? Multicultural Education for Teachers
Rewriting History	11. Recognizing Diversity within a Common Historical Narrative 12. South Carolina Unrevised		
Self-Identification	20. Self-Identification, Pan-Ethnicity, and the Boundaries of Group Identity 37. Invisibility		
Social Context of Multicultural Education	1. New Vision for City Schools 2. Ethnicity and Adolescent Achievement 3. Developmental Strategy to Prevent Lifelong Damage 4. End of Integration 5. Putting Tongues in Check 19. Families and Schools 25. Proposal: An Anti-Bias and Ecological Model 26. Beyond Socialization and Multiculturalism 30. Resurgence of Ethnic Nationalism in California and Germany 31. Telling Stories 32. Teaching Homeless Children 37. Invisibility 40. Knocking on Heaven's Door	Technology and Multicultural Education	36. Multicultural Education and Technology
		Tolerance	23. Inside Story 24. Respect, Cultural Sensitivity, and Communication 25. Proposal: An Anti-Bias and Ecological Model 29. Teaching: The Challenge of Change
		Urban Education	1. New Vision for City Schools 4. End of Integration 21. Counseling for Dropout Prevention 32. Teaching Homeless Children 40. Knocking on Heaven's Door
Social Studies Education	11. Recognizing Diversity within a Common Historical Narrative 12. South Carolina Unrevised 26. Beyond Socialization and Multiculturalism 27. Multiculturalism	Vision and Voice	36. Multicultural Education and Technology 37. Invisibility 38. Home Was a Horse Stall 39. Turning the Tide 40. Knocking on Heaven's Door
Socialization and Multuralism	26. Beyond Socialization and Multiculturalism 28. Who Needs Multicultural Education?		

The Social Contexts of Multicultural Education

We cannot ignore the power of culture in shaping persons' conceptions of social reality and the phenomenology of their visions of their own lives and the lives of others around them. Every person needs to develop their own social vision of life as it relates to actual cultural realities in their society.

The United States is becoming an ever more multicultural nation. Canada is also experiencing major changes in its cultural composition due to its very generous immigration policies. Some demographic projections indicate that within five years a majority of the total American elementary and secondary school student body will be composed of people of color, the children of the rainbow coalition—Native American, African American, Asian American, and Latino American.

Multicultural national communities have special challenges associated with the dynamics of daily life among the diverse cultural groups that comprise them. Such societies also have unique opportunities to develop truly great culturally pluralistic civilizations in which the aesthetic, artistic, literary, and moral standards of each cultural group can contribute to the creation of new standards. They can learn from one another, they can benefit from their respective strengths and achievements, and they can help one another to transcend problems and injustices of the past. There are several other multicultural national social orders worldwide, and they can also learn from and help each other more than they have in the past. We ought, therefore, to see the multicultural national fabric that is our social reality as a source of promise, hope, and pride. However, we are heirs to destructive social conditions yet to be rectified. As we work with children and young adults in our schools, we must ask ourselves certain very important questions. Are they safe? Are they hungry? Are they afraid? Are they angry? Do they have a sense of angst; are they filled with self-doubt and uncertainty as to their prospects in life? For far too many children and adolescents from all socio-economic groups, social classes, and cultural groups, the answers to these questions are "yes." Far greater numbers of children from low-income minority groups answer "yes" to at least some of these questions than do children from higher socioeconomic groups.

As educators and civic leaders, we ought to ask ourselves a few other questions. What are the purposes of schooling? Are schools limited to their acknowledged mission of intellectual development? Or are schools also capable of advancing, as classical Greek and Roman educators did for the children of their citizens, the traits of honor, character, courage, resourcefulness, civic responsibility, and social service? This latter concept of the mission of schooling is still today the brightest hope for the full achievement of our great promise as a multicultural society in an interdependent world community of nations.

What are the problems we face in achieving this end? We need to enable each child to advance intellectually in school as far as may be possible for that child. We need to do this at the same time that we help develop each child's self-respect and pride in his or her own cultural heritage as part of a national community. As educators, we need to do what we can to help each student to develop a sense of honor that will lead them to want to serve, help, and heal the suffering of others in their adult years. We need intellectually curious and competent graduates who are both knowledgeable about their own ethnic heritages and committed to social justice for all, in their own nation as well as in the community of nations.

The problems we face in achieving such intellectual and social ends are significant. Developing multicultural curriculum materials for schools and integrating them into course content and activities of the school day and year can help to sensitize all students to the inherent worth of all persons. All youth deserve the opportunity to learn about their own cultural heritages, and they deserve to understand that heritage from an objective, scientific perspective that cannot be seen through the lenses of Eurocentric perspectives alone.

UNIT 1

There have been dramatic demographic changes in the characteristics of the world's population and in the interdependence of the world's nations in a global economy. We must reconsider how we develop human talent in our schools, for our young people will be our most basic resource for the future. Young adults should be aware that ethnic struggles continue in many locations throughout the world in spite of the great advances that democracy has made in recent years, and young persons need to be able to accept and to value cultural diversity. The social context of multicultural education encompasses vigorous and continuing debate over how best to integrate it into existing curricula and to what extent.

These unit essays are relevant to courses in cultural foundations of education, educational policy studies, multicultural education, social studies education, and curriculum theory and construction.

Looking Ahead: Challenge Questions

What should every student learn about cultural diversity and her or his own cultural heritage?

What facets of the history of the human struggle for civil rights should be taught to students?

What ought students to learn about other nations and other democratic traditions?

How can the mass media more effectively inform the public on issues related to cultural diversity?

What can educators do to help students better understand the social contexts in which they live?

What ought every student to know about cultural diversity and equality of opportunity?

What role does bilingual education play in most American schools? In your view, should that role be expanded?

—F.S.

A new vision for city schools

DIANE RAVITCH & JOSEPH VITERITTI

Diane Ravitch is a senior research scholar at the School of Education of New York University. Joseph Viteritti is a research professor at NYU's Robert F. Wagner Graduate School of Public Service.

YES, there is hope for urban education. A wave of reform is spreading from city to city and state to state. Rather than aiming to alter isolated practices or to fix one piece of a jerry-built system, these changes are meant to transform the basic character of public schooling. When taken together, the ambitious range of initiatives currently under way can be structured into an integrated program for reforming urban education—one that shifts from a bureaucratic system that prizes compliance to a deregulated system that focuses on student performance.

A century ago, progressive reformers reshaped big-city schools according to the era's widely shared vision of efficient administration. To get schools "out of politics," they created tightly controlled bureaucracies. At the apex of authority were "professional experts," who managed a top-down system designed to impose uniform rules on teachers and students alike. The model for this system was the factory, which, at that time in history, was considered the acme of scientific management. The raw materials for these educational factories were the children of immigrants, who were pouring into American cities in unprecedented numbers, in need of instruction in literacy, hygiene, and basic Americanization. The workers in these factories were teachers, whose views about what or how to teach were not solicited. Nor did the experts see any need to consult parents about anything regarding their children, since many of them were barely literate.

These turn-of-the-century efforts to create what historian David Tyack called "the one best system" were remarkably effective for at least the first half of the century. Big-city schools offered unparalleled educational opportunity to millions of children and helped to generate a vast middle class. At mid-century, the nation's urban schools were considered to be a great success. But no more. The system that transformed an earlier generation of impoverished children into prosperous adults has become sclerotic; the bureaucratic organization created to impose efficiency and order has grown tired and inefficient, tangled helplessly in rules and regulations devised by the courts, state governments, federal government, union contracts, and its own minions.

In city after city, reports of corruption, disorder, neglect, and low educational achievement are legion. Urban education is in deep trouble, in part because of inept big-city bureaucracies inherited from the past, but also because the public's expectations for the schools are higher now than they were earlier in the century. Fifty years ago, the public was neither surprised nor alarmed by the large numbers of young people who did not graduate from high school; they believed that the numbers would continually improve over time. Today, the public expects a large majority of students to complete high school, especially since the jobs available for high-school dropouts are diminishing.

Convinced that the structure of public education contributes to its ineffectiveness in educating a larger proportion of students, imaginative leaders in cities and states across the country are implementing systemic changes. The new reforms proceed on the conviction that the century-old bureaucratic structures of urban education cannot succeed in today's society. The century-old system of schools cannot work today because it was designed to function in a very different society, with different social mores and different problems, where supervisors instructed teachers, teachers instructed students, and parents expected their children to mind what they were told.

The factory is no longer a useful model for urban education; teachers and children are not interchangeable parts to be moved around to fit the requirements of administrators. The reforms that are now being enacted in many cities incorporate such principles as diversity, quality, choice, and accountability. Instead of a system that regulates identical schools, reformers seek a system in which academic standards are the same for all but where schools vary widely. In the new reform vision, the schools are as diverse as teachers' imagination and will; students and their families choose the school that best meets their needs and interests; and central authorities perform a monitoring and auditing function to assure educational quality and fiscal integrity. In such a reconfigured system, the role of the local superintendent shifts from regulating behavior to auditing results. The bottom line is not whether everyone has complied with the same rules and procedures but whether children are learning.

Charter schools

Not since the beginning of the twentieth century has there been such a burst of bold experimentation in the organization and governance of schools as there has been in just the last half decade. Among the most notable initiatives on the current scene are charter schools, the contracting of instructional services, and a variety of school-choice programs. These innovations are driven by demands from parents and elected officials for higher levels of educational success. However, few of these innovations are based on hard evidence that they will succeed. But that is the nature of innovation: one purpose of these experiments is to identify what will work and what will not. Most of these initiatives, however, are based on well-documented evidence that the current institutional arrangement does not work very well for large numbers of children.

One of the most promising ideas to appear on the national horizon is charter schools. Charter schools are semi-autonomous, public entities that are freed from most bureaucratic rules and regulations by state and local authorities in return for a commitment to meet explicit performance goals. They are established under a contract between a group that manages a school and a sponsoring authority that oversees it. The contractor might consist of parents, teachers, a labor union, a college, a museum, or other nonprofit or for-profit entities. The sponsor might be a school board, a state education department, a state university campus, or a government agency. In Arizona, the legislature has created a special governing body authorized to grant or deny a request for a charter; thus such power is not limited to the state or local school boards, which may have a stake in restricting the number of these institutions.

Charter schools may be either new schools or existing ones. Their development will contribute to both the number and variety of quality institutions.

1. New Vision for City Schools

In Detroit, the Drug Enforcement Administration is creating a residential school for 200 at-risk students; a school called Metro Deaf serves the hearing impaired in St. Paul. In Wilmington, Delaware, five corporations and a medical center have cooperated in a joint venture to run a new high school for math and science. Boston University runs a school for homeless children in Massachusetts; and the Denver Youth Academy was created for at-risk, middle-school children and their families in Colorado. The possibilities seem endless.

A charter serves as a negotiated, legal agreement that sets standards and expectations for the school. School professionals are authorized to manage their own budget and to choose their own staff, but the degree of autonomy varies from state to state. The Education Commission of the States, in conjunction with the Humphrey Institute at the University of Minnesota, recently completed a survey of 110 charter schools in seven states. It found that educators at these schools are quite willing to be held more accountable for improved student performance, so long as they are permitted to enjoy more autonomy. A majority of these schools focus their attention on at-risk populations.

Presently 19 states have charter-school laws. Minnesota passed the first one as recently as 1991, with eight schools participating; there are now 40 participating. California approved the establishment of 100 charter schools in 1992. Michigan has 30. Among the states that grant the most autonomy to charter schools are Arizona, California, Colorado, Delaware, Massachusetts, Michigan, Minnesota, New Hampshire, and Texas. (The other states with charter laws are Alaska, Arkansas, Georgia, Hawaii, Kansas, Louisiana, New Mexico, Rhode Island, Wisconsin, and Wyoming.)

Charter schools are public schools. They are accountable to a public authority. In fact, the charter, which defines academic expectations and other legal responsibilities, often serves as a more powerful instrument for accountability than anything that exists for most ordinary public schools. If a charter school fails educationally or misuses its funds, the charter can be revoked, as was the case with one Los Angeles school last year. Most charter schools must accept any student who applies, or they select students by lottery if there are more applicants than places. All are bound by the usual state laws and regulations requiring schools to be nondiscriminatory and protective of civil rights.

Contracts for performance

Unlike charter-school laws, which begin as state initiatives, contracting-out arrangements usually originate with a local school board. It is not unusual for school boards to contract with private vendors for the performance of non-instructional functions—e.g., transportation, food, supplies, facilities, and custodial and administrative services. What is novel about recent developments is for school boards to arrange to have instructional programs provided by outsiders. This approach has given rise to new entrepreneurial organizations on the education scene. Educational Alternatives, Inc. (EAI), for example, is under contract to run nine public schools in Baltimore, as well as a single school in Duluth. It will also overhaul six schools in Hartford (eventually all 32) and assume general responsibility for the management of that district. The Edison Project has contracted to operate individual schools in Wichita, Kansas, Mt. Clemens, Michigan, Sherman, Texas, and Boston. Washington, D.C., has recently contracted with Sylvan Learning Systems to offer remedial reading for a limited number of students; and Sabis, an International group, runs a school in Springfield, Massachusetts.

These arrangements are similar to charter schools in that they are brought into being by a performance agreement between a school organization and a public authority. Some contracts allow more autonomy than others. EAI, for instance, ran into great difficulty implementing changes in Baltimore after it agreed to hire all the existing teachers in what were supposed to be reconstituted schools; moreover, the teachers' union was antagonistic to the project from the beginning. And some argue that EAI committed a major strategic error when it took on general responsibility for running the entire Hartford school district. The approach adopted by the Edison Project, involving the development of new schools, one at a time, with a staff that it has hired and trained, seems to hold more promise.

As with most innovations in public education, the more profound changes exacted through contracting tend to generate the strongest opposition. Wilkinsburg, Pennsylvania, a working-class suburb of Pittsburgh, where 78 percent of the children qualify economically for a free-lunch program, is a case in point. It became the scene of an intense political and legal battle when a newly elected, reform-minded school board announced its intention to contract with Alternative Public School Strategies to operate one of its three elementary schools. The local teachers' union and the National Education Association fiercely opposed its reform proposals: an extended school year, new after-school programs, merit pay for teachers.

Some observers have confused the contracting approach with privatization. Contract schools are public institutions, supported with public funds, accountable to a public authority—usually a local school board. As is the case with charter schools, they are expected to meet specific standards of academic performance defined in a legal agreement. If they do not perform adequately, they can be put out of business. When Baltimore Mayor Kurt Schmoke became dissatisfied with student performance at EAI-operated schools in Baltimore, he said he would rethink the contract. It is a rare occurrence for a city public school to be shut down for poor performance, regardless of its record over time. Contracting arrangements, whether they result from state charter laws or local initiatives, mark a new threshold of aspiration and accountability for public education.

Dimensions of choice

Choice programs are designed to enhance the options made available to parents in selecting a school for their children. The most common form of choice program allows parents to choose a public school that lies outside the ordinary range of geographical options. The objective is to improve the chances for students to be placed in settings that suit their needs. It is also assumed that giving parents choice will induce competition among schools. Minnesota adopted the first statewide inter-district choice program in 1985. By 1991, 10 states had approved some form of open-enrollment program; and now, more than two-thirds of the states have enacted public school-choice programs. The first city-wide choice program was developed in 1981 in Cambridge, Massachusetts; perhaps the most celebrated success story at the local level is found in District 4 of East Harlem.

The basic shortcoming of public school-choice programs is that those jurisdictions that have the greatest need for expanding opportunities usually offer the fewest number of satisfactory options. For example, in Massachusetts, where voluntary inter-district choice has existed since 1991, only 25 percent of the districts participate, and none of the 29 on the suburban rim of Boston is included in this group. Supposedly, New York City has had a city-wide choice program since 1992; but, in reality, choice is permitted in only six of 32 districts, and the availability of space is extremely limited. Without measures designed to increase the total number of quality institutions, public school choice promotes competition among parents and children, not educators. It raises expectations but often leads to disappointment.

In 1990, Wisconsin passed innovative legislation that would expand parental choice among low-income parents in Milwaukee. Families who met income criteria ($18,000 or less) were given a state voucher for $2,987, which they might use in either a public school or a participating private school. By the end of the 1994–1995 school year, there were 1,500 children participating in the program that involved 12 nonpublic schools. Last spring, the legislation was amended to increase the value of the voucher to $3,600 and to permit schools with religious affiliations to participate. By next year, 15,000 low-income students are expected to take advantage of this unusual opportunity.

Similarly, last spring, the Ohio legislature enacted a law that will permit up to 2,000 low-income students in Cleveland to use a $2,500 state voucher in a school of choice—public, private, or sectarian. As in Wisconsin, the law was passed at the urging of minority parents dissatisfied with the quality of education in inner-city public schools. Like parents in Milwaukee, they had been frustrated with court-imposed integration plans that led to longer bus rides, rather than better schools. For the first time, many poor children whose life chances would have been determined by assignment to a failing public school were given the opportunity for real choices that gave them access to quality institutions (choices that were formerly available only to the middle class). In the meantime, the Milwaukee program is being challenged in state court, and a legal contest is expected in Cleveland.

Opponents of these programs claim that they violate requirements for the Constitutional separation of church and state. But there is nothing in the First Amendment of the Constitution that prohibits parents who want to send their children to religious schools from receiving public support. Since 1983, rulings by the Supreme Court have held that such support is legally permissible provided that aid goes directly to the parents (not the school), that the choice of school is freely made by parents, and that the system of funding is neutral. Cognizant of these rulings, opponents of choice have resorted to legal arguments based on provisions found in state law, many of which may be incompatible with federal Constitutional standards.

Some critics of choice fear that providing families with private-school options will spell the doom of public education. They predict a mass exodus of children and dollars from public schools. This is highly unlikely, indeed impossible, since the number of children permitted to participate has been limited. Let us keep in mind that every choice program that has gotten serious consideration by policy makers thus far—including those in Wisconsin and Ohio—has targeted a limited portion of the school population, those on the lowest rung of the economic ladder. Most public-school children were not even eligible according to these criteria.

Traditionally, school reformers have asked how we can improve the existing system; today, many ask, instead, what we can do that is in the best interest of students who are at risk of failing. Since the ground-breaking work by the late sociologist James S. Coleman and his colleagues at the University of Chicago in 1982,[1] there is evidence that private and parochial schools are more educationally effective than public schools. Some scholars have attributed the difference to the selectivity of private schools. However, more recent research on Catholic schools by Bryk, Lee, and Holland[2] indicates that the differences are more the result of characteristics identified within the schools themselves, e.g., high standards, a strong academic curriculum, autonomy, an orderly environment, and a sense of community. Other studies by Coleman, Greeley, and Hoffer[3] have demonstrated rather persuasively that Catholic schools have been particularly effective in educating at-risk, inner-city students who have performed poorly in public schools.

An agenda for change

In light of the wide range of reforms currently under way in cities across the country, we propose a six-point agenda to improve educational opportunities for all children. Some of these proposals will require strong legislative action at the state level. Implementation will require an "hourglass strategy," allowing schools to escape one by one from the bureaucratic system. The best schools would function as charter schools and the worst schools would be replaced by institutions with performance contracts. Over time, more and more schools will seek the autonomy and performance agreements that charter schools have, and educational authorities will incrementally replace ineffective schools with new schools that have committed themselves to meet performance goals. The net effect of this approach would be to increase the number of desirable schools that children can attend.

1. Setting Standards. What matters most is whether children are learning, and this can only be assured by having real accountability at the school level. Each school district should establish clear performance standards and administer regular assessments to determine whether students are learning what they should at each grade level. By standards, we mean objective outcome measures that prescribe what should be expected from every school at regular intervals. For example, we would focus on such items as test scores in reading and math, attendance rates, and dropout rates. We would be especially interested in measuring "value added" or "gain scores"—the progress made over a given academic year—rather than unfairly comparing schools with children from vastly different social circumstances. We would not involve district-level administrators in defining basic inputs like instructional approaches or building specifications beyond code requirements designed to protect safety.

2. School Closings. The public school that once served as a gateway of opportunity for immigrant populations now serves as a custodial institution for disadvantaged children. Even as national achievement-test scores creep slowly upward, the gap between black and white students' scores remains shamefully wide, and those of Hispanic children are actually declining. As a matter of public policy, no child should be forced to go to a failing school. We cannot ask parents of children who are trapped in floundering institutions to be patient while we work things out. Educators and political leaders should not expect poor parents to accept educational standards for their children that the middle class would not tolerate for their own.

Any school that shows a consistent record of failure over several years should be a candidate for closure. The first step must be to define objective standards for placing a school on probation. Most school systems already have the basic data needed to develop appropriate criteria. A combination of attendance rates, test scores, dropout rates, improvement ratings, and similar markers will identify those schools that must be placed on probation or eventually closed.

3. School Autonomy. Schools that are working well should receive a performance contract and control over their budget and personnel. Subject to due process, principals should be able to select and remove staff. They should be allowed to purchase supplies and support services of their choosing, though central authorities will audit these purchases.

All schools, whether autonomous or not, should be liberated from unnecessary and cumbersome mandates. In New York, the state Education Department recently identified more than 120 regulations that are not related to health, safety, or civil rights. California, Michigan, and Florida have taken the lead on regulatory reform; their governors have called for sunsetting the entire education code and starting over, enacting only those regulations that are essential. Illinois is one of 10 states that has set up a procedure where local school districts can request waivers from outdated requirements. School superintendents should conduct a top-to-bottom review of local regulations to eliminate those that are not necessary. The goal should be to minimize the burden on teachers and principals. and to grant schools greater independence in providing education.

Many school systems in the United States are experimenting with site-based management that moves decision making out of the administrative structure of the bureaucracy down to the school level. When implemented seriously, site-based management can improve both flexibility and accountability. However, a key question is whether central school authorities will actually concede the power to which they have become accustomed. A recent evaluation of the Los Angeles autonomy program by McKinsey & Company identified significant delays at the district level in implementing the reforms. Several years ago, New York City launched a modest experiment in school-based management without reducing the power of the central bureaucracy. It resulted in neither real autonomy for participating schools nor increased accountability for student performance.

Worth consideration is the city of London's opt-out program, in which a majority of parents in a school can vote to remove the school from the supervision of the local school district. Independence means that the school gets control over its own budget and a portion of the administrative overhead, so long as it continues to meet well-defined performance standards based on the national curriculum and national tests. All big-city school districts should have a similar plan, enabling schools to "opt out" of the present bureaucratic structure. We would propose, however, that approval require a majority vote of both parents and teachers. Teachers are important members of the school community, and their support is essential for success.

Not all schools are ready for such autonomy. But, if the parents and professionals at a school apply for approval as a charter school, then such a request should be evaluated by the local superintendent, the state education commissioner, or by an independent chartering agency on the basis of established criteria. In exchange for autonomy, the school administration would be required to sign a contract defining educational and financial standards to which the school would be held accountable. Greater autonomy would permit the school to hire staff, choose its teaching materials, set its fiscal priorities, and decide where it wants to purchase supplies and support services. Decisions about what to buy and where to buy it would be made by educators at the school level, not bureaucrats at central headquarters.

4. New Schools. If we intend to close failing schools, we need to provide alternatives to students who attend them. School superintendents should be given the power to solicit proposals for new institutions, either to replace failing schools or to grant contracts for increasing the total number of quality institutions. Proposals would be received from groups of teachers or parents, universities, libraries or museums, nonprofit organizations, or private entrepreneurs who demonstrate a professional capacity to administer a school. They may be progressive schools, family-style schools, Outward Bound schools, single-sex schools, back-to-basics schools, classical academies: The range is as vast as the imagination of creative educators.

These should, of course, be schools of choice. If they attract enough students, they will succeed; if they don't, they won't. These new schools would be established under the same terms as the charter schools described above. They would be granted autonomy in exchange for signing a compact outlining the educational and financial standards to which they would be held accountable. But, if the marketplace prevails, parents will become the ultimate judges of success or failure at the school level.

5. Central Administration. In a recent article in the *Wall Street Journal*, Peter Drucker predicts that in 10 to 15 years, most organizations will be "outsourcing" all of their support activities to specialist groups, thus allowing executives to avoid distractions and focus on functions that are directly related to their central mission. We share a similar vision for public education, where the role of central authorities will be transformed. Over time, the central administrative institution will significantly reduce its role as a provider of support services to schools. It would not be in charge of supplies, leasing, meals, building repairs, transportation, personnel, and other functions that can be performed better by others. Depending on the outcome of the competitive market, support services will either be provided by a private vendor or administered by an appropriate municipal agency. Marriot, for example, already provides food services to schools in Baltimore and Salt Lake City; and most municipal governments are well equipped to assume responsibility for such functions as personnel administration, procurement, transportation, or building maintenance.

According to our plan, the central school administration will become a monitoring agency with clearly focused and limited responsibilities. It will be responsible for educational standards, city-wide assessments, fiscal accountability, capital improvements, the authorization of new schools, and negotiation of union contracts that are specific enough to protect members' rights but flexible enough to permit school-by-school variations. The school system's chief executive should concentrate on setting standards, monitoring performance, and identifying those schools that either should be put on probation or closed. The chief executive would also be responsible for financial monitoring to protect against corruption and malfeasance. In a system where every school has its own budget, this is a formidable task, and it will probably require some form of administrative decentralization.

6. Real Choice for the Poor. Parents whose children attend the worst schools—those targeted for closure—should be given scholarships on a means-tested basis to use in any accredited school, be it public, private, or religious. Middle-class parents exercise such options for their children all the time; poor children should have the same. Priority for financial aid should go first to children in failing institutions whose families are on public assistance. The amount of a scholarship should not exceed the per capita cost of sending a child to public school. Schools receiving scholarship students should accept the award as a full fee for tuition. Students who get public scholarships should be regularly tested to assess their progress, in order to assure accountability and to exclude inadequate schools from participation.

Schools for the twenty-first century

We believe that these proposals, taken together, will strengthen and energize public education—freeing professionals and students from counterproductive regulations, shifting resources from the district level to the schools, providing alternative means for the delivery of vital support services, assuring choice for the students who now receive the least educational opportunity, rewarding success, encouraging creativity, requiring accountability for results, phasing out schools that are not conducive environments for teaching or learning, and placing institutions on the line by putting students first.

The public education system as currently structured is archaic. It cannot reform itself, nor can it be reformed by even the most talented chief executive. Trying to do so would be like trying to convert an old-fashioned linotype machine into a word-processor: It can't be done. They perform the same function, but their methods and technologies are so different that one cannot be turned into the other. Instead of a school system that attempts to impose uniform rules and regulations, we need a system of schools that is dynamic, diverse, performance based, and accountable. The school system that we now have may have been right for the age in which it was created; it is not right for the twenty-first century.

Notes

1. James S. Coleman, Thomas Hoffer, and Sally Kilgore, *High School Achievement: Public, Catholic, and Private Schools* (New York: Basic Books, 1982).
2. Anthony B. Bryk, Valerie E. Lee, and Peter B. Holland, *Catholic Schools and the Common Good* (Cambridge: Harvard University Press, 1993).
3. Andrew M. Greeley, *Catholic High Schools and Minority Students* (Rutgers: Transaction, 1982); Thomas Hoffer, Andrew M. Greeley, and James S. Coleman. "Achievement Growth in Public and Catholic Schools," *Sociology of Education* 58 (1985): 74–97.

Ethnicity and Adolescent Achievement

BY LAURENCE STEINBERG
WITH B. BRADFORD BROWN AND SANFORD M. DORNBUSCH

An important new book offers fascinating summertime reading for anyone interested in trying to unravel the reasons underlying the relatively poor performance of American students. Entitled Beyond the Classroom, *the book's authors argue that out-of-school factors have enormous, perhaps decisive influence on student achievement. Drawing in large part from survey data gathered from 20,000 high school students over a three-year period, the authors examine student attitudes and values—what they think of school and learning, how they use their nonschool time, the norm of "getting by." The authors look at the role of parents and peers and culture. The article that follows is excerpted from this compelling new work.* —Editor

ONE OF the many strengths of our study was the ethnic variety in our sample. Unlike most research on adolescent development, which is based on samples of White youngsters (and middle-class White youngsters at that), our sample is ethnically and socioeconomically heterogeneous. Research on such varied populations is extremely important because, by the end of this century, ethnic minority youth will make up about one-third of the adolescent population. Although our sample was not deliberately recruited to reflect exactly the national population of teenagers, more than one-third of the participants in our study were minority youth, approximately evenly divided among youngsters from African-American, Asian-American, and Hispanic-American families.

Laurence Steinberg is professor of psychology at Temple University in Philadelphia. B. Bradford Brown is professor of educational psychology at the University of Wisconsin-Madison and research scientist in the Wisconsin Center for Education Research. Sanford M. Dornbusch is Reed-Hodgson professor of human biology and professor of sociology and education, emeritus, at Stanford University.

Although we did not intend our study to focus primarily on ethnic differences in achievement and other aspects of adolescent development, we were struck repeatedly by how significant a role ethnicity played in structuring young people's lives, both inside and outside of school. Youngsters' patterns of activities, interests, and friendships were all influenced by their ethnic background. Moreover, we could not ignore the fact that students from different ethnic groups experienced markedly different degrees of success and failure in school. Like other investigators, we found that students of Asian descent are doing far better in school than are members of other ethnic groups, and that Black and Latino adolescents are doing significantly worse. We cannot attribute these patterns simply to ethnic differences in socioeconomic status—even *within* a specific social class, Asian students outperform White students, who in turn outperform Black and Latino students. This is not to say, of course, that there aren't plenty of exceptions to this pattern—Asians who are doing poorly, and Black and Latino students who are doing very well. But the general pattern of ethnic differences was marked and consistent across the nine schools we studied.

Venturing into the realm of ethnic differences in achievement is a difficult and delicate matter today, with racial divisions in this country at an extremely high level, and with heated and often uninformed debates in the popular press about genetic bases for ethnic and racial differences in intelligence and behavior. There will be readers who will be angry at what I say, if not simply at my colleagues and me studying ethnicity and achievement at all. That ethnic differences in achievement persist even after we take into account differences in social class only makes matters worse, because this suggests that the patterns cannot be dismissed as mere reflections of differences in economic resources. But our findings on ethnicity and achievement are just too important to ignore. Moreover, as you will read, they inform the more general issues of the declining achievement of American youth. Until we really understand the causes of this problem, we will not be able to solve it.

A Few Words About Ethnicity

A few preliminary words are in order about what we mean by ethnicity. We deliberately use the term "ethnicity," and not race, because we see it as a measure of individuals' cultural background rather than their biological ancestry. In keeping with other social scientists who study ethnicity, we use the term "ethnic group" to refer to a group of individuals who share certain fundamental patterns of culture, history, values, and beliefs.

In grouping youngsters by ethnicity, we employed a categorization scheme similar to that used by other social scientists, namely, one that asks individuals to classify themselves into one of seven categories: Asian, Black, Latino, non-Hispanic White, American Indian, Middle Eastern, or Pacific Islander (the specific instruction was "Select the one major ethnic group that best describes you"). We had insufficient numbers of students in our study from three categories (American Indian, Middle Eastern, and Pacific Islander) to draw statistically reliable conclusions about any of these ethnic groups, so in analyses designed with ethnic comparisons in mind, these youngsters were not included. Thus, when I write about ethnic differences or similarities in one or another aspect of adolescent development, I am referring to youngsters in one of four major ethnic groups: Black, Asian, Latino, or White. In analyses in which ethnicity was not a consideration—for example, if we simply wanted to examine the relation between school achievement and time spent in extracurricular activities—all of the students in our sample were included.

Any attempt to group individuals into categories defined by ethnic background is necessarily imperfect, even if individuals are classifying themselves. Any superordinate ethnic category necessarily mixes groups of individuals who come from various cultural backgrounds. The category we call "Asian," for example, combines individuals of Chinese, Japanese, Filipino, Korean, Southeast Asian, and South Asian descent—cultures that in numerous respects are quite diverse. Similarly, the category we call "Latino" is composed of students whose relatives come from Cuba, Puerto Rico, Central America, Mexico, and South America—again a rather varied group of backgrounds. The White youngsters in our sample generally were of European descent (in our study, "White" refers to non-Hispanic White youth), but this, of course, includes individuals from backgrounds as different from each other as Great Britain, Poland, and Greece.

We made the decision to use these broad categories knowing full well their limitations. But in our judgment, the alternatives—using more fine-grained categories or ignoring ethnicity entirely—were equally problematic. Further divisions of the groups into smaller categories (e.g., classifying youngsters in terms of their family's specific country of origin, or using concrete indicators such as fluency in one or another language, or adherence to certain cultural customs) is also imperfect, since even these categories frequently combine individuals from different cultural origins (e.g., rural versus urban Mexico, northern versus southern China, Protestant versus Catholic Irish, African individuals born in Africa versus African individuals born in America). Moreover, using a more fine-grained classification scheme would result in having very small numbers of individuals in any given category, rendering statistical analyses virtually impossible.

There are those who might argue that in light of these difficulties we should not have used ethnicity as a classifying variable at all. Indeed, had our study been conducted several decades earlier, when social scientists downplayed ethnicity in favor of socioeconomic status, we might not have studied ethnicity. Today, however, ethnicity is an exceedingly important variable in social science research as well as public life generally. In contemporary America, ethnicity emerges as just as important a factor in defining and shaping individual experience as does social class or gender. Whether we like it or not, individuals use ethnicity in everyday life to classify themselves and others in an attempt to organize and understand their world. And, especially given the well-documented and widely reported findings concerning ethnic differences in achievement in this country, it would have been foolish, if not scientifically dishonest, to ignore this variable in our research.

This is not to say that we ignored other relevant information about individuals' ethnic background. Our surveys included detailed questions not only about the adolescent's self-categorization, but about the specific ethnic background of the adolescent's parents or stepparents, the family's immigration history, the languages spoken by the adolescent and the significant people in his or her life, and the adolescent's feelings and beliefs about his or her ethnic identity. These questions permitted us to perform more detailed analyses—examining, for example, how students whose families have recently come to the United States differ from youngsters of the same ethnic background, but whose families have been in America for several generations, or how different patterns of language use are related to school achievement among Latino or Asian youngsters.

Ultimately, the classification system we employed made the most sense in light of the particular research problem we were studying—adolescent achievement in American high schools in the late 20th century. Dividing the world into the four-way scheme we ended up with—Asian, Black, Latino, and White—made sense, not only to us as researchers, but to the adolescents, their parents, and school personnel. A different research question, or one studied at a different time or in a different setting, might well have required a different basis for classification. In the final analysis, the utility of the categorization scheme we employed is borne out by the fact that it helps to account for differences in patterns of behavior. If the scheme were unreasonable, or foolhardy, or wrong, the findings it yielded would be less consistent and less interpretable.

1. THE SOCIAL CONTEXTS OF MULTICULTURAL EDUCATION

Why Study Ethnicity?

One might think that studying ethnicity and achievement is the same as studying group differences in scholastic performance. Our investigation into ethnic differences in achievement was not primarily a documentation of differences in levels of achievement, however. The ethnic differences in achievement we found had been reported by numerous investigators long before we began our study. Our approach was aimed at understanding *why* such differences exist. What is it about Asian students that helps account for their above-average record? Why are Black and Latino students faring worse in school than their White or Asian peers? How can we account for individual students who are not performing as well as, or as poorly as, other members of their ethnic group? Are the factors that explain achievement similar or different as we move from one ethnic group to another?

The answers to these questions, it turns out, are far more complicated than the simple stereotypes that are so often (and often erroneously) casually exchanged. More important, in taking on these questions—questions about the underlying causes of ethnic differences in achievement—we were able not only to illuminate the issue of ethnicity and school performance, but to better understand the factors that affect *all* students' achievement. All of us, regardless of our personal background, have much to learn by examining why some groups are succeeding in school at far higher rates than others, and, as well, why some groups are performing so poorly.

Let me begin with a summary of what we found when we contrasted the school performance of students from different ethnic groups.

Ethnic Differences in Student Achievement and Engagement

One of the most consistent observations reported by social scientists who study school achievement in this country is that Asian-American students perform, on average, substantially better than their White peers, who in turn outperform their Black and Latino counterparts. This finding has emerged over and over again, whether the index in question is based on school grades or performance on standardized tests of achievement. What is especially remarkable about the ethnic group comparisons of achievement is that they hold up even after taking into account other factors that might contribute to ethnic differences in performance, such as differences between ethnic groups in family income, household composition, or parental education.

We find precisely the same pattern of ethnic differences in our sample as other researchers have reported. That is, even when we compare students from identical social backgrounds, we still find that Asian students are outperforming their classmates who attend the very same schools, and that both Asian and White youngsters are achieving more than Black or Latino students. Although there are social class differences in school performance *within* every ethnic group—differences that favor, as one would expect, children from wealthier, more educated families—the differences *between* ethnic groups are not simply due to ethnic differences in income or parental education. That is, Asian students from low-income homes outperform comparably disadvantaged white, Black, and Latino students, and low-income white students score higher than comparably disadvantaged Black or Latino students; middle-class Asian students outperform middle class whites, who, in turn, outperform middle-class Black and Latino students; and so on. In other words, even though Black and Latino students are more likely to come from less advantaged backgrounds than White or Asian students, this difference in family resources does not fully explain the difference in the groups' school performance.

Nor can the difference be attributable to differences in the schools youngsters attend, since we find these ethnic differences even among youngsters enrolled in the very same schools. In fact, the relative standing of ethnic groups in their school performance was virtually identical across each of the nine schools we studied—in schools in both Wisconsin and California; in urban, suburban, and rural schools; in predominantly white and in predominantly minority schools. Across these very different settings, students of Asian descent were succeeding at a higher rate than all other students, and students of Black and Latino descent were achieving at a lower rate.

How large are the achievement differences we see when we compare ethnic groups, however? Whereas the average Asian students in our study were earning a mixture of A's and B's in school, other students were averaging grades of B's and C's, with White students earning more B's than C's, and Black and Latino students earning more C's than B's. Although these differences may not seem large at first glance, differences in grades of this magnitude clearly have genuine and important implications for how youngsters fare after completing high school. Put concretely, a student who graduates with a mixture of A's and B's on his or her transcript stands a much better chance of being admitted to a selective university than one with more C's than B's.

Group averages tell only part of the story. It is also important to look at the distribution of grades in each ethnic group, to get a sense of the range of student performance. After all, a group can end up with an overall average of C by having a high proportion of students earning C grades, or by having large numbers of students earning both A's and F's. How did the ethnic groups fare when we looked at their grades in this fashion?

White students' grades, in general, are tightly distributed around a B average, with two-thirds of the white students in our sample earning grades somewhere between B– and A–. What this means, therefore, is that relatively few white students are earning either very high *or* very low grades. Among Asian students, in contrast, close to 55 percent had grade-point averages of A or A–, compared with 35 percent of White students, 19 percent of Latino students, and 16 percent of Black students. At the other end of the spectrum, fewer than 10 percent of the Asian students had averages of C or lower, as opposed to 20 percent of the White students, 34 percent of Black students, and 38 percent of the Latino students.

We can look at this pattern in yet another way, by asking how the grades given out within a school are distributed across the ethnic groups. Here again we see the same basic pattern: Although Asian youngsters represented only 13 percent of our sample, they accounted for 27 percent of the students in our sample with straight-A averages, and 20 percent of the students with A− averages. Whites, who account for a little more than 60 percent of our sample, account for the same proportion of students with A or A− averages. In contrast, although Black and Latino students made up nearly one-fourth of our sample, they accounted for only 7 percent of the students with straight-A averages. Black and Latino students accounted for more than 40 percent of all the students in our sample with grade point averages of C− or below.

These ethnic differences, as I mentioned earlier, were quite consistent within each of the different schools in our research, a finding that argues against the idea that the ethnic differences we observed are actually differences between schools or communities. If, for example, all of the Asian students were attending schools in which grading practices were liberal, and all of the Latino students were attending schools in which grading practices were more stringent, we could not tell if any observed ethnic difference in grades was really due to ethnicity or, instead, to the different schools' grading policies. For this reason, it was important to see if the ethnic differences in grades observed in the sample as a whole were also reported within each school. And they were.

Specifically, in every single high school community we studied, Asian students were earning a far higher proportion of the A's given out than would be expected by the sheer number of Asian students alone. In one school, for example, although Asian students accounted for only 8 percent of the student body, they accounted for nearly one-third of the students with straight-A averages! In contrast, Black and Latino students were always underrepresented among students with high averages, and always overrepresented among students with grades of C− or lower. White students were almost always clustered in the middle of the distribution, overrepresented among students earning B's, and underrepresented among those earning either very high or very low grades.

I noted earlier that the differences in school grades we observed among ethnic groups are large enough to make a difference in youngsters' future educational and occupational careers. We can also place ethnic differences in grades in perspective by comparing them to the differences we find when we contrast students regarding other demographic variables, such as gender, social class, household composition, or mother's employment status. For each of these demographic variables, we calculated the "net" effect of the variable in question after taking into account all of the other variables. Thus, we were able to estimate how much ethnicity "matters" after taking into account social class, household composition, gender, and maternal employment. Similarly, we were able to ask how much household composition matters after taking into account ethnicity, class, gender, and maternal employment, and so on.

2. Ethnicity and Adolescent Achievement

As one would expect based on previous research, all of these factors are related to students' school performance. On average, girls earn higher grades than boys; youngsters from more affluent families earn higher grades than those from poorer households; students whose parents have never divorced earn higher grades than those who reside with a single parent or in a stepfamily; and students (especially boys) whose mother is employed full-time earn slightly lower grades than students with a mother who is not employed or works only part-time. Many of these findings have been reported by other investigators, and none of them is especially surprising.

Here's the big surprise, though: of all the demographic factors we studied in relation to school performance, ethnicity is the most important. For example, even after we take into account the other demographic variables that make a difference, we find that the gap in grades between Asian students and Black or Latino students is nearly twice as big as the gap between students from the poorest families in our sample and those from the most affluent. Similarly, the gap between students from divorced and nondivorced homes is substantially smaller than the gap between the grades of White and Black or White and Latino students, and less than a third of the size of the gap between Asian and either Black or Latino students. In terms of school achievement, then, it is more advantageous to be Asian than to be wealthy, to have nondivorced parents, or to have a mother who is able to stay at home full-time.

Asian students are not merely distinguished from students of other backgrounds by their superior school grades and scores on standardized tests of achievement, however. Asian students also are significantly more engaged in school than their classmates—not really a surprise, since stronger engagement both leads to and results from higher grades.

Consider students' scores on some of the markers of engagement that we used in our study. Asian students spend more time on homework than other students. They cut class less often, report higher levels of attention and concentration during class, and report less mind-wandering. They report being confused less often but challenged more often—a combination that certainly suggests emotional engagement in the classroom. On our measure of overall orientation toward school, which assesses how important a priority students think school is, Asian students outscore all other groups by a wide margin. In contrast, Black and Latino students spend significantly less time on homework than White or Asian students do, and this is not due to the fact that Black and Latino students are assigned less homework. Rather, Black and Latino students are more likely to report that they do not do all of the homework they are assigned.

That we find ethnic differences in engagement, as well as in achievement, is extremely important. Some commentators have suggested that one reason for the greater success of Asian students, compared with White, Black, or Latino students, is their superior native intelligence. Our results suggest that this is unlikely. (Interestingly, other studies directly examining the genetic explanation have failed to support the view that Asian academic success is due to genetic advantages in intelligence.) A more reasonable reading of the evidence is that Asian students perform better in school because they work harder, try harder, and are more invested in achievement—the very same factors that contribute to school success among *all* ethnic groups. Indeed, as one of my colleagues once quipped, if Asian students were truly genetically superior to other students, they would not be spending twice as much time on homework each week as their peers in order to outperform them.

These strong and consistent ethnic differences in school achievement and engagement shed important light on the ongoing debate over school reform. One interpretation of our findings is that perhaps the school reform under consideration in some quarters is not the key. After all, the Asian students in our study were achieving high grades and maintaining strong engagement in the classroom despite the alleged deficiencies of their schools.

Similar conclusions have been reached in other studies. In one widely cited piece of research, the social scientists examined the achievement of Asian youngsters from Indochinese refugee families. These students came to the United States under enormously dif-

Although many social critics believe that overt discrimination against Black and Latino students by teachers is rampant, the scientific evidence for this view is not strong.

ficult conditions, with few economic resources and limited proficiency in English. All of the participants in the research went to school in poor, metropolitan areas—environments, as the researchers pointed out, that are hardly known for producing academic success. Indeed, these are the "disadvantaged urban schools" identified in so many reports as having the lowest levels of average student achievement in the country. Yet, despite all of these hardships, the Indochinese refugee children performed exceptionally well in school and on standardized tests of achievement, bettering in many cases their non-Asian counterparts for whom English was their native tongue. Whatever the faults of American schools—even those in the inner city—apparently some students are able to succeed in them. While this observation, of course, does not justify the continued existence of poor-quality schools, it does suggest that factors other than school quality must play an important role in determining student achievement.

Explaining Ethnic Differences

To what can we attribute the relative superiority of Asian students in school and the relatively poor showing of Black and Latino students? As I have suggested, we cannot explain these differences away as an artifact of other differences in background, such as social class or household composition. And, because we find the same pattern of ethnic differences *within* schools as we do in the sample as a whole, we can be confident that the differences are not due to youngsters from different ethnic groups being enrolled in different schools. But what about discrimination within schools? Could it be the case that the lower grades of Black and Latino students are a product of teachers' discrimination, and that the higher grades of Asian students are due to teachers' favorable biases toward them?

Although many social critics believe that overt discrimination against Black and Latino students by teachers is rampant, the scientific evidence for this view is not strong. For example, studies show that the assignment of students to higher or lower tracks in high school is not heavily biased in terms of ethnicity, and track assignment is surely an instance where racial discrimination, if strong, would be manifested. Rather, research shows that students tend to be assigned to tracks on the basis of their past performance, and not their social background.

Nor do we see much evidence for the "prejudiced teachers hypothesis" in our own data. For instance, we asked students to report how often teachers at school were "unfair or negative" to them because of their ethnic background. In every ethnic group, reports of discrimination by teachers were rare. Although ethnic minority students in our study (and especially Black students) reported slightly more unfair or negative treatment by teachers than White students did, ethnic differences in levels of reported discrimination by teachers were much smaller than ethnic differences in achievement. Second, our analyses found that ethnic differences in school grades persist—and, in fact, are just as strong—after we take ethnic differences in perceived discrimination into account. In other words, whether we look separately at the group of students who report high levels of discrimination or separately at the group of students who report no discrimination, we see the same pattern of ethnic differences in school performance. Finally, and perhaps most significantly, Asian students and Latino students report identical levels of discrimination from teachers, even though the groups' grades are, as we have seen, quite far apart.

On the face of it, it would seem difficult to attribute ethnic differences in school performance to blatantly unfair or biased treatment by teachers. But there is a different version of the "discrimination hypothesis" that is frequently invoked, one concerning discrimination outside of school, in the broader society. Specifically, some writers have suggested that ethnic differences in school performance are due to differences in youngsters' perceptions of their chances for economic and occupational success as adults. This is one version of what has been called the "glass-ceiling hypothesis."

The Glass-Ceiling Hypothesis

One popular view is that school success is linked to students' perceptions about the likely economic rewards of academic accomplishment. An extension of this view is that ethnic differences in school achievement are due to ethnic differences in students' beliefs about the importance of doing well in school. One widely cited theory, for example, is that Black and Latino students do not achieve as much success in school as other students chiefly because they do not believe that academic success will have a significant payoff. According to this view, because Black and Latino students anticipate discrimination and prejudice in the labor force, they have little faith that scholastic success will actually lead to concrete economic rewards, and, as a consequence, they exert relatively less effort in school.

Is the higher level of achievement seen among Asian students, and the lower level of achievement seen among Black and Latino students, due to their having different beliefs about the payoff for academic success? That is, are Asian students more engaged in school because they are more likely than other students to have faith that doing well in school will pay off? Do Black and Latino students succeed less often because they do not share this belief?

The answer, interestingly enough, is no. When we examined students' responses on questions concerning the likely economic and occupational rewards of school success, we found no ethnic differences in how students answered these questions. In other words, Asian, Black, Latino, and White students are all equally likely to say that getting a good education (that is, going far enough in school) will have a genuine payoff down the road. And despite the popular belief that students have lost faith in the value of school to their futures, we found very few students—of any color—who do not believe that getting a good job is dependent on how many years of school one completes.

Where students did differ, however, was in their beliefs about the consequences of *failing* in school. We not only asked students if they thought that getting a good education would lead to a good job; we also asked if they thought that *not* getting a good education would hurt their chances in the labor force. It was in response to this latter question that we found the most striking ethnic differences.

By a substantial margin, Asian students were more likely than other students to believe that not doing well in school would have negative consequences for their future. In contrast, non-Asian students were less likely to hold this belief—they were far more cavalier about potential negative effects of doing poorly in school. If anything, then, Asian students are successful not because of their stronger belief in the payoff for doing well, but because they have greater fear of the consequences of not doing well. It is undue optimism, not excessive pessimism, that may be holding Black and Latino students back in school. Their problem isn't that they have lost faith in the value of education; the problem is that many Black and Latino students don't really believe that doing poorly in school will hurt their chances for future success. The truth, of course, is that academic failure *does* affect the occupational and economic success of Black and Latino students, just as it does among their White and Asian peers.

Beliefs About the Causes Of Success and Failure

Having students believe that it is worth investing time and energy in school is a necessary condition for academic achievement, but it is not sufficient by itself. In order to succeed, students also must believe that they have some control over how well they do in school, that their performance is somehow related to their effort, and that trying harder will lead to an improvement in their grades and test scores.

For some time now, psychologists have studied the ways in which we try to make sense out of what happens to us and, in particular, in the ways in which we explain our successes and failures. In the research literature, these explanations for success and failure are referred to as *achievement attributions*.

In our study, we carefully measured students' achievement attributions. We asked whether they believed the grades they received were due to personal factors (for instance, ability or effort) or to external factors (for example, the teacher's attitude, the difficulty of the material) and, as well, whether they attributed their performance to factors they had some control over (e.g., effort) versus those that they did not (e.g., luck). We asked these questions about both good and bad grades. Based on students' responses to these questions, we were able to classify them as having basically healthy or unhealthy attributional styles.

Students with healthy attributional styles believe that their performance in school is due to personal factors that are under their own control. They view success as the product of hard work, and failure as the result of insufficient effort. Although they are confident in their abilities, these students do not view their performance as fixed by their intelligence. More important, students with a healthy attributional style do not attribute their performance to external factors, such as how hard or easy the material is, whether their teachers like or dislike them, or whether they have good or bad luck.

At the other extreme are students with an unhealthy attributional style. These students downplay the role of effort in school success and failure. When they succeed, they view their accomplishment as the result of innate ability, an easy assignment, favorable treatment by teachers, or just plain good luck. When they fail, they attribute their performance to unfair teachers, bad luck, low innate ability, or having to confront an exceptionally difficult test, all factors over which they have no personal control.

Our studies, as well as a good deal of other research, clearly show that a student's attributional style is significantly predictive of his or her performance in school. Successful students, on average, are more likely to attribute their academic accomplishments to hard work and their occasional failures to a lack of effort. Unsuccessful students, in contrast, are more likely to see their performance as due to factors that are beyond their personal control.

What is especially interesting about our findings on achievement attributions, however, is the pattern of ethnic differences we observed. Asian students are significantly more likely than Black, Latino, or White students to have a healthy attributional style—that is, to see their success and failure as directly linked to how hard they work. Conversely, Asian students are less likely than other students to see success or failure as resulting from things outside their personal control, such as luck or the favoritism of teachers. This view—that effort is what really counts—is an important part of the belief system among youngsters (and adults) in Asian countries as well. Our study suggests that this cultural difference in beliefs is likely to be one reason for the superior showing of Asian students, both here and abroad.

The problem of unhealthy achievement attributions is pervasive within the United States. Compared with individuals from other cultures, Americans are far more likely to believe that success in school is dependent on native intelligence, that intelligence is fixed—either by genes or early experience—and that factors in the emotional and social realms play only an insignificant role in students' academic success. When we observe differences in students' test scores, we are likely to attribute both successes and failures to differences in students' talents, and we are likely to convey this message in the ways that we speak about success and failure in school (e.g., "You're just not good at science, honey"; "You've always been good at languages"; "You've done well in algebra because you're such a 'math whiz'").

These messages about the immutability of talent take hold in our children's minds at an early age. I saw this a few years ago in our son's account of why he received a B on a math test. To put this in proper perspective, Ben had just transferred to a new school that, unlike his old one, gave letter grades on students' exams and assignments. At his old school, his teachers had corrected students' homework and examinations, but had not graded them per se. Ben had been at his new school for about six weeks when he brought home a math test on which he received a B.

I asked Ben if he knew why he had gotten the grade that he had received and, more important, if he knew what he could have done to have gotten a better grade. He looked at me, obviously upset at his performance and still trying to figure out how much his grades meant to his parents. "Suppose I'm just a B student?" he asked. "Then this is what I would expect to get."

I tried to explain to him that there was no such thing as a "B student"—that the grade he had received referred to his *exam*, not to him. But all the while I wondered how he could have so quickly transformed an evaluation of his work into a statement about his ability. Clearly, the message we give to students—you are what your grades say you are—is dangerously strong and salient, from a very early age.

Students, teachers, and parents in other parts of the world are far less likely than Americans to use the language of ability when discussing student performance. They are more likely to attribute differences in achievement to differences in students' motivation (how much they want to succeed), effort (how hard they exert themselves), or behavior (how much time they devote to their studies). Success, in their eyes, is not the outcome of inborn talent, but the product of systematic, motivated, hard work.

It is ironic that in the United States, a country that prides itself so much on its national "work ethic," we should place so little faith in hard work and so much in native ability. I suspect that one reason for the popularity of *The Bell Curve* is that its central premise—that intelligence, and therefore success, is fixed by genetic inheritance—is widely accepted as part of American folk "wisdom," even though the evidence for this belief is very weak. As you'll read later in this article, our findings concerning the drop in achievement that occurs as ethnic minority youngsters become acclimated to the American way of life indicate that school achievement is unlikely to be genetically determined.

The Myth of Asian-American Misery

About 10 years ago, *The New York Times* published an op-ed piece I wrote on the achievement gap between our students and Japan's. In that brief essay, I argued that the achievement gap was real, that it was indeed something to worry about, and that we had better address it. What were some of the "radical" suggestions I made? That American students spend more time on their studies and less time slinging hamburgers in fast-food restaurants, shopping, and partying with their friends; and that parents become more involved in their children's education. Shortly after the essay appeared, I heard from a 10th-grade social studies teacher from a school district in upstate New York. He had asked his students to read the essay and send me their responses.

The 10th-grade students' letters (which, incidentally, were written at about the sixth- or seventh-grade level) were uniformly critical of my piece. Yes, it is true, they wrote, that Japanese students outperform us in matters of achievement. But, they countered, how well rounded were those Japanese students? They might be *smarter*, one student wrote, but we're *happier*. And "everyone" knows about the high suicide rate among Japanese adolescents.

The notion that Asian students' academic success has taken a toll on their mental health and personal happiness is often used by American adolescents and parents to argue against steps we might take in this country to raise our own students' level of scholastic accomplishment. Yet it may come as a surprise to learn that the stereotype of the miserable Asian achiever is without foundation.

For example, contrary to popular belief and media hyperbole, the adolescent suicide rate today is higher in the United States than in Japan—and it has been higher for nearly 20 years. The notion that suicide is rampant among Japanese adolescents was valid 40 years ago, but is no longer so today. The suicide rate among Japanese adolescents peaked in 1955 and has declined steadily since then. Among American adolescents, during this same time period, the suicide rate has more than *quadrupled.* Japanese adolescents may feel more pressure on them to do well in school than American adolescents, but this does not appear to have resulted in an increase in suicide.

The difference in mental health between Japanese and American adolescents, favoring Japanese youngsters, is also seen when less serious indicators of psychological disturbance than suicide are examined. A recent report from the University of Michigan cross-cultural study of achievement indicates, for example, that minor signs of psychological distress are also more common among American than among Japanese students. The researchers surveyed over 1,000 students in each country and collected measures of stress, depression, anxiety, aggression, and some somatic complaints (e.g., headaches, fatigue, sleep difficulties, gastrointestinal problems). Contrary to widespread belief, the American students reported *more* stress, *more* depression, *more* anxiety, *more* aggression, and *more* somatic complaints than did their Japanese counterparts.

Stereotypes to the contrary, it is simply not the case that Japanese students are made miserable by the more intense academic environment in which they grow up. Yet this same argument—that high achievement necessarily comes at a cost to one's mental health—has also surfaced in discussions about the achievement gap between Asian students and other students *within* the United States. The argument is familiar: Asian-American students may be achieving more, but they are paying a price with their mental health. Is there any truth to this assertion?

Because we collected extensive data on youngsters' mental health, we were able to compare Asian-American students with their peers on some of the same indices used by the Michigan researchers in their comparisons of American and Japanese students. Compared with their White counterparts, the Asian-American students in our sample reported significantly *less* psychological distress (depression and anxiety), *less* somatic distress (headaches, sleep problems, etc.), *less* delinquency (aggression, troubles with the law), and *less* drug and alcohol use than other students. A different set of researchers, studying junior high school students, reached the same conclusion: "Contrary to the common belief...Asian students' academic success [is] NOT at the expense of their social adjustment."

When we look a bit closer at the correlates of positive adolescent mental health—within *any* ethnic group—it is not difficult to see why Asian students report fewer psychological problems, "despite" their superior academic performance: in all ethnic groups, students who do well in school report better mental health and fewer behavioral problems than students who do poorly in school. In fact, academic success is one of the strongest predictors of psychological adjustment in childhood and adolescence.

This is not, as many individuals believe, because positive mental health facilitates academic success. This, interestingly, was the erroneous assumption behind the movement in some educational circles to raise youngsters' self-esteem—that is, it was wrongly believed that enhancing the way students feel about themselves would lead to improvements in their school performance. We now know that success in school leads to more positive self-esteem, not the other way around. Artificially inflating youngsters' feelings of competence does little to promote genuine achievement and probably impedes it, since it erodes youngsters' sense of standards. Paradoxically, if we are genuinely concerned about improving the mental health of American youth, we ought to take steps to see that they are genuinely challenged and achieve more in school.

The High Costs of Americanization

Only a portion of the Asian and Latino youngsters currently attending school in the United States have parents who were born in this country. Any study of ethnic differences within the contemporary United States must therefore take into account the variation that exists both between and within different ethnic groups into which individual students and their parents were born. Because we collected data on youngsters' immigration histories, we were able to do this.

Most of us expect that individuals would have an especially tough time when they first arrive in a new country, and that, as a consequence, children who are recent immigrants would exhibit more distress and difficulty than their counterparts whose families have been living in the new country for some time. Given the fact that few nonnatives arrive in the United States fluent in English or acclimated to American customs and habits, one would expect that school would present a particularly demanding set of challenges for recent immigrants and their children. We would hypothesize, therefore, that students born outside the United States would be doing worse in school than those who are native Americans, and that native Americans whose families have been in this country for several generations would be faring better than their counterparts who arrived more recently.

Surprisingly, just the opposite is true: the longer a student's family has lived in this country, the worse the youngster's school performance and mental health. Consider some of the following findings from our study. Foreign-born students—who, incidentally, report significantly more discrimination than American-born youngsters and significantly more difficulty with the English language—nevertheless earn higher grades in school than their American-born counterparts. Although some commentators have speculated that the reason for this is economic—that families who are able to immigrate to the United States are from a higher social class than ethnic minority families who have been living here for several generations, and thus, more likely to succeed in school—our findings don't sup-

1. THE SOCIAL CONTEXTS OF MULTICULTURAL EDUCATION

port this interpretation. The differences in school performance favoring immigrants over native Americans remain just as large even after we take family background into account.

It is not simply that immigrants are outperforming nonimmigrants on measures of school achievement. On virtually every factor we know to be *correlated* with school success, students who were not born in this country outscore those who were born here. And, when we look only at American-born students, we find that youngsters whose parents are foreign-born outscore those whose parents are native Americans.

The more Americanized students—those whose families have been living here longer—are less committed to doing well in school than their immigrant counterparts. Immigrants spend more time on homework, are more attentive in class, are more oriented to doing well in school, and are more likely to have friends who think academic achievement is important. Immigrants also are more likely to have the sort of healthy attributional style that is correlated with school success: in accounting for their scholastic successes and failures, they downplay the significance of luck, native ability, and other factors that are out of one's control; instead, immigrants see effort as the critical influence on achievement.

Differences between immigrants and nonimmigrants are also apparent when we look at various manifestations of mental health. Immigrant adolescents report less drug use, less delinquency, less misconduct in school, fewer psychosomatic problems, and less psychological distress than do American-born youngsters.

The adverse effects of Americanization are seen among Asian and Latino youngsters alike (that is, within each of the two largest populations of immigrant youth in this country), with achievement decreasing, and problems increasing, with each successive generation. Instead of finding what one might reasonably expect—that the longer a family has been in this country, the better their child will be faring in our schools—we find exactly the reverse. Our findings, as well as those from several other studies, suggest that becoming Americanized is detrimental to youngsters' achievement, and terrible for their overall mental health.

How can we account for this? One theory is that immigrant youngsters grow increasingly skeptical about the American system with each generation. Many Asian and Latino families arrive in the United States optimistic about their future and committed to the belief that the "land of opportunity" does in fact offer chances for economic and social advancement through schooling. Under these conditions, immigrant parents probably communicate to their children the need to work hard in school and instill in their youngsters a strong drive to achieve. Over time, however, youngsters discover that the actual opportunities are not as plentiful as they had been told, and that individuals of color often face prejudice and discrimination as they make their way through school and into the labor force. With each generation, therefore, ethnic minority youngsters become increasingly skeptical about the American dream and, consequently, increasingly disengaged from school.

An alternative explanation (although entirely consistent with the first) is that immigrant youngsters' values and attitudes about the relative importance of education are transformed as they become more and more Americanized. Since American adolescents do not typically value academic excellence, the more that immigrant youth acculturate to mainstream American values, the less they see school achievement as important. In other words, the declining achievement of immigrants with each successive generation is not the product of disenchantment in the face of limited opportunities, but a result of the *normative* socialization of ethnic minority youth into the mainstream's indifferent (or at least, ambivalent) stance toward school success. Because part of what it means to be an American teenager in contemporary society is adopting a cavalier attitude toward school, the process of Americanization leads toward more and more educational indifference.

Although we cannot settle this issue definitively with our data, it looks like the second explanation (the socialization of indifference) is more likely to be true than the first (the "dashed hopes" hypothesis). When we look at youngsters' beliefs about the importance of school success for their future occupational careers, we find no differences between recently arrived immigrants and first- or second-generation Americans. Nor do we find differences between these groups in their beliefs about the consequences of doing poorly in school. If the "dashed hopes" hypothesis were true, we ought to see it reflected in youngsters' answers to these questions about the importance of school (that is, recent immigrants should have more faith in the value of schooling than their native counterparts).

This is not the case, however. Instead, it looks as if the longer a family has lived here, the more its children resemble the "typical" American teenager, and part of this package of traits is, unfortunately, academic indifference, or even disengagement. Americanized ethnic minority youngsters—Asian and Latino alike—spend significantly more time hanging out with friends, more time partying, more time dating, more time on nonacademic extracurriculars, and more time with peers who value socializing over academics. In essence, the broader context of what it means to be an American teenager in the contemporary United States pulls students away from school and draws them toward more social and recreational pursuits.

Our findings on the costs of Americanization teach us a different, but equally important, lesson about genetic explanations of ethnic differences in achievement and school performance. If in fact the superior performance of Asian students, or the poor performance of Latino students, were entirely due to genetic factors, we would not expect to find that student performance and behavior in school varied within these ethnic groups as a function of students' or parents' country of birth. The fact that students who have been brought up in the United States achieve less, are less interested in school, are more likely to engage in problem behavior, and are more interested in socializing than their nonnative counterparts from the same ethnic group points to a very strong environmental influence on achievement. It also says something very disturbing about the process of Americanization.

The Importance of Peers

One clear reason for Asian students' success is that Asian students are far more likely than others to have friends who place a great deal of emphasis on academic achievement. Asian-American students are, in general, significantly more likely to say that their friends believe it is important to do well in school, and significantly less likely than other students to say that their friends place a premium on having an active social life. Not surprisingly, Asian students are the most likely to say that they work hard in school to keep up with their friends.

Asian students' descriptions of their friends as hardworking and academically oriented are corroborated by information we gathered independently from the friends themselves. One of the unique features of our study was our ability to match information provided by adolescents with information provided directly by their friends. This provided us with a more accurate assessment of each adolescent's social network than would have been possible had we been forced to depend on adolescents' *perceptions* of their friends' behavior, since such perceptions can be erroneous (like adults, adolescents tend to overstate the degree of similarity that exists between their friends and themselves).

When we look at friends' activity patterns for adolescents from different ethnic groups, we see quite clearly that the friends with whom Asian students socialize place relatively greater emphasis on academics than other students do, whereas the opposite is true for Black and Hispanic teenagers. Specifically, Asian students' friends have higher performance standards (that is, they hold tougher standards for what grades are acceptable), spend more time on homework, are more committed to education, and earn considerably higher grades in school. Black and Hispanic students' friends earn lower grades, spend less time on their studies, and have substantially lower performance standards. White students' friends fall somewhere between these two extremes on these various indicators.

When I first saw these findings, my presumption was that they were due entirely to racial segregation in adolescent peer groups. In other words, if Asian students are performing better in school than other students, and Black and Hispanic students worse, and if peer groups are constituted mainly along ethnic lines, it necessarily follows that Asian students will have friends who are doing better in school, and Black and Hispanic students will have friends who are doing more poorly.

It turns out that the segregation argument is only partly true. While it is certainly the case that adolescent peer groups are characterized by a high degree of ethnic segregation—about 80 percent of White and Black students, and more than half of Asian and Hispanic students have best friends from the same ethnic group—there are sufficient numbers of cross-racial friendships in any school to ask whether the pattern described above holds for students who travel in integrated circles. The answer is that it does, at least for the most part. Even if we look solely at youngsters whose best friends are from a different ethnic background, we still find that Asian students' friends place a greater emphasis on doing well in school, and Black and Hispanic students' friends, rela-

---

Because Asian students find it more difficult than White students to break into the more socially oriented crowds, they drift toward academically focused peer groups.

---

tively less. Once again, White students fall somewhere in between.

Peer pressure among Asian students and their friends to do well in school is so strong that any deficiencies in the home environment—for example, parenting that is either too authoritarian or emotionally distant—are rendered almost unimportant. It is, of course, true that Asian students from authoritative homes perform better in school than those from disengaged ones. But an Asian student who comes from a less-than-optimal home environment is likely to be "saved" from academic failure by falling in with friends who value academic excellence and provide the necessary support for achievement.

Why is it so likely that an Asian student will fall into an academically oriented peer crowd and benefit from its influence? Ironically, Asian student success is at least partly a by-product of the fact that adolescents do not have equal access to different peer groups in American high schools. Asian students are "permitted" to join intellectual crowds, like the "brains," but the more socially oriented crowds—the "populars," "jocks," and "partyers"—are far less open to them. For example, whereas 37 percent of the White students in our sample were members of one of these three socially oriented crowds, only 14 percent of the Asian students were—even though more than 20 percent of the Asian students said they *wished* they could be members of these crowds (slightly less than one-third of the White students aspired to membership in one of these crowds). In essence, at least some Asian students who would like to be members of nonacademically oriented crowds are denied membership in them.

A similar argument has been advanced by several Asian social scientists in explaining the extraordinary success of Asian-American students. They have noted that academic success is one of the few routes to social mobility open to Asians in American culture—think for a moment of the relative absence of Asian-American en-

1. THE SOCIAL CONTEXTS OF MULTICULTURAL EDUCATION

tertainers, athletes, politicians, and so on. For Asian youngsters, who see most nonacademic pathways to success blocked off, they have "no choice" but to apply themselves in school. This is why Asian students are so much more likely than other youngsters to subscribe to the belief that academic failure will bring terrible consequences. When individuals believe that there are few opportunities to success through routes other than education, doing well in school becomes that much more important.

Because Asian students find it more difficult than White students to break into the more socially oriented crowds, they drift toward academically focused peer groups whose members value and encourage scholastic success. The result of this drift is that a large number of Asian students, even those who are less academically talented than their peers, end up in crowds that are highly oriented toward success in the classroom. Once in these crowds, Asian students benefit tremendously from the network of academically oriented peers. Indeed, one of the striking features of Asian student friendships is how frequently they turn to each other for academic assistance and consultation.

The opposite is true for Black and Latino students, who are far more likely than other students to find themselves in peer groups that actually devalue academic accomplishment. Indeed, peer pressure among Black and Latino students *not* to excel in school is so strong in many communities—even among middle-class adolescents—that many positive steps that Black and Latino parents have taken to facilitate their children's school success are undermined. In essence, much of the good work that Black and Latino parents are doing at home is being undone by countervailing pressures in their youngsters' peer groups. As a consequence, parental efforts in these ethnic groups do not have the payoff that we would expect.

This is true not only in racially integrated schools, but in segregated schools as well. In one well-known study of an all-black, inner-city high school, for example, the researchers found that students who tried to do well in school were teased and openly ostracized by their peers for "acting White." Students were criticized—accused of acting as if they were "better" than their peers—if they earned good grades, exerted effort in class, or attempted to please their teachers. Those who wished to do well academically were forced to hide their success and to develop other means of maintaining their popularity among classmates in order to compensate for being good students, such as clowning around in class or excelling in some athletic activity. Why would Black and Latino peer groups demean academic success? In many minority peer groups, scholastic success is equated with "selling out" one's cultural identity, as some sort of surrender to the control of White, middle-class America.

I found this so interesting that I asked an extremely bright African-American undergraduate in one of my seminars at Temple University, who was familiar with our research, to help me better understand this phenomenon. The student said that the finding rang true for her. She had been raised in dire poverty within inner-city Washington, D.C., and she was the only one of her school friends to have made it out of the ghetto; as she explained, all of her former schoolmates were either on drugs, in jail, on welfare, or raising an infant. She was torn about where she would settle after graduation from college; the pull to return to her home community was very strong, but she felt that she could not face her former friends. Whenever she returned home during school vacations, she was taunted for thinking too highly of herself and teased for not yet having given birth to a child. She said that the pressure her friends put on her over the years to drop out of college and return to her roots was enormous. In fact, she said, her friends intimated that the only reason she had gone off to college and avoided early pregnancy was because she was not physically attractive enough to interest a man.

Why is succeeding in school equated in some circles with "acting White" or "selling out?" As Signithia Fordham and John Ogbu, two African-American social scientists who have studied this phenomenon explain:

> [W]hite Americans traditionally refused to acknowledge that black Americans are capable of intellectual achievement, and ... black Americans subsequently began to doubt their own intellectual ability, began to define academic success as white people's prerogative, and began to discourage their peers, perhaps unconsciously, from emulating white people in academic striving, i.e., from "acting white."

One of my colleagues at the University of Georgia, Layli Phillips, points out that this message—that academic success is somehow incompatible with a healthy Black identity—is perpetuated by a mass media that emphasizes and glorifies low-income African-American peer culture, making it attractive even to middle-class African-American youngsters. African-American parents who want their children to succeed in school are not only battling the force of the Black peer culture (which in many circles demeans academic success), but are fighting a difficult battle against the very powerful images of anti-intellectual Black youth portrayed as normative in music, movies, and television.

We heard variations on the "acting White" theme many, many times over the course of our interviews with high schools students. The sad truth is that many students, and many Black students in particular, are forced to choose between doing well in school and having friends. Although there are crowds within each high school in which academic success is valued and in which successful students are respected, these crowds tend to be dominated by White students, and peer groups in American high schools are so ethnically segregated that it is extremely difficult for Black and Latino students to join these crowds. Thus, in many schools, there is a near-complete absence of identifiable peer groups that respect and encourage academic success and are genuinely open to Black and Latino students. As a consequence, it is far more difficult for a talented African-American student than it is for a comparably skilled Asian or White student to find the necessary peer support for achievement.

Among the high-achieving Black students in our sample, for example, only 2 percent said their friends were members of the "brain" crowd, as opposed to 8 percent of the White students and 10 percent of the Asian students with the same grades in school. Interestingly, the proportion of the high-achieving Black students who said they *wished* they were members of the "brain" crowd (6 percent) was about the same as it was for the White students (5 percent). Thus, while just as many Black students as White students aspire toward membership in the "brain" crowd, membership in this group is more open to White than to Black students.

It is important to understand that the pressure against academic excellence that is pervasive within Black and Latino peer groups is not unique to these ethnic groups. Rather, what we see in these peer groups is an extreme case of what exists within most White peer groups as well. As noted earlier, the prevailing norm in most adolescent peer groups is one of "getting by without showing off" —doing what it takes to avoid getting into trouble in school, but at the same time shunning academic excellence. The chief difference appears to be not in the different ethnic groups' avoidance of excellence—this is common among all but the Asian youngsters—but in how the different ethnic groups define academic "trouble."

We measured students' perception of this "trouble threshold" by asking them what the lowest grade was that they could receive without their parents getting angry. The students' answers to this question confirmed our suspicion: Among Black and Latino students, not until their grades dipped below a C– did these adolescents perceive that they would get into trouble. Among White students, however, the average "trouble threshold" was one entire letter grade higher—somewhere between a B and a C. And among Asian students, the average grade below which students expected their parents to become angry was an astounding A–! One reason for the relatively poorer school performance of Black and Latino students, then, is that these students typically have different definitions of "poor" grades, relative to their White and Asian counterparts. And because peer crowds tend to be ethnically segregated, different normative standards develop within Black and Latino peer groups than in other crowds. Conversely, one reason for the remarkable success of Asian students is that they have a much stricter, less forgiving definition of academic failure than their Black, White, and Latino peers, and this definition shapes peer norms.

Our findings suggest, then, that . . . at a time in development when children are especially susceptible to the power of peer influence, the circle of friends an adolescent can choose from may make all the difference between excellent and mediocre school performance.

A Developmental Strategy to Prevent Lifelong Damage

David A. Hamburg

Over the past twenty-five years, Carnegie Corporation has devoted much attention and a great deal of its resources toward better understanding of child and adolescent development and toward ways of fostering positive outcomes for youth in the face of drastic changes in the American family and society. Through the grant process and the sponsorship of special study groups, the Corporation has sought to strengthen the knowledge base in child and adolescent development, to raise public awareness of the developmental needs of young people, and to offer practical solutions for improving their life chances.

Two crucially formative and comparatively neglected phases in the life span have been the object of deep concern by the foundation in the past decade. These are the first three years of life, beginning with the prenatal period, and early adolescence, covering ages ten through fourteen. Work on these two periods has resulted in several syntheses of the best available knowledge from research and practice, leading to recommendations for action by key institutions of society. The culminating reports, *Starting Points: Meeting the Needs of Our Youngest Children* (1994) and *Great Transitions: Preparing Adolescents for a New Century* (1995), have been widely disseminated to the public, and their recommendations are beginning to take effect in policies and programs throughout the nation.

Most recently, the Corporation has established a new task force to promote healthy development and education in the years from three to ten. It will examine the current condition of primary grade education, paying particular attention to strategies for making improvements in disadvantaged communities, where the need is greatest. The final report of the task force will be issued in September 1996.[1]

With this latest initiative, the Corporation's programs now cover the entire spectrum of early life, from before birth through age fourteen. Phase by developmental phase, the programs provide the basis of a cohesive developmental strategy for ensuring the health and well-being of America's children and youth.

NOTE: *The president's annual essay is a personal statement representing his own views. It does not necessarily reflect the foundation's policies.*

3. Developmental Strategy

What are the essential requirements for healthy development, and what are the principal opportunities for meeting these requirements? In what ways can families be strengthened to meet the developmental needs of the nation's young? What extra-familial influences can help to meet them? Finally, what information, skills, and professional services can be brought to bear in ensuring healthy development under contemporary American conditions?

The Changing American Family

From time immemorial, the family has been the fundamental unit responsible for the health, education, and general well-being of children; indeed, the family has been the central organizing principle of societies everywhere. But in the United States, the structure and function of families have undergone profound changes in just the past thirty years. Some of these changes represent new opportunities and tangible benefits. Others place the well-being of children in such jeopardy as to pose a major problem for the entire society.

Today, stable, close-knit communities where people know each other well and maintain a strong ethic of mutual aid are not as common as they once were. For growing children, the intellectual and social tasks they must master are far more complex than they were in the small, simple societies of their ancestors. Young people having children are less experienced in child care than were any of their predecessors. Many start a new family without the knowledge, skills, or confidence to carry out the enduring responsibilities of competent parenthood.

In this time of accelerated change, family life has been subjected to severe strains. By 1990, more than half of all mothers of very young children, preschool as well as school-age, held jobs outside the home. Many, if not most, parents are having difficulty integrating work and family responsibilities. Close to half the children of married parents have lived through divorce by the time they reach age sixteen. The majority of American children have spent at least part of their childhood in a single-parent family. Compared with other countries, the United States has come to exhibit a kind of revolving-door pattern of repeated marriages and divorces, and of multiple attachments and disruptions, that is placing the development of children and adolescents at serious risk of long-term damage.

An additional strain on families is the diminished time that parents spend with their children. Not only are mothers at home much less than they were thirty years ago, but there is very little evidence that fathers are devoting more time to their children to compensate. Moreover, only about 5 percent of American children see a grandparent regularly. Children spend a vast amount of time during their years of most rapid growth and development gazing at the violence-drenched mixture of reality and fantasy presented by television. Young adolescents often lack the leadership, mentorship, and support of responsible, caring adults that they still need — and say they want.

With such dramatic shifts in the nature of family life, it is not surprising that surveys of public opinion indicate that American parents across all social classes are troubled about raising their children. Two-thirds of them report they are less willing than their own parents were to make sacrifices for the next generation.

A major consequence of this metamorphosis has been that children are becoming a responsibility shared by members of the family with other individuals and institutions. Just as the economic functions of the family moved out of the home early in the Industrial Revolution, so is child care to a large extent moving beyond the home. A child's development is less and less under parents' and grandparents' direct supervision and more and more in the hands of near strangers. The people who can meet the fundamental developmental needs of children and adolescents are still largely available within the young person's immediate or extended family. But other adults — health care providers, teachers, community and church workers, even business leaders — are increasingly being called upon to help provide the necessary conditions for healthy development.

1. THE SOCIAL CONTEXTS OF MULTICULTURAL EDUCATION

The Conditions for Fostering Healthy Development

A good start marks the beginning of hope. A poor start can leave an enduring legacy of impairment, and the high costs may show up in the various systems of health care, education, and juvenile justice. We call these impairments by many names: disease, disability, ignorance, incompetence, hatred, violence. By whatever name, such outcomes entail severe economic and social penalties for the nation.

During their earliest years of growth and development, children need dependable attachment to parents or other adult caregivers; they need protection, guidance, stimulation, nurturance, and skills to cope with adversity. Infants in particular need caregivers who can promote attachment and thereby instill the fundamentals of decent human relationships throughout the life span. Young adolescents, too, need to connect with people who can guide their momentous transition to adulthood with sensitivity and understanding.

In an ideal world, all children grow up in an intact, cohesive family, dependable in every crunch. They flourish in a multifaceted parent–child relationship with at least one parent who is consistently nurturing and loving and able to enjoy child rearing, teaching, and coping. They inhabit a reasonably predictable adult environment that fosters gradual preparation for adult life. They have extended family members who are available to lend a hand. They are part of a supportive community or larger group beyond the family, whether it be a neighborhood, religious, ethnic, or political group.

Conditions such as these greatly enhance the odds that young people will pursue lifelong learning, acquire constructive skills, be in good health, develop valued human attributes, including prosocial behavior, and have a tangible basis for envisioning an attractive future in which they can recognize and seize opportunities.

Approximating these optimal conditions is an immense task for the parents or other caregiver in any family. For families struggling alone, the challenge is exceedingly difficult. Child raising takes time and care, protection and guidance, experimentation, and learning from experience. Above all, it is an enduring commitment—one that is fundamentally rewarding, if often frustrating.

The institutions beyond the family that have the greatest influence on child and adolescent development are the schools, community organizations including religious ones, health care institutions, and the media. Are there a few essential requirements for healthy development that most families can meet with the support of these pivotal institutions?

Within the scientific and professional communities, an important consensus has, in fact, emerged on ways that parents and others can cooperate in coping with the developmental needs of children and young adolescents. Evidence is accumulating that a range of preventive interventions involving frontline institutions can set a young person onto the paths toward healthy, constructive adulthood. Beginning with early and comprehensive prenatal care, these measures include well-baby medical care, emphasizing disease prevention and health promotion; home visits by human service professionals, especially in homes with very young children; parent education to strengthen competence and build close parent–child relationships; parent support networks that provide mutual aid in fostering health and education for their children and themselves; child care of high quality outside the home, especially in day care centers; preschool education, modeled on Head Start, that combines parental involvement with disease prevention and the stimulation of cognitive and social skills; and enhanced elementary education and middle grade education—education that is developmentally appropriate, that fosters fundamental skills, and that encourages good health practices.

Altogether, such opportunities have strong potential to prevent damage of many kinds as reflected in indices of health and education. A few selected interventions are highlighted below.

Preventing Damage in the Earliest Years

PRENATAL CARE

Prenatal care — now absent or inadequate for at least a quarter of pregnant American women — has a powerful capacity to prevent fetal damage, including brain damage, which can lead to so many tragic outcomes. At its best, prenatal care is a two-generation intervention that serves both children and parents, provides social supports, and incorporates vigorous efforts to reach young women early.

In addition to medical care for the mother and the developing fetus, an essential component of good-quality prenatal care is education of the parents. Prenatal education makes use of the distinctive motivation of the pregnant mother as well as the new father to strengthen their knowledge and skill in caring for themselves and their prospective baby. In combination with social support services, which can link clients to job training and formal schooling, among other benefits, it can substantially improve prospects for the future of the young family.

Especially in poor communities, young parents need a dependable person who can provide social support for health and education through the months of pregnancy and beyond. This can be organized as a systematic intervention drawing upon women who are from the community and who have relevant experiences in child rearing. When given a modicum of training and supervision, these women can offer personal support and practical guidance to poor young mothers.

CHILD CARE

As child rearing moves beyond the home, the quality of outside care becomes crucial. The vast majority of responsible parents are eager to ensure that such care facilitates their child's healthy development. The crucial factor in quality of care is the nature and behavior of the caregiver. Just as parents want a competent doctor to foster their child's health, so they desire a capable caregiver who can understand and meet their child's developmental needs. In practice, this is difficult to achieve, even for affluent parents.

With the surge in demand for child care, those trying to provide it have eagerly sought to develop competent caregivers. But even with the best of intentions, this field has been characterized by low pay, low respect, minimal training, minimal supervision, and extremely variable quality. Although most child care workers try very hard to do a decent job, the plain fact is that many of them do not stay in their positions very long, and this in itself puts a child's development in jeopardy. Especially in settings for young children, in which dependable long-term caretaking relationships are essential, high staff turnover is all too common.

In 1994 the Corporation's task force report, *Starting Points*, underscored the importance of four basic approaches to meeting the needs of the youngest children: preparation for responsible parenthood; preventive health care; the enhanced quality and availability of child care — for example, through cooperative networks and professional training; and stronger community supports for families.

The report suggests ways of mobilizing intersectoral cooperation within communities toward the well-being of children — a difficult but not impossible task. Agents of change that can potentially cooperate include family–child resource centers; federal, state, and local councils for children; and educational institutions and businesses. Together they can assess specific needs and formulate ways of meeting them; seek ways to integrate educational, health, and social services in communities; and promote the direct involvement of local businesses, media organizations, and key professions in children's healthy development.

Early Adolescence: A Time of Opportunity and Risk

Early adolescence is one of the most striking developmental experiences in the entire life span. What does this transition mean? It means going beyond childhood toward the distant goal of becoming an adult. There is a chasm between these two great phases of life, and it takes a mighty leap to get across. How do our children learn to make the leap? What help do they need in making it? Who helps — or fails to help — in this risky process? Why do so many fall into the chasm, never making it to healthy, constructive, productive adult life?

It is a disturbing fact that about one quarter of our youth are at high risk for rotten futures from educational failure, serious injury, disease, and economic incompetence. Another quarter are at moderate risk for such outcomes. Some of the risks, like the crashes of drunken driving, are rapidly translated into damage. Other risks are like a time bomb set in youth that explodes later, as in cancer and heart disease, which follow from risk-taking habits shaped in adolescence.

The Carnegie Council on Adolescent Development, formed in 1986, illuminated this sadly neglected but fateful phase of life, sounding a powerful alarm for the nation in its concluding report, *Great Transitions*. Most of the report describes practical measures that can feasibly be taken to prevent the damage now crippling so many lives.

The council was composed of leaders from different sectors of American society who drew together the most reliable information about adolescent development, focusing on health, education, and the social environment. It tackled serious adolescent problems by seeking preventive interventions based, to the extent possible, on systematic research and also on careful assessment of creative innovations.

The problems adolescents face are occurring across all segments of the youth population; no part of the society is exempt from the casualties. Among the more disquieting signs is the emergence in younger adolescents of very high-risk behaviors that were once associated with older groups: smoking, alcohol use, sexual activity, alienation from school, even involvement with deadly weapons.

Early adolescence is a time of profound biological transformation and social transition characterized by exploratory behavior, much of it adaptive and expected for this age group. But carried to extremes, and especially if it becomes habitual, such behavior can have lifelong consequences. Many dangerous patterns, in fact, commonly emerge during these years.

Initially, adolescents explore these new possibilities tentatively, with the experimental attitude that is typical of adolescence. Before damaging behavior is firmly established, therefore, there is a unique opportunity to prevent lifelong casualties.

What does it take to become a healthy, problem-solving, constructive adult? Young adolescents on an effective developmental path must

▶ Find a valued place in a constructive group.

▶ Learn how to form close, durable human relationships.

▶ Earn a sense of worth as a person.

▶ Achieve a reliable basis for making informed choices.

▶ Express constructive curiosity and exploratory behavior.

▶ Find ways of being useful to others.

▶ Believe in a promising future with real opportunities.

▶ Cultivate the inquiring and problem-solving habits of the mind necessary for lifelong learning and adaptability.

▶ Learn to respect democratic values and responsible citizenship.

▶ Build a healthy lifestyle.

The work of the council has consistently addressed ways in which these requirements can be met by a conjunction of frontline institutions that powerfully shape adolescent development, for better and worse. They begin with the family but include schools, the health sector, community organizations, and the media. How can we move the balance of these influences from worse to better? The council's recommendations for each of these institutions are not utopian or hypothetical. Working models can be observed in some communities, a few of which have been scrutinized by evaluative research. The challenge is to expand them to meet the nation's needs.

STRENGTHENING FAMILIES FOR ADOLESCENT DEVELOPMENT

Parental involvement in school activities declines steadily as children progress to middle school and later to high school. School personnel often discourage such involvement, and many parents consider it inappropriate after a child reaches middle school age, or they do not make the time. Schools should regard the families of students as allies and cultivate their support. Together with other community institutions, they can create parent support groups, parent education programs, and education for prospective parents. Parents, for their part, must recognize the need to remain actively engaged in their adolescents' education.

Additionally, employers, both public and private, can pursue more family-friendly policies for parents with young adolescents. Health professionals should also be more active in helping parents understand ways of renegotiating their relationship with their developing adolescent, so that they remain deeply interested and supportive while accepting more adult-to-adult modes.

CREATING DEVELOPMENTALLY APPROPRIATE SCHOOLS

Research has shown the value of developmentally appropriate education for children and young adolescents, which means that the content and process of learning should mesh with the interests and capacities of the child. Specifically, it means the creation of schools of small units, or schools within schools, which can offer sustained individual attention to the developing adolescent in the context of a supportive group. In such schools, students learn decent human relations through the techniques of cooperative learning and supervised community service. Curiosity and thinking skills are stimulated through study of the life sciences. Education and health are linked, each nourishing the other.

The life sciences, emphasizing a distinctively human biology, can provide a salient organizing principle for middle grade education. These sciences can tap into the natural curiosity of young adolescents, who have good reason to be particularly interested in development since they are experiencing the early adolescent growth spurt. A curriculum focused on human biology should naturally include the scientific study of behavior, particularly behavior that bears strongly on health throughout the life span. Connected to life-skills training and social supports, courses in the life sciences can diminish the likelihood that a young person will engage in health-damaging behaviors.

SCHOOLS AS HEALTH-PROMOTING ENVIRONMENTS

Middle grade schools should provide clear examples of health-promoting behavior, means of social reinforcement for such behavior, and encouragement of healthful habits. They should clarify the nature of good nutrition in the classroom and serve well-balanced meals in the cafeteria. They should be smoke free and offer programs to help students and adults stop smoking. Demonstrating the effects of alcohol and illicit drugs on the brain and other organs should be an integral part of education and school practices.

Physical fitness should be a matter of pride for all in the school community. Opportunities for exercise and athletics should not be limited to varsity competition between different schools. Schools should join with parks and recreation departments to provide a variety of physical activities, so that every student can participate actively.

Schools must be safe places. Stopping violence, drug dealing, and the carrying of weapons in and around schools are an urgent challenge. Nonviolent conflict resolution should become a vital part of curriculum and school practices. Indeed, the curriculum and school practices should be closely allied over the whole range of health-relevant behavior.

1. THE SOCIAL CONTEXTS OF MULTICULTURAL EDUCATION

ENSURING ACCESS TO HEALTH SERVICES

There is a serious unmet need for accessible health care among young adolescents. Health clinics may be established at the schools or, if nearby, functionally connected with the school. Such services should be clearly recognizable to middle grade students and be user friendly. Local option is important in order to recognize and respect the diversity that exists among American communities. Though sexual behavior is controversial, reproductive health is a modest but significant part of adolescent health. This cannot be avoided in an era of AIDS and adolescent pregnancy.

It is essential to train health and education professionals with a thorough understanding of the developmental needs and behavior-related problems of adolescents. Historically, the relevant professions have skimped in preparing for the specific needs and opportunities of this crucially formative phase.

LIFE-SKILLS TRAINING

Middle grade schools can provide their students with the knowledge and skills to make informed, deliberate decisions. Such information, combined with training in interpersonal skills and decision making, can help students resist pressure from peers or from the media; relieve distress without engaging in dangerous activity; learn how to make friends if they are isolated; and develop and use conflict resolution skills to avoid violence, yet assert themselves effectively. Such life skills are pertinent to a wide range of health-relevant behavior, especially to the prevention of smoking and other substance abuse in early adolescence.

SOCIAL SUPPORTS IN EARLY ADOLESCENCE

A variety of organizations and institutions can provide supplements or surrogates for parents, older siblings, and relatives. Across the country, there are many examples of such interventions. Some are based in churches, such as the initiatives of the Congress of National Black Churches; some are based in community organizations, like the Girls Clubs. Others involve youth service, like the Campus Compact based in colleges and universities; still others are based in minority organizations. The central point is that churches, schools, community organizations, and businesses can build constructive social support networks that attract disadvantaged youngsters. These networks can foster young people's health, their education, and their capacity to be accepted rather than rejected by the mainstream society and can offer them healthy alternatives to substance abuse and violent gang membership.

OPPORTUNITIES IN THE NONSCHOOL HOURS

Communities must seek to provide attractive, safe, growth-promoting settings for young adolescents during the out-of-school hours — times of high risk when parents are often not available to supervise their children. More than 17,000 national and local youth organizations, including those sponsored by religious groups, now operate in the United States, but they do not adequately serve the needs of this age group.

These organizations must now work to expand their reach to youth in all communities, offering more activities that convey information about life chances, careers, and places beyond the neighborhood, and engaging them in community service and other constructive opportunities that foster education and health.

CONSTRUCTIVE POTENTIAL OF THE MEDIA

The undeniable power of the media could be used far more constructively than it is in the lives of young adolescents. Families, schools, and community organizations can help young people become "media literate" so they can examine media messages thoughtfully and critically. Public and professional organizations can work with media organizations in developing health-promoting programming and media campaigns for youth. Such organizations can support social actions that discourage the media from glamorizing violence and sex as well as drinking, smoking, and other drug use. Independent experts in child and adolescent development, health, and education can link up with news and entertainment leaders, striving for accurate, informative, and constructive portrayals of youth in the media.

ADDITIONAL STEPS

In the final chapter of *Great Transitions*, the Carnegie Council challenges the powerful sectors of society with ideas for what they can do to implement the recommendations of the report. Government at all levels, businesses, universities, and scientific and professional organizations will in the end have to offer substantial, sustained help to the frontline institutions, or the casualties will keep increasing and the nation will suffer altogether. Most of the efforts sketched in this essay could be strengthened by changes in science policy that would place a high priority on research on adolescent development, on the risk factors associated with early adolescence, and on preventive interventions.

Concluding Comments

Those institutions that have a major shaping influence on the young — families, schools, the health sector, community organizations, and the media — must join forces in adapting to the transforming requirements of the late twentieth century. Much could be achieved in this vast, heterogeneous nation of ours if we thought of our entire population as a very large extended family, tied by history to a shared destiny and requiring a strong ethic of mutual aid. The central question is: Can we do better than we are doing now?

In the long run, the vitality of any society and its prospects for the future depend on the quality of its people — on their knowledge and skill, their health and vigor, and the decency of their human relations. Preventing much of the damage now occurring would, therefore, have powerfully beneficial social and economic impacts, resulting in a more effective work force, higher productivity, lowered health costs, lowered prison costs, and so much relief of human suffering!

In an era when there is well-founded concern about losing a vital sense of community, the initiatives sketched here can also have the profound collateral benefits of building national solidarity, a mutual-aid ethic, and a reasonable basis for hope among people of all ages. What can bring us together better than our children? If there were any mission more important, I wonder what it could be.

PRESIDENT

Note

[1] The Carnegie Task Force on Learning in the Primary Grades was created in January 1994 with a membership of twenty-three leaders in child development, education, business, government, and the media. It is cochaired by Dr. Shirley M. Malcom and Admiral James S. Watkins, both trustees of Carnegie Corporation. The executive director is Antony Ward.

References

Carnegie Council on Adolescent Development. 1995. *Great Transitions: Preparing Adolescents for a New Century*. Concluding report of the Carnegie Council on Adolescent Development. New York: Carnegie Corporation of New York.

Carnegie Task Force on Meeting the Needs of Young Children. 1994. *Starting Points: Meeting the Needs of Our Youngest Children*. Report of the Carnegie Task Force on Meeting the Needs of Young Children. New York: Carnegie Corporation of New York.

Hamburg, David A. 1992. *Today's Children: Creating a Future for a Generation in Crisis*. New York: Times Books, Random House.

THE END OF INTEGRATION

A four-decade effort is being abandoned, as exhausted courts and frustrated blacks dust off the concept of "separate but equal"

JAMES S. KUNEN

IN ROOM CCII (MAKE THAT 202) OF Martin Luther King Latin Grammar Middle School in Kansas City, Missouri, Ms. Dickerson's rhetoric students are engaged in a public-speaking contest. Sixth-grader Jo Ann Carter, dressed in the school uniform of white blouse and plaid skirt, has chosen a speech by the school's eponym: "If something isn't done, and in a hurry, to bring the colored peoples of the world out of their long years of poverty, their long years of hurt and neglect," she declaims forcefully, "the whole world is doomed."

Jo Ann's mother Catherine Carter looks on approvingly. Jo Ann has earned all A's except for a B in phys ed, and her mother's got the report cards in her pocketbook to prove it. "I was lucky to get her into this school," says Carter, a medical secretary. King, a one-story brick building in a ramshackle area well east of Troost Avenue—Kansas City's approximate racial dividing line—offers an enriched program of classical language and related subjects such as rhetoric. "Well, not lucky— I lied. She didn't get in the first time, so I applied again and said she was white."

This is what things have come to in the latter days of school desegregation in Kansas City. For the sake of desegregation, blacks are sometimes barred from the most popular schools on account of their race, lest they tilt the enrollment too far from the goal of 35% white students. Like most urban systems, the Kansas City, Missouri, School District (KCMSD) has lost white students to the suburbs in droves, which has made the task of achieving racial balance nearly impossible. After deciding that inner-city students could not be bused out to the suburbs as part of a mandatory desegregation plan, a federal district court ordered the state and KCMSD to spend $1.7 billion to create a topnotch system, in part to lure suburban whites. Then, last June, the Supreme Court decreed that the district court had no authority to order expenditures aimed at attracting suburban whites.

When the history of court-ordered school desegregation is written, Kansas City may go down as its Waterloo. Said to be the nation's most ambitious and expensive magnet plan, Kansas City's effort is unlikely to be matched anywhere. In fact, the high court's action has accelerated the pace at which cities across the country are moving to undo mandatory desegregation (*see map*). And the federal judiciary, which long staked its authority on the enforcement of desegregation orders, appears eager to depart the field. Chris Hansen of the American Civil Liberties Union in New York City observes, "The courts are saying, 'We still agree with the goal of school desegregation, but it's too hard, and we're tired of it, and we give up.'"

After two decades of progress toward integration, the separation of black children in America's schools is on the rise and is in fact approaching the levels of 1970, before the first school bus rolled at the order of a court. Nationally, fully a third of black public school students attend schools where the enrollment is 90% to 100% minority—that is, black, Hispanic, Asian and Native American. In the Northeast, the country's most segregated region, half of all black students attend such schools. "We have already seen the maximum amount of racial mixing in public schools that will exist in our lifetime," says University of Indiana law professor Kevin Brown, an expert on race and education. The combination of legal revisionism and residential segregation is effectively ending America's bold attempt to integrate the public schools.

This historic reversal has been welcomed by many in the African-American community. In some cities—Denver, for example—the dismantling of mandatory desegregation has been initiated by black leaders, since it is often black children who bear the brunt of such plans—forced to travel long distances to schools where they may not be welcome. In Yonkers, New York, late last year the local leader of the N.A.A.C.P. was suspended by the national organization for declaring that busing had outlived its usefulness. Clinton Adams Jr., a black attorney who is sufficiently abrasive to qualify as a militant in Kansas City—a town so even-tempered that car horns are blown only to warn of impending collisions—takes an even harder line. "The most egregious injustice is the situation where suburban white kids get priority over resident African-American kids, who are the adjudicated victims of segregation," he says. "That's atrocious. Just to try to achieve some kind of mythical benefit that black kids will receive by sitting next to a white kid?"

HOMER A. PLESSY, DESCRIBED IN COURT papers as "of mixed descent, in the proportion of seven-eighths Caucasian and one-eighth African blood," bought himself a

4. End of Integration

1954, TOPEKA Linda Brown attends segregated Monroe Elementary School after being denied admission to a white school. The Supreme Court's *Brown v. Board of Education* decision later declared dual school systems unconstitutional

first-class ticket from New Orleans to Covington, Louisiana, and took a seat reserved for whites on the East Louisiana Railway. He was jailed for violating an exquisitely even-handed, race-neutral statute that forbade members of either race to occupy accommodations set aside for the other—with the exception of "nurses attending the children of the other race." Plessy insisted he was white, and when that failed, argued that criminal-court judge John H. Ferguson had violated his constitutional right to the equal protection of the laws.

In its ruling on *Plessy v. Ferguson*, announced May 18, 1896, the Supreme Court declared laws mandating that "equal but separate" treatment of the races "do not necessarily imply the inferiority of either race," and cited the widely accepted propriety of separate schools for white and colored children. In dissent, Justice John Harlan remarked, "The thin disguise of 'equal' accommodations ... will not mislead any one, nor atone for the wrong this day done."

But the thin disguise endured for a half-century, until a series of school-segregation cases culminating in *Brown v. Board of Education of Topeka*. "Separate educational facilities are inherently unequal" and violate the Constitution's equal-protection guarantee, a unanimous Supreme Court ruled on May 17, 1954. A year later, the court ruled that school districts must admit black students on a nondiscriminatory basis "with all deliberate speed" and instructed the federal district courts to retain jurisdiction "during this period of transition."

THE NATION IS STILL IN THAT period of transition, observes Kenneth Clark, 81, the black sociologist upon whose work the *Brown* decision in part relied. "I didn't realize how deep racism was in America, and I suppose the court didn't realize it either," he says. Ten years after *Brown*, when only 2% of black children in the South attended schools with whites, the court announced, "The time for mere 'deliberate speed' has run out." In 1968 the court declared that discrimination must be "eliminated root and branch." In 1971, noting that about 40% of American schoolchildren routinely rode buses to and from school anyway, the court held in *Swann v. Charlotte-Mecklenburg Board of Education* that the federal courts could order busing to desegregate schools.

Busing broke the back of segregation in the South, where 36.4% of black students attended majority-white schools by 1972. But Chief Justice Warren Burger's opinion in *Swann* also opened the door for the federal courts to get out of the integration business. Once legally enforced segregation was eliminated, he wrote, single-race schools would not offend the Constitution unless some agency of the government had deliberately resegregated them.

Since the end of World War II, as blacks have streamed into the cities in search of work, whites have streamed out—in search of greener lawns and whiter neighbors. Anytime blacks were able to breach the wall of restrictive covenants, brokers' steering and mortgage redlining to begin to integrate a neighborhood, white flight and resegregation quickly followed. By 1970, with the white birthrate plunging, Northern urban school districts, which seldom extend beyond city limits, lacked enough white children to desegregate.

A dearth of whites led a federal court to order the city of Detroit to integrate its schools with those of 53 surrounding districts. In 1974 the Supreme Court struck down that order, holding in *Milliken v. Bradley* that suburban districts could not be ordered to help desegregate a city's schools unless those suburbs had been involved in illegally segregating them in the first place. Justice Thurgood Marshall warned in dissent that the court had set a course that would allow "our great metropolitan areas to be divided up each into two cities—one white, the other black ..."

That is exactly what happened. School segregation exacerbated residential segregation, as whites chose not to live in neighborhoods served by predominantly minority schools. Detroit's public school system is now 94% minority. By 1990, in the 18 largest Northern metropolitan areas, blacks had become so isolated that 78% of them would have had to move in order to achieve an evenly distributed residential pattern. The *Milliken* ruling, says Indiana University's Brown, "eliminated all hope of meaningful desegregation in most of the country's major urban areas."

This was the state of affairs when, in 1976, the Federal Government threatened to cut off funds to the KCMSD because it had maintained a dual system of segregated schools. Pro-integration kitchen-table activists who had won control of the KCMSD school board responded by suing suburban school districts and the State of Missouri, arguing that they had worked to confine blacks to the inner city.

Until the *Brown* decision, schools were segregated by law in Missouri; after it, the state allowed desegregation at the discretion of local school boards. Many of the suburban districts (parts of which extended into the city) had not allowed blacks to attend high school, forcing black families to move into central Kansas City in search of education. As the city's minority population grew, the KCMSD redrew school-attendance zones hundreds of times and bused some black children far from their neighborhoods in order to keep the races apart.

Federal District Judge Russell G. Clark, a conservative Democrat, ruled that the state and KCMSD had violated the Constitution, but he dropped the outer districts from the case, finding insufficient proof that they had acted illegally—a decision he would have cause to regret. "The very minute I let those suburban school districts out, I created a very severe problem for the court and for myself, really, in trying to come up with a remedial plan to integrate the Kansas City, Missouri, School District," the judge reflected years later. "The more salt you have, the more white you can turn the pepper. And without any salt, or with a limited amount of salt, you're going to end up with a basically black mixture."

KCMSD's only remaining hope for racial balance was a system of magnet schools designed to lure whites back from private schools and the suburban districts. In 1986 Judge Clark ordered such a plan. After the KCMSD's enrollment became majority black in 1970, the district's voters, who remained majority white, had allowed the schools to literally fall apart, rejecting funding initiatives 19 times while pipes burst and ceilings collapsed. In addition to smaller classes and higher teacher salaries, Judge Clark's order required renovation of 55 schools and construction of 17. When the school district failed to come up with its quarter of the cost—Clark had laid three-quarters of the bill on the state—the judge took the unusual step of doubling the local property tax. The money bought, among other things, a planetarium, radio and TV studios, and 1,000 computers for Central High School's 1,069 students. Central, which before Clark's order was awash in broken toilets and overrun by rodents, now occupies a $32 million building that resembles a small city's airline terminal and features an Olympic-size swimming pool.

The KCMSD's annual per-pupil expenditure, excluding capital costs, reached

1. THE SOCIAL CONTEXTS OF MULTICULTURAL EDUCATION

$9,412 last year, an amount exceeded by perhaps 40 of the nation's 14,881 school districts. All together, as of this February, $1.7 billion has been spent under court order in Kansas City.

Sugar Creek Elementary is a French-immersion school. An integrated teaching staff of native French speakers recruited from France, Belgium, Canada, Haiti, Egypt and Cameroon keep the children speaking only French, from the Pledge of Allegiance (*"Je déclare fidélité au drapeau des Etats-Unis..."*) through recess to the end of the day. The kids even talk out of turn in French. "They're so eager to learn everything, they pick it up like a sponge," says Kindergarten teacher Janet Lawrence.

A third of the students are white, and a third of those come from outside the district—transported by parents such as Virgil Adams. (The state stopped paying for transportation into the district this year).

1957, LITTLE ROCK National Guard troops called out by Arkansas Governor Orval Faubus kept black students out of Central High School. A court ordered the Guard withdrawn, and President Eisenhower sent federal troops to escort the black kids in

Adams or his wife makes a 28-mile round-trip drive twice a day from Blue Springs, a suburb of tidy lawns and two-car garages, so that Sarah can go to second grade and William to third at Sugar Creek. They were drawn by the foreign-language instruction, but Adams, an FBI agent based in Kansas city, sees the social mix itself as an important advantage. "Somewhere on the news one night the word nigger was used," he recalls. "My son asked me what it meant. I thought that was great; if he'd been around my dad three or four days in a row, he'd have known. We didn't want to bring up our kids that way.

For all its moral appeal, however, the Kansas City plan's achievements appear modest when weighed against its enormous expense. The number of out-of-district white children enrolled at the magnet schools peaked at 1,476 last year. Standardized test scores have registered slight gains. White flight, while substantially slowed, has not been reversed: in 1985, the

---

THE NEED FOR A TOUGHER KIND OF HEROISM

By J. ANTHONY LUKAS

AT THE CREST OF BOSTON'S BEACON Hill, a bronze monument portrays Colonel Robert Gould Shaw leading the black soldiers of the 54th Massachusetts Volunteer Infantry in their assault on Fort Wagner, South Carolina, in July 1863—a battle that cost the young aristocrat and nearly a hundred of his troops their lives. When the Union army asked for his body, a Confederate officer replied, "We have buried him with his niggers," Shaw's sacrifice—memorialized by the poet James Russell Lowell as a "death for noble ends"—has become an emblem of the lofty idealism that inspired New England's 19th century abolitionists and their 20th century descendants in the civil rights and school-desegregation battles.

In the 1960s and 1970s, those movements enlisted the energies of some of that generation's finest young whites, eager to express their altruistic impulses, to live and, if necessary, to die for noble ends. But from the late '60s on, the role of white liberals was circumscribed by the rise of black nationalists, who suspected that Northern whites were as eager to put their own virtue on display as to seek self-determination for Southern blacks. After all, the Shaw monument portrays the young colonel with his patrician features, astride his prancing steed, while his swarthy soldiers follow obediently. As the 20th century moved toward its close, most American blacks no longer saw this as the model for relations between the races.

Now the relentless tides of demographic change in most large American cities have eroded the gains made during the school-desegregation era. In 1972—the year blacks sued to desegregate Boston's schools—some 90,000 students were enrolled in the public system, 54,000 of them white. As of September 1995, some 63,000 students remained, barely 18% white. What does it mean to say that one is for integration in a school system so configured?

The *Milliken v. Bradley* decision laid the groundwork for today's desegregation conundrum. Had Boston's federal district court been able to embrace the school systems of such storied American communities as Concord and Lexington, there would have been more whites with whom to integrate and less criticism that Judge Arthur Garrity's order did little more than mix "poor blacks" with "poor whites." But it would be naive to imagine that most suburban whites would obediently put their children on the bus to the inner city. Suburban families might have thrown fewer rocks than did the working-class whites of Charlestown and South Boston, but I suspect that when the dust settled, many would have put their children in private or parochial schools, or found other means of evading the order.

Ultimately, it is futile to debate what might have been. I still believe in desegregating schools by both class and race. But since it won't happen in many places, what goal realistically remains for those who fought so bravely for desegregated schools in Little Rock, Arkansas, Boston, New Orleans and Denver? To what vision of the good society can they dedicate themselves?

As a Boston school official told me last year, "Our task is to educate the kids who're here, instead of yearning for those who have left. And, who knows, perhaps if we do a good enough job, some of those who have left may start trickling back." Call her naive, if you wish, but that strikes me as the only realistic alternative: to make the urban public schools work for whatever clientele remains. It will be a long, slogging, incredibly difficult task. Those who demonstrated their virtue with marches and vigils must now do the harder thing of raising taxes and committing public resources, which may require more genuine heroism than the theatrics of the old integration story.

J. Anthony Lukas' book on the Boston busing wars, Common Ground, *won a Pulitzer Prize in 1986.*

4. End of Integration

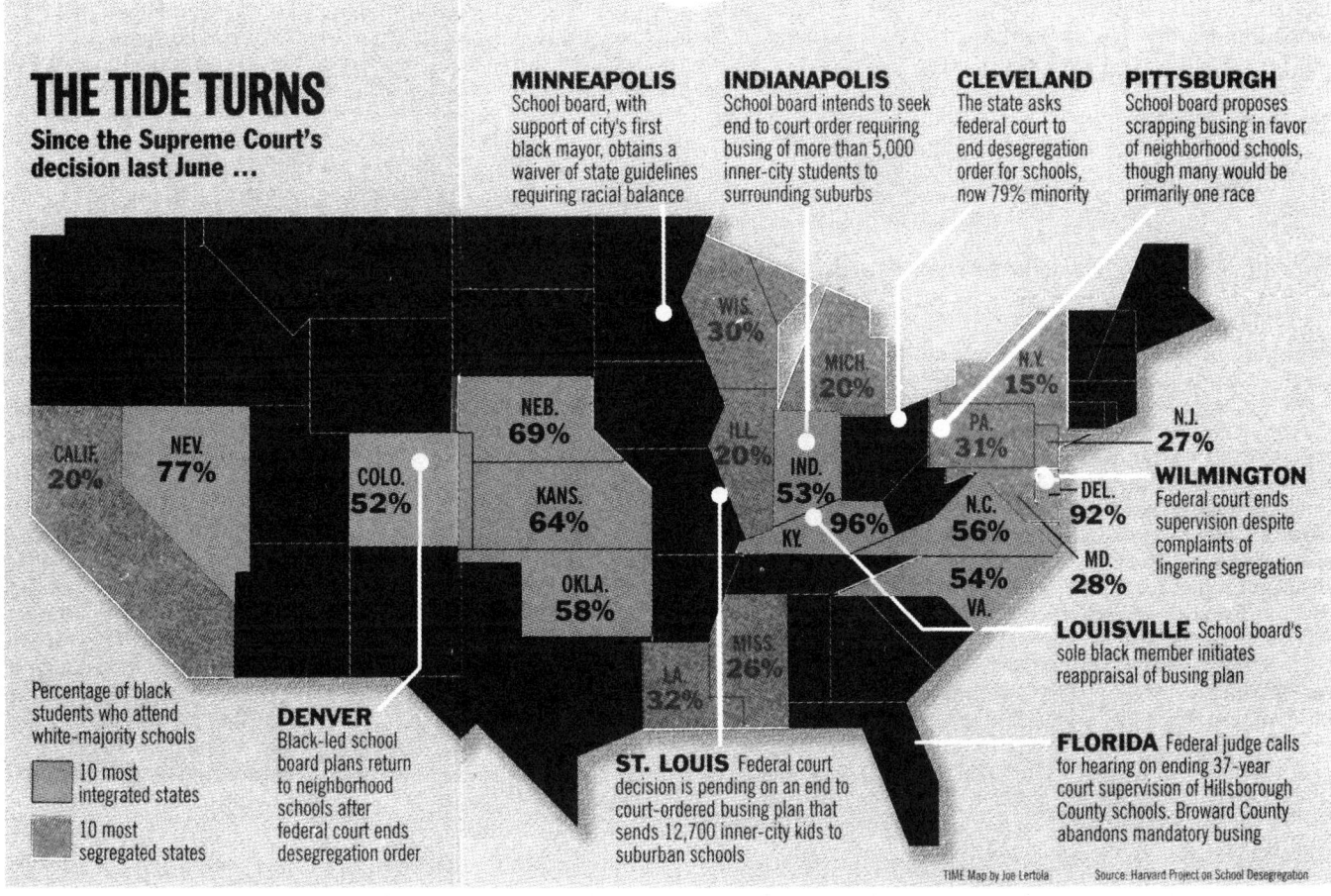

year before the magnet plan began, the district was 73.6% minority; this year it is 75.9% minority. If nothing else, horrible school facilities have been replaced with nice new ones, and for some that is justification enough. "I bet a lot of kids in Kansas City are enjoying their childhood more now that they don't have to go to schools that smell," says author Jonathan Kozol, a longtime chronicler of educational injustice. "A good society would consider that money well spent."

HIS IS NOT THE PREVAILING view in Missouri, where for the past decade candidates for just about any office have been running against what much of the electorate perceives as Judge Clark's liberal-from-hell spending spree. Attorney General Jay Nixon expresses outrage that the state has spent $2.6 billion on court-ordered school desegregation in metropolitan St. Louis and Kansas City. He is seeking "unitary status"—that is, an end to court supervision based on a judicial finding that the system is desegregated—in both cities. "I'm a Democrat, and I want to help kids' educations," he says. "But to see the fencing team in Kansas City sent to Hungary because it showed up good in the focus groups and the whites would think it's cool, is just ridiculous."

The U.S. Supreme Court evidently agrees. In *Missouri v. Jenkins*, the court held last June that Judge Clark had no authority to order the state and district to pay for a plan aimed at attracting suburban students. Chief Justice William Rehnquist pointedly reminded the district court that its ultimate goal was not to achieve racial balance but "to restore state and local authorities to the control" of the school system. Once the lingering effects of legally enforced segregation were eliminated, it would be perfectly legal for the district to run schools that happened to be all black or all white. As Justice Clarence Thomas explained, "The Constitution does not prevent individuals from choosing to live together, to work together, or to send their children to school together, so long as the State does not interfere with their choices on the basis of race."

For the KCMSD, *Missouri v. Jenkins* portends a big reduction in the state's extraordinary desegregation payments. For court-ordered desegregation generally, the decision's implications could be dire. Says associate director of the NAACP Legal Defense Fund Ted Shaw, who argued the Kansas City case before the high court: "If the courts say unitary status means school districts just have to get to the point where a desegregated snapshot can be taken, and then they can go back to the segregating school assignments they had before—if that's all *Brown* has done, it's been a big charade."

If resegregation is indeed the wave of the future, then the future can be glimpsed in Norfolk, Virginia. Norfolk won federal court approval of a return to neighborhood schools back in 1986, for the stated purpose of increasing parental involvement and arresting white flight. Black parents had sued to block the new plan because it would immediately render 10 elementary schools, many of them serving housing projects, 100% black. Sociologist David Armor, retained as an expert witness by the school board, predicted that if Norfolk's crosstown busing continued, the whole school system would soon become 75% black, making racial balance impossible. "Civil rights groups have always discounted the importance of whites," he says today, "which has always been a mystery to me. It's as though their goal were some abstract equity thing, as opposed to actual integration." The court accepted Armor's argument.

"It was turning back the clock. It was like being told you have to go to the back of

1. THE SOCIAL CONTEXTS OF MULTICULTURAL EDUCATION

the bus," recalls Lucy Wilson, then an associate dean at Old Dominion University and one of two black school-board members who initially voted against the plan. When the federal court's ruling rendered the return to neighborhood schools inevitable, Wilson and the other dissenter changed their votes in exchange for a commitment that the all-black schools would be targeted for extra resources, though Wilson doubts the promise will be kept forever. (As Harvard School of Education sociologist Gary Orfield has observed, "A less powerful group isn't going to get disproportionate resources for a very long time from a more powerful group. It requires that water flow uphill.") For the 1993-94 school year, the district's average expenditure per pupil in the black "target" elementary schools was $736 higher than at Norfolk's other elementaries, while class size averaged 20 pupils, two or three fewer than at the other schools.

Still, test scores dropped at the 10 target schools after the end of busing. In 1991 black third-graders in the target schools scored 5 percentage points lower than black third-graders in the remaining integrated elementaries on a battery of tests. Last year black third-graders in the target schools tested 10 percentage points lower.

Young Park Elementary occupies a well-kept building set among the barracks-like structures of Norfolk's Young Terrace public housing project. Of its 341 students, 98% are black and 94% are poor enough to qualify for the free-lunch program. This year so far, the parents or guardians of 60 to 70 kids have joined the PTA. "Some of the children arrive at school not knowing their full name; they just know their nickname," says principal Ruby Greer, who has managed to improve test scores and attendance. "They don't know how to hold a pencil or a book. And it seems like you never catch up."

A five-minute drive away from Young Park stands Taylor Elementary. This is the neighborhood school of white children from the large houses on the surrounding tree-lined streets; and of black children from nearby, mostly working-class neighborhoods. Sixty-one percent of Taylor's 433 children are white, and only 30% qualify for the free-lunch program. One hundred percent of the children's parents are in the PTA, which runs 22 committees. In 1994, 88% of Taylor's fourth-graders surpassed national norms on standardized tests. At Young Park, 7% did.

"The whole discussion of desegregation is corrupted by the fact that we mix up race and class," says Harvard sociologist Orfield. "You don't gain anything from sitting next to somebody with a different skin color. But you gain a lot from moving from an isolated poverty setting into a middle-class setting." National statistics provide suggestive evidence that desegregation raises blacks' academic achievement (without lowering whites'), despite its apparent failure in such high-profile cases as Yonkers—where middle-class flight left low-income students concentrated in high-poverty schools. A massive 1993 Department of Education study of Chapter One, the compensatory-education program for poor children, found that recipients of Chapter One services in schools where at least three-quarters of the children were poor scored substantially lower in math and reading than recipients attending schools where fewer than half were poor.

And, in fact, since the onset of widespread desegregation in 1971, black 17-year-olds have closed roughly a third of the reading-score gap that separated them from whites. A soon-to-be-released study by Debora Sullivan and Robert L. Crain of Teachers College, Columbia University, reports that among 32 states, the gap between black and white fourth-grade reading scores is narrowest in West Virginia and Iowa, where blacks are least isolated from whites, and largest in Michigan and New York, where blacks are the most racially isolated.

Crain and others have found, however, that academic-achievement tests are only one measure of what schools offer—another important one being what researchers call "life chances." The "great barrier to black social and economic mobility is isolation from the opportunities and networks of the middle class," Crain says. School desegregation puts minority students in touch with people who can open doors to colleges and careers.

In 1966 a randomly selected group of kindergarten-through-fifth-grade low-income students in Hartford, Connecticut, nearly all of them black, were offered the opportunity to attend school in a dozen virtually all-white suburbs. Sixteen years later, researchers tracked down more than a thousand of those who had been tapped for the program and a like number of those who had not. Crain found that males in the test group were significantly more likely to have completed two or more years of college and less likely to have dropped out of high school or got in trouble with the police, and females were less likely to have had a child before age 18.

School desegregation also leads to housing desegregation, not only by promoting tolerance but also, to put it bluntly, by making it impossible to avoid an integrated school by choosing where you live. According to a study by Louisville's Fair Housing Council, Jefferson County's school-desegregation program reduced residential segregation to such an extent that by 1990, though only 17% of the area's residents were black, a mere one-quarter of 1% of the population lived in a census tract without black neighbors.

But in the case of Louisville, a great desegregation success story, the city and suburbs are in a single school district. In most Northern cities, white flight has undermined even the best efforts at racial balance, and the measurable benefits of desegregation programs have been spottier—while the burdens, particularly on black students, have often been enormous. There has always been some preference in the black community, as in the white, for neighborhood schools (though these may be more an ideal than a reality for the children of the poor, who tend to move, or be moved, a great deal). And there is a realistic pessimism about the prospects for integration. Says the Legal Defense Fund's Shaw: "My sense is a lot of people are saying, 'We're tired of chasing white folks. It's not worth the price we have to pay.' "

EDWARD NEWSOME, AN AFRICAN-American lawyer in the real estate business who himself attended a segregated school in Texas, is a leader of the anti–magnet plan coalition that has dominated the Kansas City school board since 1994. He feels the underlying assumptions of desegregation are patronizing to blacks—as does Justice Thomas. "It never ceases to amaze me," wrote Thomas in his *Missouri v. Jenkins* concurrence, "that the courts are so willing to assume that anything that is predominantly black must be inferior."

Says Newsome: "I welcomed the Supreme Court decision. I saw it as an opportunity for the first time in years to focus on removing the vestiges of segregation. For 10 years we've concentrated on bringing in white kids. There's been no Afrocentric-themed magnet school because it doesn't appeal to white folks."

The J.S. Chick Elementary School represents the kind of school Newsome thinks there should be more of. Chick, whose African-centered program was fashioned by its enterprising principal, Audrey Bullard, occupies a bleak, brown brick building in a rundown east-side neighborhood of Kansas City. Ninety-eight percent of Chick's 327 students are black. "With a Eurocentric curriculum, it appears one race is

---

1975, LOUISVILLE Antibusing demonstrators battle police on the first day of court-ordered busing between city and suburbs. Now Jefferson County schools are among the nation's most integrated, but some parents are disenchanted with a system that requires long, arduous bus rides to school

4. End of Integration

superior over the others," says Bullard. "The African-centered curriculum makes them feel, 'I'm a part of this. I'm not on the outside looking in.'" Something must be working: Chick's students outscore some of the magnet schools' pupils on standardized tests.

On a recent morning in Lola Franklin's third-grade class, the kids are wearing paper crowns signifying their status as African kings and queens, and they are standing one after another to shout out a dizzying variety of facts. "Welcome to Guinea-Bissau! The official language is Portuguese."

"The main religion is Islam!"

"Sheep, cattle and goats are the principal animals!"

"Who can name an African-American comedian?" inquires Franklin.

"Eddie Murphy!" "Bill Cosby!"

"And some American comedians?"

"Whoopi Goldberg!"

"No, an *American* comedian," she corrects them.

"Roseanne!" a boy calls out.

"Good," says Franklin.

Clint Bolick, litigation director for the libertarian Institute for Justice in Washington, predicts court-ordered desegregation schemes will be gone in 10 to 15 years. Their fatal error was in making racial balance a goal, which eventually led to admissions preferences for whites, "turning *Brown* on its head," says Bolick. "What all this shows is that social engineering doesn't work."

But a great deal of social engineering went into creating school segregation in the first place, points out William Taylor, a Washington lawyer who has worked on civil rights cases for 40 years. Taylor laments what he sees as the courts' "peculiar notion that segregation is the natural condition and desegregation goes against the natural order of things. The court's own finding in *Brown* was that segregation had been imposed by law and practice for many years. Missouri is a good example. You have racially restrictive covenants, racially restrictive ordinances. The notion that somehow segregation came about all because of people's individual preferences is wrong."

Engineered or not, American society is facing "awesome demographic changes," says Harvard's Orfield. "In around 2050 there's going to be about half nonwhites in the total population, in 2020 about half nonwhites in the school population. We have to figure out how to run our institutions in that kind of a society. 'Separate but equal' is the most well-tried experiment in American history. It was policy for 60 years, and we have no evidence that it can work, given the distribution of power and resources in our society."

Four decades after his research helped decide the case that was supposed to change everything, perhaps Kenneth Clark still puts the issue most succinctly: "Talk about 'separate but equal,'" he says. "If they're going to be equal, why are they separate?"

といった # Putting Tongues in Check

Should bilingual schooling be silenced? Critics think so, yet a new study shows that it works

MARGOT HORNBLOWER
WESTMINSTER

IN THE SUNNY SUBURBAN SPRAWL OF Westminster, California, a city of 72,000 southeast of Los Angeles, the first-grade classrooms of the Neomia B. Willmore School offer two distinct recipes for the American melting pot. In room B-3, an English-immersion class, teacher Judy Nguyen plinks on the piano. Winsome, if off-key, her 29 charges launch into "My country 'tis of thee," fading away uncertainly as they reach the line "Land of the Pilgrims' pride." About half the children are native Vietnamese speakers; nine are Hispanic. But the book box holds the Berenstain Bears and Dr. Seuss; cheery posters list the days of the week and the months of the year—in English only. At day's end the lesson is about "contours." With crayons, the children are to outline a picture of an apple. Most comply easily, but six-year-old Tuyen, uncomprehending, gaily colors the inside of the fruit.

In Room A-2, a bilingual class, 30 first-graders, all Latinos, belt out their favorite song, *El Rancho Grande*. In the book corner: *Los Tres Cochinitos*—The Three Little Pigs. On the wall: the seasons, the months, the days, in both Spanish and English. In a mock interview, teacher Marina Williams asks Fabiola, a gap-toothed charmer, *"Señora Presidente,* what should children do in school?" Fabiola shoots back, *"Aprender inglés!"*—learn English. But one small boy has another idea: *"Bailar!"*—dance. The teacher takes the hint, winding up the day with a session of *"la quebradita,"* a sort of Mexican jitterbug.

At Willmore, 78% of the students do not speak English well enough to follow a standard American curriculum. Like thousands of public schools across the country, Willmore faces a dilemma: Should immigrant children be instructed entirely in English? Or should they be taught academic subjects in their native language while gradually learning English? For three decades, researchers have debated the complex cognitive issues.

Now, however, arguments have moved beyond pedagogy. Bilingual education is exploding into one of the nation's most divisive political issues, fueled, on one hand, by a backlash against immigration and affirmative action and, on the other, by the failures and ideological strictures of some existing bilingual programs. Last fall, for example, when Westminster officials pushed teachers to take Spanish and Vietnamese classes or face a transfer, the teachers' union organized a takeover of the school board, voting in three new members who have vowed to phase out bilingual classes such as Marina Williams'. "It is unconstitutional to force American citizens to learn a foreign language in order to keep their job," says Michael Verringia, the new school-board president.

The issue has taken on national dimensions. Last month Senate majority leader Robert Dole injected it squarely into the presidential campaign, declaring, "We must stop the practice of multilingual education as a means of instilling ethnic pride or as a therapy for low self-esteem." The red-meat rhetoric pleased conservatives, and Dole plans to introduce legislation this month declaring English the nation's "official language." But in an interview Friday, he said he will not seek to end bilingual programs so long as they "ensure that people learn English in a timely fashion." Some pending bills, however, would virtually dismantle the Federal Government's 27-year support for bilingual schooling. Congressional budget proposals would slash current bilingual education funding as much as 66%.

Leaping into the fray last week, President Clinton told a thousand cheering supporters at a Congressional Hispanic Caucus dinner, "The issue is whether or not we're going to value the culture, the traditions of everybody and also recognize that we have a solemn obligation to let these children live up to the fullest of their God-given capabilities." But the issue does not divide purely along partisan lines. Although House Speaker Newt Gingrich and G.O.P. presidential hopefuls Richard Lugar and Patrick Buchanan back the English-only movement, G.O.P. Governor George Bush of Texas left popular bilingual programs untouched in his recent school reforms. In Florida, another key primary state, politically powerful Cuban Americans—most of whom are Republicans—were dismayed by Dole's stance. "Attacking bilingual education here is like attacking Mom and apple pie," says Mercedes Toural, head of Dade County's bilingual programs.

Nationwide, of the 43.6 million children attending public school, some 2.6 million are non-English-speaking—an increase of 76% in the past decade. As new waves of immigrants pour in, conflict grows over how to assimilate them. In New Jersey, Massachusetts, Michigan, New York, the District of Columbia and California, bilingual programs have recently been challenged by parents, teachers and school boards. Three-quarters of the young newcomers live in five states: California, New York, Florida, Texas and Illinois. Nonetheless, 43% of U.S. school districts have at least some non-English-speaking children. One in six U.S. teachers has non-English speakers in the classroom. In Columbus Junction, Iowa, where a third of the students are the offspring of Hispanic pork packers, principal Becky Furlong fears that federal budget cuts will wipe out her bilingual kindergarten. Meanwhile, at the elementary school in De Queen, Arkansas, principal Cindy Hale has no plans to teach the Latino children of local poultry workers—now a quarter of her students—in Spanish. "The quicker they adapt to speaking English, the better off they are," she says.

Twenty-one years ago, a U.S. Supreme Court decision established the constitutional precedent for bilingual education when it found that San Francisco had discriminated against 1,800 Chinese children by failing to help them overcome their linguistic handicap. Last month the legal issues seemed to come full circle as a group of Brooklyn par-

5. Tongues in Check

ents filed suit against the New York State commissioner of education, claiming that tens of thousands of children are "languishing" in poorly run bilingual programs. The suit charges that American-born children with Latino surnames and low test scores are consigned to Spanish-language classes even if their dominant language is English. Fearful of losing federal and state bilingual funds, schools allegedly pressure children to remain in bilingual classes far longer than necessary. "I missed out on three years of work," says 13-year-old Ariel Peña, who tried unsuccessfully to opt out of his school's bilingual class. Children from grades 5 through 8 were mixed in one classroom. "We had the same math book, back to page one, for two years in a row," adds Peña, a plaintiff in the suit. The state will fight the suit on the grounds that many children need more than three years of bilingual classes, but it will now review cases more carefully.

New York City schools have experienced a 49% increase in non-English-speaking immigrants in six years. Besides Spanish, classes are now taught in Chinese, Haitian Creole, Russian, Korean, Arabic, Vietnamese, Polish, Bengali and French. A few schools offer a full program in the student's native language, but most give at best an hour of native-language assistance, along with an hour of instruction in English as a Second Language (ESL). At Daniel Carter Beard Junior High in the borough of Queens, teacher Michael Cao faces a daunting task. His seventh-graders, most of whom speak little or no English, spend most of the day in mainstream classes. And then, in just 45 minutes, Cao must speed them through the baffling vocabulary they have encountered. *Energy, gasoline, electron, molecule, dilute, bubble, wave, atom*—all new words to be explained in Mandarin. And, for a slender youth in the front row, in Cantonese. In three years, under state rules, newcomers are to be fluent enough to graduate into all-day mainstream classes. In practice, few are—and schools are caught between researchers who decry the unrealistic expectations and parents who blame the bilingual programs for not fulfilling them.

WHILE PUBLIC OPINION seems polarized between sink-or-swim nostalgics and politically correct diversitarians, serious research increasingly points toward a consensus: children learn English faster and are more likely to excel academically if they are given several years of instruction in their native language first. In a 1991 study endorsed by a National Academy of Sciences research team, David Ramirez, now a professor at California State University, followed 2,000 Latino schoolchildren. "It is a myth that if you want children to learn English, you give them nothing but English," says Ramirez. Both English-immersion and bilingual methods will fail, however, if classes are too crowded, taught by unqualified teachers, lacking in appropriate materials, or filled with the wrong combination of students—conditions that are all too common.

Later this year two George Mason University professors will release the largest study ever conducted on bilingual education, comparing the performance of 42,000 non-English-speaking students over 13 years. Although states such as Massachusetts and Illinois now push students out of bilingual classes within three years, the researchers found that children who had six years of bilingual education in well-designed programs performed far better on standardized English tests in 11th grade. Even with bilingual classroom aides and ESL training, children who are plunged into an English environment before they are fluent "are just left out of the discussion in their mainstream classes," according to Professor Virginia Collier. "It shows up in the long term, when the academic going gets tough."

The George Mason study also underscores the value of bilingual education's most avant-garde experiments. The highest achievers were children at "two-way" schools, where English-language children and non-English speakers are mixed together, with half the curriculum taught in a foreign language and half taught in English. In Chicago five years ago, there were three such schools teaching in Spanish and English; today there are 20. In the District of Columbia, the Oyster Bilingual Elementary School is a pioneer in two-way education. Its student body is 58% Hispanic, 26% white, 12% black and 4% Asian, and after six years of Spanish-English curriculum, its sixth-

THE RISE OF ENGLISH ONLY

Which of these statements is closest to your views on bilingual education?

	Sept. 1993	Sept. 1995
Public schools should teach all children in English	40%	48%
Public schools should teach children in their native language only until they know enough English to join regular classes	48%	39%
Public schools should teach children in their native language as long as it helps the children learn or improves their self-esteem	11%	10%

Do you think there should be a law making English the official language of this country?	Yes 65%	No 31%

From a telephone poll of 1,000 adult Americans taken for TIME/CNN on Sept. 27-28 by Yankelovich Partners Inc. Sampling error ±3%.

ENGLISH DEFICIENCY

Top school districts having students with limited English ability, 1993-94

- Number of students with limited English proficiency in thousands
- Percent of students with limited English proficiency

District	Number	Percent
Los Angeles	292	46%
New York City	155	15%
Chicago	58	14%
Dade County, Fla.	55	13%
Houston	51	25%
Santa Ana, Calif.	34	69%

Source: National Clearinghouse for Bilingual Education

1. THE SOCIAL CONTEXTS OF MULTICULTURAL EDUCATION

graders score at a ninth-grade level in reading and a 10th-grade level in math. At a two-way Chinese-English program in Public School 1 in New York City's Chinatown, three eight-year-olds—a Hispanic, a Chinese and an African American—last week recited a poem they had written together in Cantonese and English. Patricia Nixon, a Manhattan resident who has sent her third-grader Anita there since kindergarten, boasts that the child can read storefront signs in Chinese and converse in the language. "She has a great opportunity," says Nixon, beaming.

Not all communities are braced for the challenge of multilingualism. At Salina Elementary School in the shadow of the hulking Ford Rouge auto plant in Dearborn, Michigan, 90% of the students are native speakers of Arabic. Academically, many of them lag far behind other students in the district. Earlier this year, spurred by the possibility of a five-year, $5 million federal grant, school superintendent Jeremy Hughes proposed forming a two-way Arabic-English program. Not only was the proposal rejected by the local board of education after heated public criticism, but it opened the way for a wholesale attack on bilingual education, directed at the city's Arab population. "This is America. Public money for public education should be used for English only," says Stephen Kovach, a medical-supplies consultant.

In California, home to 45% of the nation's non-English-speaking students, the magnitude of demographic change is breathtaking. Thirty years ago, California's schools were more than three-quarters non-Latino white. Today the proportion has dropped to 44%. A quarter of the state's 5 million public-school students—more than 1 million children—"do not speak English well enough to understand what is going on in a classroom," according to the 1993 report of a state watchdog agency. That agency charged that California's bilingual bureaucracy had "calcified into a self-serving machine ... an ideologically based program more concerned with the intrinsic virtues of bilingualism and biculturalism" than with teaching English.

While many California school districts embrace bilingualism, others, such as Stockton, Oakland and Westminster, have defied the imposition of native-language instruction, and the state has threatened to cut off millions of dollars in school aid. The debate heated up this summer as the state board of education, prompted by calls for more local control, made it easier for districts to opt out of bilingual programs. Westminster, which had hired only nine certified bilingual teachers—far fewer than the 90 required by the state to service its 4,000 Vietnamese and Spanish speakers—is now applying for permission to eliminate native-language instruction entirely. If granted, that will mean classes such as Marina Williams' will soon disappear. And in the squat, brick Willmore school, for better or worse, no one will be dancing *la quebradita*.

—*With reporting by Ann Blackman/Washington, Cathy Booth/Miami, Wendy Cole/Dearborn and Jenifer Mattos/New York*

ONE NATION, ONE LANGUAGE?

Would making English the nation's official language unite the country or divide it?

For a Sherman Oaks, Calif., election worker, the last straw was hanging campaign posters in six languages and six alphabets. For a taxpayer in University Park, Texas, it was a requirement that all employees of the local public utility speak Spanish. For a retired schoolteacher from Mount Morris, N.Y., it was taking her elderly and anxious mother to a Pakistani doctor and understanding only a fraction of what he said.

As immigration, both legal and illegal, brings a new flood of foreign speech into the United States, a campaign to make English the nation's official language is gathering strength. According to a new *U.S. News* poll, 73 percent of Americans think English should be the official language of government. House Speaker Newt Gingrich, Senate Majority Leader Bob Dole and more than a third of the members of Congress support proposed federal legislation that would make English America's official tongue; twenty-two states and a number of municipalities already have English-only laws on the books.

Like flag burning and the Pledge of Allegiance, the issue is largely symbolic. Without ever being declared official, American English has survived—and enriched itself from—four centuries of immigration. It is not much easier for today's Guatemalan immigrant to get a good education and a good job without learning English than it was for his Italian, Polish or Chinese predecessors. And at best, eliminating bilingual education might save about a dollar per student per day. But many Americans are feeling threatened by a triple whammy of growing economic uncertainty, some of it caused by foreign competition; rising immigration, much of it illegal; and political pressure to cater to the needs of immigrants rather than letting them sink or swim. "Elevating English as an icon," says author and bilingual expert James Crawford, "has appeal for the insecure and the resentful. It provides a clear answer to the question: Who belongs?"

Nation of strangers. There is no question that America is undergoing another of its periodic diversity booms. According to the Census Bureau, in 1994 8.7 percent of Americans were born in other countries, the highest percentage since before World War II. More tellingly, at least 31.8 million people in the United States speak a language other than English at home. Of the children returning to urban public schools this fall, a whopping one third speak a foreign language first. "It blows your mind," says Dade County, Fla., administrator Mercedes Toural, who counts 5,190 new students speaking no fewer than 56 different tongues.

English-only advocates, whose ranks include recent immigrants and social liberals, believe that accommodating the more than 300 languages spoken in the United States undercuts incentives to learning English and, by association, to becoming an American. Massachusetts offers driver's tests in 24 foreign languages, including Albanian, Finnish, Farsi, Turkish and Czech. Federal voting rights laws provide for ballots in multiple translations. Internal Revenue Service forms are printed in Spanish. And in Westminster, Calif., members of Troop 2194 of the Boy Scouts of America can earn their merit badges in Vietnamese. "It's completely insane," says Mauro Mujica, the chairman of the lobbying group U.S. English and himself an immigrant from Chile. "We are not doing anybody any favors."

Pulling the plug. The proposed official-

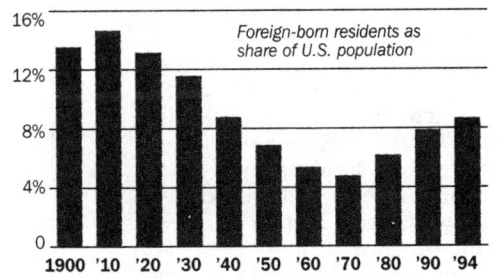

A LANDSLIDE FOR OFFICIAL ENGLISH

Coming to America. *An immigrant family at Ellis Island in 1920*

A rising tide
A larger share of Americans were foreign born earlier in this century, but the percentage is again on the rise.

Foreign-born residents as share of U.S. population

USN&WR – Basic data: U.S. Census Bureau
ROBERT KEMP – USN&WR

■ **American voters who favor making English the official language of government (for instance, printing government forms only in English):**

FAVOR: 73%   OPPOSE: 23%

■ **Voters who favor legislation that would prohibit bilingual election ballots and swearing-in ceremonies:**

FAVOR: 50%   OPPOSE: 43%

U.S. News poll of 1,000 registered voters conducted by Celinda Lake of Lake Research and Ed Goeas of the Tarrance Group on Sept. 11-13, 1995. Margin of error: plus or minus 3.1 percent. Percentages may not add up to 100 because some respondents answered, "Don't know."

1. THE SOCIAL CONTEXTS OF MULTICULTURAL EDUCATION

English laws range from the barely noticeable to the almost xenophobic. A bill introduced by Missouri Republican Rep. Bill Emerson would mandate English for government use but provide exceptions for health, safety and civil and criminal justice. Although it is the most viable of the bunch, it would change the status quo so little that it begs the question of why it is needed at all. The most extreme official-English measures would pull the plug on what their sponsors consider linguistic welfare, ending bilingual education and bilingual ballots.

Advocates of official-English proposals deny that their measures are draconian. Says U.S. English's Mujica: "We are simply saying that official documents should be in English and money saved on translations could go to help the people learn English. We're saying you could still take a driver's test in another language, but we suggest it be temporary till you learn English."

U.S. English, which reports 600,000 contributors, was founded by the late U.S. Sen. S. I. Hayakawa, a Japanese-American linguistics professor, and boasts advisory board members such as Saul Bellow and Alistair Cooke. The group was tarred eight years ago when its founder, John Tanton, wrote a memo suggesting that Hispanics have "greater reproductive powers" than Anglos; two directors quit, Tanton was forced out and the group has been rebuilding its reputation ever since. Its competitor, English First, whose founder, Larry Pratt, also started Gun Owners of America, is more hard-line.

Defenders of bilingual education, multilingual ballots and other government services ask whether legal immigrants will vote if there are no bilingual ballots. If foreign speakers can't read the street signs, will they be allowed to drive? Such thoughts bring Juanita Morales, a Houston college student, to tears. "This just sets up another barrier for people," she says. "My parents don't know English, and I can hardly speak Spanish anymore and that's painful to me."

Go it alone, the hard-liners reply, the way our grandfathers did. But these advocates don't mention that there is little, if any, evidence that earlier German or Italian immigrants mastered English any faster than the current crop of Asians, Russians and Central Americans. And it's hard to argue that today's newcomers aren't trying. San Francisco City College teaches English to 20,000 adults every semester, and the waiting list is huge. In De Kalb County, Ga. 7,000 adults are studying English; in Brighton Beach, N.Y., 2,000 wait for a chance to learn it.

The economic incentives for learning English seem as clear as ever. Yes, you can earn a good living in an ethnic enclave of Chicago speaking nothing but Polish. But you won't go far. "Mandating English," says Ron Pearlman of Chicago, "is like mandating that the sun is going to come up every day. It just seems to me that it's going to happen."

What worries many Americans are efforts to put other languages on a par with English, which often come across as assaults on American or Western culture. Americans may relish an evening at a Thai restaurant or an afternoon at a Greek festival, but many are less comfortable when their children are celebrating Cinco de Mayo, Kwanzaa and Chinese New Year along with Christmas in the public schools. In Arlington, Va., a classically trained orchestra teacher quit the public school system rather than cave in to demands to teach salsa music.

But diversity carries the day. The U.S. Department of Education policy is not simply to promote learning of English but also to *maintain* immigrants' native tongues. And supporters of that policy make a good case for it. "People ask me if I'm embarrassed I speak Spanish," says Martha Quintanilla Hollowell, a Dallas County, Texas, district attorney. "I tell them I'd be more embarrassed if I spoke only one language."

Language skills. That may be what's most disturbing about the English-only sentiment: In a global economy, it's the monolingual English speakers who are falling behind. Along with computer skills, a neat appearance and a work ethic, Americans more and more are finding that a second language is useful in getting a good job. African-Americans in Dade County, now more than half Hispanic, routinely lose tourism positions to bilingual Cubans. Schoolteachers cry foul because bilingual teachers earn more money while monolingual teachers are laid off. "There is no way I could get a job in the Los Angeles public schools today," says Lucy Fortney, an elementary school teacher for 30 years.

The proliferation of state and local English-only laws has led to a flurry of language-discrimination lawsuits and a record number of complaints with the U.S. Equal Employment Opportunity Commission. Ed Chen, a lawyer with the San Francisco office of the American Civil Liberties Union, says clients have been denied credit and insurance because they don't speak English. But courts increasingly have endorsed laws that call for exclusive use of English on the job. Officials at New York's Bellevue Hospital, where the vast majority of nurses are Filipino, say an English-only law was necessary because nurses spoke Tagalog among themselves.

Other employers have wielded English-only laws as a license to discriminate, giving rise to fears that a national law would encourage more of the same. A judge in Amarillo, Texas, claimed a

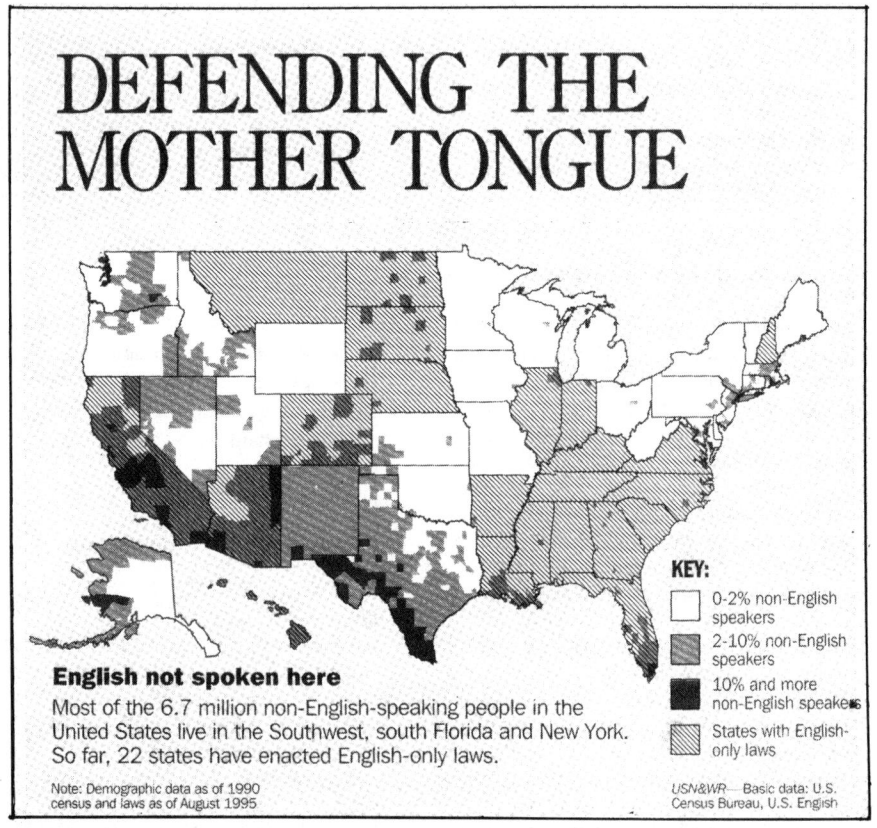

DEFENDING THE MOTHER TONGUE

English not spoken here
Most of the 6.7 million non-English-speaking people in the United States live in the Southwest, south Florida and New York. So far, 22 states have enacted English-only laws.

Note: Demographic data as of 1990 census and laws as of August 1995

KEY:
- 0-2% non-English speakers
- 2-10% non-English speakers
- 10% and more non-English speakers
- States with English-only laws

USN&WR—Basic data: U.S. Census Bureau, U.S. English

6. One Nation, One Language?

mother in a custody case was committing "child abuse" by speaking Spanish to her child at home. Another Texas judge denied probation to a drunk driver because he couldn't benefit from the all-English Alcoholics Anonymous program. In Monterey Park, Calif., a citizens' group tried to ban Chinese signs on businesses that served an almost all-Asian clientele. In Dade County, a since-repealed English-only law was so strict that it forbade using public funds to pay for court translations and bilingual signs to warn metrorail riders against electrocution.

Though it is not intended as such, the English-first movement is a reminder of a history of prejudice toward speakers of foreign tongues. Many American Indians were prohibited from speaking their own languages. The Louisiana Legislature banned the use of Cajun French in public schools in 1912, but instead of abandoning their culture, many Cajuns dropped out of school and never learned English. French was finally allowed back in the schools in the 1960s. As recently as 1971, it was illegal to speak Spanish in a public school building in Texas, and until 1923 it was against the law to teach foreign languages to elementary school pupils in Nebraska. At Ellis Island, psychologists tested thousands of non-English-speaking immigrants exclusively in English and pronounced them retarded.

Champions of diversity say it's high time Americans faced the demographic facts. In Miami, with leading trade partners Colombia and Venezuela, businesses would be foolish to restrict themselves to English. If emergency services suffer because of a shortage of foreign-speaking 911 operators, it is downright dangerous not to hire more. As for embattled teachers, Rick Lopez of the National Association of Bilingual Education says: "Why should we expect students to learn a new language if teachers can't do the same? We have to change the product to fit the market. The market wants a Toyota and we're still building Edsels."

Many Americans still value the melting pot: General Mills's new Betty Crocker is a digitized, multiethnic composite. But Skokie, Ill., educator Charlene Cobb, for one, prefers a colorful mosaic. "You don't have to change yourself," she says, "to make a whole thing that's very beautiful." The question is whether the diverse parts of America still make up a whole.

BY SUSAN HEADDEN WITH LINDA RODRIGUEZ BERNFELD AND SALLY DENEEN IN MIAMI, MISSY DANIEL IN BOSTON, MONIKA GUTTMAN IN LOS ANGELES, BARBARA BURGOWER HORDERN IN HOUSTON, SCOTT MINERBROOK IN NEW YORK, DEBRA A. SCHWARTZ IN CHICAGO AND JILL JORDAN SIEDER IN ATLANTA

THE IMMIGRATION BATTLE

Closing the golden door

California Gov. Pete Wilson's bid for re-election last year was in trouble. Polls had him behind by as much as 23 percent. Then the Republican discovered Proposition 187, a ballot measure that sought to cut off most government services for illegal immigrants. Wilson's popularity soared, and he breezed to victory in November.

Many politicians are now trying to appeal to the nation's uneasiness about immigrants. "When we got here," says White House aide Rahm Emanuel, "the border looked like swiss cheese. We've spent two years plugging holes." But some legislators and presidential hopefuls want to reduce the flow of legal, as well as illegal, immigrants. In June, the U.S. Commission on Immigration Reform concluded that reducing legal immigration is in the "national interest." President Clinton surprised immigration advocates by calling the commission's findings "consistent with my views."

Congress, too, is following the commission's lead. The House Judiciary Committee this week considers a bill by Republican Rep. Lamar Smith of Texas that would crack down on illegal immigration—through steps such as doubling the Border Patrol and stiffening penalties for bogus documents—and would reduce legal immigration by about 20 percent, to 535,000 a year. GOP Sen. Alan Simpson of Wyoming held hearings last week on legislation that closely resembles Smith's bill.

Undue burden? Critics say there is no evidence that legal immigrants are placing an undue burden on society. Frank Sharry of the National Immigration Forum, a pro-immigration group, says the commission "is still trying to come up with a rationale for their cuts." Michael Fix of the Urban Institute says data on the costs and benefits of legal immigration are scarce and unreliable. As a result, he says: "These limits are culturally or politically driven choices."

Still, Smith and Simpson think the numbers are on their side. "Over the past 12 years, the number of legal immigrants applying for supplemental security income has increased by 580 percent," Smith says. Simpson, meanwhile, feels the country needs a "breathing space" to absorb a recent uptick in new residents. Indeed, the Census Bureau reported last month that 20 percent of the country's foreign-born population arrived in the past five years.

The Smith and Simpson bills also would eliminate several visa categories. Both give priority to "nuclear family" members—spouses and minor children of current citizens and legal residents—but parents, siblings and adult children would no longer be eligible for permanent residency. Last week Doris Meissner, head of the Immigration and Naturalization Service, said the Clinton administration opposes that strategy: "We are arguing for parents to be in the scheme, along with adult married and unmarried children, so that the core family unit is maintained."

A crackdown on illegal immigration is a virtual certainty; restrictions on legal immigration are not so certain. More than 100 co-sponsors have signed on to Smith's bill. But House Majority Leader Dick Armey of Texas believes legal immigration is good for the economy, and other prominent Republicans such as Jack Kemp and Texas Gov. George W. Bush also support legal immigration. The battle is just beginning.

DAVID BOWERMASTER

Tongue-tied in the schools

Bilingual education began as a good idea. Now it needs fixing

Javier Sanchez speaks English like the proud American he is. Born in Brooklyn, N.Y., the wiry 12-year-old speaks English at home, and he speaks it on the playground. He spoke it in the classroom, too—until one day in the third grade, when he was abruptly moved to a program that taught him in Spanish all but 45 minutes a day. "It was a disaster," says his Puerto Rican-born mother, Dominga Sanchez. "He didn't *understand* Spanish." Sanchez begged the teacher to return her son to his regular class. Her request was met with amazement. "Why?" the teacher asked. "Don't you feel proud to be Hispanic?"

Along with crumbling classrooms and violence in the hallways, bilingual education has emerged as one of the dark spots on the grim tableau of American public education. Started 27 years ago to help impoverished Mexican-Americans, the program was born of good intentions, but today it has mushroomed into a $10 billion-a-year bureaucracy that not only cannot promise that students will learn English but may actually do some children more harm than good. Just as troubling, while children like Javier are placed in programs they don't want and may not need, thousands more children are foundering because they get no help with English at all.

Bilingual education was intended to give new immigrants a leg up. During earlier waves of immigration, children who entered American schools without speaking English were left to fend for themselves. Many thrived, but others, feeling lost and confused, did not. Their failures led to Title VII of the Elementary and Secondary Education Act, which ensured supplementary services for all non-English-speaking newcomers to America.

Armenian to Urdu. Significantly, the law did not prescribe a method for delivering those services. But today, of the funds used to help children learn English, 75 percent of federal money—and the bulk of state and local money—goes toward classes taught in students' native tongues; only 25 percent supports programs rooted in English. That makes bilingual education the de facto law of the land.

Historically, Hispanics have been the largest beneficiaries of bilingual education. Today, however, they compete for funding with new immigrant groups whose urge to assimilate, some educators say, may be stronger. Further, not many school districts can offer classes in such languages as Armenian and Urdu. So for practical reasons, too, children of other nationalities are placed in English-based classes more often than children of Hispanics. The problem, as many see it, is that students are staying in native-language programs far too long. In a typical complaint, the mother of one New York ninth grader says her daughter has been in "transitional" bilingual education for nine years. "We support bilingual education," says Ray Domanico of the New York Public Education Association. "But it is becoming an institutionalized ghetto."

Learning Chinese. In theory, bilingual education is hard to fault. Students learn math, science and other "content" subjects in their native tongues, and they take special English classes for a small part of the day. When they are ready, ideally within three or four years, they switch to classes taught exclusively in English. The crucial advantage is that students don't fall behind in their other lessons while gaining competence in English. Further, supporters claim, bilingual education produces students fluent in two languages.

That would be great, if it were true. Too often it is not. What is sometimes mistaken for dual-language instruction is actually native-language instruction, in which students hear English for as little as 30 minutes a day. "Art, physical education and music are supposed to be taught in English," says Lucy Fortney, a third-grade teacher from Sun Valley, Calif. "But that is absolutely not happening at all."

Assignments to bilingual programs are increasingly a source of complaint. Many students, parents say, are placed in bilingual classes not because they can't understand English but because they don't read well. They need remedial, not bilingual, help. Others wind up in bilingual programs simply because there is no room in regular classes. Luz Pena says her third-grade son, born in America, spoke excellent English until he was moved to a bilingual track. Determined to avoid such problems with her daughter, she registered her for English kindergarten—only to be told the sole vacancies were in the Spanish class.

In some cases, the placements seem to defy common sense. In San Francisco, because of a desegregation order, some English-speaking African-Americans end up in classes taught partly in Chinese. Chinese-speakers, meanwhile, have been placed in classes taught partly in Spanish. Presented with evidence that blacks in bilingual programs scored well below other blacks on basic skills tests, school officials recently announced an end to the practice.

Whether a child is placed in a bilingual program can turn on criteria as arbitrary as whether his name is Miller or Martinez. In Utah, federal records show that the same test scores that identified some students as "limited English proficient" (LEP) were used to identify others as learning disabled. The distinction depended on the student's ethnic group: Hispanics were designated LEP, while Native Americans who spoke Navajo or

7. Tongue-Tied in the Schools

Ute were labeled learning disabled. In New York City, where public schools teach children in 10 different languages, enrollment in bilingual education has jumped by half since 1989, when officials raised the cut-off on a reading test. Critics say that 40 percent of *all* children are likely to fail the test—whether they speak English or not.

Misplacement, however, is only part of the problem. At least 25 percent of LEP students, according to the U.S. Department of Education, get no special help at all. Other children are victims of a haphazard approach. In Medford, Ore., LEP students received English training anywhere from three hours a day, five days a week to 30 minutes a day, three days a week. The results? Of 12 former LEP students reviewed by education department officials, seven had two or more F's and achievement scores below the 20th percentile. Four more had D's and test scores below the 30th percentile. In Twin Falls, Idaho, three high-school teachers had no idea that their students needed any help with English, despite their obvious LEP background and consistently failing grades.

Poorly trained teachers further complicate the picture. Nationwide, the shortage of teachers trained for bilingual-education programs is estimated at 170,000. The paucity of qualified candidates has forced desperate superintendents to waive some credentialing requirements and recruit instructors from abroad. The result is teachers who themselves struggle with English. "You can hardly understand them," said San Francisco teacher Gwen Carmen. In Duchesne, Utah, two teachers' aides admitted to education department inspectors that they had no college credits, no instructional materials and no idea what was expected of them.

What all these problems add up to is impossible to say precisely, but one statistic is hard to ignore. The high-school dropout rate for Hispanic students is nearly 30 percent. It remains by far the highest of any ethnic group—four times that of whites, three times that of blacks—and it has not budged since bilingual education began.

Although poverty and other problems contribute to the disappointing numbers, studies suggest that confining Hispanic students to Spanish-only classrooms also may be a significant factor. A New York study, published earlier this year, determined that 80 percent of LEP students who enrolled in English-immersion classes graduated to mainstream English within three years, while only half the students in bilingual classes tested out that quickly. A similar study released last fall by the state of California concluded that students stayed in native-language instruction far too long. It followed an independent investigation in 1993 that called native-language instruction "divisive, wasteful and unproductive."

Not everyone agrees. More than half of American voters, according to a new *U.S. News* poll, approve of bilingual education. Jim Lyons, executive director of the Bilingual Education Association, says the recent studies are flawed because they fail to measure mastery of academic content: "They don't even pretend to address the issue of the *full* education," he says. Learning English takes time, insists Eugene Garcia of the education department. "And it's well worth the wait."

Practical approach. The alternative to native-language instruction is to teach children exclusively in English, pulling them out of class periodically for lessons in English as a second language. Lucy Fortney taught exclusively white American-born children when she started her career 30 years ago; now her classroom is almost entirely Vietnamese, Cambodian and Armenian. "I can't translate one single word for them," she says, "but they learn English."

Today, bilingual education is creeping beyond impoverished urban neighborhoods to rural and suburban communities likely to expose its failings to harsher light. Until now, no constituency has been vested or powerful enough to force the kind of reforms that may yet come with civil-rights lawsuits. "Everybody's appalled when they find out about the problems," says Linda Chavez, onetime director of the Commission on Civil Rights and a dogged opponent of bilingual education, "but the fact is, it doesn't affect their kids." That may have been true in the past. But as a rainbow-hued contingent of schoolchildren starts filling up the desks in mostly white suburbia, it is not likely to be the case for long.

BY SUSAN HEADDEN

A COSTLY SURGE IN BILINGUAL COURSES

A growth industry
About 3 million students are designated as limited English proficient (LEP), 45% of them in California. Some $156 million in federal money supports an estimated 600,000 LEP students; others are funded by states and local agencies.

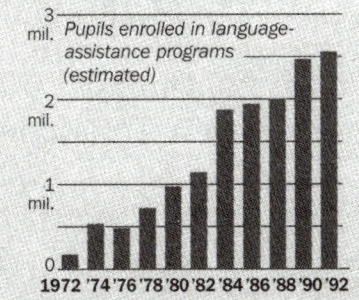

Pupils enrolled in language-assistance programs (estimated)
1972 '74 '76 '78 '80 '82 '84 '86 '88 '90 '92

USN&WR–Basic data: U.S. Dept. of Education
ROBERT KEMP–USN&WR

English, Spanish and others
Of the students in the nation's two largest cities, the native languages spoken are—

New York: 1.03 million total students
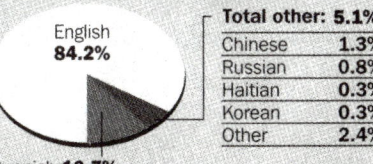
English 84.2%
Spanish 10.7%

Total other: 5.1%	
Chinese	1.3%
Russian	0.8%
Haitian	0.3%
Korean	0.3%
Other	2.4%

Los Angeles: 632,973 total students
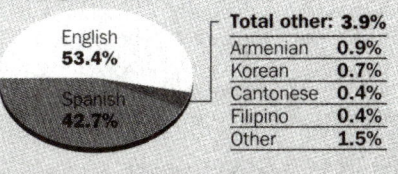
English 53.4%
Spanish 42.7%

Total other: 3.9%	
Armenian	0.9%
Korean	0.7%
Cantonese	0.4%
Filipino	0.4%
Other	1.5%

USN&WR–Basic data: California Dept. of Education; New York City Board of Education

■ U.S. voters who say bilingual education programs should be continued so children don't fall behind in other subjects **55%**	■ Voters who say bilingual education programs slow down learning English and should be eliminated **35%**	■ Even if bilingual education slows down the learning of English, is it valuable in order to preserve a student's heritage? **YES: 49% NO: 44%**

GO NORTH, YOUNG MAN

We all speak of North America. But has anyone ever actually met a North American? I know one.

Richard Rodriguez

Richard Rodriguez, an editor with Pacific News Service in San Francisco, is the author of Days of Obligation *(Penguin). He delivered an earlier version of this essay at an international gathering of writers, "A New Moment in the Americas," sponsored by the United States Information Service.*

TRADITIONALLY, AMERICA HAS BEEN AN EAST-WEST COUNTRY. WE HAVE read our history, right to left across the page. We were oblivious of Canada. We barely noticed Mexico, except when Mexico got in the way of our westward migration, which we interpreted as the will of God, "manifest destiny."

In a Protestant country that believed in rebirth (the Easter promise), land became our metaphor for possibility. As long as there was land ahead of us—Ohio, Illinois, Nebraska—we could believe in change; we could abandon our in-laws, leave disappointments behind, to start anew further west. California symbolized ultimate possibility, future-time, the end of the line, where loonies and prophets lived, where America's fads necessarily began.

Nineteenth-century real estate developers and 20th-century Hollywood moguls may have advertised the futuristic myth of California to the rest of America. But the myth was one Americans were predisposed to believe. The idea of California was invented by Americans many miles away.

ONLY A FEW EARLY VOICES FROM CALIFORNIA EVER WARNED against optimism. Two decades after California became American territory, the conservationist John Muir stood at the edge of California and realized that America is a finite idea: We need to preserve the land, if the dream of America is to survive. Word of Muir's discovery slowly traveled backward in time, from the barely populated West (the future) to the crowded brick cities of the East Coast (the past).

I grew up in California of the 1950s, when the state was filling with people from New York and Oklahoma. Everyone was busy losing weight and changing hair color and becoming someone new. There was, then, still plenty of cheap land for tract houses, under the cloudless sky.

The 1950s, the 1960s—those years were our golden age. Edmund G. "Pat" Brown was governor of optimism. He created the University of California system, a decade before the children of the suburbs rebelled, portraying themselves as the "counterculture." Brown constructed freeways that permitted Californians to move farther and farther away from anything resembling an urban center. He even made the water run up the side of a mountain.

By the 1970s, optimism was running out of space. Los Angeles needed to reinvent itself as Orange County. Then Orange County got too crowded and had to reinvent itself as North County San Diego. Then Californians started moving into the foothills or out to the desert, complaining all the while of the traffic and of the soiled air. And the immigrants!

Suddenly, foreign immigrants were everywhere—Iranians were buying into Beverly Hills, the Vietnamese were moving into San Jose; the Chinese were taking all the spaces in the biochemistry courses at UCLA. And Mexicans, poor Mexicans, were making hotel beds, picking peaches in the Central Valley, changing diapers, even impersonating Italian chefs at Santa Monica restaurants.

The Mexicans and the Chinese had long inhabited California. But they never resided within the golden myth of the state. Nineteenth-century California restricted the Chinese to Chinatowns or to a city's outskirts. Mexicans were neither here nor there. They were imported by California to perform cheap labor, then deported in bad economic times.

The East Coast had incorporated Ellis Island in its myth. The West Coast regarded the non-European immigrant as doubly foreign. Though Spaniards may have colonized the place and though Mexico briefly claimed it, California took its meaning from "internal immigrants"—Americans from Minnesota or Brooklyn who came West to remake their parents' version of America.

8. Go North, Young Man

But sometime in the 1970s, it became clear to many Californians that the famous blond myth of the state was in jeopardy. ("We are sorry to intrude, señor, we are only looking for work.") Was L.A. "becoming" Mexican?

Latin Americans arrived, describing California as "el norte." The "West Coast" was a finite idea; el norte in the Latin American lexicon means wide-open. Whose compass was right?

Meanwhile, with the lifting of anti-Asian immigration restrictions, jumbo jets were arriving at LAX from Bangkok and Seoul. People getting off the planes said about California, "This is where the United States begins." Californians objected, "No, no. California is where the United States comes to an end—we don't have enough room for you." Whose compass was truer?

IT HAS TAKEN TWO MORE DECADES FOR THE EAST COAST TO GET THE point. Magazines and television stories from New York today describe the golden state as "tarnished." The more interesting possibility is that California has become the intersection between comedy and tragedy. Foreign immigrants are replanting optimism on California soil; the native-born know the wisdom of finitude. Each side has a knowledge to give the other.

Already, everywhere in California, there is evidence of miscegenation—Keanu Reeves, sushi tacos, blond Buddhists, Salvadoran Pentecostals. But the forces that could lead to marriage also create gridlock on the Santa Monica freeway. The native-born Californian sits disgruntled in traffic going nowhere. The flatbed truck in front of him is filled with Mexicans; in the Mercedes next to him is a Japanese businessman using a car phone.

PUERTO RICANS, MEXICANS: EARLY IN THIS CENTURY WE WERE immigrants. Or not immigrants exactly. Puerto Ricans had awakened one day to discover that they suddenly lived on U.S. territory. Mexicans had seen Mexico's northern territory annexed and renamed the southwestern United States.

We were people from the South in an east-west country. We were people of mixed blood in a black and white nation. We were Catholics in a Protestant land. Many millions of us were Indians in an east-west country that imagined the Indian to be dead.

Today, Los Angeles is the largest Indian city in the United States, though Hollywood filmmakers persist in making movies about the dead Indian. (For seven bucks, you can see cowboys slaughter Indians in the Kevin Costner movie—and regret it from your comfortable chair.) On any day along Sunset Boulevard you can see Toltecs and Aztecs and Mayans.

Puerto Ricans, Mexicans—we are the earliest Latin American immigrants to the United States. We have turned into fools. We argue among ourselves, criticize one another for becoming too much the gringo or maybe not gringo enough. We criticize each other for speaking too much Spanish or not enough Spanish. We demand that politicians provide us with bilingual voting ballots, but we do not trouble to vote.

Octavio Paz, the Mexican writer, has observed that the Mexican-American is caught between cultures, thus a victim of history—unwilling to become a Mexican again, unable to belong to the United States. Michael Novak, the United States writer, has observed that what unites people throughout the

> ALREADY, EVERYWHERE IN CALIFORNIA, THERE IS EVIDENCE OF MISCEGENATION—KEANU REEVES, SUSHI TACOS, BLOND BUDDHISTS, SALVADORAN PENTECOSTALS. EACH SIDE HAS A KNOWLEDGE TO GIVE THE OTHER.

There are signs of backlash. Pete Wilson has become the last east-west governor of California. In a state founded by people seeking a softer winter and famous internationally for being "laid back," Californians vote for Proposition 187, hoping that illegal immigrants will stay away if there are no welfare dollars.

But immigrants are most disconcerting to California because they are everywhere working, transforming the ethos of the state from leisure to labor. Los Angeles is becoming a vast working city, on the order of Hong Kong or Mexico City. Chinese kids are raising the admission standards to the University of California. Mexican immigrant kids are undercutting union wages, raising rents in once-black neighborhoods.

Californians used to resist any metaphor drawn from their state's perennial earthquakes and floods and fires. Now Californians take their meaning from natural calamity. People turn away from the sea, imagine the future as existing backward in time.

"I'm leaving California, I'm going to Colorado."

"I'm headed for Arizona."

After hitting the coastline like flies against glass, we look in new directions. Did Southern California's urban sprawl invent NAFTA? For the first time, Californians now talk of the North and the South—new points on our national compass.

"I've just bought a condo in Baja."

"I'm leaving California for Seattle."

"I'm moving to Vancouver. I want someplace cleaner."

Go North, young man.

Americas is that we all have said goodbye to our motherland. To Europe. To Africa. To Asia. *Farewell!*

The only trouble is: Adios was never part of the Mexican-American or Puerto Rican vocabulary. There was no need to turn one's back on the past. Many have traveled back and forth, between rivals, between past and future, commuters between the Third World and First. After a few months in New York or Los Angeles, it would be time to head "home." After a few months back in Mexico or Puerto Rico, it would be time to head "home" to the United States.

We were nothing like the famous Ellis Island immigrants who arrived in America with no expectation of return to the "old country." In a nation that believed in the future, we were a puzzle.

We were also a scandal to Puerto Rico and Mexico. Our Spanish turned bad. Our values were changing—though no one could say why or how exactly. "Abuelita" (grandmother) complained that we were growing more guarded. Alone.

There is a name that Mexico uses for children who have forgotten their true address: "pocho." The pocho is the child who wanders away, ends up in the United States, among the gringos, where he forgets his true home.

THE AMERICAS BEGAN WITH A CONFUSION ABOUT MAPS AND A JOKE about our father's mistake. Columbus imagined himself in a part of the world where there were Indians.

We smile because our 15th-century "papi" thought he was in India. I'm not certain, however, that even today we know

1. THE SOCIAL CONTEXTS OF MULTICULTURAL EDUCATION

where in the world we live. We are only beginning to look at the map. We are only beginning to wonder what the map of the hemisphere might mean.

Latin Americans have long complained that the gringo, with characteristic arrogance, hijacked the word "American" and gave it all to himself—"the way he stole the land." I remember, years ago, my aunt in Mexico City scolding me when I told her I came from "America." Pocho! Didn't I realize that the entire hemisphere is America? "Listen," my Mexican aunt told me, "people who live in the United States are norteamericanos."

Well, I think to myself—my aunt is now dead, God rest her soul—I wonder what she would have thought a couple of years ago when the great leaders—the president of Mexico, the president of the United States, the Canadian prime minister—gathered to sign the North American Free Trade Agreement. Mexico signed a document acknowledging that she is a North American.

I predict that Mexico will suffer a nervous breakdown in the next 10 years. She will have to check into the Betty Ford Clinic for a long rest. She will need to determine just what exactly it means that she is, with the dread gringo, a norteamericana.

Canada, meanwhile, worries about the impact of the Nashville music channel on its cable TV; Pat Buchanan imagines a vast wall along our southern flank; and Mexican nationalists fear a Clinton bailout of the lowly peso.

We all speak of North America. But has anyone ever actually met a North American? Oh, there are Mexicans. And there are Canadians. And there are so-called Americans. But a North American?

I know one.

Let me tell you about him—this North American. He is a Mixteco Indian who comes from the Mexican state of Oaxaca. He is trilingual. His primary language is the language of his tribe. His second language is Spanish, the language of Cortés. Also, he has a working knowledge of U.S. English, because, for several months of the year, he works near Stockton, Calif.

He commutes over thousands of miles of dirt roads and freeways, knows several centuries, two currencies, two sets of hypocrisy. He is a criminal in one country and an embarrassment to the other. He is pursued as an "illegal" by the U.S. border patrol. He is preyed upon by Mexican officers who want to shake him down because he has hidden U.S. dollars in his shoes.

In Oaxaca, he lives in a 16th-century village, where his wife watches blond Venezuelan soap operas. A picture of la Virgen de Guadalupe rests over his bed. In Stockton, there is no Virgin Mary, only the other Madonna—the material girl.

He is the first North American.

A JOURNALIST ONCE ASKED CHOU EN-LAI, THE CHINESE PREMIER UNDER Mao Zedong, what he thought of the French Revolution. Chou En-lai gave a wonderful Chinese reply: "It's too early to tell."

I think it may even be too early to tell what the story of Columbus means. The latest chapter of the Columbus saga may be taking place right now, as Latin American teenagers with Indian faces violate the U.S. border. The Mexican kids standing on the line tonight between Tijuana and San Diego—if you ask them why they are coming to the United States of America, they will not say anything about Thomas Jefferson or *The Federalist Papers*. They have only heard that there is a job in a Glendale dry cleaner's or that some farmer is hiring near Fresno.

They insist: They will be returning to Mexico in a few months. They are only going to the United States for the dollars. They certainly don't intend to become gringos. They don't want anything to do with the United States, except the dollars.

But the months will pass, and the teenagers will be changed in the United States. When they go back to their Mexican village, they will no longer be easy. They will expect an independence and an authority that the village cannot give them. Much to their surprise, they will have been Americanized by the job in Glendale.

For work in the United States is our primary source of identity. There is no more telling question we Americans ask one another than "What do you do?" We do not ask about family or village or religion. We ask about work.

The Mexican teenagers will return to Glendale.

MEXICANS, PUERTO RICANS—MOST OF US END UP IN THE UNITED States, living in the city. Peasants end up in the middle of a vast modern metropolis, having known only the village, with its three blocks of familiar facades.

The arriving generation is always the bravest. New immigrants often change religion with their move to the city. They need to make their peace with isolation, so far from relatives. They learn subway and bus routes that take them far from home every day. Long before they can read English, they learn how to recognize danger and opportunity. Their lives are defined by change.

Their children or their grandchildren become, often, very different. The best and the brightest, perhaps, will go off to college—become the first in their family—but they talk about "keeping" their culture. They start speaking Spanish, as a way of not changing; they eat in the cafeteria only with others who look like themselves. They talk incessantly about "culture" as though it were some little thing that can be preserved and kept in a box.

The unluckiest children of immigrants drop out of high school. They speak neither good English nor Spanish. Some end up in gangs—family, man—"blood." They shoot other kids who look exactly like themselves. If they try to leave their gang, the gang will come after them for their act of betrayal. If they venture to some other part of the city, they might get shot or they might merely be unable to decipher the freeway exits that speed by.

They retreat to their "turf"—three blocks, just like in their grandmother's village, where the journey began.

ONE OF THE THINGS THAT MEXICO HAD NEVER ACKNOWLEDGED about my father—I insist that you at least entertain this idea— is the possibility that my father and others like him were the great revolutionaries of Mexico. Pocho pioneers. They, not Pancho Villa, not Zapata, were heralds of the modern age in Mexico. They left for the United States and then they came back to Mexico. And they changed Mexico forever.

A childhood friend of my father's—he worked in Chicago in the 1920s, then returned one night to his village in Michoacán with appliances for mamasita and crisp dollars. The village gathered round him—this is a true story—and asked, "What is it like up there in Chicago?"

The man said, "It's OK."

That rumor of "OK" spread across Michoacán, down to Jalisco, all the way down to Oaxaca, from village to village to village.

Futurists and diplomats talk about a "new moment in the Americas." The Latin American elite have condos in Miami and send their children to Ivy League schools. U.S. and Canadian businessmen project the future on a north-south graph. But for many decades before any of this, Latin American peasants have been traveling back and forth, north and south.

Today, there are remote villages in Latin America that are among the most international places on earth. Tiny Peruvian villages know when farmers are picking pears in the Yakima valley in Washington state.

I am the son of a prophet. I am a fool. I am a victim of history. I am confused. I do not know whether I am coming or going. I speak bad Spanish. And yet I tell Latin America this: Because I grew up Hispanic in California, I know more Guatemalans than I would if I had grown up in Mexico, more Brazilians than if I lived in Peru. Because I live in California, it is routine for me to know Nicaraguans and Salvadorans and Cubans. As routine as knowing Chinese or Vietnamese.

My fellow Californians complain loudly about the uncouth southern invasion. I say this to California: Immigration is always illegal. It is a rude act, the leaving of home. Immigration begins as a violation of custom, a youthful act of defiance, an insult to the village. I know a man from El Salvador who has not spoken to his father since the day he left his father's village.

> IMMIGRATION IS ALWAYS ILLEGAL. IT IS A RUDE ACT, THE LEAVING OF HOME, A VIOLATION OF CUSTOM, A YOUTHFUL ACT OF DEFIANCE. BUT IMMIGRANTS HAVE ALSO BEEN OUR CIVILIZATION'S PROPHETS.

Immigrants horrify the grandmothers they leave behind.

Illegal immigrants trouble U.S. environmentalists and Mexican nationalists. Illegal immigrants must trouble anyone, on either side of the line, who imagines that the poor are under control.

But they have also been our civilization's prophets. They, long before the rest of us, saw the hemisphere whole.

Teacher Education in Multicultural Perspective

At a time when minority students are beginning to approach 50 percent of the elementary and secondary school population, few minority students are preparing to be teachers. This social reality within teacher education programs in the United States only underscores the need for multicultural education, as well as for course work in specific cultural study areas in the education of American teachers.

Multicultural educational programming of some sort is now an established part of teacher education programs, but there are still major issues as to how it can be integrated effectively into these programs. The National Council for the Accreditation of Teacher Education (NCATE) has established a multicultural standard for the accreditation of programs for teacher education in the United States. The demographic changes in the population characteristics of Canada and the United States ensure that many North American teachers will have students from a wide array of differing cultural heritages.

Many teachers of European ethnic heritage have difficulty understanding the importance of the fact that national cultures in North America are becoming more culturally pluralistic. From a multicultural perspective, one of the many things course content seeks to achieve is to help all prospective teachers realize the importance of becoming learners themselves throughout their life. The knowledge base of multicultural education is further informed by the history of the struggle for civil rights in North American societies. Multicultural educational programming in teacher education programs seeks to alter how prospective teachers perceive society as a whole, not just its current minority members. Culturally pluralistic themes need to be apparent throughout teacher education programs and integrated into the knowledge bases of teacher education. Broadly conceived, multicultural education seeks to help members of all ethnic, cultural backgrounds to appreciate one another's shared human concerns and interrelationships; it should not be conceived as simply the study of minority cultural groups. Teachers need to be prepared in such a manner that they learn genuine respect for cultural as well as personal diversity.

Teachers will have to consider how each student's development is shaped by the powerful force of the values prevailing in his or her home and community. Preservice teachers need exposure to case studies that exemplify and report on the differing learning styles that develop in differing cultural contexts. Different styles of teaching can be learned from differing cultural traditions in childrearing, entry into adulthood (rites of passage), and differing cultural styles of child-adult interaction in school settings.

By the year 2000 about 5 billion of the projected 6 billion people on Earth will be persons with a non-Eurocentric conception of the world. Scholars in the social sciences, humanities, and teacher education in North America who study minority-majority relations in the schools now realize that the very terms "minority" and "majority" are changing in the context of the demographic realities of most major urban and suburban educational systems. This is also true when we consider minority-majority relations in vast isolated rural or wilderness areas where those of western or northern European descent can be minorities in the midst of concentrations of indigenous peoples.

There is still much misunderstanding as to what multicultural education is within the teacher education establishment. This will continue as long as many of its opponents consider it a political rather than an intellectual or educational concept. Multicultural educational should not be politicized. It should be a way of seeing the world as enriched by cultural and personal diversity.

The essays in this unit explore why it is important to see multicultural education not as a political concept, but rather as an area of critical inquiry from which we can all learn alternative styles of teaching appropriate to the learning styles and cultural backgrounds of students.

This unit's articles are relevant to courses that focus on introduction to the cultural foundations of education, educational policy studies, history and philosophy of education, and curriculum theory and construction, as well

UNIT 2

as methods courses in all areas of teacher education programs.

Looking Ahead: Challenge Questions

Why is multicultural education so frequently seen as an isolated, segregated part of teacher education programs?

What are the reasons for so much resistance to course work in the area of multicultural education in teacher education programs?

What can we learn about teaching styles and methods from case studies of teachers from cultures other than our own?

Why can it be said that our understanding of the relevance of multicultural perspectives on teacher education emerged from the struggle for human rights in general?

What seem to be the major points of disagreement about the role of multicultural education in teacher education programs?

What attitudes need to change in much discussion about multicultural education?

—F.S.

Accommodating Cultural Differences and Commonalities in Educational Practice

By Ronald Gallimore & Claude Goldenberg

Taking account of diversity in schools is a major challenge in a multicultural society. On one level the issue is simple: Everyone's heritage is due respect, and differences should be regarded as strengths on which to build rather than deficits to be stigmatized or overcome. But on another level there is an often unrecognized paradox: too exclusive a focus on group differences can "all too easily become the basis for creating stereotypes..." that blind educators to qualities that students have in common (Fillmore, 1982, p. 24).

How can educators be responsive to cultural differences and avoid stereotypes that mask commonalties shared by different cultural groups? One way is to distinguish between different functions of culture. In this essay we distinguish between the group-defining function and other adaptive functions to show why educators need to accommodate cultural commonalities as well as differences.

Some Functions of Culture

Culture evolves over time in response to adaptive challenges. One result of this evolutionary process is beliefs and practices that help us adapt to persistent as well as changing circumstances. These beliefs and practices are organized as models or schema about how things work, what

Ronald Gallimore is a faculty member at the University of California, Los Angeles and Claude Goldenberg is a faculty member at California State University, Long Beach.

is ideal, and which practices are proper and help individuals or groups survive and prosper (LeVine, 1977). Cultural models are so familiar and mundane that their functions and effects are often unseen, invisible, unnoticed. The evidence of their workings are often most apparent in everyday routines in communities, homes, workplaces, play yards, and schools. What activities are carried out, why they are valued, who should participate, and the rules of interaction are coded into our cultural models.

Cultural features—models of belief and practice and their associated activities—are neither static nor rigid. As circumstances and environments change, our understanding of how things work and how to respond are modified and changed to meet new challenges. We change just enough to make things work—we are satisfiers rather than maximizers, happy with just good enough. The more our environments change, the more we try to keep things the same. The more we try to keep them same, the more we have to change (Edgerton, 1992). Beliefs and practices are borrowed from others with whom we come in contact or share an ecological niche; alternative ways of organizing daily activities are tried, adapted, and adopted.

In the modern world this process is accelerated by technologies that amplify direct contact, distanced communication, and social and commercial exchange. Changes are made slowly, gradually, and are built on existing beliefs and practices.

For example, natives of Spain, Turkey, and Morrocco gradually adopted beliefs and practices encountered in Northern Europe after migrating to obtain employment (Roosens, 1994). Culture is not a straitjacket or a cake of custom, it is a storehouse of adaptive solutions to the challenges of existence (Weisner, Gallimore, & Jordan, 1988).

Some cultural features—beliefs, practices, and everyday activities—mark boundaries among groups—clans, tribes, ethnic, and reference groups. Which features mark boundaries are a product of many different historical circumstances. Sometimes two groups occupied the same ecological niche, or monopolized different territories or resources. In some cases ethnic boundaries arose from the interdependence of two groups, with each providing services or goods to the other, sometimes voluntarily, sometimes coerced by the more powerful group. A critical function of boundary markers is to distinguish between "us" and "others."

For example, some scholars have concluded that the function of kosher dietary laws was to differentiate the Jews from their "gentile" neighbors (Harris, 1985, p. 337). Ethnic boundaries help an individual identify who is a fellow member of the "in" group, who is and is not a person with shared perceptions and understandings. (Barth, 1969, p. 15). The borders between ethnic groups define both self and group identity, feelings of belonging, and conti-

9. Accommodating Cultural Differences

nuity through time; shared meanings and traditions; self-ascribed genealogical and social filiation, including related forms of family and group bonds (Roosens, 1994).

In contemporary human history, an important function of boundaries is the political and economic advantage that ethnic unity can achieve. In the United States, for example, ethnically defined groups succeeded in building coalitions to pass legislation requiring equity in school funding, hiring, mortgage granting, etc. **The unified political action which ethnic groups can muster means, paradoxically, using ethnic categories to rid society of inequities arising from ethnic distinctions** (Wright, 1994). Ron Edmonds, advocate of effective schools for minority students, wrote that poor and ethnic groups "are far more likely to be served by politics than by any equity interests to be found in the educational research establishment" (Edmonds, 1978, p. 34). To unify a group for effective political action, ethnic identity must remain relatively impervious to changing circumstances. Otherwise, membership would wax and wane, and the advantages of collective action would be threatened.

One reason ethnic boundaries persist is that they are marked by only a limited set of cultural features the particularities of which are often a product of historical and ecological circumstances (Barth, 1969). What features mark boundaries do not depend on their persistance, or their resistance to change in many domains of belief and practice. This allows for very substantial differences among individuals within an ethnic group—differences that do not affect those features that define the boundary between "us" and "others."

This flexibility regarding most beliefs and practices permits a group to remain unified around core features while allowing great variation within the group on thoughts, feelings, and behavior (LeVine, 1984, p. 68). Individuals within a group can maintain their group identity and still enjoy the adaptive advantages of many beliefs and practices, even those borrowed from the "others." The borrowing and loaning of cultural features are often a two-way process between groups.

This brings us to a key idea. Two well-differentiated ethnic groups living in the same ecological niche are likely to share many cultural beliefs and practices in common (Barth, 1969; Edgerton, 1971; LeVine, 1977). For example, many individuals emigrated from Spain, Sicily, Morocco, and Turkey to work in the factories and mines of Northern Europe (Roosens, 1994). Many in these groups sharply differentiate themselves, and are treated as different by co-resident Northern Europeans, as distinct ethnic groups. Yet the boundaries between groups, that is, what differentiates them, are limited cultural features such as tastes in clothing and food, home furnishing styles, male and female role norms, and

> **Cultural features...are neither static nor rigid. As circumstances and environments change, our understanding of how things work and how to respond are modified and changed to meet new challenges. We change just enough to make things work...**

religious beliefs (Roosens, 1994). These immigrants come to share, however, many other cultural features with their new Northern European neighbors.

Even those who intend to return to their native land adopt cultural beliefs and practices which give them an adaptive advantage in their new, even if possibly temporary, Northern European homes: They use modern medicines and technologies, take new kinds of jobs, learn new skills, aspire to higher education for their children, seek and attain material abundance, and subscribe to public social security systems, some of which entail adoption of beliefs and practices not present in their native lands.

Adapting Instruction to Culture

The behavior of immigrants to Northern Europe reflects a fundamental principle: Individuals living in the same ecologies will adopt cultural models of adaptation if they offer advantage. What has this principle to do with adapting instruction to cultural variability within groups? It suggests that educators may expect to find many **commonalties** as well as **differences** among the ethnic groups that attend America's schools.

Our two-pronged argument is this:

(1) Schools must deal with students from many different groups and should therefore be aware of potential discontinuities between home and school—*e.g.*, attitudes toward discipline, beliefs about how children learn, the nature and quality of learning experiences in the preschool years and beyond—and design programs that will foster common understandings and complementary efforts.

(2) But at the same time, schools should not assume that ethnic diversity always implies broad-based cultural differences among groups, or conversely homogeneity within groups. Different groups living in the same ecological niche can be expected to have **many** cultural features—beliefs and practices—in common. Schools therefore should also build on commonalties between schools and families—*e.g.*, beliefs about the value of formal schooling, school achievement, good behavior, and parent support and involvement. Building on commonalties is no less important than being sensitive to differences in forging productive relationships with families.

Discontinuities and Complementarities

Families who emigrate from Mexico to the United States are ethnically different and distinct from other families in this country. Racially, historically, psychologically, they identify with others whose families hail from central and northern Mexico who also speak Spanish and share Indian and Spanish ancestors. These are the people Carey McWilliams (1948, 1968) wrote about a half-century ago. Our longitudinal studies in a California community suggest that on some dimensions of belief and practice immigrant Mexican parents are different from their fellow residents (Goldenberg & Gallimore, 1995; Reese, Balzano, Gallimore, & Goldenberg, 1995).

For example, they subscribe to a cultural model of preschool child development that places a higher emphasis on moral development than on school readiness skills, a pattern exhibited by groups with origins in small-scale agrarian communities where earning a living depends on face-to-face interactions and the cooperative work of family members (LeVine & White, 1986). For the immigrant Mexican parents, it is vital that a child learn the difference between right and wrong, obedience and respect for elders, and to be a full participant in family life. They place less emphasis in the preschool years on the uses of language and print than families in which literacy is both a means of earning a living and an important child development goal (Goldenberg & Gallimore, 1995). This difference matters because the amount of preschool literacy experience is a significant precursor of early reading development in early elementary school. Children with lots of preschool literacy experience have an advantaged in early elementary school (Adams, 1990).

On the other hand, some of the cultural models of child development held by the immigrant Mexican families differ little from other Americans: The Mexican immigrant parents value schooling, are available to the children, and are interested in and capable of providing literacy-enhancing experiences, particularly when children are younger. Activities involving literacy are more frequent than suggested by many stereotypes of low income Spanish-speaking families.

Indeed, we found in our studies that the within group variability was substantial. While some families, by their own report and researchers' observations, do not always provide certain experiences, they are motivated to help their children, and eagerly adopt new models of and opportunities for child development and learning. With few exceptions, parents eagerly respond to materials, activities, and suggestions from their school. In one study, over 40 percent of all observed learning activities involved use of materials from school. Once their children entered school the range and frequency of literacy was greatly increased by parents' taking advantage of new materials and ideas the children brought home. In short, many have already adopted beliefs and practices available in the ecological/cultural niche of urban United States and exhibited adaptive flexibility (Goldenberg & Gallimore, 1995).

Yet for all their variability and willingness to adopt new beliefs and practices that benefit their children, the families are not abandoning their ethnic identity. Almost without exception we found a strong endorsement of what the families consider traditional Mexican values of *educación*, that include family solidarity, knowing right from wrong, and obedience, and respect for elders. These parents are strongly identified with their heritage.

One father said: "We Mexicans come from an old tradition, a tradition of the *ranchos* where the father and mother are respected. Regarding siblings, the younger ones respect the older ones" (Reese, et. al., 1995). One mother complained that in the United States children are given too much freedom which results in gangs, drugs, and other urban woes. She said "One cannot tell [young people] anything because [they say] they are going to call the cops on you....

We Mexicans are not like that. This is one of the customs that I don't want them to learn." She described immigrant Mexican families who have educated their children in the same way that they had been educated in Mexico. The result were hardworking young adults who stayed out of trouble, which she said was not always true when parents gave their children too much freedom and autonomy. For many of the families in our study, their adherence to traditional values is a boundary they believe distinguishes them and their group from other groups in their communities.

Yet, even as ethnic identity remains strong, changes in cultural belief and practice were evident in the more than ten years we have been interviewing and observing in homes of immigrant Latino families:

> ...*educación* for these immigrant parents has a much stronger component of "formal schooling." The immigrant parents in our sample clearly wish to maintain many of the traditional family values of responsibility and respect taught to them by their own parents, our target children's grandparents. But with its greater emphasis on formal schooling—for both boys and girls—these immigrant parents' cultural model of *educación* is itself undergoing change. It is adapting to the exigencies of life in a society where education—in the English sense of the word—[both matters and is more available]. (Goldenberg & Gallimore, 1995)

As they adapt to a new society they may be reaching out and adopting cultural models and practices that provide advantages to themselves and their children. But they are not abandoning all they brought with them.

Commonalties and Collaboration

Ethnic differences, therefore, should not obscure cultural compatibilities. In a study of Latino immigrants and their kindergartners, we found that teachers' attempts to involve parents in children's literacy development led both to greater parent satisfaction and to enhanced student achievement (Goldenberg & Arzubiaga, 1994 April; Goldenberg and Gallimore, 1995), suggesting again that parents and teachers shared many values and beliefs about educating children. The more teachers attempted to involve parents in children's academic learning—by sending home activities or through messages or phone calls home—the more satisfied parents were with both the academic content of their child's classroom and with the extent to which they felt involved in their children's learning.

In addition, teacher attempts to involve parents also predicted children's literacy development at the end of kindergarten. The more teachers attempted to involve parents in children's learning, the higher were children's end-of-year literacy scores. There was no relationship between teacher parent-involvement efforts and beginning of year achievement, so we ruled out the explanation that teachers involved were more likely to reach out to parents of higher achieving students. Furthermore, there was a striking relationship between teachers' parent involvement attempts and changes in child achievement in relation to other kindergartners across the year ($r=.58$; $p<.01$).

In other words, the more the teacher attempted to involve a child's parents in his or her academic learning in kindergarten, the more a child gained in relative achievement standing from the beginning of the year to the end. Students whose teachers took the initiative to involve parents in children's learning gained ground in comparison to peers; students whose teachers did not take the initiative to involve parents, slipped back in their relative achievement standing.

These results illustrate an important continuity between Latino parents and children's teachers: An interest in children's academic achievement and a belief in the importance of parents' playing a productive role in promoting it. When teachers take advantage of this continuity by facilitating parent involvement, the results are greater parent satisfaction and improved learning by children. When children move on to first and second grade, we have found the relationships hold between teachers' parent involvement efforts and parents' satisfaction. For these older children, parents are more satisfied when their child receives homework they feel is of high quality and that promotes learning and motivation.

Parents are also more satisfied when they feel informed of their child's progress and when the academic content of the classroom is high. This is clearly in keeping with the values and beliefs we have heard parents express for the past ten years. They want their child's school experience to be academically challenging. Indeed, as we have reported before, on occasion parents will comment that United States schools are less demanding than those in their native countries (Goldenberg & Gallimore, 1991; Reese, *et al.*, 1995).

Surface and Reality in Cultural Commonalties and Differences

In the introduction to this essay we developed the idea that only a few cultural beliefs and practices mark the boundary between groups. Yet in many contexts these limited differences are so compelling at first analysis that they may obscure substantial commonalties. Indeed, the perspective we presented in the first part of this essay would predict this—that all of us are inclined to notice those differences that mark boundaries between groups, because of the social and political functions they serve. But as Fillmore (1982) and Ogbu and Matute-Bianchi (1986) warned, this very predictable human response can, when allowed to operate freely in educational settings, produce a surface response that is insensitive to underlying realities.

In the study on the effects of kindergarten teachers' parent involvement efforts on parent satisfaction and children's achievement (Goldenberg & Arzubiaga, 1994 April), half the teachers were Latinas who spoke Spanish fluently, and the other half were Anglos with varying degrees of skill in Spanish. When we compared the achievement change of children taught by Latinas and Anglos, there was a significant difference. Those taught by the Latina teachers improved from fall to spring, whereas the Anglo teachers' children declined. At first glance this suggests the bridging of discontinuities between child and school cultures (in the form of Latina, fluent-Spanish teachers) improved children's achievement—a result that is inconsistent with previous findings that teacher ethnicity is **unrelated** to Latino children's achievement (Vierra, 1984).

However, further analyses of our data suggested a more complex interpretation was required. Because they were rated much higher at promoting parent-involvement, Latina teachers were benefiting from this powerful effect on children's achievement. When we statistically removed the contribution of parent-involvement, the effect of teacher ethnicity disappeared. The critical variable affecting student progress was teachers' parent-involvement efforts, not teacher ethnicity and language *per se*. No doubt teacher ethnicity and language contributed to communication and rapport between teachers and parents, but it was not the fact of these shared qualities. It was how teachers behaved that mattered, not their ethnic status.

The importance of teacher action over teacher status was also the argument of one the Latina teachers, Ms. Delgado—an argument she presented to us **prior** to the study. While she recognized that many children have less access to academic learning opportunities than others, Ms. Delgado also maintained a strong belief (supported by educational research) that children of immigrant Latinos, like other children, can be taught what they need to know in order to be successful in school:

[Some] teachers think these kids are deprived so [they think] all we need to let them do is play all day here. That really makes me mad because I came from [an immigrant Latino] background like this.... These kids can learn but they have to be taught. If more teachers realized this and did what they were supposed to do, more of these kids would go on to college (Goldenberg, 1994, p. 185).

Conclusion

Our examples and analyses raise an intriguing possibility: Is accommodating to culturally different children a matter of making changes in teaching, staffing, or curriculum that are sensitive to differences? Or can we also accommodate to culturally different children by recognizing similarities and consistencies, as well as differences and discontinuities, across groups? Cultural accommodation cuts both ways—making changes if needed but recognizing similarities when they exist and not allowing ourselves to see only the cultural features that distinguish a group from others. Ignoring one kind of accommodation over the other is not in the best interest of children or families.

As we confront the challenges posed by this most recent wave of immigrants to the United States, educators must be aware of discontinuities that must be skillfully and sensitively handled. At the same time, they must be equally sensitive to what the families, children, teachers, and administrators share.

References

Adams, M. (1990). *Beginning To Read: Thinking and Learning about Print*. Cambridge, MA: MIT Press.

Barth, F. (1969). Introduction. In F. Barth, (ed.) *Ethnic Groups and Boundaries: The Social Organization of Culture Difference* (pps. 9-38). London, United Kingdom: George Allen & Unwin.

Edgerton, R.B. (1971). *The Individual in Cultural Adaptation: A Study of Four East African Peoples*. Berkeley, CA: University of California Press.

Edgerton, R.B. (1992). *Sick Societies: Challenging The Myth of Primitive Harmony*. New York: Free Press.

Edmonds, R. (July, 1978). A discussion of the literature and issues related to effective schooling. Paper prepared for the National Conference on Urban Education, St. Louis, MO.

Fillmore, L.W. (1982). Cultural Perspectives on Second Language Learning. *TESL Reporter* 14(2): 23-31.

Goldenberg, C. & Gallimore, R. (1991). Local knowledge, research knowledge, and educational change: A case study of first-grade Spanish reading improvement. *Educational Researcher, 20* (8), 2-14.

Goldenberg, C. (1994). Promoting early literacy achievement among Spanish-speaking children: Lessons from two studies. E. Hiebert (Ed.), *Getting Reading Right From the Start. Effective Early Literacy Interventions* (pp.171-199). Boston, MA: Allyn & Bacon.

Goldenberg, C. & Arzubiaga, A. (1994, April). The effects of teachers' attempts to involve Latino parents in children's early reading development. Paper presented at the annual meeting of the American Educational Research Association, New Orleans, LA.

Goldenberg, C. & Gallimore, R. (1995). Immigrant Latino parents' values and beliefs about their children's education: Continuities and discontinuities across cultures and generations. In Pintrich, P.R. & Maehr, M. (Eds.). *Advances In Motivation and Achievement: Culture, Ethnicity, and Motivation, Vol 9* (pp. 183-228). Greenwich, CT: JAI Press.

Harris, M. (1985). *Good to Eat: Riddles of Food and Culture*. New York: Simon & Schuster.

LeVine, R. A. (1984). Properties of culture: an ethnographic view. In R.A. Shweder & R.A. LeVine, (Eds.) *Culture theory: Essays on Mind, Self, and Emotion* (pps. 67-87). Cambridge, United Kingdom: Cambridge University Press.

LeVine, R. (1977). Child rearing as cultural adaptation. In P. Leiderman, S. Tulkin, & A. Rosenfeld (Eds.), *Culture and Infancy* (pp. 15-27). New York: Academic Press.

Levine, R. & White, M. (1986). *Human Conditions: The Cultural Basis of Educational Development*. New York: Routledge & Kegan Paul.

McWilliams , C. (1948, 1968). *North from Mexico: The Spanish-speaking People of the United States*. New York: Greenwood Press.

Ogbu, J.U. & Matute-Bianchi, M.E. (1986).Understanding Sociocultural Factors; Knowledge, Identity, and School Adjustment. In *Beyond Language: Social and Cultural Factors in Schooling Language Minority Students*. Bilingual Education Office, California State Department of Education (eds)(Pps. 73-142). Los Angeles, CA: Evaluation, Dissemination and Assessment Center, California State University, Los Angeles

Reese, L., Balzano, S., Gallimore, R., & Goldenberg, C. (1995). The Concept of Educación: Latino family values and American schooling. *International Journal of Educational Research*, 23, 1, 57-81.

Roosens, E. (1994, November). Education for living in pluriethnic societies. Paper presented at Carnegie/Jacobs Foundation Conference "Frontiers in the Education of Young Adolescents, November 3-5, 1994, Marbach Castle, Germany.

Vierra, A. (1984). The relationship between Chicano children's achievement and their teachers' ethnicity. *Hispanic Journal of Behavioral Science*, 6, 285-290.

Weisner, T. S., Gallimore, R., & Jordan, C. (1988). Unpackaging cultural effects on classroom learning: Hawaiian peer assistance and child-generated activity. *Anthropology and Education Quarterly*, 19, 327-353.

Wright, L. (1994) One drop of blood. *The New Yorker*, July 25, pp. 46-55.

Of Pigs & Wolves at the OK Corral

By Tonya Huber

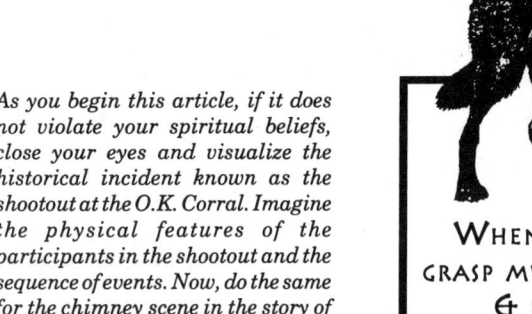

WHEN WE CAN CLEARLY GRASP MULTIPLE PERSPECTIVES & DIFFERENCES IN WORLDVIEW, WE ARE ON OUR WAY TO DEVELOPING CULTURALLY RESPONSIBLE PEDAGOGY.

As you begin this article, if it does not violate your spiritual beliefs, close your eyes and visualize the historical incident known as the shootout at the O.K. Corral. Imagine the physical features of the participants in the shootout and the sequence of events. Now, do the same for the chimney scene in the story of the "Three Little Pigs." Take these images with you into this reading.

IN A RECENT BOX-OFFICE HIT, *Tombstone* (1993), a true legend of the American West is retold in the ultimate Western showdown known most popularly as *Gunfight at the O.K. Corral*, the title of one of the earliest (1957) movie versions. On the heels of the popular Val Kilmer/Doc Holliday, Kurt Russell/Wyatt Earp dramatization followed the lengthier, reputedly more historical, version starring director Kevin Costner as Wyatt Earp, Gene Hackman as Earp's father, and an emaciated Dennis Quaid as Doc. Consideration of brief clips from these three films, along with scenes from two other early versions, John Ford's 1946 *My Darling Clementine* and the 1967 version *Hour of the Gun*, can catapult viewers into lively discussion about what **really** happened at the O.K. Corral on October 26, 1881. Did the Earp brothers take the law into their own hands or enforce it? Were the Clanton's and McLaury's a lawless gang or victims? Was Doc Holliday a dedicated, selfless friend, or a blood-thirsty, drunken killer?

That a 30-second gunfight could still create interest a century later merits discussion itself; but the topic most deserving our discussion focuses upon the difference in perspectives taken from the moment of the event through today—an issue of differing perspectives and, as such, a model for exploring the significance of multiple perspectives.

When we can clearly grasp multiple perspectives and differences in worldview, we are on our way to developing culturally responsible pedagogy. This awareness of perspectives, or paradigms, is necessary for an educator to be **responsive** to diversity and **responsible** for curriculum and instruction that reflects an understanding of diversity.

Understanding & Shifting Paradigms

A paradigm as defined by Maykut & Morehouse (1994) is "a set of overarching and interconnected assumptions about the nature of reality" (p. 4). To fully explore the concept of paradigms, shifting paradigms, and multiple perspectives, is a course unto itself, but at least a rudimentary understanding of the scope of the concept must be gained for those who would interact meaningfully in educational settings with others who operate from **different** paradigms.

Another way to explore paradigms that adds a deeper layer of culture to historical perspective, the aspect most clearly depicted in the O.K. Corral scenarios, is to explore a commonly accepted "reality" from other regional, lingual, cultural perspectives. I have found real enjoyment in applying this approach to the well-known story, "The Three Little Pigs." When I ask students in my teacher education courses or participants in staff development sessions to recall the story, most immediately offer that there were three pigs, they each built a different type of house, a big, bad wolf destroyed the first two houses, but the third house, built more carefully and with

---

Tonya Huber is a professor in the Department of Curriculum and Instruction at Wichita State University, Wichita, Kansas.

—OR—
THE EMERGING ALTERNATIVE PARADIGM & THE CONSTRUCTION OF KNOWLEDGE

brick, stood the wolf's attack and saved the pigs. Participants in this experience are quick to recognize the vestiges of the Protestant work ethic at play and the moral intended for the young ears listening to the story— work hard, invest wisely, and you will be rewarded. Other perspectives on the plot suggest varied worldviews and paradigms. I like to call this exploration, with all due respect to Steinbeck,[1] "Of Pigs and Wolves."

While many of us recall a less brutal ending to the huffing and puffing, in at least one popular retelling, we read:

> Just as the wolf was coming down the chimney, the little pig took the cover off the pot, and in fell the wolf. The little pig quickly put on the cover again, boiled up the wolf, and ate him for supper. (Galdone, 1970)

The justification, implicitly, is that since the wolf has already eaten the first two little pigs, he deserves to be eaten—an application of the "eye for an eye" retribution theory.

In Milliken's *3 Piggy Opera* by Carol Kaplan and Sandi Becker (1987), the angry wolf sneaks down the chimney, burns his tail, and runs away, never to bother the pigs again—a "friendlier" plot climax, more developmentally appropriate for young children than the murder and killing involved in other versions.

Jon Scieszka turns the tale inside out with the wolf's version of the story in *The True Story of the 3 Little Pigs* (1989). The first two pigs are accidentally killed when the sick wolf sneezes and blows their houses down, and believing in "waste not, want not," eats the remains. The rude third pig, smarter than the two brothers, survives because the police arrive and take the wolf to the "pig pen." The play, with words and the "other perspective," is a delightful way to explore multiple perspectives. However, we have thus far in the comparison only reflected on difference in perspective. An awareness of cultural differences further enhances our ability to grasp the significance of paradigm and worldview.

In two of my favorite retellings of the story, the events are different. In the Southwestern adaptation of the story, told by Susan Lowell and illustrated by Jim Harris, the geographical setting is the Sonoran Desert, and the characters are representative of Native American and Mexican cultures: three little javelinas and a coyote who sneaks down the adobe roof stove pipe to find a lighted fire. The story concludes:

> The three little javelinas lived happily ever after in the adobe house. And if you ever hear Coyote's voice, way out in the desert at night...Well, you know what he's remembering! (Lowell & Harris, 1992)

Similarly, David Vozar casts the story within another cultural setting when he retells the story in Black vernacular as a nursery rap:

> Paw over paw Wolfie climbs up the shack
> To slide down the chimney in a sneak swine attack.
> Halfway down clothes are soilin', and Wolfie's recoilin'.
> In the fireplace below, the pigs' soup is boilin'.
> He pops out the chimney, hits the ground with a **boink**.
> The pigs shout, "Yahoo!" but it sounds more like **oink**.
> —Vozar & Lewin, 1993

In both of these versions, the antagonist learns his lesson when two brothers and a sister stick together and protect each other. The implication is not only a different paradigm than the more familiar retribution version, but the cultural settings imbue the retellings with contexts that enlighten as they educate about people and places, cultures and regions.

The exploration of an historical event from more than 100 years ago and a child's fairy tale provide comfortable avenues for exploring the import of recognizing and respecting difference in learners. Maxine Greene (1993) suggests that **when the learners' stories converge with other stories, they will be compelled to reach beyond themselves**—to question, to search, and ultimately to bring about change. Greene further speculates on the need for schools to provide settings that encourage such exchanges:

2. TEACHER EDUCATION IN MULTICULTURAL PERSPECTIVE

It is a matter of overcoming the silences, of creating schools that are **natural habitats of learning**, schools on the way to becoming the kinds of miniature communities that embody possibility. Only under such conditions can we avoid misreading children's styles and abilities; only in this manner can we come in touch with what the young hope for themselves, how they think about what they want to be. Attending to them in their difference, we may invent ways of moving them to devise their own existential projects as they begin to articulate their stories. (p. 12)

One way of incorporating **natural habitats of learning** may involve the incorporation of multiple perspectives, multicultural worldviews, multiple intelligences, and the construction of knowledge in quality learning experiences. I propose that educators and leaders of educators must become cognizant of their own stories, overcome the silence that separates us in our different perceptions of reality, and shift our paradigms to ever more culturally responsible levels.

Research Paradigms & Education

Recall that **paradigm**, as defined by Maykut & Morehouse (1994), "has come to mean a set of overarching and interconnected assumptions about the nature of reality" (p. 4). First introduced into the history and sociology of science by Thomas Kuhn (1962), the concept of paradigm can, and should, be applied to the research methods of other disciplines. When applied to the research in education, review of the professional literature supports the focus given to what has been called in science the **traditional method**, or the **traditional paradigm**. As with other fields, the field of education has been dominated by the traditional paradigm—a belief in "objective observation, quantifiable data and verifiable truths" (Maykut & Morehouse, 1994, p. 7). Because of this perceived **domination**, the concept has also been termed the **dominant paradigm**.

In *Naturalistic Inquiry*, Yvonna Lincoln and Egon Guba (1985) challenged the traditional, or dominant, paradigm as the only or most appropriate way of doing research, offering instead an **emerging paradigm** based on qualitative research. Naturalistic inquiry and the exploration of sociocultural knowledge assist the learner/educator in beginning the dialogue on questions of **why** and **how** that have for so long gone unanswered by the traditional research model that more often provides numerical or positivist answers to the questions of **which** and **what**. Expanding upon the work of Lincoln and Guba in their work *Beginning Qualitative Research*, Maykut & Morehouse (1994) have called this new set of assumptions and/or postulates the **alternate paradigm**. The differences between the two paradigms affect both the general approach to research and particular practices within each research tradition.

The **dominant paradigm**, impacted by the positivist position on research, establishes complete intellectual control over experience in terms of precise rules (Polanyi, 1958). These precise rules need only be followed to negotiate the world. The implication for education, clearly, is that a set of rules, a set of answers, a teacher's edition exists and is the ultimate authority. Research on education, from this position, posits a hypothesis and its null, then sets about to disprove one and prove the other—a simplistic, dichotomous interpretation of the world, issues, and events that.

The **emerging paradigm**, impacted by the naturalistic, qualitative approach to research, perceives knowledge as a construction of the knower. The researcher, or the knower, cannot stand independently from that which is known. The qualitative researcher seeks patterns and themes that emerge from the data, just as the learner seeks patterns and themes to construct meaning. As Maykut and Morehouse (1994) explain: "If reality is multiple and constructed, it follows that the causal links will be mutual (that is, **constructed**) and that in terms of what an event of action means, the event is not unidirectional but multidirectional" (p. 11). The implication for education, clearly, is that the teacher/educator/facilitator constructs meaning **with** the learners. Research on education, from the alternate/emerging approach, can be characterized by a close examination of people's words, actions, and documents.

The significance of the emerging paradigm to the discussion of multicultural education is at least two-fold: (a) greater importance must be assigned to qualitative, anthro-ethnographic, case study research than has heretofore been given, particularly in understanding cultural and cross-cultural concepts and ultimately in unlocking the door to sociocultural knowledge; (b) the constructionist perspective of knowledge, a corollary of the emergent paradigm, must be developed to balance the traditional positivist position on peoples, nations, and their cultures that has ignored microculture voices, experiences, and histories.

The constructionist perspective is rooted in the notion that for humans knowing is a result of continual building and rebuilding (Garcia, 1994) and that knowledge is always acquired by an individual through his or her cognitive filter. (It is not the intent of this article to review the development of new historicism, ethnohistory, or constructionist theory). The constructionist approach to education is founded on the recognition of the learners' language and culture, in the school, the home, and the community (Spindler, 1982). This interpretation of the learning process precludes the implicit curriculum of ready-made materials that all students learn the same way, at the same time, on the same day, with the same strategy, through the same modality, in the same cultural style, with the same strengths. Rather, the tenets of anthro-ethnographic and constructionist perspectives respect individual difference while promoting understanding to achieve social, political, economic, and educational equity.

The Impact of Paradigms on Teaching Multicultural Education

Conceptualization of the emergent paradigm provides a key to unlocking the door to education that is culturally responsible and equitable. More traditional, linear, positivist thinking is frustrated by a perspectival response that does not provide the objective yes/no, true/false, right/wrong dichotomous answer being sought. Students enter teacher education and, in many colleges, graduate from teacher education programs, without having their traditional paradigm perspective challenged.

In multicultural education courses, the very nature of the content challenges their mechanical, linear, positivist worldview. In fact, to even begin to comprehend qualitative research and the ethnography of schooling, the history of oral tradition cultures, and the literature of people of color and women, the student of culture must leave the world of numbers, hypotheses, and proofs to journey with a multiple-perspectives worldview that hears words and discovers and builds meaning anew. This constructionist perspective of the world separates the successful student of multicultural education from the student who is expecting to prove his answer right by matching it to the teacher's edition answer key. In the emergent paradigm, no such answer key to life exists.

Because the focus of multicultural education courses is on developing the knowledge base for culturally responsible pedagogy, such courses frustrate the student who enters class believing the content will teach how to "treat" black children, the "correct" way to interact with Hispanic children, "how to," "what," "when to" *ad nauseam*—all in simple true/false and matching pairs that will insure easy test grades. Student frustration stems, in part, from lacking a conceptual foundation to approach issues of diversity. This frustration may be compounded by the admonition that major parts of the knowledge base come from data bases that a positivist worldview does not acknowledge.

Recently in a graduate-level multicultural course, a student challenged data on second language acquisition. When he queried what research supported the interpretations, several case studies were offered as supporting documentation. He retorted: "I didn't think it was real research." It seems that before we can teach multicultural education and develop empathy for others' worldviews, we must first empower ourselves to understand the alternate emerging paradigm of research and constructivist theory of knowledge. Without this open-window structure, the parameters of the knowledge base bounce off the closed doors of the positivist mind. To paraphrase Gandhi, we need to allow the winds of other lands to blow through our house, but not be knocked off of our foundation by them. Thus it must be the multiculturalist who is to construct meaning from the complexity of multiple world views.

While most educational reform challenges have acknowledged that the restructuring agenda for the 21st century should focus on the increasing diversity of America's students, the traditional response "has always been to accommodate student diversity within a preexisting framework designed from a mainstream perspective with little or no regard for diversity" (Brown, 1992, p. 10). This has often translated into an "Indians[2] at Thanksgiving, Black History in February" approach to diversity, also referred to as the "foods, festivals, fashions and famous people" approach to multiculturalism. As we focus on the relationship of human diversity to the knowledge base for teaching and teacher education, the restructuring must go beyond surface culture issues to explore deep structure dilemmas inherit in diversity and cross-cultural understanding. Rather than a divisive and negative process, as its adversaries have called it, truly **multicultural** efforts recognize multiple perspectives and different strengths as a growth process for a country that is beginning to ask serious questions about where it has been and where it is going.

The melting pot theory is finally being debunked as an ideology that was never operative in American society, nor in the educational system that mirrored that society. Equally, women, differently-abled peoples, lesbian and gay individuals, and the elderly have been assuming more active, creative roles in the shaping of the American mosaic. A reclaiming of history and voice by misrepresented and disenfranchised peoples continues to reshape the American identity.

The point to be made is that we face a very different set of issues than any educational paradigm has encountered heretofore. What is needed is a culturally sensitive and responsible pedagogy for **all** students in American education. The issue is not a color-bound, nor a language-specific one. Culturally responsible pedagogy subsumes **all** diversities to insure sensitivity to and responsibility for all students as learners. Rather than a goal of assimilation to the present order, the main purpose of education becomes one of maximizing learning for every student and determining how each learner can best achieve his or her potential creating anew rather than reproducing the old. Based on this inclusive orientation, G. Pritchy Smith has identified "Parameters of the Knowledge Base for Culturally Responsible and Responsive Teacher Education"[3] (in press), as the framework for structuring content in multicultural education courses. Smith posits:

> Some educators argue that there is no knowledge base for culturally responsible/responsive teacher education, that is, that there is no solid body of theory and research literature. Saying that "there is no knowledge base" is more of a statement about the limitations of the speaker's knowledge base than it is a statement about the reality of the knowledge base, and usually means that the speaker's reading has been restricted to the mainstream, generic literature that undergirds most traditional education programs. (Smith, 1992)

Notes

1. A reference to Steinbeck's classic novel, *Of Mice and Men*.
2. The term "Native American" is preferred by the author to indicate aboriginal or native claim to the country known as America. To enunciate that "American" is a label denoting citizenship rather than ethnic heritage, the author has avoided hyphenated-Americans.
   American Indian, often used synonymously, reflects a misnomer—the result of Columbus' mistaken belief that he had reached the shores of India. When citing other authors, original terminology has, of course, been maintained. The terms "Native American," "American Indian," "Native," and "Indian," therefore, are used interchangeably.
3. For a more complete review of the integration of the parameters in a teacher education program see Huber, T., Kline, F.M., Bakken, L., & Clark, F. L. (in press). From Traditional teacher education to culturally responsible pedagogy: Moving a graveyard. In King, Hayman, & Hollins (Eds.) *Meeting the challenge of cultural diversity in teacher preparation*.

References

Garcia, E. (1994). *Understanding and meeting the challenge of student cultural diversity*. Boston, MA: Houghton Mifflin Company.

Greene, M. (1993). The passions of pluralism: Multiculturalism and the expanding community. *Educational Researcher*, 22(1), 13-18.

Kuhn, T. (1962). *The structure of scientific revolutions*. Chicago, IL: University of Chicago Press.

Lincoln, Y.S., & Guba, E.G. (1985). *Naturalistic inquiry*. Beverly Hills, CA: Sage.

Maykut, P., & Morehouse, R. (1994). *Beginning qualitative research: A philosophic and practical guide*. London, United Kingdom: The Falmer Press.

Polanyi, M. (1958). *Personal knowledge: Toward a post-critical philosophy*. Chicago, IL: The University of Chicago Press.

Smith, G.P. (in press). Parameters of the knowledge base for culturally responsible and responsive teacher education.

Spindler, G. (1982). *Doing the ethnography of schooling: Educational anthropology in action*. Prospect Heights, IL: Waveland Press.

Article 11

Recognizing Diversity within a Common Historical Narrative

The Challenge to Teaching History and Social Studies

By John Wills & Hugh Mehan

The current debate about the history and social studies curriculum has been concerned primarily with the appropriate course content in these areas of study. Essentially, the debate has turned on these questions: Should courses in United States schools present a common narrative, one that presumably unites all citizens by celebrating the achievements of Western Civilization and United States History and that emphasizes values and standards derived from Western Civilization? Or, should schools open up the historical narrative to include the contributions of people who have been omitted, most often women and minorities? And/or, should schools participate in the struggle for cultural justice and seek to advance civil rights and democratic public life?

It is our contention that the current debate about the curriculum masks deeper issues, the most fundamental of which are: How is a society constituted? What differences make a difference in constituting a society? Or, a little more specifically: Who are we as Americans? Who do we include in the narrative of the history of American society?

There is also a debate about epistemology lurking beneath the surface of this discussion. On the one hand, those educators who call for a common historical narrative often treat history (that is, knowledge) as natural, fixed, context-free, and

John Wills is a faculty member at the University of Rochester and Hugh Mehan is a faculty member at the University of California, San Diego.

timeless. On the other hand, multiculturalists who call for an expanded view of history introduce alternative and competing narratives, which in turn lead to a different conception of history—one that is perspectival, constructed, and relative to historical setting and context.

It is our understanding that school knowledge, including historical knowledge, is socially constructed. The teaching and learning process has often been informed by a cultural transmission model in which teachers transmit school knowledge, located in the curriculum, to passive students who consume this knowledge with varying degrees of accuracy. In opposition to this unidirectional understanding of teaching and learning, we argue that school knowledge emerges in the interaction between teachers, students, and a variety of school texts that are used in instruction. While the determination of what counts as school and historical knowledge is a social and cultural accomplishment, this negotiation is not an even or level process. Teachers and other state-sanctioned officials have more authority in defining what counts as legitimate or useful knowledge in classrooms than do students.

We provide some orienting details concerning the current debate about the curriculum, pointing out that precious few of the participants in the debate have been very helpful in guiding teachers about how to teach history and social studies. Despite this lack of guidance from the national debate concerning what to teach on Monday, teachers have been working hard to

inject previously missing groups into their social studies and history curricula. Unfortunately, teachers have fallen into a number of traps when they have attempted to diversify their curriculum.

After reviewing the consequences of those difficulties, we propose an alternative perspective on the teaching of history and social studies that maintains the continuity of a unifying historical narrative (albeit one that emphasizes the struggle for civil rights instead of a celebration of a democracy achieved, a possession that must be protected and revered) while including previously omitted voices as active participants in significant historical events.

The Current Debate about the Curriculum

A significant group of educators in the current curriculum debate assert that the fundamental purpose of education is to unify society. According to these educators, in order to unify the citizenry, a common core curriculum and a common historical narrative is needed, and should be taught to all United States students. In the current debate, Hirsch (1987) and Bloom (1987) were among the first to call for a common core curriculum. They lamented the loss of a shared set of cultural facts, images, and allusions that enabled U.S. citizens to communicate effectively and understand each other. Hirsch (1987) traced the decline in shared knowledge to the adoption of value neutral and value relative curriculum in the 1960s, while

Bloom blamed elite universities for setting the current generation of students adrift on a sea of superficial and naive moral relativism. Education, they said, is no longer used to teach moral values. The way to overcome this value relativism, they said, is to teach a core set of ideas and facts to all American elementary and secondary students.

The relevant texts in Hirsh's proposal to regain "cultural literacy" would be drawn from Western Civilization, the core political values from American democracy, the ethical values from a secularized version of the Judeo-Christian tradition, coupled with industriousness, honesty, tolerance of others. The legal concepts would be drawn from the English legal tradition. The language for instructing students in cultural literacy would be English only.

This call for a common core curriculum occurred when the economic condition of the country was worsening. It was supported by many members of the Reagan and Bush administrations, including former Secretary of Education William Bennett (1992), former Assistant Secretary of Education Diane Ravitch (1990), former Assistant Secretary of Education Chester Finn (1991), and Chairman of the National Endowment of the Humanities Lynne Cheney (1995)—all of whom cited the numerous national and international academic surveys which showed U.S. students not doing as well as their German and Japanese counterparts. U.S. society is threatened, these commentators reasoned, because students are not accumulating the necessary knowledge to enable the U.S. to compete against Japan and Germany in the global economy.

Members of the Republican party transformed the common core curriculum position in an intellectual debate into a concrete course of action. President Bush included suggestions from the National Governor's Conference in "America 2000," which called for national curriculum standards and a regimen of testing to see how well states, schools, and K-12 students were mastering skills in basic courses of study (Bush, 1991). At the same time, the National Center for History in the Schools (Crabtree & Nash, 1994a, 1994b) developed a preliminary proposal for national standards for the teaching of United States and World History. After considerable controversy over the content of the draft standards, a final recommendation that emphasizes student inquiry, research, and interpretation has been produced (Crabtree & Nash, 1996).

A group of educators and researchers who have come to be called "multiculturalists" have criticized the existing curricula in history and social studies and the call by Hirsh and Bloom for a common core curriculum because ethnic minorities, women, people with disabilities, and gays have been excluded from the historical narrative (Sleeter & Grant, 1988; Banks, 1989; Nieto, 1992; Banks & Banks, 1995). Multicultural educators favor a robust plu-

> ...we propose an alternative perspective on the teaching of history and social studies that maintains the continuity of a unifying historical narrative...while including previously omitted voices as active participants in significant historical events.

ralism—which in its most extreme form, may include cultural separatism—but in general, favors diversified, highly contextualized curricula, those which not only include the standards of western culture, but also the historical and cultural experiences unique to the backgrounds of students (Massaro, 1993).

Multicultural educators want the historical narrative to include the contributions of outgroups whose histories have been trivialized, misstated, or omitted. Doing so, they claim, would give a richer, fuller, less romantic and sanitized view of history. As a result, students would learn that life, liberty, and the pursuit of happiness may be foundational principles of American society, but racism, sexism, and other forms of prejudice make it harder for some groups to compete equally for these goals. Unless the facts of gender, ethnic, and racial discrimination are acknowledged, they argue, then their harmful effects cannot be ameliorated and goals of liberty and justice will not be achieved.

In the process of calling for a more inclusive historical narrative, multicultural educators tend to reject universal and foundational claims to truth, value, and beauty. Instead, they adopt a form of anthropological relativism that argues that morality is rooted in a particular culture's history, conventions, practices, and beliefs. Therefore, they reason, the moral standards of one society can not be subjected to criticism from the point of view of an other culture's standards or by appeal to one transcultural standard.

Multicultural educators have been joined by advocates of "critical pedagogy" in their criticism of the way in which history and social studies are taught (see especially Aronowitz & Giroux, 1985; Darder, 1991: McLaren, 1991; Giroux, 1992; Giroux & McLaren, 1989; 1994; Apple & Beane, 1995; Sleeter & McLaren, 1995). Convinced that equality, justice, and social responsibility are the baseline conditions for a just society, they criticize the unequal distribution of economic and educational resources among groups, and say schools should participate in the struggle for cultural justice and should seek to advance civil rights and democratic public life.

Advocates of critical pedagogy share with multiculturalists the view that systemic and pervasive discrimination plays an important part in American culture. Conflict, not merit, choice, or personal effort often explains the gap between white and non-white, rich and poor. They agree with multicultural educators that curricular innovations are necessary to achieve equity, but educational changes are hardly sufficient, critical theorists assert, because the underlying inequalities in the society at large must be addressed if a just society is to be realized.

The call for multicultural education has not been universally or calmly accepted, however. It has been challenged by educators and parents who think education should teach respect for authority and emphasize foundational skills. The multicultural movement has also been lambasted by religious fundamentalists who think schools should teach Bible values, the constitution, and patriotism (Delfatorre, 1992).

Basically, its critics contend that the multicultural approach to education is politically and culturally divisive. Because multiculturalism sees race, ethnicity, class (and other **group** categories) as determinative of social action, Ravitch (1990) and Schlesinger (1991) say multicultural education encourages separatist tendencies. They cite Afrocentric curriculum as a particularly threatening case in point. In their enthusiasm to include omitted groups and achieve social justice, D'Souza (1991) fears universities are becoming bastions of political correctness. Cheney (1995) says multicultural education's move to diver-

2. TEACHER EDUCATION IN MULTICULTURAL PERSPECTIVE

sify the canon trivializes "the great works of Western Civilization" because some lesser texts are included under the guise of a quota system.

Furthermore, multicultural education has been criticized because it relativises beauty, reason, truth, and merit. Educators and parents who believe that there are a set of values derived from "Western Civilization" that persevere, that transcend, argue against the anthropological idea incorporated within multiculturalism that measures of human achievement are bound by history, culture, and context. Cheney (1995: 25) is particularly vitriolic in her condemnation of the relativism she sees contained in the National History Standards because they engage in the "systematic denigration of America's Western heritage." Aspects of Western Civilization, starting from Hellenic Greece and continuing through industrialization, are presented in negative light, while aspects of Chinese, African, and Aztec cultures are celebrated, she says. Cheney is particularly upset that the draft standards (Crabtree & Nash, 1994a, 1994b) would encourage students to consider the architecture, labor systems, and agriculture of the Aztecs, but not their practice of human sacrifice, and the gathering of wealth by an African king would be celebrated but denigrated when practiced by railroad barons. In lieu of this "post modern" "politically correct" dogma, Cheney (1995: 29) wants to install a "celebratory history" in the schools, one that reminds students of the "true glory" of Western Civilization and United States history.

Traps and Pitfalls When Recognizing Diversity in the Curriculum

The debate about the curriculum (and its more foundational issues concerning the constitution of society and historical knowledge) is not just an abstract and general argument among academics and policy wonks. Educators in elementary, high school, and college classrooms have been wrestling with the best way to recognize diversity in their history and social studies curricula.

We have examined middle school classrooms in which teachers have attempted to present multicultural histories of the United States (Wills, 1996, 1994; Mehan, Lintz, Okamoto & Wills, 1995) and we have made more casual observations of the efforts by elementary and secondary school teachers to construct more inclusive versions of United States and world history. As these educators have attempted to recognize diversity in the curriculum, they have fallen into a number of traps. After we describe some of the pitfalls, we propose an alternative approach which can help teachers avoid these traps.

The Culture Trap in Reforming the Curriculum

"Cultural tourism" is one trap that awaits teachers who attempt to construct a more inclusive history. Cultural tourism results when underrepresented groups are treated as "cultural representatives" and not as "social" or "historical" actors. Cultural tourism also occurs when students are invited to study the cultural attributes of specific groups as static and fixed, rather than establishing the presence of members of cultural groups as social actors in particular historical events in American history. Like tourists, students are invited to travel to "foreign lands" and learn about exotic people and places, and then return home to a place in which these people have no relevance in their daily lives. And yet, the cultures that students are studying are not foreign to American history, but a part of it. When the approaches to including diverse groups in American history situate these groups outside of history, then students' knowledge of these groups becomes that of a tourist—knowlege of an exotic people, an "other," who have no bearing on their own lives, or our history. As a consequence, students may conclude incorrectly that certain people, being members of cultural groups, have fixed cultural attributes, perhaps with a unique culture or way of life and a unique and "different" perspective on the world.

For example, one eighth grade United States history teacher had her students conduct research on a variety of Native American tribes located in the Eastern Woodlands during the Colonial period of American history. Students produced "Fact or Fiction" books based on this research which addressed the material culture, religion, family life, clothing, social and political organization, and artistic expressions of selected Native American tribes.

The results of this engaging activity were a success as far as generating cultural information about Native American tribes, but this work failed to locate these Native American tribes within American history, or portray them as social actors within any specific historical events. For example, the students studying the Mohawk Indians reported that Mohawk children wore no clothing whenever possible, that the Mohawk did not live in teepees, that the Mohawk were skillful and fierce warriors, and that Mohawk Indians built bridges and skyscrapers in the United States and Canada because they had no fear of heights. But Mohawk actions in particular historical events, such as the French-American War, were never mentioned. As a result, the Mohawks seem to exist outside of any narrative structure, sometimes in an elusive past, sometimes in an elusive present (e.g., gangs of Mohawk Indians building skyscrapers and bridges), but never in the events and happenings that constitute American history.

Brief essays that these students wrote on the origins of the United States reinforce our conclusion that they did not see Native American tribes as part of American history. Seldom did the students mention Native Americans during the colonial period in their origin narratives, even though they spent a number of weeks studying and talking about Native American cultures during this historical period. The information they had learned about the **cultures** of Native American tribes was simply not relevant to the **history** of colonial America.

Because these Native Americans exist outside of history, students have no knowledge of them as social actors in colonial America. What they thought of the White settlers, their interactions with these settlers, and the effects this had on their way of life are dormant topics. Even though these Native Americans can serve as "cultural representatives" of the Mohawk, Delaware, or other tribes studied, they cannot serve as examples of Native Americans as social or historical actors. If they were assigned the role of historical actors, then students would have an opportunity to understand the history of Native American-White relations in the United States which, in turn, is potentially useful knowledge for thinking about these relations in the present.

Other activities carried out in this classroom also fall victim to "cultural tourism" because they focus on cultural attributes rather than history or social action. The students read a novel, *The Light in the Forest* (Richter, 1953), about True Son, a white child abducted in a raid and raised by the Delaware Indians. As a young man, True Son is forcibly returned to his white family but refuses to renounce his Delaware heritage and attempts to return to his tribe. In a class discussion, students were asked to decide, having learned about Native American cultures, whether they would want to live with the Whites or with the Native Americans if they found themselves in a similar situation as True Son. The class discussion is telling, because students explain that they would rather live with the Indians because they are "better people" with "better moral values," while Whites are "kind of jerks" who like to "take over the land" and "control it." While this discussion is an opportunity for the students to explore their stereotypes concerning Native Americans, the discussion is in fact about deciding what kind of people Native Americans are, and what kind of people Whites are. The students conclude that Native Americans and Whites are distinct kinds of people, because they have unique cultures, which determine their outlook on the world and actions in it.

This incipient cultural determinism is also evident in a number of "Point of View" exercises that this eighth grade teacher conducted with her students. The exercises, revolving around *The Light in the Forest*, emphasize how culture influences the different outlook of Native Americans and Whites to the world—whether to adapt to the land or adapt the land to your needs, how Fort Pitt would seem like an "ugly, treeless prison" to Native Americans but a "safe home" to Whites, and the like. These activities and exercises are useful in establishing the cultural differences between Native Americans and White settlers. But these activities are not useful in explaining the role these differences played in shaping the interactions between Native Americans and Whites in colonial history.

This multicultural approach to recognizing diversity in history can lead teachers away from history; none of the exercises or activities dealing with Native Americans were focused on historical events, and so they failed to place Native Americans into American history. To the extent that Native Americans are present they are present as cultural representatives. While this multicultural approach exemplifies a way of life and perspective on the world which is different from that of Whites, it tells students little to nothing about the role of Native Americans in American history, their actions in specific events, and their interactions with other groups present in the colonial period. While these Native Americans are virtually present in the classroom, they are not actually present in American history.

The Pitfalls of Including Diverse Groups in History

Critics of "traditional" American history have pointed to the absence of women and people of color as evidence of the politics behind what counts as good history. They have noted women and minorities appear and disappear from the narrative, appearing during historical periods or in events of concern to Whites. Chinese Americans work on the railroad, African Americans are enslaved during the Civil War, Native Americans are obstacles to be removed during Westward Expansion. But they remain virtually absent from the remainder of American history (cf. Banks, 1989; Sleeter & Grant, 1991; Sleeter & MacLaren, 1995).

Many teachers attempt to recognize women and people of color by highlighting their contributions and accomplishments and allowing their previously missing voices to be heard. But these efforts can be flawed, because they unintentionally situate or position women and people of color outside the historical narrative being constructed, or outside the specific historical events being examined. As a consequence, diverse groups (or more accurately their representatives) are rarely constituted as social actors in history, but instead exist outside of history as shining examples of their gender/race/ethnicity, or as gendered or racialized commentators who are supposed to speak for their "people."

The troubles that can develop when teachers attempt to animate history with women and people of color is evident in a 4th grade musical recounting the history of California. Beginning with Spanish exploration and ending in the present, this musical has all the children in unison narrating the history of California and singing portions of popular songs related to the historical periods covered, interspersed with brief skits in which small groups of students act out specific historical events.

The Native American presence in California is noted early in the musical. Specific attention is paid to the culture of Indians, with the Chumash being identified by name. The sequence includes the establishment of the mission system (it notes that the Padres, who were "well-intentioned," nevertheless "neglected and misunderstood the Indian ways of life"), the movement westward into California, the discovery of gold, statehood for California, the establishment of the transcontinental railroad, the San Francisco earthquake, the rise of the Hollywood film industry, and the agricultural wealth of California. This history of California is "traditional" in that women and people of color are virtually absent, except for the mention of being thankful for "Chinese hard labor" in finishing the railroad.

The students conclude the musical by noting the contributions great individuals have made to California. They begin by naming great (male) authors such as Mark Twain, Jack London, Robert Louis Stevenson, and others. Suddenly, students in the chorus loudly ask: "But what about the women?" and are rewarded with the names of three women authors: Helen Hunt Jackson, Mary Austin, and Ina Coolbirth. This challenge opens the door to include other women—Isadora Duncan, the mother of modern dance; Lillian Gilbreth, an engineer and mother of 12; Dorothea Lange, a photographer; and Amelia Earhart—and a few men—Jackie Robinson, a baseball player; Luther Burbank, a naturalist and experimenter; and Cesar Chavez, whose claim to fame is not mentioned—in this conclusion to the musical.

What is significant about this inclusion of women and people of color is their location in this musical. The achievements and contributions of individual women and people of color are recognized **outside** and **after** the narrative of California history constructed by the musical. It is only at the end of the musical, after the story of California finally arrives in the present, that these individuals appear on the stage, are introduced, and their accomplishments are recognized. The students—and their parents and families in the audience—witness history being made by others in the brief skits, while these notable individuals gathered on the stage in the conclusion are mere "add-ons" after the fact, after the story has been told. While these representative individuals are present on stage, they are not present in American history.

Another common multicultural approach used by teachers is to include women and people of color in history by allowing them to present their points of view in discussions of historical events. In role playing activities, for example, small groups of students adopt the role of a notable figure in history, and then comment on historical events from their unique perspective. Unlike the example of the musical on California history, this approach goes beyond the mere display of notable individuals by allowing individual women and people of color to discuss historical events, thereby providing them a somewhat more active role in the history curriculum. It is also useful in providing students with an understanding of history that is multiperspectival, allowing them to see how specific historical events were interpreted differently by different people.

This approach appeared in a discussion of the Boston Tea Party in an eighth grade United States history classroom. Small groups of students were assigned the role of important historical figures—King George, Samuel Adams (a radical patriot), John Dickinson (a moderate colonist), Abigail Adams (a female colonist), Logan (an Iroquois Indian), Crispus Attucks (an African American). After reading some information on their figures and the group they represented, students were asked to comment on the Boston Tea Party from the perspective of these people. Specifically, they were to address how they felt about what happened in this event, and what they thought about the actions of the men in this significant historical event.

There are a number of problems which

made this activity difficult for the students. The information the students have to work with is primarily biographical, and yet these voices are supposed to represent the perspective of their respective communities, about which the students have little or no information. Students lack much of the historical information necessary to successfully reanimate these voices. Additionally, having one individual speak for an entire community masks or obscures the diversity within communities; if Crispus Attucks speaks for all African Americans, then why did some African Americans support the colonists while other African Americans supported the British?

The absence of historical knowledge can plague any such role playing activity. In terms of creating a more inclusive history, however, the most significant problem with this activity concerns the situation of these individuals as speakers. The selection of the events to be discussed are "traditionally" important events. Individuals such as Logan and Attucks must speak about events that they themselves did not participate in. Logan and Attucks, unlike Samuel Adams, are not speaking as participants in the Boston Tea Party. Rather, both Logan and Crispus Attucks are asked to comment as representatives of the Native American and African American communities on the actions of radical patriots, such as Samuel Adams. In contrast, Adams gets to respond that "I think we did the right thing," speaking as an active participant in the Boston Tea Party.

Perhaps more importantly, the focus of this activity is not on history—on explaining what happened, who was involved, who did what, and the different perspectives that help to understand and explain their actions—but rather on getting the responses of people of color or women to give opinions on events that have already happened. This activity is not about explaining and understanding historical events. Instead, it is a lesson about multiple perspectives. As a result, individuals such as Logan and Attucks are positioned **outside** of history and constituted as commentators on the actions of others, individuals like Samuel Adams who exist as actors **inside** important historical events. Finally, other activities in the classroom confirm the role of patriots, loyalists, and moderates as historical actors, as the students read the Declaration of Independence, Paine's "Common Sense," and other important documents. These are the people who are quoted, pictured, and talked about in the students' textbook and other curriculum during this period in American history. Again, while diverse individuals such as Logan and Attucks are present in the classroom, they are not present in history.

The Discontinuity Trap

The *National Standards for History* (Crabtree & Nash, 1996) and the *California Framework for History and Social Studies* (State Department of Education, 1990) recommend that history be taught in such a way that students can use history to interpret current events. But when history is taught as discontinuous events, diverse groups appear in and then disappear from the narrative in unexplained ways. Therefore, students have difficulty relating the relevance of the past to current events.

For example, one eighth grade class spent a total of eight weeks studying the Civil War period, which included a detailed study of the experiences of African Americans as slaves in the South. The students learned a considerable amount about the brutalities, indignities, and injustices suffered by enslaved African Americans during this period in American history, which presented them with clear lessons about the immorality of slavery. And yet, when this teacher asked her students to connect the injustices experienced by African Americans under slavery to possible injustices experienced by African Americans in Los Angeles in the Spring of 1992—her students could not see the relevance of history in contemporary race relations.

These students had difficulty using the past to understand the present because their knowledge of the injustices experienced by African Americans in American history was anchored in slavery. Other than their presence as slaves during the Civil War, African Americans were virtually absent from the United States history they studied. The only injustices these students thought African Americans experienced were associated with their enslavement. To these students, moreover, slavery was a problem that was "solved" many years ago. Therefore, these students did not see history to be relevant in thinking about the possible injustices suffered by African Americans in contemporary United States society. Slavery was an historically specific event and, therefore, the injustice was also historically specific. Without a continuous history of African American experiences in the United States, connections between past and present injustices remained elusive.

Recognizing Diversity within a Common Historical Narrative

As we've suggested above, efforts to include diverse groups in history have fallen into some unforeseen traps. Calls for cultural diversity have unintentionally led many teachers to focus their attention on cultural attributes and not on social action in history. While culture is certainly a resource or tool which mediates social action, the task of history is not to appreciate cultural diversity (although an appreciation of cultural diversity will be a natural byproduct of history that is well taught). **The purpose of history is to understand and explain the past so that we can better understand contemporary relations in our increasingly diverse society.**

The Need For a Sociological Perspective

Focusing on cultural attributes often leads to the study of groups ahistorically, statically, and in isolation, rather than the study of groups in interaction. History is made in interaction. If history is to provide any lessons for the present, then students need to examine and understand these relations in the past. In addition, teaching history involves constructing an historical narrative (Zinn, 1980).

With this conception of history in mind, the criteria for including diverse groups becomes more clear. Women and people of color must be visible in specific historical events to be visible in history. Furthermore, they must appear as active participants, that is, social actors who made sense of their circumstances and orient their actions to others around them.

In what follows, we revisit the examples we presented above in order to construct an approach to history that includes women and people of color as participants in specific historical events. Our sociological approach avoids the traps and pitfalls of previous efforts and is more likely to achieve the goals that both common-culturalists and multiculturalists espouse. On the one hand, it recognizes diversity in the curriculum. On the other hand, it treats history as a common unifying theme, the struggle for civil rights. An added benefit of this sociological approach is that it doesn't necessarily require new curricular materials, only a shift in perspective, one which would enable teachers to make better use of the materials already at hand.

Recall the research on Native American cultures during the colonial period and the teacher's emphasis on cultural difference and point of view. Shifting the focus to an examination of social relations between Native Americans and White settlers would allow this teacher to get the same points about culture across, as well as construct a more usable history of the colonial period. The novel the students read, *The Light in the Forest*, is ripe with information on the relations between the White settlers and the local Native American tribes. With more attention to this aspect of the novel, class discussions on point of view and cultural difference would look quite different. Students could use these differences in outlook and world view to explain the actions of Native Americans and White settlers in this period of American history. **In this revised approach, the question is no longer whether culture makes a difference, but what difference did cultural difference make in the interactions between Native Americans and White settlers.**

The students' "Fact or Fiction" books could be made a more useful activity with a shift toward our sociological perspective. Rather than studying the cultural attributes of Native American tribes in isolation, attention could be redirected to examining facts concerning Native American-White relations during the colonial period, as well as the changes Native American-white contact wrought in the way of life and outlook of these Native American tribes.

The focus on groups in interaction in specific historical events would also facilitate the meaningful integration of diverse groups into the history of California recounted in the fourth grade musical. Recall that women and people of color were only showcased at the conclusion of the musical. At a minimum, shifting to a sociological perspective would make obvious the need to always situate individuals or groups in history, and to portray what they were doing in concert with others. In this instance, the relations between Native Americans and the Spanish missionaries would not simply be mentioned but acted out. A similar change would occur with the Chinese labor used to build the railroads. Diverse groups would appear uniformly throughout the American historical narrative, such as Native Americans, Chinese, and Mexican Americans in California during the Gold Rush. Shifting attention away from cultural attributes and toward social life would help students understand how history is made as diverse peoples came together in specific times and places.

Finally, this shift to a sociological perspective would affect the approach to integrating or recognizing multiple perspectives in the discussion of historical events. When teachers recognize that history consists of social actors, then teachers would be encouraged to choose certain kinds of events rather than others for discussion. Teachers would want to be careful to include events in which women and people of color could authentically speak as active participants in them. In the case of the Boston Tea Party, for example, Crispus Attucks could debate Samuel Adams, a radical patriot, and Thomas Peters, an African American contemporary who allied himself with the British, about whether or not African Americans should support the colonists or the British in the Revolutionary War. Juxtaposing Attucks, Peters, and Adams would not only constitute African Americans as actors in history, but would also demonstrate to students the diversity of opinion within cultural/racial/ethnic groups. This approach does not mean that a representative of every cultural/racial/ethnic group would necessarily have to speak as a participant in every event; but, when representatives of groups do appear, they would appear in appropriate historical events, thus constituting them as participants in history, speakers inside rather than outside the narrative of American history.

Our sociological approach to teaching history adds a new dimension to what Banks (1989) has called the "transformative approach" to multicultural education. In Banks' approach, the curriculum is changed to enable students to view concepts, issues, events, and themes from the perspective of diverse ethnic and cultural groups. Central to his approach is the infusion of various frames of reference that provide students with a more complex understanding of United States society.

In fact, the "multiple perspective" activities implemented in the classrooms we studied could be seen as examples of Banks' transformative approach. In the "Point of View" exercises in particular, students were not simply exposed to the view of European colonists; they were asked to view issues and events from the cultural standpoint of different communities within colonial America.

As we've seen, however, a multiple perspective approach is not as transformative as one might imagine, because women, Native Americans, and African Americans are not situated as actors in American history. Students learned about the existence of diverse perspectives to be sure, but these were divorced from any examination of the specific actions taken by these groups in specific historical events. While students learned about distinct cultural points of view, they did not learn how the actions of distinct groups, informed by their unique perspectives, contributed to our common history. The lesson is that a transformative approach can be inclusive, but it is not necessarily inclusive in any meaningful way unless the people who hold diverse perspectives are rendered as active participants in history.

11. Recognizing Diversity

Studying Social Life In History

The emphasis in our sociological approach to history is on social life. We believe that history should prepare and enable students to think critically about contemporary society by providing them relevant lessons from the past. To do this, history must help students understand and explain the interactions between diverse groups in specific historical events and during particular historical periods because these events constitute our common history.

There are a number of features in our sociological approach that will enable teachers to successfully recognize diversity in their history curriculum. First, the focus is on society, which means students should not study groups in isolation, but rather groups in interaction. Society—whether equal or unequal, just or unjust—is constituted in this interactional space between groups. If students are going to learn lessons from history that are relevant to the present, then this is where the lessons are going to be found. Therefore, diverse groups must always be situated in society. They must always be constituted as social actors who are interacting with others. The focus of inquiry within history and social studies must be on explaining and understanding these actions.

A second recommendation that emerges from our approach is situating diverse groups in time and space. Commentators who disagree on other points (such as Crabtree, Nash, and Cheney) agree that history is, or should be, in the words of the *National Standards for History* and the *California History-Social Studies Framework*, a "story well told." History, as a well-told story, is a sequence of events about the struggle for civil rights that adds up to the story of America. Teachers need to recognize that along with their students, they are constructing a narrative of events about the struggle for rights which constitutes American history. This story about the struggle for rights tells us who we are as Americans (Gitlin, 1995). If diverse groups are to be meaningfully included in the curriculum, then they need to exist in this civil rights narrative. To do so means situating them as social actors, as active participants, in specific historical events and periods.

Third, our sociological approach to teaching history is necessarily conversational and, therefore, multiperspectival. The goal in learning about American history is to understand and explain historical events. Why did this event turn out this way and not some other way? Explaining historical events necessitates including all the participants in them. Consider, for example, the Revolutionary

2. TEACHER EDUCATION IN MULTICULTURAL PERSPECTIVE

War. Students will gain a deeper and richer understanding of this event if the views of women, African Americans, and Native Americans are included along with the views of those that are usually presented, White male colonists and the British. After all, Native Americans were a force to be reckoned with in the colonial period. It mattered to the British and the colonists who they decided to support. Similarly, African Americans did fight on both the British side and the colonists' side. Therefore, understanding their participation will enrich students' understanding of this crucial and significant event in American history. Studying history as social interaction then not only tells us about African Americans and Native Americans, but also the views of the White colonists as well. A conversational or multiperspectival approach provides us the opportunity to learn about all the parties involved (Zinn, 1980).

This sociological approach is evident in one sixth grade teacher's approach to studying Ancient Civilizations. Faced with the problem of meaningfully including the civilizations of India and China in the more traditional study of Egypt, Greece, and Rome (i.e., Western Civilization), this teacher developed a curriculum that focused on society and social life, rather than exploring the cultures of these groups. This teacher did not simply teach the food, clothing, music, and art of these groups, which is the approach so often taken by teachers attempting to include diversity in their curriculum (Cochran-Smith, 1995; Sleeter & Grant, 1987). Instead, she organized her students into small groups to research either the daily life, religion, political organization, economic organization, or science and technology of one of these civilizations. Students had to work on different civilizations throughout the year. Therefore, the group that reported on daily life in China would study the political organization in Egypt, science in China and India, etc.

In this way, the students became familiar with different aspects of all five civilizations and were able to recognize the contributions and accomplishments of each. For example, the Egypt and China research groups each declared that they were the first to make paper. This led to a comparison of dates to establish who was actually first, followed by a discussion of the nature of history, and how history gets written. Similar discoveries occurred throughout the year as students discovered equivalent scientific and technological accomplishments shared by these diverse civilizations. Because students continually studied all of these civilizations—rather than studying Egypt, Greece, and Rome (Western Civilization), and then adding on the study of India and China if time permitted—India and China were recognized as equally significant civilizations in the ancient world.

Students discovered the social interactions that existed between these civilizations during their investigations. When entering this class, these students had perceived each civilization to be distinct, existing in isolation, with one civilization dying as another one rose to take its place. By the end of the school year, the students had gained the sense that these civilizations inhabited the same world over a period of many years and interacted with one another through trade, warfare, and cultural exchange. Instead of seeing these civilizations as distinct cultural groups, students came to realize, often on their own, the interconnectedness of these civilizations, and the mutual influences they had on one

References

Apple, Michael W. & J.A. Beane. 1995. *Democratic Schools*.
Aronowitz, Stanley & Henry A. Giroux. 1985. *Education Under Siege: The Conservative, Liberal and Radical Debate Over Schooling*. Hadley, MA: Bergin & Garvey.
Banks, James A. 1989. Multicultural Education: Characteristics and Goals. In: James A. Banks & Cherry A. McGee Banks (Eds.), *Multicultural Education: Issues and Perspectives* (pp. 2—26). Boston, MA: Allyn & Bacon.
Banks, James A. & Cherry A. McGee Banks (Eds.). 1995. *Handbook on Research on Multicultural Education*. New York: MacMillan.
Bennett, William J. 1992. *The De-Valuing of America: The Fight for our Culture and Our Children*. New York: Summit Books.
Bloom, Alan. 1987. *The Closing of the American Mind: How Higher Education Has Failed Democracy and Impoverished the Souls of Today's Students*. New York: Simon & Schuster.
Bush, George. 1991. *Goals 2000: An American Educational Strategy*. Washington. DC: U.S. Department of Education.
California State Department of Education. 1990. *Framework for History and Social Studies*. Sacramento, CA: Department of Education.
Cheney, Lynne V. 1995. *Telling the Truth: Why Our Culture and Our Country Have Stopped Making Sense—and What We Can Do About It*. New York: Simon & Schuster.
Cochran-Smith, Marilyn. 1995. Color Blindness and Basket Making Are Not the Answers: Confronting the Dilemmas of Race, Culture, and Language Diversity in Teacher Education. *American Educational Research Journal* 32 (3): 493—522.
Crabtree, Charlotte & Gary B. Nash. 1994a. *National Standards for United States History: Exploring the United States Experience, Grades 5—12*. Los Angeles, CA: National Center for History in the Schools.
Crabtree, Charlotte & Gary B. Nash. 1994b. *National Standards for World History: Exploring the Paths to the Present, Grades 5—12*. Los Angeles, CA: National Center for History in the Schools.
Crabtree, Charlotte & Gary B. Nash. 1996. *National Standards for Teaching History: Basic Edition*. Los Angeles, CA: National Center for History in the Schools.
Darder, Antonia. 1991. *Culture and Power in the Classroom: A Critical Foundation for Education*. New York: Bergin & Garvey.
Delfattore, Jean. 1992. *What Johnny Shouldn't Read*. New Haven: Yale University Press.
D'Souza, Dinish. 1991. *Illiberal Education: The Politics of Race and Sex on Campus*. New York: Free Press.
Finn, Chester. 1991. *We Must Take Charge*. New York: Basic Books.
Giroux, Henry A. & Peter L. McLaren (Eds.). 1989. *Critical Pedagogy, The State and Cultural Struggle*. Albany, NY: State University of New York Press.
Giroux, Henry A. & Peter McLaren (Eds.). 1994. *Between Borders: Pedagogy and the Politics of Cultural Studies*. New York: Routledge & Kegan Paul.
Gitlin, Todd. 1995. *The Twilight of Common Dreams: Why America Is Wracked by Culture Wars*. New York: Henry Holt.
Hirsch, E.D., Jr. 1987. *Cultural Literacy: What Every American Needs to Know*. Boston, MA: Houghton Mifflin..
MacLaren, Peter L. 1991. Critical Pedagogy, Multiculturalism and the Politics of Risk and Resistance. *Journal of Education* 173 (3): 109-139.
Massaro, Toni Marie. 1993. *Constitutional Literacy: A Core Curriculum for a Multicultural Nation*. Durham, NC: Duke University Press.
Mehan, Hugh, Angela Lintz, Dina Okamoto & John S. Wills. 1995. Ethnographic Studies of Multicultural Education in Classrooms and Schools. In: James A. Banks & Cherry A. McGee Banks (Eds.), *Handbook on Research on Multicultural Education*. New York: MacMillan.
Nieto, Sonia. 1992. *Affirming Diversity: The Sociopolitical Context of Multicultural Education*. White Plains, NY: Longman Publishers.
Ravitch, Diane. 1990. Multiculturalism: E Pluribus Plures. *The Key Reporter* 56 (1): 1-4.
Richter, Conrad. 1953. *The Light in the Forest*. New York: Knopf.
Schlesinger, Arthur, M. Jr. 1992. *The Disuniting of America*. New York: Norton.
Sleeter, Christine E. & Carl A. Grant. 1987. An Analysis of Multicultural Education in the United States. *Harvard Educational Review* 57 (4): 421—444.
Sleeter, Christine E. & Carl A. Grant. 1991. Mapping Terrains of Power: Student Knowledge vs. Classroom Knowledge. In: C. E. Sleeter (Ed.), *Empowerment Through Multicultural Education*. Albany, NY: State University of New York Press.
Sleeter, Christine E. & Peter L. McLaren. 1995. *Multicultural Education, Critical Pedagogy and the Politics of Difference*. Albany, NY: State University of New York Press.
Wills, John S. 1994. Popular Culture, Curriculum, and Historical Representation: The Situation of Native Americans in American History and the Perpetuation of Stereotypes. *Journal of Narrative and Life History* 4 (4): 277—294.
Wills, John S. 1996. Who Needs Multicultural Education? White Students, U.S. History, and the Construction of a Usable Past. *Anthropology and Education Quarterly* 27 (3): xx—yy.
Zinn, Howard. 1980. *A People's History of the United States*. New York: HarperCollins.

another. Locating these civilizations on a timeline and establishing their location in the world, students were surprised to discover that Egypt, Greece, and Rome shared the Mediterranean world, and that India and China shared the Himalayan Mountains on their borders. The end result of this teacher's sociological approach to the teaching of history was the construction of a narrative of the ancient world, a common story that united Egypt, Rome, and Greece without marginalizing the civilizations of India and China. **Perhaps more importantly, the students learned that history is about explaining and understanding social life, not on evaluating the "cultural worth" of civilizations.**

Conclusions

Critics have complained that the introduction of multiple perspectives in the curriculum makes history radically relativistic. Students will no longer be able to evaluate the merits of competing points of view about contentious historical events such as the Holocaust, the Vietnam War, or the Civil Rights movement. Or, if students study the social organization of the Upic, the Americans, and the Mexicans, and learn that one cultural system is as functional as another, then how do students judge the superiority of any one society? Our response to this criticism is that the purpose of history is to explain, not to evaluate. When a multi-perspectival history is taught well, it will provide students with the grounds upon which they can make judgments and evaluations about significant historical events.

Another important result of our sociological approach to the teaching of history is it invites us to rethink the relationship between identity and society. Multicultural approaches—as they exist in practice in actual classrooms—begin with peoples' ethnic or racial identity, which relegates society to a residual status. We suggest beginning with society, which, of necessity, will turn our attention to how racial and ethnic identities are constituted in social life. Identity is not a fixed characteristic of individuals and groups. It is not always a relevant attribute that affects interactions in particular ways. Identity is instead a fluid process that emerges in interaction. Such features as race, ethnicity, and gender **may** be relevant in a variety of ways, **may** be relevant in some situations, but not in others. Furthermore, the "identity politics" that emerge from multiculturalism celebrates membership in a racial, ethnic, or gendered group, which deflects attention away from the civic identities that are needed to maintain a democratic, civil society (Gitlin, 1995).

The question to address, then, is not simply what difference does cultural difference make, because this approach can fall into the essentialist trap of assuming that race, ethnicity, and gender are ascribed, indeed permanent characteristics of people. The question to address is: What differences make a difference in specific historical events and periods?—an approach that assumes identities are fluid and ever-changing, something that is achieved, constructed, and constituted in and through social interaction. This sociological view of identity in relationship to society necessitates a different kind of work in the history classroom, one which we have tried to outline above. In this approach the relevance of diversity in history is always an empirical question, and the focus of attention is always on society, out of which identity emerges.

We accept the premise that the teaching of history requires a common narrative, although we believe that the common core of this narrative is the struggle for civil rights, not the celebration of inevitable progress. We also accept the critique that the historical narrative often taught in schools is Eurocentric, has excluded the voices of minorities and women, and has neglected or suppressed issues of injustice. We also recognize that the task of teaching history is a complex one: how to construct and teach a narrative that tells us who we are as Americans while being inclusive and honest about institutional racism, exploitation, and discrimination.

If we begin the teaching of history with an inclusive narrative about the struggle for civil rights, then students will draw upon it unconsciously. The inclusive narrative will provide them "naturally" with a diverse view of what it means to be an American. **When an inclusive narrative is the taken-for-granted starting point, then issues concerning social justice, equality, and discrimination are more easily raised, because everyone is present, everyone is an active participant, and everyone is a speaker in the conversation about the constitution of American society.**

South Carolina Unrevised

Portrayals of Race in Current South Carolina History Textbooks

By Alan Wieder

Introduction

It has been over twenty years since James Banks' work began questioning the treatment of race and ethnicity in social studies textbooks. Journals like *The Social Studies*, *Social Education*, *Theory and Research*, *The Journal of Negro Education*, and *Equity and Excellence* have addressed this issue but there has not been a great deal of scholarship on the topic. Especially when we consider the quantity of recent writing on multicultural education. This study is a modest attempt to address this issue by analyzing the books currently used to teach South Carolina history.

Eighth grade students in South Carolina are required to take a course in South Carolina history. At the present time two textbooks, Lewis P. Jones's *South Carolina: One of the Fifty States* and Archie Vernon Huff Jr.'s *The History of South Carolina In the Building of the Nation*, are the approved texts for the course.[1] The purpose of this study is to describe and analyze the treatment of race in both of these books. This is important within the context of both the historical and present reality of race relations in the state. It has to be remembered that South Carolina is

Alan Wieder is a professor in the College of Education at the University of South Carolina, Columbia. Another version of this article appeared in Journal of Thought, Volume 30, Number 1.

the only state in the nation that still flies the Confederate Flag above the state capitol. Consideration of the history of the state that South Carolina children learn through their South Carolina history textbooks might help clarify the large and adamant support of many South Carolinians for continuing to fly the flag. It might also help to explain the white racism that is an historical and present part of life in South Carolina and the rest of the nation. This essay will begin with some background material and a brief review of the textbooks that proceeded the current texts. Frances Fitzgerald's book, *America Revised: History Schoolbooks in the Twentieth Century*, will provide the theoretical foundation for this essay. Fitzgerald's work will be integrated throughout the body of this essay and will offer valuable insights in the conclusion.

Background

The South Carolina legislature passed laws in 1896 that mandated curriculum for public schools in the state. These laws followed the 1895 Constitution which is critically referred to as South Carolina's Black Codes of 1895. The state legislature's decree requiring the teaching of South Carolina history put the state in accord with the rest of the country at this time as most states were beginning to require history classes as part of the school curriculum. Fitzgerald designates the 1890s "as

the Quatrocento of American-history text writing."[2] Fitzgerald's book offers an important insight for this essay in that Fitzgerald was particularly sensitive to the significance of tone in the texts that she reviewed.

> In some general sense, this may be the truth of the matter: what sticks to the memory from those textbooks is not any particular series of facts but an atmosphere, an impression, a tone. And this impression may be all the more influential just because one cannot remember the facts and arguments that created it.[3]

Jones's and Huff's textbooks were preceded by four turn-of-the-century textbooks and six editions of the state's most famous South Carolina school history book, the Simms/Oliphant book. This list includes John J. Dargan's *School History of South Carolina*, John Langdon Weber's *Fifty Lessons in the History of South Carolina*, John Chapman's *School History of South Carolina*, and Henry Alexander White's *The Making of South Carolina* from the turn of the century and the Simms/Oliphant texts that were used in the state from 1917 to 1970.[4]

Throughout these textbooks we find examples of the racism that Fitzgerald documents in her study. Each of the textbooks provides portraits of slaves and freedmen who loved, adored, and were loyal to white South Carolinians. None of the books addressed the harshness and inhumanity of slavery, and, in fact, each of the books portrayed the good treatment of white South Carolinians towards their slaves. Consider two examples: The first is from the 1917 Simms/Oliphant book:

> As we shall hear much a little later on about the evils of slavery, it should be said now that the slave owners in South Carolina, as a rule, treated their negroes with the greatest kindness, fed them well and clothed them comfortably. **A negro slave cost money and a slave owner would no more have thought of mistreating a slave and making him unfit to work than he would have thought of abusing a fine horse.**[5]

Thankfully the horse analogy was left out in later editions of the book although the tone continued through the 1970 edition. The second example is from the Dargan book and explains that slavery in South Carolina benefitted the slave:

> As to the effect on the slave, it must be admitted that slavery did for the negro what nothing else could have done—it brought him here and partially civilized him. Whoever else may abhor the institution, the negro everywhere should turn to it with gratitude.[6]

The early books also provided racist representations of Reconstruction. Carpetbaggers, Scalawags and Black politicians are depicted as evil and the emancipated slave is presented as a dupe of white Northerners and white southern opportunists. Both the turn of the century texts and Simms/Oliphant praise the Ku Klux Klan as a necessary organization to protect law abiding white South Carolinians. The following paragraph on Reconstruction from Dargan is not unlike the characterization in the Simms/Oliphant texts:

> So there came early into this field, to ply their nefarious arts; the "carpet-bagger"—the soulless oppressor from the North—and the "scalawag"—the soulless plunderer from the South—and for nearly ten years in South Carolina 'they robbed while they pretended to rule; they plundered while they professed to protect.' until the State became so reduced in material strength and so dispirited under the heavy weight of such conditions that it was known as the "Prostrate State."[7]

The tone that the early textbooks took on both slavery and Reconstruction is quite clear. Interestingly, we learn from Frances Fitzgerald, that it was a tone that was representative of American history textbooks throughout the country. Fitzgerald provides a composite text of pre-1970 American history textbooks' writings on Reconstruction:

> According to these books, Radical Reconstruction was an unmitigated disaster. The Reconstruction governments were imposed on the South with federal bayonets and were run by a lot of unscrupulous 'carpetbaggers' and 'scalawags.' Instead of reconstructing the region, they pillaged it. The legislatures—filled with ignorant Negroes who obeyed the dictates of the carpetbaggers and scalawags—engaged in an 'orgy of spending.' The legislators embezzled funds and voted themselves huge gold watches, imported perfume, and champagne. The tremendous corruption of these governments, combined with the anarchy caused by bands of Negroes roaming the countryside, finally forced Southerners to take action. The use of violence by the Southerners was deplorable, but the Northerners could not have expected the Southerners to submit to Negro rule, and the Ku Klux Klan had a worse reputation than it deserved.[8]

Fitzgerald then explains that American history textbooks' treatment of race went through a complete change in the midsixties and early seventies. She provides a second composite on Reconstruction which is a 180-degree change from the above quote. Although it is quite long, it is necessary that we quote it at length as a bridge to our discussion of the present texts.

> The Reconstruction state legislatures were dominated not by former slaves (only in South Carolina did the blacks have majority, and there in the lower house alone) but by people the white Southerners called carpetbaggers and scalawags, some of whom were adventurers but many of whom were sincere reformers. Corruption existed in these governments but it existed in the South both before and after Reconstruction, and it was just as prevalent in the North during that period. Public spending was enormous mainly because there was so much to be done to help the freedmen and to rebuild the devastated economy of the South. White Southerners formed a number of secret societies to oppose the Reconstruction governments, one of which was the Ku Klux Klan. To prevent the freedmen from voting, the Klan waged a campaign of terror against the blacks which included arson, beatings and murder.[9]

Fitzgerald's composite might serve as a barometer for the current textbooks' portrayals of race. What follows is a description and analysis of these texts.

The Current Texts—Introduction

South Carolina: One of the Fifty States by Lewis P. Jones and Archie Vernon Huff, Jr.'s *The History of South Carolina In the Building of the Nation*, like both the turn of the century texts and the Simms-Oliphant books, deal with both slavery and Reconstruction. Both of the current texts also devote time to Jim Crow and of course both books deal with 20th century issues and the civil rights movement in South Carolina. The styles and the spirits of the texts, however, are very different. Jones, a history professor at Wofford College, and his editors at Sandlapper Publishing have produced a glitzy Madison Avenue textbook in the new tradition that Frances Fitzgerald describes in *America Revised*. Jones's book is not one of the textbooks that Fitzgerald tells us are imitating *Architectural Digest* or *Vogue*, but its graphics and illustrations are much more sophisticated than the texts we have introduced above as well as the Huff book which is its contemporary. While Fitzgerald's conclusion is an exaggeration when comparing the Jones and Huff texts, it is worth presenting.

> Whereas in the 1950s the texts were childish in the sense that they were naive and clumsy, they are now childish in the sense that they are polymorphous-perverse. American history is not dull any longer; it is a sensuous experience.[10]

Marketing modernism aside, it is the Jones text, more than Huff's, that continues the tradition of racism in South Carolina history textbooks. Style is ironic in this situation because the Huff book is in the tradition of 1950s textbooks stylistically and is dedicated to Mary C. Simms Oliphant. Although the book is by no means a sensitive multicultural textbook, it does do a more thoughtful and equitable job in its dealing with race in South Carolina. This will become apparent as we review both books' portrayals of race in South Carolina history.

The Current Texts—Slavery

Huff's depiction of slavery begins with a description of the slave trade and offers

2. TEACHER EDUCATION IN MULTICULTURAL PERSPECTIVE

an interesting characterization of African diversity:

> Few of the slaves brought directly from Africa knew English. They belonged to many tribal groups. For example, some were Ebos, some Angolans, and others Gambians. They spoke many African dialects; some spoke Arabic. Many worshiped the spirits of their ancestors in the African tradition.[11]

This passage as well as Huff's book in general offers no great insights on race in South Carolina. Passages like this, do, however, offer possibilities of teachers infusing African and African-American culture and history as part of South Carolina history.

Jones' writing on slavery begins with the early 19th century. He introduces abolitionist voices including the Grimke sisters and does short biographies of two pro-slavery preachers—James Thornwell and Ben Palmer.[12] Jones uses bold outlined and shaded boxes throughout the text for special effect. Many of these are subtly or not so subtly racist. I will return to these boxes as we proceed and it will become apparent that the tone of the anti-slavery boxes and the boxes about white South Carolinians is very different.

Both Jones and Huff address slave rebellions and white South Carolinian's fear of blacks. The Stono Rebellion in Charleston, John Brown, and Denmark Vesey are discussed by each author but the books promote different responses. Jones stresses the justification of white fear and it is in his discussion of the slave rebellions that he begins to create a tone of blameless white South Carolinians. It is this attitude that gives the book a racist undertone and it continues as Jones discusses Reconstruction and the beginnings of Jim Crow. Consider this brief portrait of John Brown:

> In 1859, a fanatic drove the South into a frenzy. John Brown, **an unbalanced abolitionist**, with a tiny 'army' launched a rebellion at Harper's Ferry, Virginia, and called for slaves to rise and join the movement. John Brown's raid was quickly nipped in the bud and was not supported by the North. But it convinced Southerners of their worst fears concerning slave rebellions and abolitionists.[13]

Jones continues by comparing southerners' view of Brown with northerners' view of Simon Legree, thus, again implying that there was no right or wrong when it came to slavery, just differing points of view. Huff discusses white fear but he doesn't award it as much justification as Jones. There is a painting of Denmark Vesey on page 206 and the Grimke sisters are pictured on 207. Instead of emphasizing white fear Huff spends time discussing the 1840 laws that were enacted to further suppress blacks. Even when he compares northern and southern views of John Brown there is a different tone. "To the Southerners he was a symbol of the desire of the North to end slavery. To Northern abolitionists Brown was a saint and martyr."[14]

Both books also briefly describe the lives of slaves in South Carolina. Huff uses chapter ending sections titled "Eyewitness to History" to present short biographical sketches. One of these sections is a letter written in 1875 by an emancipated slave named Sancho Cooper.[15] The subtitle is "Sancho Cooper Becomes A Slave" and the letter discusses life as a slave and the importance of religion. Huff devotes two other pages to describing the life of the slave. Jones's book is more descriptive with a four page section depicting slave's life on the plantation. Although he does not write that slave's life was difficult for blacks, he writes a rather lengthy paragraph on the burdensome life of the overseer:

> Normally a crude and uncultured person, the overseer was the key individual in disciplining and managing plantation slaves. Seeking to please the owner and yet not to oppress the slaves, he couldn't win. If he drove the slaves too hard, they would rebel. He could not supervise every detail of every slaves life and be everywhere at once. He rarely had time away from his task, and hence it is not surprising that on many plantations there were frequent turnovers of overseers.[16]

Jones certainly doesn't glorify the overseer but his presentation of the trials and tribulations parallels his writing on the difficulty of life for innocent white South Carolinians preceding, during and after the Civil War.

Both Jones and Huff discuss white South Carolina leaders like Calhoun and their relationship to race and they both also discuss abolitionism. Huff bemoans the lack of leadership in the country—meaning that Clay, Webster, and Calhoun were gone and they were replaced by "southern fire-eaters" and "northern abolitionists."[17] In his chapter introduction to "Life in the Antebellum Years," he writes, "Planters dominated the state, but small farmers, poor whites, and African Americans made major contributions to society."[18] He introduces Massachusetts free black abolitionist David Walker and, of course, William Lloyd Garrison as well as the Grimke sisters. Jones introduces abolitionism as a force that fortified the white South Carolinians that advocated slavery.

> The more the Abolitionists up North screamed, the more the Southerners fell back on rationalizing or excusing. **Extremism always gives birth to extremism.**[19]

It is another case of Jones failing to place responsibility at the feet of white South Carolinians. The discussion of abolitionism provides the beginning of the **Fan the Flame** bold faced and shaded boxes that were introduced above. The effect is extremely racist because what stands out as bad is either black or northern, always under the title of **Fan the Flames**, and the remaining boxes—the ones that don't Fan the Flames—record the sensitivity of South Carolina whites. This first box is titled; "The Grimke Sisters Fan the Flames: 1839." The text inside the box introduces the Grimke's book, *Slavery As It Is: The Testimony of A Thousand Witnesses*. Jones writes that the sisters had scanned newspaper articles in the south for articles on the cruelties of slavery. He adds that it wasn't fair because it had made the South testify against itself.[20] Maybe Jones should have used more of the testimony if he had wanted an honest appraisal of South Carolina history?

Two pages after the Grimke sisters box is another titled "Opinion-Makers Fan the Flames." Jones explains that famous writers "added their voices and influence to the abolitionist movement."[21] Inside of the box is the poem, "The Slave Ships," by John Greenleaf Whittier. On the following page Calhoun's speech, "Africanization of the South," is quoted in reference to the need to stop the antislavery movement.[22] Jones then uses Harriet Beecher Stowe's *Uncle Tom's Cabin* as an illustration of a book that hardened the southerners views on slavery. This is especially troubling, especially the following quote: "More and more the South then sought to defend slavery as a good system blessed and desired by God."[23] For Jones it is another example of extremism producing extremism and it allows Jones, and thus eighth-grade students who read his texts, to elude their responsibility to critically analyze history.

Huff spends very little time on slavery during the Civil War with only some discussion of black troops and an introduction to Robert Small. Jones produces another **Fan the Flames** box, this one titled "Blacks Fan the Flames." Included in the box are short passages condemning slavery but the title is more important than the content in that it again sets up anti-slavery people as the trouble makers.[24] There is one more **Fan the Flames** box titled "Northerners Fan the Flames." Compare these with a box titled "A Southern Conscience." The content of the latter is inconsequential because the contrast of the titles is so extreme. Jones uses Mary Chesnut's *Diary From Dixie* as a continual source and presents a thoughtful discussion of white missionaries' positive view of the emancipated slaves before moving to a discussion of Reconstruction.

As stated above, Huff's portrait of race and slavery is not particularly insightful or thoughtful. Neither is it condemning of African Americans nor does it elevate white South Carolinians as did the earlier texts. Jones, also, does not present a lofty portrait of white South Carolinians during times of slavery. He spends very little time describing slavery or individual African-Americans but there is a major flaw in his work on slavery. That flaw, which continues in his discussion of Reconstruction, is that he doesn't condemn white South Carolinians and slavery. On the contrary, he provides reasons and excuses for the continuing support white South Carolinians, leaders and others, conferred upon slavery.

The Current Texts—Reconstruction

Huff and Jones keep their same differing tones in their chapters on Reconstruction. Huff begins with a very brief discussion of black inclusion and reprints the disparaging Thomas Nast cartoon of a carpetbagger as well as a painting of the Ku Klux Klan attacking three African Americans. Next to Nast's cartoon is the question: "What was Nast's view of carpetbaggers?"[25] Below the Klan picture is the following description of the organization. "The Ku Klux Klan began as a social club and soon became an organization spreading terror among black freedmen."[26] Huff's explanations are clear as is his chapter on Reconstruction. Huff discusses the same themes that are discussed in most American history textbooks—carpetbaggers, scalawags, emancipated slaves, education, the black church, and moderate and extreme white reactions to Reconstruction. Like the historians that preceded him, Huff documents Wade Hampton coming to power and he labels 1877-1890 as the conservative years:

> In South Carolina white conservatives were in power from 1877 to 1890. At first, they followed Hampton's moderate racism, but later they sought ways to keep blacks out of politics. The Conservatives kept the memory of the "Lost Cause" alive while they welcomed the industrial age they called the New South.[27]

Huff is honest in his appraisal of Wade Hampton and although he doesn't examine any of the blacks who participated in Reconstruction in any depth, with the possible exception of Robert Small. Although it would be stretching the truth to call Huff's representation of Small an extensive portrait, he does quote Small's speech at the Constitutional Convention of 1895.

> My race needs no special defense, for the past history of them in this country proves them to be the equal of people anywhere. All they need is an equal chance in the battle of life.[28]

Although Robert Small is mentioned in Lewis P. Jones's book, there is no mention of the speech cited above. Jones's Reconstruction chapter continues with the same tone that was evident in the section on slavery—the continuing conflict between north and south. Again, it was northern attitudes that lead to southern resentment. "The victors were determined not so much to reconstruct the South as they were determined to stifle (suppress) antebellum attitudes and policies in the South."[30] He creates a negative picture of the emancipated slaves and then blames Reconstruction for the continuance of white racism at the present time. Does this connect to the **Fan the Flames** boxes? Is the white racism that exists in South Carolina in the late 20th century the result of Northern and black influences during Reconstruction? As preposterous as it appears, that is what Jones alludes to. Might descriptions of the emancipated slaves, like those that Jones supplies in his text, be a more probable cause for South Carolina racism at the present time? Consider his description:

> Unprepared for their new status, lacking education needed to improve their role in society, frustrated by being downtrodden in a region now itself crushed and poverty-ridden, blacks faced a bleak future despite their new freedom in their 'Day of Jubilee.'[30]

This isn't presented to deny that there isn't some truth in Jones's description. Personally, I would have preferred the Robert Small speech that Huff quotes because it is a more honest example of possibilities for blacks when given a chance. The problem with Jones's analysis is that it presents a totally negative view of the emancipated slave and implies blame on northern whites and black people themselves rather than providing an honest presentation of the horrors of slavery or the coming horrors of Jim Crow.

Jones continues with an informative discussion on the carpetbaggers and provides thoughtful portraits of two blacks—Richard Cain and Martin Delaney. He quotes a black politician on the responsibility of blacks in power not to become scoundrels. Interestingly he perceives no need for the same warning for white politicians. Again, Jones makes interesting choices of what is important for his readers. He covers the general topics that we listed above and concludes the chapter with what would be insightful historiography if taken at face value, unfortunately it is a direct contradiction to both his account of slavery and Reconstruction. It is necessary to quote at length:

> For half a century, most accounts of the period were biased and often inaccurate. Many were written to stir fears and to strengthen white determination to prevent any change in the society which they had redeemed by ending the political reconstruction....The manner in which later generations learned their history, the views and the ideas that people had about 1865-1877, affected their thinking, their attitudes, their prejudices, their actions. People's understanding of reconstruction thus was more important than was Reconstruction itself, because it has had so much influence on the years since 1877. Studying history, you see, puts real responsibility on the reader or the student. Much of the grief of South Carolina in the last hundred years has come from its own misreading of its history. For a state with so much decency, it should have been spared that.[31]

Jones's quotation which concludes his writing on Reconstruction left me speechless upon first reading. All that I could think of was whether or not he even realized that much of his description of both slavery and Reconstruction were prime examples of **Fanning the Flame**.

The Current Texts—Jim Crow

Both textbooks begin this section with chapters on Tillmanism. Huff's is titled "Tillman and the Rise of Farmers" while Jones's chapter has the interesting title "Tillmanism: A Political Departure."

2. TEACHER EDUCATION IN MULTICULTURAL PERSPECTIVE

Whether or not Jones's title is historically accurate is open to debate, but the chapter does present a thoughtful and critical description of the oppression of African Americans. The 1895 Black Codes are presented as is a discussion on the increase of lynchings. Jones presents statistics on black illiteracy and poverty and describes black life in a section titled, "Less Happy Side of Life: Bleakness for Blacks." This is followed by a section on black leadership which presents South Carolinians in the tradition of Booker T. Washington. The text discusses black emigration to the north and Jones concludes the chapter in two ways. First he uses a box to explain why he had to present so much on race. This is interesting because I didn't think he gave race enough exposure. Finally, he finishes with a conversation on racism and stereotyping. As in all preceding discussions, Jones cannot put the blame squarely on the shoulders of white South Carolinians. He again has to equivocate:

> Too long in South Carolina, both whites and blacks have lacked the patience for that kind of approach. And all have been the worse for it. As a wise person put it once, the only way to keep another person down in a ditch is to get down in the ditch with that person.[32]

Huff's chapter presents the 1895 all-white primary, *Plessy versus Ferguson*, and Booker T. Washington as the consummate role model. It is important to stress, however, that throughout the book Huff's tone places much of the blame for slavery and racism on white South Carolinians. He presents ideas from Tillman's inaugural speech.

> In his inaugural address he urged a law against lynching, that is, mob violence against blacks. But he also made very clear his views on race. Jefferson was wrong when he said all men were created equal. Blacks were not equal. 'The whites have absolute control of the State Government,' Tillman said, 'and we intend...to retain it.'[33]

Although the contrast between the two books is not as great when discussing Jim Crow, there are examples of the same differences in tone as are found in the two preceding sections. Huff is harder on white South Carolinians and offers a more compassionate picture of blacks in the state. Jones, again, finds it impossible to declare white South Carolinians responsible for racism.

The Current Texts— The Civil Rights Movement

There is very little mention of race in either text's review of the 20th century up until the civil rights movement. Some black leaders like Benjamin Mays and Mary Mcleod Bethune are introduced but the treatment is at best cursory. Both texts introduce the Brown decision and white resistance and they both discuss civil rights sit-ins and Judge Waties Waring's decision against the state's white primary. Both Jones and Huff also present Governor Byrnes's attempt to build new black schools to satisfy the equal part of "separate but equal." Huff has a section that is titled "James F. Byrnes and The Battle For Segregation." Included is a picture of a new black school with the caption, "Why were so many black schools built." Huff's style, just like the rest of his text, is rather boring, but he is willing to ask some direct questions about racism and occasionally offers quotations from white South Carolina leaders that are somewhat incriminating:

> He blamed 'the politicians in Washington' and 'Negro agitators in South Carolina' for the state's problems. He warned that South Carolina would 'abandon the public school system' rather than desegregate.[34]

Jones begins his chapter "South Carolina Since 1945: Changing Social Patterns" with a photograph of African-American ministers marching in Orangeburg. He describes the realities of segregation and explains that court cases quickly brought important changes. This page has a photograph of Harvey Gantt and the caption tells us that he was the first black student at Clemson and later the mayor of Charlotte. It might be added that Gantt lost a close senatorial race to Jesse Helms in the early 1990s. Jones's tone is slightly different in this chapter but there are some statements that are related to the general view of the text that absolves white South Carolinians for responsibility in race relations in the state. The following passage follows a paragraph on Martin Luther King and passive resistance:

> Passive resistance and the underlying threat of violence began to win speedy results in many places. It also antagonized many supporters of white supremacy whose reaction often resulted in widespread collisions, violence and bloodshed. Not since the Civil War had the nation seemed so close to the brink of chaos. Amid all of the rioting of the 1960s, many fearfully saw the disrupted nation as approaching anarchy. The cords which held society together seemed to be snapping apart.[35]

The rest of the chapter is pretty straightforward, with Jones taking the position of a cheerleader for both black and white South Carolinians in his discussions of school integration and race relations in the state. Huff, of course, is also straightforward but he chooses to elaborate on the white forces that fought very hard against integration in the state—besides Governor Byrnes; Senator Thurmond, the Gressette committee, and Governor Timmerman's white supremist actions are discussed as is the legislature passing a law for racially pure blood banks and the firing of University of South Carolina College of Education dean Chester Travelstead. Dean Travelstead was fired for challenging the state's attempts to end state mandated schooling.

There are also differences in the author's discussions of school integration. Jones was very positive:

> When schools opened in the fall of 1970, all districts were at least 'legally and technically' complying, and by the mid-1970s were complying generally and willingly. Utopia had not arrived—it rarely does. But sanity had been preserved. In some respects, it seemed like a miracle—like unscrambling an egg. It was an accomplishment which broke with the traditions 300 years old.[36]

This discussion is preceded by a photograph of local civil rights leader Modjeska Simkins (a photograph of Governor Byrnes is on the same page) and followed by a section titled "Forces Working Toward Desegregation" which briefly discusses individuals and groups in the state that worked very hard for better race relations and the end of racism.

The Orangeburg Massacre (not so named in Jones's book) is discussed as part of a paragraph, but what is astounding is that there is no mention of the school integration battle in Clarendon County which was part of the Brown decision. Huff on the other hand discusses this battle for school integration and introduces Reverend DeLaine's heroic acts. However, he is not insensitive to successes and he gives credit to white South Carolinians when discussing Harvey Gantt enrolling in Clemson as well as the beginnings of school integration in Greenville. He also acknowledges whites working for better race relations and tells the story of Governor Russell's 1963 Inaugural Barbecue for all South Carolinians—white and black.

So while Jones's tone is better, the reality of racism by white South Carolinians is still avoided. Blacks are good if they go through the system quietly and whites in the state will come through in the end because they have good manners and morals. Consider this passage concerning the NAACP:

> It early made the important decision to concentrate the fighting in the courts and in a dialogue with the white power structure to avoid direct hostile and physical collision. News of that quiet dialogue began to come out only later. The results of seeking dialogue instead of confrontation were positive.[37]

Both Lewis P. Jones and Archie Vernon Huff, Jr. provide their readers with a fairly extensive review of modern race relations in the state of South Carolina. Huff is again harder on white South Carolinians than Jones, but Jones does not place blame on everyone except white South Carolinians as much as he has in his discussions of slavery, Reconstruction, and Jim Crow. If Huff has a shortcoming in this section it is that he doesn't provide enough detail on the struggles of African Americans in their fight for civil rights in South Carolina. While Jones is too generous in his praise of white South Carolinians working for race relations, his major flaw is the omission of Reverend DeLaine and the battle for school integration in Clarendon County. Ironically, both Huff and Jones conclude by telling their readers how far we have come regarding race relations in both South Carolina and the rest of the nation. Without disputing progress and success, one wonders if Huff and Jones allow their young readers to finish both texts without questions about the segregation and racism that still exists in both South Carolina and the nation.

Conclusions

This paper has reviewed the tone and content in the treatment of race in the two South Carolina school history textbooks that are currently approved by the state—Lewis P. Jones's *South Carolina: One of the Fifty States* and Archie Vernon Huff, Jr.s' *The History of South Carolina in the Building of the Nation*. Although neither book is an exemplary multicultural textbook, it is apparent from both the description and analysis presented in this essay that there is great disparity in the books' presentations of race. Frances Fitzgerald's two composite portraits (which were quoted earlier in this essay) of American history textbook's characterizations of Reconstruction provide us with a useful measuring stick. If you recall, Fitzgerald explained that pre-1970s texts presented Reconstruction as a time of evil northerners who exploited the south and used the "ignorant freedmen." They also depicted the Ku Klux Klan as a southern "civic organization." The post-1970s texts did a 180 degree turn and presented Reconstruction as thoughtful and utilitarian.

Jones's book does not follow Fitzgerald's model. Although the book isn't as extreme as Fitzgerald's pre-1970 portrait, it corresponds to that composite more closely than to the post-1970 version. Northerners, Abolitionists, and Blacks are presented as "Fanning the Flames" while white South Carolinians are viewed as victims throughout Jones's chapter on Reconstruction. Huff's writing on Reconstruction is closer to the post-1970 composite. He is extremely critical of the Klan and he softly discusses the racism of white South Carolinians.

The author's tones are very different and this is the case throughout each text's discussions of race in South Carolina. Jones's text seeks to absolve white South Carolinians of their 19th and early 20th century racism, their more recent racism during the civil rights movement, and the racism that currently operates in the state. While Huff's text is more honest concerning race, both past and present, it doesn't dig deeply into the racial hatred and the struggle for racial equality that are both part of South Carolina's story. Huff's book is usable in that teachers can build on the topics Huff introduces concerning race by bringing in outside sources that provide both more depth and description in portraying race as a major element in South Carolina history. Jones's book is only usable if eighth-grade South Carolina history teachers want to use it as an example of current white racism in South Carolina.

In final analysis, neither text offers eighth-grade students a desirable picture of race in South Carolina. Huff tries, but his book doesn't ask hard questions or probe deeply into historical or present race relations. Jones's book is racist in that it provides both denials of and excuses for white racism—both past and present. Unfortunately, neither book will help to change young South Carolinians' views of the history of race relations and racism in the state. What is even more unfortunate is that because the textbooks fail to help young South Carolinians address their history, they also fail to help young people in the state confront the racist reality that exists today.

Notes

1. Lewis P. Jones, *South Carolina: One of the Fifty States* (Orangeburg, SC: Sandlapper Publishing, 1985); Archie Vernon Huff, Jr. *The History of South Carolina in the Building of the Nation* (Greenville, SC: Furman, 1991)
2. Frances Fitzgerald, *America Revised: History Schoolbooks in the Twentieth Century* (Boston, MA: Little, Brown and Company, 1979) p. 52.
3. *Ibid.*, p. 18.
4. The textbooks include: John J. Dargan, *School History of South Carolina* (Columbia, SC: The State Company, 1906); John Langdon Weber, *Fifty Lessons in the History of South Carolina* (Boston, MA: Ginn and Company, 1891); John Chapman, *School History of South Carolina* (Richmond, VA: Everett Waddey, 1895); Henry Alexander White, *The Making of South Carolina* (New York: Silver, Burdett & Company, 1906); William Gilmore Simms (revised by Mary C. Simms Oliphant), *The History of South Carolina* (Columbia, SC: The State Company, 1917, 1922); Mary C. Simms Oliphant, *The Simms History of South Carolina* (Columbia, SC: The State Company, 1932, 1940); Mary C. Simms Oliphant, *The History of South Carolina* (River Forest, IL: Laidlaw Brothers, 1958, 1970)
5. Simms/Oliphant, *The History of South Carolina*, (1917) p.140.
6. Dargan, *School History of South Carolina*, p. 126.
7. *Ibid.*, p. 151.
8. Fitzgerald, *America Revised*, p. 86.
9. *Ibid.*, p. 88.
10. *Ibid.*, p. 16.
11. Huff, *The History of South Carolina*, p. 70.
12. Jones, *South Carolina*, p. 377.
13. *Ibid.*, p. 454.
14. Huff, *History of South Carolina*, p. 251.
15. *Ibid.*, pp. 98,99.
16. Jones, *South Carolina*, p. 426.
17. Huff, *History of South Carolina*, p.248.
18. *Ibid.*, p. 213.
19. Jones, *South Carolina*, p. 428.
20. *Ibid.*, p. 454.
21. *Ibid.*, p. 456.
22. *Ibid.*, p. 457.
23. *Ibid.*, p. 458.
24. *Ibid.*, p. 460.
25. Huff, *History of South Carolina*, p. 281.
26. *Ibid.*
27. *Ibid.*, p. 295.
28. *Ibid.*, p. 336.
29. Jones, *South Carolina*, 504.
30. *Ibid.*, p. 505.
31. *Ibid.*, pp. 525-527.
32. *Ibid.*, p. 597.
33. Huff, *History of South Carolina*, p. 333.
34. *Ibid.*, p. 404.
35. Jones, *South Carolina*, p. 659.
36. *Ibid.*, p. 664.
37. *Ibid.*, p. 667.

Article 13

CORRESPONDENCE IN COOPERATING TEACHERS' AND STUDENT TEACHERS' INTERPRETATIONS OF CLASSROOM EVENTS

LUZ E. GONZALEZ

Associate Professor and Chair of the Department of Chicano & Latin American Studies at California State University, Fresno. Also Director of the Faculty Mentoring Program (FMP). One of the many components of the FMP is to assign incoming Freshmen and Transfer students to faculty mentors and to support and assist them as they develop a strong mentoring relationship.

KATHY CARTER

Professor at the School of Education, Division of Teaching and Teacher Education at the University of Arizona, Tucson.

Abstract—Using the concept of well remembered events, we examined how members of 13 elementary school cooperating teacher student teacher dyads interpreted the same teaching events. Members of a dyad remembered the same events and the same "visible" students but thought about them in qualitatively different ways. These differences are discussed in terms of expert-novice studies, a conception of teachers' knowledge as event-structured, and recent inquiry into personal narrative in teaching. Particular attention is given to the consequences of these differences for communication between cooperating teachers and student teachers and for understanding the process of learning to teach.

The purpose of the study reported in this article was to examine cooperating teachers' and student teachers' interpretations of the same teaching events. The premise underlying this analysis was that cooperating teachers and their students teachers often have shared experiences but not necessarily a shared understanding of what that experience means. These differences may have powerful consequences for communication between cooperating teachers and student teachers and, ultimately, for the process of learning to teach.

An early version of this paper was presented at the annual meeting on the American Educational Research Association, Boston, April, 1990.

It has been known for some time that cooperating teachers have a substantial influence on the development of student teachers' orientations, dispositions, conceptions, and classroom practices (see, e.g., Griffin, 1986; Olson & Carter, 1989; Zeichner, 1986; Zimpher, 1987). However, considerably less is known about the dynamics of this relationship and the processes by which such influence might occur.

The present study grew out of an attempt to combine three lines of inquiry into teachers' understandings of their work: expert-novice studies, a conception of teachers' knowledge as event-structured, and recent inquiry into the power of personal narrative in learning to teach, Expert-novice research (e.g., Borko & Livingston, 1989; Carter, Sabers, Cushing, Pinnegar, & Berliner, 1987; Leinhardt & Smith, 1985; Peterson & Comeaux, 1987) has documented that expert teachers comprehend, interpret, and predict classroom events more accurately and efficiently than novices. In extending our understanding of these differences, Carter and Doyle (1987, 1989; see also Carter & Gonzalez, 1993), have argued that experienced teachers' knowledge of curriculum and pedagogy is event-structured. That is, what teachers come to know through experience is constructed around the events they encounter in classroom settings. Finally, recent studies focusing on teachers' biographies suggest that teachers' understandings of teaching are deeply grounded in their personal narratives of experience (see Carter & Doyle, in press).

These lines of reasoning suggest that there should be essential differences between expert and novice teachers' personal understandings of the same classroom events. However, few attempts have been made to date to study student teachers' or cooperating teachers' memories for and explanations of student teachers' salient teaching events.

The basic analytical framework for this study was the concept of well remembered events. A well-remembered event is an incident or episode a teacher observes or experiences in a school situation and considers, for his or her own reasons, especially salient or memorable (see Carter, 1994). Through interviews with members of cooperating teacher and student teacher dyads, attempts were made to examine if similar events and details were recalled and if these events were accounted for in similar ways. Because individual criteria were used for selecting memorable events, an attempt was also made to gain access to teachers' personal narratives as interpretive frames for teaching experiences.

Data Sources and Method

The results reported in this paper are part of a larger effort designed to explore student teachers' acquisition of event-structured knowledge (see Carter, 1994). Data for the present report were collected from structured interviews with members of 13 elementary school cooperating teacher student teacher dyads. Seven of the student teaching experiences took place in the fall and six in the spring of one academic year.

Student teachers who participated in the study were in their last year of their teacher preparation program. Four of the student teachers indicated previous teaching experience (e.g., as teacher aides or parent volunteers). Cooperating teachers, who taught in three different school districts in the Western U.S.A., had an average of 12 years of teaching experience.

The student teachers were interviewed four times each, at 4-week intervals, during their student teaching. The first three interviews focused on: (a) what teaching events they remembered, (b) how they understood them, (c) what changes these events created in their teaching, and (d) generally how they thought about teaching at the time of each interview. The fourth interview covered the entire student teaching experience and focused on their memory for its three most salient events. Cooperating teachers were interviewed at the end of their student teachers' teaching experience. These interviews focused on the cooperating teachers' reflections on and interpretations of what they considered to be the three most salient teaching events of their student teachers.

The central purpose of the study was to examine the nature of possible differences between cooperating teachers and student teachers at the level of classroom events. Do cooperating teachers see a different world in classrooms than their student teachers or do they see the same worlds and simply interpret them differently? To avoid cuing cooperating teachers to attend more than usual to classroom events, the investigators decided to delay their interviews until the end of student teaching. This design decision led to differences in the timing and content of the two sets of interviews, differences which may have influenced how the events were interpreted. Although this possibility certainly existed, our sense of the data, given the congruence between cooperating teachers and student teachers in the events remembered, is that such influence was minimal.

A three-stage iterative analysis of the transcribed interviews for each dyad was conducted. In the first stage of the analysis, all four interviews for each student teacher were examined, and special attention was given to the identification of specific episodes that appeared and reappeared throughout the interviews. In addition, the salient teaching events identified by the cooperating teachers were extracted from the transcriptions and summarized. In the second stage, teaching events from cooperating teacher/student teacher dyads were compared and analyzed for similarities and differences. In the third and final stage, a comparison was made of the cooperating teachers' and student teachers' explanations of the same teaching events.

During the course of data collection, weekly classroom observations of the student teachers were made. These observations consisted of running accounts of the stream of behavior in the classrooms. In preparing final versions of these accounts, descriptions were framed into event segments following conventional procedures in ecological analyses (see Doyle, 1986). The observations did not always coincide with the events reported in interviews, but when they did they were quite useful in grounding researchers' understandings of the events described by cooperating teachers and student teachers.

Results and Discussion

Findings are summarized in the form of three propositions representing qualitative differences that appeared to exist between cooperating teachers' and student teachers' accounts of the same teaching events. Each proposition is followed by excerpts from interviews that help instantiate the findings.

Proposition 1: Members of a dyad remembered the same teaching events but thought about them differently.

Of particular interest to this study was the congruence between the classroom events that cooperating teachers remembered observing and those that their student teachers remembered experiencing. In the analysis it became clear that members of a dyad remembered the same events as a result of a key incident that occurred within the event that either made a negative or positive impact or, in some cases, both.

The garden event. For example, the cooperating teacher and the student teacher in Dyad #9 both remembered "the garden event." During the spring the cooperating teacher decided to have her student teacher do an activity in which the students planted and cared for a vegetable garden. The student teacher was instructed to have the students plant an assortment of spring vegetables in a 6 by 6 foot plot of land outside the classroom. After the seeds had been planted, she was to take the students out every other day and have them water and weed the garden.

Observation notes indicated that the student organization and management went through three different phases. At first, the students were all allowed to work in the garden, but they began to push and shove each other. On subsequent days, only a handful of students were allowed to work in the garden, and the rest were instructed to sit on the outskirts of the garden quietly. Soon the latter group began to run around the outside of the garden and in the school halls. Finally, the student teacher brought out school work for those that were waiting to work in the garden.

For both the cooperating teacher and the student teacher, the organization and management of students was the central issue that made this a salient event. They differed, however, in how they talked about this issue. For the student teacher this event indicated "how different the kids are whenever they are not in their normal surroundings" and, thus, "how much harder [it is] having control over [them]." Little mention was made of the organization of the activity or the work students were to accomplish.

In contrast, the cooperating teacher pointed to the organizational properties of the work students were given in the garden. For example, she noted that the student teacher "didn't have some of the detail ... that you don't put six kids in a 6 by 6 [foot] plot," and that it was necessary to plan "what to do with the kids that were running around." For the cooperating teacher, in other words, student misbehavior was the result of improper planning for the specific nature of the activity.

The place value event. Similarly, the student teacher and cooperating teacher in Dyad #7 both recalled an event in which the student teacher was teaching place value. In this event, the student teacher taught two examples of how to solve place value problems on the board and then asked the students to solve several place value problems on slates at their desks. After the students were done, she asked them to raise their slates so she could see their answers. She then selected four slates, two with correct answers and two with incorrect answers, and discussed them with the whole class.

The student teacher recalled her vigorous efforts during this event to "get through" to the students and especially the discussion she had after the class with the cooperating teacher. By her account, the cooperating teacher was upset that she was "demeaning" students during the lesson by making their wrong answers public. She, in turn, felt "real bad" and "embarrassed" by having hurt the students' self-esteem. She also heard the cooperating teacher tell her to "monitor and adjust with the kids" better but she did not understand what this meant.

In her interview, the cooperating teacher felt that the exposing of wrong answers was improper but saw this as only a symptom of much more serious issues. She was primarily concerned about the lesson itself, especially the lack of student involvement, the exceptionally slow pacing, poor monitoring and adjustment by the student teacher, and the fact that the students did not seem to learn very much. In several respects, what was "figure" in the student teacher's interpretation was clearly "ground" in the cooperating teacher's memory of the same event.

The science experiment. The members of Dyad #13 remembered a whole-class science demonstration in which the student teacher was teaching wave motions. For this lesson, the student teacher set up a large fish tank filled with water on top of a table in the back of the classroom. She had the 32 students in the class gather around the table to observe her as she conducted the experiment. Unfortunately, the lesson failed in part because the students could not see and in part because the experiment itself did not work.

For the student teacher, this event was "terrible." She had read the experiment through in the book the night before but had not tried it out before the lesson. She concluded, therefore, that "you can't trust books," and "ended up telling the kids, 'I guess we proved science wrong today 'cause it wasn't working ...'"

The cooperating teacher also noticed the failure of the experiment, the student misbehavior, and the lack of preparation. But in her discussion of this event she concentrated on the need to stop the event sooner and redirect the students to another activity so that the class would not get out of control.

Discussion. These and similar accounts of the same teaching events by cooperating teachers and student teachers revealed that the parties both saw the same events as salient and had similar general attitudes and emotions toward the events. Cooperating teachers, however, were quick to express their concerns for pacing, timing, student ability, involvement, and achievement. In addition, they appeared to be able to pull from their rich store of classroom knowledge to diagnose classroom problems and prescribe possible solutions for them.

In contrast, student teachers tended to give raw descriptions of events they had experienced, but they seldom focused on the work students were accomplishing or the interactions of students and the curriculum within the classroom environment. Rather, they seemed to be concerned with the particulars of the events and how these particulars affected them personally.

Proposition 2: Members of dyads differed in their verbal descriptions of teaching events.

The analysis indicated qualitative differences in the nature of the verbal descriptions of remembered teaching events. In general, student teachers tended to use a quite brief description to summarize an event. Examples include: (a) "a couple of students were not paying attention in that second reading group," (b) "always with manipulatives it's louder," (c) "trying to get their attention was crazy," or (d) "when we were doing handwriting I felt very stiff and uncomfortable." If any explanation was offered at all, it tended to be succinct and uncomplicated: (a) "I didn't model," (b) "I didn't explain," (c) "it is not at their level of ability," (d) "they're looking at me as the new kid on the block," or (e) "I finally got up and taught them and they were gonna test me and they did!"

For example, the student teacher in Dyad #2 was observed teaching a lesson on "fact and opinion" to a second grade class when she was 8 weeks into her student teaching experience. The student teacher first explained the difference between a fact and an opinion by using students and objects in the classroom as examples. For instance, the student teacher said,

"Joe has a blue shirt; this is a fact."
"Joe is a nice person; this is an opinion."
"This is a desk; this is a fact."
"This desk is pretty; this is an opinion."

This activity went smoothly and the students reliably answered the teacher's questions correctly.

After the explanation, students were divided into groups of five and asked "to construct five facts and opinions sentences from a reptile or a mammal and then write a paragraph with a topic sentence." The students found this task much more difficult. The activity flow slowed down as students asked a number of questions about the assignment and delayed in getting started on their work. Only five students actually completed the work.

The student teacher felt that "I bombed really well" primarily because "I didn't model it well enough or... I didn't explain it thoroughly enough..."

Cooperating teachers, on the other hand, seemed to use their experience and domain-specific knowledge of pedagogy, students, and the curriculum to make sense of an event. They typically embedded in their descriptions clear connections across students, the nature of assigned tasks, the resources available to get the academic work done, and especially how these aspects came together and affected student outcomes. The cooperating teacher in Dyad #2, for instance, explained the event in terms of the nature of the work students were asked to do, paying particular attention to the issues of transferring their newly acquired knowledge of fact and opinion, the domain knowledge of mammals and reptiles that was required, and the shift from "yes and no" answers to constructing their own fact, opinion, and topic sentences. Cooperating teachers also tended to focus on pacing and timing as key factors in maintaining students' participation in classroom events. Dimensions such as work demands or pace were noticeably absent from the accounts offered by student teachers.

Proposition 3: Members of dyads remembered the same "visible" students in teaching events, but viewed the import and impact of these students differently.

Cooperating teachers and student teachers tended to recall the same visible students across several teaching events. Visible students were those that student teachers mentioned frequently in their event descriptions throughout the four interviews. It was clear that student teachers attributed much of what happened in the classes to these students. Cooperating teachers, in contrast, mentioned these students briefly and revealed quite different understandings about their impact on classroom events. The difference between student teachers' and cooperating teachers' views were often related to the power individual students were thought to have over classroom events.

The following excerpts from Dyad #10 provide a particularly dramatic case of a visible student. Cynthia, the student teacher in this dyad, repeatedly talked about Bob, a student in the class, in all four of her interviews. In the first interview, she described Bob as a student who "intrigued" her not only because he seemed to be a "really smart kid" but also because of the "power" he seemed to have over the class. She felt the other students "follow and looked up to him" and "look for his approval" and that he "sets the mood in the class." Indeed, Bob's mood seemed very important to her: "If he comes in with a good mood the class is in a good mood, if he comes in with a bad mood the class is in a bad mood."

Very early in her teaching, Cynthia felt that Bob's support would be essential to her control of the class. As a result, she reported focusing often on Bob in her planning and teaching. Indeed, her tentative explanation for Bob's power in the class was that the cooperating teacher "gives him too much attention" in order to keep the class in control. "She may be doing it [to keep] the class in control, because if she... keeps [Bob] in a good [mood] maybe it will help the rest of the class stay in a good [mood]."

In her second interview, Cynthia reported that she increased the pace of a lesson because Bob was making her nervous by showing a lack of interest. She felt his impact quite personally: "I felt a little bit like he was doing it just because it was me." In the process of attending to Bob, she forgot to use a planned activity with the class.

By the third interview, Bob was a key figure in Cynthia's planning and teaching and he was having a substantial impact on the class. She argued that this attention to Bob was necessary because of his power over the class:

> I did tend to call on Bob a lot more to keep him happy. I've felt like I had to keep him happy... I had to talk with him a few times about... how things were going, I [told him] they weren't going as well as I [was] hoping and that I needed his cooperation. It was like, he's like the center of attention in this classroom and I didn't... want [it] to be that way, but... I felt like that would be easier for me.

In contrast, Bob was remembered by the cooperating teacher but not given special status in the classroom. For her, Bob was one of several strong personalities in the class who pushed Cynthia to increase the pace of her lessons.

Themes in Student Teachers' and Cooperating Teachers' Interviews

In addition to these three broad propositions, the analysis revealed several themes that recurred across the interviews with student teachers and cooperating teachers.

Four themes emerged from the student teachers' interviews. First, student teachers were primarily concerned with classroom events that had a negative impact on them. Although, they did mention successful events, the focus of their descriptions was clearly on those that they felt were flawed. Second, student teachers were also concerned that they did not know how to deal with diverse student abilities. They consistently wanted all of their students to understand what they were teaching, but did not always reach this goal or know what to do to achieve it. Third, managing whole class instruction was problematic for the student teachers. They felt generally comfortable with small group instruction, but struggled with lessons before the entire class. Finally, 10 of the student teachers reported having repeated confrontations with a particular student, and these confrontations contributed greatly to their feeling of success or failure.

In addition to pacing, curriculum, academic work, and student achievement, three themes emerged from the analysis of the interview with cooperating teachers. First, teachers who reported a lesson as having gone "well" usually noted that the lesson had been discussed with the student teacher prior to its implementation. In some cases, this meant that the cooperating teacher had a major role in planning the entire lesson. In no instance in which a lesson was seen as problematic was it also reported that the lesson had been discussed prior to the performance, although some cases may well have occurred. Second, if the student teachers' performance was viewed to be in alignment with the teaching style of the cooperating teacher, the cooperating teacher tended to view the lesson or overall performance of the student teacher as successful. These themes suggest that cooperating teachers' judgments are embedded in their own personal understandings of their teaching practice.

Finally, cooperating teachers' shared the view that knowledge of teaching was best acquired through trial and error and experience. As a rule, cooperating teachers tended to attribute student teachers' poor classroom performance to their need to develop a "trained eye" and to become more "observant" through experience. As a result, they felt that the most they could do was model for a student teacher what a good lesson should look like and give them abbreviated suggestions (e.g., "you should walk around and monitor").

Discussion

This analysis of student teacher and cooperating teacher dyads indicates that members recognize the same events as salient in a student teacher's experience but interpret these events in quite different ways. At one level, this finding suggests that there is a common ground for cooperating teachers and student teachers to discuss teaching in quite specific terms. At another, however, it means that the differences which have been found between experts and novices in teaching play themselves out in the core student teaching relationship. Fundamentally, it appears that cooperating teachers and student teachers do not share interpretive practices. Thus, communication between these two participants is likely to be demanding and perplexing for both parties (see Griffin, 1986).

There were several instances in the present data that pointed to such communication or "miscommunication" problems. In particular, the cryptic remarks made by cooperating teachers sometimes had unintended consequences. For example, in the case of Dyad #7, the cooperating teacher thought that by saying the students had "brains like sieves," the student teacher would realize that "students need to have things repeated to them." Instead, the student teacher thought the cooperating teacher was calling the students "dummies" and did not know how to deal with this typification. Such instances obviously make the process of learning to teach difficult.

Given the differences that show up in the sense that is made of the same events, it would seem critical for cooperating teachers and student teachers to communicate more fully their understandings to one another. The fact that such rich communication is not often the case points to a more basic issue of the frames that cooperating teachers and student teachers bring to this relationship and its conversations.

Recent work that focuses on personal narratives and life histories in learning to teach (see Carter & Doyle, in press; see also Kagan, 1992; Knowles, 1992) provides insight into the frames that novice and experienced teachers bring to teaching. This literature suggests that novices enter teacher education programs with richly formulated, deeply personal, and quite persistent understandings of what it means to teach. These understandings, derived from being pupils in classrooms, serve as theoretical frameworks within which novices interpret and judge suggestions by educational faculty or classroom teachers and invent a personal meaning for the experiences they have in the field. Experienced teachers also have strongly formulated personal understandings of their teaching, but these are grounded in accumulated experiences over the span of several years. As a result, their explanations reflect a narrative of classroom events.

This framework readily explains the differences in narrative structures that we found between student teachers' and cooperative teachers' descriptions and explanations of events. Cooperating teachers had a broader and more fully elaborated narrative frame for salient events than student teachers. As a result, student teachers' descriptions of classroom events, about which they had limited experience, were terse and their explanations simple. They lacked a narrative of classroom experience with which to structure their talk about events.

One obvious contrast between cooperating teachers and student teachers in the present study was in the area of pace and timing as critical dimensions of classroom events. Clandinin (1989) notes, for example, that rhythm is central to a teacher's personal understanding of teaching practice and, thus, a central element in learning to teach. The student teachers in the present study had not yet acquired this lens with which to see their teaching.

The literature on personal narrative also suggests that novices' understandings are grounded in their experiences as students and thus, they tend to judge the practices in terms of whether they or students they have known would find these practices motivating and helpful (see Holt-Reynolds, 1992). It is not surprising, then, that they keyed on students as powerful agents in shaping classroom events. One also suspects that, in the absence of a classroom narrative, they were singling out students who were salient from their own personal narratives of schooling, that is, students they were like or would have liked to be.

Finally, studies suggest that novices' personal understandings tend to "shatter" when they enter student teaching, in part because they are based on incomplete narratives of classroom events (see Cole & Knowles, 1993). It is highly likely that our interviews picked up some of this effect as we asked student teachers to account for classroom events. Classroom events are the least developed area of their personal understandings. It is important, therefore, not to interpret their cryptic answers as indicating an absence of strong personal theories of teaching. We simply did not provide them with much opportunity to reveal their personal understandings.

What, then, does this personal narrative approach say about communication in student teaching dyads? At one level, this discussion suggests that the differences are real and not easily bridged. There are, to the best of our knowledge, no substitutes for classroom experience in understanding classroom events. Indeed, life history studies indicate that it takes about 4 years for beginning teachers to come to a comfortable understanding of classroom situations and their management (see Huberman, 1993; Nias, 1989; Sikes, Measor, & Woods, 1985). At another level, however, this literature on personal narrative provides a context for moving cooperating teacher and student teacher conversations forward. In particular, it suggests that student teachers should have the opportunity to discuss openly their personal histories and understandings of teaching, in part to facilitate communication and in part to help them understand what drives their interpretations and decisions in classroom contexts. In addition, it indicates that cooperating teachers need to have a rich understanding of the frames that novices bring to teaching so they can address these preconceptions and avoid miscommunicating their intentions and insights. Finally, this analysis suggests that cooperating teachers can do more than simply provide models or experiences or brief suggestions to fix lessons. They can also reveal the underlying narrative structure of their understandings of teaching events. It is in these shared narratives that the members of student teaching dyads might capitalize on their common awareness of classroom events and thus learn for each other.

We would especially underscore the importance of the last point. Narratives of experience obviously come from experience and there are limits to what can be learned from the experiences of others (see Munby & Russell, 1994). At the same time, having access to the underlying narrative structure of an experienced teacher's understandings of a classroom event one has actually lived through would seem to be a grounded and quite powerful way to learn how to think about teaching. Moreover, such a conversation can only happen between a cooperating teacher and a student teacher in that they share a common awareness of salient teaching events in a specific setting. Thus, this conversation represents a unique dimension of learning to teach in student teaching. Certainly, this possibility warrants further inquiry if we are to move beyond simply noting that novices and experts differ and move towards forms of pedagogy that might make learning to teach a richer and less painful experience.

This study, and others like it, obviously call attention to issues of the role of preservice preparation. Why, for instance, does it seem that preparatory courses fail to produce sophisticated thinking among candidates for teaching? Is experience the only real teacher of teachers? How can teacher preparation be improved so that graduates think like experts?

In large measure these issues are shaped by the expert-novice framework itself. Comparing beginners and seasoned veterans in any field is likely to underscore differences that result primarily from experience, that is, differences that can be bridged largely by more experience. Expertise as defined within this context will always be an elusive goal for preservice teacher preparation. But preservice preparation can point novices in the right direction by orienting them to the kinds of event knowledge that experts in our study, and in many others, seem to rely on to interpret situations and make decisions. Our sense is that conversations between cooperating teachers and student teachers are an ideal place for such orienting to occur.

References

Borko, H., & Livingston, C. (1989). Cognition and improvisation: Differences in mathematics instruction by expert and novice teachers. *American Educational Research Journal, 26,* 473–498.

Carter, K. (1994). Preservice teachers' well-remembered events and the acquisition of event-structured knowledge. *Journal of Curriculum Studies, 26,* 235–252.

Carter, K., & Doyle, W. (1987). Teachers' knowledge structures and comprehension process. In J. Calderhead (Ed.), *Exploring teachers' thinking* (pp. 147–160). London: Cassells.

Carter, K., & Doyle, W. (1989). Classroom research as a resource for the graduate preparation of teachers. In A. E. Woolfolk (Ed.), *Research perspectives on the graduate preparation of teachers* (pp. 51–68). Englewood Cliffs, NJ: Prentice-Hall.

Carter, K., & Koyle, W. (in press). Personal narrative and life history in learning to teach. In J. Sikula, T. J. Buttery, & E. Guyton (Eds.), *Handbook of research on teacher education* (2nd ed.). New York: Macmillan.

Carter, K., & Gonzalez, L. (1993). Beginning teachers' knowledge of classroom events. *Journal of Teacher Education, 44*(3), 223–232.

Carter, K., Sabers, D., Cushing, K., Pinnegar, S., & Berliner, D. (1987). Processing and using information about students: A study of expert, novice, and postulant. *Teaching and Teacher Education, 3,* 147–157.

Clandinin, D. J. (1989). Developing rhythm in teaching: The narrative study of a beginning teacher's personal practical knowledge of classrooms. *Curriculum Inquiry, 19,* 121–141.

Cole, A. L., & Knowles, J. G. (1993). Shattered images: Understanding expectations and realities of field experiences. *Teaching and Teacher Education, 9,* 457–471.

Doyle, W. (1986). Classroom organization and management. In M. C. Wittrock (Ed.), *Handbook of research on teaching* (3rd ed.). New York: Macmillan.

Griffin, G. (1986). Issues in student teaching. A review. In J. Raths & L. Katz (Eds.), *Advances in teacher education* (Vol. 2, pp. 239–274). Norwood, NJ: Ablex.

Holt-Reynolds, D. (1992). Personal history-based beliefs as relevant prior knowledge in course work. *American Educational Research Journal, 29,* 325–349.

Huberman, M. (1993). *The Lives of teachers* (J. Neufeld, Trans.). New York: Teachers College Press.

Kagan, D. M. (1992). Professional growth among preservice beginning teachers. *Review of Educational Research, 62,* 129–169.

Knowles, J. G. (1992). Models for understanding preservice and beginning teachers' biographies: Illustrations from case studies. In I. F. Goodson (Ed.), *Studying teachers' lives* (pp. 99–152). New York: Teachers College Press.

Leinhardt, G., & Smith, D., (1985). Expertise in mathematics instruction: Subject matter knowledge. *Journal of Educational Psychology, 77,* 247–271.

Munby, H., & Russell, T. (1994). The authority of experience in learning to teach: Messages from a physics methods class. *Journal of Teacher Education, 45,* 86–95.

Nias, J. (1989). *Primary teachers talking: A study of teaching as work.* London: Routledge.

Olson, P., & Carter, K. (1989). The capabilities of cooperating teachers in USA schools for communicating knowledge about teaching. *Journal of Education for Teaching, 15,* 113–121.

Peterson, P. L., & Comeaux, M. A. (1987). Teachers' schemata for classroom events: The mental scaffolding of teachers' thinking during classroom instruction. *Teaching and Teacher Education, 3,* 319–221.

Sikes, P. J., Measor, L., & Woods, P. (1985). *Teacher careers: Crises and continuities.* London: Falmer.

Zeichner, K. (1986). Individual and institutional influences on the development of teacher perspectives. In J. Raths & L. Katz (Eds.), *Advances in teacher education* (Vol. 2, pp. 135–163). Norwood, NJ: Ablex.

Zimpher, N. (1987). Current trends in research on university supervision of student teaching. In M. Haberman & J. Backus (Eds.), *Advances in teacher education* (Vol. 3, pp. 118–150). Norwood, NJ: Ablex.

Submitted 14 July 1994
Accepted 3 May 1995

Why Do We Need This Class?
Multicultural Education for Teachers

Ms. Pang's main goal is to help teachers create a classroom that is effective for all children. To accomplish that goal, she encourages teachers to examine issues of race, class, and gender that may serve as barriers to equal opportunity to learn.

Valerie Ooka Pang

VALERIE OOKA PANG is an associate professor of teacher education at San Diego State University.

IT WAS THE first day of class. A new group of teachers conversed noisily as I looked for my attendance sheet. I could hear a loud voice saying, "Why do we have to take *this* class? I'm not prejudiced. I don't need to be in here. I like all kids." I could hear someone else answer in a low voice, "I don't need it either. This is going to be a waste of time."

I smiled to myself and thought, "There are always doubting Thomases or Tomasitas. That's great. They will make my work easier."

After calling names on the class roster, I said, "I want to welcome you to the class. I am excited that I will have the opportunity to get to know you over the next 15 weeks. I realize that some of you feel the class will be a waste of time because you aren't prejudiced. Let's talk a little about this."

I turned to a broadly built woman with horn-rimmed glasses who was chatting in the back of the classroom. With a smile I said gently, "Joan, I was just wondering why you don't think you need this class."

Many of the teachers had been talking while I read through the class roster, but all of a sudden the room was quiet. The teachers turned toward Joan, waiting to see what she would say. Joan didn't want to back down. Just like the children in her classroom, she was cool and stood her ground. "Well, I just don't need to hear about prejudice and discrimination. I'm tired of hearing about the things we have done to blacks and Indians."

I smiled and replied, "I realize that many of you have thought a lot about prejudice and that you would never knowingly discriminate against any of your students." Joan's broad shoulders relaxed. "Let's hear from someone else. Why do you think we have this class?" I asked.

A tall male student wearing a gray sweat suit said, "I want to know how to teach black kids."

I looked at Larry in a puzzled way. "You need to respect, care, and believe in every student," I ventured.

"No, that's not what I mean," Larry said, his forehead wrinkling in frustration. "I want you to tell me about black culture. You know — their music, history, foods. Things like that."

"Why do you think you need information about black culture?" I asked.

"Because then I will appreciate their culture more," Larry said, smiling.

"What do you know about your own culture?" I asked.

This was the beginning of another wonderful semester in multicultural education. And I knew that this class would be exciting because these teachers were already willing to share their honest views with one another. We were off to a great start.

Preparing Teachers for Diversity

Preparing teachers for a culturally diverse society is one of the most exciting and rewarding endeavors in education. I love what I do because most teachers are caring and dedicated people. I see teachers as America's national treasures. They do not go into teaching to get rich. Many teachers feel that teaching is more than a job; it is a commitment and a calling.

In my semester-length class on multicultural education, I try to model the kind of classroom that I hope the teachers in my class will create. I believe that modeling is the most powerful strategy in teaching. I try to create a learning atmosphere that says to each teacher, "You are a precious and worthy person. All of us in the class need your input to grow. Help us be the best people we can be." During the first class session, I begin memorizing the names of each teacher. I learn the teachers' names quickly because I want each one to know that he or she is an important member of our team.

I also try to create an interesting and lively classroom climate. If I expect teachers to motivate their students, I must get teachers involved in their own learning. Though the content and the activities I use in a college class are different from those in a fourth-grade classroom, I can still get teachers excited about learning. Teachers can become enthusiastic and animated about the ideas and solutions they develop to solve classroom problems.

I have developed my class around some of the beliefs of Paulo Freire, the Brazilian educator. I asked myself, "How can I develop a community of learners where everyone works together to create a free and just society?" I like Freire's idea of "problem-posing education," which means centering learning on social issues and problems. He thinks that students who are truly free bring what they know into the classroom. Students make connections between their lives, others' lives, and themes in society. True freedom occurs when teachers and young people tackle a problem and come to collective decisions about what action can be taken. The teacher does not act as the person in control; rather he or she shares leadership and the responsibility for learning. The "light bulb" goes on in both teachers' and students' minds, because through their dialogue they struggle together to arrive at solutions to social problems.

In contrast Freire sees most teachers making deposits in the minds of children. In this "banking" approach to education, students are passive learners, receiving and memorizing information so that they can recite it back to the teacher.¹ This passive role, Freire believes, conditions students to accept the status quo. Because the environment of the classroom teaches students not to challenge ideas or to create new ways to think, they will blindly accept the unfairness of society.

I attempt to provide a challenging and engaging learning environment by using lots of dialogue. I believe that the teachers in my classes learn more from one another than from me. In this shared learning process, they ask one another many questions, which forces them to clarify their values. They also ask me difficult, soul-searching questions.

Since I believe in "problem-posing" or issues-centered education, I know it is crucial to get teachers to talk about their ideas. I try to create a classroom in which we trust and respect one another, a place of caring.² It is a safe place where mistakes are the "fertilizer of success." I believe that every teacher should have the opportunity to find his or her "voice" and to express it. I explain to my teachers that we need each person's input because we will not grow as individuals or as a learning community unless we help one another see new aspects of issues. This point is extremely crucial in a class like multicultural education, which deals with a complex mix of emotions, attitudes, misconceptions, and ignorance about race, class, gender, and other cultural differences. I want my teachers to be "hooked" on dialogue so that their classrooms will become "think tanks" of committed students who work together. Each classroom can reflect a democratic community in which each student is an active and respected learner.

14. Why Do We Need This Class?

Three Phases of Instruction

My main goal is to help teachers create a classroom that is effective for all children. Teachers need to know that multicultural education is the study of schooling aimed at providing all children with an equal opportunity to learn in a culturally affirming and caring environment.³ I help teachers look at issues of race, class, and gender that may serve as barriers to that goal. In building my class I divide the instruction into three phases.

1. *Who am I? Am I prejudiced?* In the beginning of the class, I want teachers to better understand themselves. I ask them to examine who they are by identifying their own values and goals. I am convinced that no matter how much information I give teachers about other cultural groups, if they are not prepared to understand others, they will not be ready to hear and receive the information.

Since most of those who enter the teaching profession are white and middle class, we read the book *White Teacher*, by Vivian Gussin Paley.⁴ This book is a wonderful resource because Paley writes about her own prejudices and the mistakes she made as a kindergarten teacher. Reading this book helps teachers examine their own biases in a nonthreatening way; they look at racism in schools while learning effective teaching strategies that worked for Paley in her classroom.

I believe that teachers do not want to be prejudiced, but, because prejudice is often part of the hidden curriculum, they may be acting or thinking in ways that limit their own growth or that of their students. For example, a teacher might say, "I don't know why those black kids can't sit still." Then I ask the teacher, "Do you hear what you are saying? Do you also say, 'I don't know why those white kids can't sit still'?" Another teacher may point out the first teacher's unconscious prejudices by noting the tone of voice and the use of the term "those" children.

2. *What do I think about culturally diverse communities?* The second phase of my class focuses on getting to know culturally diverse neighborhoods. I ask the teachers, "Do you hold stereotypes about different communities? Do you believe that Mexican parents from low-income areas do not care about their children? And do you believe that rich white parents from Beverly Hills are more concerned than black parents about their youngsters? Where did you get those ideas?" In order to help teachers think

about their misconceptions, I take my class on field trips and require teachers to donate time to a community organization of their choice.

I believe that teachers will feel more connections with children in their classes when they know the school neighborhood and the issues that are most important to the community. In large urban areas, teachers may live in the suburbs and commute an hour to their schools in the inner city. Yet in teaching children, teachers can be more effective when they can make connections between the school curriculum and students' lives.

On one of our field trips, I take my classes to visit a community center in San Diego. The center serves several hundred low-income families. The drug traffic in the community has been limited because the neighbors worked with the police and forced the drug pushers out. I want the teachers to get to know the community and to learn that the parents and children in this neighborhood have the same desires for education, homes, and jobs as the teachers do.

At one point in the semester, we put on a learning carnival. The teachers set up booths with science experiments, math games, reading activities, and art projects. In discussions after the carnival, one teacher said, "I expected the kids from this neighborhood to be rude and wild. But they were all polite. In fact I was surprised that so many older siblings — some only as old as 6 — were taking younger brothers and sisters from booth to booth making sure that they had fun and got prizes. Many of the younger kids spoke only Spanish and so their older brothers or sisters translated and encouraged them to try each booth. I never knew how much family meant to some children."

Though the teachers thought they had created the carnival for the community, they benefited too. Members of the class began to feel personal connections with parents and children from low-income African American and Mexican American families — people whom they had initially seen as so different and separate from themselves. The walls of isolation were slowly crumbling.

During the debriefing discussion, Joan, one of the teachers in the class, mentioned, "There's a family in the neighborhood with two boys in junior high. These boys aren't going to school because they don't have any shoes. Is there anyone willing to donate so the community center can buy them shoes?"

The teachers generously contributed. We then began to discuss what kinds of shoes the kids wanted. Larry commented, "I know that my students are very label-conscious. Do you think we should put any stipulations on how expensive the shoes are that the center buys for the boys?"

A teacher who was usually quiet raised her hand and said, "Just because these boys are poor, why should they want anything less than other children?" Several other teachers agreed. Though we hoped the money would be spent in a reasonable way, we felt that the students and the center would know what was best.

The social worker called me several weeks later to thank us for the donation. He told me that he had taken the boys to the store, and they had decided not to buy the designer tennis shoes but to buy a more moderately priced brand, because that would leave them a few dollars to buy new shirts too.

Since we all went on the field trip and were part of the carnival, everyone could share observations about our common experiences. One of the most damaging assignments a college professor can give teachers in a multicultural education class is to send them to various gatherings in ethnic communities — for example, services at black churches, Vietnamese festivals, or Latino political rallies — which may reinforce stereotypes that outsiders hold about culturally different groups. I have heard teachers come back from an African American Baptist church service and say, "Those people are so warm. I was scared to go to the church, and I didn't want to leave my car on the street, but the people made me feel so accepted. And the people are great gospel singers." Many times teachers need a chance to talk about what they have observed so that their encounters with other cultures do not become "zoo" experiences. Going to view another neighborhood can be dangerous if teachers do not understand what they are seeing. Many cultural traditions are rooted in deep values, but these values may not be obvious because of differences in dress and behaviors.

I want teachers to go beyond knowing that "we are all people" or being satisfied with only superficial contact with members of other communities. In a community service project, such as tutoring children after school or teaching English to newly arrived adult immigrants, teachers are able to have real discussions of ideas and to learn about the world view of people who are culturally different from themselves, because they visit the neighborhoods of those people repeatedly. In addition, teachers are more likely to see beyond cultural stereotypes and learn about individual differences. Again, dialogue with their peers is crucial because it gives teachers the opportunity to clarify their beliefs and to better understand what they felt and saw.

3. *What does multicultural education look like in a classroom?* In the third portion of the semester we explore the teaching of multiculturalism. I help teachers to look at what happens in the classroom by asking such questions as, What is multicultural education? What do you know about the historical experience of women, Native Americans, Asian Americans, Latino Americans, and African Americans in the United States? Why is a child's home language important to keep? What strengths does culture give children? What impact does culture have on learning? What does racism, sexism, or classism look like in schools?

Many teachers do not realize that culture can affect the learning environment. Students bring beliefs from home to school. One teacher asked a Vietnamese student to work with a new Cambodian immigrant. The Vietnamese student told the teacher, "I don't think he will accept my help." The teacher dismissed his concerns, believing that, since both students were from Southeast Asia, they would have natural connections. "I don't think you will have any trouble," she told the Vietnamese student.

Soon after this exchange, the Cambodian student came to the teacher with fire in his eyes and said, "I respect you because you are the teacher, but I won't work with a Vietnamese." This teacher learned that animosities from the past affected her classroom. After this incident, she did not assume that all Asian students got along well.

In addition to bringing up the questions listed above, I encourage teachers to incorporate ethnic content into their curriculum. Teachers are often unsure how to begin. One said, "I'm afraid I'll offend a Navajo student by talking about Navajo culture, because I don't know much about the culture." I suggest that they begin by getting to know each student as a person.

A teacher can also use literature to provide windows into the lives and cultures of others. In order to model the importance of literature, I read to my students almost every week. Since I am a former first-grade teacher, reading stories is one of my greatest pleasures. My teachers are just like young students. Their eyes sparkle when I read *The Knight Who Was Afraid of the Dark* or *Honey, I Love*. Their faces become clouded with sadness when I read *The Children We Remember* — a book about the Holocaust — or *Teammates*, which tells about the pain Jackie Robinson and Pee Wee Reese endured fighting racism. Teachers feel the desperation in Langston Hughes' poems "Dream Deferred" and "American Heartbreak." The book *Grandfather's Journey* helps them sense the closeness of family and understand the emotional bonds we have to our country.[5] I discuss how to choose multicultural literature that can enrich the curriculum and how to use it in the classroom. I believe that literature is one of the most wonderful gifts we can share with our students.[6]

Another aspect of curriculum that I focus on is how to build a problem-posing unit. I ask teachers, "How can you provide ways for your students to look at a social issue? What questions can you ask students that will let them investigate and come to their own conclusions?" Older students might examine the civil rights movement as they consider the question, Are there times when people should challenge their government? Other students might examine the importance of diversity in the United States, seeking to answer the questions, Do you think the emphasis on cultural diversity separates Americans or brings them together? Why? Younger children can struggle with the question, What is fairness? Or they might be asked, Why do children call each other mean names? Wise teachers create lessons on issues that their students have chosen to investigate.

On the last day of class, after most of the teachers had left, a young teacher named Delia sat down next to me. "This has been the most difficult and yet most fun class I've had. You made me think. I learned more about who I was in this class. I never knew I had so many preconceived notions about people from other cultures. Sometimes I went home from class with a terrible headache. I had to own up to my prejudices and ignorance. I want to make a difference with all kids, and now I know I should never deny any children their culture."

Teachers like Delia created a real family of learners because they shared themselves with their peers and with me. I celebrate the important work that she and the other teachers do because they care for our most precious people, our children.

14. Why Do We Need This Class?

1. Paulo Freire, *Pedagogy of the Oppressed* (New York: Herder & Herder, 1971).

2. Nel Noddings, *The Challenge to Care in Schools* (New York: Teachers College Press, 1992).

3. The phrase "study of schooling" was taken from the wonderful book by John Goodlad, *A Place Called School: Prospects for the Future* (New York: McGraw-Hill, 1984). I use the phrase because Goodlad documents the importance of looking at the entire ethos of schools in order to better understand what reforms must be undertaken.

4. Vivian Gussin Paley, *White Teacher* (Cambridge, Mass.: Harvard University Press, 1979).

5. Barbara Shook Hazen, *The Knight Who Was Afraid of the Dark* (New York: Dial Books, 1989); Eloise Greenfield, *Honey, I Love* (New York: Thomas Y. Crowell, 1977); Chana Abells, *The Children We Remember* (New York: Greenwillow Press, 1986); Peter Golenbock, *Teammates* (New York: Harcourt Brace Jovanovich, 1990); Langston Hughes, *The Panther and the Lash* (New York: Alfred A. Knopf, 1967); and Allen Say, *Grandfather's Journey* (Boston: Houghton Mifflin, 1993).

6. The Council on Interracial Books for Children published a pamphlet called "10 Quick Ways to Analyze Children's Books for Racism and Sexism," which has been reprinted in Bill Bigelow et al., eds., *Rethinking Our Classrooms: Teaching for Equity and Justice* (Milwaukee: Rethinking Schools, 1994). For lists of children's books that are multicultural and appropriate for the discussion of social issues, see Ronald Evans and Valerie Ooka Pang, "Resources and Materials for Issues-Centered Social Studies Education," *The Social Studies*, May/June 1992, pp. 118-19; and Valerie Ooka Pang et al., "Beyond Chopsticks and Dragons: Selecting Asian-American Literature for Children," *Reading Teacher*, November 1992, pp. 216-24.

Multicultural Education as an Academic Discipline

A spirited dialogue is occurring among scholars in multicultural education on the future directions and philosophical foundations of this field of study. The essays in this unit reflect the results of some of this dialogue. How best can multicultural education be integrated into professional educational studies so as to achieve its objectives?

Multicultural education developed out of the social upheavals of the 1960s and the concerns of many scholars with the critical need for research-based knowledge of the cultural contexts of education. Much of our initial knowledge came from important research in anthropology and sociology, as well as psychiatric studies of the impact of prejudice and victimization on targeted racial and cultural minorities, from the 1920s on. These studies examined intercultural relations in all sorts of urban, suburban, and rural settings in the United States. These field studies used ethnographic inquiry methods initially developed by anthropologists and later used by some sociologists and educators. Studies from the 1920s through the 1950s focused on such concerns as child-rearing practices, rites of passage into adulthood, perceptions of other cultural groups, and the social stratification systems of communities and neighborhoods. Studies in the 1930s and 1940s showed how victimized and involuntarily segregated racial and cultural groups responded to being targeted for discriminatory treatment. This body of social science knowledge became important documentation for the plaintiffs in *Brown v. Board of Education of Topeka* in 1954, the historic U.S. Supreme Court case that declared segregation on the basis of race to be unconstitutional.

As the civil rights movement begun in the 1950s in the United States grew in momentum throughout the 1960s, anthropological and sociological inquiry about the education of minority youth continued to develop. Out of the urban and other social crises of the 1960s emerged a belief among educators concerned with questions of racial and cultural justice that there was a serious need for an area of educational studies which would specifically be focused on the study of intercultural relations in the schools from a "multi-" cultural perspective. They envisioned studies that would challenge the by-then traditional Eurocentric "melting pot" visions of how one became "American." The problem with the Eurocentric melting pot was that it was a very exclusionary pot; not everyone was welcome to jump in. Many cultural groups were excluded from it. The philosophy of a culturally pluralist democracy in which all cultural heritages would be treasured and none rejected became attractive to those of us who witnessed the arbitrary and cruel effects of racial and cultural prejudice in schools, as well as in other areas of life in "mainstream" society.

The belief that all teachers should respect the cultural heritages of their students and that all students have the right to know their cultural heritages as well as to develop self-esteem and pride in them began to spread among socially concerned educators. Studies conducted on intercultural relations among teachers and students by the early 1970s clearly demonstrated the need for an academic discipline that would specifically focus on building knowledge about our multicultural social reality as well as on how to teach about other cultural heritages and to improve the quality and the pedagogical effectiveness of instruction in multicultural school settings. Many of us realize today that all young Americans of our social present and future need to know about this nation from a perspective that rejects and transcends the old Anglo and Eurocentric presuppositions of melting pot and theories of assimilation into American social life.

As part of the movement for civil rights, people from non-English-speaking countries also sought to guarantee that their children would be given the opportunity to grow up both bilingual and bicultural. By the time the U.S. Supreme Court handed down its decision in *Lau v. Nichols* in 1974, there were dozens of federal court cases pending at various stages of development concerning this matter. The issues of bilingual education and English as a second language were being argued.

The academic leadership of the nation's cultural minorities and many other concerned scholars have forged a competent community dedicated to the task of setting standards of practice for multicultural education as a discipline. There is spirited dialogue in the field about what these standards should be as well as about what academic qualifications people ought to have in order to conduct multicultural education. James A. Banks, at the University of Washington, and others are concerned about the survival and development of multicultural education as an academic discipline that must maintain its focus on classroom practice as well as defensible theoretical constructs.

Multicultural education must develop an ongoing cadre of competent leaders to direct the development of the field as well as to ensure that attempts to merely add multicultural content to existing teacher education course content dilutes neither the academic quality of multicultural education content nor the quality of standards of practice in the field. Banks argues that merely adding mul-

UNIT 3

ticultural education content to existing teacher education course work must be resisted, and in his essay he identifies 5 dimensions of multicultural education: content integration, knowledge construction process, prejudice reduction, equity pedagogy, and empowering school culture and structure. Multicultural education is an interdiscipline that draws from anthropology, sociology, social history, and even psychiatry. Focused, adequately prepared specialists in this new interdiscipline are necessary if it is to maintain its academic integrity.

The essays in this unit reflect concerns regarding academic standards and goals for multicultural education as the field continues to develop and to enter a new period in its history. The authors of these essays raise important issues that must be addressed as the time approaches when a majority of Americans will be from "minority" cultural heritages and when traditional conceptions of "minority" and "majority" relations in the United States will have little meaning.

The essays in this unit are relevant to courses in curriculum theory and construction, educational policy stud-

ies, history and philosophy of education, cultural foundations of education, and multicultural education.

Looking Ahead: Challenge Questions

What should be some minimal standards of practice in the field of multicultural education?

What should be the qualifications for people who wish to become specialists in multicultural education?

It has been argued that all American students should learn the multicultural reality of our nation. Do you feel that this is true? How might it be accomplished?

What does it mean to speak of multicultural education as an interdiscipline?

What ought all American students to know about racism and prejudice by the time they graduate from high school?

How do we help people learn to accept cultural diversity? What sorts of things can teachers do to foster acceptance of cultural differences?

—F.S.

Multiculturalism and Multicultural Education in an International Perspective

Lotty Eldering
Leiden University

In many countries with a population of mixed ethnicity and culture, some form of multicultural education is given. Comparisons between the various approaches to multicultural education in these countries are hampered by a lack of conceptual clarity and by differences in social context and views on cultural diversity. In this article the concept of multiculturalism is explored and several approaches to multicultural education are discussed, drawing examples from North America, Europe, and Australia. This conceptual framework is used to describe and analyze the current state of affairs in these fields in the Netherlands.

As a member of two committees advising the Dutch Minister of Education and Science on the state of multicultural education, I have visited several countries on the European and North American continents and have perceived that transnational comparisons are hampered at two levels, first, by differences in the kind of diversity in each society and, second, by differences in the connotation attached to the concepts of multiculturalism and multicultural education. In this article the dimensions of multiculturalism and multicultural education are explored and a contextual approach that enables transnational comparisons to be made is presented. In the second part of the article the current state of affairs regarding multiculturalism and multicultural education in the Netherlands will be analyzed, using the conceptual framework developed in the first section.

Multiculturalism

To analyze the nature of multiculturalism in a society, one must distinguish the following dimensions or levels:

- objective reality,
- ideology,
- official policy,
- process or practical implementation. [Fleras and Elliott 1992]

Multiculturalism as an objective reality concerns the coexistence of different ethnic or cultural groups in one country (state). These groups often differ in history, numbers, social position, power, culture, and ethnic/racial origins. Ethnic and cultural diversity in a society is usually the result of (colonial) expansion, slavery, or immigration. Each multicultural society has its own genesis and, consequently, its own diversity. Northwestern European countries, for instance, have experienced immigration from a variety of continents and countries, as a result of decolonization and economic expansion after the Second World War (Eldering and Kloprogge 1989). The immigrants in these countries comprise no more than ten percent of the total population, whereas the populations of traditional immigration countries like Canada, the United States, Israel, and Australia consist predominantly of immigrants and their descendants. Besides their numerical strength, the power relations between ethnic/cultural groups are an important factor. Ethnic groups that are a majority in the numerical sense may have no political weight in nondemocratic societies, as was formerly the case in South Africa.

A second dimension of multiculturalism concerns the ideology with regard to the identity of society and how cultural differences between groups are to be dealt with. The ideology may fluctuate between the extremes of assimilation and pluralism. Assimilation means the merging of ethnic/cultural groups into a dominant group, culturally as well as structurally. Pluralism in its extreme form implies that the society is comprised of groups whose distinctive cultures are maintained by structural pluralism. Cultural pluralism cannot exist without duplication of institutions and hence without structural pluralism, according to sociologist Van den Berghe (1967). Many varieties exist between the extremes of assimilation and pluralism. In the political debate between interest groups, the identity and culture of a society are always the object of discussion. Views on the identity of a society or the desirable degree of cultural diversity may change over the course of time. One of the relevant issues in the current political debate in Europe is the compatibility of two values: equality of opportunity and a person's right to maintain his or her cultural identity. In his book *Race and Ethnicity* (1986), Rex discusses how to resolve the conflict between these values. He concludes that a society with equality of opportunity in the public domain and multiculturalism in the private domain would appear to be the ideal situation. In a later publication, he distances himself from this point of view, mainly for sociological reasons (Rex 1991), arguing that according to the functionalist theory in sociology and anthropology, the various institutions constituting a sociocultural system are all necessarily interrelated and that in this theory there is no place for the idea of two separate sociocultural domains. The public and private domains are interacting subsystems. Schools, for instance, have a function in preparing children for their public role, but at the same time, by transmitting cultural values they have an impact on the private lives of the pupils and their families (Eldering 1993). For their values to be accepted in the public domain, ethnic and cultural minorities should organize themselves and negotiate with other interest groups in society. In addition to the official ideology, which is at best the result of a negotiation process between political parties and other interest groups, other ideologies may exist in society. A popular "man in the street" ideology or a teachers' ideology on cultural diversity may not coincide with official ideology; indeed, they may even contradict that ideology and hamper the implementation of official policy.

The terminology used in the description of a society's objective reality is often ideologically colored and is often influenced by history and policy. In the Netherlands, for instance, the terms *guest workers, immigrants, minorities,* and *allochthones* have been used successively in past decades. Guest workers refers to the predominantly male workers recruited in the 1950s and 1960s from Mediterranean countries to work in the mines and expanding industries. This term emphasizes the temporariness of the workers' stay in the host country. The right of their families to come to the Netherlands has long been an issue on the policy agenda. *Minorities,* a term introduced at the end of the 1970s and currently in general use, refers to immigrant groups that occupy a low socioeconomic position (Ministry of Internal Affairs 1983). Because of the negative connotations and stigmatizing effects of that term, the neutral *allochthones,* referring to immigrants from outside the Netherlands up to and including the third generation, was proposed by the Wetenschappelijke Rand voor het Regeringsbeleid, or Scientific Council for Governmental Policy (WRR 1989). *Immigrants* and *minorities* are currently used in many northwestern European countries, with the exception of Germany, a country that officially does not admit that the migrants have become immigrants and continues to call the foreign workers and their families *Gastarbeiter.*

Allochthon and *autochthon* are also applied in Canada. The Inuit (Eskimos) and Indians are autochthons, also recently called *First Nations.* The allochthonous English- and French-speaking groups form the dominant majority. In the United States, a similar situation exists. Here, however, the Indian groups are called *natives* or *American Indians,* and *allochthon* and *autochthon* are rarely used. Autochthons form a numerical minority in Canada and the United States and the majority in countries such as the United Kingdom, France, Germany, Netherlands, and Belgium.

As in the Netherlands, *minorities* is used in Canada and the United States, but with different connotations. Whereas in the Netherlands the term refers to groups with a low socioeconomic position, Canadian and U.S. use of this term emphasizes mainly the cultural "deviation" from the majority (in terms of language, religion, art, music, behavior, etc.) or racial characteristics ("visible minorities" in Canadian policy documents). U.S. opinion is rather divided as to which groups should be rated as "mainstream." Some consider only Anglo-American groups to belong to the mainstream (see, for example, Banks 1988); others opine that all groups of European origin belong to it (Spindler and Spindler 1990). In Canada, only the "Charter Groups," the groups of English and French origin, are considered as such (Fleras and Elliott 1992). This results in immigrants of German origin being considered a minority in Canada, whereas in the United States they may or may not be called a minority, depending on personal opinion. Chinese groups are considered to be minorities in both Canada and the United States, but not in the Netherlands since they do not have a low socioeconomic position there.

Minorities is usually preceded by an adjective that indicates another distinguishing feature of the group concerned (e.g., "racial minorities"). The choice of this adjective reflects the ideological perspective from which the problems are examined. In the United States and the United Kingdom, the racial perspective dominates. Relationships between the majority and minorities are often described in terms of color and race. Troyna and Edwards (1993) state that the specific U.K. terminology can become a problem in European research since, on the European continent, differences in culture are emphasized (mostly in terms of language and religion), rather than differences in ethnicity or race.

As to the policy dimension of multiculturalism, a distinction must be made between immigration policy and minorities policy. Immigration policy primarily regulates the categories of immigrants which are accepted and the conditions of immigration. Canada and Australia, for instance, have populations of predominantly northwestern European origin (mainly British and French) because of their selective immigration policy. The immigrant population of many northwestern European countries largely consists of foreign workers from Mediterranean countries and their families and of immigrants from former colonies. If it reacts at all, a country often reacts slowly to demographic changes, for example, by formulating a minorities policy. A minorities policy in principle reflects a country's official ideology. In its elaboration and implementation, however, there may be discrepancies—for instance, when values and goals are incompatible or when one goal is given priority, as I will show regarding the Netherlands.

Approaches to Multicultural Education

The lack of clarity surrounding concepts and the controversy regarding the term multicultural education (also known as *intercultural education, multiethnic education, or antiracist education*) complicate comparative research. A number of researchers have tried to bring order to the multitude of views on and approaches to multicultural education (Baker 1983; Banks 1983, 1988; Cummins and Danesi 1990; Fleras and Elliott 1992; Gollnick and Chinn 1990; Ogbu 1987, 1992; Sleeter and Grant 1987; Troyna and Edwards 1993). Using this literature, I have developed the following scheme of multicultural education (see Table 1). Multicultural education is considered in a broad sense here and is defined as being education that takes into account in some way the ethnic/cultural differences between pupils. The scheme is based on two principles of order: the target groups at which multicultural education is aimed and the approach from which this occurs. Multicultural education can be limited solely to pupils from ethnic/cultural groups (a particularist approach) or can be directed at all pupils (a universalistic

3. MULTICULTURAL EDUCATION AS AN ACADEMIC DISCIPLINE

Table 1
Approaches to Multicultural Education (Eldering 1994)

Approach	Target groups	
	Pupils from ethnic groups	All pupils
Disadvantage	– attunement of education to development level – second-language education – bilingual education – culturally responsive education	
Enrichment	monocultural courses aimed at – language – literature – geography – religion – history – art	multicultural courses aimed at – language – literature – geography – religion – history – art
Bicultural competence	bicultural education	bicultural education
Collective equality groups	private schools	multicultural curriculum

approach). Multicultural education can be approached from various perspectives according to the position of the minority cultures in the curriculum and the attention paid to individual or collective inequality.

The Disadvantage Approach

The assumption underlying multicultural education with a disadvantage approach is that pupils from ethnic/cultural groups have educational arrears that pupils from the majority group do not have. Multicultural education under this approach is aimed at removing these disadvantages. The educative activities in this framework are intended solely for pupils from ethnic/cultural groups of low socioeconomic position. Catching up on disadvantages occurs with an eye to gaining better school achievements and realizing equality of opportunity. The degree to which account is taken of the specific cultural characteristics of the pupils depends on the perception and appreciation of cultural differences. If one begins with a deficit approach, no account is taken of the cultural features of the pupil, but if one has a positive attitude toward the culture of the pupils concerned, then the cultural features of the pupils such as their home language, communication and learning style may serve as education's point of departure ("culturally responsive teaching") (Erickson 1987; McDermott and Goldman 1983; Ogbu 1987). Under the disadvantage approach, the removal of the disadvantage comes first, and the ethnic culture plays a sustaining and temporary role at most. Different forms of multicultural education can be placed under this heading, varying from the immersion model, in which education is exclusively in the second language, to bilingual education with a transitional character (Extra and Vallen 1989).

The Enrichment Approach

The assumption behind this approach is that cultural diversity implies an enrichment of society, which should be reflected in education (in Canadian terms, "celebrating diversity"). Multicultural education under this approach may be aimed at pupils from specific ethnic/cultural groups; it may also be for all pupils, irrespective of ethnic/cultural origin.

Monocultural courses are set up for a variety of reasons: as an acknowledgement of the language and culture of the ethnic communities ("heritage-language courses" in Canada), as a means for making pupils from ethnic/cultural groups aware of the contribution made by their group to the establishment of society ("black studies," followed later by "Mexican American studies" "American Indian studies," and "Asian studies" in the United States), or as a preparation for returning to the country of origin (the Netherlands and Germany) (Banks 1988; Eldering 1989; Seller 1992).

Multicultural courses are intended for all pupils, irrespective of ethnic/cultural background. The most important objective is for pupils from all groups to become acquainted with each other's cultures, learn to appreciate them, and learn how to relate to each other (the *human relations approach*, also known as the *intergroup approach* or *multicultural education*). The assumption of multicultural education is that knowledge of each other's cultures leads to mutual appreciation and respect and to a better understanding. The culture elements dealt with in the curriculum mostly concern language, literature, history, geography, and religion. It is evident that the culture of the various groups within the multicultural courses will receive only marginal attention if the pupils in a school come from a number of ethnic groups. Although recommended by several governments, multicultural courses have never become an integral part of the curriculum. (For the United Kingdom see Education for All 1985; Troyna and Edwards 1993; for the Netherlands see CEB 1994; Eldering 1989). This approach has some serious shortcomings. No theoretical connection has been sought in psychological theories on intergroup conflicts and prejudice, and the cultural content of these courses is usually not based on empirical research on the culture of the groups concerned (Ogbu 1992; Sleeter and Grant 1987; Vedder 1993).

The Bicultural Competence Approach

Multicultural education under this approach goes one step further than the previous approach and is mainly intended to make pupils from ethnic/cultural groups competent in two cultures through bicultural education. Education in the culture of the ethnic/cultural groups aims at the preservation of the cultures (including languages) concerned. According to Banks (1988), bicultural education should not be limited to pupils from ethnic/cultural groups, but all pupils and teachers should at least have bicultural competence and preferably be cross-culturally competent. Bicultural education for ethnic minority pupils rarely occurs in practice. It requires at least a sufficient number of pupils from one ethnic/cultural group, like the Finns in Sweden or the Mexican Americans in the U.S. Southwest (see, for example, Warren 1983).

The Collective Equality Approach

The approaches discussed so far are limited to mostly minor adaptations of the existing curriculum. The education system itself, the structure of society, and the mechanisms that support inequality are not questioned in these approaches. But this happens to be the case in multicultural education under the collective equality approach. This approach emphasizes the collective equality of groups or cultures rather than the equality of individuals. Two approaches can be distinguished. The first approach assumes the equal rights of the diverse ethnic/cultural groups in society. Supporters of this view strive for a society that is pluralistic in cultural and structural sense (Van den Berghe 1967). Canada with its French and English school system, Belgium with its French and Flemish school system, and the Netherlands with its denominational school system ("pillarization") are examples of this approach.

In the second approach, the objective is to make the existing school system more multicultural: not just the curriculum but also the teaching methods, the staff, and the representative bodies. Some supporters hold the view that the inequality of ethnic/cultural groups cannot be regarded separately from other inequalities in society. Within multicultural education, attention must also be paid to other social categories in an unequal position such as women, low socioeconomic groups, the handicapped (Banks 1988; Cummins and Danesi 1990; Gollnick and Chinn 1990; Troyna and Edwards 1993).

Summary of the Approaches

As we have seen, multicultural education has several approaches and many modalities. These do not occur equally often in practice. Multicultural education is usually aimed at pupils from ethnic/cultural groups. Multicultural education for all pupils still has not properly got off the ground in practice and is often limited to an ideological discourse. In most cases, multicultural education exists merely as an addition to or a minor adaptation of the regular curriculum. Multicultural education therefore tends to lean toward assimilation rather than toward cultural pluralism. This is hardly surprising, given the population ratio of the majority to the minorities, and the social position of both categories in many countries. Recurring points in the discussion on multicultural education are the questions of how far cultural diversity threatens the unity of a society, and to what degree cultural diversity hampers or encourages the realization of equality of opportunity for all pupils, as will be shown by the case of the Netherlands.

The Case of the Netherlands

In this section the state of affairs of multiculturalism and multicultural education in the Netherlands will be described and analyzed, using the conceptual framework presented in the previous sections. The first question is whether Dutch society is multicultural in an objective, ideological, and political sense. The second concerns the approaches to multicultural education in this country.

A Multicultural Society?

The Dutch government officially stated in 1983 that the Netherlands is a multicultural society and acknowledged that most migrants from former colonies (the Moluccans, Surinam, and the Dutch Antilles) and Mediterranean countries (predominantly Turkey and Morocco) had become immigrants. Today these immigrants compose about six percent of the total population of 14 million, and they live mainly concentrated in cities with more than 100,000 inhabitants. For the population in these cities, the multicultural nature of Dutch society is a daily reality, whereas people living in other parts of the country, particularly in rural areas, are only incidentally confronted with the changed character of Dutch society.

The ideological discourse concerning immigrants centers around two basic values of Dutch society: equality of opportunity and equivalence of cultures. Equivalence of cultures (religions), a value with a long tradition in the Netherlands, has been the basis of the compartmentalization manifest in many sectors of Dutch public life. The "school battle" in 1917 resulted in a state-supported school system compartmentalized along religious lines. About two-thirds of pupils currently attend private state-funded denominational schools. The religious segregation in other sectors of public life (health care, trades unions, broadcasting corporations) has slowly eroded in recent decades. With the arrival of large numbers of Muslims from Morocco, Turkey, and Surinam, the question arises whether a new Muslim "pillar" will be formed. It appears that Islam has become institutionalized in the Netherlands. There are currently about 380 mosques (separate ones for Moroccan, Turkish, Surinamese, and Pakistani Muslims) in the country. About one-quarter of the Muslim children attend Qur'an lessons at these mosques. Provisions have been made for ritual slaughter, and Muslim adults and children have the right to take days off to celebrate their religious festivals (Shadid and Van Koningsveld 1995). Although the constitutional right to establish schools is also given to immigrants, only four percent of pupils with an Islamic background currently attend schools based on Islamic principles. The low numbers of the Muslims and the national and religious differences among Muslims hamper the formation of a new religious compartment and the establishment of an Islamic school system (CEB 1994; Eldering 1993).

In 1979, the Netherlands Scientific Council for Government Policy (WRR) advised the government to create a minorities policy (WRR 1979). In its report, the council recommended that the idea of a temporary residence for all migrant groups be abandoned and that a policy aimed at integration should be outlined in order to prevent migrant groups from becoming ethnic minorities. Dutch government proposed a two-track ethnic minorities policy, aiming at "integration without loss of cultural identity." The WRR, evaluating the situation ten years later, concluded that, despite the minorities policy, the socio-

3. MULTICULTURAL EDUCATION AS AN ACADEMIC DISCIPLINE

economic position of ethnic minorities had worsened and advised concentrating efforts on education and the labor-market position of minorities and to abandon the culture track of this policy (WRR 1989). Currently, target groups of Dutch minorities policy show unemployment rates four times as high as those for the Dutch majority.

The Dutch government has opted for a minorities policy that aims at integration of ethnic minorities as well as preservation of their cultural identity. How this two-track policy works out in the field of education will be explored in the next section.

Educational Minorities Policy

The Dutch Ministry of Education and Science launched a minorities policy plan in 1980. In consonance with the general minorities policy, this plan stipulated that educational practice should aim at equality of educational opportunity as well as equivalence of cultures. To realize equal opportunities for all pupils, the Educational Priority Policy came into effect in 1985. In this policy, priority (i.e., additional funds) is given to geographical areas and schools with a high percentage of disadvantaged children from ethnic-minority and Dutch backgrounds. Pupils are rated according to ethnicity and parents' educational level. Thus, pupils from ethnic-minority parents with a low educational level are given a weight of 1.9, and pupils from disadvantaged Dutch backgrounds, 1.25, compared to 1.0 for middle-class Dutch children. This weighting forms the basis for assessing the school score. High-scoring schools receive much more additional funding than low-scoring ones (Eldering 1989). About seventy percent of the primary schools received extra funds in 1993 (SCP 1994). The Educational Priority Policy is accompanied by a longitudinal evaluation. About 40,000 pupils are assessed every two years on school achievements (mainly reading and mathematics). Recent outcomes of this evaluation have shown that ethnic-minority pupils, in particular those of Moroccan and Turkish origin, still have serious arrears in secondary education and that more than eighty percent of these arrears originate in primary education (Kloprogge and Walraven 1994).

Policy (i.e., extra funding) is therefore concentrating on primary education and recently also on the preschool period, although the evaluation of preschool programs has not yet revealed that this is having any major effects (see Eldering and Vedder 1993).

Besides this policy aimed at eliminating educational arrears, there is a cultural policy, composed of monocultural courses (lessons in the language and culture of the country of origin) for minority pupils and multicultural education—called intercultural education in the Netherlands—for all pupils. Ethnic-minority children from Mediterranean countries are entitled to courses in the language and culture of their home country in primary education for $2\frac{1}{2}$ hours per week during school hours.

The range of financial aid for the activities indicates the relative weight of both approaches. Eliminating educational arrears (fostering equality of opportunity) has the highest priority in primary education. Although under the 1985 Primary Education Act schools must prepare children for life in a multicultural society, so far no financial aid has been made available for multicultural education. Strikingly, the budget available for the respective elements of the Educational Priority Policy is inversely proportional to the regulations concerning its spending. The lion's share of available monies is allocated for combating the educational arrears of disadvantaged children. The allocation of these funds, however, rarely corresponds to recommendations on how they should be spent. Schools are not even obliged to spend this money exclusively on the target groups. Most schools use it to reduce the number of pupils per class. In view of the disappointing effects of the Educational Priority Policy on school achievement, discussions are currently in progress on whether the system of input financing should be replaced by a system of output financing, thereby forcing schools to pay more attention to equality of outcomes than to equality of opportunity.

The situation regarding multicultural, or intercultural, education is the exact reverse. This education is surrounded by policy memoranda and documents containing indications of what schools should do, whereas no funds are given to realize its implementation.

Regarding education in the language and culture of the country of origin, the Dutch government has pursued an ambiguous policy. Originally set up as education to prepare children from Mediterranean groups for return to their home country, its psychological functions (fostering the self-concept and the well-being of these children) were stressed in the 1980s (Eldering 1989). In the 1990s the Ministry of Education has stated that this education should primarily support the learning of Dutch. Despite these changes in official policy, however, the content of the lessons in the language and culture of the home country has changed only marginally over the past decades (CEB 1994).

Implementation

The number of pupils receiving education in the language and culture of their country of origin has increased considerably since 1982. About eighty percent of the Turkish and seventy percent of the Moroccan pupils participate in this education. Most pupils (85%) receive this education during school hours. The lessons are largely made up of language activities, followed by geography, history, and religion. Most teaching methods are oriented toward the home countries; only a few reflect the multicultural reality in the Netherlands. About ninety percent of the teachers have obtained their teaching qualification in their country of origin (CEB 1994). This situation reflects the original objective of this education (preparing children for return) rather than the current policy aim of supporting the learning of Dutch. Education in the language and culture of the country of origin has remained an isolated part of the curriculum. School staff are on average not interested in this education; they see these lessons as the sole responsibility of the ethnic-minority teachers. Many ethnic-minority teachers have a poor command of Dutch and have little contact with the Dutch teachers about the content of their lessons or the pupils. Changing the educational content toward current official goals would require a huge investment from both school staff and ethnic-minority teachers.

An issue currently being debated is whether it would not be better to hold these lessons outside school hours. The first reason might be that about half of the ethnic-minority pupils miss lessons in Dutch and other cognitive subjects because they clash with lessons in the language and culture of their home country. This poses the question of the compatibility of equality of opportunity and equality of cultures. Second, most ethnic-minority children are second- or even third-generation immigrants, and their home country is the Netherlands rather than Turkey, Morocco, Surinam, or the Moluccan Islands. Third, if given outside school hours, this education could retain its original function of preserving cultural heritage (cf. "heritage language courses" in Canada) rather than support the learning of Dutch (CEB 1994). Several political parties now argue for removing this education from the regular curriculum.

The 1985 Primary Education Act prescribes that schools prepare pupils for life in a multicultural society through multicultural, or intercultural, education. Multicultural education must be given to all pupils by all schools, regardless of the presence of ethnic minority children. At the end of the 1980s, policy makers at the Ministry of Education and at national educational organizations reached consensus on the objectives and content of multicultural education. According to them, multicultural education is neither a subject nor a separate part of the curriculum. The whole curriculum should reflect society's cultural diversity. Multicultural education should also have implications for school policy, staff ethnicity, and ethnic-minority parent representation on school boards. Its main objectives are that children acquire knowledge of each other's cultures, learn to live harmoniously together, and be free of prejudice, discrimination, and racism (Ministry of Education and Science 1987). To what degree does daily practice reflect this ambitious consensus?

The Committee for the Evaluation of Primary Education (CEB) recently analyzed the state of multicultural education (CEB 1994). This analysis showed that multicultural education has been integrated in the curriculum in only 20 percent of Dutch schools. This occurred proportionally more often in public (i.e., nondenominational) schools, in schools in large cities, and in schools with more than 20 percent ethnic-minority pupils. In 40 percent of the schools no steps have been undertaken since 1985 to make education more multicultural; 30 percent of the schools—again mostly schools in large cities with more than 20 percent ethnic-minority pupils—said that they were preparing to make the curriculum more multicultural. Multicultural education is almost nowhere the result of a well-thought-out school policy; rather, it depends on individual teachers' initiatives. In only one-third of Dutch schools has multicultural education been a topic on a staff meeting since 1985. Although school principals are of the opinion that the prevention of prejudice, discrimination, and racism is the most important objective of multicultural education, only a few schools have a formalized nondiscrimination code. This code concerns pupils only, not teachers or parents.

This short overview shows that there is a big gap between policy makers' ideological discourse and daily school practice. This is due to several factors. An important one is that multicultural education does not correspond to the daily life situation of many schools. More than 75 percent of Dutch schools have no or only a few pupils from ethnic minority backgrounds. They feel no need to make the curriculum more multicultural and tend to associate multicultural education more with educational problems than with educational enrichment. Multicultural education is more often reactive education, in the sense that teachers only react to interethnic or multicultural incidents or conflicts in their classroom. Although there are no indications that teachers have a negative attitude toward pupils from ethnic-minority backgrounds, teachers are not trained in coping with interethnic situations and conflicts. Research shows that the reactions of teachers who are not expert in this area may have the effect of encouraging rather than preventing prejudice (Troyna and Edwards 1993). As already mentioned, multicultural education has no solid theoretical basis. Nor has the concept of culture been defined and empirically tested. No research has been done so far in the Netherlands on interethnic and multicultural classroom situations and conflicts, and on the way in which teachers deal with these. This is a serious omission, as teachers in multiethnic classrooms are expected to teach pupils how to cope with ethnic and cultural differences.

Summary of Multiculturalism in the Netherlands

Ethnic minorities comprise only six percent of the population in the Netherlands. Despite this low percentage, the Dutch government officially stated in 1983 that the Netherlands is a multicultural society. To realize the ideological goal of "integration with preservation of their own culture," a "two-track" minorities policy was developed about fifteen years ago. In terms of government funding, however, equality of opportunity has been given a much higher priority in the policy's implementation than equality of cultures has been. Although the Dutch constitution permits the establishment of institutions based on religious principles, it is unlikely that Muslims will develop their own infrastructure and form an Islamic pillar.

The unequal priority of equality of opportunity and equality of cultures is also reflected in educational policy and practice. The elimination of educational disadvantages receives more funding and more attention from schools and teachers than cultural activities. Compared with many other countries, the Netherlands may be a front-runner in laying down statutory standards concerning the multicultural character of Dutch society and multicultural education, but in policy practice the emphasis lies more on integration of immigrants than on preservation of their original culture. Moreover, the gap between official policy and day-to-day practice remains great, particularly regarding the labor market and the educational system.

Conclusion and Discussion

The first part of this article discussed levels of multiculturalism and various approaches to multicultural education and then presented a contextual approach for international comparisons. The second part used this conceptual framework to describe and analyze multiculturalism and multicultural education in the Netherlands. The conceptual framework makes it possible to compare across societies and to generate issues for discussion. I conclude this article with some remarks on the relationship between the various dimensions of multiculturalism.

3. MULTICULTURAL EDUCATION AS AN ACADEMIC DISCIPLINE

It will be clear that, although many societies consider themselves to be multicultural, multiculturalism has not permeated all the dimensions distinguished. Multiculturalism is often limited to the objective level of coexistence of ethnic-cultural groups in society and an ideological discourse about society's cultural identity. Monoculturalism prevails at the level of policy and its implementation.

The various dimensions of multiculturalism are only indirectly related. The presence of various ethnic-cultural groups in a society generally stimulates a public discussion on the society's cultural identity but does not necessarily lead to a multicultural policy and multicultural practice in its institutions, as is illustrated by the case of multicultural education in the Netherlands. The discrepancy between objective reality and ideology/policy may be caused by the imbalance of power between the ethnic-cultural interest groups in society, whereas the discrepancy between multicultural policy and practice may be due to several factors, such as the failure of policy to be geared toward implementation in practice. Only a minority of Dutch primary schools, for instance, has made multicultural education a structural part of its regular curriculum, although this education is prescribed in the 1985 Primary Education Act. Policy makers at the Dutch Ministry of Education and at national educational organizations have reached consensus about the principles and global content of multicultural education after many years of discussion about culture and the enrichment of contacts between cultures. They have, however, neglected to define the key concept of culture and to prepare guidelines for multicultural activities to teachers who have to deal with classes of pupils from various ethnic-cultural groups with different levels of acculturation or who teach monocultural classes. These questions arise in other countries too.

The concept of culture has been neglected not only by policy makers dealing with multicultural education but also by cultural anthropologists—for whom it is the raison d'etre of their discipline. Fortunately the discussion on this concept has recently been reopened (Borofsky 1994). I hope that educational anthropologists will follow this example and make this concept more workable for educational practice.

Lotty Eldering is a professor in intercultural pedagogics at Leiden University, in the Netherlands. She has published on immigrant families (particularly Moroccan families) and their children's education.

References Cited

Baker, Gwendolyn C. 1983. Planning and Organizing for Multicultural Instruction. Reading, MA: Addison-Wesley Publishing.

Banks, James A. 1983. Language, Ethnicity, Ideology and Education. *In* Multicultural Education: A Challenge for Teachers. Lotty van den Berg-Eldering, Ferry J. M. de Rijcke, and Louis V. Zuck, eds. Pp. 33–51. Dordrecht: Foris Publications.

― 1988. Multiethnic Education. Theory and Practice. Boston: Allyn and Bacon.

Borofsky, R., ed. 1994. Assessing Cultural Anthropology. New York: McGraw-Hill.

CEB (Commissie Evaluatie Basisonderwijs). 1994. Onderwijs Gericht op een Multiculturele Samenleving. The Hague: SDU.

Cummins, James, and Marcel Danesi. 1990. Heritage Languages. The Development and Denial of Canada's Linguistic Resources. Toronto: Our Schools/Our Selves Education Foundation and Garamond Press.

Education for All. 1985. Education for All. The Report of the Committee of Inquiry into the Education of Children from Ethnic Minority Groups. London: Her Majesty's Stationery Office.

Eldering, Lotty. 1989. Ethnic Minority Children in Dutch Schools: Underachievement and its Explanations. *In* Different Cultures Same School. Ethnic Minority Children in Europe. Lotty Eldering and Jo Kloprogge, eds. Pp. 107–136. Amsterdam: Swets & Zeitlinger.

― 1993. Cultuurverschillen in een Multiculturele Samenleving. Comenius 49:9–26.

― 1994. Benaderingen van Multicultureel Onderwijs. *In* Christelijk Onderwijs in Ontwikkeling. S. Miedema and H. Klifman, eds. Pp. 30–44. Kampen, Netherlands: Kok.

Eldering, Lotty, and Jo Kloprogge, eds. 1989. Different Cultures Same School. Ethnic Minority Children in Europe. Amsterdam/Lisse: Swets & Zeitlinger.

Eldering, Lotty, and Paul Vedder. 1993. Culture Sensitive Home intervention. The Dutch HIPPY Experiment. *In* Early Intervention and Culture. Preparation for Literacy. Lotty Eldering and Paul Leseman, eds. Pp. 231–252. Paris: UNESCO Publishing, Netherlands National Commission for UNESCO.

Erickson, Frederick. 1987. Transformation and School Success: The Politics and Culture of Educational Achievement. Anthropology and Education Quarterly 18:335–357.

Extra, Guus, and Ton Vallen. 1989. Second Language Acquisition in Elementary School: A Crossnational Perspective on the Netherlands, Flanders and the Federal Republic of Germany. *In* Different Cultures Same School: Ethnic Minority Children in Europe. Lotty Eldering and Jo Kloprogge, eds. Pp. 153–188. Amsterdam: Swets & Zeitlinger.

Fleras, Augie, and Jean Leonard Elliott. 1992. Multiculturalism in Canada. The Challenge of Diversity. Ontario: Nelson Canada.

Gollnick, Donna M., and Philip C. Chinn. 1990. Multicultural Education in a Pluralistic Society. New York: Merrill, Macmillan Publishing.

Kloprogge, Jo, and Guido Walraven. 1994. Vernieuwde Kaders, Veranderende Structuren. Notitie over het Onderwijsvoor rangsbeleid 1993. The Hague: Stichting Onderzoek Onderwijs.

McDermott, Ray P., and Shelley V. Goldman. 1983. Teaching in Multicultural Settings. *In* Multicultural Education: A Challenge for Teachers. Lotty van den Berg-Eldering, Ferry J. M. de Rijcke, and Louis V. Zuck, eds. Pp. 145–165. Dordrecht: Foris Publications.

Ministry of Education and Science, Netherlands. 1987. Intercultureel Onderwijs Verder op Weg [Verslag miniconferentie]. Zoetermeer, Netherlands: Ministry of Education and Science.

Ministry of Internal Affairs, Netherlands. 1983. Minderhedennota. The Hague: Staatsuitgeverij.

Ogbu, John U. 1987. Variability in Minority School Performance: A Problem in Search of an Explanation. E. Jacob and C. Jordan, eds. Explaining the School Performance of Minority Students. Anthropology and Education Quarterly (theme issue) 18:312–334.

― 1992. Understanding Cultural Diversity and Learning. Educational Researcher 21(8):5–14.

Rex, John. 1986. Race and Ethnicity. Milton Keynes: Open University Press.

― 1991. The Political Sociology in a Multi-Cultural Society. European Journal of Intercultural Studies 2(1):7–19.

Seller, M. 1992. Historical Perspectives on Multicultural Education. What Kind? By Whom? For Whom? And Why? Paper presented at the American Educational Research Association Annual Meeting, San Francisco, April.

Shadid, W. A. R., and P. S. van Koningsveld. 1995. Religious Freedom and the Position of Islam in Western Europe: Opportunities and Obstacles in the Acquisition of Equal Rights. Kampen, Netherlands: Kok Pharos.

Sleeter, Christine E., and Carl A. Grant. 1987. An Analysis of Multicultural Education in the United States. Harvard Educational Review 57:421–444.

SCP (Sociaal Cultureel Planbureau). 1994. Sociaal en Cultureel Rapport. Rijswijk, Netherlands: Sociaal en Cultureel Planbureau.

Spindler, George, and Louise Spindler. 1990. The American Cultural Dialogue and Its Transmission. London: Falmer Press.

Troyna, Barry, and Viv Edwards. 1993. The Educational Needs of a Multiracial Society. Coventry, England: University of Warwick.

Van den Berghe, Pierre L. 1967. Race and Racism. A Comparative Perspective. New York: Wiley.

Vedder, Paul H. 1993. Intercultureel Onderwijs Vanuit Psychologisch Perspectief. Leiden: Rijksuniversiteit, Sectie Interculturele Pedagogiek.

Warren, Richard L. 1983. The Application of Ethnographic Research in Multicultural Education. *In* Multicultural Education: A Challenge for Teachers. Lotty van den Berg-Eldering, Ferry J. M. de Rijcke, and Louis V. Zuck, eds. Pp. 121–135. Dordrecht: Foris Publications.

WRR (Wetenschappelijke Raad voor het Regeringsbeleid). 1979. Etnische Minderheden. The Hague: SDU.

― 1989. Allochtonenbeleid. The Hague: SDU.

Multicultural Education and Curriculum Transformation

James A. Banks

James A. Banks, Center for Multicultural Education, University of Washington-Seattle*

In this, the text of the 1995 Charles H. Thompson Lecture, the author describes five dimensions of multicultural education, focusing on the knowledge construction process. This dimension is emphasized to show how the cultural assumptions, frames of reference, and perspectives of mainstream scholars and researchers influence the ways in which they construct academic knowledge to legitimize institutionalized inequality. The process by which transformative scholars create oppositional knowledge and liberatory curricula that challenge the status quo and sanction action and reform is also described. This process is endorsed as a means of helping students become effective citizens in a pluralistic, democratic society.

The racial crisis in America, the large number of immigrants that are entering the nation each year, the widening gap between the rich and the poor, the changing characteristics of the nation's student population make it imperative that schools be reformed in ways that will help students and teachers to re-envision, rethink, and reconceptualize America. Fundamental changes in our educational system are essential so that we can, in the words of Rodney King, "all get along." The nation's student population is changing dramatically. By 2020, nearly half (about 48%) of the nation's students will be students of color. Today, about 31% of the youth in the United States under 18 are of color and about one out of every five students is living below the official poverty level (U.S. Bureau of the Census, 1993).

It is imperative that schools be reformed in ways that will help students and teachers to re-envision, rethink, and reconceptualize America.

Multicultural education, a school reform movement that arose out of the civil rights movement of

3. MULTICULTURAL EDUCATION AS AN ACADEMIC DISCIPLINE

Teachers play an important part in helping students understand how knowledge is created and how it can be influenced by race, ethnic, and social class. (Photo by Steve Takatsuno)

the 1960s and 1970s, if implemented in thoughtful, creative, and effective ways, has the potential to transform schools and other educational institutions in ways that will enable them to prepare students to live and function effectively in the coming century (Banks & Banks, 1995a). I will describe the major goals and dimensions of multicultural education, discuss knowledge construction and curriculum transformation, and describe how transformative academic knowledge can be used to re-invent and re-imagine the curriculum in the nation's schools, colleges, and universities.

Multicultural Education and School Reform

There is a great deal of confusion about multicultural education in both the popular mind and among teachers and other educational practitioners. Much of this confusion is created by critics of multicultural education such as Schlesinger (1991), D'Souza (1995), and Sacks and Theil (1995). The critics create confusion by stating and repeating claims about multiculturalism and diversity that are documented with isolated incidents, anecdotes, and examples of poorly conceptualized and implemented educational practices. The research and theory that have been developed by the leading theorists in multicultural education are rarely cited by the field's critics (Sleeter, 1995).

The critics of multicultural education often direct their criticism toward what they call multiculturalism. This term is rarely used by theorists and researchers in multicultural education. Consequently, it is important to distinguish what the critics call multiculturalism from what multicultural education theorists call multicultural education. Multiculturalism is a term often used by the critics of diversity to describe a set of educational practices they oppose. They use this term to describe educational practices they consider antithetical to the Western canon, to the democratic tradition, and to a universalized and free society.

Multicultural education is an educational reform movement that tries to reform schools in ways that will give all students an equal opportunity to learn.

Multiculturalism and multicultural education have different meanings. I have conceptualized multicultural education in a way that consists of three major components: an idea or concept, an educational reform movement, and a process (Banks, 1993a). As an idea or concept, multicultural education maintains that all students should have equal opportunities to learn regardless of racial, ethnic, social-class, or gender group to which they belong. Additionally, multicultural education describes ways in which some students are denied equal educational opportunities because of their racial, ethnic, social-class, or gender characteristics (Lee & Slaughter-Defoe, 1995; Nieto, 1995). Multicultural education is an educational reform movement that tries to reform schools in ways that will give all students an equal opportunity to learn. It describes teaching strategies that empower all students and give them voice.

Multicultural education is a continuing process. One of its major goals is to create within schools and society the democratic ideals that Myrdal (1944) called "American Creed" values—values such as justice, equality, and freedom. These ideals are stated in the nation's founding documents—in the Declaration of Independence, the Constitution, and the Bill of Rights. They can never be totally achieved, but citizens within a democratic society must constantly work toward attaining them. Yet, when we approach the realization of these ideals for particular groups, other groups become victimized by racism, sexism, and discrimination. Consequently, within a democratic, pluralistic society, multicultural education is a continuing process that never ends.

The Dimensions of Multicultural Education

To effectively conceptualize and implement multicultural education curricula, programs, and practices, it is necessary not only to define the concept in general terms but to describe it programmatically. To facilitate this process, I have developed a typology called the dimensions of multicultural education (Banks, 1993b, 1995a). This dimensions typology can help practitioners identify and formulate reforms that implement multicultural education in thoughtful, creative, and effective ways. It is also designed to help theorists and researchers delineate the scope of the field and identify related research and theories. The dimensions typology is an ideal-type construct in the Weberian sense. The dimensions are highly interrelated, and the boundaries between and within them overlap. However, they are conceptually distinct.

A description of the conceptual scope of each dimension facilitates conceptual clarity and the development of sound educational practices. As Gay (1995) has pointed out, there is a wide gap between theory, research, and practice in multicultural education. The practices within schools that violate sound principles in multicultural education theory and research are cannon fodder for the field's critics, who often cite questionable practices that masquerade as multicultural education to support the validity of their claims. Although there is a significant gap between theory and practice within all fields in education, the consequences of such a gap are especially serious within new fields that are marginal and trying to obtain legitimacy within schools, colleges, and universities. Thus, the dimensions of multicultural education can serve as benchmark criteria for conceptualizing, developing, and assessing theory, research, and practice.

In my research, I have identified five dimensions of multicultural education (Banks, 1995a). They are: (a) content integration, (b) the knowledge con-

3. MULTICULTURAL EDUCATION AS AN ACADEMIC DISCIPLINE

struction process, (c) prejudice reduction, (d) an equity pedagogy; and an (e) empowering school culture and social structure. I will briefly describe each of these dimensions.

Content integration describes the ways in which teachers use examples and content from a variety of cultures and groups to illustrate key concepts, principles, generalizations, and theories in their subject area or discipline. The knowledge construction process consists of the methods, activities, and questions used by teachers to help students understand, investigate, and determine how implicit cultural assumptions, frames of reference, perspectives, and biases within a discipline influence the ways in which knowledge is constructed. When the knowledge construction process is implemented, teachers help students understand how knowledge is created and how it is influenced by the racial, ethnic, and social-class positions of individuals and groups (Code, 1991; Collins, 1990).

The prejudice reduction dimension of multicultural education relates to the characteristics of students' racial attitudes and strategies that teachers can use to help them develop more democratic values and attitudes. Since the late 1930s, researchers have been studying racial awareness, racial identification, and racial preference in young children (Clark & Clark, 1939; Cross, 1991; Spencer, 1982). This research is too vast and complex to summarize here; however, studies indicate, for example, that both children of color and White children develop a "White bias" by the time they enter kindergarten (Phinney & Rotheram, 1987; Spencer, 1982). This research suggests that teachers in all subject areas need to take action to help students develop more democratic racial attitudes and values. It also suggests that interventions work best when children are young. As children grow older, it becomes increasingly difficult to modify their racial attitudes and beliefs (Banks, 1995b).

An empowering school culture and social structure conceptualizes the school as a complex social system.

An equity pedagogy exists when teachers modify their teaching in ways that will facilitate the academic achievement of students from diverse racial, ethnic, cultural, and gender groups (Banks & Banks, 1995b). A number of researchers such as Au (1980), Boykin (1982), Depit (1995), Kleinfeld (1975), Ladson-Billings (1995), and Shade and New (1993) have described culturally sensitive (sometimes called culturally congruent) teaching strategies whose purpose is to enhance the academic achievement of students from diverse cultural and ethnic groups and the characteristics of effective teachers of these students. This research indicates that the academic achievement of students of color and low-income students can be increased when teaching strategies and activities build upon the cultural and linguistic strengths of students, and when teachers have cultural competency in the cultures of their students. Kleinfield, for example, found that teachers who were "warm demanders" were the most effective teachers of Indian and Eskimo youths. Other researchers maintain that teachers also need to have high academic expectations for these students, to explicitly teach them the rules of power governing classroom interactions, and to create equal-status situations in the classroom (Cohen & Lotan, 1995).

An empowering school culture and social structure conceptualizes the school as a complex social system, whereas the other dimensions deal with particular aspects of a school or educational setting. This dimension conceptualizes the school as a social system that is larger than any of its constituent parts such as the curriculum, teaching materials, and teacher attitudes and perceptions. The systemic view of the schools requires that in order to effectively reform schools, the entire system must be restructured, not just some of its parts. Although reform may begin with any one of the parts of a system (such as with the curriculum or with staff development), the other parts of the system (such as textbooks and the assessment program) must also be restructured in order to effectively implement school reform related to diversity.

A systemic view of educational reform is especially important when reform is related to issues as complex and emotionally laden as race, class, and gender. Educational practitioners—because of the intractable challenges they face, their scarce resources, and the perceived limited time they have to solve problems due to the high expectations of an impatient public—often want quick fixes to complex educational problems. The search for quick solutions to problems related to race and ethnicity partially explains some of the practices, often called multicultural education, that violate theory and research. These include marginalizing content about ethnic groups by limiting them to specific days and holidays such as Black History month and Cinco de Mayo. A systemic view of educational reform is essential for the implementation of thoughtful, creative, and meaningful educational reform.

Knowledge Construction and Curriculum Transformation

I will focus on only one of the dimensions of multicultural education: knowledge construction. In my latest book, *Multicultural Education, Transformative Knowledge, and Action* (1996), I describe a typology of knowledge that consists of five types: (a) personal/cultural, (b) popular, (c) mainstream academic, (d) transformative academic, and (e) school knowledge. I will discuss only two of these knowledge types: mainstream academic and transformative academic.

Mainstream Academic Knowledge

Mainstream academic knowledge consists of the concepts, paradigms, theories, and explanations that constitute traditional and established knowledge in the behavioral and social sciences. An important tenet within mainstream academic knowledge is that there is a set of objective truths that can be verified through rigorous and objective research procedures that are uninfluenced by human interests, values, and perspectives. Most of the knowledge that constitutes the established canon in the nation's schools, colleges, and universities is mainstream academic knowledge.

Today, the West paradigm in American history and culture is powerful, cogent, and deeply entrenched in the curriculum of the nation's institutions of learning.

The traditional conceptualization of the settlement of the West is a powerful example of the way in which mainstream academic knowledge has shaped the paradigms, canons, and perspectives that become institutionalized within the college, university, and school curriculum. In an influential paper presented at a meeting of the American Historical Association in 1893, Frederick Jackson Turner (1894/1989) argued that the frontier, which he regarded as a sparsely populated wilderness and lacking in civilization, was the main source of American democracy and freedom. Although Turner's thesis is now being criticized by revisionist historians, his paper established a conception of the West that has been highly influential in American scholarship, popular culture, and school books. His ideas, however, are closely related to other European conceptions of the Americas, of "the other" (Todorov, 1982), and of the native peoples who lived in the land that the European conceptualized as "the West." Turner's paradigm, and the interpretations that derive from it, largely ignore the large number of indigenous peoples who were living in the Americas when the Europeans arrived (Thornton [1995] estimates seven million). It also fails to acknowledge the rich cultures and civilizations that existed in the Americas, and the fact that the freedom the Europeans found in the West meant destruction and genocide for the various groups of Native Americans. By the beginning of the 20th century, most American Indian groups had been defeated by U.S. military force (Hyatt & Nettleford, 1995). Their collective will, however, was not broken, as evidenced by the renewed quest for Indian rights that emerged during the civil rights movement of the 1960s and 1970s.

Today, the West paradigm in American history and culture is powerful, cogent, and deeply entrenched in the curriculum of the nation's institutions of learning. As such, it often prevents students at all levels of education from gaining a sophisticated, complex, and compassionate understanding of American history, society, and culture. The West paradigm must therefore be seriously examined and deconstructed in order for students to acquire such an understanding. Students must be taught, for example, that the concept of the West is a Eurocentric idea, and they must be helped to understand how different groups in American society conceptualized and viewed the West differently.

For example, the Mexicans who became a part of the United States after the Treaty of Guadalupe Hidalgo in 1848 did not view or conceptualize the Southwest as the West. Rather, they viewed the territory that Mexico lost to the United States after the war as Mexico's "North." The Indian groups living in the western territories did not view their homelands as the West but as the center of the universe. To the various immigrants to the U.S. from Asia such as those from Japan and China, the land to which they immigrated was "the East" or the "land of the Golden Mountain." By helping

3. MULTICULTURAL EDUCATION AS AN ACADEMIC DISCIPLINE

students view Eurocentric concepts such as the West, "the Discovery of America," and "the New World" from different perspectives and points of view, we can increase their ability to conceptualize, to determine the implicit perspectives embedded in curriculum materials, and to become more thoughtful and reflective citizens.

Transformative Academic Knowledge

Teachers can help students acquire new perspectives on the development of American history and society by reforming the curriculum with the use of paradigms, perspectives, and points of view from transformative academic knowledge. Transformative academic knowledge consists of the concepts, paradigms, themes, and explanations that challenge mainstream academic knowledge and that expand the historical and literary canon (Banks, 1996). It thus challenges some of the key assumptions that mainstream scholars make about the nature of knowledge as well as some of their major paradigms, findings, theories, and interpretations. While mainstream academic scholars claim that their findings and interpretations are universalistic and unrelated to human interests, transformative scholars view knowledge as related to the cultural experiences of individuals and groups (Collins, 1990). Transformative scholars also believe that a major goal of knowledge is to improve society (Clark, 1965).

Louie Psihoyos—Woodfin Camp

Transformative Scholarship and the Quest for Democracy

Within the last two decades, there has been a rich proliferation of transformative scholarship developed by scholars on the margins of society (Banks & Banks, 1995a). This scholarship challenges many of the paradigms, concepts, and interpretations that are institutionalized within the nation's schools, colleges, and universities. Much, but not all, of this scholarship has been developed by scholars of color and feminist scholars. For example, in this book, *Margins and Mainstreams: Asians in American History and Culture,* Gary Okhiro (1994) argues that groups on the margins of society have played significant roles in maintaining democratic values in American society by challenging practices that violated democracy and human rights. Okhiro notes that America's minorities were among the first to challenge institutionalized racist practices such as slavery, the forced removal of the American Indians from native lands, segregation, and the internment of Japanese Americans during World War II. By so doing, they helped to keep democracy alive in the United States.

As I point out in my most recent book, transformative scholars and transformative scholarship have long histories in the United States (Banks, 1996). Transformative scholars and their work have helped to maintain democracy in the academic community by challenging racist scholarship and ideologies that provided the ideological and scholarly justification for institutionalized racist practices and policies. This lecture honors Charles H. Thompson, a transformative scholar and educator who was founding editor of the *Journal of Negro Education.* The *Journal* was established to provide a forum for transformative scholars and researchers to publish their findings and interpretations related to the education of Black people throughout the world. Much of their research challenged mainstream research and contributed to the education and liberation of African Americans.

Transformative scholars and their work have helped to maintain democracy in the academic community by challenging racist scholarship and ideologies.

In his editorial comment in the first issue of the *Journal,* entitled "Why a Journal of Negro Education?" Thompson (1932) advocated Black self-determination. He believed that the *Journal* would provide African Americans with a vehicle for assuming a greater role in their own education. As Thompson stated:

> ... leadership in the investigation of the education of Negroes should be assumed to a greater extent by Negro educators ... [yet there is] no ready and empathetic outlet for the publication of the results of [the Negro's] investigations.... Thus, it is believed that the launching of this project will stimulate Negroes to take a greater part in the solutions of the problems that arise in connection with their own education. (p. 2)

Black self-determination is as important today as when Thompson penned these words. The first issue of the *Journal of Negro Education* was published in April 1932. The *Journal* has continued its transformative tradition for 63 years. Other transformative journals founded by African American scholars include the *Journal of Negro History,* founded by Carter G. Woodson in 1916, and *Phylon,* founded by W. E. B. DuBois at Atlanta University in 1940. Prior to the founding of these journals, transformative scholars had few outlets for the publication of their works. The mainstream academic community and its journal editors had little interest in research and work on communities of color prior to the 19690s, especially work that presented positive descriptions of minority communities and that was oppositional to mainstream racist scholarship. When we examine the history of scholarship in the United Stats, it is striking how both racist scholarship and transformative scholarship have been consistent through time. Near the turn of the century, research and theories that described innate distinctions among racial groups was institutionalized within American social science (Tucker, 1994). A group of transformative scholars including thinkers as DuBois, Kelly Miller, and Franz Boas seriously challenged these conceptions (Banks, 1996).

The relationship between transformative and mainstream social science is interactive; each influences the other. Over time, transformative knowledge influences mainstream knowledge, and elements of tranformative knowledge become incorporated into mainstream knowledge. For example, the conceptions about race that were constructed by transformative scholars near the turn of the century became the accepted concepts and theories in mainstream social science during the 1940s and 1950s. Nevertheless, a group of scholars continued to invent research and construct ideas about the inferiority of particular racial groups.

Prior to the civil rights movement of the 1960s and 1970s, the White mainstream academic community ignored most of the scholarship created by African American scholars.

The history of research about race in America indicates that theories about the racial inferiority of certain groups—and challenges to them from transformative scholars—never disappear (Tucker, 1994). What varies is the extent to which theories of racial inferiority and other theories that support inequality attain public legitimacy and respectability. Since the beginning of the 20th century, every decade has witnessed the development of such theories. The extent to which these theories, and the individuals who purported them, experienced public respectability, awards, and recognitions has varied considerably. The amount of recognition that transformative scholars who challenged these theories have received from the public and academic communities has also varied considerably through time.

Prior to the civil rights movement of the 1960s and 1970s, the White mainstream academic community ignored most of the scholarship created by

3. MULTICULTURAL EDUCATION AS AN ACADEMIC DISCIPLINE

(Photo: AP/Wide World/Carlos Osorio)

Teachers can help their students learn new perspectives on American history and society development through curriculum reformation.

African American scholars. Most African American scholars had to take jobs in historically Black colleges. Most of these colleges were teaching institutions that had few resources with which to support and encourage research. Professors at these institutions had demanding teaching loads. Nevertheless, important research was done by African American and by a few White transformative scholars prior to the 1960s. Yet, because this research was largely ignored by the mainstream academic community, it had little influence on the knowledge about racial and ethnic groups that became institutionalized within the popular culture and the mainstream academic community. Consequently, it had little influence on the curriculum and the textbooks used in most of the nation's schools, colleges, and universities.

Although it was largely ignored by the mainstream community, a rich body of transformative scholarship was created in the years from the turn of the century to the 1950s. Much of this research was incorporated into popular textbooks that were used in Black schools and colleges. For example, Carter G. Woodson's *The Negro in Our History*, first published in 1930, was published in a 10th edition in 1962. John Hope Franklin's *From Slavery to Freedom*, first published in 1947, is still a popular history textbook in its seventh edition. Scholarly works published during this period included *The Philadelphia Negro* by W. E. B. DuBois (1899/1975), *American Negro Slave Revolt* by Herbert Aptheker (1943), *The Negro in the Civil War* by Benjamin Quarles (1953), *The Free Negro in North Carolina, 1790–1860*, by John Hope Franklin (1943), and Woodson's *The Education of the Negro Prior to 1861* (1919/1968).

The Need for a Transformative, Liberatory Curriculum

Prior to the 1960s, African American scholars and their White colleagues who did research on the African American community remained primarily at the margins of the mainstream academic community. Most of the paradigms and explanations related to racial ethnic groups that became institutionalized within the mainstream academic community were created by scholars outside these groups. Most of the paradigms, concepts, and theories created by mainstream scholars reinforced the status quo and provided intellectual justifications for institutionalized stereotypes and misconceptions about groups of color. An important example of this kind of scholarship is *American Negro Slavery* by Ulrich B. Phillips, published in 1918. Phillips described slaves as happy, inferior, and as benefiting from Western civilization. His interpretation of slavery became the institutionalized one within American colleges and universities, and he became one of the nation's most respected historians.

Phillips's view of slavery was not seriously challenged within the mainstream scholarly community until historians such as Stanley M. Elkins (1959), Kenneth M. Stampp (1956), John Blassingame (1972), and Eugene D. Genovese (1972) published new interpretations of slavery during the 1950s, 1960s, and 1970s. Transformative scholarship that presented other interpretations of slavery had been published as early as 1943, when Aptheker published *American Negro Slave Revolts*. However, this work was largely ignored and marginalized by the mainstream community partly because it was inconsistent with established views of slaves and slavery.

More recent research on the cognitive and intellectual abilities of African Americans indicates the extent to which antiegalitarian research is still influential in the mainstream academic community. In 1969, for example, the prestigious *Harvard Educational Review* devoted 123 pages of its first issue that year to Arthur Jensen's article on the differential intellectual abilities of Whites and African Americans. Papers by transformative scholars who embraced paradigms different from Jensen's were not published in this influential issue, although comments on the article by other scholars were published in the next issue of the *Review* (Kagan et al., 1969). Even though Jensen's article occupied most of the pages in an issue of a well-known scholarly journal, he experienced much public scorn and rejection when he appeared in public lectures and forums on university campuses.

Published nearly a quarter century after Jensen's article, *The Bell Curve* by Herrnstein and Murray (1994) received an enthusiastic and warm reception in both the academic and public communities. It was widely discussed in the public media and remained on the *New York Times* bestseller list for many weeks. Although it evoked much discussion and controversy (Jacoby & Glauberman, 1995), it attained a high degree of legitimacy within both the academic and public communities.

The publication of *The Bell Curve*, its warm and enthusiastic public reception, and the social and political context out of which it emerged provide an excellent case study for discussion and analysis by students who are studying knowledge construction. They can examine the arguments made by the authors, their major assumptions, and find out how these arguments and assumptions relate to the social and political context. Students can discuss these questions: Why, at this time in our history, was *The Bell Curve* written and published? Why was it so widely disseminated and well-received by the educated public? Who benefits from the arguments in *The Bell Curve*? Who loses? Why do arguments and theories about the genetic inferiority of African Americans keep re-emerging? How do such arguments relate to the social and political climate?

The work of transformative scholars indicates that the quest for human freedom is irrepressible.

Stephen Jay Gould (1994) responded to the last question in a *New Yorker* article by noting the following:

> *The Bell Curve*, with its claim and supposed documentation that race and class differences are largely caused by genetic factors and are therefore essentially immutable, contains no new arguments and presents no compelling data to support its anachronistic social Darwinism, so I can only conclude that its success in winning attention must reflect the depressing temper of our time—a historical moment of unprecedented ungenerosity, when a mood for slashing social programs can be powerfully abetted by an argument that beneficiaries cannot be helped, owing to inborn cognitive limits expressed as low IQ scores. (p. 139)

The publication and public reception of *The Bell Curve* is a cogent example of the extent to which much institutionalized knowledge within out society still supports inequality, dominant group hegemony, and the disempowerment of marginalized groups. *The Bell Curve*, its reception, and its legitimacy also underscore the need to educate students to become critical consumers of knowledge, to become knowledge producers themselves, and to be able to take thoughtful and decisive action that will help to create and maintain a democratic and just society. Works such as *The Bell Curve,* and the public response to them, remind us that democracies are fragile and that the threats to them are serious. Fortunately, the work of transformative scholars indicates that the quest for human freedom is irrepressible.

*Presented November 1, 1995, at Howard University. The speech has been slightly modified for publication.

James A. Banks is a professor of education at the University of Washington-Seattle and director of its Center for Multicultural Education. A past president of the National Council for the Social Studies, Banks has over 20 years of experience in the multicultural education field, serving as a professor and consultant to school districts, professional organizations, and universities throughout the United States and internationally. He has written over 100 articles and authored or edited 18 books, the most recent being *Multicultural Education, Transformative Knowledge, and Action* (1996), and the landmark *Handbook of Research on Multicultural Education* (1995). His other publications include *Curriculum Guidelines for Multicultural Education, Teaching Strategies for Ethnic Studies, Multicultural Education: Issues and Perspectives* (with Cherry A. McGee Banks), *Multiethnic Education: Theory and Practice, Teaching Strategies for the Social Studies,* and *An Introduction to Multicultural Education.* His achievements have earned him considerable recognition, including the 1986 Distinguished Scholar/Researcher on Minority Education and 1994 Research Review awards of the American Educational Research Association, and an honorary Doctorate of Humane Letters from the Bank Street College of Education in 1993.

References

Aptheker, H. (1943). *American Negro slave revolts.* New York: International Publishers.
Au, K. H. (1980). Participation structures in a reading lesson with Hawaiian children. *Anthropology and Education Quarterly, 11*(2), (91–115).
Banks, J. A. (1993a). Multicultural education: Characteristics and goals. In J. A. Banks & C. A. M. Banks (Eds)., *Multicultural education: Issues and perspectives* (2nd ed.) (pp. 3–28). Boston: Allyn & Bacon.
Banks, J. A. (1993b). *Multiethnic education: Theory and practice* (3rd ed.). Boston: Allyn & Bacon.
Banks, J. A. (1995a). Multicultural education: Historical development, dimensions, and practice. In J. A. Banks & C. A. M. Banks (Eds.), *Handbook of research on multicultural education* (pp. 3–24). New York: Macmillan.
Banks, J. A. (1995b). Multicultural education: Its effects on students' racial and gender role attitudes. In J. A. Banks & C. A. M. Banks (Eds.), *Handbook of research on multicultural education* (pp. 617–627). New York: Macmillan.
Banks, J. A. (1996). *Multicultural education, transformative knowledge, and action.* New York: Teachers College Press.
Banks, J. A., & Banks, C. A. M. (Eds.). (1995a). *Handbook of research on multicultural education.* New York: Macmillan.
Banks, J. A., & Banks, C. A. M. (1995b). Equity pedagogy. An essential component of multicultural education. *Theory into Practice, 34*(3), 152–168.
Blassingame, J. W. (1972). *The slave community: Plantation life in the antebellum south.* New York: Oxford University Press.

Boykin, A. W. (1982). Task variability and the performance of Black and White school children: Vervistic explorations. *Journal of Black Studies, 12,* 469–485.
Clark, K. B. (1965). *Dark ghetto: Dilemmas of social power.* New York: Harper & Row.
Clark, K. B., & Clark, M. P. (1939). The development of consciousness of self and the emergence of racial identification in Negro preschool children. *Journal of Social Psychology, 10,* 591–599.
Code, L. (1991). *What can she know? Feminist theory and the construction of knowledge.* Ithaca, NY: Cornell University Press.
Cohen, E. G., & Lotan, R. A. (1995). Producing equal-status interactions in the heterogeneous classroom. *American Educational Research Journal, 32*(1), 99–120.
Collins, P. H. (1990). *Black feminist thought: Feminist theory and the construction of knowledge.* New York: Routledge.
Cross, W. E., Jr. (1991). *Shades of Black: Diversity in African American identity.* Philadelphia: Temple University Press.
Delpit, L. (1995). *Other people's children: Cultural conflict in the classroom.* New York: The New Press.
D'Souza, D. (1995). *The end of racism: Principles for a multicultural society.* New York: The Free Press.
DuBois, W. E. B. (1940). Apology. *Phylon, 1*(1), 3–5.
DuBois, W. E. B. (19750. *The Philadelphia Negro: A social study.* Millwood, NY: Kraus-Thomson Organization Limited. (Original work published in 1899)
Elkins, S. M. (1959). *Slavery: A problem in American institutional and intellectual life.* Chicago: The University of Chicago Press.
Franklin, J. H. (1943). *The free Negro in North Carolina, 1790–1860.* New York: Russell & Russell.
Franklin, J. H. (1947). *From slavery to freedom: A history of Negro Americans.* New York: Knopf.
Gay, G. (1995). Curriculum theory and multicultural education. In J. A. Banks & C. A. M. Banks (Eds.), *Handbook of research on multicultural education* (pp. 25–43). New York: Macmillan.
Genovese, E. D. (1972). *Roll, Jordan, roll: The world the slaves made.* New York: Pantheon.
Gould, S. J. (1994, November 28). Curveball. *The New Yorker, 70*(38), 139–149.
Hernstein, R. J., & Murray, C. (1994). *The bell curve: Intelligence and class structure in American life.* New York: The Free Press.
Hyatt, V. L., & Nettleford, R. (Eds.). (1995). *Race, discourse, and the origin of the Americas: A new world view.* Washington, DC: Smithsonian Institution Press.
Jacoby, R., & Glauberman, N. (Eds.). (1995). *The Bell Curve debate: History, documents, opinions.* New York: Times Books/Random House.
Jensen, A. R. (1969). How much can we boost IQ and scholastic achievement? *Harvard Educational Review, 39*(1), 1–123.
Kagan, J. S., Hunt, J. M., Crow, J. F., Bereiter, C., Elkin, D., & Cronbach, L. (1969). Discussion: How much can we boost IQ and scholastic achievement? *Harvard Educational Review, 39*(2), 274–347.
Kleinfeld, J. (1975). Effective teachers of Eskimo and Indian students. *School Review, 83,* 301–344.
Ladson-Billings, G. (1995). Toward a theory of culturally relevant pedagogy. *American Educational Research Journal, 32*(3), 465–491.
Lee, C., & Slaughter-Defoe, D. T. (1995). Historical and sociocultural influences on African American education. In J. A. Banks & C. A. M. Banks (Eds.), *Handbook of research on multicultural education* (pp. 348–371). New York: Macmillan.
Nieto, S. (1995). A history of the education of Puerto Rican students in U.S. mainland schools: "Losers," "outsiders," or "leaders"? In J. A. Banks & C. A. M. Banks (Eds.), *Handbook of research on multicultural education* (pp. 388–411). New York: Macmillan.
Myrdal, D. (with R. Sterner & A. Rose). (1944). *An American dilemma: The Negro problem in modern democracy.* New York: Harper.
Okhiro, G. (1994). *Margins and mainstreams: Asians in American history and culture.* Seattle, WA: University of Washington Press.
Phillips, U. B. (1918). *American Negro slavery.* New York: Appleton.

Phinney, J. S., & Rotherman, M. J. (Eds.). (1987). *Children's ethnic socialization: Pluralism and development.* Beverly Hills, CA: Sage Publications.

Quarles, B. (1953). *The Negro in the Civil War.* Boston: Little, Brown.

Sacks, D. O., & Theil, P. A. (1995). *The diversity myth: "Multiculturalism" and the politics of intolerance at Stanford,* Oakland, CA: The Independent Institute.

Schlesinger, A., Jr. (1991). *The disuniting of America: Reflections on a multicultural society.* Knoxville, TN: Whittle Direct Books.

Shade, B. A., & New, C. A. (1993). Cultural influences on learning: Teaching implications. In J. A. Banks & C. A. M. Banks (Eds.), *Multicultural education: Issues and perspectives* (2nd ed.) (pp. 317–331). Boston: Allyn & Bacon.

Sleeter, C. A. (1995). An analysis of the critiques of multicultural education. In J. A. Banks and C. A. M. Banks (Eds.), *Handbook of research on multicultural education* (pp. 81–94). New York: Macmillan.

Spencer, M. B. (1982). Personal and group identity of Black children: An alternative synthesis. *Genetic Psychology Monographs, 106,* 59–84.

Stampp, K. M. (1956). *The peculiar institution: Slavery in the ante-bellum south.* New York: Vintage.

Thompson, C. H. (1932). Editorial comment: Why a journal of Negro education? *Journal of Negro Education, 1*(1), 1–4.

Thornton, R. (1995). North American Indians and the demography of contact. In V. L. Hyatt & R. Nettleford (Eds.), *Race, discourse, and the origin of the Americas: A new world view* (pp. 213–230). Washington, DC: Smithsonian Institution Press.

Todorov, T. (1982). *The conquest of America: The question of the other.* New York: Harper Collins.

Tucker, W. H. (1994). *The science and politics of racial research.* Urbana, IL: University of Illinois Press.

Turner, F. J. (1989). The significance of the frontier in American history. In C. A. Milner, II (Ed.), *Major problems in the history of the American West* (pp. 2–21). Lexington, MA: Heath. (Original work published in 1894)

U.S. Bureau of the Census. (1993). *We, the American children.* Washington, DC: U.S. Government Printing Office.

Woodson, C. G. (1930). *The Negro in our history.* Washington, DC: The Associated Publishers.

Woodson, C. G. (1968). *The education of the Negro prior to 1861.* New York: Arno Press. (Original work published in 1919)

Multicultural A Movement in Search of Meaning

Leonard Davidman

Leonard Davidman is a Professor of Education with the University Center for Teacher Education at California Polytechnic State University, San Luis Obispo.

Introduction

When teacher educators responsible for conveying the meanings and rationales for multicultural education sit down to plan their courses, there are many questions to ponder. For example, several of the questions listed below are likely to be considered:

1. How many conceptions or definitions of multicultural education will I present, and whose conceptual framework will receive the most emphasis?
2. Should I begin the course with one or more definitions of culture, ethnicity, cultural group, ethnic group, minority group, etc., and if so, which definitions should be employed?
3. Which essays, texts, and on-and off-campus activities should be included?
4. Will students be expected to engage in some form of ethnic and/or cultural self-analysis and self-disclosure, and if yes, why?
5. What are the central objectives of this course of study? Am I primarily concerned with knowledge exchange, attitude formation (including commitment to multicultural education), and/or modelling how to implement multicultural education in a given setting (the school, classroom, community, or a specific level of education—elementary or secondary), or all of the above?
6. How will I perceive (label) and relate to my students, and how do I want them to perceive and relate to me?

The process of delineating these questions reminds me of the complexity professors of multicultural education face as they design their courses. It reminds me also of the need for an infusion approach to multicultural teacher education, one in which concepts and activities critical to an understanding of multicultural education are spread throughout all the courses and phases in a program. But, even with an infusion approach, it is likely that one or more courses will be given the special responsibility of introducing the topic of multicultural education. Therefore, some faculty will have to contemplate several of the questions enumerated above.

As might be expected, I have a point of view about each of the questions listed. All have been grappled with for over 15 years as I have created separate multicultural education courses for elementary, secondary, and graduate students at my university.

Three related beliefs have guided me in my planning:

(1) I believe that courses which cover topics related to multicultural education should involve knowledge exchange and growth, attitude formation and reformation, and modeling of strategies related to multicultural education.

(2) I also believe that prospective and inservice teachers at an early and later point in a program should have the opportunity to study and discuss themselves as individuals with a cultural identity, and, further, that these discussions should occur in small, diverse cooperative groups. This implies that students will receive instruction regarding various competing meanings of specific concepts like culture, ethnicity, race, cultural group, ethnic group, racial group, minority group, ethnic minority group, macroculture and microcultures, and core values. This also implies a flexible instructor, one who will not tell the candidates who they are, as in "You are White, lower-middle class, women with little awareness of the importance of your Whiteness," but will genuinely engage students in a process of self-exploration, self-defini-

Education: and Positive Connections

tion, self-discovery, and self-disclosure, a process informed by the idea that the concepts used and knowledge gleaned in this self-analysis activity are socially constructed. This process might wind up with the instructor politely challenging the self-definitions of a group of candidates, who, for example, refuse to see the social meaning of their own color or anyone else's color or ethnicity, but this will come after a degree of rapport has developed and will be carried out in a thoughtful, respectful way.

(3) Finally, I believe that a logical place to begin an inquiry about the design of multicultural teacher education courses is with the meaning or meanings of multicultural education. A cursory review of the multicultural education literature will show that I am not alone in making this assumption.

Most writers begin their discussion of multicultural education by sharing one or several meanings of multicultural education. One recent example of this is found in the work of Brian M. Bullivant (1993); his work will be used as a point of departure as I try to indicate why a very broad and pluralistic conception of culture and cultural group will work to the advantage of multicultural teacher educators in general, and particularly those who make use of some form of ethnic and cultural self-disclosure in their courses. After this attempt I will discuss: my definition of "cultural group;" the implications which this definition holds for multicultural education; and the importance of teachers developing a positive attitude toward multicultural education in general, and more specifically the idea of beginning a journey into the field of multicultural education. I will close this essay by taking a closer look at ethnic and cultural self-disclosure, and in this final section will provide examples of the questions I use to initiate the process of ethnic and cultural self-disclosure in my classes.

The Meaning(s) of Multicultural Education

In his attempt to clarify the meaning of multiculturalism and multicultural education, Bullivant took the seemingly logical approach of breaking the word multicultural down into its constituent parts, prior to doing an analysis of each of the parts—"multi-" and "cultural." Because the meaning of multi-, or many, is obvious, his main analytical work was with "cultural," and for Bullivant this meant determining, in the context of multicultural education, the truest or best meaning for the term "culture." After examining several alternative meanings Bullivant defined culture "...as a social group's design for survival in and adaptation to its environment," (1993, p. 29) and with this definition in mind went on to add that one aim of multicultural education would be "...to teach about the many social groups and their different designs for living in a pluralist society."

I am concerned about the narrowness of Bullivant's definition and his general approach to defining the meanings and aims of multicultural education, particularly as this term and reform movement has evolved in the American (U.S.A.) context. While analyzing the term "multicultural," or more specifically "culture," to shed light on the meaning of multicultural education appears logical, the approach is ahistorical and somewhat presumptuous in assuming that there is one meaning of multicultural education out there. This approach would have had a stronger rationale if the early "American" creators of the multicultural education movement had moved directly from a definition of culture to their conceptions and operationalizations of multicultural education.

But, this is not what happened, at least not within the American historical context. As James A. Banks (1992) and others have pointed out, the educational movement(s) now called multicultural education was initially a set of individual and group responses to economic inequality, racism, and sexism in American culture. And, these responses, by and large, were initially located in the 20th century Negro (and now African-American) community. Indeed, in retrospect, it can be seen that all of the individuals and groups struggling for greater equality and opportunity for members of oppressed groups were laying the groundwork for the educational reform movement which in America would later be called multicultural education.

Given these realities, first, that the roots of multicultural education preceded early definitions of multicultural education, and second, that the early definitions of multicultural education did not have a one-to-one correspondence with a specific definition of culture, it may prove profitable to reverse Bullivant's procedure. Instead of selecting or creating a definition of culture to shed light on the aims of multicultural education, we can examine a pivotal goal and early influential definition of multicultural education to see what it might imply about the meaning of "cultural" in the term multicultural education. The goal referred to is educational equity; analysis of this goal will make three things clear.

First, from its beginning in the American context, multicultural education was concerned with a range of cultural and ethnic groups; second, the groups which initially fell under multicultural education's umbrella of concern were different in kind, and finally these differences can have important implications for the way we invite prospective teachers, students, parents, and lay people to enter into the conversation about multicultural education.

The influential definition referred to above stated that "Multicultural education [is] an educational reform movement that is concerned with increasing educational equity for a range of cultural and ethnic groups" (Banks, 1981). We see with this definition that educational equity has always been a pivotal concern for leading advocates of multicultural education, and further, that a central proposition in this enterprise has been the idea that **all** students regardless of gender, social class, **degree of learning handicap, linguistic background, or ethnic, cultural, or religious identity should have an equal opportunity to learn in school and, by extension,** society. Put another way, in school students should not be penalized because of the various labels and social groups which together shape their "social identity." We see also that for teachers, multicultural education could mean learning as much as possible about a range of cultural and ethnic groups so as to be better able to create equitable learning environments for members of these groups.

In other words, the adjective multicultural in the term "multicultural education" refers to various social, cultural, and ethnic groups which exist within America's macroculture (total culture), and a major concern for advocates of multicultural education is equity (and excellence) for all members of these groups. To the extent that studying these different groups and their "...designs for living or program for survival" can provide ideas for maximizing the learning of members of these cultural groups, Bullivant's description of aims for multicultural education reinforces the equity focus of multicultural education. But, it is noteworthy that many groups of concern to multicultural education practitioners do not have a "survival program" which is widely shared by group members. Ironically, in Bullivant's use and definition of the term "culture," these groups lack culture, and yet in the eyes of multicultural practitioners these cultureless groups are important cultural groups. And this means that these groups—the "poor," the "homeless," learners who are "at risk," the "English learner," "women," and the "learning disabled" or "gifted" learners—do have a culture, or rather are part of a macroculture.

One Meaning of Cultural Group

At this point, it may prove helpful to discuss my understanding of the term "cultural group." As I use them the terms "social group" and "cultural group" are synonymous; if a specific social group has an identity or label which is recognized or created in a macroculture (from within or outside the social group—exonymously or autonymously), like "Gay-Americans" or "developmentally disabled/mentally retarded," "recovering alcoholics," or "African-American," then that social group can also be accurately described as a cultural group, and possibly as an ethnic or racial group as well.

This is true because in a macroculture any group that has a publicly recognized identity (label) becomes a cultural group within the macroculture; this is the case because its identity and label are facts which are negotiated or given meaning within that specific macroculture. In other words, any group in a macroculture that fits or fits itself into that macroculture's definition of "group" becomes, automatically, a cultural group.

Furthermore, cultural groups that exist in one macroculture like the "gifted" or "at-risk learners" or the "criminally insane" or "Mexican-Americans" or the "homeless" may not exist in some other macroculture. Or, if a group such as "developmentally disabled learners" does exist as a category in one macroculture, the developmentally disabled learners in this macroculture may by bureaucratic definition have different characteristics than the developmentally disabled learners in a second macroculture.

Implications for the Multicultural Education Conversation

As indicated earlier, this discussion about the meaning of culture, cultural group, and multicultural education has implications for the way we can invite future teachers, parents, students, and lay people into the multicultural education conversation. To begin with, it reminds us that multicultural education is about cultural groups of all kinds (cultural, ethnic, racial, and socio-economic) as well as culture, and that the key cultural groups of concern in one macroculture (nation) may differ from those in another. In addition, in a given society the focus of multicultural education may broaden from one decade to the next as new groups enter a society (the Hmong from Laos and Viet Nam) or are invented by legislative or bureaucratic definition (the at-risk learner or the "English learner," formerly called the limited English proficient student), or are "rediscovered" as a group which is uniquely disadvantaged by power relationships within a society (women).

This expansive meaning of cultural group, if accepted, may also have positive implications for multicultural teacher educators who are trying to help prospective and veteran teachers see that:

(a) as individuals with a cultural identity they are a part of multicultural America and the multicultural education equation; and

(b) multicultural education, broadly construed, is about equity, and empowerment, and intergroup harmony, and cultural pluralism for teachers as well as students.

In short, multicultural education is for and by teachers, as well as their students, parents, and other stakeholders.

Developing a Positive Attitude Towards Multicultural Education

In many cases when teacher educators responsible for conveying the meanings and rationales for multicultural education face their university audience, mainly prospective and in-service teachers, the majority of the group, often up to 70 or 90 percent, are White Americans or Americans of European Descent (depending on your label preference), and the majority of this group are women, particularly in elementary education classes. In addition, the students "of color" in the class, Americans of African, Asian, American Indian, Hispanic, and Pacific Island descent, often have overlapping values and social characteristics with the White Americans as well as differences. In short, the students of color and their white colleagues have commonalities and points of divergence just like most of the classes they encounter, or will encounter, in K-12 settings.

One of the commonalities pertains to their preliminary understanding or misunderstanding about multicultural education. Like many others, these students often confuse multicultural education with ethnic studies, and for many, both of these topics appear to be exclusively or largely concerned with the social and academic problems of "people of color." While somewhat understandable given the origins of multicultural education and the recent contentious public and university debate about multiculturalism, ethnic studies, and multicultural education, this perception is both erroneous and counter-productive in terms of getting a group of largely White teacher candidates and their non-white colleagues to develop a positive connection with multicultural education; and I mean here multicultural education construed as a powerful model of curriculum and instruction which addresses the aspirations and learning needs of all students, as well as their parents and teachers.

I believe that a major objective of a course or sequence of courses on multicultural education should be to develop in teacher candidates a positive personal connection with the content and goals of multicultural education. If this objective is to be realized, the course(s) should have certain characteristics. To begin with the course content should be historically accurate, reveal that multicultural education is for and about the candidates and their individual and group needs as well as groups they are not a part of, and should provide a forum in which candidates can safely explore and publicly speculate about their tentative cultural, ethnic, and racial group connections.

In addition, at the beginning of such a course the instructor should make clear that the attempt to comprehend multicultural education in all its facets is a lifelong journey. And, further, that at the beginning of such a journey it is inevitable that many students will discover that there is a lot they don't know about African-American history, Mexican-American history, inequality in American life, and so on, and much to learn. But, that is the point of the journey and the course(s); it is the attitude toward the lifelong journey that is critical and practical, rather than the unrealistic hope that the candidates can master a substantial part of the increasing "multicultural" body of knowledge prior to student teaching or that they will have developed a set of correct attitudes by the end of a ten or 14 week course.

Ethnic and Cultural Self-Disclosure

In the context of such a course the opportunity to explore, describe, and share one's cultural, ethnic, and racial connections can have a positive enduring effect. Instructors and students sometimes overlook and bypass the rich diversity—religious, gender, ethnic, racial, S.E.S., age, life style, work and life experience, language, and experience with handicapping conditions—that exists in almost any classroom, as they make a sustained effort to cover some part of the traditional curriculum. But, a positive experience with cultural and ethnic self-exploration and disclosure can make a strong impression on prospective and in-service teachers.

If such teachers, working in small, diversely structured, cooperative discussion groups (five or six students to a group), can see that their efforts to study and communicate with fellow teachers are en-

---

Self-Disclosure Questions

1. Your name.

2. Geographically, where are you from? Where do you live now?

3. Your mode of abode (I live with my friends, family, etc.). **This is optional**.

4. How long has your family or ancestors been on this continent?

5. Where did your family or ancestors come from before joining the drama "of the Americas"? Or, were they always here?

6. How many generations of your family, on both sides, have lived in the U.S.A.? In California?

7. What languages were or are spoken in your (childhood) home? What languages are spoken in your current domicile?

8. Please identify a favorite author, book, film, or ritual you value or have especially enjoyed, and/or a significant event in your life. An important book in your life like the Bible, Koran, or Torah, etc., should also be mentioned.

9. Given our opening definitions of race, ethnicity, ethnic group, culture, and cultural group, would you be comfortable in describing yourself as a member of a racial, ethnic and/or cultural group? If so, which **groups** would you say you are a part of at this point in your life?

10. Have you ever experienced interpersonal conflict because of your race, ethnicity, gender, cultural group, or an organization you were active in? If so, please describe one or more of these conflicts. Was this conflict resolved in any way, and if so, how?

11. Do you feel your racial, ethnic, and/or cultural group membership (and the latter includes gender) has been a positive feature in your life? If so, briefly explain why.

12. At this point in your teacher education (or graduate school) program, do you have any opinions about multicultural education which you'd like to share? If yes, please list below.

13. Do you have a favorite hobby? If so, please identify.

14. If currently employed, please describe where and what your current responsibilities are.

15. When you have the license or credential you are seeking, in what organization and region would you like to begin, or continue, your career?

3. MULTICULTURAL EDUCATION AS AN ACADEMIC DISCIPLINE

hanced because of the prior knowledge gained from the teachers' self-disclosure, it is quite possible that these same teachers will be more likely to create opportunities for their students to discover each other as sources of cultural information and insight.

Part of the value of self-disclosure derives from the realization that the cultural information shared in small groups sets the stage for a deeper type of trust and rapport building in a classroom community. It is noteworthy that this trust and rapport is linked to the broad conception of "cultural group" discussed earlier. I want my candidates to see that their values and self-perceptions lead them to culturally connect with selected groups, and, I want them to know I am interested in all their cultural connections, just as I want them to be interested in their students' full cultural biographies.

Thus, in my courses the term "cultural group" is taken to mean any collection of people in the macroculture who share a public identity and sense of commonality. This sense of commonality is not the same as a sense of unity, or the strong sense of affinity which is felt by members of some ethnic, racial, and cultural groups. The sense of commonality merely suggests that members of the group understand that: (a) they have something in common with all members of that group, and (b) the group has a public identity or label which can be shared. A vegetarian, for example, may share some norms and behavior patterns with all other vegetarians, and may read articles and books about vegetarians, but may not, at a given point in time, know other vegetarians in his or her community, or be interested in spending time with other vegetarians. And the fact that the vegetarian's spouse and children do not choose to share vegetarianism is inconvenient but not critical.

Of course, it is likely that there are vegetarians who take their lifestyle and group more seriously; such individuals may be vegetarians on an individual as well as a group level. They may pay dues to a vegetarian organization, write articles about vegetarianism, and attend local and state meetings of vegetarians. Still, this organization-oriented vegetarian may be more connected to a healthy lifestyle and social movement than to other vegetarians as a "people." And, if he or she should desire, it would be fairly easy to stop being a vegetarian. And vegetarians have not suffered oppression because of their belief system, physical characteristics, language background, or place of origin, although being a vegetarian in some agricultural-oriented contexts could be delicate. In this sense, vegetarians are very far from being an ethnic group, a cultural group with a sense of peoplehood, shared history, common ancestry, and a common set of political and economic interests.

Nevertheless, this cultural connection should be treated seriously and respectfully; in no way should it be dismissed as a "mere" lifestyle identity. I have learned that being a vegetarian, or a divorced, working single parent, or a conservationist, or a pacifist, or a recovering alcoholic can be a critical part of a student's cultural identity for the short or long term. More importantly, this identity can become the lens through which a candidate better perceives the similarities and differences between himself or herself and others who have different types of cultural identities; furthermore, in an accepting environment the identities students start with serve as a catalyst for deeper insights into their full cultural biographies.

A key point to remember is that when I ask teachers and prospective teachers to engage in cultural and ethnic self-exploration and disclosure, I want them to report on **all** the cultural groups they see themselves as part of, and not just the important ones that are traditionally and still a major concern of multicultural education. This strategy is consistent with the idea of starting your teaching where your students are, and not where you'd have them be. Furthermore, because we encourage students to define themselves and then proceed to value those initial self-perceptions, it is also consistent with cultural pluralism, a major goal of multicultural education.

Finally, and quite significantly, this strategy builds positive relationships between advocates (and models) of multicultural education and our next generation of teachers. Although I have not studied this claim in a systematic way, my qualitative impression is that these positive human relationships help to produce candidates who have a more positive attitude towards the content and goals of multicultural education. If such attitudes are part of what we are after in our introductory multicultural education courses, then I think the self-disclosure strategy discussed above is worthy of more discussion, adaptation, and research.

To promote such discussion I will close by enumerating the set of questions which students respond to in the latest version of my ethnic and cultural self-disclosure form. Parenthetically, in my university courses I use the self-disclosure data in a variety of ways. For example, at the beginning of the course I use the self-disclosure data to help form heterogeneous discussion groups. The self-disclosure reports, made in the small groups, also helps each student see the rich diversity that exists in a class that could be perceived as fairly homogeneous (80-90 percent White women).

References

James A. Banks (1981). *Multiethnic Education: Theory and Practice*. Boston, MA: Allyn and Bacon, p. 32.

James A. Banks (1992), "African American Scholarship and the Evolution of Multicultural Education," *The Journal of Negro Education*, Vol. 61, No. 3, pp 273-286.

Brian M. Bullivant (1993). "Culture: Its Nature and Meaning for Educators," in *Multicultural Education: Issues and Perspectives*, 2nd edition, James A. Banks and Cherry A McGee Banks, eds., Boston, MA: Allyn and Bacon, p. 29.

Bridging Multicultural Theory and Practice

Geneva Gay

Geneva Gay is a professor of education and an associate with the Center of Multicultural Education at the University of Washington, Seattle, Washington.

The current state of multicultural education is at once exciting and troubling. A significant part of this dilemma—and the one of interest here—results from disparities in the developmental growth of its theory and practice. Ideally, educational theory and practice develop in tandem, and the relationship between them is complementary, reciprocal, and dialectic. This is not yet happening, in any systematic way, in multicultural education. Its theoretical development is far out-stripping its practical development, and its further refinement is stimulated more by proposals of what should be than by lessons learned from what is.

Multicultural theory is becoming more thorough, complex, and comprehensive, while its practice in K-12 and college classrooms continues to be rather questionable, simplistic, and fragmentary. This gap is growing exponentially; it fuels much of the current debate because critics fail to distinguish between the two in their critiques; and it limits the overall effectiveness of multi-cultural reform efforts.

These divergent growth patterns also make it difficult for multicultural advocates in different aspects of the educational enterprise to engage in constructive dialogue, and to work as collaboratively as they might for the achievement of common goals. As a result, multicultural classroom instruction is often not synchronized with curriculum development. Policy statements governing school practices may specify that multiculturalism must be included in instructional materials and program designs, but routinely fail to make similar requirements for hiring personnel and for assessing the performance of students and teachers. Yet, theorists consistently argue that for multicultural education to be maximally successful, all parts of the educational system must be responsive to and inclusive of cultural diversity.

The gaps between multicultural theory and practice present some serious challenges and opportunities for future directions in the field. In this discussion, I will offer some thoughts about why these gaps exist, and make some suggestions for how the challenges they present might be addressed.

INVERSE GROWTH PATTERNS

According to George Beauchamp (1968), an essential function of educational theorizing is to constantly search for new conceptual ideas, understandings, and principles to describe, explain, and predict issues of interest or study. He adds that the theorist "seeks out new relationships by combining sets of events into a new universal set and then [proceeds] with the search for new relationships and new laws in a new theory" (p. 19). This search has both internal and external dimensions. It analyzes the components of an existing paradigm to achieve greater depths and clarity of meanings, while simultaneously bringing ideas and insights from other sources to bear upon the phenomenon being studied.

For example, multicultural education was initially conceptualized as a discrete program of studies with heavy emphasis on teaching factual content about the histories, heritages, and contributions of groups of color. Over the last 25 years, this conceptualization has been re-examined, revised, and refined so that now multicultural education is conceived more as a particular ideological and methodological approach to the entire educational enterprise than a separate curriculum or program *per se*.

The relationships between culture, ethnicity, and learning, which are so central to multicultural education are continually analyzed and reinterpreted. Different ways to systematize the implementation of commonly-agreed-upon elements of multicultural education are constantly being proposed by various scholars. In the rhetoric of today's educational thinking, these processes might be coded as self-reflection, critical interrogation, knowledge reconstruction, meta-analysis or meta-cognition, and multiple perspectives. Thus, the evolvement of educational theory from inception to maturity is a self-renewing, regenerative process. One of its natural effects is the creation of subsidiary theories and conceptual models.

Even a quick and cursory look at the scholarship of leading multiculturalists (see, for example, Banks & Banks, 1993, 1995; Hollins, King, & Hayman, 1994; Bennett, 1995; Sleeter, 1992; Sleeter & Grant, 1995; Foster, 1991) provides persuasive evidence of these processes taking place. Senior scholars are revisioning and elaborating on some of their earlier thinking, as well as using knowledge and interpretive filters from other disciplines to enrich, elaborate, and extend the conceptual contours, attributes, and principles of multicultural education.

Several specific examples illustrate this trend. In a recent publication, Gay (1994) explained the relationship between canonical principles of general education commonly endorsed by United States schools and those of multicultural education. She argued that these are fundamentally the same, with the only differences being in context and constituency. Multicultural

3. MULTICULTURAL EDUCATION AS AN ACADEMIC DISCIPLINE

education merely translates general educational principles to fit the specific contexts of ethnic and cultural diversity. James Banks (1995) is now exploring intersections between feminist theory, knowledge reconstruction, and multicultural education, as well as ideological antecedents to it found in the thinking of early 20th century African American educators. Christine Bennett (1995) and Sonia Nieto (1992), along with Banks and many others, evoke democratic principles and ethics to support their claims about the multicultural imperative in education. Carl Grant, Christine Sleeter, Joyce King, Gloria Ladson-Billings, and Antonia Darder (1992) incorporate ideas from critical theory, post-modernism, social reconstructionism, and political empowerment into their explanations of the essential goals, purposes, and anticipated outcomes of multicultural education. Other theorists are beginning to establish direct linkages between economic development, international diplomacy, and being responsive to cultural diversity in the educational process.

This "conceptual webbing" is producing both encouraging and disturbing results for multicultural education. It is stimulating and enriching discussions among theorists about the necessities, contours, and potentialities of multicultural education. The thoughts and ideas which result from these discussions are at increasingly higher levels of sophistication, abstraction, and complexity. In this sense, the field is developing the way it should, from the perspective of theory development. As any kind of educational theory matures, its ideological contours become more complex and abstract, and thus moves further and further away from direct and immediate translation to classroom application.

Ironically, its theoretical strengths are also the nemesis of multicultural education practice. Rather than enlightening practitioners and stimulating them to higher levels of instructional action, complex theoretical explanations often have the reverse effects. They can intimidate, confuse, overwhelm, and incapacitate classroom teachers. The language used to expressed key ideas and concepts become more esoteric, thereby making them less clear to everyone except other theorists with similar developmental status and understanding. More attention is devoted to conceptualizing than to actualizing multicultural components and characteristics. That is, as theorists prescribe and visualize what **should be done,** they speak increasingly in terms of ideals without clearly articulating directions for how these are to be operationalized in practice.

This situation is complicated even further by differences in the ideological ideas disciplinary emphases, and maturational levels of theorists themselves. Some multiculturalists are influenced heavily by history and sociology, while others speak through the conceptual and linguistic filters of politics, psychology, anthropology, and pedagogy. Consequently, classroom teachers and school administrators are left to their own devices to translate theory to practice. Frequently what they do in practice is inconsistent with or even violates what is meant by the theory.

Thus, while multicultural theorists argue that cultural diversity should be infused into the learning experiences of all students regardless of the ethnic demographics of specific school and classroom sites, practitioners still tend to make its implementation contingent upon the presence of specific ethnic groups of color. If there are no African-American, Latino, Native-American, or certain Asian-American students enrolled in their schools, they find it difficult to see the relevance of doing multicultural education. When theorists propose that the K-12 educational process be **transformed** by cultural diversity, they mean the most fundamental and deeply ingrained values, beliefs, and assumptions which determine all educational policies, content, procedures, and structures schooling will be **revolutionalized** by being culturally pluralized.

However, their college and university counterparts do not necessarily conceive of transformation in the same way. They, as well as many K-12 practitioners, use a more restricted notion of transformation as simply "change." They assume that multicultural transformation is accomplished by merely including information about ethnically diverse individuals and achievements into the content of instruction, or disciplinary canons. In this sense, the curriculum of a United States literature course is thought to have been transformed when writings by authors of color and females are routinely included for study. These conceptions and practices fail to realize that curriculum involves more than content, that the educational enterprise is not analogous to curriculum, and that the mere presence of ethnic information is not enough to constitute transformation.

These kinds of discrepancies in meanings between theorists and practitioners, are understandable, given their differential levels of mastery of and maturity in the field. But they also are confusing and can have negative effects on the overall advancement of multiculturalism in all levels of the educational enterprise. They place both the practitioners and the theorists in reactive, rather than pro-active positions. The practitioners are faced with having to explain away their unintended misinterpretations and possible accusations that theorists are too esoteric in their explanations of key multicultural ideas. The theorists feel the need to re-examine and re-explain their intended original meanings to avoid future misinterpretations. This "back-stepping" slows down the forward thrust and continuous development of multicultural education in both theory and practice.

A strongly endorsed theoretical idea that is often misunderstood and is another powerful illustration of the lack of **operational bridging** between multicultural educational theory and practice is **infusion.** Virtually every multicultural theorist supports the idea that cultural diversity should be an integral part of the total educational experiences of all students in all school settings. This means it should impact the contexts and structures of teaching and learning as well as their content and text. Stated somewhat differently, all policies, programs, and procedures in school curriculum, instruction, administration, guidance, assessment, and governance should be responsive to cultural diversity. This responsiveness is multidimensional, too, including recognition, knowledge, acceptance, respect, praise, and promotion. But, very few theorists explain how to actually do these all-encompassing mandates in the various dimensions of the educational enterprise.

What do school principals do to multiculturalize the different tasks which comprise their administrative and leadership functions? What are the operational steps and decision-making points involved in multiculturalizing the curriculum creation process? How can these general principles be specified to different domains of learning such as math, science, reading, and social studies? How does one make the content as well as the administrative styles of student assessment culturally pluralistic? These are the kinds of questions that remain after most theoretical pronouncements are made regarding multicultural education infusion. They must be answered more precisely in order to establish better connections between theory and practice.

The few attempts that are made to create these bridges often are unsuccessful because they tend be "finished or product examples" of what infusion looks like, instead of clearly articulated and functional explanations of the **processes** of infusion itself. For example, theorists may present illustrations of multiculturally-infused reading units, but fail to explain how decisions about their specific components were made, or why they embody and personify different principles of multicultural education.

Consequently, these samples are of limited value in empowering other educators to create similar ones, and thereby continuing to advance the development of multicultural education practice. This places practitioners in a situation of trying to imitate or replicate the sample lessons without being sufficiently informed about how the original decisions were made. The results are not very successful which can cause instructional program designers to become frustrated and discouraged. This frustration then becomes a convenient excuse for them to abandon future efforts to implement multicultural education in their classrooms.

Another tension between multicultural theory and practice is the fact that many application models suggested for classroom use are **decontextualized.** They are not connected in any systematic way to what teachers routinely do in the day-to-day operations of their curricula and classrooms. Excellent books which present authentic and accurate portrayals of different ethnic groups' cultures, contributions, and experiences are now available. A wide variety of richly textured and significant learning activities have been developed for teaching various aspects of multicultural education, such as prejudice reduction, ethnic identity development, intergroup relations, and self-esteem.

Despite their inherent worth, decontextualized multicultural activities are of limited use in classrooms because the authors do not explain where and how they fit into typical instructional tasks and responsibilities. If, for example, designers were to demonstrate how learning non-pejorative terms for ethnic groups can be incorporated into standard vocabulary lessons in reading instruction, how ethnic population statistics can be used in teaching math skills such as proportions, ratios, and graphing, and how participating in inter-ethnic group social exchanges approximate some of the skills social studies teach about international diplomacy classroom teachers may be more willing and capable of using them.

Without this **functional contextualization,** teachers are likely to continue to perceive multicultural education as an intrusive addition to an already over-burdened workload, or something that requires extra efforts and special skills. It then becomes very easy for them to dismiss the idea of cultural diversity without due consideration because they "don't have time to teach anything else," or because "it jeopardizes other important things that must be taught, such as basic literacy skills."

Another occurrence common to a profession which causes a split between theory and practice is variability in the positional responsibilities of the membership. Educational theorists tend to be more highly specialized in selected aspects of a discipline than school practitioners. They have the luxury of concentrating their professional activities on fewer things, and becoming more thoroughly involved in exploring even deeper conceptual parameters and possibilities of their areas of expertise.

By comparison, school practitioners tend to be more generalists than specialists, and are more engaged in applying than creating new knowledge. The more deeply involved they are in a pedagogical field, the more devoted they become to improving its practical applications. It seems only natural that these positional emphases would produce more divergent than convergent developments. As the field of study advances, both groups grow in clarity and coherency, but in opposite directions—practice seeks increasing conciseness, while theory searches for greater complexity. These kinds of developments support the need for specialists who can translate theory to practice.

These **patterns of professional participation** are evident in the field of multicultural education. Most nationally-known multiculturalists are scholars and specialists whose units of study and analysis are precollegiate educational programs, processes, and practices. Their suggestions and proposals are **ideal prescriptions** about what cultural education should be.

By comparison, most school practitioners are specialists in something other than multicultural education, such as reading, history, math, or science instruction. They are concerned more with **realistic and functional descriptions** of what to do, and how—about cultural diversity in relation to their other pedagogical responsibilities.

When these different professionals appeal to each other to satisfy their respective needs, they are often disappointed, and may even doubt the value of each other's contributions because their quality may not be readily apparent in other domains of operations. Thus, when multicultural practitioners appeal to theorists for suggestions on how cultural diversity should be taught, they expect procedural specificities, but get conceptual guidelines instead. They are advised to be integrative, authentic, and transformative. These are great principles, but they do not have any action directives.

Conversely, when theorists look to practitioners for evidence of the application of conceptual ideas in classroom actions they expect composites and systems of varieties of methods, materials, and tools, since concepts embed a multitude of action possibilities. Instead, they frequently see isolated activities and fragmented events.

These situations are understandable from the perspective of both the theorist and the practitioner. Multicultural theorists should be pursuing deeper conceptual understandings and explanations of the field, and practitioners should be looking for more pragmatic ways to implement cultural diversity in the classroom. It does little toward advancing both theory and practice for either to indict the other for not being maximally accountable for quality performance. Theorists should not be expected to perform as practitioners do; nor should practitioners be held accountable for being theorists. Both should be valued for their respective skills and functions. Yet, the need to establish better linkages between multicultural education theory and practice is imperative. Therefore, individuals who can translate theoretical ideas to the functional operations of actual classroom instruction can contribute significantly to the overall development of the field.

BUILDING BETTER BRIDGES BETWEEN THEORY AND PRACTICE

Two ideas are discussed here to illustrate how multicultural education theory and practice can be linked closer together. One involves approaches to multicultural education implementation, and the other

3. MULTICULTURAL EDUCATION AS AN ACADEMIC DISCIPLINE

has to do with the personal and professional empowerment of teachers in cultural diversity. Hopefully, they are instructive of the kinds of opportunities this challenge offers for enriching current developments in the field, as well as adding new dimensions of growth in the future.

All major multicultural scholars have developed models of different approaches to implementing cultural diversity in classroom curriculum and instruction. In some form or another, they include variations of **inclusion, infusion, deconstruction,** and **transformation.** The progression of these is from teaching information about ethnic groups in rather fragmentary, haphazard, and additive ways; to incorporating cultural pluralism throughout the educational process systemically and systematically; to using culturally pluralistic knowledge, perspectives, and experiences as criteria for re-examining the basic premises and assumptions on which the United States educational system is grounded; to creating new educational and social systems that are based upon the ethics, morality, and legalities of cultural diversity.

Embedded in all of these models are ideas of historical context, developmental growth, and increasing referential and conceptual complexity. Each model also conveys the message that some approaches to dealing with cultural diversity are inherently better than others, and everyone should aim to adopt these. It will help to establish closer and more functional linkages between multicultural theory and practice if these conceptualizations were reconsidered to be more developmental than hierarchical.

Rather than continuing to argue that there is **a single best** way to do multicultural education to which everyone should adhere, it is more feasible, pragmatic, inclusive, and empowering to legitimize multiple levels appropriateness in participation. Currently the theoretical message is that efforts to do multicultural education are inadequate if they are not at least at the infusion and preferably the transformation level. To impose these expectations on everyone is unrealistic. Educators just entering the field of multiculturalism simply do not have the background information, the pedagogical skills, or the personal confidence needed to fully understand what infusion and transformation are, least of all how to translate these ideals to practice. When they try to do so, the results are disastrous for everyone concerned—the professionals, the students, and the field.

The theoretical ideas of **developmental progression and appropriateness** have far greater potential for improving the quality of participation of educators at various stages of personal growth and professional positions in the promotion of multicultural education, as well as closer synchronizing its theory and practice. Developmental progression means that people's understanding of and capabilities in multicultural education move through different stages of conceptualization and practice; that each stage has inherent worth and legitimacy; and that the emergence of more advanced stages are contingent upon the development of earlier, more basic stages. It also means that there is growth potential within each stage.

While the inclusion of ethnic content into selective curriculum lessons or units of instruction is a more rudimentary and basic approach to multicultural education than transforming the entire schooling enterprise, it has conceptual value and practical utility. Educators have to master this approach before they move on to more advanced levels of implementation. They have to learn how to do good multicultural lessons before they can design effective units on cultural diversity, or redesign topics in other subjects so that they include multicultural perspectives. Teachers most certainly cannot deconstruct the cultural hegemony ingrained in their instructional styles, or make them multiculturally responsive until they have learned a great deal about how cultural elements of different ethnic groups are embedded in the rituals and routines of teaching and learning.

Viewing multicultural education theory and practice as developmental and progressional enfranchises more people to be active advocates. Relatively few educators are ready now to actually transform the educational system so that it reflects cultural diversity in all of its content, values, and structures even though they may believe this is necessary. Therefore, if its practice were solely dependent upon them, very little would be accomplished. As others engage in practical actions at other levels of conceptualization the numbers of advocates who promote diversity increases significantly. The field needs these numbers to create a critical mass of change agents who can impact the educational system at multiple levels and in diverse ways. Diversified personnel with differentiated abilities and skills are imperative to operationalize the multicultural mandate of **systemic reform.**

This idea of individuals involved at various levels of complexity, and using a variety of techniques to incorporate cultural diversity in the educational enterprise, is highly consistent with the nature of the field. The heart of multicultural education is diversity and plurality. Just as advocates demand that these principles be applied in teaching students about cultural differences, the field should apply similar criteria to itself. If it does, then both multicultural theory and practice must provide opportunities for educators in various stages of professional development to be involved in a variety of ways in promoting cultural diversity that are legitimized and compatible with their capabilities. They also should have the chance to improve the quality of their present state of being before they are expected to move to new planes of performance. These ideas evoke the learning principles of readiness and prerequisites. Just as classroom teachers use them to help guide their students' learning, similar applications should be made to the professional growth of teachers in cultural diversity.

More systematic ways to **empower practice** are needed within each of the developmental stages of multicultural education theory. These can be accomplished by carefully analyzing essential components of teaching functions endemic to each stage, and then demonstrating how these can be modified to illustrate stage related principles of multicultural education. Four brief examples will suffice to illustrate this point. A powerful feature of the **inclusion** stage of multicultural education theory and practice is the concept of heroism. Students are introduced to a host of ethnic individuals who have made major contributions to their own cultural groups, as well as to United States society and humankind. The theoretical idea of selecting authentic ethnic individuals and artifacts to be taught can be applied in practice by teachers understanding what is a cultural hero or heroine according to the standards of different ethnic groups. Using these as criteria to select candidates for this distinction will help educators to avoid using their own cultural standards to select heroes and then imposing them upon students from other ethnic groups. Understanding cultural standards of heroism and how different candidates manifest them thus empowers teachers and curriculum designers to select better examples of ethnic heroes and contributions to teach to students.

At the **infusion** level of multicultural education, implementation educators can be empowered in practice by demonstrating how the typical components of curriculum development can be culturally diversified. For example, how can sensitivity to cultural diversity be embedded in a curriculum rationale, statement of goals and objectives, content and learning objectives, and students' performance assessment? Other natural infusion opportunities can be identified by analyzing the teaching act to determine things that teachers routinely do, and then changing them to be responsive to cultural diversity. The notions of impacting that which is habitual, routine, and fundamental in the educational process are central to the multicultural education infusion. Because teacher talk is a major component of instruction, and it affects culturally diverse students differently, it should be a primary target for multicultural infusion. But, in order to do this well, how teachers talk needs to be carefully analyzed, and then changed accordingly. This analysis might include the kinds of questions asked of which students, turn-taking rules, wait time for responses, and mechanisms used to convey praise and criticism to students.

At the essence of **deconstruction** approaches to multicultural education is what is often referred to as critique, interrogation, and knowledge reconstruction. In practice this means that students are groomed to be healthy skeptics who are constantly questioning existing claims to social and academic truths and accuracy in search of new explanations, and to determine if the perspectives of different ethnic and cultural groups are represented. Nothing is considered sacrosanct, infallible, perfect, totally finished, or purely objective. Students are taught how to discern authors' biases, determine whose story is being told and validated from which vantage point, how to engage in perspective taking, as well as how to be self-monitoring, self-reflective, and self-renewing, especially in relation to issues of cultural diversity. These are the behavioral or practical manifestations of such deconstructive principles as multiple perspectives, giving voice, and the positionality of knowledge.

In practice, **transformative** approaches to multicultural education focus on constructing new realities, new systems, and new possibilities. They are the **action response** to deconstructive processes. Whereas deconstruction focuses on thinking and imagining new explanations of culturally pluralistic social situations, transformation takes the revisioning processes to its ultimate conclusion by acting upon the mental constructions. This building of new systems that are fully culturally pluralistic may include models, facsimiles, simulations, and actual creations. In creating them students are engaged in various forms of social and political actions, both within and outside of schools, which symbolize their moral and ethical commitments to freedom, equality, and justice for culturally diverse peoples.

CONCLUSION

The challenges posed by the need to bridge multicultural education theory and practice require that one is able to think analytically about current developments to explicate their most salient intersecting possibilities. With some careful thinking from individuals with the necessary expertise, it is possible to generate a whole new body of research and scholarship in multicultural education which demonstrates, with operational clarity, how theoretical principles can be translated into actual practices in schools and classrooms.

However, the act of creating these strategies will prompt yet another generation of multicultural theorizing. But, this evolving vitality and potential should not be seen as a problem to the field. As long as multicultural education has the regenerative power to create new thoughts, critiques, possibilities, and proposals for its own refinement, it is alive and well both as a theoretical endeavor and a practical necessity.

REFERENCES

Banks, J. A. (1995). The historical reconstruction of knowledge about race: Implications for transformative teaching. *Educational Researcher,* 24 (20), 15–25.

Banks, J. A., & Banks, C. A. M. (Eds.). (1993). *Multicultural education: Issues and perspectives.* Boston, MA: Allyn & Bacon.

Banks, J. A., & Banks, C. A. M. (Eds.). (1995). *Handbook of research on multicultural education.* New York: Macmillan.

Beauchamp, G. A. (1968). *Curriculum theory* (2d. ed.). Wilmette, IL: Kagg Press.

Bennett, C. I. (1995). *Comprehensive multicultural education: Theory and practice* (3rd ed.). Boston, MA: Allyn & Bacon.

Darder, A., (1991). *Culture and power in the classroom: A critical foundation for bicultural education.* New York: Bergin & Garvey.

Foster, M. (Ed.). (1991). *Readings on equal education. Volume 11: Qualitative investigations into schools and schooling.* New York: AMS Press.

Gay, G. (1994). *At the essence of learning: Multicultural education.* West Lafayette, IN: Kappa Delta Pi.

Hollins, E. R., King, J. E., & Hayman, W. C. (Eds.). (1994). *Teaching diverse populations: Formulating a knowledge base.* Albany, NY: State University of New York Press.

Nieto, S. (1992). *Affirming diversity: The sociopolitical context of multicultural education.* New York: Longman.

Sleeter, C. E. (Ed.). (1991). *Empowerment through multicultural education.* Albany, NY: State University of New York Press.

Sleeter, C. E., & Grant, C. A. (1995). *Making choices for multicultural education: Five approaches to race, class, and gender* (2d ed.). Columbus, OH: Merrill.

Identity and Personal Development: A Multicultural Focus

We have known for several decades that all human affective behavior (emotional response, values assessment, and so on) is learned behavior. Anything that can be learned can be unlearned or modified. There is no more important task for human beings than learning how to define themselves as persons within a cultural as well as global societal context. People are influenced by many social forces as they interact with others in the process of forming themselves as individuals. Multicultural education can help both students and teachers to identify those social forces that affect their personal development.

The preschool, elementary, and secondary school years are ones in which each of us learns critically important cognitive and affective strategies for defining ourselves, others, and the world. Multicultural education seeks to help people develop intellectual and emotional responses to other people that will be accepting and empathic. There has been much psychological and psychiatric research over the past few decades on the differences between prejudiced and tolerant personalities. Educators have the opportunity as they work with students to provide good examples of accepting, tolerant behavior and

UNIT 4

to help students develop positive, affirmative views of themselves and others. Gordon A. Allport, in his classic book, *The Nature of Prejudice,* commented that we could be "doubly sure" that early instruction and practice in accepting diversity is very important in directing a child toward becoming a tolerant person. Thus, we take up the topic of personal identity development in this unit.

As teachers, we must be aware of the interconnections among such factors as gender, social class position in society, racial or ethnic heritage, and cultural values in informing the way people see the world and themselves. We need to be sensitive to their visions of who they are and to "see our clients whole." It is vital for teachers to set positive examples of empathy, compassion, and concern for the well-being of each student.

Self-definition can be integrated and effectively achieved within the intellectual mission of the school. One way to do this is by encouraging students to critically interpret and evaluate the texts they read and to discuss issues in class openly and actively. Identity development is an ongoing process. Each student needs to be able to explore the boundaries of his or her intellectual strengths and weaknesses and the social boundaries encountered inside and outside of school.

Cultural values are of primary importance in the process of a person's conceptualization of him- or herself. This unit's articles explore various models of human interaction and the psychosocial foundations for the formation of students' knowledge. How students form social groups in culturally integrated school settings is explored, along with the behavioral differences among members of social groups in desegregated school settings. The ways in which students define themselves as they move beyond or are trapped within social boundaries they perceive in school and community settings are explored. How educators can take advantage of the knowledge of minority families in assisting minority students to achieve better social integration into school settings is also examined. The multiple social roles students must frequently play in and out of school are another social phenomenon in personality development that receives analysis in these essays.

Students live in a hierarchy of social contexts in which their racial, cultural, gender, and social class backgrounds, and the degree of their personal identification with each of these factors, influence their choices and individual decisions. Research on how teachers can achieve more effective intercultural socialization is also considered. Helping students to learn from the cultural perspectives of other groups is one of the tasks of multicultural education. Another purpose is to teach tolerant, accepting attitudes toward others of differing cultural backgrounds. Educators are *not* powerless in the face of the prejudiced views that many students bring to school from their homes.

The essays in this unit are relevant to courses in educational policy studies and leadership, cultural foundations of education, sociology or anthropology of education, history and philosophy of education, and curriculum theory and construction, among others.

Looking Ahead: Challenge Questions

What are the primary gender issues in multicultural school settings?

What should children learn about the cultural heritages and values of other children in their schools?

How do class differences relate to misunderstandings among students from different social positions in a community?

What can educators learn from open communication with the families of their students?

What challenges do minority students encounter that majority students in a desegregated school do not encounter?

How does community structure affect adolescent identity development?

What can teachers do to foster positive personal identity development in their students?

—F.S.

Families and Schools
Building Multicultural Values Together

Kevin J. Swick, Gloria Boutte and Irma Van Scoy

Kevin Swick is Professor, Gloria Boutte is Assistant Professor and Irma Van Scoy is Assistant Professor, Early Childhood Education Program, College of Education, University of South Carolina, Columbia.

A society's culture encompasses its citizens' efforts to develop meaning about individual and collective values, beliefs and actions (Slonim, 1991). It serves as a continuing reference point through which people construct their perceptions about and reactions to the environment. Families and schools in a democratic, multicultural society must promote a positive climate in which children learn to appreciate not only their own culture, but also cultures of other people (Fu, Stremmel & Treppte, 1992).

Indeed, the current social context throughout the world suggests an urgent need for multicultural learning. The rise in hate groups, distorted perceptions of people of different cultures, ethnic-related crime and many other antisocial patterns must be countered by families and schools working together to build a social fabric that values cultural diversity (Swick, Van Scoy & Boutte, 1994). Before a proactive multicultural learning environment can be developed, parents and teachers must recognize both its importance, and the barriers that prevent its achievement.

The Rationale for Multicultural Citizens

Csikszentmihalyi (1993) challenges the myopic view that multicultural learning is only important for minority populations. He notes that progressive societies succeed because their people can "transcend themselves" and relate to the environment in more sensitive and humane ways. This challenge is relevant to the growth and development of everyone in the global community. Pursuing unity through diversity calls for total involvement. Gary Howard (1993) stresses, "The future calls each of us to become partners in the dance of diversity, a dance in which everyone shares the lead" (p. 17). Multicultural learning must begin at birth and be continually nurtured through intentional family-school efforts.

Most important cultural understandings are shaped during the early childhood years. Thus, adult modeling of proactive multicultural values is critical for children. Hohensee and Derman-Sparks (1992) note that:

Numerous research studies about the process of identity and attitude development conclude that children learn by observing the differences and similarities among people and by absorbing the spoken and unspoken messages about these differences. The biases and negative stereotypes about various aspects of human diversity prevalent in our society under-cut all children's healthy development and ill-equip them to interact effectively with many people in the world. (p. 1)

Barriers to a Proactive Multicultural Learning Framework

Many individual and cultural variables interact to impede the development of culturally sensitive individuals, including: cultural stereotypes, social isolation, tradition and excessive conformity. All of these factors have a powerful influence on children's understanding of racial, ethnic and cultural perspectives and behaviors (Banks, 1993).

Cultural stereotypes arise from incomplete and often distorted conceptions of people and events. They tend to emerge when people are insecure, have low self-esteem and are isolated from people of other cultures (Hilliard, 1992). Such contexts often create intergenerational racism and/or culturally destructive attitudes. Isolation and tradition often serve to reinforce ignorance and, thus, further exacerbate prejudices (Derman-Sparks, 1991). Social isolation reduces children's opportunities to learn about culturally different people. Tradition may actually even encourage the continuation of erroneous beliefs. Without understanding the need to become multicultural, many people conform to long-lasting beliefs that are racist, sexist or highly prejudicial.

Barriers of cultural conformity, tradition and related exclusionary practices daily convey a distorted and inequitable picture of people from different backgrounds and contexts. Men, for example, still hold most leadership positions while many women are subtly isolated from mainstream political life. Minorities still compose a disproportionate segment of low-paying positions. Television often presents incomplete and distorted views of minority cultures, offering prime-time programs filled with sexist humor, distorted ethnic characterizations and superficial presentations of illnesses like AIDS (Diaz, 1992).

These barriers are maintained and reinforced by individual, family, school and community patterns (Ramsey & Derman-Sparks, 1992). The family learning system, for example, may distort a child's images of people from other cultures (Slonim, 1991). Insecure adults pass on their distorted views to their children through the family socialization process. Insecure and fearful children are likely to form rigid conceptions of people different from themselves.

Schools also need to recognize the effect they have on children's multicultural development (Boutte, La Point & Davis, 1993). Some teachers have limited understanding of their students' cultural backgrounds. The resulting erroneous beliefs must be transcended through staff development, personal reading and enrichment, and through personal growth experiences. Institutional practices of tracking, ability grouping and rigidly defined graded systems need to be replaced with more inclusionary strategies such as multiage grouping, cross-cultural peer learning and more personalized instruction. Unquestioned rituals and policies imprison culturally different children within an inequitable and insensitive environment (Swick, Van Scoy & Boutte, 1994). For example, the failure to use bilingual teaching strategies and resources can impede academic and social growth (Diaz, 1992). Inappropriate and inaccurate labeling has led many children to years of academic failure.

A Developmental Framework for Multicultural Learning

Learning new concepts, attitudes, skills and behaviors requires awareness, exploration and experimentation, systematic development, and integration of newly acquired knowledge (Hohensee & Derman-Sparks, 1992). Family-school collaboration is essential to actualizing these processes in ways that create meaningful multicultural learning.

Awareness. The initial step in this learning process is awareness of desired outcomes and potential barriers (Hohensee & Derman-Sparks, 1992). Critical questions to ask are: What kind of citizens do we need to foster a truly proactive multicultural society? And, what conditions support the development of this kind of person? We must be aware of the need for a multicultural learning vision and the strategies for achieving it (Gay, 1992).

Permeating this awareness process is our understanding of the cultural values and behaviors that we model for children and parents (Hilliard, 1992). Other important aspects of the awareness process include:

- *Examining how self-esteem is developed:*
  How do people feel about themselves?
  What do they know about their own culture?
- *Probing people's perceptions of different cultures, lifestyles and contexts:*
  What do people know about other cultures?
  What are their attitudes toward people from diverse cultures?
  What stereotypes and biases do people have about other cultures?
- *Examining the ingrained cultural habits of a society, particularly with regard to inequities in jobs, roles, salaries, status symbols and related rituals:*
  Are people from different cultures equitably represented in public roles?
  Do the housing and living patterns in our community reflect patterns of discrimination?
  Do employers, schools and business practice systematic discrimination?

What kind of citizens do we need to foster a truly proactive multicultural society?

4. IDENTITY AND PERSONAL DEVELOPMENT: A MULTICULTURAL FOCUS

- *Analyzing the ways families socialize children about culture:*
  Are parents educating children about their cultural heritage in appropriate ways?
  Are parents modeling culturally sensitive and enriching behaviors and attitudes for children?
- *Probing the substance of school and classroom practices relative to multicultural learning:*
  Are staff exemplary models of multicultural learning?
  Do school artifacts, policies and learning activities reflect equity and proactive multicultural learning?
- *Studying the biases, inequities and related issues of cultural distortion that may pervade our daily lives:*
  Are families providing equitable and respectful roles and relationships?
  Are schools providing quality learning arrangements for all children?
  Are communities actively seeking policies that support equity and justice for all citizens?

Awareness depends upon a climate of openness that can be created to strengthen attitudes, knowledge and skills that foster more sensitive and enriching interrelationships (Banks, 1993). Family and school frameworks need to encourage open discussion and analysis of cultural understanding, behavior patterns and relationship patterns.

Dialogue about how we live with and relate to each other should also include an assessment of specific family, school and community habits (Hilliard, 1992). For example, parent education could help adults assess the ways they teach their children to view themselves and others, especially people from different cultural contexts. Teachers can enrich this process by using proactive multicultural teaching methods.

Exploration and experimentation. Exploration and experimentation with new ways of building multicultural learning environments is the second step in a multicultural learning process (Hohensee & Derman-Sparks, 1992). Attempts to gain everyone's involvement in culturally sensitive activities are typical of this effort. Parents and teachers can involve children in volunteer activities, for example, that broaden their cultural understanding and increase their self-efficacy. These activities might include service at a homeless shelter, participation in programs that serve special populations and social awareness field trips.

Teachers might develop regular activities that enrich children's perspectives, such as highlighting a "culture of the week," visiting community cultural events, involving parents and children in multicultural social and educational activities, hosting parent study groups that focus on multicultural issues, and offering teacher development programs on curriculum issues and community awareness activities that bring people of different cultures together in meaningful ways (Boutte & McCormick, 1992).

This exploratory phase of multicultural learning stimulates interest in learning about others in a positive and enjoyable way. The main focus in this effort is to help people realize the importance and enrichment possibilities of living in a multicultural environment (Banks, 1993).

Systematic development. Systematic multicultural development is the phase in which communities of people intentionally recognize and act on a transformational vision. The community focuses on building multicultural learning communities in which beliefs, perceptions and actions create a flow of cultural habits that help people understand, value, support and learn from each other (Csikszentmihalyi, 1993). Formalized family and school collaboration incorporates planning, design and implementation of multicultural learning systems into daily life.

The initial step in this development phase is to review, refine and integrate proactive multicultural attitudes, knowledge and skills into all facets of the family-school-community learning system (Banks, 1993). Clearly, the major impediment to a fully functioning multicultural world is the lack of accurate representation and involvement of diverse peoples. Hilliard (1992) notes the pervasiveness of this impediment in global actions:

Those who have studied worldwide liberation struggles know that the manipulation of information, including propaganda and misinformation, are primary tactics employed in the domination process. Oppressive populations defame, stigmatize, stereotype and distort the reality of dominated populations. Ultimately, if the curriculum is centered in truth, it will be pluralistic, for the simple fact is that human culture is the product of the struggles of all humanity, not the possession of a single racial or ethnic group. (pp. 157-158)

In this context, it is critical that families and schools assess all aspects of their cultural functioning. For example, families need to examine how they relate to each other in terms of multicultural learning (Swick, VanScoy & Boutte, 1994). At school, classroom content, teacher-child interactions and significant processes and rituals (such as grouping patterns, treatment of all children, involvement of families and the overall school culture) should be continuously reviewed for accuracy, cultural inclusion and degree of collaboration and individuality (Derman-Sparks, 1991).

Some specific actions that can promote this systematic effort include:

- Joint parent-teacher planning of activities and strategies that integrate multicultural learning into children's daily experiences
- Teacher assessment and refinement of instructional and curricular content, process and actions relative to providing accurate and comprehensive multicultural experiences
- School ecology team actions to develop policies that promote equity, cultural enrichment and individual sensitivity to cultural differences and commonalities.

Formalized planning brings systematic attention to all aspects of multicultural learning in order to promote accurate representations of culturally diverse people and promote a proactive multicultural orientation within family, school and community (Hilliard, 1992). Planners must develop goals, an action plan, strategies and tools for continually monitoring and refining the entire system. Nothing less than a comprehensive and collaborative approach to addressing multicultural learning needs can achieve the goal of a more sensitive and nurturing citizenry.

Swick, Van Scoy and Boutte (1994) suggest five "opportunities for multicultural learning" that can be initiated with children from birth through age 7: 1) educating parents about their role in building children's self-esteem, 2) helping children explore their own culture through family and school activities, 3) training parents and teachers to assess their multicultural competence, 4) supporting families' and schools' development of skills and strategies for promoting multicultural learning and 5) initiating intense teacher education about multicultural learning. The

Positive multicultural learning relies upon a foundation of being valued within the family, meaningfully guided in school and engaged in helpful community rituals.

following sampling of strategies highlights the importance of a comprehensive approach:

- Teachers can share multicultural information with parents by lending them relevant books, articles and videos; posting information and suggestions on parent bulletin boards; offering monthly parenting programs; and publishing newsletters that report on multicultural activities within the school and community.
- Classroom displays should represent diverse ethnic, racial and cultural backgrounds. Also, these displays should include children's personal work. Parents can participate by helping to acquire materials and by volunteering in the classroom.
- Teachers can ask families to share pictures, family recipes, dramatic play props, family experiences, books and other print materials, stories and other artifacts that reflect their cultures.

Integration of multicultural learning. This step is necessary to build a cooperative and proactive society (Byrnes & Kiger, 1992). This phase of multicultural development filters every aspect of social functioning through the lenses of equity, sensitivity, understanding and cultural enrichment. Families and schools will eventually internalize multicultural values so that these filtering actions become natural and sustaining behaviors. Four behavior patterns are essential: 1) nurturing authentic and positive self-esteem; 2) promoting a sharing, nurturing and positive self-other relationship syndrome; 3) nurturing the cultural strengths of all people and 4) promoting collaborative relationships among different cultures (Swick & Graves, 1993).

Low self-esteem is the most prevalent obstacle to building proactive multicultural communities (Slonim, 1991). Children and adults need contexts that build self-esteem. Positive multicultural learning relies upon a foundation of being valued within the family, meaningfully guided in school and engaged in helpful community rituals. The secure and valued "self" is the basis for cultural competence (Neugebauer, 1992).

Learning about others through nurturing, sharing and positive relationships can foster critical prosocial skills (Hilliard, 1992). Regular opportunities for people to meet, and learn from, culturally diverse people in positive ways must be available. Cooperative learning, cross-age grouping and networking activities are strategies that support this process.

Culturally different people are too often viewed from the perspective of the dominant culture, which is often deficit-focused (Neugebauer, 1992). An attitude of strength through diversity, by contrast, celebrates the multiple talents of all people. Likewise, collaborative relationships are critical to sustaining proactive multicultural learning (Oliver & Howley, 1992).

Systematic effort can facilitate integration of multicultural learning into family, school and community habits. This process must be revisited frequently to combat the often subtle forms of prejudice, racism, sexism and classism (Boutte, La Point & Davis, 1993).

Collaboration and Advocacy Is Essential
Every effort to promote a culturally sensitive and enriching world is empowering. Family-school collaboration, however, enables people to transform themselves in ways that can extend multicultural constructs toward full societal implementation. This collaboration process can occur in many ways: within the family, in collaboration between family and school and in societal planning and advocacy activities (Hilliard, 1992).

Collaborative schemes work best in small social units (e.g., teams of teachers, neighborhood action teams and community innovation groups). The power of small groups is evident in school events that focus on cultural celebrations, antibias committees and multicultural learning teams (Banks, 1993). Face-to-face interactions bring about the most powerful transformations and understandings. It is only through working together that we really come to understand one another. The important elements of these small social action units are: commitment to a common goal, continuous membership, specific roles for members, a detailed plan on how to achieve identified goals and a system for continued nurturance of the group's original mission (Csikszentmihalyi, 1993). Creating networks with like-minded groups can increase each group's influence, if system flexibility within the smaller units is maintained.

Advocacy is critical to the long-term promotion of multicultural values. Families, schools and communities need to monitor their systems to ensure cultural accuracy and to maintain supports that foster integrative multicultural learning habits. For example, education programs can highlight multicultural learning experiences that families can carry out on a regular basis. Schools and community groups can serve as anti-bias watchdogs. The best hope for cultural harmony that respects positive individuality is collaborative advocacy. We must be continually reminded of the urgency and need for attention to our cultural knowledge, attitudes and skills.

◆

References
Banks, J. (1993). Multicultural education for young children: Racial and ethnic attitudes and their modification. In B. Spodek (Ed.), *Handbook of research on the education of young children* (pp. 236-251). New York: Macmillan.
Boutte, G. S., La Point, S., & Davis, B. (1993). Racial issues in education: Real or imagined? *Young Children, 49*(1), 19-22.
Boutte, G., & McCormick, C. (1992). Authentic multicultural activities: Avoiding pseudomulticulturalism. *Childhood Education, 68,* 140-144.
Byrnes, D., & Kiger, G. (Eds.). (1992). *Common bonds: Anti-bias teaching in a diverse society.* Wheaton, MD: Association for Childhood Education International.
Csikszentmihalyi, M. (1993). *The evolving self.* New York: HarperCollins.
Derman-Sparks, L. (Ed.). (1991). *Antibias curriculum: Tools for empowering young children.* Washington, DC: National Association for the Education of Young Children.
Diaz, C. (Ed.). (1992). *Multicultural education for the 21st century.* Washington, DC: National Education Association.
Fu, V., Stremmel, A., & Treppte, C. (Eds.). (1992). *Multiculturalism in early childhood programs.* Urbana, IL: ERIC Clearinghouse on Elementary and Early Childhood Education.
Gay, G. (1992). Effective teaching practices for multicultural classrooms. In C. Diaz (Ed.), *Multicultural education for the 21st century* (pp. 38-56). Washington, DC: National Education Association.
Hilliard, A. (1992). Why we must pluralize the curriculum. *Educational Leadership, 49*(4), 157-160.
Hohensee, J., & Derman-Sparks, L. (1992). *Implementing an anti-bias curriculum in early childhood classrooms.* Champaign, IL: ERIC Clearinghouse on Early Childhood Education. ED 351146.
Howard, G. (1993). Whites in multicultural education: Rethinking our role. *Phi Delta Kappan, 75*(1), 36-41.
Neugebauer, B. (Ed.). (1992). *Alike and different: Exploring our humanity with young children.* Washington, DC: National Association for the Education of Young Children.
Oliver, J.-P., & Howley, C. (1992). *Charting new maps: Multicultural education in rural schools.* Charleston, WV: ERIC Clearinghouse on Rural and Small Schools. ED 348196.
Ramsey, P., & Derman-Sparks, L. (1992). Multicultural education reaffirmed. *Young Children, 47*(2), 10-11.
Slonim, M. (1991). *Children, culture, and ethnicity.* New York: Garland.
Swick, K., Van Scoy, I., & Boutte, G. (1994). Multicultural learning through family involvement. *Dimensions of Early Childhood, 22*(4), 17-21.
Swick, K., & Graves, S. (1993). *Empowering at-risk families during the early childhood years.* Washington, DC: National Education Association.

Article 20

Self-Identification, Pan-Ethnicity, and the Boundaries of Group Identity

by Dag McLeod

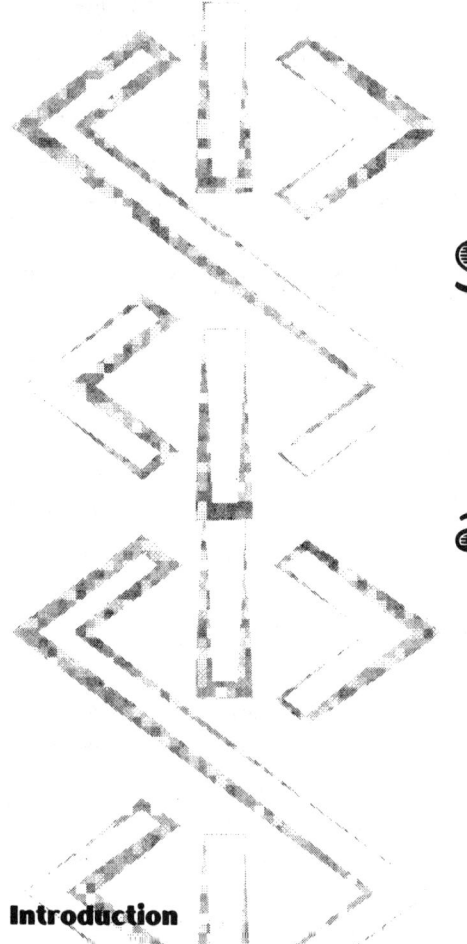

Introduction

W. I. Thomas, one of the most important sociologists of the early 20th century, once asserted that "If men define situations as real, they are real in their consequences." The Thomas theorem, as it has come to be known, captures nicely a truth that has been verified most dramatically in the hard sciences by the placebo effect. Our beliefs about the world are not lifeless interpretations of reality. Instead, we often change, even create important aspects of that reality through our understanding—or misunderstanding—of it.

At the same time, the Thomas theorem is obviously overstated. Not everything that we define as real has real consequences. Nor can the consequences of our definitions be easily determined in advance. And, even accepting the importance of mental images, it is common for groups to disagree about the correct definition of a situation. In these cases, whose definition should we expect to prevail?

Although Thomas used the word

Dag MacLeod is a graduate student in the Department of Sociology at The Johns Hopkins University, Baltimore, Maryland.

"men" in its traditional sense to mean "people," his theorem might actually have been more accurate had he applied it exclusively to men: specifically, white men. Certainly in his time, the vast majority of history, literature, science and art was produced by such men.

Today, it is precisely these definitions that have come under the scrutiny of groups that were previously excluded from participating in the cultural and scientific production through which we define our world. In the struggles between competing definitions of the world, perhaps none is more interesting than that of identity. At first glance, the question of identity appears to be an intensely personal one. What, after all, could be more private than our "self"?

In fact, researchers have long recognized that identity is formed and maintained through interaction between our selves and the social world. Not only is the way that we identify ourselves fluid, shifting subtly with our surroundings, but identity is strongly influenced by inter-group relations and power differentials that exist between groups in the wider society. As such, identity needs to be understood as a product of both individual and social definitions; it is a changing, individual framework within which we place our experience of the social world and attempt to give it meaning.

This multi-level understanding of identity begins to explain why members of dominant groups often have trouble understanding the importance of defining identity. As the framework constructed in the family is applied to progressively larger spheres of society—to the neighborhood, the community, society at large—members of majority groups usually encounter a relatively good fit between their experience of the world and the definitions they encounter in the mass media or in cultural symbols and representations.

Where our experience of the world is consistent with the norms of society at large the frame of identity tends to blend in with the background and disappear. In contrast, minority groups are often forced to adjust their understandings of the world to accommodate the majority perspective. Not only are the practices and understanding of minority cultural systems interpreted from a majority viewpoint, but the very boundaries that are used to classify different minority groups are often imposed from without with little regard for the ways in which members of these groups view themselves.

4. IDENTITY AND PERSONAL DEVELOPMENT: A MULTICULTURAL FOCUS

Two of the most conspicuous examples of the arbitrary imposition of minority group boundaries are the growing use in recent years of the pan-ethnic labels "Asian" and "Hispanic." Although a Japanese Buddhist and a Pakistani Muslim share neither language nor culture, both become Asian when they arrive in the United States. They are treated as part of the same ethnic group by social service agencies catering to the needs of the "Asian" community and thrown into the same symbolic soup by the dominant institutions of society.

Hispanic—literally referring to "the people, culture, or language of Spain"—was adopted by the US Census in 1980 to help categorize the large numbers of recent immigrants from Latin America. Yet, despite a common language and the dreams of continental unity held by thinkers such as Bolivar, little in the history of the region suggests that "Latin Americans" have much in common. Not only are different national groups deeply divided amongst themselves—Argentines against Chileans, Ecuadorans against Peruvians, and Costa Ricans against all other central Americans—many Latin American countries are themselves poorly integrated.

In Guatemala, a majority indigenous population descended from the Mayans has little in common with the white and mestizo populations of Guatemala City and other metropolitan areas. Nonetheless, upon arrival to the United States, these distinct groups all become part of the same symbolic whole.

Consistent with the Thomas theorem, studies of Asian and Hispanic pan-ethnicity have shown that these names are not irrelevant window dressing. However, the causal ordering is more complex than Thomas suggested and the consequences of lumping groups together under all-inclusive designations can be counter-intuitive and contradictory.

Under certain conditions, pan-ethnic labels may encourage minority groups to forge coalitions among themselves. Where the rewards or punishments offered by the majority in society are directed at an imagined community, these groups may very well coalesce around that identity. A less encouraging outcome of pan-ethnic labeling has been the adoption of these identities by children of immigrants who lack a strong co-ethnic community and are not well integrated into U.S. society. In this case, the pan-ethnic label may be an indicator of marginality and possibly a predictor of future failure.

Asian-American and Hispanic Solidarity

The most thorough study of Asian American pan-ethnicity[1] points to a number of factors that have made the label "Asian American" real in its consequences. Yen Le Espiritu shows how the failure of social services to differentiate between distinct Asian groups in the allocation of public welfare led Japanese and Chinese Americans to coordinate their activities, in effect, to become Asian Americans. Not just belief, but real material incentives provided to the various groups that were lumped under this heading played a crucial role in fostering pan-ethnic solidarity. In the words of Espiritu:

> A community that relies upon outside funding must define its problems and needs in terms its sources can understand and with which they can concur…. Because funding sources often expect people of various ethnic origins to speak with a common voice, Asian American groups have had to unite to be competitive in the funding game.

Similarly, Felix Padilla has documented the emergence of a pan-ethnic coalition of Puerto Ricans and Mexicans in Chicago in response to the incentives offered by Affirmative Action.[2] As with Asian-American solidarity, Latino unification required the provision of actual material benefits—in this case, job opportunities—to the minorities who had been grouped together.

However, the provision of material incentives to a group being lumped together may not, by itself, be sufficient to unite diverse peoples around a single identity. Instead, some trigger may be required to awaken a potential unity. In the case studied by Padilla, this stimulus was provided by an official of the Illinois Bell phone company who stated publicly that the company was reluctant to employ Spanish-speaking workers. Incited to action by the statement, the Puerto Rican and Mexican communities of Chicago united in defense of the opportunity for employment with Illinois Bell.

As further evidence that the emergence of pan-ethnic solidarity may require more than the carrots provided by Affirmative Action or social welfare, Espiritu has also documented the formation of Asian-American solidarity in response to the stick of anti-Asian violence. In the early 1980s, in the midst of a deep recession and the phenomenal success of Japanese imports, two Detroit men attacked and beat to death a man who they thought was Japanese. In fact, their anger had been unleashed on a Chinese American named Vincent Chin. When neither of the

Identity Chosen by Second Generation Children of Latin-American Origin

	American	Hyphenated American	Non-Hyphenated Latin Nationality	Hispanic
Home Ownership				
Yes	22.4%	41.1%	18.2%	18.4%
No	11.2%	29.4%	27.5%	31.9%
Class Self-Identification				
Upper Middle-Class	21.5%	36.4%	20.3%	21.8%
Lower Middle-Class	16.2%	36.1%	22.7%	25.0%
Working-Class or Poor	10.4%	32.9%	26.9%	30.0%
Knowledge Of English				
Not Well	0.0%	14.3%	44.5%	41.2%
Well	10.7%	30.5~	25.6%	33.2%
Very Well	21.3%	39.5%	19.7%	19.6%
National Origin				
Cuban (Private School)	33.1%	59.2%	4.1%	3.6%
Cuban (Public School)	19.8%	52.8%	19.0%	8.4%
Colombian	19.9%	27.2%	26.2%	26.7%
Mexican	2.7%	36.5%	24.6%	36.2%
Dominican	26.8%	2.4%	32.9%	37.9%
Nicaraguan	9.1%	12.6%	35.3%	43.0%

men received a prison term and, instead, were fined $3,000 and sentenced to three years' probation, Detroit's Asian American community coalesced. Although the combined Chinese and Japanese population of Detroit was barely one quarter of the total Asian population in the city, these two groups spearheaded the creation of a multiethnic group for the defense of Asian-American rights, the American Citizens for Justice.

Far from a simple confirmation of the Thomas theorem, pan-ethnic identification appears to depend, at the very least, upon some objective basis for group unification. In addition, a triggering incident may be required to set in motion a latent group identification. This may begin to explain why attempts by liberals in this country to forge broad progressive coalitions under all-inclusive banners such as "people of color" have had little real success in uniting diverse groups. Without first feeling real consequences of a common identity, people may simply fail to define themselves as part of a larger group.

Downward Mobility and Hispanic Identification

Pan-ethnic identification, however, need not be associated with the positive assertion of group rights identified by Espiritu and Padilla. In both of these authors' studies it is primarily more affluent groups that unite around a pan-ethnic label to gain the benefits that numbers provide. A more recent study of immigrant children in Miami and San Diego casts doubt upon the generally favorable results of pan-ethnicity.[3] In this study, children who identified themselves as Hispanic were generally less affluent and had a weaker grasp of English than those children who identified themselves as either Americans, or as hyphenated Americans.

In a survey administered to second-generation immigrants, 5288 eighth and ninth graders were asked how they identified themselves. The question was open ended allowing for any possible response but offered illustrations of possible answers, such as: Anglo, African-American, Hispanic, American, Cuban, Cuban-American, Jewish, Irish, Mexican-American, etc. Of the 2633 students of Latin American heritage, the majority, approximately 35 percent, identified themselves as hyphenated Americans, such as Cuban-American, or Mexican-American with another 17 percent of the sample identifying themselves simply as Americans. Most of the remainder, roughly 25 percent of the total, identified themselves with the pan-ethnic label, Hispanic.

When these data on ethnic identification were cross tabulated with other information on the children, a number of disturbing patterns emerged (See Table 1). Home ownership, which can be used as a rough approximation of class, was strongly associated with a rejection of the Hispanic label. Of those whose parents owned their own home, only 18 percent identified themselves as Hispanic compared to 22 percent who identified themselves as American and 41 percent who identified themselves with a hyphenated American identity. Similarly, 30 percent of those children who described themselves as "working class or poor" identified themselves as Hispanic, compared with only 10 percent of those who chose the label "American."

Here, the relationship between class and self-identification is more complicated. Of the children who described themselves as Upper Middle-Class, the largest percentage identify themselves as hyphenated Americans. However, this same group makes up 32.9 percent of those children identifying themselves as poor, or, almost three percent more than the children who identify themselves as Hispanic.

Of the children who report speaking English very well, only 19 percent identified themselves as Hispanic compared with 21 percent of those calling themselves American, and 39 percent of those who use the hyphenated-American label to identify themselves. In this category, those children who identify themselves with a non-hyphenated Latin-American identity appear to be quite similar to children who adopt the Hispanic label. Over 80 percent of the children who report poor knowledge of English fall into these two categories while they contain less than 40 percent of the children who report knowing English very well.

Finally, correlations of specific national-origin groups and self-identification show that the use of the Hispanic label depends very much upon ethnic background. Cubans in both public and private schools in Miami were by far the least likely to identify themselves as Hispanic. At the other extreme, Nicaraguans, also primarily concentrated in the Miami area, were the most likely to adopt the Hispanic label.

Something within the national culture of these groups appears to make some groups more prone to use the pan-ethnic label while making other groups less inclined to use it. Interestingly, the group of second-generation immigrants that appears to be the best positioned to succeed in the United States is not those who identify themselves as "American," but rather, those who identify themselves as hyphenated Americans. This group makes up the bulk of those whose parents own their home, contains the largest percentage of those who identify themselves as "upper middle-class" and the largest percentage of children who report knowing English "very well."

Unlike the cases described by Espiritu and Padilla, here we find that it is the children in the most marginal positions who have adopted the pan-ethnic label. Although adolescence is a particularly volatile period in the process of identity formation, it is also a period during which impressions are formed that are likely to endure.

We can only speculate about why these specific children would gravitate toward the pan-ethnic identity. One explanation might be that the lack of a strong co-ethnic community from which to forge a distinct and positive identity leads the most vulnerable children to adopt a label that is growing in usage in the mainstream but whose content is unclear. Without the instrumental advantages of Affirmative Action or public spending, it is the more marginal groups that adopt this ambiguous pan-ethnic identity.

A slightly different interpretation would draw upon the data for which nationalities choose the Hispanic label. Because the Cuban population in Miami has attained a position of power and prestige that is unique for immigrant groups it is possible that even at a young age, immigrant children have begun to appreciate the advantages of symbolic association. Cuban-American children may wish to retain the status associated with their specific ethnicity, thus rejecting the Hispanic label. Nicaraguan-American children, on the other hand, may adopt the pan-ethnic label in an attempt to associate themselves with the Cubans by placing themselves into the same symbolic category.

Conclusion

As Shakespeare noted some 400 years ago, that which we call a rose, by any other name would smell as sweet. But flowers don't actively participate in choosing their names or interpreting what they mean. It is our interaction with others that defines us and, in large part accounts for the extreme malleability of identity. At the same time it is the internalization of these roles, the adoption of these relationships as integral to who we are that returns the question of identity to the personal level.

This dual significance has made the question of identity especially important to social scientists. Explanations of social phenomena such as participation in social movements, voting patterns, even state formation must all return at some point to the way in which individuals come to define themselves either as members of or in opposition to larger groups. Indeed, this paradox of identity appears to be contained within the very definition of the word which denotes both "absolute sameness"—as the term is still used in algebra—and "individuality, personality."

This apparent contradiction begins to resolve itself when we recognize that the groups to which we adhere through some claim of sameness are frequently defined oppositionally, as "not" some other group; belonging to a particular group makes us both the same and different, together and apart. Ultimately, the boundaries of all groups contain a certain element of fiction. Foundational myths have been created to help cement fractious tribes into single nations just as the United States itself adopted an entire public-school curriculum in the latter part of the 19th century in order to incorporate large numbers of immigrant children into the "American" way of life.

The point is not that some groups are more real than others, or that all ethnic distinctions are mere fantasy. Instead, ethnic identification—whether in larger or smaller groups—can have both positive and negative consequences. Perhaps the real challenge is to find ways to resolve the contradictions inherent in identity itself: to recognize that it is the diversity of different groups that makes them the same; just as they can join together by respecting those things that set them apart.

Notes

1. See Yen Le Espiritu, *Asian American Panethnicity*. Philadelphia, PA: Temple University Press, 1992.
2. See "Latino Ethnicity in the City of Chicago," in *Competitive Ethnic Relations*, Susan Olzak and Joane Nagel, eds. New York: Academic Press. 1986.
3. See Alejandro Portes and Dag MacLeod, "What Shall I Call Myself: Hispanic identity formation in the second generation," *Ethnic and Racial Studies*, forthcoming.

Counseling for Dropout Prevention: Applications From Multicultural Counseling

Jerry Trusty

Jerry Trusty is an assistant professor in the Department of Counseling and Guidance, East Texas State University at Commerce. Correspondence regarding this article should be sent to Jerry Trusty, Department of Counseling and Guidance, East Texas State University, Commerce, TX 75429.

> Although high school dropout rates have declined over the past several years, rates remain high for many segments of our population. Most of the attention devoted to dropout prevention counseling has focused on group counseling or programmatic issues, whereas individual counseling has largely been ignored. This article draws on commonalities between multicultural counseling and dropout prevention to produce a general framework for individual counseling with students who have potential to drop out of high school.

According to recent national educational studies and 1990 national census data, high school dropout rates have steadily declined over the past 20 years. Rates have fallen faster for African Americans than they have for other major ethnic groups, but rates for Hispanics and students living in inner cities have not declined. Among Hispanic subgroups, rates are much higher for Mexican Americans and Puerto Rican Americans than they are for Cuban Americans. Also, children from low socioeconomic status (SES) families continue to drop out at much higher rates than do children from middle or high SES families. These studies and data indicate that of the low-income youths, ages 16 to 24, 26.5% have not completed high school. Rates for middle-income and high-income youths who have not completed high school are 11.8% and 2.7% (Kaufman, McMillen, & Bradby, 1991). The pervasive effects of SES or social class on educational achievement (Ornstein & Levine, 1989) and school dropout (Frase, 1989; Kaufman et al., 1991; Rumberger, 1983, 1987) have been well documented.

Pedersen (1991), in conceptualizing culture and multicultural counseling, suggested that counselors accept a broad definition of culture. Culture then has broader applicability in counseling, and variables such as social class, or even school dropout, may be viewed as cultural variables. There is support for the viability of this perspective both from the dropout prevention literature and from the counseling literature. From the dropout prevention literature, Pittman (1986) and Beck and Muia (1980) saw school dropout as resulting from conflicts between the student's culture and the school's culture. From multicultural counseling literature, Carter (1991) and Goldstein (1994) indicated social class differences in clients' and students' values and functioning regardless of race or ethnicity. Because social class or SES is axiomatic in the dropout process and multicultural counseling is based on accommodating various cultural value orientations or worldviews (Sodowsky & Johnson, 1994), multicultural counseling seems naturally applicable to dropout prevention.

The purpose of this article is to demonstrate the applicability of multicultural counseling structures to individual counseling for dropout prevention. Parallels between these structures and existing dropout prevention interventions are explained and recommendations for counseling practice are detailed.

BACKGROUND LITERATURE

Most literature on counseling for dropout prevention has focused on one or more of the following

4. IDENTITY AND PERSONAL DEVELOPMENT: A MULTICULTURAL FOCUS

counseling roles: (a) consultant, (b) educational change agent, or (c) group counselor. The consultation and change agent functions, which should involve the school (Blum & Jones, 1993; Rose-Gold, 1991), the parents (Cranston-Gingras & Anderson, 1990; Rose-Gold, 1991), and the community (Rose-Gold, 1991; Streeter & Franklin, 1991), are salient to dropout prevention. Robinson (1992, 1993) effectively demonstrated how an appreciation of differences in social class, gender, and race can produce educational practices that promote positive development in at-risk students. Group counseling also seems effective (see Blum & Jones, 1993; Muha & Cole, 1991; Praport, 1993). Individual counseling strategies for this population, however, have received little attention from the dropout prevention literature and multicultural counseling literature.

Cognitive Approaches

In reviewing the literature, cognitive-behavioral techniques were suggested most often as intervention methods for students who have potential to drop out of school. Sapp (1990) suggested combining academic counseling with cognitive-behavioral strategies for improving students' academic self-concepts, thereby improving academic achievement. Counseling could facilitate at-risk students in disputing cognitive distortions related to their perceptions of self and school. A study by Phillips (1984) supported the efficacy of cognitive-behavioral interventions for low-income students.

Through a naturalistic study of low SES adolescents, Brantlinger (1990) found frequent cognitive distortions. Regarding school achievement, students exhibited a defeatist attitude. Although students admitted to exerting little effort in school, they tended to attribute their lack of success to low levels of ability. Students often vacillated between rejection of their own social status and acceptance of subordinate status. Many students thought that people are poor because of deficits in personal capacities. Brantlinger described the process of status formation: "While low-income students are socialized to accept inequities during school they are also conditioned to expect a similar status later in life, and to hold themselves personally responsible for this outcome" (p. 321).

This attribution pattern is consistent with the external locus of control/internal locus of responsibility (EC-IR) worldview presented in the multicultural counseling model of Sue (1978). Basically, the EC-IR person attributes control over his or her life to external forces and attributes blame internally. There are similar attributional patterns in early stages of the minority identity development model of Atkinson, Morten, and Sue (1983). The Black and White racial identity models of Helms (Carter & Helms, 1992; Helms & Carter, 1991; Helms & Piper, 1994) are also similar. In the early stages of identity development, a combination of self-depreciation and dominant group appreciation naturally produces a distorted, defeatist attitude. In subsequent stages of the Atkinson et al. and Helms's models, a self-appreciation/dominant group depreciation pattern emerges. This produces resistance. From the dropout prevention literature, Fine and Rosenberg (1983) found school dropouts not to be "losers," but resisters to inequity. Other research (Cairns, Cairns, & Neckerman, 1989; Pittman, 1986, 1991; Rumberger, 1987; Tidwell, 1988) pointed toward student resistance as a major variable in the dropout process. Bowditch (1993) demonstrated how school personnel interpret this resistance and cognitively construct the label "troublemakers" for students. These cognitive distortions—on the part of educators—seem to reinforce students' distortions and to result in a negative spiral of mutual resentment.

Cognitive and Cultural Styles

Research on learning styles has revealed similarities between dropout prevention and multicultural counseling. Students' learning styles seem to be related to their (a) dropout potential (Gadwa & Griggs, 1985; Griggs, 1991; Nunn & Parish, 1992), (b) ethnicity (Dunn, Gemake, Jalali, & Zenhausern, 1990; Griggs, 1991; Griggs & Dunn, 1989), and (c) SES (Goldstein, 1994). Support for the existence of cultural influences on cognition also comes from research on testing. Sedlacek (1994) reported that the abilities of nonmainstream individuals are not adequately assessed by college admissions tests, and Miller-Jones (1989) asserted that measurement of cognitive skills may be more strongly related to cultural contexts than to innate qualities.

Although research may be inconclusive (see O'Neil, 1990), many educators (Allen & Boykin, 1992; Blum & Jones, 1993; Griggs, 1991; Griggs & Dunn, 1989; Haynes & Gebreyesus, 1992; Vatterott & Yard, 1993) contend that matching teaching styles to the learning styles of students produces positive gains. Similarly, there is support for the contention that when counselors match the learning styles (cognitive styles) of clients, positive outcomes result (Goldstein, 1994; Griggs, 1991; Griggs & Dunn, 1989; Ibrahim, 1991).

Other authors have broadened the concept of counselor or educator adaptation to include dimensions of client or student functioning other than purely cognitive processes. Sue (1978, 1990) suggested that counselors match the communication style of the client. Ivey, Ivey, and Simek-Morgan (1993) referred to style shifting in accommodating clients. Still others (Carter & Helms, 1992; Goldstein, 1994; Ibrahim, 1991; Ramirez, 1991) referred to the advantages of counselors' matching the client's preferred styles. Regarding school dropouts, Heldman (1984) stated that, "educators may have to reevaluate their own settled responses to such things as bureaucratic structures before they can be useful aids to the dropout" (p. 360). Lack of counselor flexibility may be one of the reasons for underuse of services by those who are culturally different (Atkinson, Casas, & Abreu, 1992) or at-risk educationally (Chodzinski, 1994; Hafner, Ingels, Schneider, & Stevenson, 1990).

Mismatch between value orientations of clients/students with institutions/schools is also a problem. Mismatch results in lower levels of belonging, and therefore alienation (Ramirez, 1991). Alienation from school is claimed by many to be a means for understanding the dropout process (Ensminger & Slusarcick, 1992: Finn, 1989; Trusty & Dooley-Dickey, 1993). Finn (1989) described identification with school, the inverse of alienation or withdrawal. Identification has two dimensions, belonging and valuing. Belonging is the student's feeling that she or he is part of the school environment. Valuing is the student's perceived relevance of school goals or norms. Students' feelings (belonging) and thinking (valuing) determine levels of school identification.

Cognitive and Cultural Flexibility

Downing and Harrison (1990) proposed a *small wins* approach to prevent students with potential to drop out from dropping out of school. Because school dropout is such a complex phenomenon, a focus on practical, segmented steps or hurdles leading toward school completion is helpful to students. To overcome obstacles to school completion, many students must, as Downing and Harrison suggested, " 'kiss a lot of frogs' " (p. 71). In other words, a student's view of the world will often be different from the school's view of the world, and therefore students need flexibility in adjusting to the status quo.

In viewing this model, similarities between dropout prevention strategies and multicultural counseling emerge. First, multicultural counseling is based on counselors' understanding of their own worldviews, of the worldviews of clients, and how these fit into the dominant culture (Sodowsky & Johnson, 1994). Dropout prevention is based on understanding worldviews of students, counselors, and schools (Downing & Harrison, 1990). Second, the counseling task of helping students adjust to the status quo has parallels in multicultural counseling. Axelson's (1993) *compromising* with mainstream values, or Ramirez's (1991) *cultural flexibility*, are examples of pragmatism (coping) that is fostered in clients. Ramirez (1989, 1991) suggested that (a) teachers should accommodate the personality styles of students, (b) counselors should adjust to the styles of clients, and (c) students and clients should develop flexibility in their cognitive and cultural styles. According to Ramirez, *cognitive flex* (flexibility), *cultural flex*, and *personality flex* help students and clients function more effectively. The products of flex are *bicognition* and *biculturalism*.

Cognitive flex has its roots in the field theory of Kurt Lewin (Ramirez, 1991). Lewin's contributions to social psychology and education are far reaching, and predate contemporary educational thought by 40 or 50 years. Lewin's work is applicable to contemporary (a) educational reform, (b) educational research, (c) multicultural education, (d) cooperative learning, and (e) conflict resolution (Maruyama, 1992). For the purposes of this article, however, the focus will be on Lewin's field independent and field sensitive (field dependent) cognitive styles, and modern and traditional cultural styles.

Ramirez (1991) conceptualized cultural differences in terms of cognitive style (field independent and field sensitive) and cultural style (traditional or modern). Modern families and communities use socialization processes that foster the development of analytical or field independent cognitive styles, whereas traditional families and communities use socialization processes that foster relational or field sensitive cognitive styles. Cognitive and cultural styles influence motivation, communication, and relationships (see Ramirez, 1989, 1991, for a more thorough explanation of cognitive and cultural styles). Ramirez (1991) did not view these dichotomies (field independent vs. field sensitive, traditional vs. modern) as mutually exclusive. Individuals will concurrently operate in both field independent and field sensitive modes, and will hold traditional and modern values. People generally will, however, have preferred or dominant styles.

Evidence supporting this framework of cognition and cultures comes from research on cooperative learning. There seem to be strong links between culture and cognitive style (Allen & Boykin, 1992), and students from traditional cultures tend to respond positively to cooperative learning structures (Haynes & Gebreyesus, 1992). Multicultural counseling literature (Axelson, 1993; Hoare, 1991; Ivey et al., 1993; Sue, 1990) supports the existence of an individual philosophy in modern cultures and a social or a relational philosophy in traditional cultures.

RECOMMENDATIONS

The following recommendations are intended as a general perspective or framework for individual counseling with students who have potential to drop out of high school. Because the causes and corollaries of dropout are multifarious, a more specific framework may be limited in applicability.

Counselor and Student Perceptions

Counselors must first examine their own perceptions. Before counselors can effectively address student perceptions, they must examine their own attitudes, beliefs, and values regarding education and school dropout. Quite naturally, we are perceived as the status quo (Chodzinski, 1994). We, as counselors and educators, are "educated." We operate from and are rewarded by a system whose goal, to some degree, is to transform students into people like us. Through our identification with the educational system, we are often perceived as inculcators and assimilators, even if we are not. Our worldviews are foreign, especially to many students who are of low SES or are educationally at risk. Furthermore, we are perceived as devaluing students' worldviews and, thereby, as devaluing students. In this paradigm, teaching is perceived as indoctrination, counseling as inculcation, encouragement as pressure, empathy as sympathy, and therefore responsibility is internalized and status formation (Brantlinger, 1990) is accomplished. Without citing specific examples, this seemingly necessary initial step in helping students who are educationally at-risk is often overlooked.

Flexible counseling perspectives positively influence student perspectives. Counselors must genuinely demonstrate that they are not inculcators and assimilators. This is accomplished by various means. Downing and Harrison (1990) promoted a collaborative model in which the counselor and the student join forces against the system. Goldstein (1994) fostered *prescriptive* counseling. Instead of following a unidimensional philosophy of counseling, counselors should tailor their interventions to the student in his or her personal, interpersonal, and environmental contexts. Prescriptive counseling requires counselor flexibility, and therefore, stereotypical perceptions of counselors by students are eliminated. Matching models (Axelson, 1993; Goldstein, 1994; Ramirez, 1991) and advocacy roles (Atkinson, Thompson, & Grant, 1993; Nunn & Parish, 1992; Svec, 1987) are both useful in altering students' perceptions of counselors and educators. Matching the student's preferred styles and assuming an advocacy role also seem to be mutually reinforcing.

Counselor Understanding

Counselors must understand students' worldviews. Once initial trust and cooperation have been established, the counselor needs to learn the various experiences and contexts of the student's (or the dropout's) life. This process or task is common to many multicultural counseling models (e.g., Axelson, 1993; Ivey et al., 1993; Ramirez, 1991) as well as to counseling models and theories in general (see Egan, 1994). In the particular case of the dropout or the potential dropout, the counselor should explore the student's world and her or his perceptions of that world. This can be accomplished through various counseling structures. A life history (Ramirez, 1991) could be assessed, or the counselor could operate from a worldview basis (Axelson, 1993; Ibrahim, 1991; Sodowsky & Johnson, 1994). The counselor's goal would be to determine those assumptions, values, and personal constructs with which the student or the client interprets his or her would.

Counselors assess student-school match and mismatch and levels of alienation from school. Every student brings an accumulation of preferred styles to school. The school is equipped to accommodate a particular range of those preferred styles. Some degree of match and mismatch will result. Match and mismatch may be in terms of cultural style, cognitive style, or both (Ramirez, 1991). Mismatch results in feelings of being different or of alienation from school. An understanding of specific reasons for alienation should lead counselors toward effective strategies (Chodzinski, 1994).

Areas of match and mismatch should emerge from information on students' experiences. Likes and dislikes related to parents, teachers, administrators, peers, and the school should reveal preferences for and differences in communication, social, and cognitive styles. Students' styles are also determined by socialization processes (Carter, 1991; Ramirez, 1991), and these should guide counselors toward an understanding of student and school mismatch and alienation.

Facilitating Students' Flexibility

Counselors carefully facilitate students' cognitive and cultural flexibility. What seems most salient in the alienation process is that schools themselves should have goals and norms that are relevant to students. It seems inherently unfair that students should be expected to adjust to the status quo. We, however, do not live in a totally culturally homogeneous, culturally sensitive, or socioeconomically equitable world (Fine & Rosenberg, 1983); and, therefore, practicality, flexibility, and adaptation on the part of students is warranted (Downing & Harrison, 1990). Nevertheless, counselors should exercise caution in promoting flexibility in students. That is, students should have a firm sense of acceptance of their unique selves before counselors expect them to adapt. Fostering adaptability in students may seem like assimilation to counselors. However, if counselors see fostering students' adaptability as promoting their autonomy, then fostering adaptability seems less like cultural assimilation.

Counselors facilitate students in developing multicultural coping mechanisms. Ramirez (1991) outlined his cognitive and cultural flex theory of personality. Personality flex requires that clients be developed in each dichotomy of cognitive (field independent and field sensitive) and cultural (modern and traditional) style. To promote flexibility, counselors facilitate clients to shuttle between poles of cognitive style and between poles of cultural style. Clients are encouraged to combine modern and traditional value orientations and thinking styles to evolve new styles. These new styles, or multicultural coping mechanisms, are then integrated into a multicultural identity.

In dropout prevention, cognitive styles and teaching styles are readily applicable to the aforementioned structure. Other aspects of schooling are also applicable. For example, low SES children experience parenting and disciplinary styles that are different from mainstream styles (Goldstein, 1994). These variations reflect differences between traditional and modern cultures. Students' understanding of these differences and flexibility in response to these styles would increase coping and, therefore, decrease alienation. Additionally, communication styles (Goldstein, 1994; Monroe, Borzi, & Burrell, 1992) and related aggressive behavior (Baker, 1991; Cairns et al., 1989) seem to be highly associated with school success. Students might be helped to gain flexibility in cognitive (Ramirez, 1989, 1991) and communication styles (Goldstein, 1994) and to learn new methods for problem solving and coping (Chodzinski, 1994; Goldstein, 1994).

CONCLUSION

In short, counselors can help students to develop a multicultural identity, that is, to become bicognitive and bicultural. There are varying views of biculturalism, acculturation, and identity development (cf. Atkinson et al., 1993; Hoare, 1991; Ramirez, 1991; Reynolds & Pope, 1991; Sedlacek, 1994). Developing cultural flexibility seems to require, at least, a great deal of courage. Darder (1991), in a poem on biculturalism, demonstrated the many conflicts and complexities involved in the bicultural and minority identity process. A segment of that poem follows (pp. 79–80):

> i sit in meetings with harvard-ites
> as i sit with the barrio folks
> on lazy afternoons in the park,
>
> the sounds of spanish beckon my soul
> as the sounds of english move my mind,
>
> i am fed by multicolored mothers,
> i am caressed by multicolored fathers.
>
> and all of these
> i contain within
> the complex borders
> of my double-vision
> of my two worldness,
> of my twin beings,
> of this place where
> i am never who
> i appear to be.

For students who feel alienated from school, however, these conflicts may not be as difficult or as pervasive as in other areas of life; and the rewards for flexibility and adaptability may be more immediate in schools.

This article has identified several philosophical, theoretical, and practical commonalities between dropout prevention counseling and multicultural counseling, drawing from dropout prevention literature as well as from counseling literature. There are, and there will undoubtedly be more commonalities. Because there is such a need for counseling in the area of dropout prevention (Chodzinski, 1994; Svec, 1987; Tidwell, 1988), it is hoped that more and expanded structures for dropout prevention counseling will emerge.

The aforementioned framework was designed for dropout prevention with high school students. However, it may be relevant for college students, or any student who might feel alienated, isolated, or different—for whatever reason. It seems that the fourth force (multiculturalism), as described by

4. IDENTITY AND PERSONAL DEVELOPMENT: A MULTICULTURAL FOCUS

Pedersen (1991), is generic rather than exotic and does recognize the complexities of social systems. At least in the case of dropout prevention, culture seems to be a useful metaphor.

REFERENCES

Allen, B. A., & Boykin, A. W. (1992). African-American children and the educational process: Alleviating cultural discontinuity through prescriptive pedagogy. *School Psychology Review, 21,* 586–596.

Atkinson, D. R., Casas, A., & Abreu, J. (1992). Mexican-American acculturation, counselor ethnicity and cultural sensitivity, and perceived counselor competence. *Journal of Counseling Psychology, 39,* 515–520.

Atkinson, D. R., Morten, G., & Sue, D. W. (1983). *Counseling American minorities; A cross-cultural approach.* Dubuque, IA: Brown.

Atkinson, D. R., Thompson, C. E., & Grant, S. K. (1993). A three-dimensional model for counseling racial/ethnic minorities. *The Counseling Psychologist, 21,* 257–277.

Axelson, J. A. (1993). *Counseling and development in a multicultural society* (2nd ed.). Pacific Grove, CA: Brooks/Cole.

Beck, L., & Muia, J. A. (1980). A portrait of a tragedy: Research findings on the dropout. *The High School Journal, 64,* 65–72.

Blum, D. J., & Jones, L. A. (1993). Academic growth group and mentoring program for potential dropouts. *The School Counselor, 40,* 207–217.

Bowditch, C. (1993). Getting rid of troublemakers: High school disciplinary procedures and the production of dropouts. *Social Problems, 40,* 493–509.

Brantlinger, E. (1990). Low-income adolescents' perceptions of school, intelligence, and themselves as students. *Curriculum Inquiry, 20,* 305–324.

Cairns, R. B., Cairns, B. D., & Neckerman, J. J. (1989). Early school dropout: Configurations and determinants. *Child Development, 60,* 1437–1452.

Carter, R. T. (1991). Cultural values: A review of empirical research and implications for counseling. *Journal of Counseling & Development, 70,* 164–173.

Carter, R. T., & Helms, J. E. (1992). The counseling process as defined by relationship types: A test of Helms's interactional model. *Journal of Multicultural Counseling and Development, 20,* 181–201.

Chodzinski, R. T. (1994). Dropout intervention and prevention: Strategies for counselors, a multicultural perspective. In P. Pedersen & J. C. Carey (Eds.). *Multicultural counseling in schools* (pp. 1–18). Boston, MA: Allyn & Bacon.

Cranston-Gingras, A., & Anderson, D. J. (1990). Reducing the migrant student dropout rate: The role of school counselors. *The School Counselor, 38,* 95–104.

Darder, A. (1991). Poems: A bicultural riddle. *Journal of Education, 173*(2), 78–84.

Downing, J., & Harrison, T. C., Jr. (1990). Dropout prevention: A practical approach. *The School Counselor, 38,* 67–74.

Dunn, R., Gemake, J., Jalali, F., & Zenhausern, R. (1990). Cross-cultural differences in learning styles of elementary-age students from four ethnic backgrounds. *Journal of Multicultural Counseling and Development, 18,* 68–93.

Egan, G. (1994). *The skilled helper* (5th ed.). Pacific Grove, CA: Brooks/Cole.

Ensminger, M. E., & Slusarcick, A. L. (1992). Paths to high school graduation or dropout: A longitudinal study of a first-grade cohort. *Sociology of Education, 65,* 95–113.

Fine, M., & Rosenberg, P. (1983). Dropping out of high school: The ideology of school and work. *Journal of Education, 165,* 257–272.

Finn, J. K. (1989). Withdrawing from school. *Review of Educational Research, 59,* 117–142.

Frase, J. D. (1989). *Dropout rates in the United States: 1988. Analysis report.* (Report No. NCES–89–6090). Washington, DC: National Center for Education Statistics. (ERIC Document Reproduction Service No. 313 947).

Gadwa, K., & Griggs, S. A. (1985). The school dropout: Implications for counselors. *The School Counselor, 33,* 9–17.

Goldstein, A. P. (1994). Teaching prosocial behavior to low-income youth. In P. Pedersen & J. C. Carey (Eds.) Multicultural counseling in schools (pp. 157–175). Boston, MA: Allyn & Bacon.

Griggs, S. A. (1991). *Learning styles counseling.* Washington, DC: Office of Educational Research and Improvement. (ERIC Document Reproduction Service No. 333 308).

Griggs, S. A., & Dunn, R. (1989). The learning styles of multicultural groups and counseling implications. *Journal of Multicultural Counseling and Development, 17,* 146–155.

Hafner, A., Ingels, S., Schneider, B., & Stevenson, D. (1990). A profile of the American eighth grader: NELS:88 student descriptive summary (NCES Publication No. 90–458). Washington, DC: U.S. Government Printing Office.

Haynes, N. M., & Gebreyesus, S. (1992). Cooperative learning: A case for African-American students. *School Psychology Review, 21,* 577–585.

Heldman, C. G. (1984). Promoting the autonomy of another person: The difficult case of the high school dropout. *Educational Theory, 34,* 355–365.

Helms, J. E., & Carter R. T. (1991). Relationships of White and Black racial identity attitudes and demographic similarity to counselor preferences. *Journal of Counseling Psychology, 38,* 446–457.

Helms, J. E., & Piper, R. E. (1994). Implication of racial identity theory for vocational psychology. Journal of Vocational Behavior, 44,] 124–138.

Hoare, C. H. (1991). Psychosocial identity development and cultural others. *Journal of Counseling & Development, 70,* 45–53.

Ibrahim, F. A. (1991). Contribution of cultural worldview to generic counseling and development. *Journal of Counseling & Development, 70,* 13–19.

Ivey, A. E., Ivey, M. B., & Simek-Morgan, L. (1993). *Counseling and psychotherapy: A multicultural perspective* (3rd ed.). Boston, MA: Allyn & Bacon.

Kaufman, P., McMillen, M. M., & Bradby, D. (1991). *Dropout rates in the United States: 1991.* Washington, DC: National Center for Education Statistics. (ERIC Document Reproduction Service No. ED 351 421).

Maruyama, G. (1992). Lewin's impact on education: Instilling cooperation and conflict management skills in school children. *Journal of Social Issues, 48,* 155–166.

Miller-Jones, D. (1989). Culture and testing. *American Psychologist, 44,* 360–366.

Monroe, C., Borzi, M. G., & Burrell, R. D. (1992). Communication apprehension among high school dropouts. *The School Counselor, 39,* 273–280.

Muha, D. G., & Cole, C. (1991). Dropout prevention and group counseling: A review of the literature. *The High School Journal, 74,* 76–80.

Nunn, G. D., & Parish, T. S. (1992). The psychosocial characteristics of at-risk high school students. *Adolescence, 27,* 435–440.

O'Neil, J. (1990). Making sense of style. *Educational Leadership, 48*(2), 4–9.

Ornstein, A. C., & Levine, D. U. (1989). Social class, race, and school achievement: Problems and prospects. *Journal of Teacher Education, 20*(5), 17–23.

Pedersen, P. B. (1991). Multiculturalism as a generic approach to counseling. *Journal of Counseling & Development, 70,* 6–12.

Phillips, R. H. (1984). Increasing positive self-referent statements to improve self-esteem in low-income elementary school children. *Journal of School Psychology, 22,* 155–163.

Pittman, R. B. (1986). Importance of personal, social factors as potential means for reducing high school dropout rate. *The High School Journal, 70,* 7–13.

Pittman, R. B. (1991). Social factors, enrollment in vocational/technical courses, and high school dropout rates. *Journal of Educational Research, 84,* 288–295.

Praport, H. (1993), Reducing high school attrition: Group counseling can help. *The School Counselor, 40,* 309–311.

Ramirez, M. (1989). A bicognitive-multicultural model for a pluralistic education. *Early Child Development and Care, 51,* 129–136.

Ramirez, M. (1991). *Psychotherapy and counseling with minorities: A cognitive approach to individual and cultural differences.* New York: Pergamon.

Reynolds, A. L., & Pope, R. L. (1991). The complexities of diversity: Exploring multiple oppressions. *Journal of Counseling & Development, 70,* 174–180.

Robinson, T. (1992). Transforming at-risk educational practices by understanding and appreciating differences. *Elementary School Guidance & Counseling, 27,* 84–94.

Robinson, T. (1993). The intersections of gender, class, race, and culture: On seeing clients whole. *Journal of Multicultural Counseling and Development, 21,* 50–58.

Rose-Gold, M. S. (1991). Intervention strategies for counseling at-risk adolescents in rural school districts. *The School Counselor, 39,* 122–130.

Rumberger, R. W. (1983). Dropping out of high school: The influence of race, sex, and family background. *American Educational Research Journal, 20,* 199–220.

Rumberger, R. W. (1987). High school dropouts: A review of issues and evidence. *Review of Educational Research, 57,* 101–121.

Sapp, M. (1990). Psychoeducational correlates of junior high at-risk students. *The High School Journal, 73,* 232–234.

Sedlacek, W. E. (1994). Issues in advancing diversity through assessment. *Journal of Counseling & Development, 72,* 549–553.

Sodowsky, G. R., & Johnson, P. (1994). World views: Culturally learned assumptions and values. In P. Pedersen & J. C. Carey (Eds.), *Multicultural counseling in schools* (pp. 59–79). Boston, MA: Allyn & Bacon.

Streeter, C. L., & Franklin, C. (1991). Psychological and family differences between middle class and low income dropouts: A discriminant analysis. *The High School Journal, 74,* 211–219.

Sue, D. W. (1978). Eliminating cultural oppression in counseling: Toward a general theory. *Journal of Counseling Psychology, 25,* 419–428.

Sue, D. W. (1990). Culture-specific strategies in counseling: A conceptual framework. *Professional Psychology: Research and Practice, 21,* 424–433.

Svec, H. (1987). Youth advocacy and high school dropout. *The High School Journal, 70,* 185–192.

Tidwell, R. (1988). Dropouts speak out: Qualitative data on early school departures. *Adolescence, 23,* 939–954.

Trusty, J., & Dooley-Dickey, K. (1993). Alienation from school: An exploratory analysis of elementary and middle school students' perceptions. *Journal of Research and Development in Education, 26,* 232–242.

Vatterott, C., & Yard, G. J. (1993). Accommodating individual differences through instructional adaptations. *Middle School Journal, 24,* 23–28.

Problems Caused for Mental Health Professionals Worldwide by Increasing Multicultural Populations and Proposed Solutions

Thomas L. Chiu

Thomas L. Chiu is a staff psychiatrist in the Sunset Park Mental Health Center of The Lutheran Medical Center, Brooklyn, New York. Correspondence regarding this article should be sent to Thomas L. Chiu, 14 Chaucer Street, Hartsdale, NY 10530.

Psychiatric disorders on a global scale, combined with rapid national population diversification, demand that mental health professionals worldwide become more informed about the realities of diagnosing and treating a multicultural patient population. Recommendations are offered to enable such professionals to most efficaciously diagnose and treat patients from diverse sociocultural backgrounds.

Psychiatrists and other mental health professionals in most countries today need to be more aware of cross-cultural differences in psychiatric patients than they have ever been before. The need for heightened awareness of patient behaviors and backgrounds among mental health professionals is due to their increasingly being called on to diagnose and treat an unprecedented number of patients from foreign cultures. For a variety of reasons that are discussed and illustrated in this article, diversity in multicultural patients poses challenges and causes problems for mental health professionals involving diagnosis and treatment that can be minimized through education and experience.

The major purposes of this article are to illustrate the types of diagnostic and treatment problems that are caused for mental health professionals by a multicultural patient population and to propose ways in which the mental health profession can minimize such problems.

THE CAUSE OF INCREASING DIAGNOSTIC AND TREATMENT PROBLEMS

The reason that mental health professionals in nations around the globe have been increasingly confronted by an unprecedented number of foreign patients during the past several decades is the rapid growth rate of worldwide population migration. This migration has not only added to a nations' population heterogeneity resulting from sociodemographic factors such as age, sex, and religion, but it has greatly increased the importance of the existence and the treatment of mental health problems in a heterogeneous population.

The recent rapid growth rate of international population migration has been the result of revolutionary events around the globe, the most important being (a) the demise of the Soviet Union and the fall of the Berlin Wall; (b) the refugee problems in many parts of the world, especially in Africa and Eastern Europe; (c) the reduced cost of international travel, which is encouraging masses of people to take up residence in foreign countries for varying periods; and (d) the ongoing spread of multinational corporations around the globe, which has necessitated millions of workers to reside in foreign nations for long periods.

22. Problems Caused for Mental Health Professionals

The unprecedented population heterogeneity within nations of the world is bound to continue at an even more rapid rate into the twenty-first century because of the continuation of the aforementioned trends, and also because of the proliferation of international free trade that will be brought about by the General Agreement on Tariffs and Trade (GATT) and the North American Free Trade Agreement (NAFTA).

Associated with the rapid growth rate of worldwide heterogeneous population are three factors that have increased diagnostic and treatment problems for mental health professionals: (a) the universality of psychosis, depression, and other mental health problems, (b) the higher rate of mental health problems among immigrants compared with those who stay in their homelands, and (c) people from different cultures tend to act out or behaviorally express the same underlying psychiatric problem differently, as well as to relate to mental health professionals, medication, and treatment differently.

With respect to the ubiquity of mental health problems, people within every nation have serious mental and emotional disorders that often differ by type and by frequency, depending on the nation. This fact has been well documented in the literature (Currer, 1984; Harrison, Holton, Neilson, & Owens, 1989; Killian, & Killian, 1990; Ruiz, 1985; Sachdev, 1990; Sanua, 1989).

Regarding psychosis, for example, many studies have shown that this disorder exists in so-called primitive as well as in advanced industrial societies, including Colombia, Czechoslovakia, India, Nigeria, Russia, Japan, Denmark, Great Britain, and America (Jablensky, Sartorius, Ernberg, Anker, 1992), Croatia (Folnegovic & Folnegovic, 1992), Sri Lanka (Chandrasena, 1987), Trinidad and Tobago (Neehall, 1991), Asia (Gupta, 1991), the Carribean (Harrison et al., 1989), Sarawak (Chiu & Schmidt, 1967), Ireland (Keatinge, 1985), and Italy (Munk & Tansella, 1986).

In addition, depression, other mood disorders, and neurotic disorders have also been reported to exist in nations on all continents, including China, Japan, and Korea (Kua, 1990; Nakane, Ohta, Radford, & Yan, 1991; Nakane, Ohta, Uchino, & Takada, 1988), Spain and Senegal (Hanck, Ayuso-Gutierrez, & Ramos-Brieva, 1981), Australia, Nigeria, and Switzerland (Shader, 1984), Ethiopia (Tafari, Aboud, & Larson, 1991), Greece and Germany (Fichter, Elton, Diallina, & Koptagel, 1988), and Finland (Lehtinen et al., 1990).

These two facts in combination, namely, high rates of population migration and universal prevalence of mental health problems, increase the chance of mental health professionals in most nations being likely to be confronted by more patients from foreign cultures with mental health problems than they were in previous decades. This phenomenon is exacerbated by the facts that people from different cultures tend to define health and illness differently and that a disproportionate number of migrants have mental health problems, as indicated in various studies. For example, Fichter et al. (1988) assessed the mental health of an immigrant population of 453 females and 414 male Greek adolescents in Germany and compared the findings with a local population of 445 female and 1,255 male Greek adolescents in Greece and 1,584 female and 1,196 male Turkish adolescents in Turkey. The study found, among other things, that Greeks and Turks in their homelands scored significantly higher in mental health than did Greeks in Germany. With the exception of the "social dysfunction" factor, that is, difficulty adjusting to the social environment, Greeks in their homeland had significantly higher mental health scores than did Greeks in Germany. According to the researchers, the findings supported the hypothesis of selective migration, which states that Greek adolescents in Germany constitute a positive selection with respect to increased risk of mental illness.

The fact that mental health professionals are more likely to be confronted by more patients from foreign cultures with mental health problems than they were in the past would not, in itself, necessarily cause problems for the professionals involving diagnosis and treatment. The cause of such diagnostic and treatment problems is, to summarize the discussion thus far, that individuals from different cultures vary greatly in the ways that they act out or behaviorally express the same underlying pathology, such as in schizophrenia; and in how they relate to initial help-seeking, the authority of physicians, medicine-taking, and treatment follow-up, among other factors (Angel & Thoits, 1987; Chiu, 1994; Moffic, 1983). In addition, patients from diverse sociocultural backgrounds, as a result of their different norms, values, and beliefs, tend to define health and illness differently and to attribute the cause of their mental health problems to a wide array of factors.

This fact of cross-cultural variation in patient behaviors was acknowledged by Moffic (1983), who attributed such differences to child rearing, cognitive styles, social networks, gender roles, symptom expression, and concepts of mental health and illness. According to Moffic, sound principles of "cultural psychiatry" require that practitioners be aware of patient differences in verbal and in nonverbal communication to prevent misunderstandings. In addition, Moffic suggested that cultural self-analysis by the clinician is necessary to alleviate counter-transference problems.

4. IDENTITY AND PERSONAL DEVELOPMENT: A MULTICULTURAL FOCUS

What, exactly, are the types of problems that mental health professionals experience as a result of a multicultural patient population? This question is answered through examples based on my own experience and on the available literature.

EXAMPLES OF TREATMENT AND DIAGNOSTIC PROBLEMS

Treatment Problems Resulting From Sociocultural Diversity

A vivid example of how a patient's cultural and religious background can cause the patient to reject a seemingly valid medication for psychosis comes from my experience as a psychiatrist, working as part of a mental health team from a mobile crisis unit (MCU; Chiu & Primeau, 1991) operated by Gouverneur Hospital, on the Lower East Side of Manhattan. The case involved Mr. S, a man with schizophrenia, who lived alone on the Lower East Side.

When we came to treat him, Mr. S was 57 years old, single, unemployed, and an orthodox Jew, who was referred by the rabbi of his synagogue. The rabbi reported that the patient was not eating, was extremely depressed, and would not leave his apartment. During the initial visit, Mr. S presented paranoid ideation and vegetative signs of depression. We heard from the rabbi that the suddenness of the onset of illness coincided with the anniversary of the death of his brother of a heart attack, in the same synagogue Mr. S attended.

Mr. S at first refused any kind of medication, and the MCU team and the rabbi tried to persuade him to change his mind. The rabbi spoke directly to him in Yiddish, and we basically pointed out to Mr. S that the congregation needed him. Apparently this was the key statement for gaining his compliance, and he finally accepted an injection of a neuroleptic.

Mr. S's condition improved in a few days, and he started attending the synagogue and coming to our clinic for follow-up. The following year, sometime during Passover—an important Jewish holiday—Mr. S relapsed into a similar psychotic state. The rabbi again contacted us and tried to communicate with Mr. S. We initiated a treatment consisting of a neuroleptic and an antidepressant. Two days later, we were hastened back to Mr. S's apartment and were made aware of a problem involving the 50 mg antidepressant pill that we had prescribed. Both the rabbi and the patient had consulted a Hebrew pharmaceutical book and found that the 50 mg pill was not Kosher because of the way it was prepared (with wheat or barley); however, the 25 mg pill was kosher and acceptable. During Passover, the preparation of the 50 mg pill was not in keeping with the Jewish Law. "Everyone agreed with this," the patient told us. We complied with the patient's wish by prescribing two of the 25 mg pills. Improvement was gradual and progressive.

The case of Mr. S. illustrates well some of the ways in which sociocultural factors affect psychiatric illness and treatment. Each time the MCU team was called to see Mr. S, it seemed to be a religiously heightened time for the patient. In the first instance, the onset of illness coincided with the anniversary of the death of his brother, who died in the synagogue, and the second time the illness occurred during Passover. It is thus suggested, in this context, that mental health professionals should pay greater attention to susceptible patients during emotionally heightened times, especially those who can be stimulated by religious or by other sociocultural events involving basic realities such as family, God, and "roots."

Diagnostic Problems Resulting From Patients' Nationalities

Patients' nationalities can sometimes adversely affect how they are perceived and diagnosed by mental health professionals. This problem of diagnosis is illustrated in two studies by Nakane et al. (1988, 1991). In the first study, Nakane et al. (1988) investigated depressive disorders in three Asian countries: the People's Republic of China, the Republic of Korea, and Japan, with the goal of showing the effects of culture on reported cases. The findings showed that in Nagasaki, psychiatrists' diagnoses tended toward an affective psychosis depression, whereas in Shanghai diagnoses tended toward a neurotic disorder. Nakane et al. (1991) further investigated prevalence rates and symptoms of depressive disorders in 100 patients from Japan, 100 patients from China, and 111 patients from Korea. Although prevalence rates of depression were similar in all three centers, differences in symptoms were noted. Most Korean patients were diagnosed as having neurotic depression, Japanese patients were diagnosed as having major depression, and Chinese patients were diagnosed as having either neurotic depression or as having major depression.

The findings from these two studies by Nakane et al. are directly pertinent to the thesis of this article: the studies—by showing how mental health professionals in different cultural settings can diagnose the same problem differently, depending on their own and on their patients' backgrounds—herald the need for more awareness of the effect of culture on the diagnosis and treatment of mental and emotional disorders by mental health professionals.

Diagnostic Problems Caused by Cultural Norms, Beliefs, and Customs

Just as variation in nationality can cause problems of diagnosis, so can variation in cultural norms, beliefs, and customs. This problem was illustrated in the work of Pages-Larraya (1977), who conducted a 5-year psychiatric study of the 593 remaining Siriono aborigines of Bolivia and observed a high rate of acute psychosis as well as incidents that could be described as "epidemic madness." The latter is best explained, according to the investigator, by the cultural and mythical structure of the people. Supporting the main thesis of the current article, Pages-Larraya emphasized that, in an alien culture, the psychiatrist must have a clear understanding of the people's beliefs and customs to distinguish psychiatric problems from behavior that is reasonable to the society.

This point, that mental health professionals need to understand people's beliefs and customs to avoid misdiagnosis of psychiatric problems, was also reported by Jenkins (1988), who examined the nature and the meaning of *nervios*, a notion used by Mexican-American families to understand the schizophrenic illness of a relative. In Jenkins's study, 61 relatives of schizophrenics completed open-ended and forced-choice questionnaires about the nature of the problem and its emotional and symbolic meanings. The respondents also gave an open-ended description of nervios. Results from the study led Jenkins to suggest that a cultural preference for the term *nervios* is linked to the efforts of family members to reduce the stigma associated with a mental illness. By using the concept of nervios, family members often made it difficult for mental health professionals to accurately understand and diagnose the nature of the patient's condition.

Problems of Patients' Resistance to Treatment Caused by Sociocultural Values and Nationality

Psychiatrists and other mental health professionals can encounter resistance from patients who may lead the practitioners to become perplexed or frustrated, and this can adversely affect their continuing treatment strategy and approach. By understanding that such resistance may be culturally normative for a particular group, however, based on the group's values, the mental health professional can have the patience and wisdom to most efficaciously diagnose and treat such patients.

Kinzie (1985) discussed this problem regarding the basic values of Indo-Chinese refugee patients, showing how their values may conflict with prevailing values of U.S. psychotherapists and inhibit the use of mental health services. According to Kinzie, Southeast Asians, although of various ethnic groups, generally reflect an interdependent and holistic Eastern culture with traditional family values and a fear of mental illness. Their approach to medical problems and mental illness follows both the scholarly tradition of China and the local folk tradition. No cultural analogy to psychological therapy exists, and the decision to see a psychiatrist is made only after other treatment options have been exhausted. For such patients, Kinzie advocated a medical approach for treatment, with emphasis on thorough history taking before treating the symptoms. A long-term supportive approach to therapy was considered the most helpful.

Suggestions by Kinzie were based on data from over 350 Indo-Chinese refugees who visited a university psychiatric clinic. Their continuing attendance at the clinic convinced Kinzie that when appropriate treatment approaches are used, along with the support of trained mental health counselors, the Indo-Chinese will use psychiatric services.

Brodsky (1988) conducted a study that suggested why individuals from foreign nations might pose problems of treatment for some mental health professionals but not for others. In her study, Brodsky surveyed 151 immigrants to the U.S. from the former U.S.S.R., to examine sources of assistance that the participants would turn to if confronted with mental health problems. The participants completed a questionnaire in response to vignettes that featured childhood behavior disorder, alcoholism, anxiety neurosis, compulsive phobic disorder, simple schizophrenia, and paranoid schizophrenia. Results showed that the participants preferred doctors and medical facilities as mental health resources over social workers and social service agencies, which were not the preferred resource in any of the vignettes. According to Brodsky, this reflected an attitude exhibited by other ethnic and racial groups. She suggested that a preference for medical resources as sources of mental health assistance may be due to ideological stigma attached to mental illness in the U.S.S.R.

4. IDENTITY AND PERSONAL DEVELOPMENT: A MULTICULTURAL FOCUS

Problems Involving Mislabeling of Patients and Patients' Resistance to Treatment

Another study that has implications for understanding why foreign patients may often resist seeking treatment from mental health professionals was conducted by Flaskerud (1984). She compared the perceptions of difficult behavior and the suggested management of those behaviors by six minority groups composed of 159 individuals and 68 mental health professionals. The minority participants included Chinese Americans, Mexican Americans, Filipino Americans, Native Americans, Black Americans, and Appalachians. The mental health professionals were from Pennsylvania, Louisiana, and California. All of the participants were interviewed using a structured interview schedule. The findings showed that there were significant differences between minority and mental health professional groups, both in the labels placed on difficult behaviors and in the suggested management of the behaviors.

Another study that indicated how the national and racial characteristics of patients can result in diagnostic mislabeling, among other problems in the practitioner-patient relationship, was shown by Adams, Dworkin, and Rosenberg (1984). The researchers used clinical data from 1,752 ambulatory patients between the ages of 17 and 91, who were treated at five public mental health clinics to test hypotheses concerning the diagnoses and psychopharmacotherapy of Hispanic patients compared with Anglos and Blacks. The results of their study showed that Hispanics were less likely than the other two groups were to be labeled as "schizophrenic," but they were more likely to be diagnosed as having other mental illnesses. Hispanics were also less likely to receive medication than were the other two groups. When pharmacotherapy was used, however, there were no significant differences among groups in the number of medications prescribed and no differences in dosages prescribed among the groups were found.

SUMMARY, CONCLUSION, AND RECOMMENDATIONS

This article argues that, in most nations today, more mental health professionals experience increased problems involving patient diagnosis and treatment than they did in the past. This is because mental health professionals see more patients from many diverse cultures than they ever have before, and patients from different cultures tend to express their symptoms differently, behave differently in their interactions with health care professionals, and have different norms, values, and beliefs regarding medication and treatment plans. The sociocultural differences among individuals pose special challenges for mental health professionals working in a multicultural setting.

Specifically, sociocultural factors such as religion and nationality influence the way that patients think about their mental illness, act out their mental illness, relate to medication, treat mental health professionals, and follow through on treatment modalities, including visits to clinics and hospitals in their neighborhoods. Because of sociocultural differences among patients, treatment strategies must inevitably vary from one sociocultural group to another.

A vivid example of this was presented earlier in this article, in the case of the orthodox Jewish patient, Mr. S. This case study showed that the "wrong" medication can be prescribed by a mental health professional because it violates not medical but religious proscriptions.

As we enter the twenty-first century, more mental health professionals worldwide will be diagnosing and treating more patients from diverse cultures. It is imperative that the mental health profession take active steps to minimize the frequency and the negative consequences of such problems. Toward this end, the following recommendations are offered both to executives and professors in mental health organizations, such as universities, graduate schools, and hospitals, and to individual practitioners working in the field:

1. Mental health professionals should develop sound principles of what Moffic (1983) called "cultural psychiatry." This requires that practitioners learn to be aware of patients' differences in verbal and nonverbal communication to prevent misunderstandings, and that practitioners engage in cultural self-analysis to alleviate countertransference of problems.
2. Mental health professionals should practice taking a thorough patient history, including religious and cultural norms, beliefs, and values, especially when seeing patients whose values and understanding of health are shaped by local folk culture, before initiating treatment.
3. Mental health professionals should make it part of their ongoing practice to read articles and books that describe and analyze the impact of cross-cultural factors on mental health.
4. Mental health professionals should make it part of their ongoing practice to discuss the

impact of sociocultural variables on mental health with their peers.
5. Medical schools, graduate schools, and other educational organizations that train mental health professionals should establish more educational courses and workshops that instill heightened awareness as to how people from different nations experience and exhibit mental and emotional disorders.

Through ongoing educational activities and field experience, mental health professionals can be better prepared to diagnose and to treat the diverse patient populations that they will increasingly confront in the rapidly changing world at the end of the twentieth century.

REFERENCES

Adams, G., Dworkin, R., & Rosenberg, S. (1984). Diagnosis and pharmacotherapy issues in the care of Hispanics in the public sector. *American Journal of Psychiatry, 141*(8), 970–974.

Angel, R., & Tholts, P. (1987). The impact of culture on the cognitive structure of illness. Culture, *Medicine and Psychiatry, 11*(4), 465–494.

Brodsky, B. (1988). Mental health attitudes and practices of Soviet Jewish immigrants. *Health and Social Work, 13*(2), 130–136.

Chandrasena, R. (1987). Schneider's First Rank Symptoms: An international and interethnic comparative study. *Acta Psychiatrica Scandinavica, 76*(5), 574–578.

Chiu, T. (1994). The unique challenges faced by psychiatrists and mental health professionals working in a multi-cultural setting. *The International Journal of Social Psychiatry, 40*(1), 61–74.

Chiu, T., & Primeau, C. (1991). A psychiatric mobile crisis unit in New York City: Description and assessment, with implications with mental health care in the 1990s. *The International Journal of Social Psychiatry, 37*(4), 251–258.

Chiu, T., & Schmidt, K. (1967). *A research study in Sarawak: A comparative survey of mental illness among the Ibans, Malays and Chinese.* Unpublished manuscript.

Currer, C. (1984). Pathan women in Bradford: Factors affecting mental health with particular reference to the effects of racism. *International Journal of Social Psychiatry, 30*(1–2), 72–76.

Fichter, M., Elton, M., Diallina, M., & Koptagel, G. (1988). Mental illness in Greek and Turkish adolescents. *European Archives of Psychiatry and Neurological Sciences, 237*(3), 125–134.

Flaskerud, J. (1984). A comparison of perceptions of problematic behavior by six minority groups and mental health professionals. *Nursing Research, 33*(4), 190–197.

Folnegovic, Z., & Folnegovic, S. (1992). Schizophrenia in Croatia: Interregional differences in prevalence and a comment on constant incidence. *Journal of Epidemiology and Community Health, 46*(3), 248–255.

Freeman, H., & Alpert, M. (1986). Prevalence of schizophrenia in an urban population. *British Journal of Psychiatry, 149*, 603–611.

Gupta, S. (1991). Psychosis in migrants from the Indian subcontinent and English-born controls. A preliminary study on the use of psychiatric services. *British Journal of Psychiatry, 159*, 222–225.

Hanck, C., Ayuso-Gutierrez, J., & Ramos-Brieva, J. (1981). Clinical forms of depression in African and in Spanish cultural communities: A new comparative study. *Acta Psychiatrica Belgica, 81*(5), 437–443.

Harrison, G., Holton, A., Neilson, D., & Owens, D. (1989). Severe mental disorder in Afro-Caribbean patients: Some social, demographic and service factors. *Psychological Medicine, 19*(3), 683–696.

Jablensky, A., Sartorius, N., Ernberg, G., & Anker, M. (1992). Schizophrenia: Manifestations, incidence and course in different cultures: A World Health Organization ten country study. *Psychological Medicine, 20*(97), 18–20.

Jenkins, J. (1988). Ethnopsychiatric interpretations of schizophrenic illness: The problem of nervious within Mexican-American families. *Culture, Medicine and Psychiatry, 12*(3), 301–329.

Keatinge, C. (1985). Schizophrenia in rural Ireland: A community comparison of tolerance of mental illness, level of social support and attitudes toward psychiatric facilities. *Dissertation Abstracts International, 46*/09B, p. 3220.

Killian, T., & Killian, L. (1990). Sociological investigations of mental illness: A review. *Hospital and Community Psychiatry, 41*(8), 902–911.

Kinzie, J. (1985). Cultural aspects of psychiatric treatment with Indochinese refugees. *American Journal of Social Psychiatry, 5*(1), 47–53.

Kua, E. (1990). Depressive disorder in elderly Chinese people. *Acta Psychiatrica Scandinavica, 81*(4), 386–388.

Lehtinen, V., Joukamaa, M, Lahtela, K., Raitasalo, R., Jyrkinen, E., Maatela, J., & Aromaa, A. (1990). Prevalence of mental disorders among adults in Finland: basic results from the Mini Finland Health Survey. *Acta Psychiatrica Scandinavica, 81*(5), 418–425.

Moffic, S. (1983). Sociocultural guidelines for clinicians in multicultural settings. *Psychiatric Quarterly, 55*(1), 47–54.

Munk, J., & Tansella, M. (1986). Hospital and community based psychiatry: A comparative study between a Danish and an Italian psychiatric service. *International Journal of Social Psychiatry, 32*(2), 6–15.

Nakane, Y., Ohta, Y., Radford, M., & Yan, H. (1991). Comparative study of affective disorders in three Asian countries. Differences in prevalence rates and symptom presentation. *Acta Psychiatrica Scandinavica, 84*(4), 313–319.

Nakane, U., Ohta, Y., Uchino, J., & Takada, K. (1988). Comparative study of affective disorders in three Asian countries: Differences in diagnostic classification. *Acta Psychiatrica Scandinavica, 78*(6), 698–705.

Neehall, J. (1991). An analysis of psychiatric inpatient admissions from a defined geographic catchment area over a one-year period. *West Indian Medical Journal, 40*(1), 16–21.

Pages-Larraya, F. (1977). Investigation of the last remaining Siriono of eastern Bolivia: A study of cross-cultural psychiatry. *Acta Psiquiatrica y Psicologica de America Latina, 23*(4), 247–266.

Ruiz, R. (1985). The minority patient. *Community Mental Health Journal, 21*(3), 208–216.

Sanua, V. (1989). Studies in mental illness and other psychiatric deviances among contemporary Jewry: A review of the literature. *Israel Journal of Psychiatry and Related Sciences, 26*(4), 187–211.

Sachdev, P. (1990). Mental health and illness of the New Zealand Maori. *Transcultural Psychiatric Research Review, 27*(2), 85–111.

Shader, R. (1984). Epidemiologic and family studies. University of California, Los Angeles Department of Psychiatry and Biobehavioral Sciences at the 137th annual meeting of the American Psychiatric Association: Panic disorders: Clinical update 1984. *Psychosomatics, 25*(10, Suppl.), 10–15.

Tafari, S., Aboud, F., & Larson, C. (1991). Determinants of mental illness in a rural Ethiopian adult population. *Social Science Medicine, 32*(2), 197–201.

THE INSIDE STORY

Counseling for tolerance in the early years means paying attention to the way children think and feel about the world — and themselves.

DAVID ARONSON

"Hey, what is this, *One Flew Over the Cuckoo Nest?*" It was Meredith Kimber's first meeting with a 6th grade class she would be counseling as part of her year-long internship with Inventing the Future, a racism-prevention project, and Kimber was encountering more than the usual dose of suspicion. The students were from predominantly Irish families in a blue-collar Massachusetts town with a reputation for insularity and xenophobia. Kimber's project was to help children address the inner source of the violence and racism that seem to surge in the middle school years.

A graduate of Harvard Divinity School, Kimber was shocked by the attitudes she encountered among many of the children. "These kids had derogatory names for everyone," she recalls. "They used to ride the subway searching for black kids to pick fights with. They'd come in punching each other, calling each other 'fag.' " They initially had little interest in pursuing an inner exploration of their own biases.

Still, Kimber persisted. "We didn't ever tell the children what was right or wrong. Instead, we asked them how they felt about things, trying to get them to change. If someone said 'fag,' we said, 'OK, here's the homosexuality issue again.'" Kimber's hope was that by getting the children to disclose their beliefs, values and fears, she and the other counselors on her team could help the children overcome the irrational thinking underlying their prejudice.

"By the end of the year, a lot of the kids had come to accept us and were relying on us to help them think through a lot of issues about racism, sex and violence."

Increasingly, for school counselors and psychologists, helping students become more tolerant and accepting means starting at the very earliest ages. Even then, however, racism may already have sprouted its first insidious roots. Debra Van Ausdale, a doctoral student in sociology at the University of Florida, witnessed a disturbing number of racial incidents when she worked as a teacher's aide at Gainesville Day Care Center in Gainesville, Fla.

"When a white girl became weary pulling an Asian girl in a wagon one day, the Asian girl hopped out and offered to pull," Van Ausdale recalls. "The white girl said, 'You can't pull the wagon. Only white people can pull the wagon.'" It was, says Van Ausdale, an incident that crystallized for her just how well her students understood the power of racial identity.

"We often think of the early years as an age of innocence," says Dr. Kevin Dwyer, assistant executive director of the National Association of School Psychologists. "In fact, prejudice is probably developed before children enter school — as is a predisposition to violence.

School counselors, because of their unique position, can intervene against prejudice at every level.

Teaching About "Same" and "Different"

A primary source of prejudice stems from how we make sense of the world. Kids, says Don Locke, a professor of counseling at North Carolina State University, especially want the world divided into easy pieces: Good and Bad, Black and White, Boy and Girl. And they want to assign fixed meanings to each of these categories: Boys never cry; all Chinese are good at math; girls play with dolls.

"Because kids think in such absolute terms," Locke says, "they have trouble understanding how people can be similar in some ways and different in others."

One counselor was able to get at the issue of categorization in a simple way. She tells of a second grade classroom where children had begun to use racial epithets like "whitey" and "darky." She had all the children form a circle and thrust their left hand into the middle. "The extraordinary variety of shades took them all aback," she says. "They realized you couldn't just divide people into two or three racial categories, but that there was a whole rainbow of skin tones and that everyone was unique." The racial epithets immediately ceased.

During their many visits to classrooms, Locke and his colleagues have designed a more extended program that delights children while subtly changing the way they think.

This activity, aimed at younger, elementary-age children, develops children's appreciation for cultural differences through four engaging activities that build on each other. Since school counselors and psychologists are usually scheduled to visit classrooms only periodically, this one is designed to work even if the counselor's class sessions are widely spaced. All that's required is to review the previous session at the start of each new one.

Begin each session by setting rules for speaking and listening: 1. We listen to and respect one another's thoughts, ideas and feelings. 2. We share, when comfortable, our own ideas, thoughts and feelings. 3. Anyone can pass a turn if they wish. Provide a supportive environment so that the students will leave the session feeling good about being like some of their classmates while also feeling good about being different from others.

• Bring in three clear bowls—one containing salt; the second, yellow corn meal; and the third, flour. Do not tell the students the contents of the containers. Ask the children to describe how each substance looks in turn. Then place the words "same" and "different" on the blackboard and write down how the contents are similar to each other and how different. Now have them do the same exercise but this time focus on how the contents *feel*.

Summarize the discussion and ask the students what other things they know about that are the same and different. Ask them to think of things that are the same and that are different for the next scheduled session. (For example, foods all nurture our bodies but have many different tastes; clothes keep us warm but are made in different styles and colors.)

• Have the students discuss what they remember from the last session, and have them share some of the things that they discovered to be the same and different.

Next, distribute plenty of play dough or plasticine of different colors to each child. Tell the children they can make anything they want. Then go around in a circle and have the students describe what they have made. Have them discuss one way in which their item is similar and one way in which it is different from the preceding child's creation.

At the end of the session, point out that there are a lot of ways in which things are similar and a lot of ways in which they are different. Point out that every child's creation is made from the same material, yet it is different from all the others.

• Bring in two play phones. Have pairs of children take turns in front of the class making believe that it is after school and they are calling each other to discuss an imaginary new classmate. How is that child similar to them and how is he or she different? Discuss how sameness and difference affect the children's descriptions of their new classmate.

• This time, pair the students up and have them discuss themselves. Ask them for three self-descriptions, for example, "I am tall; I have a big sister; I like to read." Do the students have some traits in common and some that are unique to themselves?

Ask the students how they felt about being different from each other and how they felt about being the same. Encourage students to remember a time when they felt like they were different from others and ask them to describe their feelings. Ask them how they get along with classmates they perceive as the same and as different.

Have the students tell how they are going to work to appreciate those students whom they see as different from themselves. They may resolve to invite them to play in their game or to share in some discussion.

These activities should help the students understand how sameness and difference are part of life, and that all people are the same in some ways and different in others. In our diversity, we have strength as a community.

School forces children together who might not have had the chance to exhibit that sort of anti-social behavior before they arrive."

The psychological development of prejudice in children was brilliantly illuminated 40 years ago in the work of Gordon Allport (*see Box* "The Ages of Intolerance"). Today, school counselors have developed an effective approach to reducing prejudice in the crucial early years, when the direction of the child's emotional and psychological growth can be set for life. This approach relies less on proselytizing than on changing the way young children make sense of the world–and themselves.

Because of their training, counselors have a better understanding than most about how young children form opinions, feelings and personalities around what they see and experience. And because of their position—their "beat" is typically an entire school—counselors can intervene at every level, from advising the troubled child who may have violently expressed his or her prejudice, to developing teacher training programs, to working with parents on addressing racial tensions in the community.

Successful early intervention efforts are based on the premise that hatred and prejudice are tools of the subconscious that ease the feeling of insecurity by offering

4. IDENTITY AND PERSONAL DEVELOPMENT: A MULTICULTURAL FOCUS

the illusion of superiority. Counselors try to offer more responsible ways to achieve emotional security.

"Giving children a positive experience of themselves, teaching them to recognize the validity of human differences, and providing them with the tools to express their emotions — all these are ways that intolerance can be counteracted," says Pat Schwallie-Giddis, associate director for the American Counseling Association.

Like strands in a rope, the various elements that Schwallie-Giddis speaks about — self-awareness, self-expression and self-esteem — are all widely recognized as intertwined aspects of the tolerant person. Children cannot freely express their emotions or feel secure with others unless they feel secure with themselves. And they can't feel good about themselves without having some understanding of who they are. Though any effort to separate these elements is necessarily artificial, they do build on and strengthen each other and can be thought of sequentially.

A child's failure to identify and express feelings leads to frustration and self-defeating behavior.

Self-Awareness and Self-Expression

School counselors can help foster children's self-awareness through exercises designed to help children see themselves and others for who they are, apart from the expectations and stereotypes that can easily color their thinking.

In one activity, called "The Me Bag," children are each given a plain brown grocery bag that they may decorate any way they choose. Then they are encouraged to fill the bag at home with things they value, things that represent what they love and feel proudest of. The next day, children get to show off what they've brought in. A recent immigrant from Bolivia may come in with an embroidered doll, for example, and another student may bring an LA Lakers cap.

Although each bag looks different, they all contain precious items. Children learn that the things that make them unique are as valuable as the things that they have in common. They learn to appreciate differences rather than fear them. And they learn to see themselves as others might see them: as individuals with their own enthusiasms and cultural traditions, neither better nor worse than others.

With an awareness of themselves as distinct individuals, children can better learn how to express their emotions in responsible and appropriate ways. The ability to articulate feelings is one of the most difficult things for children to learn, says Kevin Dwyer of the National Association of School Psychologists — yet it is absolutely critical. "So much depends on it: how well you're able to work as a team member, how well you resist acting on impulse, how you deal with the problems you're having."

Because it is often easier to make sense of other people's feelings than of one's own, educators have found that one of the best ways to develop children's emotional expressiveness is by asking them to think about the experiences of fictional characters. Through specially designed reading programs, children learn how failing to identify and express feelings can lead to increasing frustration and self-defeating behavior. Consider the following scenarios, taken from two popular reading programs in schools today, *PUMSY: In Pursuit of Excellence* and *Kids Have Feelings, Too*.

In the first, Pumsy the dragon is having a terrible day. While her friends are out picnicking on the beach, having the best times of their lives, Pumsy is moping under a tree. Usually, her best friend Steve would come tell her to stop feeling sorry for herself. But today, he's decided to let her make her own decisions.

In the second, a little girl from the picture book *Sometimes I Feel Awful* is also having a pretty rotten time. She has invited her best friend, David, over to play. But David just sits around playing with a puzzle, while she wants to go outside and climb a tree. Maybe a good swift punch will bring him around—but, of course, that only makes David want to leave. Now the little girl—who is never given a name, and who might, therefore, be any child—is lonelier than ever.

Children listening to these stories are encouraged to think about the consequences of the characters' actions and to offer alternatives. The little girl in *Sometimes I Feel Awful* explodes in anger because she isn't able to express to David how frustrated she is feeling. One group of children in Florida had very definite ideas about how she should behave.

"She should tell him!" called out one tousle-headed boy.

"We respect individuals not because they are from another race or culture, but because they are individuals."

"Tell him what?" the boy was asked.

"That she wants to go play in the tree!" he shouted, with the certainty of a 4-year-old.

The goal of these programs is for the children to take the insights they've learned from others and apply them to their own lives. Programs that develop children's powers of self-expression give them a feeling of control over their environment and make them less likely to lash out in violence and anger.

In Hillsboro County, Fla., an early childhood program has as its guiding image a stop sign. Bright red stop sign stickers, plastered everywhere in the classroom, emphasize children's power as decisionmakers. By teaching children to stop and think before they act, the "stop sign" program encourages "smart behavior."

"So much in our society encourages children to act on impulse," Dwyer notes. "Get out a watch and time how long any single camera angle lasts in a TV show. There's rarely more than three or four seconds between cuts. Teaching kids to slow down, not to go after the immediate gratification, is essential to reducing violent outbursts, which express the very worst kind of intolerance."

Self-Esteem

Self-awareness and self-expression are steppingstones for self-esteem. "Those persons with high self-esteem have fewer inhibitions and can relate to and accept others far more easily than those who do not," says Schwallie-Giddis. "By contrast, vengeful, intolerant behavior reflects poor self-esteem."

Self-esteem is a complicated subject that is easy to parody: "I'm OK and you're OK, but you got an 'F' on the test." And some self-esteem programs can focus so much on affirming the child's self-identity that they seem to ignore the child's own perceptions and experiences. It takes more than simply asserting the child's worth for the child to feel worthy.

True self-esteem develops out of a variety of experiences. A vital ingredient is the attention, acceptance, approval, acknowledgment and affection that a child receives from parents, primarily, but also from teachers, friends and counselors.

From these "Five A's" come feelings of competence, security, social responsibility and self-

---

The Ages of Intolerance

In *The Nature of Prejudice,* first published in 1954, social scientist Gordon Allport developed a powerful explanation of the psychological roots of prejudice.

Allport says that from a startlingly young age children begin learning the lessons of tolerance or intolerance—recognizing certain differences, for example, while still in diapers. There's nothing intrinsically worrisome about this. The 10- or 12-month-old baby who cries at the approach of a stranger is doing exactly what he or she is biologically programmed to do: alert Mom or Dad to the presence of a potential source of danger.

But if the parents are themselves prejudiced, the infant's reaction to a stranger of a different skin color or different physical features may be subtly reinforced, generating an apparently seamless education in bigotry that justifies itself as "natural." "My baby just doesn't like people of such and such a color," some parents may report, oblivious of their own role in shaping the child's perceptions.

By age 3 or 4, children begin to pick up on more explicit clues about in-groups and out-groups from their own family, the media and their peers. Children at this age are at the cusp of racial awareness and may be extremely curious about physical differences. Although they may use derogatory remarks, they often have little idea what they mean. And while they may utter racist sentiments, and even use race and gender to exclude others, their opinions and attitudes haven't yet gelled.

Of all influences on the child's ideas at this age, the family is clearly the most important. "The family," wrote Allport, "supplies a constant undertone of acceptance or rejection, anxiety or security." Even parents who avoid making overt racist comments may teach their kids negative racial values. The parent's lightening grip around the child's hand or the sound of the car doors being locked shut when a group of teenage males of a different race or ethnicity passes by—these communicate the parent's attitudes about others as clearly as words do.

By age 6 or 7, children have begun to recognize that there are distinct categories of people—that the janitor belongs to a different social class from the doctor, for example. And they've also begun to understand that many of these identities, such as race, gender and ethnicity, are fixed. They recognize that social status and positive or negative qualities can be ascribed to people based on their affiliation within these groups. And they've begun to make the connections between their individual identity and their group identity.

Often the lessons children learn at this age are as much about societal hypocrisy as they are about race. Parents who mutter something about the "wrong section of town" and then deflect their child's questions about what they meant aren't teaching their child that racism is bad; they are teaching the child to be cautious about speaking his or her mind on issues of race.

By age 10 or so children may start consistently excluding others who belong to an out-group, or , if they are themselves members of a minority, to develop a complex of attitudes that include defiance, self-doubt and hostility. Children this age are an excellent barometer of societal attitudes, for, in contrast to their elders, they tend to voice racial stereotypes quite freely.

A final stage comes in the teenage years, when the child learns those subtler rules of etiquette that govern relations between people. They've learned that "prejudiced talk and democratic talk are reserved for the appropriate occasions," Allport writes. What is said between friends in the mall may never be voiced in an official forum like a classroom. "It takes the entire period of childhood and much of adolescence to master the art of ethnocentrism," Allport concludes.

4. IDENTITY AND PERSONAL DEVELOPMENT: A MULTICULTURAL FOCUS

discipline, as well as strongly held values. Positive self-esteem, in other words, isn't just "feeling good about yourself." Rather, it's feeling that your life matters to others and to yourself. With that feeling comes the capacity to get along with others and the desire to conform to the rules of society.

An effective self-esteem program gives children the opportunity to learn about themselves in an environment that nurtures their growth and validates their feelings. Activities that promote self-esteem begin by teaching children to recognize the thought patterns and emotional habits that have a negative impact on their self-concept. As an alternative, such programs offer affirmations of the child as a unique being whose perceptions and feelings are valuable and appreciated. Eventually, it is hoped, the child internalizes that affirmation. No longer insecure or dissatisfied, the child is able to recognize his or her own worth and respond to the worth of others.

Some counselors have used self-portraits as a way to bring out the best in children. They ask the children to draw portraits of themselves. Then, without discussing the pictures, they have each child personally compliment the others in his or her group of six to eight fellow students ("I like your smile," "I like your shoes," etc.). Then they have the children draw their self-portraits once again, and ask them what was different this time around. Did they draw happier, prettier pictures? How did it make them feel to receive compliments from others? Did receiving compliments affect their self-portraits?

"Learning to respect yourself as an individual is, in an odd sort of way, one of the best ways to learn to respect other people and other cultures," says Jackie Allen, a school counselor who works in two bilingual elementary schools in California. "That's what it's about, ultimately, respecting individuals not because they are from another race or culture, but because they are individuals."

Counseling for the Future

School counselors, therapists and psychologists already have an extraordinary range to cover. With their many other responsibilities and involvements, it's no wonder that most feel stretched too thin. They have been lobbying for greater funding to place more counselors and psychologists in the schools.

They're needed because many of the same intervention techniques that promote tolerance can help children avoid other problems, as well: violence, drug abuse, suicide, teenage pregnancy. The whole

RESOURCES

- The World of Difference Institute of the Anti-Defamation League sponsors workshops promoting diversity awareness in the classroom. The Institute's *Elementary Study Guide* is an outstanding resource packed with activities and insights to address diversity.

    Anti-Defamation League
    1100 Connecticut Ave.,
    Suite 1020
    Washington, DC 20036
    (202) 452-8310

- The two volumes of *Thinking, Feeling, Behaving: An Emotional Education Curriculum for Children* ($25.95 each) are compendiums of classroom activities based on the principle that thinking things through rationally is one of the best ways to overcome problems. The activities focus on developing the children's emotional intelligence. (Grades 1-6 and 7-12)

    Research Press
    2612 N. Mattis Ave.
    Champaign, IL 61821
    (217) 352-3273

- *The Best Self-Esteem Activities for the Elementary Grades* ($24.95) offers an excellent overview of the theory behind self-esteem and emotion management for children, as well as strategies for promoting children's sense of personal agency and self-fulfillment.

    Innerchoice Publishing
    P.O. Box 2476
    Spring Valley, CA 91979
    (619) 698-2437

- *Counselor in the Classroom* ($19.95) gives counselors the keys to integrating the fundamental lessons of people-skills into enjoyable learning activities designed for all children.

    Innerchoice Publishing
    P.O. Box 2476
    Spring Valley, CA 91979
    (619) 698-2437

- *PUMSY: In Pursuit of Excellence* ($210) is an 8-week self-esteem program featuring a cuddly dragon puppet and a variety of workbooks, posters and other supporting material. This structured program develops children's emotional skills by involving them in the trials and tribulations of Pumsy, the dragon who sometimes acts up. (Ages 6-9)

    Timberline Press
    P.O. Box 70187
    Eugene, OR 97401
    (503) 345-1771

- *Sometimes I Feel Awful* ($8.95) is an affecting book about a young girl who's having a lousy day. The accompanying teacher's guide ($8.95) gives practical suggestions for helping children identify and express their emotions. (Ages 4-8)

    Fearon Teacher Aids
    P.O. Box 280
    Carthage, IL 62321
    (800) 242-7272

raft of social ills that manifest themselves with such virulence in today's schools, and that speak to the existence of so much pain and emotional distress, are to varying degrees addressed by focusing on psychological issues in early childhood.

Forty years ago, at the end of his analysis of prejudice, Gordon Allport arrived at a penetrating insight: Those who hate, he told us, are hurting. By giving children the tools to overcome the pain they feel, by listening to, caring for and comforting them, by helping to build healthier and stronger psyches, counselors can play a crucial role in arresting the dismaying rise in hatred and violence.

Like a sport that requires the coordination of various skills and muscle groups, tolerance is by its nature a complex undertaking. By isolating and strengthening the fundamental psychological components of self-esteem, self-awareness and self-expression, counselors and psychologists hope to encourage children to become healthier, more tolerant human beings.

Respect, Cultural Sensitivity, and Communication

Promoting Participation by Asian Families in the Individualized Family Service Plan

"When I was growing up, what did my family say about people from different cultures?"

Jinhee K. Hyun
Susan A. Fowler

Jinhee K. Hyun, *Doctoral Student, and* **Susan A. Fowler** *(CEC Chapter #51), Professor and Head, Department of Special Education, University of Illinois at Urbana-Champaign.*

ASKING YOURSELF A QUESTION LIKE THIS AND EXPLORING YOUR ANSWERS MAY GO A LONG WAY TOWARD HELPING YOU UNDERSTAND YOUR OWN CULTURE. THIS IS AN IMPORTANT FIRST STEP IN LEARNING ABOUT THE CULTURES OF THE PEOPLE YOU SERVE IN EARLY INTERVENTION PROGRAMS. TEACHERS, ADMINISTRATORS, SOCIAL WORKERS, HEALTH AND CHILD CARE PROFESSIONALS—ALL ARE CLOSELY INVOLVED WITH THE FAMILIES IN THEIR PROGRAMS, AND ALL CAN BENEFIT FROM GREATER AWARENESS OF CULTURAL DIVERSITY.

This article provides suggestions for enabling families with different cultural and linguistic backgrounds to participate fully in early intervention programs. Because Asian Americans have emerged as the fastest-growing ethnic minority group in the United States (Chan, 1992), we have based most examples on the Asian culture. In addition, we recognize that diversity exists within a cultural group. Variables such as socioeconomic status, educational level, and length of residence in the United States may affect people's beliefs as much as culture itself. Therefore, each family should be viewed as a unique unit that is influenced by its culture, but not defined by it (Wayman, Lynch, & Hanson, 1990).

We hope that this article will lead to a better understanding of the ways in which cultural diversity can be acknowledged, respected, and valued in the individualized family service plan (IFSP) process. The first step is to enhance our own cultural awareness.

Enhancing Cultural Awareness

We may enhance cultural self-awareness by (a) exploring our own cultural heritage and (b) examining the attitudes and behaviors that are associated with our own culture. Listening to or recollecting stories of the eldest members of a family, such as grandparents or great-grandparents, is a first step. Examining family genealogical records, family albums, or church records is invaluable in exploring our own heritage.

One illuminating way to examine some of the behaviors, values, and attitudes identified with our own cultural heritage is to recount common sayings (e.g., "Make do with or do without" and

"Where there is a will, there is a way") and identify the values behind these sayings. For example, if you are from the Euro-American culture, which values individualism and independence, you may want to examine how these values affect your attitude toward an Asian family who values harmony and interdependence in a family. Moreover, if you have been raised in beliefs like "Where there is a will, there is a way," your views about disabilities may be very different from those of a person who has heard that "It's God's will" or "It's my fate."

A question like the one at the beginning of this article—"When I was growing up, what did my family say about people from different cultures?"—may also clarify your own attitudes toward people from diverse cultures. This self-awareness can help us discover potent but pervasive biases that may affect intercultural interactions.

Learning about other cultures is a lifelong process, involving the following:
- Reading books or magazines about different cultures.
- Watching films or videotapes about diverse cultures.
- Interacting with friends, colleagues, or neighbors from different cultures.
- Participating in gatherings like celebration of holidays of other cultures.

Dealing with language barriers effectively can enrich your own understanding and speed the communication process.

Overcoming Language Differences—Obvious Barriers to Communication

If a family has limited English conversational skills, invite an interpreter to conferences and meetings. Ideally, the interpreter should be trained in cross-cultural interpretation, have knowledge about the early intervention system, and be proficient in both the language of the family and your language. In addition, you need to be sensitive to the family's choice of who should act as an interpreter, because the interpreter will be translating potentially confidential or privileged information by the family. In many Asian families, family matters involving a child with a disability are considered private concerns, not openly discussed with others.

Early Intervention and Cultural Issues

Public Law 99-457 places the family in the center of the early intervention system. A major intent of the law is to foster meaningful parent-professional partnerships to support the optimal development of infants and toddlers (Summers et al., 1990).

The issues on which families and professionals focus in providing services for these very young children often are closely related to the families' beliefs, values, and child-rearing practices (Hanson, 1992). This may present a challenge when professionals and families are from different cultures. Important issues include the following:

- The family-centered perspective may not be shared by all cultures (Hanson, Lynch, & Wayman, 1990).
- Recommendations and child-rearing practices may be misunderstood by either party (Lynch, 1992).
- Parents with different cultural and linguistic backgrounds may respond differently to the individualized family service plan (IFSP) process, depending on their understanding of the educational process and the number of barriers they encounter to their participation.
- Even though the concept of uniqueness of each family is generally acknowledged, it may not be always considered in the design of all early intervention programs (Chandler, Fowler, & Lubeck, 1986).

A leader of the cultural community can be a rich resource for understanding the culture; because of his or her position, a community leader is usually trusted and respected by the family. In the Korean-American culture, for example, a clergyman or a priest may be a good source for a cultural mediator or guide because "between 60% and 70% of Korean-Americans are affiliated with Christian churches" (Chan, 1992, p. 196).

Other specific suggestions for effective cross-cultural communication with many Asian families include the following courtesies:

- Using Mr., Mrs., or Miss with the family name (e.g., Mr. Chen, Mrs. Lee), because only close friends in the same peer group use first names.
- Learning greeting words or other simple words (e.g., hello, thank you) in the family's language.
- Using written forms and letters in the family's language for important communications, such as information about parent rights and community resources.

Asian language is characterized by indirect and nonverbal communication styles, whereas Anglo-American language focuses on direct and verbal styles (Lynch, 1992). Many Asian families convey a lot of information through nonverbal communication, using silence and eye contact. Maintaining silence in a conversation often indicates an expression of respect. However, if silence follows active verbal responses by the family, it may indicate disagreement. Direct eye contact is usually avoided. Especially, direct eye contact with the elder is viewed as disrespectful. Given the differences in communication styles, listen carefully—and, when unsure, ask parents for clarification. Developing your listening skills is especially important in parent-professional conferences with families from diverse cultures.

Holding Effective Family Conferences

Include time for preconference preparation and consider the schedule, room arrangement, and number of participants. Families should have an opportunity to participate at the level they find comfortable. Provide alternatives to facilitate parent participation and then let the parents decide on their level of participation.

Careful preconference preparation can influence actual IFSP conference success. Consulting with other service providers or mediators who are familiar with and knowledgeable about the families' cultural and linguistic community should be the first step.

Helpful strategies include the following:

- Decide with the parents the time and location of the meeting and who will participate.
- Encourage parents to bring people who are important to them, such as relatives, friends, or religious leaders.
- Send a written notice of the meeting in the family's primary language.
- Determine whether families need assistance with logistics, such as child care or transportation.

We can express respect for the family by scheduling adequate time for the meeting and arranging it at times convenient for the family (Summers et al., 1990). The location of the meeting is another consideration. If meetings are conducted at home, professionals should be sensitive to different customs. In most Asian homes, it is common courtesy to remove one's shoes upon entering. If older persons or grandparents are present, it is a courtesy to greet them with a slight bow and, when seated, to avoid crossing one's legs. Asian families are likely to provide a snack or beverage, because it is their custom to offer food when visited. You may decline the offered snack or beverage, but you should express thanks for the offering.

When meetings are conducted at a center or in a public location, you should select a quiet, private place with comfortable chairs. To promote the sense of professional-parent partnership, provide all participants with adult-sized chairs; and do not sit behind a desk, separated from the parents (deBettencourt, 1987). Privacy is essential if you expect families to feel comfortable discussing personal concerns (Kroth, 1985).

In addition, consider the number of people present at the conference. Parents may feel overwhelmed and outnumbered by too many professionals at the IFSP meeting (Able-Boone, Sandall, Loughry, & Frederick, 1990), particularly if families are from cultural backgrounds different from others present at the meeting (Lynch & Hanson, 1992). Meetings in which the professionals don't outnumber the family representatives are likely to be more comfortable and conducive to exchange of ideas for Asian families.

Developing Family Outcomes in the IFSP

We should always respect family preferences and concerns in the development of family outcomes. The family outcomes should be written in clear and nonintrusive language, considering the family's cultural background. Meaningful family involvement requires culturally acceptable family outcomes. To identify culturally acceptable family outcomes, consider the following issues:

- Who is the primary caregiver?
- What are the family's beliefs about disability?
- Who is the decision maker? (Hanson et al., 1990).

In addition, ask about daily routines, such as eating practices or sleeping patterns. Some practices may be unique to the culture; if so, the cultural values must be respected when choosing those routines for intervention. For example, if one outcome is that a child will increase her ability to feed herself, keep in mind that an Asian family whose main meal is rice and soup usually doesn't encourage very young children to self-feed but instead provides assistance during mealtime. The professional can recommend self-feeding during snack time when finger feeding is possible, rather than emphasizing self-feeding during mealtime. Professionals should also ensure that the proposed outcomes are important to the family and are realistic for them.

If outcomes involve sleeping patterns, consider that the mother-infant interaction is often characterized by close physical contact in many Asian families (Chan, 1992). Infants rarely sleep alone, and it is not unusual that children under school age sleep with their parents in the same room. If you recommend that the child sleep alone, the outcome is not likely to be acceptable to the family.

If families have a different understanding of the family outcomes, or if their view of their roles in implementation differs from yours, the potential for conflict may emerge. For example, a reverent regard for teachers is firmly established in Asian culture. Professionals are viewed as respected figures with the expertise and ability to offer assistance (Chan, 1992). As a result, some Asian parents may assume a dependent role rather than active partnership. Accordingly, even if family members believe that family outcomes are of no importance, they are not likely to contradict your selection of outcomes, out of respect for your opinion as a professional. However, the family may not implement the plan, if the outcomes are not important goals for the family.

By frequently reviewing the outcomes and holding informal interviews with the

---

Promoting Communication Between Parents and Professionals

Cultural sensitivity, clear language, and active listening are critical to ensuring shared communication in the IFSP process. Cultural sensitivity involves respecting family values, beliefs, and customs that differ from our own (Wayman et al., 1990). To infuse cultural sensitivity into all aspects of our programs, we need to do the following:

- Be aware of the extent to which our own opinions are driven by cultural values (Randall-David, 1989).
- Learn about the values of families with whom we work (Lynch, 1992).
- Whenever possible, identify members of the family's linguistic or cultural community to serve as a resource for translation or mediation (Anderson & Goldberg, 1991).

family, you can recognize the family's perceptions about the outcomes. Your patient and sincere attitudes toward the family may facilitate the family in being frank, addressing problems, and making decisions. Once the outcomes are realistic and acceptable for the family, they will work very hard to achieve the outcomes.

Conclusion

The extent to which parents will participate as partners with professionals in the development and implementation of the IFSP must be determined by the family itself. We must recognize and respect the individual preferences and cultural values of each family. The IFSP must be flexible to be acceptable by families. If we are to attain the collaboration and meaningful partnership intended by the IFSP, we must cultivate and maintain respect for families, for their diversity, and for their choices.

We must have *culturally sensitive* early interventions. In this article, we have suggested strategies for enabling Asian parent participation. However, each family is different, and culture-specific information cannot be assumed to apply in every situation. *The information should not be used to make generalizations that stereotype families.* Acquiring cross-culturally competent skills and attitudes can be a long process; however, a desire and willingness to learn about different people is certainly a rewarding pursuit (Lynch, 1992). *Enthusiasm, openness, and willingness* are the most important characteristics that support meaningful partnership between professionals and culturally diverse families.

References

Able-Boone, H., Sandall, S. R., Loughry, A., & Frederick, L. L. (1990). An informed, family-centered approach to Public Law 99-457: Parental views. *Topics in Early Childhood Special Education, 10*, 100–111.

Anderson, M., & Goldberg, P. F. (1991). *Cultural competence in screening and assessment: Implications for services to young children with special needs ages birth through five.* Chapel Hill, NC: National Early Childhood Technical Assistance System. (ERIC Document Reproduction Service No. ED 370 313)

Chan, S. (1992). Families with Asian roots. In E. W. Lynch & M. J. Hanson (Eds.), *Developing cross-cultural competence: A guide for working with young children and their families* (pp. 181–257). Baltimore: Paul H. Brookes.

Chandler, L. K., Fowler, S. A., & Lubeck, R. C. (1986). Assessing family needs: The first step in providing family-focused intervention. *Diagnostique, 11*, 233–245.

deBettencourt, L. U. (1987). How to develop parent relationships. *TEACHING Exceptional Children, 19*, 26–27.

Hanson, M. J. (1992). Ethnic, cultural, and language diversity in intervention settings. In E. W. Lynch & M. J. Hanson (Eds.), *Developing cross-cultural competence: A guide for working with young children and their families* (pp. 3–18). Baltimore: Paul H. Brookes.

Hanson, M. J., Lynch, E. W., & Wayman, K. I. (1990). Honoring the cultural diversity of families when gathering data. *Topics in Early Childhood Special Education, 10*, 112–131.

Kroth, R. L. (1985). *Communicating with parents of exceptional children: Improving parent-teacher relationships.* Denver, CO: Love.

Lynch, E. W. (1992). Developing cross-cultural competence. In E. W. Lynch & M. J. Hanson (Eds.), *Developing cross-cultural competence: A guide for working with young children and their families* (pp. 35–57). Baltimore: Paul H. Brookes.

Lynch, E. W., & Hanson, M. J. (1992). Steps in the right direction: Implications for interventionists. In E. W. Lynch & M. J. Hanson (Eds.), *Developing cross-cultural competence: A guide for working with young children and their families* (pp. 355–370). Baltimore: Paul H. Brookes.

Randall-David, E. (1989). *Strategies for working with culturally diverse communities and clients.* Washington, DC: Association for the Care of Children's Health. (ERIC Document Reproduction Service No. ED 325 559)

Summers, J. A., Dell'Oliver, C., Turnbull, A. P., Benson, H. A., Santelli, E., Campbell, M., & Siegel-Causey, E. (1990). Examining the Individualized Family Service Plan process: What are family and practitioner preferences? *Topics in Early Childhood Special Education, 10*, 78–99.

Wayman, K. I., Lynch, E. W., & Hanson, M. J. (1990). Home-based early childhood services: Cultural sensitivity in a family systems approach. *Topics in Early Childhood Special Education, 10*, 56–75.

Curriculum and Instruction in Multicultural Perspective

Curriculum and instruction includes all concerns related to subject matter content to be taught and pedagogical theory. Any pedagogical theory is informed by underlying philosophical assumptions regarding what is worth knowing and what actions are good. Every school curriculum is the product of specific choices among all those available. Since classroom teachers are the "delivery systems" for any curriculum, along with whatever texts are used, they have the opportunity to interpret and add their own insights regarding what they teach.

It is through curriculum and instruction in elementary and secondary schools, as well as in teacher education curricula, that a fundamental transformation must occur to sensitize all young people, including those living in isolated communities, to the multicultural reality of our national civilization. There are several different approaches

UNIT 5

to multicultural education in use today. Some school systems merely include the study of minority groups living in their area in elective or required courses. This is not the approach to multicultural education that current leaders in the field favor. Today, most experienced multicultural educators favor a more holistic, inclusive approach to the subject—the infusion of multicultural themes into the entire life of the school and all possible course content. Such an inclusive approach to multicultural education seeks to help students and teachers to develop a sense of social consciousness. The sense of social consciousness, coupled with a more global and integrated conception of our social reality, will empower them to assess more critically than most citizens have in the past such distinctions as the disparity between public democratic rhetoric and the reality that some social groups still have difficulty being accepted into society's mainstream.

The National Council for the Social Studies (NCSS), through its Task Force on Ethnic Studies, has developed comprehensive curriculum guidelines for the implementation of multicultural education in elementary and secondary schools. A revised version of these guidelines was published in 1991. They reflect the thinking of many educators who have been involved in the implementation of multicultural programming in school systems and teacher education programs. An important focus of multicultural education is that a democratic nation has a moral responsibility to prevent minority ethnic, cultural, or religious groups from being socially isolated or marginalized. What students learn informally in their communities about groups different from themselves can be misleading or incorrect. This is how our past sad heritage of racism and negative stereotyping evolved. There has been much progress in the area of civil rights in the past 40 years, but there has also been resurgent racism and intercultural misunderstanding. School is the one place children and adolescents go each day where it is possible for them to learn an objective view of the culturally pluralistic national heritage that is both their current and future social reality. When students leave high school to go into military service, attend college, or begin careers in the corporate sector, government, or the arts, they may encounter a multicultural world very different from that of their local community or cultural group.

Teachers can help their students to recognize and respect ethnic and cultural diversity and to value the ways in which it enhances and enriches the quality of our civilization. Children and adolescents should also be made aware that each of them has the right to choose how fully to identify with his or her own ethnic or cultural group.

The essays in this unit provide a wide variety of perspectives on how to broaden the multicultural effort in our schools. The authors seek to incorporate more intercultural and global content and experiences into the main body of curriculum and instruction. Educators will find that, taken together, these essays provide a sound basis for understanding what multicultural curriculum and instruction should be about. They are relevant to course work in curriculum and instruction, curriculum theory and construction, educational policy studies and leadership, history and philosophy of education, and cultural foundations of education.

Looking Ahead: Challenge Questions

How should teachers and students deal with xenophobic reactions when they occur?

What are the similarities and distinctions between a "culture" and an "ethnic group"?

Why might it be effective to integrate multicultural content into all aspects of a school curriculum?

What are the varying ways in which multicultural education is defined? Which model of multicultural education do you prefer?

What is the rationale for multicultural education in elementary and secondary schools? Should all students be exposed to it?

How can inservice teachers be better prepared to engage in multicultural instruction and learning experiences?

—F.S.

Article 25

Proposal:
An Anti-Bias and Ecological Model for Multicultural Education

Francis Wardle

Francis Wardle is Director, Resource Development & Training, Children's World Learning Centers, and Adjunct Faculty, University of Phoenix, Arizona.

The early childhood community has led efforts to develop materials and resources to support children's unique heritages and diverse experiences (Derman-Sparks, 1989; Neugebauer, 1992; York, 1991). While recognizing that education programs should validate all children and their families, educators have relied on a traditional multicultural model that limits their ability to explore the full range of diversity. It is time to propose a new model—one that recognizes the differences among traditional racial and cultural groups, acknowledges the variability within these groups and enables us to explore the uniqueness of people whose heritages and experiences do not fit into any traditional racial or cultural category.

Traditional Model
The traditional model of anti-bias and multicultural education views the child as the product of culture (Figure 1). Or, to put it another way, children's sets of experiences and their world outlook are totally predetermined by their culture. "Culture forms the prism through which members of a group see the world and create shared meaning" (Bowman, 1989, p. 2). Children's values, traditions and expectations are predetermined by their religion, attitudes about family and, sometimes, a long history of persecution and oppression.

Children are then viewed as a product of their community's culture: African American, Native American, Asian, Hispanic or European. According to this model, all black children are supposedly the products of a collective black cultural context and Native American children all "see the world" in the same way. This model stresses culture, group membership and shared attributes. Individual identity and self-esteem are based on a sense of belonging to and pride in one's cultural group.

The traditional multicultural education model in the United States teaches children about the values, celebrations, histories, traditions and art forms of five traditional cultural groups: European, African American, Latino, Asian American and Native American (Ramirez & Ramirez, 1994). Teachers are urged to help each child connect with his/her heritage, and to help each child feel positive about the group to which he/she belongs. Multicultural curricula include books and other materials that reflect each of these groups (Ramirez & Ramirez, 1994). The child develops a sense of self-esteem and identity through knowledge of and identification with his/her cultural group.

This traditional model has many shortcomings. It perpetuates stereotypes: if every child from the same culture sees the world through the same prism, then all children from one culture must be the same. The traditional model does not allow for the tremendous diversity to be found within traditional cultural groups (Wardle, 1994a; West, 1992). A child who can trace his/her heritage directly to the original Spanish settlers of northern New Mexico has a different cultural context from a Latino child living in inner-city Los Angeles. A black child whose family has just immigrated to the United States from Belize has a very different set of experiences from a child of black college professors at Harvard.

Many Latin Americans have parents who are German, Polish, Austrian or Swiss. They speak Spanish and live in a Hispanic culture, yet are blond and have blue eyes. A member of Argentina's current national soccer team, for example, is a third-generation Irish descendent with red hair and freckles. Other residents of these Hispanic countries belong to specific minority groups.

William Cross (1985) questions the notion that young minority children's self-esteem is based on pride in and a sense of belonging to their cultural and racial group. Cross's research shows that positive self-esteem is more likely to be based on how the child sees himself as an individual, not how he sees himself in reference to racial groups or communities. Personal identity reinforced by positive responses to the individual child is more important than group identity.

Also, it is impractical, if not impossible, to teach about the multitude of cultures in our world (Gomez, 1991). According to Valeria Lovelace (1994), this difficulty is the reason *Sesame Street*'s "Race Project" does not explore the identities of biracial children. Clearly, Lovelace adheres to the traditional model of multicultural education. Furthermore, some children's experiences do not fit into any of the traditional cultural groups. Transracially adopted children, biracial children and some foreign children, for example, cannot be placed into any of the five traditional groups (Wardle, 1988a, 1993, 1994b). Curricula that use the traditional model as the basis for classroom activities and material selection do not reflect these children's experiences, and sometimes actually force them to deny part of their heritage (York, 1991).

Many people claim multicultural education is divisive, and that it creates ethnocentric curricula, segregation and alternative histories. Most books that address multicultural education portray a power conflict between whites and people of color (McCracken, 1993; Ramirez & Ramirez, 1994). The traditional model lends itself to these criticisms, and sometimes does create hostility among students from different cultural groups. Furthermore, it gives ammunition to those who believe the sole purpose of multicultural education is to devalue the majority culture.

Finally, the problem of content must be addressed. Educators should not assume that *what* they teach is more important than *how* they teach. A traditional focus on content led to the development of state-mandated curricula and national social science texts that did not represent the backgrounds of non-white students and children of recent immigrants. Consequently, discussions about multicultural education are often debates about what content should and should not be taught (e.g., the current debate on the national standards for social science content and Colorado's new state standards).

Focusing on the content of traditional multicultural groups can result in a "tourist approach" (Derman-Sparks, 1987) to multicultural education and very inappropriate teaching methods (Bredekamp, 1987). This focus emphasizes the cultures, leading to arguments concerning which culture is most important and who is competent to teach each culture. Consider the debate about who should teach bilingual Spanish/English classes. In a California district, for example, protests erupted when bilingual teachers were hired from Spain. And what happens if a conflict exists between two minority groups? Such jockeying for a favored position tends to make the child's needs secondary, even though multicultural education's purpose is to support the total heritage of each child.

We should instead focus on recognizing the unique set of experiences each child brings to school, and learning how we can utilize those experiences to help him or her achieve the utmost self-esteem and academic success. When we let adult content and political ends become more important than children's needs, we fail as educators.

The Anti-Bias and Ecological Model

An anti-bias and ecological model requires educators to present a multicultural foundation that teaches all children to accept one another (Gomez, 1991). It should enable each child to associate positive feelings with multicultural experiences and to feel included and valued (Dimidjian, 1989). It also provides a much simpler framework for teaching with a multicultural perspective.

In this model, the child is the focus, rather than the culture. Educators should recognize the variety of contexts that affect each child's experiences and point of view. The individual child exists within his/her own dynamic context, or milieu, which includes a variety of experiences that interact with each other to produce a unique environment (Johnson, 1990). This model is built on previous models by Jones (1985) and Wardle (1992), which themselves were developed to study the psychological functioning of African Americans and biracial children, respectively.

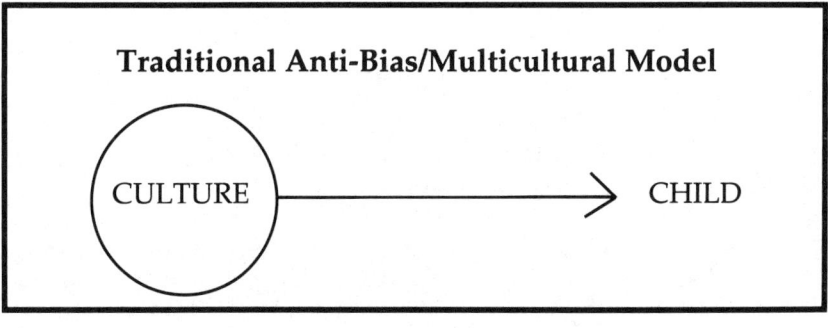

Figure 1

5. CURRICULUM AND INSTRUCTION IN MULTICULTURAL PERSPECTIVE

The resulting model recognizes that children clearly experience integrated contexts, not a series of distinct, opposing factors (Jones, 1987; Wardle, 1992). The overlapping circles depicted in Figures 2 and 3 represent the weight, or power, of each contextual factor that differs from situation to situation, from child to child, and is dependent on the interaction between two or more factors. This model assumes that children interact on their contextual environments. Thus, each child will experience the same context differently.

Factors/Contexts

Two groups of significant factors come into play. Group A factors are the traditional areas addressed in most anti-bias curricula (Derman-Sparks, 1989; Neugebauer, 1992; York, 1991): race, culture, gender and disability (see Figure 2). Our society has traditionally viewed these factors as having a preferred side, and one or more sides that can be inferior, dominated and/or persecuted. They are also individual characteristics that cannot be changed.

Group B factors are what Bronfenbrenner (1989) calls ecological components: family, community and social-economic status (S.E.S.) (see Figure 3). These factors have a powerful effect on the other factors' influence. Anti-bias activities must be directed toward these factors. Children cannot change their race, culture, gender or disability. Family, school and community, however, can help them feel positive about these personal characteristics.

It should not be assumed that A factors are more important than B factors. All the factors interact in a variety of unique ways, and their influence changes as children develop. Factors group together in different ways to affect children's development in different ways. For example, race, gender and S.E.S. can have such a strong impact on a child's development that they sometimes override other factors.

Group A Factors (Figure 2)

Race/Ethnicity. Although racial groups do not represent pure biological categories, society does attach significance to differences of physiognomy (Wilson, 1984). The assumption is that racial contexts affect an individual's identity (Wilson, 1984). Until quite recently, however, scholars studied race and culture separately. Many countries still separate race and culture (Wilson, 1984).

Culture. Culture includes family traditions, religion, holidays, heroes, music, ideals and beliefs, primary language and national origin. Cultures operate as contexts because they fix meanings over time, and each culture has the capacity to fix meaning differently (Johnson, 1990). The separation of the cultural category from the racial category allows for distinctions among American blacks, first-generation blacks from Africa and Caribbean blacks; direct descendants of original Spanish settlers, Puerto Rican immigrants in New York, first-generation immigrants from Brazil and Mestizos from Mexico; third-generation Chinese Americans and first-generation Hmongs, Cambodians and Vietnamese. It also allows us to appreciate the rich differences in the customs, religions, art, dance, houses and languages of the various Native American nations (Sample, 1993).

Gender. This distinction is obvious. Many cultures still respond very differently to girls and boys, beginning in infancy. Early childhood programs, curricula and experiences treat the genders in distinct ways (Wardle, 1990). More boys are diagnosed with learning disabilities, and girls are less likely to succeed in math and science. The students in special education programs are predominantly boys.

Disability. For the purposes of this article, disability is what a child views as a disability—in him/herself and/or others. This includes obvious physical disabilities along with speech problems, mental challenges, learning disabilities and behavioral issues.

Group B Factors (Figure 3)

Family. In the language of Johnson (1990), the family clearly is a context. The most critical influence on young children is the family (Wardle, 1992). Family diversity can mean two working parents, teen parents, adoptive parents (including transracial adoption), foster parents, single parents (male or female), blended families, interracial and interethnic families, families that combine divergent religious beliefs, extended family support, grandparents raising their grandchildren and gay families. Parenting style (authoritarian, authoritative or permissive) and family dysfunction or abuse are also included in this factor.

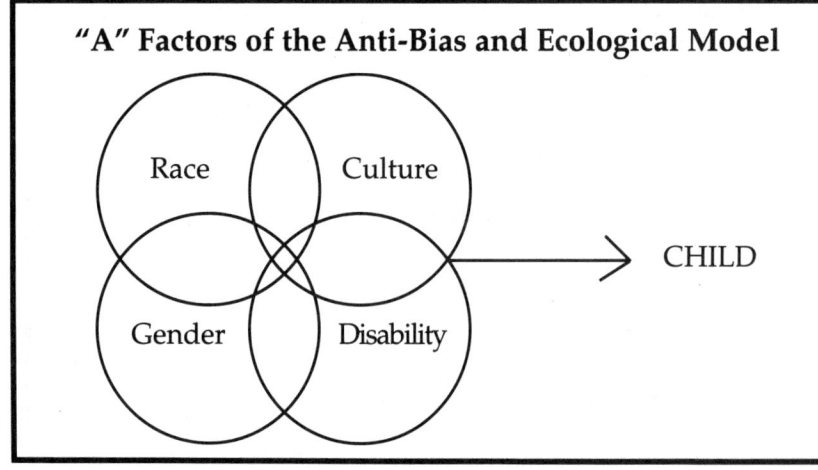

Figure 2

Technology also affects this ecological component—primarily TV, movies and music videos, but also home computers. TV's influence can be totally absent (Amish and Hutterite children and some poor children), controlled (in terms of content and amount) or uncontrolled, developmentally inappropriate and dominating.

While religion is placed under the cultural factor in this model, the family is the prime vehicle through which children receive their religious context. Families that mix religions (Jewish/Protestant, etc.) have a different effect on children from those that do not, or families that practice no religion.

Social-Economic Status. It could be argued that this factor belongs under the A factors in recognition of the tremendous discrimination that exists against the poor. It could also be argued, however, that this status can and does change, either improving or worsening.

Poverty clearly has a long-standing impact—thus the term, "culture of poverty." Welfare status, middle-class culture and professional households (regardless of income) all act as strong ecological factors. Some families have been welfare recipients for generations; others have a long heritage of college education. Homeless children's experiences are distinct from those of an Appalachian child from a poor family.

Community. Community encompasses a vast array of factors. It includes a child's geographical location and type of community (rural, urban, suburban, etc.). A Native American reservation, a bedroom community, and integrated and segregated neighborhoods represent different community contexts, as do intentional religious communities—Hutterite, Amish, Mennonite and New Age.

Schools, child care centers, churches, Head Starts, colleges, recreational opportunities, health centers, gangs and soccer teams help identify a community. Media also play a part.

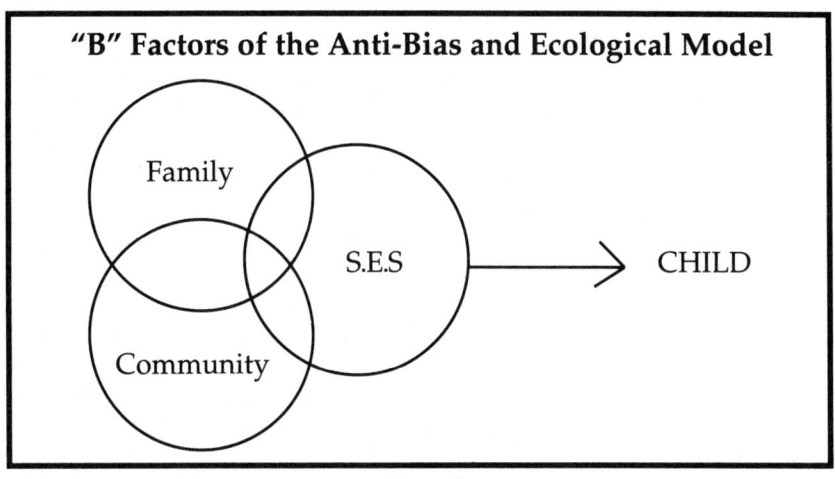

Figure 3

Advantages of the Anti-Bias and Ecological Model

The anti-bias and ecological model allows us to concentrate on each individual child. It acknowledges that every child has a unique culture (Gomez, 1991), and ensures that each child will feel included and valued (Dimidjian, 1989). By concentrating on the child, the family and the family's education expectations, we can begin to tailor and individualize multicultural programs for each child. This approach is totally consistent with the individual perspective advocated by developmentally appropriate practice (Bredekamp, 1987). It also discourages stereotyping and prevents expectations that children who belong to the same cultural groups will act the same way, share the same interests and play with children from their "group" (Wardle, 1988b).

Role of Teacher and School

How can a teacher respond to all these factors, and the range within factors? How can the school environment be arranged to support children whose set of experiences can differ so dramatically? How can we provide child care settings that are responsive to such a range of diversity? And how can we teach our children to respect and appreciate the variability of other children, both inside and outside the classroom?

We must always go back to the child. Instead of trying to learn everything about every community, culture and home, the teacher should combine an enlightened knowledge of cultural, gender and individual differences with a constant ability to "read" the child. If a child does not seem to respond to certain stories or is uneasy in certain activities, find out why.

This approach will require a radical change in teaching methods and in the way many teachers are trained. Traditionally, we expect children to adapt to the needs of the classroom, curricula and teacher. If something did not work, we tried to change the child or labeled the child with a disability (Wardle, 1990). Now we must change our entire approach. The teacher must also "read" the family and community. What encourages a family to come to the program? What keeps them away? What do they expect the program to do for their child? What materials do they want their children to use? (York, 1991).

A good teacher must be able to use the framework of this model to effectively support each child in the classroom and challenge his/her own cultural and individual framework. This model can be effectively used by a sensitive, well-trained teacher. Clearly this model challenges the notion that a black teacher is the only person who can adequately teach black children and only a Native American teacher can teach a Native

American child. That notion leads to segregated classrooms; in one instance, a Head Start teacher from one Native American tribe was considered an inappropriate teacher for children from another tribe (Wardle, 1991).

Clearly, society has strong biases toward each factor of this model—from race to income to community to religion. Thus, any program adapting this model must engage, to some extent, in anti-bias activities and consciousness raising (Derman-Sparks, 1989).

Schools and child care centers must know about the children, community and families they are serving before purchasing curriculum materials. Furthermore, because curriculum materials still tend to support socially accepted points of view, program administrators may have to develop their own materials.

Curriculum materials, classroom activities and community outings must address all seven factors in a way that conveys the variability within each factor. A lesson about communities, for example, can focus on the dynamics of a small farm community, a Native American reservation, integrated segments of a large city or a Mexican neighborhood. As part of this activity, a class might study various dwellings, including apartments, mobile homes, hogans and homeless shelters.

Equal value should be given to all aspects of any factor. When teaching about the various religions in a community, each religion—be it Quaker, Jewish, atheist or Methodist—must be taught with the same respect and deliberation. The program must support exploration of the variability within each factor, regardless of whether the program is religiously, ethnically, racially or economically homogeneous or diverse.

Conclusion

The traditional multicultural model has served well to heighten the recognition that all children should be exposed to the rich contribution of all Americans, and that we must support the history, heritage and culture of each child in our programs. We have been sensitized to the injustices and biases that have hurt people from specific cultural, gender and disability groups. We were inspired to develop curricula that celebrate each of these traditional cultures. Now, however, we must move beyond this traditional model. The anti-bias and ecological model described in this article enables us to see the child as a product of important factors, including—but not limited to—culture. We can examine every factor that affects the child's set of experiences, and allow each of our children to develop to their full potential.

◆

References

Bowman, B. T. (1989). Educating language—minority children. *ERIC Digest.* Urbana, IL: ERIC Publications.

Bredekamp, S. (Ed.). (1987). *Developmentally appropriate practice in early childhood programs serving children birth through age 8.* (rev. ed.). Washington, DC: National Association for the Education of Young Children.

Bronfenbrenner, U. (1989, April). *The developing ecology of human development.* Paper presented at the biannual meeting of the Society for Research in Child Development, Kansas City, KS.

Cross, W. (1985). Black identity: Rediscovering the distinction between personal identity and reference group orientation. In M. B. Spencer, G. K. Brooklin, & W. R. Allen (Eds.), *Beginnings: The social and affective development of black children* (pp. 155-172). Hillside, NJ: Lawrence Erlbaum.

Derman-Sparks, L. (1989). *Anti-bias curriculum: Tools for empowering young children.* Washington, DC: National Association for the Education of Young Children.

Dimidjian, V. J. (1989). Holiday, holy days, and wholly dazed. *Young Children, 44*(6), 70-75.

Gomez, R. A. (1991). Teaching with a multicultural perspective. *ERIC,* EDO-PS-91-11.

Johnson, S. (1990). Toward clarifying culture, race, and ethnicity in the context of multicultural counseling. *Journal of Multicultural Counseling and Development, 18,* 41-50.

Jones, A. (1985). Psychological functioning in Black Americans: A conceptual guide for use in psychotherapy. *Psychotherapy, 22,* 363-369.

Lovelace, V. (1994, April). Personal communication with F. Wardle.

McCracken, J. B. (1993). *Valuing diversity: The primary years.* Washington, DC: National Association for the Education of Young Children.

Neugebauer, B. (1992). *Alike and different.* Washington, DC: National Association for the Education of Young Children.

Ramirez, G., & Ramirez, J. L. (1994). *Multiethnic children's literature.* Albany, NY: Delmar.

Sample, W. (1993). The American Indian child. *Child Care Information Exchange, 90,* 39-44.

Wardle, F. (1988a). Kids benefit from exposure to other cultures. *Denver Parent, 2,* 20.

Wardle, F. (1988b). Who am I? Responding to the child of mixed heritage. *PTA Today, 13*(7), 7-10.

Wardle, F. (1990). Are we short-changing boys? *Child Care Information Exchange, 79,* 48-51.

Wardle, F. (1991). *Problems with Head Start's multicultural principles.* Unpublished paper. Denver, CO.

Wardle, F. (1992). *Biracial identity: An ecological and developmental model.* Denver, CO: Center for the Study of Biracial Children.

Wardle, F. (1993). Interracial families and biracial children. *Child Care Information Exchange, 90,* 45-48.

Wardle, F. (1994a). Diversity module. In F. Wardle (Ed.), *Staff training modules for CDA candidates in Children's World Learning Centers.* Golden, CO: Children's World Learning Centers.

Wardle, F. (1994b). What about the other kids in the neighborhood? *New People, 4*(5), 10-19.

West, B. (1992). Children are caught—between home and school, culture and school. In B. Neugebauer (Ed.), *Alike and different.* Washington, DC: National Association for the Education of Young Children.

Wilson, A. (1984). Mixed race children in British society: Some theoretical considerations. *British Journal of Sociology, 35*(1), 42-61.

York, S. (1991). *Roots and wings.* St. Paul, MN: Toys 'n Things Press.

Beyond Socialization and Multiculturalism:

Rethinking the Task of Citizenship Education in a Pluralistic Society

BRUCE GRELLE AND DEVON METZGER

Most contemporary social studies educators view their educational role as passing on or transmitting to their students the knowledge, skills, and attitudes that are shaped and determined by the status quo (Leming 1989). As Sears and Parson (1991) have observed, "Most teachers view social studies as a vehicle to promote socialization and to prepare students to conform to the existing social structure, both in the school and society" (48). This standard socialization approach to social studies education–defined as "citizenship transmission" by Barr, Barth, and Shermis (1977)–is the generally accepted and historical practice that has, for more than seventy-five years, dominated social studies classrooms throughout our nation's schools.

The following summary, based on Leming's research, offers a description of the different aspects of the socialization role played by many social studies teachers (Leming 1989, 404-405):

- Teach students to observe the mores of the community.
- Teach students to conform to the role of the good citizen, e.g., basic literacy, good work habits, self discipline, academic excellence, and personal growth.
- Prepare students for the next rung of the educational ladder.
- Help students maintain positive attitudes toward American institutions.
- Steer away from value questions and controversial issues.
- Limit student access to material that challenges the existing social structure, e.g., material that focuses on the injustices and inadequacies of economic and political institutions.
- Control knowledge to prevent the development of cynicism in students and to help achieve quiet manageable classrooms.

The prevalence of this traditional socialization approach among social studies teachers should not be surprising. After all, human communities throughout history have sought to reproduce their central institutions and patterns of life from generation to generation through the initiation of their youth into accepted beliefs, values, and behaviors (Barth 1993, 57). Leming (1992) states the same point more dramatically: "No successful society in the history of the world has failed to recognize the necessary connection between cultural survival and cultural transmission. Consistent with a respect for basic human rights, educational institutions have always had a major responsibility in all societies to pass on the existing culture to the young" (310).

The greatest single strength of the traditional socialization approach is that it recognizes the important contribution that social studies can make to the task of education for citizenship in American society.

5. CURRICULUM AND INSTRUCTION IN MULTICULTURAL PERSPECTIVE

However, a growing number of critics have expressed concern about some of the curricular, pedagogical, and ethical-political implications of the standard socialization approach to social studies education. More specifically, these critics have argued that the standard socialization approach is grounded in and perpetuates (1) an overly narrow and "Eurocentric" definition of the curriculum, (2) an overly instrumental view of teachers as technicians (along with an excessively homogeneous view of students as passive recipients of predetermined knowledge), and (3) an overly narrow and uncritical conception of American citizenship. These criticisms of the standard socialization approach to social studies education have often been gathered together under the banner of "multiculturalism."

"Multiculturalism" is a term that means different things in different settings. For present purposes, it may be defined very generally as an educational reform movement that seeks both to restructure the social studies curriculum and classroom and to rethink the task of citizenship education in a pluralistic society. Although advocates of multiculturalism are fairly united and clear in their critique of the standard socialization approach, we will see that the movement actually encompasses a range of competing perspectives and agendas when it comes to addressing the central issue of citizenship education.

In what follows, we will survey the main features of the multicultural critique of the standard socialization approach to social studies education. We will set multiculturalism in a broader historical and intellectual context so that we can better assess both the contributions and the limitations of this new philosophy and practice of teaching and learning. Finally, we will distinguish which aspects of multiculturalism are more helpful, and which are less so, for rethinking the task of citizenship education in a pluralistic society.

The Multicultural Critique of the Standard Socialization Approach to Social Studies Education
Curricular Issues

It has become commonplace to charge that the standard socialization approach to social studies education has been characterized by a Eurocentric point of view. Until quite recently, the curriculum has given pride of place to the European (and more specifically, to the white Anglo-Saxon Protestant male) origins of and contributions to American history, culture, religion, and politics. The "canon"–the authoritative collection of texts, artifacts, experiences, and events that is regarded as important enough to be worthy of study in the public schools–has been defined almost exclusively in terms of western civilization. The Eurocentric curriculum has very self-consciously served to perpetuate distinctive norms of truth, beauty, and goodness that conform to the values and inculcate the virtues of the dominant social groups in America.

Critics of Eurocentrism do not deny the importance of European origins and contributions. What critics do assert is that European origins and contributions are neither identical with nor definitive of American culture as a whole. Essentially, critics of the standard socialization approach to social studies education argue that America is not now and never has been a nation with a homogeneous people or culture. Rather, the United States has always been a pluralistic nation consisting of many different religious, racial, ethnic, and cultural groups. Advocates of multiculturalism insist that every level of the social studies curriculum should reflect this pluralistic reality. It is argued that a failure to reflect the realities of our pluralistic society in the social studies curriculum not only distorts our understanding of American history and society, it also has the damaging effect of excluding students (as well as parents and entire communities) who are not from the traditional mainstream culture. Some of the more troubling implications of this exclusion are suggested by Takaki (1993) when he asks,

What happens when historians leave out many of America's peoples? What happens, to borrow the words of Adrienne Rich, "When someone of the authority of a teacher" describes our society, and "you are not in it"? Such an experience can be disorienting–

"a moment of psychic disequilibrium, as if you looked into a mirror and saw nothing." (16)

The primary concern, which critics of the standard philosophy and practice of social studies education share, is that the traditional social studies curriculum has simply failed to adequately encompass or address the histories, experiences, and contributions of the diverse communities to which our students themselves belong. Issues of personal and historical identity are profound in the life of the student, in the classroom learning environment, in the larger school environment, and in society in general. The lack of a sense of personal identity, through the formal subtraction of a student's history, often translates into student alienation, which, in turn, can lead to isolation or arbitrary social attachments. As Cummins (1989) explains, "Transmission models exclude, and therefore, effectively suppress, students' experiences" (65).

Recent calls for rethinking the canon and restructuring the social studies curriculum are, in part, an effort to include the history and culture of all American students. In contrast to the traditional socialization or transmission approach to social studies education, multicultural education is considered a culturally additive process, a process that strives to encompass within the curriculum the diverse and often complex perspectives representing the reality of the American experience. Restructuring the curriculum so that it more adequately reflects the complexities of American history and society as well as the experiences of all Americans can make an important contribution toward providing the identity a student is seeking. However, changing the social studies curriculum may not by itself provide the remedy that is needed, according to advocates of a multicultural approach. This brings us to a consideration of the perceived pedagogical limitations of the traditional socialization approach to social studies education.

Pedagogical Issues

In addition to the problem of a narrowly interpreted curriculum, critics have claimed that the standard socialization approach is rooted in and encourages an overly instrumental conception of the role of teachers, and a passive rather than active conception of student learning. The traditional socialization or citizenship transmission approach to social studies education encourages teachers to adopt the view of "teachers-as-technicians" (Giroux 1988) whose task is to impose a predetermined body of knowledge upon passive and unsuspecting students. The classroom practice of teacher-technicians is typically more oriented toward the textbook than it is toward students. Such teaching is characterized by a never-ending race to cover content, by a willingness to allow externally developed tests to dictate curriculum, and by the imposition upon students of singular and oversimplified perspectives on what are often complex theories, concepts, and historical events. Summarizing research on textbooks, Banks (1992) concludes that

> ... textbooks present a highly selective view of social reality and give students the idea that knowledge is static rather than dynamic, and encourage students to master isolated facts rather than to develop complex understandings of social reality. These studies also indicate that textbooks reinforce the dominant social, economic, and power arrangements within society. Students are encouraged to accept rather than to question these arrangements. (11)

Concerned about the limitations of the traditional socialization approach, Engle and Ochoa (1989) suggest a very different role for social studies teachers, a role that is consistent and compatible with the instructional goals of multiculturalism:

- Involve students in the examination of social problems.
- Teach independent thinking and responsible social criticism.
- Introduce students to diverse and multiple perspectives.
- Encourage students to participate actively in the improvement of society.
- Recognize students as present and capable citizens.
- Include students as partners in curriculum and instruction decision making.
- Develop a democratic/participatory classroom.
- View knowledge as tentative, biased, and incomplete.

Advocates of multiculturalism propose that social studies teachers can better provide the identity a student is seeking by developing a classroom learning environment that allows, invites, and encourages all students to see themselves as active participants in history and society. It is argued that by encouraging all students to more fully and actively participate in the learning process, students are given the important opportunity to empower themselves. "In short, pedagogical approaches that empower students encourage them to assume greater control over setting their own learning goals and to collaborate actively with each other in achieving these goals" (Cummins 1989, 64).

It is also important to note that teachers who do not work toward student empowerment may themselves feel invisible or disempowered. Consequently, some teachers become unwitting conspirators against students. As Cummins (1989) states, "In reality, teachers are themselves being controlled and disempowered by the highest levels of educational hierarchy. They have little or no input into the content of the curriculum, nor into alternative means of achieving curricular objectives" (71). Teachers who feel disenfranchised or embittered by the educational bureaucracy or educational establishment may intentionally and actively work against using or developing instructional approaches that provide opportunities for students to empower themselves, thereby illustrating the old adage, "the pettiness of the powerless."

Ethical-Political Issues

Multiculturalism's critique of the standard socialization approach to education has been viewed by some as part of a larger "culture war" that is taking place in the United States (Hunter 1991). It is certainly true that the standard socialization approach and multiculturalism are caught up in an ongoing debate about the meaning and destiny of our life together as Americans. Who are we? What do we stand for? Where have we come from? Where are we going? How are we to tell the story of our lives as a people? Answers to these fundamental ethical and political questions have a direct bearing on our conceptions of social studies and the tasks

> *Teachers who do not work toward student empowerment may themselves feel invisible or disempowered.*

of citizenship education.

Throughout our history, the idea of "America" has not simply designated a place, a country, or a continent. It has also been associated with a set of ideals and values and with a myth or story that is charged with moral meaning and religious-political significance. This epic story that we tell about ourselves consists of a variety of themes, some of which are in tension with one another.

In its unstated assumptions, the standard socialization approach continues to be rooted in the story of America as a melting pot. As described by Israel Zangwill in his 1909 play "The Melting Pot,"

> America is God's great Crucible, the great Melting Pot where all races of Europe are melting and reforming! Here you stand, good folk, think I, when I see them at Ellis Island, here you stand in your fifty groups with your fifty hatreds and rivalries, but you won't be long like that, brothers, for these are the fires of God. A fig for your feuds and vendettas! Germans and Frenchmen, Irishmen and Englishmen, Jews and Russians–into the Crucible with you all! God is making the American . . . The real American has not yet arrived. He is only in the Crucible, I tell you–he will be the fusion of all races, the coming superman. (Zangwill 1909, 37, quoted in Gollnick and Chinn 1983, 23-24)

There are some obvious reasons why the story of America as a melting pot has proven to be so attractive to so many Americans over the years. It seems to

5. CURRICULUM AND INSTRUCTION IN MULTICULTURAL PERSPECTIVE

set forth a vision that seeks to move us beyond our differences and antagonisms by fusing people from various new and old immigrant groups into a new common and unified American society that is unlike any other the world has ever seen. Such an ideal has not only appealed to America's WASP establishment, it has also been embraced by many immigrants themselves as a viable means for becoming integrated into the mainstream of American society. Although social pressure to conform and even coercion have been constant features of the immigrant and minority experience, it must also be acknowledged that many immigrants willingly anglicized their names, strived to learn English and rid themselves of their accents, and modified or abandoned various customs and styles of dress so that they might more readily "melt" into the American mainstream (ibid., 24). Such an attitude is still frequently expressed in a colloquial fashion by any number of Americans from a variety of different backgrounds who express impatience with "hyphenated" Americanism (Irish-American, African-American, Asian-American, Mexican-American) and assert the sufficiency of a single homogenous definition of what it means to be an American.

The story of the melting pot has historically been linked to an assimilationist agenda that has sought to conform all American citizens to norms that are derived from the Western European traditions of the dominant social groups. This is why some have argued that the melting pot theory of American society is more accurately described as the Anglo-conformity theory. For as Gollnick and Chinn have explained, distinct cultural groups were never really expected to contribute equally to the making of the new and true American as idealized in the story of the melting pot. Rather, they were expected to adopt the WASP culture that historically had shaped most of the political and social institutions of the country. Compulsory school attendance helped to inculcate the language, values, traits, dress, and customs of the dominant culture (ibid., 24, 25).

Yet the story of America as a melting pot that would create the real American—a model American—has never conformed to the multiracial, multiethnic, and religiously diverse reality of America. Although some members of immigrant and minority communities chose to adopt the dominant WASP culture as their own, many others either refused or were denied the opportunity to do so. Members of some minority groups (including such religious minorities as the Amish) have been unwilling to abandon their traditions and identities in order to conform to the values, norms, and styles of mainstream American culture. Instead, they developed the institutions, agencies, services, and power structures that would enable them to maintain their own ethnic communities, enclaves, and identities within the larger society. Across America there are any number of communities—ranging from Harlem to the Little Italys, Chinatowns, and Greektowns of America's major urban areas—that reflect and help to preserve the ethnic identities of their inhabitants. Still other groups were never invited to enter the crucible of the melting pot in the first place. In Zangwill's speech, for example, there is no mention of adding American Indians, Blacks, Hispanics (other than immigrants from Spain), or Asians to the American melting pot (ibid.). Although the unmeltable groups might anglicize their names and show no signs of an accent, they were unable to rid themselves of their skin color or physical characteristics that marked them as different from the idealized model American who was supposed to emerge from the melting pot. Even when these unmeltable groups chose to be the fused American, they were not accepted, primarily because they were not white (ibid.). Thus, an irreducible cultural pluralism has always characterized the American experience.

According to its critics, it is precisely this fact of cultural pluralism that the standard socialization approach to social studies education has failed to address adequately. Rather, it has oversimplified the story of America and has ignored experiences and events that do not conform to an idealized monocultural image of American history and society. Such oversimplification not only presents an ideal that conflicts with reality (Engle and Ochoa 1989), it has also often contributed to the transmission of an overly narrow, uncritical, and chauvinistic conception of citizenship that tends to equate being a good citizen with the acceptance and defense of the status quo—a conception of what it means to be a good citizen that amounts to "my country right or wrong, love it or leave it!"

By way of contrast, multiculturalism insists that the story we tell ourselves about ourselves as Americans must take

The full impact of the revisionist project on American education did not begin to be felt until the emergence of multiculturalism in the 1980s

the fact of cultural pluralism as its starting point. In contrast to the story of America as a melting pot, multiculturalism has offered an alternative story of America as a patchwork of disparate and often conflicting experiences and perspectives. As Breitborde states, "Majority and minority students, mainstream and non-mainstream students, all need to develop the ability to see the world from more than one point of view, because that is the reality in which they live; there is more than one point of view in the world, in the United States, in the cities, and in the schools we share" (1993, 108).

Advocates of multiculturalism also endorse a more self-critical conception of citizenship that fosters and cultivates the student's ability to examine ideas, events, or values from a variety of perspectives. Such a conception of citizenship encourages students to ask questions about whether the status quo measures up to such professed American ideals and values as liberty, equality, and justice for all. In this respect, multiculturalism is correctly viewed by proponents and critics alike as a part of the wave of revisionism that began to sweep through American life and thought in the 1960s.

The single most outstanding feature of the revisionist project has been its focus on the gaps that exist between professed American ideals and values on the one hand, and actual American institutions and social realities on the other hand. Throughout the 1960s and 70s, this spirit of revisionism found expression in a variety of social reform movements that were seeking to transform some aspect of American society. Among the most significant of these was the African American liberation movement, which focused the country's attention on the issue of race in a more direct and sustained fashion than at any other time in our history since the Civil War. Both the civil rights movement, with its struggle for political empowerment, and the black power movement, with its stress on cultural self-determination and issues of cultural pride and self-esteem, played a major role in shaping the ethical-political agenda of what would later come to be known as multiculturalism.

Similarly, the women's movement, and its theoretical expression in the form of feminism, introduced the category of gender as an analytical tool for the reinterpretation of history and society, thereby calling our attention to the variety of ideological and institutional factors that have contributed to the subordination of women in America and around the world. For its part, the student movement of the 1960s questioned the balance of power between older and younger generations in American schools and universities and agitated for a greater voice in the process of decision making and institution building. And finally, the peace movement, in its opposition to the war in Vietnam, and subsequently in its opposition to the nuclear arms race and to military intervention in Latin America and elsewhere, sought to expose the contradictions between the militarism and imperialism of American foreign policy on the one hand, and America's professed commitment to peace, democracy, and the self-determination of peoples on the other hand.

These social reform movements not only had an impact on American society, law, and politics, they also had an impact on American education. One indication of this impact was the growth of such new programs as Black or African American studies, Chicano studies, and Women's studies in the 1960s and 1970s. But the full impact of the revisionist project on American education did not begin to be felt until the emergence of multiculturalism in the 1980s. Indeed, the revisionist preoccupation with issues of race and gender, liberation and empowerment, along with such additional and related issues as ethnicity, language, religion, and culture, are at the very heart of multiculturalism.

Beyond Socialization and Multiculturalism

Multiculturalism's attention to diverse experiences and perspectives and to critical questions about the status quo are clearly among its most controversial features. Liberals such as Arthur Schlesinger (1992) have accused multiculturalism of sowing seeds of division between Americans by concentrating too much on what divides them rather than on what unites them. And conservatives like William Bennett (1992) have accused multiculturalism of undermining the task of citizenship education by concentrating too much on the shortcomings rather than the accomplishments of traditional American values, virtues, and institutions. On the other hand, such figures as Gerald Graff (1992) have argued that what has led to social divisiveness and an increasingly widespread cynicism about American ideals and institutions is not multiculturalism, but rather the inequitable distribution of power and resources along the lines of class, race, gender, and ethnicity that multiculturalism has in part sought to address. Indeed, as we have argued above, multiculturalism itself is best viewed as part of a broader movement that is seeking to remedy these inequities through the intellectual and moral reformation of society.

However, one of the main challenges facing any movement for social change is the task of fashioning a discursive strategy that successfully balances the language of critique with the language of appreciation and possibility (Giroux 1988, 128). Up to this point, multiculturalism has not risen to this challenge. On the contrary, proponents of multiculturalism have too often employed a quasi-revolutionary rhetoric that seems to repudiate all traditional American ideals and institutions as morally bankrupt and devoid of the resources necessary for solving the problems of racism, poverty, and injustice. Thus, although the socialization approach has been too uncritical in its presentation and appraisal of American history, society, and culture, the discourse of multiculturalism has often been too extreme in its condemnation. We are thus forced to admit that there is much truth in the claims by such otherwise diverse critics of multiculturalism as Schlesinger and Bennett.

Up to this point, despite its own best intentions, the discourse of multiculturalism does seem to have done as much to "disunite" America as it has done to mobilize a popular movement for social justice. And it seems often to have encouraged a premature abandonment of traditional American ideals, values, and institutions without having identified or created any clear or practical alternatives. Although the need for the intellectual and moral reformation of American schools and society remains great, it is time to rethink the strategy and discourse that is most appropriate for such a project.

We believe that a growing number of social studies educators are already, or will soon become, dissatisfied with the either/or alternative presented to them by the socialization versus multiculturalism debate. Either they support the status quo in order to defend the United States and its schools against dangerous revolutionaries, or they join in an assault upon traditional American ideals, values, and institutions. Although there remain die-hard proponents of socialization and hard-core advocates of multiculturalism who are unable to see anything of value in their opponents' positions, we believe that there are many teachers who recognize that both approaches have strengths and weaknesses.

We believe a more balanced approach is warranted, an approach that preserves what is valuable while moving beyond the limitations of both socialization and multiculturalism. This alternative must recognize that both socialization and multiculturalism, despite their obvious and very real differences, are vital to education for citizenship in a democratic society.

Social studies educators must work to instill in their students a commitment and allegiance to our democratic ideals, but also teach the skills that enable students intelligently to examine those same democratic ideals within the context of their daily lives. Both the transmission of

5. CURRICULUM AND INSTRUCTION IN MULTICULTURAL PERSPECTIVE

values and knowledge and the critical examination of multiple perspectives are essential parts of education for citizenship in a pluralistic democracy.

Finding a balance between socialization and multicultural education can help to discourage polarization while encouraging critical discourse about the aims and purposes of social studies education. Only such a balanced perspective can move us beyond the socialization versus multiculturalism debate to a position that embraces both commitment and critique.

References

Banks, James A. "The Canon Debate, Knowledge Construction, and Multicultural Education." *Educational Researcher* 22 (June-July 1993): 4-14.

Barr, Robert, James L. Barth, and S. Samuel Shermis. *Defining the Social Studies*. Bulletin no. 51. Washington, D.C.: National Council for the Social Studies, 1977.

Barth, James A. "Social Studies: There Is A History, There Is A Body, But Is It Worth Saving?" *Social Education* 57 (February 1993): 56-57.

Bennett, William J. *The De-Valuing of America: The Fight for Our Culture and Our Children*. New York: Summit Books, 1992.

Breitborde, Lawrence. "Multiculturalism and Cultural Relativism After the Commemoration." *Social Education* 57 (March 1993): 104-108.

Cummins, Jim. *Empowering Minority Students*. Sacramento, Calif.: Association For Bilingual Education, 1989.

Engle, Shirley, and Anna S. Ochoa. *Education for Democratic Citizenship*. New York: Teachers College Press, 1988.

Giroux, Henry A. *Teachers as Intellectuals: Toward a Critical Pedagogy of Learning*. New York: Bergin & Garvey, 1988.

Gollnick, Donna M., and Phillip C. Chinn. *Multicultural Education in a Pluralistic Society*. St. Louis: Mosby, 1983.

Graff, Gerald. *Beyond the Culture Wars: How Teaching the Conflicts Can Revitalize American Education*. New York: W.W. Norton, 1992.

Hunter, James Davison. *Culture Wars: The Struggle to Define America*. New York: Basic Books, 1991.

Leming, James S. "Ideological Perspectives Within The Social Studies Profession: An Empirical Examination Of The 'Two Cultures' Thesis." *Theory and Research in Social Education* 3 (Summer 1992): 293-312.

———. "The Two Cultures of Social Studies Education." *Social Education* 53 (October 1989): 404-408.

Schlesinger, Arthur M. *The Disuniting of America*. New York: W.W. Norton, 1992.

Sears, Alan, and Jim Parsons. "Towards Critical Thinking As An Ethnic." *Theory and Research in Social Education* 1 (Winter 1991): 45-68.

Takaki, Ronald. *A Different Mirror: A History of Multicultural America*. Boston: Little, Brown, 1993.

Bruce Grelle is Associate Professor and Director of the Religion and Public Education Resource Center in the Department of Religious Studies at California State University, Chico. Devon Metzger is Professor of Education at California State University, Chico.

Multiculturalism: Practical Considerations for Curricular Change

TONY R. SANCHEZ

Tony R. Sanchez is an assistant professor of education at Indiana University Northwest, Gary, Indiana.

Many school districts today are jumping on the multicultural bandwagon by adopting, or at least encouraging, a more divisified curriculum. Proponents of multiculturalism call for an interdisciplinary approach that draws from and spans all subject areas, an approach that I believe is the most effective. I offer here a framework designed to be useful to teachers who want to change their personal or curricular perspective from one that is "mainstream" to one that is more "diverse" and are willing to incorporate that new perspective into whatever subject matter they teach.

Unfortunately, misconstruing the purposes or definition of multicultural education, many teachers either back off from it entirely or teach about different groups sequentially, resulting in a fragmented and isolated treatment. We do the latter when we assign specific groups to specific months (Black History Month, Hispanic Heritage Month, Women's History Month). During one of these periods, the attitude is that teachers will deal with that group for thirty days (maximum) and then return to the mainstream curriculum. Multiculturalism, however, belongs within the framework of the existing curriculum.

The Teacher's Role

By exposing our students to other cultures (whether the contributions of various groups or nonmainstream perspectives of an event or concept), we help them learn about other people's lifestyles and values. This awareness in turn may alter negative, stereotypic thinking, reduce intolerance, and promote cooperation (Cohen 1986). It will also expand *your* personal horizons as well as your students'.

As an educator interested in such an outcome, what might your creed be? I suspect something like this: *Within my course I will promote the recognition and understanding of diversity, and teach respect for it. By doing so, I hope not only to provide personal enrichment but also, through my teaching and actions, to help develop positive, productive interactions and attitudes.*

To put this creed into action, you most likely will do the following: teach the perspectives of the mainstream culture (don't assume students already know them); teach the perspectives of other cultures (with the message: they're equally valid to some); and examine similarities and differences between cultures (Hernandez 1989). This last point is certainly the most challenging; *both* similarities and differences should be addressed so that your students move from merely tolerating differences to viewing them as acceptable, desirable, and valuable (Noar 1989).

Implementing a multicultural curriculum requires specific components. These include (1) a teacher willing to critically evaluate his or her personal perspectives, (2) instructional materials that provide diverse but accurate perspectives, and (3) general goals and objectives.

Analyzing Your Attitude

As the teacher, you implement and guide the questioning, reasoning, analysis, and truth-seeking in your classroom. As such, you must consider your personal attitudes toward your subject area—negative and positive—and the fact that they can't be hidden from your students. What exactly is your level of commitment to the value of diverse perspectives?

Coming to grips with your values and attitudes, changing some, and developing sensitivity to diversity will require time—and courage. It will depend on your willingness to

5. CURRICULUM AND INSTRUCTION IN MULTICULTURAL PERSPECTIVE

work on your new perspective. Without this commitment, you may find yourself saying, "I'm not very comfortable with this diverse curriculum I'm trying out, but I think it's working out." What that really means is, "It's not working because I don't really believe in it." If that becomes the case, back off. Don't deceive yourself and your students. The payoff for this self-examination will be that the ugliness of prejudice, rejection, and exclusion—all results of ignorance and misinformation—will have no place in your classroom. You will be sensitizing your students not only to the mechanics of learning but also to their own worth and value. The rest of the process will be anticlimactic by comparison with this step.

Choosing Instructional Materials

In the next step of the process, you examine and select instructional materials that reflect accurate, quality (i.e., true) information. Choose materials that you're comfortable with, that won't require a radical change in your style (a change that many teachers needlessly fear).

Danger of Relying on Textbooks

Textbooks, as we know, account for most of the teaching/learning process (Sewall 1987). Furthermore, "Teachers tend to not only rely on, but believe in, the textbook as the source of knowledge" (Fitzgerald 1979).

Recent evaluations indicate that a diverse curriculum requires a change in this attitude. Various cultural/ethnic groups have brought attention to bear on the depiction of their respective cultures in textbooks (Garcia and Florez-Tighe 1986). The attitude shared by these groups can be summed up as follows: "The sole false perspective is that which claims to be the only one there is" (Gasset, cited in Smith and Otero 1982). The multicultural movement does *not* require abandonment of the mainstream perspective. This would only lead to isolated enclaves, fragmentation, and polarization. On the contrary, the movement promotes integrating a variety of perspectives, which must include the mainstream (Banks 1991).

Bias in textbooks appears in several forms, including stereotyping, omissions, distortions, overrepresentation in certain contexts, romanticized portrayals, token representations, and biased language. As educators, we need to examine and evaluate these materials in terms of content, language, and illustrations. Though textbook bias has been reduced in some quarters, it still remains, its manifestations sometimes blatant and other times subtle (Garcia and Florez-Tighe 1986).

How do we go about identifying such bias? We will need to explore, compare, contrast, question, and evaluate information from multiple sources (which may include students, peers, and the community). Eventually, we will strengthen our evaluative skills so that we can uncover discrepancies and contradictions. Analyzing and questioning the accuracy of the content we teach may represent a major departure for us, but it may also keep us from becoming "adults who believe everything they read—or read only what they wish to believe" (Klein 1985, 27). Passing on critical reading skills to our students may ultimately be our greatest legacy to them.

Guidelines for Multicultural Curriculum

Here are some basic guidelines to keep in mind as you purposively change your curricular perspective (Gaines 1992):

Go beyond a trivializing, "tourist" curriculum. A diversity curriculum is more than holidays, special months, food, and costumes. Rather, it means coming to know the values, viewpoints, and meaningful traditions that characterize individuals and groups (and you can still include food and costumes). These interpretations must be regular, built-in components of your subject area.

Go beyond tokenism. Do you enrich your class with African American or Hispanic perspectives simply because you have some black or Mexican students? Or, instead, do you employ multiple, unbiased perspectives because you recognize the value of alternative interpretations and want to promote acceptance and respect for different experiences and viewpoints? The former approach is characteristic of a teacher who doesn't really believe in or is uncomfortable with the notion of diversity in his or her subject area; the teacher's efforts will come off as phony. The latter approach characterizes a teacher who appreciates diversity.

Go beyond stereotyping. Give students continuous opportunities to examine images for accuracy. Too often a student's stereotypic perception goes unchallenged and therefore becomes solidified as truth. In this regard, you must expect to handle incidences of bias and ignorance that arise in the classroom. What should you do on such occasions? Here are four pieces of advice that I have found helpful:

1. *Don't ignore comments or questions that reflect misinformation.* Address the issue while a direct connection to the goals of the curriculum can still be made. Your silence on such matters can only be interpreted as confirmation.

2. *Don't excuse comments or questions that could be interpreted as culturally or racially insulting.* The students who are targets of such remarks (which can very quickly escalate into full-blown classroom incidents) will segregate themselves for protection—something that you didn't provide.

3. *Don't be afraid to step in to handle and clarify a situation.* Doing something on the spot is certainly preferable to doing nothing and allowing things to fester.

4. *Don't forget your commitment.* Your mission in establishing a diverse curriculum is to expand your students' knowledge so that they will develop more positive attitudes and behaviors that will enable them to interact effectively in our diverse society. Your responsibility in the mission is consistency.

Goals and Objectives

What learning outcomes should a multicultural curriculum promote? The following goals are frequently found in a diversified curriculum (Hernandez 1989; Kosmoski 1989):

To help students recognize and understand the values and experiences of one's own ethnic/cultural heritage

To promote sensitivity to diverse ethnicities/cultures through exposure to other cultural perspectives

To develop an awareness and respect for the similarities and differences among diverse groups

To identify, challenge, and dispel ethnic/cultural stereotyping, prejudice, and discrimination in behavior, textbooks, and other instructional materials

Goals are, of course, intended to be guidelines. A multicultural curriculum can only be effective when the teacher is given choices as to how to achieve such goals within his or her subject area or grade level. An inappropriate or too narrowly focused curriculum—a product of haste and pressure to conform—will likely result when teachers are not free to make those decisions. How to integrate a multicultural perspective into the curriculum rather than making it a blatant "add-on" is the main issue they face. Teachers usually approach this task by trial and error. Using a single, all-encompassing model to implement a diverse curriculum is not a good idea because no model can provide what is effective for all students at all times and under all circumstances. Rather, the teacher must systematically incorporate content and strategies in a comfortable balance. The process requires time, with the teacher "testing the waters" on a by-unit or by-lesson basis.

As an initial effort, many teachers employ a "cultural" unit or lesson in their standard monocentric curricula. It is usually additive instead of integral, but it serves the important purpose of "breaking the multicultural ice." Such an initial effort is almost always necessary to allow the educator to comfortably ease into a truly diverse curriculum.

Development and implementation of a multicultural curriculum must eventually be evaluated for effectiveness (California State Department of Education 1979). What must be assessed? Three chief components are (1) achievement; (2) student behavior; and (3) student attitudes (Hernandez 1989). Achievement, the primary focus of American education, can be fairly assessed through various conventional measures. Student behavior can be monitored and evaluated formally (questionnaires, surveys, discussion groups, reduced number of disruptive incidents) and informally (teacher observations of cooperative interactions, voluntary student participation and assistance, student willingness to explore cultural similarities and differences). Student attitudes are the most difficult to assess for change. The validity of evaluation is dependent on the instrument used and should always be interpreted with caution. Research indicates that attitude change as a goal of multicultural education is indeed feasible. Studies of the use of content and strategies to change cultural/ethnic/racial attitudes and reduce prejudice show positive results, even when complex, multiple variables, such as age, socioeconomic status, and social institutions, are involved (Sanchez 1991). Establishing the foundation for such change—through diverse content and teacher modeling—cannot guarantee positive attitude changes. As educators, however, we must be willing to take the chance that this endeavor will promote understanding, acceptance, and respect.

REFERENCES

Banks, J. A. 1991. *Teaching strategies for ethnic studies.* 5th ed. Needham Heights, Mass.: Allyn and Bacon.

California State Department of Education. 1979. *Guide for multicultural education.* Sacramento, Calif.: California State Department of Education.

Cohen, C. B. 1986. Teaching about ethnic diversity. *ERIC Digest* 32: 1–2.

Fitzgerald, F. 1979. *America revisited.* Boston, Mass.: Atlantic Monthly Press/Little, Brown.

Gaines, L. 1992. What you can do. *Creative Classroom* (Sept.): 115.

Garcia, J., and V. Florez-Tighe. 1986. The portrayal of Blacks, Hispanics, and Native Americans in recent basal reading series. *Equity and Excellence* 22(4-6): 72–76.

Hernandez, H. 1989. *Multicultural education.* Columbus, Ohio: Merrill.

Klein, G. 1985. *Reading into racism.* London: Routledge and Kegan Paul.

Kosmoski, G. J. 1989. *Multicultural education.* Chicago: Third World Press.

Noar, G. 1989. *Sensitizing teachers to ethnic groups.* Needham Heights, Mass.: Allyn and Bacon.

Sanchez, T. R. 1991. *The effects of knowledge acquisition about Blacks on the racial attitudes of White high school sophomores.* Ann Arbor, Mich.: University Microfilms, Inc.

Sewall, G. T. 1987. *American history textbooks: An assessment of quality.* New York: Columbia University, Teachers College, Educational Excellence Network.

Smith, G. R., and G. Otero. 1982. *Teaching about cultural awareness.* Denver, Col.: University of Denver, Center for Teaching International Relations.

Who Needs Multicultural Education? White Students, U.S. History, and the Construction of a Usable Past

John S. Wills

University of Rochester

This article evaluates the efforts of three teachers at a predominantly white middle school to create a multicultural U.S. history curriculum by focusing on the experiences of enslaved African Americans during the Civil War. I argue that this focus unintentionally undermines students' ability to use history as a resource for thinking about contemporary race relations. I conclude with some suggestions for creating a multicultural history curriculum that will benefit both white students and students of color.

The multicultural education debate has intensified in recent years, particularly around efforts to reform the history and social science curriculum to make it more multicultural. Critics (Bloom 1989; D'Souza 1991; Ravitch 1990; Schlesinger 1992) have attacked multicultural educators as radicals out of touch with mainstream American society, have argued that the emphasis on race and ethnicity in the curriculum is divisive, and have attacked multicultural curricula as intellectually weak and victim to political correctness.

An equally heated debate rages in California. In 1987 the California State Board of Education adopted a new *History-Social Science Framework* (1988). While this framework increased the history requirements, emphasized studying major historical periods and events in depth, and emphasized the use of literature and primary source documents, its call for a multicultural perspective in the teaching of U.S. and world history caused controversy. According to California's *History-Social Science Framework*, a multicultural perspective necessitates a history that "reflect[s] the experiences of men and women of different racial, religious, and ethnic groups," and also presents U.S. history as a "complex story of many peoples and one nation," an "unfinished struggle to realize the ideals of the Declaration of Independence and the Constitution" (1988:5).

After all textbooks that publishers submitted were rejected because they did not attend sufficiently to diversity, a series of textbooks for kindergarten through eighth grade published by Houghton Mifflin and an additional eighth grade U.S. history textbook published by Holt, Rinehart, and Winston were eventually approved for adoption.

Community organizations throughout California, representing many racial, ethnic, and religious groups, did not think that these textbooks were progressive and multicultural. African Americans, Asian Americans, Native Americans, Mexican Americans, Jews, and Muslims argued that the new Houghton Mifflin textbooks were biased, that events and people were omitted or misrepresented, that the achievements of whites were privileged over nonwhites, and that racial, ethnic, and religious groups were stereotyped (Banks and Trombley 1990; Drummond 1992; King 1992; Trombley 1990a, 1990b, 1991). Diverse community groups feared that these textbooks would perpetuate stereotypes and promote prejudice among the students who used them. Despite the intensity of this debate, most school districts introduced these textbooks in the fall of 1991. Now they are used in virtually all districts in California.

I will not review the California or the national debate; instead I will address two issues in relation to this debate. First is the issue of audience. Underlying much of this debate is the assumption that students of color are the primary audience for multicultural education. Although there are many different definitions and models of multicultural education (Gibson 1976; Sleeter and Grant 1987; Suzuki 1984), most writers have focused on the benefits that a multicultural curriculum holds for students of color. For example, a multicultural curriculum can enhance the academic success of minority students (Ogbu 1992), or it can provide these students with materials that foster the development of strong minority-cultural identities (McCarthy 1990). Including historical figures of color in U.S. history, as well as their perspectives on historical events, will allow students of color to see themselves in history, to hear the stories of their people, and to recognize the contributions of their ancestors to U.S. history.

While it is important to provide students of color with a history of the United States which recognizes the presence and contributions of their ancestors, it is equally important to recognize that a more inclusive, multicultural history of the United States also holds potential benefits for white students, something that has been noted (Banks 1989) but largely ignored in this debate.

Second is the issue of what counts as a multicultural history in actual classrooms. Empirical data on which to argue the pros and cons of multicultural reform in history and social science have been missing from the debate. Anecdotal evidence has been cited, and the scholarly arguments are rarely grounded in the happenings in actual classrooms. While a multicultural history curriculum in classrooms is likely to be very different from one place to another throughout the United States, there is virtually no literature on this topic (Mehan et al. 1995). Therefore it is difficult to measure the worth of arguments concerning multicultural reform of the history and social science curriculum.

I address these two issues by presenting some findings from a case study of three teachers' efforts to present a multicultural history of the United States in a predominantly white, suburban middle school. Specifically, I want to discuss one teacher's efforts to provide her students with a more inclusive, multicultural history of the United States by focusing on the experiences of African Americans through an in-depth study of southern slavery during the Civil War period. After discussing the methodology and setting of my case study, I present excerpts from a classroom discussion of the uprisings/riots in Los Angeles following the verdict in the first trial of the officers accused of beating Rodney King. I then use this discussion as a vantage point from which to present and analyze the curriculum in use in this classroom, arguing that the exclusive focus on the experiences of slaves in the Civil War South as a means of including African Americans in U.S. history and the emphasis on the immorality of slavery unintentionally undermine students' ability to effectively use history as a context for thinking and talking about contemporary race relations. Following this, I discuss the lessons we can learn from this classroom for multicultural reform of the history and social science curriculum, and then I conclude with some remarks on the value of a multicultural history for white students.

An Ethnographically Informed Discourse Analysis of the Curriculum

The "impact" that textbooks and other curriculum have on the knowledge, attitudes, and beliefs of students is complex. The reading or use of cultural texts (broadly defined) is not a simple process involving the transmission and consumption of meaning that is located "in" the text (Liebes and Katz 1990; Long 1986; Press 1991; Radway 1984; Shively 1992). It is rather a social and cultural process involving the fabrication (Griswold 1987) or construction of textual meaning, meaning that is not located in the text but in the interaction between cultural texts and their readers.

Luke, de Castell, and Luke, in a discussion of the authority of the school textbook, questioned this transmission-consumption view of the relationship between textbooks and student knowledge, and argued for

> a more interactive and pragmatic explanation of text apprehension, whereby meaning is contingent on the interaction between the reader's prior knowledge, the institutional setting within which the reading task is situated, the teacher who teaches the text, and the distinctive features of the textbook *per se.* [1983:125, italics in original; see also Apple 1993; Apple and Christian-Smith 1991; McNeil 1981]

Recent studies have found that the implemented curriculum, what teachers actually teach in the classroom, is not a simple reflection of the official curriculum (Cohen et al. 1990; Stevenson and Baker 1991) and that textbooks do not dictate the content of classroom instruction (Freeman and Porter 1989). Mediating factors influence the construction of classroom knowledge, from the teacher's perceived need to maintain order and control in the classroom (McNeil 1981, 1986) to the cultural biases and assumptions teachers and students bring with them into the classroom, biases that can affect their realization of curriculum content (Wills 1994).

In addition, the construction of knowledge in the classroom is not confined to the use of textbooks in the fabrication of historical meaning. Teachers draw upon a variety of resources, from documentary and popular films to laserdisc presentations, literature, primary source documents, role playing and cooperative learning activities, and a variety of reference materials from school and public libraries. Therefore an investigation of the impact of textbooks and other curriculum on student knowledge, attitudes, and beliefs necessitates an "ethnography of the curriculum," in which teachers' and students' use of educational and popular materials in constructing knowledge in actual classrooms is examined. In this way we can better understand the processes whereby the metaphors, modes of representation, and arguments present in the curriculum make their way into teachers' and students' discourse.

To investigate the role of curriculum in constructing students' knowledge of racial and ethnic groups in U.S. history, I spent ten months at a school that I am calling "Canyon Middle School," from September 1991 through June 1992, observing and videotaping lessons in three eighth-grade U.S. history classrooms. Canyon Middle School is a predominantly white (78%), suburban school located in San Diego County, California. The three teachers I observed—"Judy," "Ruth," and "Tom"—are white, as am I. I videotaped a total of 130 lessons in these three classrooms and transcribed the audio portion of these videotapes for analysis of classroom talk. Videotaped lessons include teacher lectures and discussions, which often draw upon the textbook and other materials, as well as documentary and popular films, laserdisc presentations and filmstrips, student presentations, skits, and cooperative learning activities.

I analyzed student work including essays, "Fact or Fiction" books on Native Americans, journal writing, Civil War newspapers, a variety of Revolutionary War projects, reports on Native American leaders, and Constitution board games created by the students. My observations were also supplemented by conversations with the teachers about specific lessons and their teaching in general, as well as formal interviews with the teachers and a small group of students in Judy's class. Finally, borrowing an idea from Wertsch and O'Connor (1994), I asked students in Judy's, Ruth's, and Tom's U.S. history classes to write brief narrative descriptions of U.S. history. Thus, through extensive observation, interviews, microanalysis of classroom discourse, and content analysis of curricular materials and student work, I was able to record not only how students came to understand the place of racial and ethnic groups in U.S. history but also the role of the curriculum, mediated by the tacit cultural knowledge of students and teachers, in the construction of their historical knowledge.

5. CURRICULUM AND INSTRUCTION IN MULTICULTURAL PERSPECTIVE

The three teachers were chosen for their very different teaching styles and interests, and their different views concerning a multicultural history of the United States. Judy, who had been teaching for six years, was interested in giving her students an understanding of the perspectives of different groups in U.S. history through cooperative learning activities and small group projects. This included making them aware of the injustices some groups have experienced in the United States. While all three teachers were using the new Houghton Mifflin textbook *A More Perfect Union* (Armento et al. 1991) for the first time, Judy was also piloting curriculum from the Teachers' Curriculum Institute in Palo Alto, California (TCI 1992), a packet of materials containing slide lectures and a variety of cooperative learning activities, including activities intended to help students see historical events from multiple perspectives.

Ruth, who had taught at Canyon Middle School since it opened 21 years ago, wanted to make her students aware of the contributions of diverse cultures and give them an appreciation of cultural diversity. Ruth favored individual and group projects, as well as role-playing activities that reenacted historical events. While her students sometimes read from the textbook during class, she viewed the textbook—like Judy—as one resource among many that the students could draw upon when working on their projects.

Tom, who had also taught at Canyon Middle School since it opened, wanted his students to learn both the good and the bad in U.S. history, and he regularly noted the "unfairness" that different groups had experienced in the United States. Unlike Judy and Ruth, Tom's teaching was centered around the textbook. He had his students read each textbook chapter for homework, answer the review questions, and then discuss the material the next day in class. Movies, student reports, and articles on historical periods or events supplemented the textbook.

The Historical Context of Contemporary Race Relations

In this section I present an excerpt from a discussion in Judy's class in which she encouraged her students to use their knowledge of the experiences of African Americans in U.S. history to think about contemporary race relations. I focus specifically on Judy's class for two reasons: this was one of the most controversial discussions concerning race relations in the three classrooms that I observed, and Judy is explicitly encouraging her students to use history as a resource in understanding contemporary events.

In May 1991, Judy's students were studying the Civil War period. Following the guidelines of the California *History-Social Science Framework,* which argues for studying major historical events and periods in depth, Judy spent eight weeks studying the Civil War period, with a specific emphasis on learning about the experiences of enslaved African Americans in the South. Judy's intention was not only to teach her students about the growing conflict between the North and the South but also to make them aware of the cruelties, indignities, and injustices African Americans had experienced under slavery.

Judy used the documentary film *Roots of Resistance: The Underground Railroad,* which depicts the resistance of slaves to slavery, the Underground Railroad, the Fugitive Slave Act, and the Dred Scott decision, as a starting point for discussing southern slavery. Her students had also read the first few chapters in *A More Perfect Union,* dealing with slavery and the growing conflict between North and South, and they were also reading *To Be a Slave* (Lester 1968), a collection of interviews of African Americans who experienced slavery firsthand.

Current events transformed a strictly historical discussion of southern slavery into an opportunity to connect history to current events. The verdict had been announced in the first trial of the Los Angeles officers accused of beating Rodney King, followed by the uprising/riots in Los Angeles. Judy asked her students to draw upon their knowledge of African Americans in U.S. history to talk about the common experiences of African Americans in U.S. society.

Judy began this discussion by emphasizing that the inequities that African Americans faced in U.S. society had not changed from the Civil War to the present. Judy stressed to her students that the uprising/riots in Los Angeles affect all of us:

(1) Teacher: I strongly encourage all of you to pay attention to this kinda stuff because, um, this problem is not that far away from us. We have ghettos and barrios right here in San Diego, where people live who are just as angry as those people in L.A., who are just as angry as those slaves who feel totally disenfranchised and feel like there is no government protection for them. They have freedom, but do they have equality? The same issue. You know, we can look at the issue today of equality: who has equality? Who has equal opportunity under the law, or under our society, as the slaves looked at once they were freed in 1860, in 1863? Same type of thing, and people in L.A. are saying the exactly same—this exact same thing. That there is no equality. We have no opportunity. We have no jobs. The number one problem that people who live in, in those neighborhoods talk about is police brutality. That they don't have the same rights under the law.

Freedom, equality, economic opportunity, brutality, equal protection, and rights under the law—these are the issues that link the common experiences and concerns of African Americans in the United States. For Judy, and also for Ruth and Tom (and, frankly, for any history teacher I have ever talked to), the point of history is that it speaks to the present. It helps us to understand the role of the past in shaping current events. Judy wanted to help her students see that the struggle for freedom, equality, equal protection, and rights under the law are common experiences that unite African Americans today with African Americans in the past. But as the discussion continues, it becomes apparent that these links between the past and the present are not at all obvious to the students:

(1) Teacher: So, you know, my question to you is: have things changed that much? Or do we still have these same kinds of issues in our society? Do we think that our society is, is—um, has equality for everybody? Or not? Carl?
(2) Carl: I don't know. I think, I think [inaudible] bring it upon themselves because—
(3) Teacher: Okay. How would they do that?
(4) Carl: 'Cause I don't—I mean. I mean, I'm not racist against black people or anything, but if you look at, like, all the minorities that we've had in our country, for the last 20

or 30 years—the Japanese and the, the, um, Philippines, and everything. They've all come to our country and they've started businesses and, it'll have, places like the black people do down in the 'hood and everything. They have their own businesses, and the Koreans have—have businesses, but I think black people—

(5) Teacher: Let me play devil's advocate with you for a minute here, and say to you, um, those people were not brought here as slaves.

(6) Carl: Well yeah, but, I mean, there are no slaves anymore, I mean. I mean—mean, there's plenty of people who are, are racist against [them], against other, other minorities, not just blacks.

(7) Teacher: Uh huh.

(8) Carl: And—but they've put up with it, and they've gone and—against odds, they've started businesses, but black people, I mean—I mean, I'm not saying all of them 'cause there are a lot of successful black people, but a lot of 'em just kind of think that everybody's against 'em, and they just stood down there and they don't have jobs and stuff, and they think that everybody's against 'em.

(9) Teacher: Okay. Patty?

(10) Patty: Well in response to what Carl said, I don't know if he thinks about this, but it's possible that a lot of blacks feel like they're—that everyone's against them because—through, I mean, through their descendants they've been told about, through the people before them they've been told about slavery. And a lot of times people, people, I guess—when you start hearing things over and over again and you—when you hear that, that you're inferior, you're gonna start to believe it. It's not—I mean, I understand what Carl's saying, but it's not, it's not that they don't wanna try, I don't think. It's just that they believe that they can't because that's what they've been told.

(11) Teacher: How many of you read *Roll of Thunder, Hear My Cry* in here? [*A few hands go up.*] And *Roll of Thunder* was written about a time during the Depression. And how were the blacks treated in that book? Were they treated as if they were equals, Patty?

(12) Patty: No.

(13) Teacher: And we're looking at a time that is roughly sixty years after the Civil War ended. So they weren't treated as equals then either, were they?

Carl responds to Judy's question by stating that he thinks African Americans "bring it upon themselves" (line 2). While assuring Judy and the other students that he's not a racist (line 4), Carl wonders why other minorities like the Japanese, Koreans, and Filipinos have started businesses and succeeded economically while African Americans have not. In response to Carl's comments Judy interjects a statement that hints at the historical experiences of African Americans: "those people [other minorities] were not brought here as slaves" (line 5). Carl responds, "Well yeah, but, I mean, there are no slaves anymore" (line 6).

Carl is correct. There are no slaves anymore. While African Americans did experience cruelty, brutality, and horrible atrocities and injustices under slavery, experiences that the students have been studying, that is a "problem" that was corrected many years ago. Slavery is "history," an event in the past that had no obvious connection to the present for Carl. As a consequence, Carl concludes that, although there are some successful blacks, a lot of African Americans simply believe that everyone is against them and, so, are not motivated to get jobs.

At this point Patty (line 10) attempts to enlighten Carl about the effects that the legacy of slavery has on present-day African Americans. It is not that African Americans do not want to succeed economically but that they believe everyone is against them and they are inferior to whites and other minority groups, because that is what they have told themselves year after year. For Patty, the condition of blacks today is the unfortunate consequence of remembering the history of their ancestors, a history that makes them believe in their own inferiority.

Judy rejoins the discussion (line 11), asking if any of the students have read Mildred D. Taylor's *Roll of Thunder, Hear My Cry* (1976), one of the selections that students can read in their literature course. Only a few of the students have read this book (and so Judy does not continue with this point), which recounts the experiences of Cassie Logan and her family, who are black, in the South during the Great Depression, experiences that expose the racism, discrimination, and injustices African Americans must endure in more recent American society. Judy's question is meant to turn attention away from African Americans themselves (i.e., what's wrong with these people?) to the issue of how blacks have been treated in American society—under slavery, during the Great Depression, and today. She is asserting that African Americans have not been treated as equals by whites, a continuous problem in race relations throughout U.S. history.

What are we to make of Carl's and Patty's comments? Why couldn't they make the connections between the past and the present that were so obvious to Judy? These are exactly the questions Judy asked herself after this lesson. She expressed to me her frustration and disappointment over her students' seeming inability to connect past and present. The discussion hadn't gone at all the way the teacher wanted it to. Why didn't this lesson work?

This question is important, not only because her lesson seemed to be a "failure" but because it can provide us with a vantage point for analyzing the curriculum in use in contemporary classrooms. Given that past histories of the Civil War period have either ignored the experiences of enslaved African Americans altogether or portrayed slavery as a benign social institution, shouldn't we embrace an approach that studies the experiences of African Americans under slavery as a much needed improvement in the teaching of U.S. history?

Frankly, I was very impressed with the work that was being done in Judy's classroom. But this lesson, and Judy's reaction to it, was my first indication that the new multicultural approach might not be all it seemed to be. How should we make sense of Carl's comments? The easy answer is that, in spite of his denials, Carl is a racist, and these racist views explain his failure to acknowledge the inequities in race relations between blacks and whites throughout U.S. history. One could simply dismiss Carl by saying he "just doesn't get it" and so he's not going to benefit from a valuable approach to including African Americans in U.S. history. We could also conclude that Carl just wasn't paying attention, he wasn't doing the readings and assignments, and so he missed the connection that Judy was trying to make.

But neither one of these explanations is very satisfying. In fact, Carl is a good student, one of the more vocal ones at that. And concluding that Carl is a racist just does not fit with my yearlong observations of him in Judy's classroom.

5. CURRICULUM AND INSTRUCTION IN MULTICULTURAL PERSPECTIVE

A more satisfying line of inquiry is to ask what is it about the curriculum in use that makes Carl's comments "sensible," given the way in which African Americans are presented in U.S. history, that is, as slaves in the Civil War South.

In fact, Carl provides a clue to this line of thinking when he notes that "there are no slaves anymore" (line 6). Stated simply, an unintended consequence of focusing on the experiences of slaves during the Civil War is that students' historical understandings of the experiences of African Americans with regards to racism, discrimination, and injustice become anchored in slavery. The injustices experienced by African Americans and witnessed by the students in classroom lessons and schoolwork are understood as a product of their enslavement. Outside the context of southern slavery, the curriculum in use provided these students with virtually no historical knowledge to draw upon for thinking about African Americans' continuous experiences of racism, discrimination, and injustice in the United States. For these students, these injustices ended with the abolition of slavery, with the end of the Civil War.

In effect, the curriculum in use provided students with a moral discourse for understanding slavery by focusing on issues such as the brutal or inhumane treatment of slaves and the indignities suffered by slaves in their everyday lives. But Judy speaks not a moral but a political discourse when attempting to use history to think about contemporary events in Los Angeles. She frames this discussion in terms of political issues—equality, economic opportunity, equal protection and rights under the law—but her students have learned to see and understand the moral dimensions of African Americans' experiences. It is no wonder that Carl and Patty have difficulty transforming a moral assessment of the past into a political critique of the present.

Studying African Americans in U.S. History

The historical presence of African Americans in U.S. history was introduced fairly early in the school year.[1] In discussions of early colonial history, both Ruth and Tom noted African Americans' presence, using a population chart ("Ethnic Population, 1775") that shows African Americans making up 20 percent of the population in colonial America. Tom provided his students with a graphic depiction of the Middle Passage and the purchase of African Americans by white colonists once they had arrived in North America. Ruth briefly discussed the conditions Africans faced on their voyage from Africa, using a model of a slave ship created by a student in a previous year, with sunflower seeds representing Africans, to show how Africans were packed into the ships. Most of the talk about African Americans was concerned with their enslavement, including their abduction and passage from Africa to North America, being sold at slave auctions, and that slaves were counted as three-fifths of a person for purposes of representation and taxation during the Constitutional Convention.

There were some exceptions to the equation of African Americans with enslavement expressed in moral terms. As part of a "colonial faire" in Ruth's class, Roy, the only African American student, brought in a replica that he built of a clock made by Benjamin Banneker, an African American man of science from colonial times. Tom discussed a few black Revolutionary War heroes with his students and asked them to write a report on a black Revolutionary War hero of their choice. This was not a great success; discovering the paucity of resources on this topic in their school and local public libraries, most students wrote very brief reports plagiarizing the little information they could find on the few individuals mentioned in their textbook—Crispus Attucks, Salem Poor, and Peter Salem (Armento et al. 1991:58, 73–74).

In fact, Crispus Attucks was the only noted African American in the colonial period. He was a "a black man who had fled slavery to become a sailor" (Armento et al. 1991:58) and the first person to die in the Boston Massacre. Both Tom and Ruth made note of Attucks in their lessons. Ruth restated what the textbook said, telling her students that Attucks was an important person to remember but never clearly explaining why. Tom also discussed Crispus Attucks, defining his two accomplishments (hence his claim to fame) as being one leader of the Boston Massacre on the American side and the first to die for the ideals of the U.S. Revolution.

The utility of Crispus Attucks as an African American in early U.S. history was also evident in Judy's class. Besides *A More Perfect Union,* the other major resource Judy used was a collection of materials published by the Teacher's Curriculum Institute (TCI 1992). In a TCI cooperative learning activity intended to show students the perspectives of different groups regarding specific colonial events, Crispus Attucks served as the voice of African Americans as students attempted to comment, from Attucks's point of view (and, by extension, the view of at least one part of the African American community), on the Boston Massacre, the Boston Tea Party, and a political cartoon commenting on the British taxation of the colonies.

The addition and elevation of Crispus Attucks to Revolutionary War hero typifies a predominant approach to multicultural curriculum reform, namely, the injection or addition of people of color and women into the existing narrative of U.S. history (Banks 1989). But this approach does not tell the whole story of African Americans in U.S. history. It does not focus on the historical experiences of these men and women. Instead, these added voices are asked to comment on events important in a white story of the United States. While African Americans were asked to comment, in the person of Crispus Attucks, on the Boston Massacre and Boston Tea Party, they were not asked to comment, for example, on debates concerning slavery in the Constitutional Convention. And while both the textbook and Tom focused on African Americans who fought on the side of the colonists in the Revolutionary War, a similar focus on African Americans who fought on the side of the British, for example, one Thomas Peters (Nash 1986), is missing.

While African Americans were present early in U.S. history, their presence was never examined in any depth. Students learned little or nothing about the experiences of African Americans in America during the colonial period. In fact, students learned very little about African Americans until their teachers began their discussion of the Civil War. The only place that African Americans really entered the narrative in more than superficial or incidental ways, was in discussions of the Civil War period, when their presence as slaves in the South is more important to the story of white America.

The Experiences of Slaves in the South

It was during the study of the Civil War period that students had the opportunity to learn about the experiences of African Americans in depth, specifically, about the experiences of enslaved African Americans in the South. In this section I focus on Judy's class because, in contrast to Ruth and Tom, she spent a considerable amount of time on the Civil War period (eight weeks in all), drawing on a wide variety of material—the students' textbook, slides, library resources, laser-disc presentations, documentary film, literature, period music, and her own supplementary reference materials—to teach her students about the growing conflict between North and South, as well as the cruelties, indignities, and injustices that African Americans experienced under slavery.

Student work in Judy's class included small group Civil War projects that students presented to the class—slide lectures, poetry recitals, reenactments of the Lincoln-Douglas debate, monologues from famous individuals of the time, point-counterpoint presentations between pro- and antislavery historical figures, reports on music from this period, and skits on Civil War events—and the completion of a final essay in which students answered one of three questions dealing with slavery.

In addition, Judy had her students read Julius Lester's *To Be a Slave* (1968), a collection of interviews of African Americans who experienced slavery firsthand. Judy instructed her students to create a dialectical journal using this book, each student choosing a few passages from each chapter to which they were then to write a personal response in their journal. The students were fairly consistent in the passages that they chose to comment upon. They repeatedly talked about the cruelty of splitting up African American families through the buying and selling of slaves, the brutality of masters who beat their slaves for small offenses, the poor living conditions of slaves, and the long hours that slaves were forced to work, even when sick or hurt or during bad weather.

One particularly moving and memorable passage concerned Paul, an escaped slave who wore an iron collar with bells attached to it, who was found hiding in a swamp by another slave. He promised to return the following Sunday with a file and other tools to remove Paul's collar, but when he returned, he found that Paul had hung himself from a sassafras tree (Lester 1968:122–126). This passage was all the more powerful because it was repeated in the documentary *Roots of Resistance: The Underground Railroad,* which Judy showed to her students. The students listened to the narrator tell the story of Paul, which ended with the image of the empty collar hanging from the tree, the bells jingling as it sways in the breeze.

This passage elicited many sympathetic responses from the students, with many of them noting that, if they were slaves, they would prefer to be killed or kill themselves rather than return to the harsh and brutal conditions of slavery. For example, Cindy noted:

I think I would kill myself if I was a slave and had escaped but was close to being captured. I would know that it is better in the heavens where there are no slaves and all are equal. I wouldn't want to be captured and taken back to be whipped and to have to go on working under someone else.

Here we can see that Cindy is sympathetic to the plight of the slaves and that she is also making an effort to identify with their experiences. The dialectical journals provided Judy's students with an opportunity to identify and sympathize with the experiences of enslaved African Americans, an opportunity that they took advantage of. Very often the students' personal responses to the *To Be a Slave* passages took the form of putting themselves in the place of the slaves and imagining how they would feel. For example, Bob responded to a passage concerning the separation of slave families due to the selling of their children by imagining his reaction to this event:

Having to leave your family on the spot or anytime for me would be painful. Families is all some of the slaves got, and sometimes that would be broken up too. To me that would be horrible.

If one goal of a multicultural history is to sensitize students to the lives and experiences of others, then Judy's curriculum was successful in this regard.

Finally, the *To Be a Slave* passages that the students read are similar to a few quotes in *A More Perfect Union,* reinforcing the lessons they have learned about the lives of African Americans under southern slavery. Here students can read Solomon Northup's description of the whippings slaves received while picking cotton (Armento et al. 1991:285). At the end of the same chapter is a literature selection containing an extended excerpt from Frederick Douglass's *Narrative of the Life of Frederick Douglass,* in which he talks about his time with Mr. Covey, a master who succeeded in breaking Douglass "in body, soul, and spirit" (1991:296–297).

By the end of their unit on the Civil War, Judy's students had become "witnesses" to the experiences of African Americans under slavery. All the work the students did and the materials they read were focused on imparting some sense, however imperfect, of the indignities, injustices, and brutalities of slave life. And the students seemed sincere, both in their writing and comments in class, in their expressions of shock and outrage at the treatment of African Americans under slavery. Slavery is immoral, and they had difficulty understanding how white slaveholders could have been so mean and cruel. African Americans experienced unimaginable cruelty at the hands of slaveholders, who considered them inferior and less than human, and this was a lesson Judy's students had learned well.

One would think that Judy's students, after studying the experiences of enslaved African Americans in such great detail, would have a depth of historical knowledge that would make them well-prepared to think and talk about the experiences of contemporary African Americans with some sensitivity. But applying this historical knowledge to contemporary events was problematic for Judy's students, because the students viewed the injustices experienced by African Americans as specific to their lives under slavery, an historically specific problem that has been solved rather than one example in a continuous history marked by racism and discrimination toward African Americans in U.S. society.

The Situation of African Americans in U.S. History

Sleeter and Grant (1991) note the power of the narrative of U.S. history text-

5. CURRICULUM AND INSTRUCTION IN MULTICULTURAL PERSPECTIVE

books to situate people of color in specific time periods or events that are important to whites. Native Americans are included as friends of the early English colonists, or in their later fights with settlers, Asian Americans are noted for their work on the railroad, and African Americans are included in slavery and the civil rights struggle (Sleeter and Grant 1991:85–86).

The bias of mainstream, white American culture, part of the "cultural baggage" that teachers and students bring with them into the classroom and that is evident in classroom lessons and curricular materials is that the Civil War South is the only proper place to study the presence of African Americans in U.S. history. It is an unquestioned assumption that slavery is the place to include African Americans in U.S. history. As currently constructed, a multicultural perspective means studying slaves and slavery in-depth, so that students gain a deep understanding of the experiences of African Americans under slavery.

But as we saw in Judy's class, this practice of situating African Americans in a particular time and place in U.S. history—in the Civil War South—and focusing on their experiences as slaves during this period has some surprising consequences. Carl's and Patty's comments suggest that this practice confines African Americans, and their experiences and concerns, to a specific time and place in U.S. history. By examining the experiences of African Americans under slavery but ignoring the experiences of African Americans outside of slavery—for example, communities of free blacks in the North and the South—is to construct a history that binds the injustices African Americans have experienced in the United States specifically to their enslavement in the South. A few examples from the work produced by Judy's students illustrates this point.

Jean, writing in her *To Be a Slave* journal, responds to a passage in the epilogue in which Thomas Hall comments that, while there are a few white men who may be all right, they will continue to talk against blacks and give them the cold shoulder due to pressure from their white friends (Lester 1968:156), in this way:

This is still quite true in the United States, which is really sad because this [slavery] was more than one hundred years ago, which was the era of racism, prejudice, and slavery.

Jean is saying that more than one hundred years ago there was an era in which enslaved African Americans experienced racism and prejudice. While Jean acknowledges that whites are still prejudiced against blacks, this "is really sad" because this problem was supposedly solved many years ago. Eric, writing on a question concerning liberty and equality in his *To Be a Slave* final essay, makes a similar point:

The worst part of slavery was that the slaves were bought and sold all the time. I think this is horrid for the slaves because they have no control over what will happen to them. Having control of your life is a major idea of liberty.
Less than 90 years later black people were the target of racism once again. In the 1950s blacks were not blessed with the same rights and privileges that the whites were.

Eric notes that 90 years after the Civil War "black people were the target of racism once again" and that blacks were not "blessed with the same rights and privileges that the whites were." Eric, like Jean, has situated African American experiences of racism and discrimination in specific historical moments—in the Civil War South and then again, for Eric, in the 1950s. While there are still problems in black-white relations, they imply there is no continuous history of racism and discrimination toward African Americans in the United States, but only problems that have periodically plagued African Americans.

Finally, Diana and Sue, both writing in their narrative descriptions of U.S. history, express the belief that slavery is a thing of the past:

My most favorite thing we did was learning about slaves. It's really hard to accept what they [white slaveowners and black slaves] did to each other. But that was the past. [Diana]
[North and South are arguing over slavery.] Soon the North and the South had begun the Civil War. Many people died. But in the end, as you know, there is no more slavery anymore. [Sue]

While it is "really hard to accept" what happened to African Americans under slavery, "that was the past," something between white slaveholders and black slaves, and, as Sue says, echoing Carl's comment above, "there is no more slavery anymore."

Recognizing this unintended "confinement" of the experiences of African Americans with racism, brutality, and injustice to those of black slaves in the South helps to explain the problems that Judy had in using her students' history to discuss the events in Los Angeles and the experiences of contemporary African Americans. When her students turn to history, all they find is slavery, a horribly brutal period for African Americans in U.S. history, but a situation that exists no more. Carl tried to understand the situation of African Americans today, but he could not see the connection between slavery and contemporary events. Patty did her best to make use of this history, positing that the legacy of slavery is an unfounded belief by blacks in their own inferiority.

Both Carl's and Patty's comments deny any continuous history of racism, discrimination, or prejudice experienced by African Americans in American society. Their only detailed knowledge of the injustices experienced by African Americans occurred during slavery, and so for Patty the only connection between the past and the present in this regard is African Americans' memory of this historical event, while for Carl there is no connection at all. There are neither contemporary analogous events nor any sequence of events between the enslavement of African Americans during the Civil War and the present, which would provide for a continuous history of common experiences shared by African Americans who lived in the United States in the past and those who live in the United States in the present.

Judy tried to move the conversation in a new direction: she tried to get her students to focus on the inequities in black-white relations. The problem is that her students had little knowledge of the history of black-white relations. What they did know, in detail, was the character of the relations between enslaved blacks and their white masters. But there are no slaves anymore, and no white masters. Slavery, it seems, was simply not a very useful vehicle for understanding the experiences of African Americans in the United States. But could it be?

Revising the Curriculum: Including Diverse Historical Voices

One reason that Judy's focus on the experiences of African Americans as slaves was less than successful in achieving her goals was because African Americans were virtually absent from the rest of U.S. history. While they were mentioned in the early colonial period, students had no detailed knowledge of African Americans in other times and places, which might have suggested to them that the injustices faced by African Americans under slavery were not specific to slavery but a feature of race relations throughout U.S. history. A stronger presence for African Americans throughout U.S. history would certainly go a long way toward addressing some of the problems we have seen in Judy's classroom.

The lesson for multicultural curriculum reform in history is one that has been argued before. The way to include diverse groups is to place them in many different times and places and study them as historical actors with political voices. The Houghton Mifflin textbook series attempts to expand the existing narrative of U.S. history by including the voices of more women and people of color. It is the inclusion of these voices, in fact, that suggests a potential means of organizing curriculum in a way that would help students connect the past and present experiences of African Americans in the United States.

One of the new, progressive features of *A More Perfect Union* is its inclusion of quotes from historical figures, not only the traditional quotes from white males but also quotes from women, African Americans, Native Americans, and others. These quotes are intended to convey the experiences, opinions, and perspectives of these often forgotten people. But there is a definite "politics of speaking" concerning these voices: limits on what they get to speak about as well as how they get to speak about it. For example, in *A More Perfect Union* white males and females (the latter a sign of progress) get to speak with a political voice, discussing issues of liberty, equality, and freedom. While students can still hear Patrick Henry's declaration to "give me liberty, or give me death" (Armento et al. 1991:66–65) or read Thomas Paine's *Common Sense* (Armento et al. 1991:666–667), they can also read a section entitled "Susan's Trial," in which Susan B. Anthony can declare (in response to her being found guilty of the crime of voting in the 1872 presidential election) that "my natural rights, my civil rights, my political rights, my judicial rights are all alike ignored" (Armento et al. 1991:276–277).

But other groups never get to speak with a political voice. Native Americans are limited to speaking with a defeated, victim's voice (on page 201, Tecumseh says, "They [whites] have driven us from the sea to the lakes—we can go no farther," and on page 425, Chief Joseph says, "I will fight no more forever,"), while African Americans are confined to addressing the immorality of slavery and the brutalities of slave life (e.g., Solomon Northup, on p. 285). In fact, it is this exclusive focus on the immorality of slavery, of showing students the "evils" of slavery if you will—mean and cruel masters, the brutal treatment of slaves, the belief in the inferiority of slaves who were less than human—that is problematic in Judy's unit on the Civil War and their study of the experiences of African Americans during this period.

While this focus on the brutality and immorality of slavery is valid and important, it provides a history that is too narrow and limited to be of much use in discussing contemporary issues. It provides very weak links to issues of racism, discrimination, and the denial of political and civil rights, the very issues that the California *History-Social Science Framework* alludes to when it talks about teaching students a history of the United States as "an unfinished struggle to realize the ideals of the Declaration of Independence and the Constitution" (1988:5) and the issues that Judy attempted to discuss with her students concerning the events in Los Angeles.

Politicizing the voices of African Americans, Native Americans, and other racial and ethnic groups has the potential to broaden the focus of the history students learn and provide themes, concepts, and issues that provide more easily realized connections between the past and the present. To illustrate my point, here is an excerpt from Frederick Douglass's *Narrative of the Life of Frederick Douglass*, which appears in the students' textbook:

(1) We were worked in all weathers. It was never too hot or too cold; it could never rain, blow, hail, or snow, too hard for us to work in the field.... Mr. Covey succeeded in breaking me. I was broken in body, soul, and spirit. My natural elasticity was crushed, my intellect languished, the disposition to read departed, the cheerful spark that lingered about my eye died; the dark night of slavery closed in upon me; and behold a man transformed into a brute! [Armento et al. 1991:296–297]

Now compare that excerpt to a quotation that did not appear in the students' textbook, an excerpt from a speech that Douglass gave on July 5, 1852, entitled "What to the Slave Is the Fourth of July?" and reprinted in the appendix of Douglass's *My Bondage and My Freedom*:

(2) The blessings in which you this day rejoice, are not enjoyed in common. The rich inheritance of justice, liberty, prosperity, and independence, bequeathed by your fathers, is shared by you, not by me. The sunlight that brought life and healing to you, has brought stripes and death to me. This Fourth of July is *yours,* not *mine. You* may rejoice, I must mourn.... To him [the slave], your celebration is a sham; your boasted liberty, an unholy license; your national greatness, swelling vanity; your sounds of rejoicing are empty and heartless; your denunciations of tyrants, brass-fronted impudence; your shouts of liberty and equality, hollow mockery; your prayers and hymns, your sermons and thanksgivings, with all your religious parade and solemnity, are to him mere bombast, fraud, deception, impiety, and hypocrisy—a thin veil to cover up crimes which would disgrace a nation of savages. [Douglass 1984:441–445, emphasis in original]

The first quote adds to the students' knowledge of the cruelties of slave life and is representative of the approach of the curriculum overall, which is to focus on the immorality of slavery. I am not suggesting that this is not worthy of study, but it seems to add to the problems faced by Judy's students in trying to make connections between the past and the present and to their difficulty in using a moral discourse to engage political issues. The second quote comes from a completely different Frederick Douglass, one who has the potential to facilitate students' abilities to connect the past to the present. This is an angry Frederick Douglass who attacks white America not simply for the cruel treatment of enslaved African Americans but for their refusal to extend "the rich inheritance of justice, liberty, prosperity, and independence" to African Americans. It is the political discourse of this second Douglass that places the experiences of African Americans under slavery within a broader political narrative of U.S. history and provides a discourse for talking about the past which connects the past with the present.

The inclusion of this second Douglass in the curriculum has potential benefits for both white and African American students. For white students, like the majority of Judy's students, the political discourse of this second Douglass provides a bridge between the past and present. The experiences of enslaved African Americans are no longer presented in terms of the immorality and brutality of slavery but as a denial of the basic political and civil liberties and freedoms embodied in the Declaration of Independence and the Constitution. It is the recognition of the denial of African Americans' civil and political rights that is crucial to understanding the experiences of African Americans in U.S. society, past and present.

This second quote from Douglass also holds benefits for African American students, for through him African American students are brought into, and become a part of, the rich political heritage of the United States. Although, as alluded to in the California *History-Social Science Framework,* the extension of the rights and liberties guaranteed in the Declaration of Independence and the Constitution has been a hard fought struggle that continues even today, women and people of color have contributed to this heritage, often in the face of great resistance and personal danger. They are part of our political community, drawing upon and contributing to our political heritage in many important ways. Understanding this struggle is also significant for white students, as it provides them with a more complete and diverse account of our political history, and the diversity of Americans who have contributed to this positive struggle. And of course, Douglass provides a wonderful role model for all students, an example of an American who stepped forward and demanded that we hold our social practices accountable to our political ideals.

The example of Frederick Douglass is not unique. The students' textbook favors apolitical, noncontroversial quotes from historical figures of color. While these figures are allowed to speak, they are not allowed to speak freely. This is one way in which the textbook contributes to a U.S. history that often obscures the connection between past and present, sometimes mentioning (Apple and Christian-Smith 1991) but rarely examining the history of injustice, discrimination, and racism which different racial, ethnic, and religious groups have experienced continuously in the United States. When African Americans such as Crispus Attucks address events important in a white story of America but never events important to African Americans themselves—such as the failure of the founding fathers to abolish slavery in the Constitution—it becomes easier to see how the new Houghton Mifflin textbooks and TCI materials may be more inclusive but are still a long way from presenting a multiperspectival, truly multicultural history of the United States.

Some Lessons for Creating a Multicultural History Curriculum

There are three general lessons for multicultural reform in history and social science that we can learn from my study of the curriculum in use in three classrooms. First, although most calls for reform are concerned with what students know (or rather, what they do not know), this case study points out the importance of looking at how students come to know history. In this case, while slavery is realized as a moral reality, it is not realized as a political reality. As a consequence, the students' knowledge of history is a less useful resource than it could be in thinking about contemporary events. I do not want to abandon a moral perspective on slavery, but I do think it is important for students to develop a political perspective on slavery. While a multicultural history should make students aware of the different perspectives and experiences of all kinds of Americans in our common past, I would argue that an emphasis on our common political history is crucial to this undertaking, because it provides students with a way of talking about history—a political discourse—that provides a bridge between the past and the present.

Second, the meaningful inclusion of women and people of color into the narrative of U.S. history means, at minimum, including them as participants in multiple historical events. The students' anchoring of the discrimination and injustice experienced by African Americans in slavery and their inability to see this as part of a larger, continuous history of black-white relations, is in large part due to the virtual absence of African Americans in other times and places in U.S. history. Teachers need to begin to examine the experiences of African Americans outside of slavery, but their ability to do this will in part depend upon the availability of good materials. For example, while *A More Perfect Union* does focus extensively on slavery, it also discusses, albeit briefly, the existence of communities of free blacks in both the North and the South (1991:193–195, 304–305). This is an opportunity, if seized by teachers, to provide their students with a more complete history of the experiences of African Americans in the United States, one that is likely to raise issues of injustice, discrimination, and racism.

Third, the history curriculum should make apparent to students that the realization of equality, whether political, social, or economic, has been a continuous struggle throughout U.S. history, involving the courageous efforts of all kinds of Americans, men and women of all races and ethnicities. This is a story that these students still have not heard, but one that schooling has a responsibility to teach them. The way to achieve this is to expand the narrative of U.S. history, both by populating traditionally important events with people whose participation has previously been ignored and by including new events that highlight the actions of these previously ignored Americans in our common history. And most importantly, we need to refuse to shy away from the kind of political critique provided by Frederick Douglass in his Fourth of July speech. Isn't it our political ideals, and our continuing struggle to achieve these ideals, that unite us as a people and a nation?

These are easy suggestions to make, but they will be difficult to achieve in practice. The problem is not simply biased curriculum, but that teachers and students bring their own biases to their reading of history—popular stereotypes of racial, ethnic, and religious groups, as well as assumptions about where and when different groups belong in U.S. history. When it comes to African Americans and U.S. history, Judy and her students know about slavery and often little else. Together, they are enacting a cultural narrative that specifies the proper place of African Americans in U.S. history. It is this tacit cultural knowledge that is central to understanding the politics of representation (Crichlow et al. 1990; Holquist 1983; Mehan and Wills 1988; Shapiro 1988): the decisions of teachers and students to privilege some representations of historical figures and events over others, surrounding the use of curriculum in the construction of historical knowledge in classrooms.

This implies that curriculum reform involves much more than simply writing "truly" multicultural texts. Constructing multicultural histories in the classroom will involve challenging the tacit biases and assumptions of teachers and students which mediate their reading of texts, even multicultural texts, and as such can undermine even the best curriculum reform efforts. A multicultural history curriculum is extremely useful for white, suburban students, who often have little contact with people of color in their everyday lives and are, therefore, much more dependent upon cultural stereotypes and assumptions when trying to imagine the situations of others in American society. These efforts are sure to be met with resistance and anger from parents, teachers, and students, as we have already seen in the debate over multicultural curriculum reform throughout the United States. These efforts are necessary, however, if we are going to prepare all our students to live together amidst the diversity of American society.

Who Needs Multicultural Education? White Students and the Construction of a Usable Past

One way of judging the utility or success of multicultural reform in history and social science is to ask how well the curriculum in use provides students with the discursive resources for positioning themselves in public debates concerning important social issues. Schools can provide students with an important space for practicing the role of active citizen, and for thinking critically about American society and culture. Conceptualized this way, efforts at multicultural curriculum reform can be critiqued in terms of whether or not they provide students with a usable past, a history that "includes the experiences and involvement of people of all classes and conditions" (Nash 1989:248) and that will "serve as a useful tool for understanding current affairs" (McNeill 1989:157).

The history constructed in the classrooms that I studied is a step forward in terms of creating a more inclusive history of the United States. Examining the cruelties and brutalities that African Americans endured under slavery during the Civil War period is worthwhile and an advancement from the past, but it is simply not enough. The focus on the history and immorality of slavery is so historically specific that it is hard to find any connections between past and present.

While the students' history does not provide them with an entirely usable or useful past for thinking about contemporary race relations, it is rife with possibilities, possibilities that I have tried to illuminate in this article. With regards to what counts as a multicultural history in the classroom, the curriculum is not as radical as some critics of multiculturalism feared, the story not much different than it was 20 or more years ago. True, the students do spend time learning about the experiences of African Americans under slavery, but the history of America is still overwhelmingly white and still populated with the same familiar historical figures and events that critics worried would be lost to future generations of students. But I also do not think proponents of reform should despair, because while the curriculum may be flawed, it is a flaw that can be fixed. By continuing to expand the narrative of U.S. history to make it more inclusive, we can create a history curriculum that is truly multicultural.

Finally, who needs a multicultural history curriculum? Certainly students of color do, but so do white students like Carl and Patty, who clearly have something to gain as well. Perhaps Carl and Patty "just don't get it," but to assume that this is due to simple ignorance or that because they are white they are incapable of understanding the experiences and perspectives of people of color is to ignore the constitutive and constructive work that has gone into their not "getting it." History is not a found reality but rather a culturally and socially constructed reality, part of a "selective tradition" (Apple and Christian-Smith 1991). Therefore, it is useful to think of history as a resource that is both enabling and constraining for students as citizens.

While the study of enslaved African Americans during the Civil War is a positive step forward, it is also at the same time something of a "trap" for white students. It provides a very limited and narrow understanding of African Americans' experiences in U.S. history, one that provides few tools for thinking critically about contemporary race relations. Oftentimes we hear comments from whites that are very similar to Carl's, comments that quickly turn a discussion of contemporary race relations into a discussion of slavery, followed by protestations that "even if my ancestors owned slaves I did not, and anyway that is a problem that was solved a long time ago." Maybe it is time to recognize these comments not as a reflection of ignorance but as the "educated," albeit incomplete, comments that they are. If race relations are not "their problem" but "our problem," then we need to think about the many ways schooling can outfit all students with the tools that they will need to deal effectively with these issues as active citizens. If history is a resource for citizens, then we can provide students with better resources than we have, and they deserve it.

John S. Wills is an assistant professor in the Margaret Warner Graduate School of Education and Human Development at the University of Rochester.

Notes

Acknowledgments. This research was supported by a Spencer Postdoctoral Fellowship from the National Academy of Education. My thanks to Hugh Mehan for his comments on earlier drafts of this article, and three anonymous *AEQ* reviewers for helpful suggestions that improved this article.

1. In California eighth-grade U.S. history goes through the end of World War I. In 11th grade students study 20th century U.S. history.

5. CURRICULUM AND INSTRUCTION IN MULTICULTURAL PERSPECTIVE

References Cited

Apple, Michael W. 1993. Official Knowledge: Democratic Education in a Conservative Age. New York: Routledge.

Apple, Michael W., and Linda K. Christian-Smith. 1991. The Politics of the Textbook. New York: Routledge.

Armento, Beverly J., Gary B. Nash, Christopher L. Slater, and Karen K. Wixson. 1991. A More Perfect Union. Boston, MA: Houghton Mifflin.

Banks, James A. 1989. Approaches to Multicultural Curriculum Reform. *In* Multicultural Education: Issues and Perspectives. James A. Banks and Cherry A. McGee Banks, eds. Pp. 195–214. Boston: Allyn and Bacon.

Banks, Sandy, and William Trombley. 1990. New Textbooks: Out with Dull, In with Diverse. Los Angeles Times, October 12: A3.

Bloom, Allan. 1989. The Closing of the American Mind. New York: Simon & Schuster.

California State Department of Education 1988 History-Social Science Framework. Sacramento: California State Department of Education.

Cohen, D. K., P. L. Peterson, S. Wilson, D. Ball, R. Putnam, R. Prawat, R. Heaton, J. Remillard, and N. Wiemers. 1990. Effect of State-Level Reform of Elementary School Mathematics Curriculum on Classroom Practice. Final Report, Office of Educational Research and Improvement. Washington, DC: U.S. Department of Education.

Crichlow, Warren, Susan Goodwin, Gaya Shakes, and Ellen Swartz. 1990. Multicultural Ways of Knowing: Implications for Practice. Journal of Education 172(2):101–117.

Douglass, Frederick. 1984[1855] My Bondage and My Freedom. Salem, NH: Ayer Publishing.

Drummond, Tammerlin. 1992. Group Opposes Stereotyping of Muslims. Los Angeles Times, October 3:B4.

D'Souza, Dinesh. 1991. Illiberal Education: The Politics of Race and Sex on Campus. New York: Free Press.

Freeman, Donald J., and Andrew C. Porter. 1989. Do Textbooks Dictate the Content of Mathematics Instruction in Elementary Schools? American Educational Research Journal 26:403–421.

Gibson, Margaret A. 1976. Approaches to Multicultural Education in the United States: Some Concepts and Assumptions. Anthropology and Education Quarterly 7(4):7–18.

Griswold, Wendy. 1987. The Fabrication of Meaning: Literary interpretation in the United States, Great Britain, and the West Indies. American Journal of Sociology 92:1077–1117.

Holquist, Michael. 1983. The Politics of Representation. Quarterly Newsletter of the Laboratory of Comparative Human Cognition 5(1):2–9.

King, Joyce. 1992. Diaspora Literacy and Consciousness in the Struggle against Miseducation in the Black Community. Journal of Negro Education 61:317–340.

Liebes, Tamar, and Elihu Katz. 1990. The Export of Meaning: Cross Cultural Readings of *Dallas*. New York: Oxford University Press.

Lester, Julius. 1968. To Be a Slave. New York: Scholastic.

Long, Elizabeth. 1986. Women, Reading, and Cultural Authority: Some Implications of the Audience Perspective In Cultural Studies. American Quarterly 38:591–612.

Luke, Carmen, Suzanne de Castell, and Allan Luke. 1983. Beyond Criticism: The Authority of the School Text. Curriculum Inquiry 13(2):111–127.

McCarthy, Cameron. 1990. Multicultural Education, Minority Identities, Textbooks, and the Challenge of Curriculum Reform. Journal of Education 172(2):118–129.

McNeil, Linda. 1981. Negotiating Classroom Knowledge: Beyond Achievement and Socialization. Journal of Curriculum Studies 13:313–328.
1986 Defensive Teaching and Classroom Control. *In* Ideology and Classroom Practice. Michael Apple and Lois Weis, eds. Pp. 114–142. Philadelphia: Temple University Press.

McNeill, William H. 1989. How History Helps Us to Understand Current Affairs. *In* Historical Literacy: The Case for History in American Education. Paul Gagnon, ed. Pp. 157–169. Boston: Houghton Mifflin.

Mehan, Hugh, Dina Okamoto, Angela Lintz, and John S. Wills. 1995 Ethnographic Studies of Multicultural Education in Classrooms and Schools. *In* Handbook of Research on Multicultural Education. James A. Banks and Cherry A. McGee Banks, eds. Pp. 129–144. New York: MacMillan Publishing.

Mehan Hugh, and John S. Wills. 1988. MEND: A Nurturing Voice in the Nuclear Arms Debate. Social Problems 35:363–383.

Nash, Gary B. 1986. Thomas Peters: Millwright, Soldier, and Deliverer. *In* Race, Class, and Politics: Essays on American Colonial Revolutionary Society. Chicago: University of Illinois Press.
1989 History for a Democratic Society: The Work of All the People. *In* Historical Literacy: The Case for History in American Education. Paul Gagnon, ed. Pp. 234–248. Boston: Houghton Mifflin Company.

Ogbu, John. 1992. Understanding Cultural Diversity and Learning. Educational Researcher 21(8):5–14.

Press, Andrea L. 1991. Women Watching Television: Gender, Class, and Generation in the American Television Experience. Philadelphia: University of Pennsylvania Press.

Radway, Janice A. 1984. Reading the Romance: Women, Patriarchy, and Popular Literature. Chapel Hill: University of North Carolina Press.

Ravitch, Diane. 1990. Diversity and Democracy: Multicultural Education in America. American Educator 14(1):16–20, 46–68.

Schlesinger, Arthur M., Jr. 1992. The Disuniting of America. New York: W. W. Norton & Company.

Shapiro, Michael J. 1988. The Politics of Representation: Writing Practices in Biography, Photography, and Policy Analysis. Madison: University of Wisconsin Press.

Shively, JoEllen. 1992. Cowboys and Indians: Perceptions of Western Films among American Indians and Anglos. American Sociological Review 57:725–734.

Sleeter, Christine E., and Carl A. Grant. 1987. An Analysis of Multicultural Education in the United States. Harvard Educational Review 57:421–444.
1991 Race, Class, Gender, and Disability in Current Textbooks. *In* The Politics of the Textbook. Michael W. Apple and Linda K. Christian-Smith, eds. Pp. 78–111. New York: Routledge.

Stevenson, David L., and David P. Baker. 1991. State Control of the Curriculum and Classroom Instruction. Sociology of Education 64(January):1–10.

Suzuki, Bob H. 1984. Curriculum Transformation for Multicultural Education. Education and Urban Society 16:294–322.

Taylor, Mildred D. 1976. Roll of Thunder, Hear My Cry. New York: Bantam Books.

TCI (Teachers' Curriculum Institute) 1992 Geography of America from Past to Present. Palo Alto, CA: Teachers' Curriculum Institute.

Trombley, William. 1990a. New Curriculum Aims to Bring History, Social Studies to Life. Los Angeles Times, July 30: A3.
1990b New History Curriculum Stirs Passionate Dissent. Los Angeles Times, October 9: A1.
1991 In Oakland, a Textbook Case of Trouble. Los Angeles Times, November 4:A3.

Wertsch, James V., and Kevin O'Connor. 1994. Multivoicedness in Historical Representation: American College Students' Accounts of the Origins of the United States. Journal of Narrative and Life History 4:295–309.

Wills, John S. 1994. Popular Culture, Curriculum, and Historical Representation: The Situation of Native Americans in American History and the Perpetuation of Stereotypes. Journal of Narrative and Life History 4:277–294.

Teaching:

*The Challenge of Change;
Reclaiming Democracy through Schooling*

Sudia Paloma McCaleb

Sudia Paloma McCaleb is Director of Teacher Education at the New College of California, 777 Valencia Street, San Francisco, California 94110

Many educators across the country are beginning to rethink old assumptions about "minority" or "non-dominant" cultures and about the ways in which we educate culturally and linguistically diverse populations. It is unlikely that there will be any real, deep, or lasting changes in public schooling until the nature of teacher education itself begins to change radically. This is the story of a small progressive college in San Francisco and a Federal grant (Title III) it received to develop and begin a new Teacher Education/Credential Program. The College had the opportunity to start from the beginning, rather than to reform or to cosmetically reorganize an already existing program.

New College of California in San Francisco made the decision to adopt as its basic teacher education program the new Bilingual, Crosscultural, Language and Academic Development (CLAD/BCLAD) credential recently developed by the state of California. This credential emphasis integrates inclusive multicultural and bilingual teaching perspectives and pedagogies.

New College has endorsed diversity and multiculturalism from its inception. Its programs emphasize innovative and interactive pedagogy and the vital importance of education to a democratic and just society. Undergraduates are encouraged to put their social principles into practice in their working lives. The college's administrators and faculty were enthusiastic and hopeful about beginning in teacher education at a time when a profound societal awareness of the need for educational change and reform exists.

We began by engaging in informal dialogues with educators across the state who represent a variety of perspectives. Our guiding question was, "What should a new teacher education program look like? What is needed?" The following summary of comments provided us with some serious beginning thoughts for the initiation of the program:

First Year Teachers
"I am learning a lot of what I need to know from other teachers in my school and 'in-services' which are covering areas I never learned about in my teacher education program. They didn't prepare me for the reality of classroom teaching."

Veteran Teachers
"I learned everything on the job, nothing in teacher education."

School Principals Receiving New Teachers
"They need classroom management and organizational skills or they'll drown."

District Superintendent
"I'm tired of the quality of teachers being sent by standard credential programs. They are not interactive and problem-posing enough. They copy what they see traditional veteran teachers doing."

Enlightened Faculty in Schools of Education
"If you're starting from scratch do it right! You know what needs to happen. Don't blow the opportunity. Don't just train the new teachers to 'fit in' to what already exists in the schools or we'll never see any change. Present the whole picture in the beginning and then return to the pieces all throughout the year."

The recent report from California Tomorrow, "Embracing Diversity" (Olsen & Mullen, 1990) gave us much to reflect on. It presents a teacher-generated summary of four major areas of competency required to teach effectively in classrooms which integrate immigrant and students born in the United States. The list included,

1. Competency in Language Development;
2. Competency in Building and Teaching an Inclusive Curriculum;
3. Competency in Establishing a Climate Supportive of Diversity;
4. Knowledge of the Cultures and Backgrounds of the Students.

As we began to create and develop our program we were also inspired and guided by Nieto's (1992) definition of multicultural education as a "process of comprehensive and basic education for all students." In interacting with a culturally diverse student population, teachers today are challenged to find ways to create partnerships in learning with their students, families, and communities. These partnerships have the potential to nurture literacy and academic achievement in the schools, while validating and celebrating students' home culture and language.

THE COLLEGE COMMITMENT TO A DIVERSE TEACHING FORCE

New College has a strong commitment to increase the numbers of culturally and

5. CURRICULUM AND INSTRUCTION IN MULTICULTURAL PERSPECTIVE

New College credential students engage in interactive science exploration. —Photo by Vincent William

linguistically diverse teachers in the profession. (At the present time, approximately 85 percent of students in the nation's teacher education programs are Anglo women). During the first year of the Teacher Credential Program, New College offered a 50 percent tuition grant to all bilingual and teachers of color who demonstrated potential for becoming excellent teachers. This comprised more than half of the beginning class of 25 candidates. State and national exams that have served as gate-keeping mechanisms for the profession were not used to exclude potential teacher candidates since these have been shown to be culturally and linguistically biased. Additional ways of evaluation, such as demonstrated commitment to youth, community service, and subject area knowledge were emphasized for entrance. Support systems were developed to assist students to pass the exams required before completing the credential.

This article describes how New College is implementing a broad multicultural vision with extensive pedagogical goals in a year-long Elementary Teacher Credential program. The article focuses primarily on innovative aspects of the program. Components of the program design which are in all standard teacher education programs are not discussed. We created innovative, integrated program structures, institutional supports, and pioneering program components to actualize our vision of the new understandings and skills teachers would need for the culturally diverse 21st century schools.

PRE-PROGRAM READER

Students are required to complete a reader before entering the program. This provides the incoming cohort of students a common text for reflection and discussion. If teachers do not have a strong philosophical vision and theoretical foundation, their practice will be shaky and their teaching direction vague. Through the readings a strong multiculturally inclusive perspective is presented and many of the current educational debates are introduced.

The reader is available approximately two months before the program starts and begins with James Baldwin's essay, "A Talk to Teachers." Also included are a series of articles about multiculturalism and diversity, language issues and bilingualism, literacy development, cooperative learning, participatory research, critical pedagogy, environmentalism and the struggle for environmental justice among people of color in urban communities. Issues of family literacy are fully developed. The reader ends with a letter by Medicine Grizzlybear, "An Indian Father's Plea," in which a Native American father introduces his son to his new teacher. He encourages the teacher to put aside any deficit assumptions concerning his child's lack of skills and get to know his son. Using this approach, the teacher discovers the multiple forms of knowledge the child possesses, knowledge gained by living close to the earth while being nurtured by the traditional cultural practices of his people.

Students are asked to write personal interpretive reflections about each article. Through their readings and writings students begin to see that education is not a politically neutral endeavor. There are many important issues to think about that

29. Teaching: The Challenge of Change

affect how children grow up and how they are educated in our schools. The dialogue among students and faculty is rich and lively from day one.

THREE WEEK INTENSIVE: A LOOK AT THE BIG PICTURE

The actual program begins in August with a Three Week Intensive session. The goal is to introduce many of the philosophical, instructional, "management", and subject content areas that will be studied in depth during the year. Students are asked to prepare for the first day of class by bringing two items; a visual item that can be hung on the wall and some kind of personal artifact. Both objects are to have personal or cultural meaning for the student and are used as a way to introduce themselves to the group—their learning cohort, with whom they will be learning and working throughout the year. This activity, and many of the subsequent activities are designed to model an inclusive pedagogical practice which connects the development of literacy in the classroom to each student's home and community.

Among the wall hangings this summer were travel and political posters, family photographs, and a painting done in kindergarten by one student and saved for 25 years by her mother. Written across the painting were the words, "I will not be quiet in class." Lucy remembered doing the drawing after being scolded by the teacher. Tara, a student artist, brought an oil painting of the kitchen of her childhood home. "When I was growing up, there were rats in my kitchen." How did the group respond to Tara's painting? How can or should teachers respond to the pain that students may bring into the classroom? Through the sharing of cultural artifacts, a group book was produced in which every student contributed an illustrated page with a descriptive sentence. The book was named, "These Are a Few Of My Favorite Things." Elisa, a native of Puerto Rico, brought a hand-crafted statue depicting a woman grinding corn. Her sentence was "*Siempre en la lucha*" [Always in the struggle] which she said represented the life force of all the women in her family.

PROGRAM VISIONS AND GOALS

During the Three Week Intensive and throughout the year everything is linked to the following seven philosophical and pedagogical goals:

1. Celebrating Diversity; Unlearning Prejudice
Teachers need to reflect on their own schooling and cultural experiences in order to acknowledge and understand the perspective that they bring to the profession. In recognizing that there are multiple perspectives which must be affirmed and embraced, teachers increase their capacity for compassion and can more equitably educate all students.

Teachers frequently display a lack of awareness about people different from themselves. They need the self understanding and the skills to be able to counteract the low self-esteem many students bring to school because of inter-

Drawing by New College credential candidate Elisa Garcia which she introduced as her artifact from Puerto Rico.

5. CURRICULUM AND INSTRUCTION IN MULTICULTURAL PERSPECTIVE

nalized oppression. Teachers must ask themselves, "What baggage am I bringing along with me? How can my own conscious or unconscious prejudice and even ignorance about 'otherness' limit my effectiveness as a teacher to all my students?"

During the first week everyone participates in two days of a "Celebrating Diversity; Unlearning Prejudice" workshop. A skilled facilitator, using a compassionate approach, helps students to share their cultural experiences and also to recognize the inequalities which members of the group have experienced in life due to race, class, or gender. The goal of the facilitator is to build allies among future educators, across groups, by helping them to recognize their commonalities and differences. This experiential process of self and group discovery is essential for those who will be working with diverse groups of students and their families.

Assumptions about Family Realities
Following the diversity training days, a set of assumptions that are commonly held by many educators about "minority" students and their families are presented. (Auerbach, 1990). One assumption is that children who do not speak English at home are at a disadvantage academically. Another is that good readers only come from homes where adults read. Students discuss these assumptions and share counter-evidence that they have found in their own experience to contradict these commonly held assumptions. It is important for future teachers to have this discussion because the views that they hold about their students and their families may not only negatively label children but also will set unjustifiably low academic expectations for them.

2. Building Communities of Learners
Teachers must learn how to humanize the teaching environment and develop their classrooms as "communities of learners" (McCaleb, 1994).

As candidates acquire deeper levels of understanding about their own past, present, and future realities they are better able to create a learning environment in their classrooms in which all students feel listened to, validated, and empowered as both individual and collaborative learners. Students who know that their realities and identities are valued at school do not have the same need to resist or reject school learning as those who feel their identities are being demeaned or excluded.

Cooperative Learning, "Complex Instruction," "Tribes"
It is clear from the research and our own work with classroom teachers and diverse student groups that children attain higher achievement levels when they learn in the context of cooperative classrooms. We must view cooperation as including not only classroom practice but also as a necessary skill for productive work and democratic citizenship in the future. During the Three Week Intensive, students are introduced to "Complex Instruction" or "Finding-Out Descubrimiento." This is a model for cooperative learning, developed at Stanford University (Cohen, 1986) which looks at power issues within groups and works towards balanced learning groups where responsibilities are clearly shared as the members work to attain a common goal. Students are also introduced to "Tribes: A Process for Social Development and Cooperative Learning" (Gibbs, 1987). Collaboration among teachers, students, and their families and communities in ways that embrace the diversity of cultures and languages that families pass onto their children is a major aspect of building communities of learners. This collaboration extends beyond the classroom and breaks down the

New College Family Literacy Program: students learn strategies to facilitate home/school literacy partnership.

—Photo by Vincent William

29. Teaching: The Challenge of Change

Mask-Making workshop at New College— learning how to integrate the arts across curriculum.

—Photo by Vincent Williams

walls between the school and the community.

3. Working with Families through Family Literacy

Teachers must gain the experience and skills needed to work with families in collaborative relationships and to develop curricula that include and affirm family concerns and cultural values. Teachers must discover that through living and observing everyone learns to read the world before reading the word (Freire, 1970). This understanding and the instructional strategies involved to translate it into practice are essential for educating all students.

One of the major innovative features of the program is the creation of a Family Literacy Center at the College. It is located in San Francisco's Mission District—home to many Mexican and Central American immigrants. The Center not only offers a service to the surrounding community and to the schools in which student teachers are working but also provides a facility where teacher education students acquire strategies for working with families around issues of literacy development. They learn the mechanics of how to create successful programs. Family literacy, as we define it, is the collaboration between the family, community, and school in support of the student's emerging literacy skills.

The Center experience is considered an essential component of the methods courses in Literacy Development and Social Studies. Sessions are also included which focus on Family Math, Hands-On Science and Ecology. Several of our first year students were talented musicians; this led to the development of a Family Literacy Band. We learned that the way in which we welcome families and the enthusiasm and generosity expressed by the program participants makes families want to return. At the end of sessions, parents shared their feelings:

"Ustedes saben porque regresamos. Es por el amor y la dedicación que sentimos aquí de los maestros en el programa y también por primera vez en la vida sentimos que como padres de familia somos importantes en la educación de nuestros hijos . . . que nosotros los padres tenemos algo importante de enseñar." [Do you know why we keep coming back? It's because of the love and dedication we feel here from the teachers in this program and also because for the first time in our lives we feel that we are important in the education of our children and that we as parents have something to teach them].

Over the course of the year, students work with parents, many who have limited years of formal schooling themselves. Teachers come to see both children and their families as writers, authors, and experts about their own lives. Sessions always integrate art, singing, and hands-on experiences with literacy development as students facilitate small groups by using children's literature as a point of departure for discussion of important common life issues and concerns.

In the first year we chose to conduct the sessions in Spanish, which is the primary language in the surrounding community. This was initially viewed by the program faculty as a way to support and raise the status of the Spanish language in the community. This helped the children to develop a strong primary language foundation in order to become potentially more successful in English. Several students felt that the Center presented a perfect opportunity to bring together the multiple cultural and linguis-

5. CURRICULUM AND INSTRUCTION IN MULTICULTURAL PERSPECTIVE

tic groups in the community and to begin to build bridges in the community with the children as the focus. They suggested that the sessions be conducted bilingually.

4. Teachers as Researchers

The concept of "teachers as researchers" must be developed through participatory or action research. This will enable future teachers to come to know and respect the communities in which they teach. Teachers cannot be expected to enter a classroom or a community with all the necessary knowledge and answers but must be co-learners along with their students, their families, and the communities from which they come.

During the Three Week Intensive students discussed the basic principles of participatory research. "Participatory research is a philosophical and ideological commitment which holds that every human being has the capacity of knowing, of analyzing and reflecting about reality so that she becomes a true agent of action in her own life" (Ada & Beutel 1991, p.8). By attempting to break down the established power roles between researcher and participants, both agents become co-participants in a dialogue.

The researcher, who in this case is the teacher, the students, or both, invites the participants to speak or write about and critically reflect on their thoughts. The participants may be other students in the classroom or members of the family or community. As teachers and students through dialogue, writing, and illustration, establish partnerships of co-researchers, more meaningful participation in the lives of all results. This classroom research is particularly appropriate for students and parents from culturally and linguistically diverse backgrounds because their voices have seldom been heard or documented.

To learn the process, during the Three Week Intensive students engage in a short research project among themselves; a community of future teachers. The current group of students formulated their own research question. "What obstacles stand in the way of teachers implementing a multicultural curriculum?" Through dialogues with each other, they explored their own cultural and educational experiences growing up and spoke of their dreams and visions as teachers. Collectively they explored the common themes and concerns that arose. On the final day of the Three Week Intensive each group presented its findings and formulated a plan for creative action as future teachers.

During the Fall semester, the candidates' research skills are expanded and their understanding of the potential instructional benefits of the process grow as they begin their second research project. They are asked to engage in dialogue with two different parents of children in the public schools. (At least one of the two is to be of a culture or language group other than their own). They are to explore three areas: (a) The educational experiences of the parents, (b) the parent's view of their child's present schooling experiences, and (c) the parent's view of the potential for building bridges between the home and the school.

Participatory research invites parents to tap into their internalized and traditional sources of knowledge and wisdom while contributing to their children's education. Teachers are acquiring the skills to listen and to seek out the experiences and opinions of the families which can help in the creation of an authentic text for classroom learning.

5. Integration of Music and the Arts

Music and the arts must be integrated into all methods courses so that future teachers may appeal to the diverse learning modes of children and teach to the whole child.

We are not all artists and musicians but as teachers we can all promote and facilitate the arts. We involve ourselves with music as a way to learn about and experience the richness of diverse cultures. Part of the New College vision is that teachers emerging from this program will be bridge builders in their schools and communities. They will be able to recognize common forms of oppression experienced by all groups that are not part of the dominant culture and will develop ways to work together for the common good of equitably educating all children.

During the Three Week Intensive we chose to focus on bringing together the African American and the Latino experiences through Afro-Cuban music and movement because it is common in urban schools to witness an ongoing struggle between the African American and the Latino populations. An Afro-Cuban musicologist presented the dual influences on Cuban music (African and Spanish) and also taught call and response songs and dances. Students also worked with a multicultural music educator who taught songs which helped future teachers to begin to build their own classroom repertoire. This approach enhances the ability to build classrooms as inclusive communities.

All credential students learn silk-screening, an empowering art form. They are asked to purchase a silk screen which becomes one of their tools of the trade. They learn a simple method for making posters with their students. The posters can speak about any theme being studied and include printed words and opinions students may wish to express. This year, most of the students during their field placements took turns borrowing additional screens from their peers and experimented in their classrooms.

6. Development of Personal Philosophy

Students need to formulate their own philosophy and vision of critical pedagogy and transformative education and see themselves as agents working towards positive change in the schools, the community, the society and the world.

The central pedagogies of transformative or critical education are dialogue and problem posing. The problems are real-life concerns that the students engage in for critical reflection. Through this process, students come to see and understand how they exist in the world. The teacher is present not only as an observer and a guide but also as a co-participant in an on-going dialogue.

Mary Poplin (1991) emphasizes that critical pedagogy is concerned primarily with ways to educate citizens to "live responsibly in a free and democratic state." In a transformative classroom students are encouraged to develop their own voices in interaction with the voices of others and to participate in the democracy of the classroom. Throughout the year, teacher candidates participate in a process which focuses on learning how to provide multiple opportunities in their classrooms for the development of student voices. Teachers must be seen as "transformative intellectuals" (Giroux, 1989) and must be given time to plan and reflect with others about the theory that informs their practice. Students need to believe that they can make a difference in the world, but first teachers must believe that they can make a difference.

7. Societal and Political Context

Teachers must understand the societal and political context of the institution of schooling and develop an understanding of how the history and structures of schooling have impacted ethnically and linguistically diverse students.

New teachers soon discover that the basic structures of roles and relationships in school systems are generally more bureaucratic than collaborative. Schools are expected to produce "winners and losers." These assumptions are reinforced by testing, tracking, and accountability practices. Cummins (1989) proposes that real changes in schools will begin to take place only when the relationships of power begin to change, that is, when the voices of parents, community, and teachers are heard and the direction of the schools reflects a collaborative vision and effort.

For transformative educators, a discussion of schools is very much intertwined with a discussion of society in general and democracy specifically. Teaching practices that include only one group's knowledge might serve to silence rather than empower the students who are living in cultural worlds that exist outside of the dominant culture. While at school, unless care is taken, these students may learn that they don't count and that their histories and ideas are unimportant.

ONGOING QUESTIONS

Several key questions guide the program:

1. How do we maintain a balance between the transmission of information and the importance of dialogue in a teacher education program when there is so much to learn and less than one year in which to accomplish it?
2. How do we engage in a reflective and in-depth learning process when many students, for economic reasons, need to continue working and thus become overwhelmed by the process itself?
3. How does the teacher education process itself become an instructional model and an inspiration for future teachers in their own work?
4. How can students gain experience in new ways of teaching when there are so few appropriate practice environments available to them?

CONCLUSION

These are the major concerns we have for the education of our teachers. Machado poetically expressed, *"Caminante, no hay camino, se hace camino al andar."* [Traveler, there is no road, we make the road by walking.] These words affirm our belief that there is no set way or formula to be followed. If we as educators fully commit ourselves to the process and respond authentically to what we see and understand emerging, we can recreate our schools and offer our students and ourselves multiple opportunities in our lives.

This process is not an easy undertaking. In our first year we made mistakes, learned, and grew a great deal from that experience. We hope that this presentation of our infant program will inspire a dialogue among teacher educators. We would appreciate hearing from you.

REFERENCES

Ada, A. F. & Buetel, C. 1991. Participatory research as dialogue for action. Unpublished Manuscript. University of San Francisco.

Auerbach, E. 1990. *Making Meaning Making Change.* Boston, MA: University of Massachusetts.

Baldwin, J. 1988. A talk to teachers. In R. Simonsons & S. Walker (Eds.), *Multicultural Literacy.* St. Paul, MN: The Graywolf Annual Five.

Cohen, E. 1986. *Designing Groupwork: Strategies for the Heterogeneous Classroom.* New York: Teachers College, Columbia University.

Gibbs, J. 1987. *Tribes; A Process for Social Development and Cooperative Learning.* Salt Lake City, UT: Publisher's Press.

Giroux, H. 1989. Rethinking education reforms in the age of George Bush. *Phi Delta Kappan,* 70, 728–730.

Lake, R. (Medicine Grizzlybear) *Teacher.* September 1990. pp. 50–53.

McCaleb, S. P. 1994. *Building Communities of Learners: A Collaboration Among Teachers, Students and Family, and Community.* New York: St. Martin's Press.

Olsen, L. & Mullen, A. 1990. *Embracing Diversity.* San Francisco, CA: California Tomorrow.

Poplin, M. 1991. The two restructuring movements: Which shall it be? Transformative or reductive? Manuscript submitted for publication.

Special Topics in Multicultural Education

Each year we try to focus in this section of this volume on selected special topics that have been of particular interest to those who work in multicultural settings. There are always areas of concern which demand our attention having to do with the stereotypes of particular cultural groups, as well as relations between cultural groups wishing to exercise their basic right to express their own voice about their experience in society. Topics are also chosen if they have a direct bearing on issues of equality of educational opportunity.

The important changes in the demographic composition of the United States referred to in the opening unit of this edition are reexamined in the light of the implications of these population changes for educators. We examine also the struggle to empower both youth and adults to develop their own visions of the world as they become literate persons defining their own understanding of their respective life situations. What children and teenagers learn from their neighborhood environments is also of interest to teachers.

One demographic change is the continuing increase in the number of intercultural marriages in the United States. Biracial families still face hostility from many people. Another dynamic is that several cultural minorities in the United States are involved in the complex and sometimes painful resolution of historic misperceptions of one another. Antagonistic stereotypes can occur among minority groups as well as between the dominant American population and people of non-European heritage. There is thus an ongoing dialogue within and among those minority groups who believe their interests to be challenged by other minorities as well as by mainstream American society.

Issues relating to interethnic and intercultural perceptions need to be dealt with as part of a response to xenophobic reactions to immigrants and migrants.

Educators who work in the area of multicultural education are concerned with research into how students can succeed in school and transcend the impact of socioeconomic inequality and feelings of powerlessness, as well as with documenting the causes of school failure. How at-risk minority students can overcome feelings of low self-esteem and develop workable strategies for solving their problems in school are matters of great importance.

The essays in this unit are relevant to courses in educational policy studies, multicultural education, and cultural foundations of education.

Looking Ahead: Challenge Questions

In what ways can texts used in schools be critically reviewed for cultural and gender biases?

Name several ways for a teacher to empower students. How can teachers help to develop social consciousness in students?

How can educators counter what many young people learn in urban ghettos?

Why did so much resegregation occur as the United States attempted to desegregate?

What should every American student know about the Holocaust? Is anti-Semitism still a major problem in America? What can be done to combat it? What are the special challenges confronting biracial families?

—F.S.

UNIT 6

Resurgence of Ethnic Nationalism in California and Germany: The Impact on Recent Progress in Education

José Macias

University of Texas at San Antonio

In a comparative study, the author examines the recent passage of California's "anti-illegal immigrant" Proposition 187, and the resurgence of hostility toward resident "foreigners" in Germany, as forms of ethnic nationalism resulting in exclusionary movements directed toward Mexicans, and Turkish and other non-German groups, respectively. Historical analysis and data from educational ethnographic studies reveal the interrelationship of historically constructed racial or ethnic ideology, intergroup experience, and education. Schools, while recent targets of exclusionary social movements, are still key sites for an education in new ways of thinking about racial and ethnic-group relations.

California, 1994: The results of the Fall general elections included the passage of Proposition 187 by a large majority of the California electorate. The state referendum proposed to withhold virtually all government services and benefits to "illegal" immigrants in the state, including support to families with dependent children, most health care, and all education to children of undocumented immigrant parents. Its proponents argued that this population does not legally qualify for the aforementioned benefits and services, and that they are too costly a burden for the taxpaying citizens of this country's largest state. Although implementation has been blocked by a series of court orders, a redefinition of ethnic group relations and the open persecution of undocumented Mexicans and other suspects was clearly established in the state, region, if not the whole of the United States. [Macias 1995:4–5]

Germany, 1992: During the course of fieldwork in September, a colleague and I sat in a restaurant in Mainz, discussing a variety of topics related to my comparative research project—migration, education, and integration of ethnic groups in Germany, as well as related "hot" topics including German reunification, the European Community, guestworkers, and the like. Midway through our main course a sudden flash of light and a deafening thud from the front of the building interrupted the tranquil evening. We were later to learn—after the initial shock, confusion, and arrival of the police squad cars—that we had just witnessed a violent attack by a German "redneck" on the Syrian restaurant in which we were dining. Fortunately no one was injured in this incident, there was minor damage to the property, and we were able to continue, as our conversation turned to the escalating German hostility and violence toward foreign residents of Germany that has been reported in recent years by the media and German government itself. [field notes]

In this article, I examine the growing phenomenon of ethnic group conflict, particularly the return of open hostility directed by a majority population toward minority ethnic groups. Two cases are the basis for this discussion: California, with its Proposition 187, the anti-illegal-immigrant referendum; and Germany, a country marked by growing hostility toward its foreign residents in recent years. One purpose here is to compare and contrast these two situations to search for the common underlying dynamics in which sociopolitically weak, "foreign" ethnic groups have been singled out for societal persecution, scapegoating, and exclusion. Another objective is to examine the role of education both as part of the discourse, as well as a potential, albeit partial solution in this kind of group conflict.

Two methodological threads are intertwined here. First, I take a diachronic perspective to outline some fundamental historical elements of the two cases over time (Brubaker 1990; Macias 1990, 1993). This approach assumes that complex phenomena follow from a series of events that need to be taken into account as part of an explanation of the present. The second line is ethnographic, in which I draw on data from two projects carried out over the last several years. From 1987 to 1991, I conducted fieldwork to study the educational experiences of Mexican immigrant students moving into a U.S. school system and within a transnational migrant stream (Macias 1990). While the overall study involved fieldwork in immigrant communities and schools in both Mexico and the United States, the data reported here depict the California situation before the current backlash.

The Mexico-U.S. project naturally involved a review of a comparative body of cases on migration, and the role of education for the integration of foreign groups in receiving nation states. Out of these, the case of Turkish guestworkers and "foreigners" in Germany presented several similarities to Mexican immigrants in the United States. Armed with a few key contacts and German language fluency, I decided to develop this comparative study, and between 1990 and 1993 I conducted fieldwork in Berlin, Hamburg, and Frankfurt. But nobody had foreseen in the late 1980s, when I was still planning the work, Gorbachev and the collapse of the Communist Bloc, the fall of the Berlin Wall, and German reunification. And few were prepared for the open return of hostility toward guestworkers and other non-Germanic ethnic populations of a kind that had not been seen since the end of World War II. The dramatic escalation of this hostility was widely documented during the fieldwork period and added a critical focus to my inquiry.

Ethnographic data presented here came from similar sources in both sites: school and classroom observations; interviews with teachers, program specialists, and school administrators; and documents describing relevant policies and programs. German fieldwork activities also included home-family observations and interviews, and interviews with government and community agencies that served guestworker and other ethnic communities.

California Ethnic Nationalism: Territorial Displacement and Structural Exclusion

The two events described in the opening of this article are each grounded in histories that can help us understand the similar evolution and common meaning of current phenomena apparently separated by geography, culture, and nation. For instance, Proposition 187 can be understood as a form of ethnic nationalism in which the majority ethnic group singled out undocumented immigrants, who represent a "foreign" ethnic group, as the source of California's recent socioeconomic problems, and who then were defined as "not belonging" in the society of which they have been a part for a century and a half. These two assumptions cleared the way for an official exclusionary movement against illegal residents, which culminated in the success of Proposition 187. But for Mexicans, the main group targeted, this is not a new experience. They know their own history in the United States, including their periodic subjection to this kind of treatment since the arrival of the United States in the Southwest.

California ethnic nationalism, as exemplified by Proposition 187, is grounded in the earliest contact between Northern European Americans and previously settled American Indians and Mexicans. The early 19th century marks the beginning of substantial contact between whites and the settled people of the Southwest. In the 1800s the "Indian problem" was being resolved through U.S. government policies of territorial displacement, cultural destruction, and genocide—a treatment that ultimately resulted in the relegation of small numbers of surviving American Indians onto a reservation system. This treatment of American Indians had been politically and morally justified by the ideology of U.S. Manifest Destiny:

> Manifest Destiny had its roots in Puritan ideas, which continue to influence Anglo-American thought to this day.... Anglo-Americans believed that God had made them custodians of democracy and that they had a mission.... Their destiny made manifest was to spread the principles of democracy and Christianity to the unfortunates of the hemisphere. [Acuna 1988:13]

But while Manifest Destiny was largely successful in the removal of American Indians, Mexicans presented another kind of problem.

When people from the United States reached Mexico in the early 1800s, they found a people struggling toward nationhood after its 300-year legacy of Spanish colonial rule. As a nation left destitute and politically chaotic from centuries of Spanish plundering and dominance, the government not only allowed but invited U.S. Americans to help Mexicans settle their northern territories (Acuna 1988). From present-day Utah to Texas, and in New Mexico, Arizona, Nevada, and California, the newcomers came in contact with Spanish creoles, Indians, and the numerically dominant mestizos, all citizens of the young Mexican nation.

But the Mexican policy of open borders and peaceful cooperation met its demise when the new settlers and their government quickly turned to Manifest Destiny and the supremely grounded right to appropriate all territory to the Pacific Ocean. To make a very long story very short, the United States pressured, threatened, made war, and then assumed this control through the Treaty of Guadalupe Hidalgo and the annexation of the northern territories of the weakened Mexican nation. Mexicans resisted this forced incorporation through both political and violent means, but to no avail. Under the new regime, U.S. Americans systematically abrogated the treaty, illegally appropriated most Mexican land-holdings, and relegated Mexicans to the lowest ranks of the political economy and social order (Acuna 1988).

Since that time, Mexicans have been subjected to a "love-hate" relationship with U.S. society. When in favor with the dominant majority, Mexicans are welcomed, employed as a needed labor force, and are allowed to make their lives peacefully in the United States. But at other times, they have been singled out for persecution, blamed for society's problems, and targeted for deportation. For example, through the early 20th century, the U.S. border with Mexico was open, and Mexicans crossed it freely, back and forth. Mexicans in this period, as today, were the largest non-European ethnic group involved in the development of the U.S. Southwest. Their skills and labor ensured the building of the transcontinental railroad, helped mine the region's natural resources, made farming a lucrative enterprise, and made ranching a traditional hallmark of U.S. American culture. In fact, the entire "cowboy" culture—for example, horses, leather, livestock, rodeos, the barbecue, chili, and the guitar-strumming, singing cowboy—was taken from the already existing Mexican "charro" subculture and ensured the successful adaption of U.S. Americans to the harsh and expansive West. But by the early 1900s a deep anti-immigrant sentiment permeated the national mood, with the most severe actions coming in the form of the Chinese Exclusion Act (Takaki 1993). With restrictions now also established for Mexicans, European immigrants came under the more generous quotas reserved for them.

A brief period of interest in Mexicans and other "Latins" took place in the 1920s and 1930s within U.S. popular culture. The oversexed "Latin lover," the saucy "hot señorita," and the uncouth "Mexican bandit" epitomize the type of superficial, romantic, and negative im-

6. SPECIAL TOPICS IN MULTICULTURAL EDUCATION

ages that dominated the cinematic, printed, and other popular media of that period. But the Mexican masses remained exotic and foreign enough to still be relegated to the lowest ranks of society and its institutions. Another flip-flop in relations occurred after the 1929 Wall Street crash that marked the beginning of the Great Depression. In 1930 Herbert Hoover began a program of deportation of Mexicans in which thousands were "repatriated" to Mexico without due process, many as legal citizens and residents of the United States. Thus, government policy to the effect that Mexicans "do not belong" in the United States coincided with a peak in immigration, economic decline, and the negative stereotyping of certain groups selected for scapegoating as the source of the nation's problems. Through the 1950s, conditions for Mexicans in the Southwest did not change substantially. For instance, Mexicans were allowed to hold only agricultural, manual labor, and service jobs that paid substandard wages under the poorest of working conditions. Those who broke this pattern often capitalized on their light skin color, changed their names, or otherwise managed to pass the barrier of being Mexican. While illegal, segregation in housing and education was systematic and effective. Their treatment at the hands of the U.S. public ranged from stereotyping to violent attack. Mexicans rejected these conditions as they have resisted their oppression since the intrusion of the United States a century and a half ago. Labor strikes were a common form of protest, as were legal challenges to school segregation. A few local victories were won, but with little systematic change.

World War II and its aftermath included a few expressions of "normal relations" between U.S. Americans and Mexicans. A labor shortage in that period led to the importation of temporary workers from Mexico through the Bracero Program, an international agreement that lasted through the 1950s. After its conclusion, many braceros who had decided to stay and work were periodically rounded up and deported by the Immigration and Naturalization Service. The societal lot of Mexicans remained marginal as a result of their systematic exclusion from opportunities for economic mobility, political power, and the education that would lead to these.

Since the 1960s, some measure of social progress has resulted from the initiatives of the Civil Rights movement, but a period of regression began in the early 1980s with two trends: (1) the return of a fundamental "American" social ideology and politics, with Californian Ronald Reagan its banner carrier and (2) a dramatic rise in illegal immigration from Mexico and other nations experiencing economic and political hard times. The present period thus represents a cyclical resurgence of a complex of dominant group beliefs about and behavior toward Mexicans that has taken place against the backdrop of U.S. national development, and within a history of intimate, conflictual experiences between the two groups.

The Cycle of Mexican Educational Exclusion, Inclusion, and Back

The chaotic World War I era marked a period of large-scale migration to the United States. Europe's conflict of empires and nations caused waves of displaced humanity to land on U.S. shores, while in America the aftermath of the 1916 Mexican Revolution pushed hundreds of thousands of Mexican nationals across the border. While reaping the benefit of abundant, cheap labor, the nation also faced the task of integrating millions of newcomers into society. Thus, systematic public schooling came to be offered to Mexicans and other immigrant groups, just as the sociopolitical ideology of "Americanization" gained dominance.

Americanization was grounded in a set of ideas current at that time. For instance, nationalistic fervor had resulted in the ethnic conflicts of World War I, but if everyone were uniformly "American," with a common national identity and loyalty, we could avoid political conflict. Also, a common socialization for work and citizenship would benefit immigrants and society. Moreover, the popular "melting pot" idea held that immigrants should give up their cultures, languages, and all other foreign attributes.

Americanization thus became the dominant policy for immigrant education. Throughout the Southwest, Mexican children attended Americanization schools to receive English instruction, citizenship training, and preparation for work. The latter curriculum stressed non-skilled job training, for example, home economics and factory work. Citizenship involved a dose of U.S. history and saluting the flag. English instruction used the "sink or swim" method and the explicit rejection of Spanish.

Beyond its logic, however, the rhetoric of Americanization was both contradictory and extreme in practice. For instance, Americanization schools or classrooms were implemented by public school districts but were segregated from "regular" ones and, thus, were inequitable in terms of resources and quality. In addition, lack of contact and interaction with peers in mainstream schools precluded a full socialization experience that would enhance students' skills and competencies in society. Since the main purpose of this program was to teach "American" cultural values and behavior, the incorporation of students' cultural knowledge and skills never was a consideration. Moreover, the informal, personal treatment given students reinforced the formal program, and teachers regularly meted out verbal humiliation and corporal punishment to students for speaking Spanish, for their ethnic behavior, for their physical appearance, in other words, for being Mexican. Ideally, Mexicans were to give up all traces of their foreign heritage in order to become "American." This brand of education was designed to culturally assimilate Mexican children, bring them under control, while preparing them to continue in the lowest strata of the socioeconomic order.

Mexican parents resisted this treatment. Individuals sometimes petitioned local schools to allow their children into the regular program; other times they took group action. The documentary film *The Lemon Grove Incident* depicts a classic case of school segregation in the 1930s wherein a Mexican community takes legal action against the local school district and wins (Espinosa 1982). A California court ruled for the parents who claimed that their children's segregated school provided an inferior education and deprived them of necessary opportunities due to all Americans. But change was slow, and Mexicans remained largely excluded from education for decades.

An upturn in the educational cycle aptly describes the progress that followed the Supreme Court school desegregation ruling of 1954. By the mid-1960s federal government policies and programs were in place that represented the first good-faith attempts to provide equitable education for ethnic minorities. For instance, programs began to address inequity and the special needs of children with social, cultural, and linguistic "disadvantages." Furthermore, the education profession generally jumped on the ethnic-minority education bandwagon and developed more inclusive philosophies, curricula, and instructional strategies. In the 1970s and 1980s "cultural difference," "learning styles," and "bilingual and multicultural education" became standard jargon in the educational lexicon.

Ironically, California was until recently in the vanguard of most initiatives to improve the schooling of ethnic minority students. For instance, port-of-entry programs specifically targeted students newly arrived in the United States. A typical example was the Newcomers Program, which I observed in the large Central Valley city of Vintageland.[1] Beginning in the late 1970s, Vintageland School District experienced a great influx of Mexican immigrants, as well as refugees from several Asian nations among its student population. These students came with distinct cultural backgrounds, limited English skills, and diverse educational backgrounds (Macias 1990, 1993).

Officially, the Vintageland program provided these newcomers with an English as a Second Language (ESL) program and a basic curriculum to prepare them for regular classrooms. But Mrs. Weiss, the program's director, added that "we provide a warm, comfortable, secure environment . . . [and] give confidence. . . . Students learn what school is about, . . . and they get one semester of credit." Moreover, the program maintained working ties with other key agencies, regularly referring students and their families for appropriate medical, dental, or social services. The program managed in these ways to mainstream and respond to the needs of its migrant, immigrant, and refugee student body.

Another example of California educational leadership was in Orchardtown, a rural community I studied on the southernmost margins of the San Francisco Bay Area. Although rapid growth and modernization has come in the form of new shopping centers and increased commuter traffic along the nearby state highway, the still viable, old downtown preserves Orchardtown's small-town feel. With agriculture still the base of the economy, much of the local population and labor pool is comprised of Mexicans, the only group in the area willing to fill this economic niche. A part of this population is settled, but a large cohort follows the seasonal migrant workstream that brings them here from April through October for work in the tomato, spinach, and other field harvests. Families represent more than one migration pattern: some former migrants have settled in the community, and others traverse Texas, Arizona, and other states; some migrate between Mexico and the United States, and others are new arrivals from Mexico. These migrant families bring about 300 school-age children with them, a number that increases by another hundred in summer.

Educators in Orchardtown School District generally knew much about the migrant experience, particularly the low-income and family stresses that detract from students' schooling. The district addressed the educational needs of students in various ways, including a dual-language emphasis, curricular rigor, and special attention to the socioeconomic and cultural situation of the students. Mary Paz, principal of Morningside Elementary, said the district philosophy holds that "kids can learn" and considers language difference a strength. The "real factor," she added, is good teachers and how they implement these ideas.

Ms. Rogelio is one of these teachers whose classroom at one school is made up of mostly "kids from Mexico" who receive "some bilingual content instruction everyday." For example, Rogelio teaches social studies in Spanish and math in English on one day and then switches languages on the next. Every school in the district had at least two classrooms that implemented a bilingual or ESL program. Another third-grade teacher, Tina Pulido, says that students with Mexican schooling tend to bring high levels of Spanish language competence: "When we write stories, the Mexican kid has a sense of what a story is: . . . organized sentences." Pulido asserts that students' advanced grounding in Spanish is generalizable to other academic subjects, although her observation does not apply to students who've had little schooling, or a poor experience in Mexico or in the United States. But positive assessments of students' skills such as these heighten teachers' expectations.

High expectations, in turn, appear to drive a general emphasis on a strong curriculum. Angela Rogelio related that her own "success hypothesis" requires that students have a quality schooling that includes a good curriculum, appropriate instruction, and appreciation of students' cultural heritage. Martin Sosa is a 7th-and-8th-grade math teacher at Rancho San Jose Junior High School who supports rigor in the curriculum. Sosa also claims that students who come with schooling from Mexico are well prepared in mathematics, with "good comprehension and problem solving skills." The point is that Sosa also tends to "push" his math curriculum to all students, since he says that even the average students are ready to handle it.

Roberto Gomez is director of the district's migrant education program, which attends to the particular needs of migrant students. Eligibility for the program requires evidence that the student's parents must move during the school year because of employment in an agriculturally related job. There has been no requirement for proof of citizenship or legal residence status; it has not been the responsibility of school personnel to verify if students or families are "legal" or "illegal."

The migrant program supports schooling in a variety of ways. Migrant students, for example, are monitored through a national system, as they move across state lines, between school districts, and through local migrant programs. For students and parents, participation in the migrant program provides information and helps facilitate entry into each new school situation. Those who periodically leave for Mexico remain eligible for the program upon their return. Meanwhile, an "individual service contract" may be drawn up between program personnel and the student, who agrees to a plan of study while away. Students are able to receive credit and keep up this way.

Parents benefit in various ways through their involvement in the program. Director Gomez says that the Mexican parents have little knowledge of U.S. schools. Through program meetings, classroom visits, and other involvement, parents receive information, suggestions, and encouragement to help their children succeed in school. Gomez believes this kind of support is especially important because the parents, as former migrant students themselves, may have little schooling in either country. Families typically hear about the migrant program and other school services through relatives and other personal sources. But one evening, I attended a multifaceted informational program that had been organized at Rancho San Jose Junior High. The well-publicized program drew about 150 parents, their children, and school personnel. "Noche Ranchera" was opened by a faculty music ensemble playing traditional Mexican music. The principal gave a brief welcome, after which the curriculum coordinator gave an overview of the school curriculum and special programs. Then another faculty member explained the district's testing program and alerted the audience to some approaching schoolwide testing dates. Then a series of activities related to the topic of parental support followed: a teacher's brief speech, a parent small-group activity, and an emotional testimonial by Martin Sosa, who shared his personal journey from migrant student to teacher and spoke of the support given him by his parents and teachers. The evening was interspersed with music throughout and appeared to succeed as an educational, social, and cultural program.

The foregoing examples illustrate some of the ways that California schools and educators have recently served students of Mexican and other immigrant origins. School-level personnel, in particular, supported these improvements not only because they work closely with students and families but also because they understand the pedagogical bases of the policies and programs that they are putting into practice. Ostensibly, a growing interest in diversity and effective schooling for ethnic-minority students would seem to characterize the education camp, if not California society as a whole. But suddenly, the direct impact of Proposition 187 would simply rid the schools of "illegal" immigrant students, making irrelevant the question of what kind of schooling they should receive. Local districts are free to make their own improvement efforts, but this is less feasible with shrinking budgets and a growing hostility from outside.

What, then, accounts for the sudden flip-flop in which California voters singled out immigrants for their illegal status and moved to deny them education? Politics is a key element in the turn of events. Public educational policies are always determined within a wider public discourse that is ultimately a political one. In California, the discourse around a number of socioeconomic problems found a political target in "illegal immigrants," their children, and state programs that provided them with benefits. While the problems have been around since the mid-1980s, the discourse escalated and finally took on a life of its own as a political, election-year movement, with education a "logical," easy target.

Recent trends within education also figured here: Since the early 1980s widespread criticism of the entire education system has dominated the public discourse, and since that time, we have been in a "back-to-basics" cycle that stresses mathematics, science, and literacy. Although nobody can disagree with the necessity of these subjects, this push deemphasizes, by default, improvement efforts in history, geography, languages, arts, and music. These are subjects in which teachers might find it relatively more straightforward to develop multicultural curricula and, concurrently, to use it as a means of including Mexican students in the instructional process. Thus, both California's serious economic downturn, in an epoch when simple politics played well and when education needed reforming anyway, and the rise of interethnic hostilities, including immigrant bashing, are elements that all came together in the form of Proposition 187.

German National Development and Racial Ideology

Germany presents another case of contemporary ethnic conflict that has received wide media coverage. Reports of harassment and violence directed toward guestworkers, refugees, and other resident foreigners, the rise of neo-Nazi groups, and a shift to nationalist, anti-foreigner politics are instantly interpreted as a resurgence of Nazi Germany, and easy comparisons to other situations are tempting. But prior to any comparisons, the German case must be seen within its own historical development.

Through World War II, Germany harbored an image of itself as an ethnically homogeneous nation, even if contrary to historical evidence (Sauer 1992). But the postwar period left a critical need for labor and led to the undeniable ethnic diversification seen in Germany today. In the 1950s Germany entered into agreements with a succession of European nations to import *gastarbeiter* (guestworkers) for the postwar economic boom (Castles 1986). Among the first to arrive were workers from Italy, Spain, and Portugal; others from Yugoslavia, Greece, and Turkey followed. Initially imported as temporary labor, by the 1970s many of these "foreigners" had brought or started families and were permanently settled in Germany (Castles 1985). Today, the Turks are the largest of these guestworker groups, numbering 1.8 million. Furthermore, since the mid-1980s increasing numbers of political refugees from around the world have taken advantage of Germany's asylum policy, the most liberal in all of Europe, to contribute to the exponential growth of the foreigner population.

Actively recruited and legally admitted by the German state, these groups have been accepted by much of the German citizenry, but continual barriers have prevented their full incorporation in German society. These barriers have included widespread cross-cultural misunderstanding, social discrimination, and residential segregation. Other barriers to full integration take the form of myriad governmental laws and policies that regulate entry and legal status, work and economic opportunities, and education and social benefits (O'Brien 1988). By the mid-1970s the German government reacted to a dramatic rise in the number of all foreigners by implementing a program for encouraging and paying Turks and other guestworkers to return to their homelands (Körner and Mehrlander 1986; Penninx 1986). The remigration policy generally failed. This population has worked, settled, and had families in Germany, with their second- and third-generation children possessing little knowledge of or experience with Turkey (Körner and Mehrlander 1986). But by the end of the 1980s "the German mood towards immigrants [had] soured.... Guestworkers in Germany in 1989, particularly Turks, [were] the subject of widespread hostility and a growing anti-immigrant political party" (Tomasi, Tomasi, and Miller 1989). That was just before the fall of the Berlin Wall. Now Germany's pressures from global economic competition, European integration and, since 1990, national reunification all have aggravated even more ethnic group tension and hostility toward foreigners.

Germany apparently has had considerably less experience with non-Germanic ethnic groups, in contrast with the United States, whose experience with racial and ethnic diversity was underway for two centuries before its existence as a nation. So, are today's observations simply a modern resurgence of the Nazi era, which is often explained away as an aberration in German history, as "Hitler's doing"? Or does a longer historical view perhaps help explain both that era and the present?

The German case reveals a set of assumptions and beliefs that crystallized in the nation-building era of 19th-century Europe. One strand in this thought derived from German Romanticism, a genre exemplified by Goethe, Schiller, and other philosophers and writers of the 18th and 19th centuries. A key part of the Romantic vision was the idealization of the natural domain: the cosmos, the natural environment, and humanity. This view pointed to nature for both practical teachings and moral guidance in human affairs. Then Darwin, with his theory of biological evolution, arrived by the middle of the 19th century. The idea of a natural hierarchy of the species in which *Homo sapiens* ruled superior, while controversial among the general populace (it challenged creation theories of the universe), provided the spark for a social darwinism built upon both Darwin's science and the idea of essential nature from German Romanticism.

German writers, thinkers, and social critics quickly attributed an ethical quality to nature. For instance, the idea that the more developed, superior species supersede and dominate the less evolved, inferior forms was evidence of the wisdom of nature to ensure the "survival of the fittest." By extension, human races also were judged to have evolved in a hierarchy, as evidenced in each group's achievements and the domination of one superior group over all others.

Thus Darwinism provided a scientific rationale for a number of assumptions that were incorporated into a romantic vision of a German race by not only the literati but also the social thinkers of the 19th-century nation-building era:

> The aesthetic and socio-historical idiom of German Romanticism was perfectly suited to the elaboration of the ethnocultural conception of nationhood. The celebration of individuality as *Einzigkeit* or uniqueness . . . of unconscious, organic growth . . . of the vitality and integrity of traditional, rooted folk cultures: . . . all of these themes were easily transported from the domain of aesthetics and cultural criticism to that of social philosophy. [Brubaker 1990:391]

German Romanticism and its philosophy had peaked at a critical time of historical transformation, and its seductive images were appropriated for the political task of nation building:

> In the social and political thought of Romanticism . . . nations are conceived as historically rooted, organically developed individualities, united by a distinctive *Volkgeist* and by its infinitely ramifying expression in language, custom, law, culture and the state. (Brubaker 1990:391]

Thus a number of related concepts, including German organic kinship, racial purity, and cultural superiority were first introduced into the German social consciousness and contributed a racial element to Germany's national ideology.

Within this historically constructed ideology, racial assumptions have defined who is and who is not German. A racial group is biologically related; thus kinship or blood ties determine who is German. The idea of racial and ethnic boundaries was extended to political boundaries and membership: "What is specific about the concept of the German nation . . . lies in the fact that it is constructed biologically. German nationals are defined by their origin; one can only be born a German" (Rathzel 1990:41).

Since 1913 until only recently, German citizenship has been legally based in the principle of jus sanguinis, or blood-kinship (Brubaker 1990). For decades, an explicit racial ideology formed part of the dominant group's social philosophy, politics, and institutional treatment of ethnic groups defined as not belonging to the German nation. The semantic category *Ausländer* (foreigners) separates those who do not "belong" from the dominant, majority German ethnic group. It was this very principle—Germany for Germans only—that supported the takeover by the National Socialists (Nazis) before World War II, as they justified ethnic cleansing as a solution to broader economic, political, and international crises (Burleigh 1991).

30. Resurgence of Ethnic Nationalism

Today we see in Germany the resurgence of ethnic hostilities not seen since the 1940s. A reactionary social climate and the popularity of nationalistic, antiforeigner politics have resulted in physical violence toward German residents in guestworker or refugee statuses. While only a very small minority of Germans is actually involved in these actions, historically minded observers cannot help but see these current hostilitiy toward Turks and other ethnic groups as a resurgence of old, stable patterns of German thinking and behavior (O'Brien 1988). Many Germans agree with this view, as they openly debate this crisis and ask themselves what kind of folk and society they want to be.

The Schooling of Foreigners, the Reeducation of Germans

Some indications are that many Germans have decided to redirect their nation's history to become a more inclusive society. For instance, large public demonstrations against racism and xenophobia have been organized in Berlin, Frankfurt, and other German cities. The Green Party and other political organizations also are working against blatant anti-foreigner politics, while the national leadership has recently taken an aggressive stance against the proliferation of extremist, neo-Nazi groups. In settings ranging from neighborhood and workplace to family, many other Germans have assumed personal responsibility for speaking out and acting concretely on these critical issues.

In all of this, education, schools, and educators appear to be key actors resisting the past and working for progressive change. This was not always the case, because German education has been marked by systematic neglect, discrimination, and exclusion of Turks and other foreigners, even into the 1980s. Turkish-German bilingualism has undergone intensive study, but no systematic initiatives have begun to address the critical issues inherent in language transition and loss, and their impact on school achievement (Pfaff 1981, 1991). Structural barriers to schooling remain, while research has documented the segregation of educational opportunity for foreigner children who, by the secondary level, cluster "at the lowest level—*the Hauptschule*—and remain there" (Baker

6. SPECIAL TOPICS IN MULTICULTURAL EDUCATION

et. al. 1985:219) to receive preparation for unskilled and semiskilled jobs (Gitmez and Wilpert 1987). The last set of issues to gain notice have been the personal experiences of students living between two worlds: the dilemma of choosing between two sets of cultural values and beliefs, the crisis of identity, or the decision whether to wear traditional or modern clothes (Saydam 1990; Springer 1992). But in Berlin and Hamburg, I interviewed and observed administrators and teachers who felt a responsibility to address issues of diversity and inclusion in their professional roles. High in the educational hierarchy are administrators such as Herr Schmidt, a Hamburg School Board administrator and also the German national representative to the education task force of the European Community. In response to the shortcomings of the past, state educational agencies now have offices to oversee policy and programs addressing the education of foreigners. The reality, says Schmidt, is that Germany is an immigration country responsible for the integration of children and youth through education. Since the late 1970s, states have responded variably through programs for newcomers, bilingual instruction, German as a second language, and vocational education.

Schmidt shared a vignette that captures the tension inherent in these attempts to reform the past. He explained that the *multikulturelle Gesellschaft* (multicultural society) is now "in" but that some theories about the multicultural society and intercultural education can be extreme. Then Schmidt told of one community in which multicultural enthusiasts insisted that Germans learn Turkish, and noted that these extreme supporters of intercultural education actually stimulated a right-wing reaction among those who countered, "We want this to be a German school."

But more successful attempts to initiate educational change can be found in progressive communities. The Hamburg suburb of Wilhelmsburg is known as a *Sozialsbrennpunkte* (social flashpoint). This is jargon for communities of both German and foreigner, working, or welfare families, who live in public housing located in areas with high levels of poverty, substance abuse, and crime. According to one teacher, families are typically afraid to let children out of their massive, impersonal high-rise apartments. At the same time, Wilhelmsburg is an historically "Red" workers' community with a population mixed along class and ethnicity, and a record of progressive action.

This progressive bent is often expressed in the attitudes and behaviors of administrators and teachers of the local *Grundschule* (elementary school). In an interview, the school principal indicated that integration is the main goal of education for the foreign students, who make up about 35 percent of her school's population. This is not a straightforward matter for Turks and other groups who suffer from stigma, discrimination, relative poverty, and related social disadvantages in Germany. The Turkish community's strong fear of losing its culture further points to the crucial role of education in providing an accepting and effective experience for Turkish students and their families.

The staff of this school explained that most of their students have grown up in Germany, unlike many newcomers at higher grade levels who are likely to have had formative experiences in Turkey or other countries of origin. But children come to school typically "not ready to learn," as the bleak neighborhood provides few stimulating environments, such as parks, museums, or wholesome recreational venues. The school's approach is to provide a safe, supportive, and enriching environment to all children, regardless of background. While staff claims to make no distinctions among students, I took note of some efforts they clearly are making on behalf of their foreign students. In the classroom, these include both the integration of culturally inclusive curricular content and bias-free instruction—elements of the typical Multi Kulti (multicultural education) approach.

Outside of school the staff takes advantage of the strong Turkish family and community systems (Gitmez and Wilpert 1987). For instance, in addition to the typical school-to-home notes and phone calls, individual teachers try to know and maintain personal contact with Turkish parents. Occasional invitations to Turkish homes are seen as opportunities to make contact, as are standing invitations by teachers for Turkish parents to visit the classroom or share a cultural activity with the class.

The director described a schoolwide project they had once organized. Wir Können Viel Zusammen Tun (We Can Do Much Together) was a parent-involvement program that, in addition to cooking, dancing, and other social activities, had as its goal consciousness raising to combat *Ausländerfeindlichkeit* (hostility toward foreigners). While the project had attendance problems due to parents' working, the need for child care, and Turkish parents' lack of facility in German, the effort had been made to change school relations with and within the community.

In one case, a teacher's interest in the community was great enough that he has become closely involved with a group of Turkish boys. Originally formed as a gang to protect against German skinheads who regularly invaded the community to beat up Turks and other foreigners, the group continues as a social club, with the German teacher acting as advisor and cultural facilitator to the Turkish adolescents. Here, progressive community attitudes attract educators who believe "they have a job to do," in one teacher's words, that is, to maximize their students' education.

In Berlin I found another site of progressive action in Frau Adler's second-grade classroom. This teacher is involved in a special Turkish bilingual, biliteracy project that has received state funding (Berlin is a city-state) for ten years. The project is in place through the collaborative efforts of a group of Free University of Berlin researchers and the school's administrators, teachers, and staff (personal communication, Carol Pfaff, 1991). The program is open to both Germans and Turks, but parents must request it.

While the ultimate goal is to teach German, Adler and the Turkish teacher who co-ops with her use what is termed *coordination* to teach both German fundamentals and Turkish basics in parallel fashion. Bilingual language instruction is the focus, but the team also teaches in the content areas. A parent-involvement component encourages the parents to come into class to cook, do arts and crafts, or other forms of cultural sharing.

While Adler admits that formal measures of achievement may not improve, she claims other benefits from this program. Children receive language training in two languages, their behavior improves, and they gain new attitudes. As second- or third-generation Turks in Germany, Adler's Turkish students know little about their own history and culture. Thus a critical benefit accrues to Turkish children as they hear and see their language used in class and as they see the involvement of their parents grow through the acceptance of Turkish language and culture. They gain a new consciousness and feeling about themselves, says Adler. But the German children benefit as well, she continues. The learning of a second language enhances their learning of German. And the German children gain another consciousness about languages, that is, that another language is just another system of communication, she adds. Adler's hope is that these new attitudes generalize to other forms of diversity with which children must be prepared to live in school and in society.

These examples are followed by a less than optimistic postscript, however. Schmidt notes that lack of resources have prevented the development of systematic improvements so far. Now with the *Sparpolitik* (budget-cutting policy) that has kicked in since reunification in 1990, state and local governments find it even more difficult to fund educational improvements. Moreover, in the current reactionary social climate, educators find it more difficult to carry out alone the changes needed to better include and school Turkish and other foreign children.

History, Ideology, Society: The Place of Education

Clearly, we need to learn more about each of the cases presented here, and to bear in mind that all things are not equal in any two situations. Still, we can begin to better understand the central problem from this kind of historical comparison. Within this view, three interrelated elements stand out in the California and German cases: ideology, experience, and education. In both cases, a resurgence of ethnocentrism, xenophobia, and nationalism can be linked to a standing ideology that rationalizes dominant-group exclusion and persecution of target groups (Arendt 1973). A particular set of beliefs has been constructed through internal processes of group development and refined over time through external contact with others. Historically, the Germanic people represented a number of different tribal heritages that needed a common identity and cohesion before a nation-state could be built. Race, a narrowly defined blood kinship, provided this organizing principle, which then came to function with other assumptions of group superiority and purity. These ideas have been part of Germany's legacy since its inception as a nation. The atrocities of World War II, the persecution, imprisonment, and genocide of unwanted groups, primarily the Jews, were the "logical" extreme expression of this ideology, and the events of today represent a return by some elements in Germany to that belief system, however modified in form.

In contrast to Germany's ideological "headstart," experience preceded ideology in the United States. For example, African slavery in the United States was initially justified on a Christian-heathen argument, but "race" became the rationale after slaves began to adopt Christianity (Takaki 1993). The enslavement of Africans and removal of American Indians provided the experiential ground in which the official policy of Manifest Destiny was cultivated to justify the territorial displacement and subjugation of Mexicans in the latter half of the last century. The standard cliché that "Americans only think through action and doing" applies, in that historical subjugation and exclusion of racial and ethnic groups became a key part of a definition of the United States as a nation. Although the development of racial or ethnic ideologies took different routes in Germany and the United States, the common point is that a similar complex of ideas has existed at some level in both places.

The identification of an ideology does not mean that a group goes about daily life thinking consciously about a related set of racist or ethnocentric beliefs, plotting how to act on them. Except for the most fundamental elements, most members of a group would not admit holding ideas that have received negative criticism in modern times. The longevity of these ideas depends on more subtle mechanisms including: the popular repackaging of imagery of Romanticism or of the Manifest Destiny of a chosen people with a great calling to fulfill; the official representation of historical events in favor of the dominant group, to the degree that the mistreatment of other groups never really happened or was not that bad, or that victim groups are actually the racists; or in the political revival of earlier, simple solutions to complex issues, a return to an idealized past when we had few problems, and "other" groups were easily dismissed by decree. Politics is clearly the arena to which elements of racial or ethnic thinking have returned, through the kind of nationalistic imagery, informational selectivity, and emotional persuasion in which politicians are skilled.

Beyond similar ideologies, other historical factors in each case have mediated their translation into practice. For example, the U.S. Constitution, with its principles of equality, democracy, and human rights, together with the concept of equal legal protection, is another way of thinking about the rights and recourse due to all, including members of minority groups. Thus, two competing ideologies have been in tension throughout U.S. history, with the result that systematic racial persecution and exclusion have been reduced over time, albeit gradually and largely through the efforts of the persecuted groups themselves. This tension has accounted in part for the periodic expression of the racial and ethnic system of thought, not only in the historical "love-hate" Mexican-U.S. relationship described earlier but in other phenomena such as racial segregation (after Emancipation), Americanization policy ("ethnic/language difference is bad"), or immigrant bashing ("get rid of them"). The manifestation of this ideology is thus cyclical, coming out at certain times in social discourse, in local and national politics, and in the treatment of target groups. In contrast, German society has been relatively less constrained in the practice of its racial beliefs. Ultimately, World War II and world condemnation were necessary to put an end to the Nazi atrocities. But an externally motivated change of behavior did not necessarily affect deeply seated German beliefs about permissible intergroup relations; they simply have been suppressed.

One way of summarizing these different conditions is that Germany has had the more explicit ideology but a shorter history of implementation and now faces external pressures to change. The United States, on the other hand, has applied a less-articulated exclusionary ideology over a longer period of time and with more groups. But the periodic return of exclusionary social phenomena appears to automatically force an internal examination of those historically grounded beliefs that are, by definition, in direct contradiction with essential democratic values. This does not imply an advantage in either nation's quest to redirect its history, for both in-

6. SPECIAL TOPICS IN MULTICULTURAL EDUCATION

ternal dialogue and external opinion would appear to be important. On the other hand, internally motivated dialogue and change would seem to be minimum requirements, and a more solid basis for lasting resolutions.

The critical point of commonality in these cases is what dominant groups have come to believe about targeted ethnic groups and what is permissible behavior toward them. An education, in the broad sense, in certain beliefs, ideas, and behavior has formed the predispositions of both individuals and groups. But it follows equally that education, or reeducation, is thoroughly implied in the redirection of the habits of the past. The role of education in the present cases illustrates how schools actually have taken responsibility for implementing policies, programs, and strategies that constructively address the group divisions at issue here. The California and German schools studied here feature curricula that incorporate students' ethnic backgrounds, instruction that utilizes their cultural knowledge and linguistic skills, and educators' concerted attention to the material and social conditions faced by their students. The ends achieved through these school improvement efforts are the enhanced inclusion of all students in the educational process, and the new conceptions of race and ethnic group relations modeled through those efforts.

But we cannot assume that formal education can solve all the problems of ethnic group interaction in either California or Germany, especially when reactionary sociopolitical movements have targeted the best efforts of schools for easy solutions. The abundance of uninformed, political, and emotionally charged solutions suggests the potential and critical role of education beyond school fences. Although Proposition 187 surfaced in the political arena, its ideas obviously found support in many other places, including families, the workplace, and the media. Parents and families must somehow be supported in their task of caring for and socializing their children and helped to gain new understandings about human differences that should not matter, such as race, and actions that are unsupportable, such as negative stereotyping and discrimination. Education continues to be a great need in the workplace, despite recent advances. Several instances of racial or ethnic discrimination have been widely reported in the media recently, involving issues that range from verbal and physical harassment to problems of hiring, promotion, and pay. The backlash against affirmative action policy reminds us that lasting social progress is ultimately dependent on popular understandings that support that change.

Political and government leaders need to understand the key role they play in the resolution of racial and ethnic conflicts, and education can help. The preparation of informed leadership will depend on the accessibility of useful information about what the real problems are, about how schools can continue to be part of a constructive solution, and about how social policy and legislation are involved. A role for anthropologists is clearly implied in all of these potential educational sites.

But neither anthropologists, nor families, nor school teachers, nor politicians, acting alone, can turn an entire nation's history around. All must contribute to such a transformation based on education. That education must be based on dialogue, a sense of responsibility to resolve common societal problems, and knowledge of our common and group histories. Only when we begin to understand the present as directly linked to the past will we be in a position to explore new ways of thinking about intergroup relations in a free democracy.

José Macias is an associate professor in the Division of Bicultural Bilingual Studies at the University of Texas at San Antonio.

Notes

Acknowledgments. The research reported here was supported by the University Research Committee, the Department of Educational Studies, and the Ethnic Studies Program, all units of the University of Utah. The author gratefully acknowledges the assistance of Elizabeth Escalera-Bell in the preparation of the manuscript.

1. All community names and personal names are pseudonyms.

References Cited

Acuna, Rodolfo. 1988. A History of Chicanos, 3rd edition. New York: Harper and Row.

Arendt, Hannah. 1973. The Origins of Totalitarianism. New York: Harcourt, Brace, Jovanovich.

Baker, David, Yilmaz Esmer, Gero Lenhardt, and John Meyer. 1985. Effects of Immigrant Workers on Educational Stratification in Germany. Sociology of Education 58(October):213–277.

Brubaker, William R. 1990. Immigration, Citizenship, and the Nation-State in France and Germany: A Comparative Historical Analysis. International Sociology 5(4):379–407.

Burleigh, Michael. 1991. Racism as Social Policy: The Nazi "Euthanasia" Programme, 1939–1945. Ethnic and Racial Studies 14(4):453–469.

Castles, Stephen. 1985. The Guests Who Stayed—The Debate on "Foreigners Policy" in the German Federal Republic. International Migration Review 19(3):517–534.

   1986. The Guest-Worker in Europe—An Obituary. International Migration Review 20(4):761–778.

Espinosa, Paul, dir. 1982. The Lemon Grove Incident. Film, VHS, 60 min. San Diego: KPBS-TV.

Gitmez, Ali, and Czarina Wilpert. 1987. A Micro-Society or an Ethnic Community? Social Organization and Ethnicity amongst Turkish Migrants in Berlin. *In* Immigrant Associations in Europe. John Rex, Daniele Joly, and Czarina Wilpert, eds. Pp. 86–125. Brookfield, VT: Gower.

Körner, Heiko, and Ursula Mehrlander. 1986. New Migration Policies in Europe: The Return of Labor Migrants, Remigration Promotion and Integration Policies. International Migration Review 20(3):672–675.

Macias, José. 1990. Scholastic Antecedents of Immigrant Students: Schooling in a Mexican Immigrant-Sending Community. Anthropology and Education Quarterly 21(4):291–318.

   1993 Forgotten History: Educational and Social Antecedents of High Achievement Among Asian Immigrants in the U.S. Curriculum Inquiry 23(4):409–432.

   1995 Proposition 187 and Racism. Ethnic Studies Program Newsletter [University of Utah] 2(2):4–5.

O'Brien, Peter. 1988. Continuity and Change in Germany's Treatment of Non-Germans. International Migration Review 22(3):109–134.

Penninx, Rinus. 1986. International Migration in Western Europe since 1973: Developments, Mechanisms and Controls. International Migration Review 20(4):951–972.

Pfaff, Carol W. 1981. Sociolinguistic Problems of Immigrants: Foreign Workers and Their Children in Germany. Review article. Language in Society 10:155–188.

   1991 Turkish in Contact with German: Language Maintenance and Loss among Immigrant Children in Berlin (West). International Journal of the Sociology of Language 90:97–129.

Rathzel, Nora. 1990. Germany: One Race, One Nation? Race & Class 32(3):31–48.

Sauer, Paul. 1992. On the History of Jews in Southwest Germany. European Education 24(4):68–72.

Saydam, Onur. 1990. Turkish Children and Youth. Western European Education 22(1):80–85.

Springer, Monika. 1992. A Conversation with Turkish Female Students: "Every Sheep Is Hung by Its Own Leg." European Education 24(3):77–82.

Takaki, Ronald. 1993. A Different Mirror: A History of Multicultural America. New York: Little, Brown.

Tomasi, Silvano, Lydio Tomasi, and Mark Miller. 1989. IMR at 25: Reflections on a Quarter Century of International Migration Research and Orientations for Future Research. International Migration Review 23(3):393–402.

Telling Stories: On Ethnicity, Exclusion, and Education in Upstate New York

Ellen Bigler

Rhode Island College

Examination of the public discourse of Euro-American senior citizens and minority speakers during a community debate on the educational needs of Latinos indicates sharply differing constructions of group identity and explanations for the social and educational status of ethnic minorities. Reasons for conflicts over multiculturalism are explored.

We are currently witnessing a struggle over public school curricula and programs. Recent projects for change challenge the assumption that all ethnic groups' stories are essentially the same and, in the process, call into question popular visions of the nation as a color-blind land of equal opportunity for all. As with other initiatives like affirmative action and federal programs intended to even out disparities between groups, resistance to bilingual and multicultural education—including a more inclusive history and literature curriculum—has been sustained in many quarters of mainstream America.

While educational policy changes may be issued at the state or national level, it is at the local level that change is supported or resisted, implemented or subverted. Thus looking to the local level, to uncover the underlying premises that structure current educational debates and to make sense of how local actors interpret and respond to proposals for change, can provide insights of vital importance.

In this ethnographic study I analyze stories told in an upstate New York community during a heated public debate regarding the necessity for multicultural and bilingual education. The stories told by two individuals—one a Latino community organizer and the other a Euro-American senior citizen, are analyzed in depth. I also construct and contrast the collective stories about "being" and "becoming" American as told by Euro-American seniors and minority speakers,[1] using discourse analysis to provide each group's interpretive framework. Analysis of this public discourse reveals sharply differing constructions of group identity and explanations for the social and educational status of minorities. These then are *telling* stories that I argue can provide important insights into what contributes to current struggles over educational programs and curricula in the nation's schools.

Studying Stories/Constructing Frameworks

The personal narratives we construct from the past events in our lives, and our reconstructions of the stories we hear growing up, are important mechanisms for revealing our "presentation of self," both to ourselves and to others (see Benmayor et al. 1988; Goffman 1959). The stories we tell help us organize and make sense of our world and where we fit into it. They have strategic value as we attempt to move others to see our own visions of ourselves and our world.

Given that one's reading of the past is shaped by present circumstances and that one's experience of the present is shaped by our knowledge of the past (Connerton 1989), we can anticipate significant differences in the narrative content of Euro-American senior stories and ethnic minority stories. For groups from differing structural locations in society, such stories come to "mean" differently, both in content and function (Benmayor et al. 1988). Therefore narratives of Euro-American seniors, Latinos, and African Americans were selected from public discourse (letters to the editor, public meetings) for analysis. These narratives, alongside other publicly printed materials and transcripts of related public speeches, interviews, and radio talk show callers' comments, were also examined in order to identify themes recurring in multiple sites. These recurring themes were taken to be indicative of content areas significant to the speakers and to reveal the semiotic building blocks of the conceptual framework through which they make sense of their worlds (Agar 1983; Woolard 1989). They thus were used to construct the interpretive frameworks through which participants understood the conflict and the community's responses.

Community Background

Arnhem,[2] the site of the conflict, is in many respects a microcosm of the larger society. Southern and eastern European immigrants flooded into the city in the early 1900s, seeking employment in its flourishing industries. By midcentury, however, Arnhem had begun to lose its

6. SPECIAL TOPICS IN MULTICULTURAL EDUCATION

industrial base. As in many such older industrial communities, it was people of color and the newest immigrants who, faced with declining opportunities in primary labor markets, moved in to work at marginal jobs. Arnhem's Puerto Rican and Costa Rican communities gained a foothold during this era.

Interviews and archival research suggest that Arnhem's Latino community was "tolerated" during the early decades of its existence, though largely excluded from access to the better jobs. Construction of the Arnhem Mall in the city center during the early 1970s—what one Latino leader refers to as the "Arnhem Wall"—further isolated many Latinos from the Euro-American population. Programs designed to meet the particular needs of the Latino community were virtually nonexistent up through the 1980s. In the city's schools, most teachers had little or no knowledge of Latino cultures or the literature on educating students with language or cultural differences.[3]

Arnhem's Latino population increased by 71 percent during the 1980s. This dramatic rise was fueled both by people coming directly from Puerto Rico and Central America, as well as by metropolitan area transplants seeking employment, a better education for their children, and relief from the drug and crime infested inner cities of the Northeast. The 1990 census put Hispanics—three quarters of them Puerto Rican—at 12 percent of the population,[4] though many locals insist that they were seriously undercounted. One third live below poverty level (three times the rate of local Euro-Americans), and the majority of adult Latinos have not completed high school.

While the numbers of Latino residents are increasing, the city's total population, now standing at 21,000, continues to decline from its all-time high of 35,000 in 1930. Many younger Euro-Americans, facing declining opportunities for gainful employment, have left the city. Seniors—most of them the children and grandchildren of the southern and eastern European immigrants—now comprise over 30 percent of the population. Most are on fixed incomes. With local taxes rapidly escalating in the past decade, they resist further increases and "special favors" for the more recently arrived minority population.

The Conflict

The conflict that generated the public discourse analyzed in the following pages erupted in 1991. John Marris, a retired Euro-American fiscal officer, had successfully run for the school board on a platform advocating extreme fiscal conservatism. Asked after his election how he felt about the strong multicultural emphasis in a report on the need for social studies reform in New York State (Sobol 1989), Marris replied that minorities who made "genuine contributions" should be included, but that some contributions "have been disasters. The Spanish people in South America, for instance, can't run a country without total chaos. You don't find that in Western civilization because people there are reasonably intelligent and know how to do things."

Local Latinos, angered by his comments, picketed the following school-board meeting and demanded an apology. Marris refused; in subsequent interviews he also made disparaging comments about Hispanic youth and police officers. Minority spokespersons then called for his resignation from the board, which in turn generated angry countercharges from a large senior-citizen cohort supporting Marris. The conflict remained front-page news for several weeks, and a heated topic of debate in letters to the editor and on radio talk shows for several months afterward. The school district held a locally televised public forum to air grievances and concerns, and New York State Education Department personnel entered the schools to investigate charges of racism.

The call for change in the schools was led by local Hispanic leaders and an African American woman; Latino college students from a nearby city also became involved. Organizing to challenge their claims was a large senior citizen cohort. As a group, seniors in Arnhem wielded considerable political power, for instance, controlling the majority of votes on the school board, and their spokespersons were regularly consulted by the local media for their opinions. As is often the case, local participants and the media both framed the conflict as a debate between two sides in polar opposition to one another,[5] Euro-American "seniors" on one side and "Hispanics" (or "minorities"), on the other. In the following sections, the term *Seniors*, when capitalized, represents the public presentation of this group's sentiments, while *Minorities* is used to represent the collective view put forward by minority speakers.

The Senior Story

Let us begin by looking at excerpts from a Senior narrative in order to develop a sense of the Senior perspective articulated in public texts. The following letter to the editor, written by a Polish American resident, appeared after two months of angry charges and countercharges in the media and at public meetings:

> To the editor:
> There is no need to debate or question which language should be spoken in these United States as the universal language. It is to the benefit of all nationalities to speak English, so that all can understand each other....
> The ambitious... built America. ... They faced ridicule and name calling and survived... [and] worked... for a few coins per hour....
> They asked for nothing. They spoke their native tongue in their homes, communities and business places. They had no modern schools, they learned to speak English from their co-workers... and [in the] streets.
> My mother taught me to read and write Polish as a child. She sent me to a one-room schoolhouse to learn to read, write and spell English....
> The Indians... [lost] their land by force. Today the Indian nation speaks English. Their native tongue (I presume) they speak among themselves....
> It should be essential that all immigrants go to school to learn English, so they can read and write, to vote and converse with their fellow men....
> [I]f language becomes an issue, there will be hard feelings amongst all.... There will be the danger of dividing these United States into sections like Europe. Stand together and be an immigrant American under one God, one government, one flag and one universal language—English. Many speak English the world over....
> Let us lay aside our personal enmities.

Visible throughout the text are widely recognized American symbols:

the immigrant "muscle" and self-sacrifice that built the nation, the one-room schoolhouse of bygone and better days, and the English language as a symbol of national unity and culture. By way of responding to Hispanics' demands for a bilingual education program—which is never explicitly mentioned—the writer presents a romantic vision of earlier European immigrants, to which he negatively contrasts, largely by implication, current Hispanic (im)migrants.

Through the use of past tense and reference to bygone days, the author attributes virtues of hard work and self-sacrifice to earlier immigrant groups. He then shifts to a discussion of today's immigrants, without attributing such characteristics to them. Immigrants of the past went to school to learn English, but immigrants today, by implication, do not. Unlike immigrants of the past, he implies, current newcomers come expecting too much, making too much of discrimination, asking for special favors, trying to change the country (language), rather than accept it and find ways to fit in. Finally, by referring to the local Hispanics as "immigrants," though 75 percent are Puerto Ricans (all U.S. citizens and many second- and third-generation mainlanders), the author situates Puerto Ricans as newcomers and, thus, as a group that has yet to earn its place and be accepted into American society. In his closing paragraph, he asks "us" to "lay aside our personal enmities," although those acting on their "personal enmities" appear to be Latinos.

A close reading of the text also reveals that, behind the author's initial statement in support of English as the universal language, are several unspoken presuppositions. The author argues that native languages should be taught and maintained only in the privacy of the home and ethnic community; *even the Indians,* wronged as they were by white settlers, speak English in public and their native tongues in private. Choosing to make language an issue, like the Hispanics who are never mentioned, will divide the nation's people and destroy America. Implicit here is the assumption that an intended outcome of bilingual education programs is the replacement of English by Spanish and that acceptance and support for maintenance of speakers' Spanish language abilities cannot coexist with acceptance of English as the "universal language." Hispanics who demand bilingual programs are threatening national unity, symbolized by the *"one* God, *one* government, *one* flag and *one* universal language" (emphasis added).

Interpretive Framework of Seniors

Several key themes apparent in this letter also recurred in much of the wider Senior public discourse. Representative statements, made by seniors over the three-month period following Marris's original statements, illustrate each theme.

Theme 1: Assimilation Keeps America Strong. Seniors voiced strong support for cultural and linguistic assimilation, maintaining that their own parents had publicly abandoned their homeland, culture, and language for the greater good. Hispanics, the newest immigrants, were censured for their alleged refusal to conform to the culture and language of the nation, which Seniors claimed was necessary for American unity. if there *is* bias against Hispanics, Seniors asserted, they bring it on themselves:

School board member, public forum: Keep your heritage and language; speak Spanish at home or with your friends. But learn to speak English in school and the outside world if you want to succeed. Whether you like it or not, this *is* an English-speaking country.

Letter to the editor: Promotion of multiculturalism as public policy is antithetical to our national ideal of unity through cultural assimilation. ... Witness the problems, the notoriously ethnocentric, acculturation resistant Hispanics have entering the American mainstream.

Theme 2: "Attitude" Problem. Senior texts frequently portrayed Hispanics as lacking in motivation and expecting handouts, in sharp contrast to Seniors' parents, who they felt had labored to make this city (nation) great and asked for nothing in return:

Talk-show caller: Enough is enough with the "gimme, gimme" attitude and "you owe me" attitude. I've had it.

Speaker, public forum: Arnhem is a wonderful city and affords many opportunities to everybody who wants them. ... [But] I can't understand why the Hispanic population doesn't *want* to be educated. ... Do you think that ... [European immigrants] were just handed everything? No, they worked hard.

Theme 3: Equivalence of Experience/Denial of Racism. Hispanics were repeatedly censured for making "a big to-do" about racism and discrimination. Seniors either denied the existence of bias, claimed they and/or their parents had faced similar bias without complaining, asserted that it was no different in Arnhem than elsewhere, and/or claimed that minorities brought it on themselves by adhering to their old ways and to each other.

Letter to the editor: To orchestrate an attempt at [Marris's] ouster is a classic example of an overreaction by a hypersensitive minority to a small and imagined slight.

Op-ed writer: Certainly we all agree these incidents (throwing racial epithets at minority students] are cruel and worthy of our contempt, but are they racist? ... Controversy sparks angry name calling. ... We have no more prejudice or racism than you will find in any similar community.

Retired teacher, public forum: If there's been racism in Arnhem School District—maybe I'm naive—I don't know about it. ... The Italians were called guineas and wops; so what's new?

Theme 4: Public Comportment. Closely related to theme 3, this theme spoke to public behaviors. Hispanics were depicted as "rowdy" and "out of line" picketing and "raising a ruckus" over issues of racism, behaviors portrayed as harming both the community's reputation and ethnic relations:

Speaker, public forum: You have a right to protest. But you also have an obligation to live peacefully within the rest of the community. So to sit down and discuss in a quiet manner. ... Wildcat demonstrations are not the way. They only tend to polarize the community.

Speaker, public forum: Now I notice today, all the rowdies aren't here. The Hispanic community is well behaved ... not like they were on the

6. SPECIAL TOPICS IN MULTICULTURAL EDUCATION

last board meeting, with signs and everything.... I sympathize with you people, but not when you're rowdy, not when you're cracking up.

Theme 5: Insider/Outsider. Seniors characterized government agencies and people from outside the city (e.g., Hispanic college students) as "outsiders," who have no business being involved:

School board member, public forum: I do *not* want to listen to anyone... not from the Arnhem School District.... This is a family matter.

Speaker, public forum: [Directed at Hispanics] Let's keep it quiet; let's keep it to ourselves.... Arnhem is a good place to work... [and] to live.

Theme 6: Dividing and Destroying Arnhem/USA. Euro-Americans, according to Seniors, made Arnhem (and the United States) great. The actions of minorities are destroying all they worked so hard for:

Speaker, school board meeting: The same people trying to get [Marris] out are the ones you see in the police report every night in the paper.

Letter to the editor: The economy... is not only the fault of our leaders but ... those who demand that the government owes us a living. Our oldsters remember how we made our own way and shouldered our own problems.

Talk-show caller: [Euro-Americans] kept the city nice.... Why do the Latinos [and other minorities]... flock in here? Again, do you realize how much is being taken out of the taxpayers' pockets, to teach so many of your people?

Seniors thus put forward as a universal model for incorporation into the American mainstream what they perceived to have worked for them (see Figure 1). Their model drew (sometimes contradictorily) upon both what social scientists have variously termed an "assimilationist," "Anglo-conformity," or "melting-pot" model, taken for so long as the appropriate metaphor to describe the "making" of the American people, and upon the self-conscious assertions of ethnic pride that reflect the "new-ethnicity" appearing among Euro-Americans by the 1970s (Novak 1971). *Conformity,* *accepting hard knocks,* and *hard work* are the ingredients that ensure *success,* which is ultimately what *made Arnhem great;* with *success* also comes *acceptance* as an *American.*

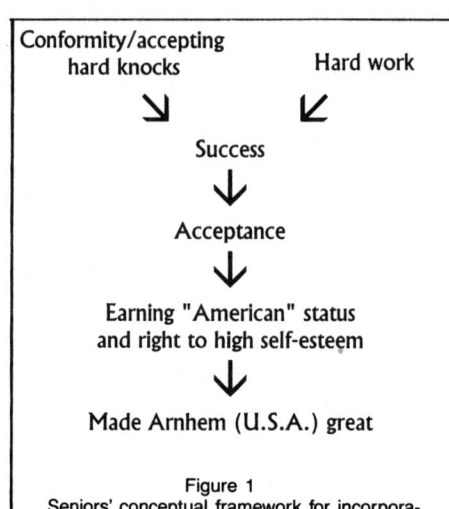

Figure 1
Seniors' conceptual framework for incorporation into American mainstream

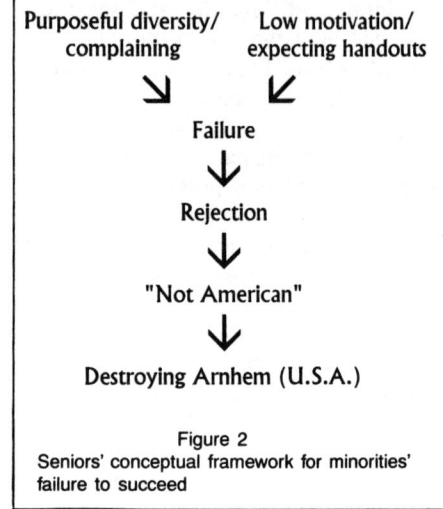

Figure 2
Seniors' conceptual framework for minorities' failure to succeed

We see in their arguments their claim to being Americans as rooted in the story they share of a struggling, self-sacrificing immigrant past and their own hard work, through which they and their children succeeded in achieving social mobility and, by extension, national greatness. As Alba's sociological study (1990) of ethnic identity among whites in a nearby metropolitan area suggests, ethnicity for Euro-Americans continues to be salient. What we are witnessing, however, is the original ethnic divisions among those of European descent being replaced or supplemented by a "Euro-American" identity, with emphasis on the shared immigrant experience and social mobility as setting them apart from "nonwhite" ethnic groups. As will become apparent, this Euro-American "national origin myth" contrasts sharply with the stories being put forward by minority spokespersons.

Taking the model depicted in Figure 1 as their basis for evaluating the minority community, Seniors positioned minorities as operating from the opposite, and negative ends of the various continua (see Figure 2). The actions of "those people," as seen by Seniors, helped explain both: troubling changes in the United States in their lifetimes and the lower social, economic, and educational status of minority groups:

The Minority Story

Minorities came back with a counterclaim. Analysis of their discourse reveals a contrasting interpretation: their difficulties achieving success are rooted in the nation's racism and exclusion of their language and culture, which they maintain to be their entitlement as Americans. This perspective was eloquently expressed by a Hispanic community activist at the public forum, where she spoke in support of calls for a school district more responsive to Hispanic students' needs. Her narrative paints a picture of the exclusion of minorities and asks the listener to consider the consequences:

My name is Virginia Colón.... *Primeramente, quiero empezar por decirles que hay mas gente en los Estados Unidos que hablan español que muchísimos países. En fin, el derecho ajeno es la obligación de todos, incluídos ustedes que están presentes aquí esta noche.* [First, I want to begin by telling you that there are more people who speak Spanish in the U.S. than in many countries. So the obligation of all, to respect others, includes you who are present here tonight.]

You know, I used to live in Kansas, and I remember the first time I went to a restaurant and I ordered my usual BLT—I love BLTs; I have a passion for BLTs—and the waitress told me, "I'm sorry, we don't serve niggers here. You'll have to go." ... What happens to kids who didn't have the skills that I had to get through that?

People have labeled this discussion ... hostile. This is called dialogue. People have labeled this ... racial preference. It's called diversity. People have ... label[ed] it un-American. It's democratic ... the foundations that this country has been built on.... Every time I hear a student have to ... [say] "I am an American," it's because we once again are not included.... Let's make sure ... all of us here today represent each star on that flag.

The speaker initially switches to Spanish, emblematic of her identification with Hispanics in the audience and affirming their right as Americans to use Spanish in public discourse. Her message, intended for Spanish speakers, is never repeated in English, though on the surface it addresses seniors. It stakes out the claim that Hispanics are here in force, they need not apologize for who they are, and they are entitled to respect. "Kansas" and "BLTs" (bacon, lettuce, and tomato sandwiches) are quintessentially "American"; Hispanics can be different and at the same time as "American" as the nation's heartland and BLTs.

Colón's narrative also depicts Latinos as being forced to confront the ugliness of racism in their most formative years. The speaker's innocence and eager anticipation when entering the restaurant are juxtaposed to the ugliness and exclusion she encounters, symbolic of immigrants' anticipation of life in the United States and their encounters with the reality of racism. Using alliteration for greater impact—"dialogue," "diversity," "democracy"—she puts forward a reinterpretation of events that Seniors have condemned, turning a positive light on them. She concludes with an appeal to all the flag represents.

Interpretive Framework of Minorities

The themes found in this narrative of (a) the United States as benefiting from diversity, (b) minority rights to "difference," and (c) the long history of racism and exclusion that has held minorities back also recurred throughout the Minority discourse.

Theme 1: Difference as Entitlement. Diversity was portrayed as a positive quality, an entitlement and something to be proud of:

Latino college student, public forum: Nowhere in the U.S. Constitution is English the official language. ... They left it open so that people who wanted to come ... didn't have to worry about speaking English to fit in.... The English Only movement in this country is only gonna damage the greater culture ... 'cause we're such a mixture of many, many cultures.

Hispanic leader: We should learn from other ethnic minorities who regret that they can't speak their native language.

Theme 2: Racism as Damaging. The racism experienced by minorities is qualitatively different from that earlier groups experienced. Prejudice, discrimination, and insensitivity have historically held minorities back and continue to do so:

Latino high school student, public forum: The self-esteem of Hispanic students is suffering in our schools, because we hear every day of negative messages about who we are and why we are here.... We want to achieve, ... to organize *as* a group, ... [to] deal with the prejudice ... constructively.

Latino high school student, public forum: I have been called "nigger" and ... [other words] I don't care to repeat.... [If you] want the children of the community to succeed, why are you continuously putting us down?

Latino college student, public forum: We [students] ... would like to propose that a stronger, cultural oriented curriculum be formulated for the purpose of educating and alleviating racial tension. We, as an oppressed people ...

Theme 3: Exclusion. Although they are as American as everyone else, White America excludes and treats minorities as the Other, in the process damaging their self-esteem.

Latino college student, public forum: For you to come here and tell us that we're not Americans ... to expect us to listen to Mr. Marris ... [and then] expect Latinos to wrap ourselves around the American flag, then maybe you have to analyze yourselves.... Stand up and support the idea of Latinos.

Hispanic community leader interview: Without that information [about ethnic contributions to the United States], children are handicapped—they are defenseless—and information about their heritage is needed to arm them.... If they hear nothing, ... then they think, "I must be nothing."

Whereas Seniors argued that the gaps between the Hispanic and Euro-American community—both in terms of ethnic polarization and also economic/educational status—were brought on Hispanics by their own doing, Minorities reversed causality: Student failure is rooted in bias and rejection that has its roots in their "Otherness" for white Americans (see Figure 3).

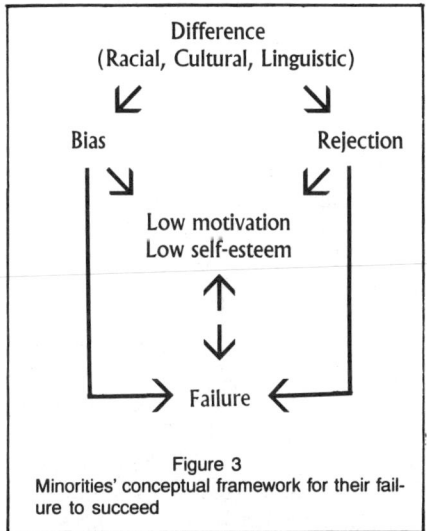

Figure 3
Minorities' conceptual framework for their failure to succeed

Difference, a stigma in the Seniors' framework, is inverted to become a positive factor, an entitlement rooted in appeals to the Constitution and the nation's longstanding espousal of the ideals of tolerance. Breaking the cycle for minority youth, then, requires a multipronged approach that severs the connections between *difference,* and *bias* and *rejection,* through education and use of the state's institutions. The *low self-esteem* of minority youth, a consequence of their experiences with bias and rejection of their cultural, racial, and linguistic differences, can be countered through positive acknowledgment of minority cultures and languages and the sense of empowerment they will experience in understanding the roots of their low status in the United States. An integral element in such a schema is the advocacy of bilingual and multicultural education programs that promote the desirability and legitimacy of linguistic and cultural diversity and the empowerment of minority youth and communities (e.g., Banks 1991; Cummins 1986; Nieto 1992). Embedded in Senior and Minority narratives and interpretive frameworks, then, are the outlines of two very different propositions about "being" and "becoming" American.

Discussion

> There's no denying that the multicultural initiative arose, in part, because of the fragmentation of American society, by ethnicity, class, and gender. To make it the culprit for this fragmentation is to mistake effect for cause. [Gates 1991:1]

There is in the construction of both the Senior story and the Minority story a dialectic operating between past and present. The history and current circumstances of the group to which the letter-to-the-editor writer belongs—descendants of southern and eastern Europeans—differ significantly from the experiences of most Latinos, African Americans, and Native Americans. In turn, significant differences, as the works of Connerton (1989) and Benmayor et al. (1988) would anticipate, emerge in the analysis of the narratives of these two groups.

Southern and eastern European immigrants and their children initially experienced prejudice and discrimination, alongside economic difficulties, up through and including the Great Depression years. On the eve of World War II, analysis of their chances for large-scale mobility would have led one to believe such a possibility was remote (Alba 1990; di Leonardo 1992). Social scientists, seeking explanations for their overall lack of upward mobility, frequently attributed their lack of rapid mobility to cultural behaviors and values such as fatalism and familism (see Steinberg 1981).

Beginning in the 1940s, however, a fortuitous set of circumstances came together, raising the living standards of this generation and catapulting their children squarely into the mainstream. A growing economy, better-funded public services, government-subsidized programs such as the GI bill, and unionized jobs greatly enhanced the likelihood of their entering the mobility queue (Davis 1986; di Leonardo 1992). Upward mobility for these groups was not the product of educational success; rather, educational success was largely the *outcome* of economic mobility. Their descendants achieved near parity with older European ethnic groups without having had to displace others of the middle class.

Seniors, raised on an ethos of ancestral sacrifice and hard work as the essential ingredients for upward mobility *and* having achieved something of the American Dream (tenuous though their hold may be on it), unproblematically link hard work and conformity to white ethnics' successes in climbing the social-class ladder. A consequence is to defend the individualistic, "up-by-their-own-bootstraps" view of the American' system. For members of struggling minority communities for whom the "rags-to-riches" story has rarely applied, stories of hardship and discrimination "mean" differently. Linking racial oppression, past and present, to contemporary ethnic/racial socioeconomic inequalities helps explain their current positions in the social hierarchy and inspires members to challenge the status quo.

What remains unacknowledged in both groups' stories is the significance of changing economic factors in explaining differing rates of upward mobility among groups in the United States. Sustained racial/ethnic oppression has historically acted to limit the mobility of people of color, but groups on the lower end of the social-class ladder today confront additional barriers. The expanding economy beginning in the 1940s that made large-scale upward mobility possible for white ethnics has drastically changed. The nation's economic structure has been transformed, moving away from a manufacturing-dominated economy toward a service-based economy. In the new deindustrializing era many employment opportunities no longer exist for groups, such as the majority of Puerto Rican citizens of this country, who were poorly positioned to take advantage of the postwar boom that lasted into the 1960s.

Decline in the manufacturing sector and corporate downsizing also translate into economic and social dislocation for many working-class and middle-class whites (Thurow 1995; Weis 1990). Those seeking to climb the social-class ladder today thus increasingly confront the downwardly mobile and those who cling precariously to a middle-class status. For many mainstream Americans, as this study suggests, the recent demographic and social changes they have witnessed during their life-times have been conflated with the nation's political and economic downswing in recent years, so that the blame for such changes is not infrequently projected onto the increasingly visible minority communities.

As growing economic inequality and racial/ethnic cleavages in the United States pose an ever graver threat to our social fabric (Bradsher 1995; West 1993), the need for concerted intervention designed to address educational and economic inequalities appears critical. Yet the federal government's commitment to a more just and equitable society has declined. Federal spending for education and training, for instance, dropped by 40 percent during the 1980s (Lind 1995). Implementing significant change in impoverished inner-city schools and communities across the nation will require greater public commitment to a more equitable distribution of economic opportunities and resources, and government support for eradicating the vast disparities in school funding that currently threaten the educational futures of a significant portion of American youth. An essential element in obtaining the support needed for such commitments will be gaining public recognition both of the structural factors that contribute to unequal opportunities in the United States and of the consequences for all Americans of leaving such potentially devastating trends unaddressed.

While multicultural education initiatives cannot singlehandedly resolve the problems of racial/ethnic inequality, they constitute an important mechanism for effecting positive social change from within schools. Culturally relevant pedagogy, a multicultural curriculum, and greater minority community involvement in their children's schooling, within the framework of "education that is social reconstructionist" (e.g., Sleeter and Grant 1987), are critical components of such initiatives.

Political activism and debate in Arnhem initiated a dialogue around equality of opportunity in the schools and community (see Bigler 1994b). It also created some initial movement toward multicultural education reform and greater minority community input and involvement in the schooling of their children. A Puerto Rican minister was elected to the school board the subsequent year, as a result of an interracial coalition of voters that organized to effect educational change; bilingual teacher aides were hired by the school district; the school administration began to send home notices in both English and Spanish; and a small number of school faculty and administrators began to seriously examine curricula, school policies, and classroom pedagogy in light of concerns raised by the New York State Education Department and community activists.[6]

Implementing such initiatives for change requires serious consideration of the perspectives of both educators and community members. Multicultural projects, as suggested in the community debate, threaten the status quo: they introduce the perspectives and practices of non-mainstream groups into school and community discourse, challenge popular assumptions about equality of opportunity, destabilize and threaten other identities, and engender resistance.

Teachers in Arnhem, not unlike their peers elsewhere (see for instance Cochran-Smith 1995; Ladson-Billings 1995), generally subscribed to the belief that the schools were meritocratic institutions and that "race" no longer significantly affected people's life chances. Minority activists contested such claims. To work more effectively with students and parents from diverse racial/ethnic and class backgrounds, teachers will require sustained opportunities to engage in critical thinking about the consequences of social inequities, to analyze their own assumptions about an unproblematic link between education and economic success, to recognize the perspectives they bring to their classrooms as raced, classed, and gendered actors, and to reexamine the purposes of education as we approach the 21st century.

While the voices of the minority community members that emerged in Arnhem reflect the differing relations of "involuntary" minorities to the schools that researchers such as Ogbu (1987) describe, at another level they also reflect their faith in the *potential* of our nation's schools. Rather than dismissing schools as important sites for the future well-being of their children, minority leaders in Arnhem argued that schools can become what they have long been in the popular imagination, sites that foster opportunities for all children to succeed. More than that, they also envision them as important sites in fostering the creation of a more democratic common culture.

The assumption that all ethnic stories are the same, that is, that the "Senior" model applies equally to all minority groups and that only the names of the groups change, has been successfully challenged by a new generation of scholars (see Nelson and Tienda 1985; Portes and Rumbaut 1990; Rodriguez 1989; Rosaldo 1989). Their historical analyses and ethnographic studies highlight the need to consider the significance of factors including race, class, educational background, changing economic conditions, communication and transportation revolutions, and the reception of immigrants in the receiving country in seeking explanations for interethnic differences in "succeeding" in the United States. But the understandings generated from such studies have yet to make their way into mainstream "folk" explanations, including, as we see in Arnhem, those holding local power. Their support—along with that of teachers—will be vitally important if substantive changes are to take place. Further, if we are to address the issues that divide Americans along ethnic lines and move toward a more equitable and just society, creating greater opportunities for dialogue and public forums for the telling of American *stories* will be essential.

Ellen Bigler is an assistant professor at Rhode Island College, with a joint appointment in anthropology and in educational studies.

Notes

Acknowledgments. This research was supported by the National Research Center on Literature Teaching and Learning at SUNY Albany. Special thanks goes to James Collins at SUNY Albany for his invaluable assistance throughout the project, and Alan Purves, John Calagione, and Pedro Pedraza, for their useful comments on the report (No. 7.2) issued through the Center.

1. The term *minorities,* rather than *people of color,* is used in the text because it was the term universally used in the community to refer to groups from non-European backgrounds.
2. Pseudonyms have been used for all persons and places.
3. All but one were Euro-American, roughly half had grown up in Arnhem, and most had attended college prior to the introduction of multicultural education programs (see Bigler and Collins 1995).
4. Hispanics comprised 17 percent of the student population, African Americans 2.2 percent, and Asian Americans 1 percent.
5. Largely missing were the views of younger Euro-Americans in the community and the sentiments of nonpolitically active minority community members. Interviews suggest that local Latinos identified strongly with the charges of discrimination. They also wanted their children to master English and maintain Spanish, and to take pride in their heritage (see Bigler 1994b).
6. The impetus for change slowed considerably the subsequent year when department chairs were eliminated, funds for educational workshops were slashed, and threats of massive layoffs shifted the focus of attention away from such issues.

References Cited

Agar, Michael. 1983. Political Talk: Thematic Analysis of a Policy Argument. Policy Studies Review 2(4):601–614.

Alba, Richard. 1990. Ethnic Identity: The Transformation of White America. New Haven, CT: Yale University Press.

Banks, James. 1991. A Curriculum for Empowerment, Action, and Change. *In* Empowerment through Multicultural Education. Christine Sleeter, ed. Pp. 125–142. Albany: State University of New York Press.

Benmayor, Rina, Ana Juarbe, Celia Alvarez, and Blanca Vazquez. 1988. Stories to Live By: Continuity and Change in Three Generations of Puerto Rican Women. Oral History Review 16(2):1–46.

Bigler, Ellen. 1994a. Talking "American": Dialoguing on Difference in Upstate New York. Report, 7.2. Albany: National Research Center on Literature Teaching and Learning, State University of New York, Albany.

1994b. Multiculturalism in Upstate New York: Contested Identities and the Schooling of Puerto Rican Youth in a Deindustrializing Economy. Ph.D. dissertation, State University of New York, Albany.

Bigler, Ellen, and James Collins. 1995. Dangerous Discourses: The Politics of Multicultural Literature in Community and Classroom. Report,

6. SPECIAL TOPICS IN MULTICULTURAL EDUCATION

7A. Albany: National Research Center on Literature Teaching and Learning, State University of New York, Albany.

Bradsher, Keith. 1995. More on the Wealth of Nations. New York Times, August 8:E6.

Cochran-Smith, Marilyn. 1995. Uncertain Allies: Understanding the Boundaries of Race and Teaching. Harvard Educational Review 65(4):541–570.

Connerton, Paul. 1989. How Societies Remember. Cambridge, England: Cambridge University Press.

Cummins, James. 1986. Empowering Minority Students: A Framework for Intervention. Harvard Educational Review 56(1):18–36.

Davis, Mike. 1986. Prisoners of the American Dream: Politics and Economy in the History of the U.S. Working Class. London: Verso.

di Leonardo, Micaela. 1992. White Lies, Black Myths. Village Voice 37(September 22):29–36.

Gates, Henry Louis. 1991. Multiculturalism: A Conversation among Different Voices. Rethinking Schools 6(1):1, 7.

Goffman, Erving. 1959. The Presentation of Self in Everyday Life. New York: Doubleday.

Ladson-Billings, Gloria. 1995. Toward a Theory of Culturally Relevant Pedagogy. American Educational Research Journal 32(3):465–492.

Lind, Michael. 1995. To Have and Have Not: Notes on the Progress of the American Class War. Harper's Magazine (June):35–47.

Nelson, Candace, and Marta Tienda. 1985. The Structuring of Hispanic Ethnicity: Historical and Contemporary Perspectives. Ethnic and Racial Studies 8 (January):49–74.

Nieto, Sonia. 1992. Affirming Diversity: The Sociopolitical Context of Multicultural Education. White Plains, NY: Longman.

Novak, Michael. 1971. The Rise of the Unmeltable Ethnics: Politics and Culture in the Seventies. New York: MacMillan.

Ogbu, John. 1987. Variability in Minority School Performance: A Problem in Search of an Explanation. Anthropology and Education Quarterly 18(4):312–334.

Portes, Alejandro, and Rubén Rumbaut. 1990. Immigrant America: A Portrait. Berkeley: University of California Press.

Rodríguez, Clara. 1989. Puerto Ricans: Born in the U.S.A. Boston: Unwin Hyman.

Rosaldo, Renato. 1989. Culture and Truth: The Remaking of Social Analysis. Boston: Beacon Press.

Sleeter, Christine, and Carl Grant. 1987. An Analysis of Multicultural Education in the United States. Harvard Educational Review 57(4):421–444.

Sobol, Thomas. 1989. A Curriculum of Inclusion: Report of the Commissioner's Task Force on Minorities: Equity and Excellence. Albany, NY: State Education Department.

Steinberg, Stephen. 1981. The Ethnic Myth: Race, Ethnicity, and Class in America. New York: Atheneum.

Thurow, Lester. 1995. Companies Merge; Families Break Up. New York Times, September 3:E1.

Weis, Lois. 1990. Working Class Without Work: High-School Students in a De-Industrializing Economy. New York: Routledge, Chapman & Hall.

West, Cornel. 1993. Race Matters. Boston: Beacon Press.

Woolard, Kathryn. 1989. Sentences in the Language Prison: The Rhetorical Structuring of an American Language Policy Debate. American Ethnologist 16(May):268–278.

Teaching Homeless Children: Exemplary Field Experience for Teacher Education Candidates

John P. Gustafson
and Stacy M. Cichy

John P. Gustafson is Associate Professor of Education at North Park College in Chicago, Illinois. His research interests include the foundations of education and the influence of social factors in the professional and personal development of teacher candidates. Dr. Gustafson is a member of the Gamma Gamma Chapter of Kappa Delta Pi.

Stacy M. Cichy has a Bachelor of Science in Elementary Education from Moorhead State University in Minnesota. She is currently seeking a teaching position. Ms. Cichy is a member of the Gamma Gamma Chapter of Kappa Delta Pi.

As a university professor, I receive many high quality assignments as partial fulfillment of course requirements. However, few are as moving as Stacy Cichy's report, which follows. This report was written at the conclusion of a student-arranged, alternative early field experience in teacher education. I encouraged Cichy to contact a school that served the children of homeless families in a metropolitan area; following a personal interview, she voluntarily served six weeks rather than the two weeks required by the university.

Cichy had participated in the South Texas Multicultural Internship during her sophomore year, working in a public school classroom half days for the entire quarter (Gustafson 1995). During her senior year, Cichy participated in three early field experiences prior to student teaching. She first spent full days for three weeks in a traditional first-grade public school classroom assisting the teacher and preparing and presenting lessons. She then worked in a team of four students teaching on five Wednesday afternoons without the supervision of the regular classroom teacher. The alternative field experience described in this manuscript was Cichy's final early field experience before student teaching. Ideally, the intent of this experience was to place the teacher candidate in a nontraditional school setting or in another geographic region.

Her reflective report focused attention on four critical areas of development during teacher preparation: racial issues, dependence cycles, classroom management, and career decisions. Cichy kept a journal of this experience, which represents the action research of a teacher candidate as researcher.

ACTION RESEARCH

According to May (1993), a practitioner of any professional field and at any level can engage in action research. Kelsay (1991) wrote that experience—with reflection—was the best teacher. Kelsay's graduate students also kept journals and recorded their thoughts and reactions to the experience. Searle (1993) described this reflection as learning from people rather than studying them. Indeed, action research seems to have endless potential to promote personal and social reflection (Llorens 1994). The participant researcher gathers data about the subjects and the context. In doing so, he or she becomes a part of the study by recording his or her reactions (Devault 1990).

Action research most often relies on qualitative or interpretive research methods to examine how participants construe their worlds (May 1993; Freeman 1995). It is always field based, "lending itself to ethnographic methods such as keeping field notes or journals, participant observation, interviewing, engaging in dialogue, audiotaping, and collecting and analyzing documents and students' work" (May 1993, 118). Action researchers also "gain a better understanding of their beliefs/practice and how these came to be," enhancing "their practice if, when, and how they see fit" (May 1993,

118). This better understanding of their own beliefs leads to teacher theorizing, aiding in establishing the link between theory and practice.

CICHY'S ALTERNATIVE FIELD EXPERIENCE

When I began my alternative experience serving the children of homeless families, I tried to enter with an open mind and without preconceived notions. My familiarity with the site was limited to a brief interview and orientation one month prior to my alternative experience.

The school served only children aged 5–12 from homeless families. School enrollment was approximately 40–45 students from four shelters in the metropolitan area. Due to the often unstable home and school background of the children, they were grouped according to age. This was done to protect the child's self-esteem; they were rarely on grade level.

Approximately 95 percent of the students attending the school moved there to escape from crowded and very dangerous conditions in the Chicago area. Because families did not know where they would be located once they found employment and permanent housing, the children attended the school during this interim period. The vast majority of the children at the school were African-Americans; only 2 percent were European-American and from other minorities. The school rarely had Native American, Asian-American, or Hispanic students because they had their own private schools that aided families in homeless circumstances in the area.

The classrooms at the school were extremely small, sometimes resulting in crowded conditions—though there was always enough room to learn and work together. The small size of the classroom seemed to set the children more at ease during this rocky period of their lives. Every room had a warm and comfortable atmosphere.

I taught only three lessons during my two-week alternative experience at the school. Recognizing the shortcomings of this time period, I continued on at the school for an additional four weeks. Never knowing for sure which children would be in the classroom each day helped me realize the importance of planning.

The school utilized two-week themed units, an attempt to accommodate the constant fluctuation of the student body. During my second two-week stint at the school, the teacher asked me to give an impromptu lesson on agriculture, especially dairy farming. The children asked me questions, and I tried to make this relatively foreign subject interesting with some farm stories. During the lesson, I realized how little the "city children" knew about farming, so I traveled home to my parent's dairy farm to do some videotaping and to get some feed and crop samples, all of which I shared with the entire school. For the first time, many students began to understand some of the extreme differences between rural and urban lifestyles. While watching the video, one child asked, "When are you going to show some people? I'm sick of all these cows."

Racial Issues

Staying beyond the required two weeks provided me with invaluable information and experience about the realities of homelessness. I had no concept of many of the difficulties these children faced every day. One important area of understanding on my part dealt with race issues. After Halloween, a group of children from a wealthy suburb brought some candy that they gathered to donate to the school. They wanted to know more about the school, so the lead teacher showed them around. Although these children had good intentions, they made the homeless children feel even less fortunate than they were. Hard feelings resulted from the way the suburban children looked at the homeless children. Following this episode, the teachers held a meeting and decided that no more groups could come into the school without some interaction between the children.

A few days later, a different group of children came in from another suburb. This time activities were planned, so the teachers informed the children of the forthcoming visitors. One student raised his hand and asked, "Are they all gonna be white?" The teacher replied, "Does it really matter? You're still breaking it down to a black/

white thing." All the student had to say in return was, "Yeah, white people aren't that bad once you get to know them." Imagine the thoughts that were racing through my head, being the only white person in the classroom. I wondered if I "wasn't that bad" because he had gotten to know me, or if I wasn't a color or race anymore, only a teacher. The teacher asked the same student if all white people were bad, and he said "no" but could not explain quite what he meant.

Within the same week, I seemed to find my answer about my racial status with these children. I was helping some students with a paragraph writing exercise that required they write complete sentences to answer the various questions asked. One of the questions was "What color are your eyes?" They read this and asked me what color my eyes were. I opened my eyes as widely as I could so they could see for themselves. They exclaimed, "They're brown! I thought your eyes were green." Within 30 seconds they all decided that I was black. The classroom teacher asked, "What do you mean she's black. She's white." They insisted, "She's black. She's got light skin, or she's mixed. She just dyed and straightened her hair." The teacher and I questioned these students for some time trying to understand exactly how they could think someone as white as myself was black. Finally, the same student who had decided white people were not "that bad" said, "She's black. She's too nice to be white." I was speechless. On the one hand, I was honored that this child would think highly enough of me to include me in his race. On the other hand, I was somewhat offended because I am white; it was awful that his experience had been such that he felt white people were mostly bad or mean. The teacher asked him if all white people were mean, and he said "no." Although the teacher tried to get him to expand, the child wanted to drop the subject.

In talking later with the lead teacher, who was one of two white teachers in the school, I learned that she had similar experiences with the children. She believed that their primary experience with white people had been with the police and that, being children, they did not understand the whole story.

The Dependence Cycle

I also learned much about the dependence of women on men. At first I thought it was only children making a big deal of boy/girl things. Then I discovered that, from kindergarten to the sixth grade, they were intent on finding me a boyfriend once they learned I was not attached to a significant other. If they saw me talking to a male teacher who was unmarried, suddenly he was my boyfriend. Another field experience student was also called my husband or boyfriend. Even though we did not talk extensively, we were both white and young—though race was not the crucial issue in finding someone for me. In my final week at the school, during general assembly, the children were sharing stories. One child told a story about how the male kindergarten teacher and the female first-second grade teacher went out, kissed, fell in love, and got married. Even kindergarten children would ask me if I had any children of my own. After I stated that I did not, they would say, "First you need a boyfriend or husband, then you need to get pregnant." I had not realized that kindergarten children knew that much about the facts of life. This really proved to me the truth about the dependence cycle. Many of the mothers of the children at the school were still children themselves. They dropped out a school, got a boyfriend to take care of them, got pregnant, and decided to keep their baby so they could have someone to love. Usually the boyfriend left them dependent on the state for support.

I had never before experienced a case of a child slipping through the cracks. One girl was placed in the sixth-grade classroom because she was 12. She stayed there for a week, and finally the teacher decided that he could not adapt his materials to meet her needs. The teacher felt she needed to go back to the first-grade level. The other teachers agreed that her academic level was probably at that grade but felt that it was too large of a jump socially. They opted instead to place her with the third- and fourth-grade children. After working one-on-one with this girl for a week, I realized that—unless she had some drastic intervention in her education—she was headed down the path of dependency. She had no reading skills, not even small sight words such as I, we, or me. Her math skills were at an early first-grade level; although she was a sweet girl, she had problems with social interactions with children of her own age and younger. I felt that she had a learning disability, but she had not been tested because her parents never stayed anywhere long enough to get through the referral process. All I could think to myself was, "Boy, I hope she gets help soon. In another year, she will be a teenager and will become interested in boys. She hasn't been successful in school thus far, so why stay in? Get a boyfriend, get pregnant, and the dependence cycle begins again. This poor girl won't even be able to get a minimum wage job if she doesn't get help, because she has no basic skills."

Classroom Management

Normal behavior management strategies that are usually successful in middle-class, public schools—giving stern looks or waiting until everyone was "ready" to participate—did not work with this population of students. In order to survive, these children had learned to be tough and to challenge authority in every aspect of their lives. They continued to do so in the classroom. Firmness and an air of confidence were definitely necessary in order to gain the students' respect; otherwise, they would not listen.

The information I had received in my college classes about group behavior was evident at the school. If the more difficult children were absent, other children who typically gave the teacher no trouble began acting-up. Many teachers commented on how children who were "model" pupils at first slowly became more troublesome. They thought, and I agreed, it was due to the disproportionate amount of time, energy, and attention that was given to students who misbehaved. Another point of information I found extremely relevant was needing a sense of community. Teachers at the school agreed that these children knew they lived in a shelter; whatever homelessness was by society's definition, they are not homeless. They all belonged at the school; they had a sense of community because everyone was in the same circumstance. The teachers also strongly believed in these children. For many children, it was the first time any teacher really cared about them. For example, class size in this school varied from 2 to 13 children. In contrast, the regular classroom teacher would have roughly 30 children to teach. Therefore, a child in the regular classroom could easily fall through the cracks. Not so at this school. No one ever gave up on these children.

Career Decisions

I often asked myself whether I would be interested in ever pursuing a job in a school of this type. At first, I had serious doubts due to the transient student body and high level of stress but, the longer I stayed, the more I realized what a difference the teachers, and even a volunteer, made in the lives of the children. So often I hear teacher candidates say that the reason they want to be teachers is to make a difference in the future and in a child's life. As a result of this experience, I believe the biggest impact will not be made in suburban, wealthy schools that offer comfortable salaries and perks. Nor is that where the highest job satisfaction is going to take place. I know now that I would not hesitate for a moment if I had the opportunity to teach in a school that reached out to help the children who need it most.

Overall, I enjoyed every aspect of working with these children of homeless families. I have learned valuable skills that I will take with me when I begin student teaching.

PLACING QUALIFIED TEACHERS

Much has been written about attracting and retaining qualified teachers for difficult assignments like the inner city. Kozol (1991, 52) reported that "on an average morning in Chicago 5700 children in 190 classrooms come to school to find they have no teacher" because even substitute teachers were in short supply. He documented similar shortages in other inner-city schools throughout the country. Retention of teachers in difficult assignments was another problem reported in the professional literature. Adams and Dial (1994) found that educational preparation influenced teacher retention. Beginning teachers with graduate degrees had a higher survival rate in urban districts than those with bachelor degrees. Problems in attracting qualified teachers to difficult assignments and retaining teachers in urban areas were clearly identified in the literature. We believe that early field experiences in these settings influence the desire to serve in and aids in the subsequent retention of teachers prepared to work in difficult assignments. Linking action research with an assignment of this nature further aids in preparing teachers to serve society's neglected children. Participant observation permits the researcher to learn from the children and the context. Such learning leads to teacher theorizing, an essential component in the professional development of a teacher.

If we in teacher education expect to prepare teacher candidates for difficult assignments, we must offer them extensive opportunities for service in those difficult positions. That experience must be in exemplary classrooms under teachers who model the best teaching practices known. This experience coupled with action research supports the preparation of teachers of society's neglected children.

REFERENCES

Adams, G., and M. Dial. 1994. The effects of education on teacher retention. *Education* 114(3): 358–63.

Devault, M. 1990. Talking and listening from women's standpoint: Feminist strategies for interviewing and analysis. *Social Problems* 37(February): 96–116.

Freeman, D. 1995. Asking "good" questions: Perspectives from qualitative research on practice, knowledge, and understanding in teacher education. *TESOL Quarterly* 29(3): 581–85.

Gustafson, J. P. 1995. A multicultural internship in South Texas for Minnesota students: A qualitative study. *Teaching and Learning: The Journal of Natural Inquiry* 10(1): 24–28.

Kelsay, K. L. 1991. When experience is the best teacher: The teacher as researcher. *Action in Teacher Education* 13(1): 14–21.

Kozol, J. 1991. *Savage inequalities: Children in America's schools.* New York: Crown.

Llorens, M. B. 1994. Action research: Are teachers finding their voice? *Elementary School Journal* 95(1): 3–10.

May, W. T. 1993. "Teachers-as-researchers" or action research: What is it, and what good is it for art education? *Studies in Art Education* 34(2): 114–26.

Searle, J. 1993. Participant observation: A way of conducting research. ERIC ED 359 259.

The Road to Auschwitz:

What's So Funny About Schindler's List?

Bernard Beck

Bernard Beck is a Professor in the Department of Sociology at Northwestern University, Evanston, Illinois, and an actor with Second City *in Chicago.*

Steven Spielberg knows how to make movies that please people, or so everyone believes. His film essay on a provocative episode of the Holocaust, *Schindler's List*, was widely praised. Even those commentators who were displeased or doubtful agreed that the movie was effective at manipulating audience sentiments. The most common criticisms, when there were any, blamed him for being too facile and effective with the techniques of popular movie making.

It was natural for educators to try to use the movie as a tool of instruction for American students about the Holocaust and all the important lessons our generation has decided it must teach us; about the horrible consequences of prejudice, hostility against minorities, uncritical conformism, indifference to the fate of outsiders, and the failure of political courage. The Holocaust is the unmatchable horror and the modern Hollywood movie is the state-of-the-art horror show. So it was a scandal when a school audience of African-American young people received the movie with hilarity. The context of multicultural education revealed some paradox in the work, a paradox unexpected after a history of winning Oscars and honors. It was all the more agonizing because it seemed to show American Black disrespect for an event regarded by American Jews as defining their peoplehood.

To belong to a people is a serious business. We use culture to represent that seriousness to ourselves and others: Treating cultural matters seriously is a way of showing respect for the people whose culture it is. Silence is one of the strongest ways of taking things seriously, and breaking silence about an important subject is one of the most daring things we can do in culture. But silence is also dangerous; it may lead us to forget and neglect that serious business.

It should not be a surprise that sacred matters present cultural paradoxes. Both to speak and to be silent are dangerous, outrageous, and intolerable. The matters that define us and preoccupy us as a definable people are sacred cultural questions, and the uniqueness of those questions is what makes a people distinctive.

Making movies, on the other hand, is a profane and irreverent enterprise—especially commercial, cosmopolitan movies addressed to whom it may concern. Especially "Hollywood" movies. Although our contemporary feeling about movies recognizes their emotional power, their capacity to impress, persuade, and move us, we are suspicious of that power in our more grown-up, responsible moods. The movies, in America, are about entertainment, about making money, about consumption of marketed pleasures. When movies are about sacred matters, they embody a fundamental contradiction. They communicate loudly, vividly, even promiscuously, about things that should be treated with respectful silence. At the same time, they present the opportunity to send a profound message out to a mass audience, a message that is most likely to be heard and attended to.

This contradiction is familiar to us through the conventions of religious movies, such as the Bible epics that were C.B. DeMille's stock in trade. The obligatory avoidance of explicit portrayals of Jesus (as in *Ben-Hur*) or God (as in *The Ten Commandments*) demonstrates how difficult it is to be reverential and entertaining at the same time. It is always safe to be suspicious of the facile, maudlin religiosity of such works. A religious movie is always a trap, as the strong reaction against Martin Scorsese's *The Last Temptation of Christ* shows.

For Jews, the Holocaust is a sacred matter on many levels. For 50 years, it has been understood to be a problem for interpretation. Those who speak about it with the greatest moral authority, the survivors, have endowed it with transcendent meaning: It may not be explained; it may not be recovered from; it may not be assimilated to ordinary theories of human action. It must be regarded as unique and unknowable. At the same time, it must be regarded as paradigmatic and instructive to all humanity. It is fundamental to the efforts of contemporary Jews to explain to themselves what it means to be Jewish. It also dominates the claims they make on the attention of non-Jews.

So Jews are concerned with any cultural representation of the Holocaust; they examine its meaning for them and its meaning to non-Jews. What does it say to us, and what does it say about us? Underlying these questions is another loaded question: Who dares to say anything about the Holocaust, what do they want, and what are they doing to us? Every year at Passover, Jews observe the season with a Seder, a ceremony that focuses on the retelling of the Exodus from Egypt, emphasizing that the story explains and confirms the existence of the Jewish people. What is formalized in the Seder is also expressed in the continuing cultural exploration of the Holocaust. It is an exploration of the meanings that Jews will give to their Jewishness. It is an exploration that each individual Jew may do, that Jews may do with (and against) one another, and that Jews may do in the presence of and for the instruction of non-Jews. A movie about the Holocaust is always an exercise in multicultural education for Jews, whatever the explicit apology for the movie may be.

Many peoples have such central themes and events that they treat as defining of their identity and their legitimacy. A significant aspect of claiming to be a people is the assertion of proprietorship over an element of culture, a form of expression, an episode of history. A vital and powerful people can demand to be consulted and respected whenever the world at large presumes to understand, explain, or participate in such a defining cultural enterprise. As the Holocaust is for Jewish self-consciousness, so is the history of slavery for African-Americans or the history of European conquest for Native Americans. For outsiders to mention it is troublesome; for insiders to deal with it is to invite criticism from their fellows.

The cultural repertoire produced about the Holocaust for half a century, often by Jews and sometimes by non-Jews, has become massive. Each generation has raised anew the questions and produced additional material, taking form as historical or scientific research, artistic and philosophical comment. There is a long and significant history of films about the Holocaust from many different countries, including Alain Resnais's *Night and Fog* from France, *The Shop on Main Street* from Czechoslovakia, and Claude Lanzmann's long and powerful documentary *Shoah*, to name a few. We can also remember popular American movies like *The Diary of Anne Frank, The Pawnbroker, Julia, Sophie's Choice,* and the television mini-series *Holocaust*.

Schindler's List is different in important ways. It is, perhaps, the most popular, successful, and effective movie ever made about the Holocaust. High on the list of reasons why people have been impressed with this movie is their belief that it will have a salutary impact on some target audience. It is not only that people have had a positive response to their own viewing of the movie but also that they expect it to make an impression on some others who need a lesson. In other words, even before it was introduced into any school curriculum, the audience for *Schindler's List* was thinking of it as a tool of multicultural education.

The Holocaust was a long, complex event involving millions of people all over the world. There are countless stories to be told about it, including the rise of modern European Anti-Semitism, the institution of the Nazi persecution of Jews, the imposition of the Final Solution, the creation and decimation of the ghettoes of Eastern Europe, the operation of the death camps, the growth of resistance, the flight of refugees, liberation, and many more. The story of Oskar Schindler is a peculiar one to occupy such a central place in our contemporary view of the Holocaust.

Many critics have wondered whether this story should be treated as so important. Why would the book about Schindler's activities make such an impression on a hugely successful, assimilated Jewish movie maker who had never before concerned himself with themes of Jewish identity or history? Why would he treat the project with the care and respect he has testified to? Why would the result be so honored in comparison to all the other cultural products dealing with the Holocaust?

Schindler was a small-scale German entrepreneur of no particular power or importance, a member of the Nazi Party who made business opportunities for himself in the midst of war and genocide. He established a successful business using the labor of Jews who were, to begin with, his slave workers. In the process, he kept them alive. At the war's end, he had managed to save an incredible number of people, at the cost of his profits from the business. Along the way, he had become a savior of Jewish victims, like some other non-Jews now called "righteous Gentiles" by Jews, but unlike most people in the Nazi world, for reasons that the book and movie explore without satisfying us with a pat explanation.

What is wrong with this picture? Although we can observe in passing some important themes, such as the injustice and inhumanity of the genocide against the Jews of Europe and their suffering and courage in the face of it, the movie is focussed on the slippery maneuvers of Schindler, his survival and the success of his enterprise under dangerous conditions, the transformation of his feelings, his complex relations with his workers and the Nazi officials who held the fate of all of them in their hands. In the midst of a great historical occurrence of death and misery to an entire people, this movie has a happy ending, one which was true but highly unusual. And the agent of this deliverance is not a member of the group that is so involved with this story that defines their contemporary identity, but an oddball member of the oppressive group. Why is he so interesting?

I do not propose to offer a clever answer to this question. Instead, I

6. SPECIAL TOPICS IN MULTICULTURAL EDUCATION

intend to present something I believe will be more useful, a discussion of some themes and issues of contemporary relevance that are raised by the movie. So a viewing of the movie can be the basis for a continuing dialogue about them.

Separation and Inclusion

This is a movie made by a Jew about a matter sacred to modern Jews. But is it a Jewish treatment of a Jewish question? Perhaps the movie can be seen as the contribution by a Jew who defines himself as a member of a multicultural, diverse, and cosmopolitan world to a dialogue about responsibility, participation, and courage. It may be a reflection of the common (although by no means universal) position of Jews in American society—prosperous, resourceful, accomplished. While Jews in America and the world must still face the challenges of minority status, hostility, prejudice, and outbreaks of hate, their moral challenges are more likely to look like Schindler's than like those facing his Jewish proteges. Spielberg has not preoccupied himself with the plight of the victims of cultural persecution, but with the obligations of someone found among those who are spared. **Living in a multicultural world raises not only questions about differentiated identity and the preservation of distinctive culture, but also the construction of common identity and the creation of a culture of mutual care.** The lessons of the Holocaust from its victims and for them may be more about forbearance and rescue than about resistance and survival. Jews are still victims in the world, but the recurrences of genocide in the modern world have involved people in Cambodia, Bosnia, El Salvador, Rwanda, Angola and other places, where anti-semitism is not the issue but where Jews, like others, may need to be involved.

Strength and Weakness

Jews have found in the Holocaust a painful challenge that has much in common with the cultural preoccupations of other minority groups in many modern societies. Focusing on injustice may bring an awareness of weakness, vulnerability, and helplessness, as well. An overriding concern of groups trying to define their own legitimacy and honor their own virtues is nowadays called "empowerment." The word suggests to us the importance of feeling strong and capable. We abhor the suggestion that we may be unable to command respect, that we may depend, like Blanche DuBois in *A Streetcar Named Desire,* "on the kindness of strangers."

Spielberg has rubbed the noses of his audience, particularly his Jewish audience, in the fact that they required the emerging good will of an unlikely friend to survive. In the midst of a cosmic tragedy, in which courage, culture, and humanity were destroyed over and over, some were saved, not by their own virtue, but by the almost whimsical intercession of a nobody. This disturbing idea is all the more disturbing to members of a triumphal capitalist, individualist, and litigious society whose deepest wisdom has transformed the Golden Rule into "when the going gets tough, the tough get going."

Who Is the Hero?

Movies are popular entertainments that are more concerned with sentiment than with history. They have more in common with parables than reports. We emerge from the movie theater more responsive to an experience than to information. And the experience is as though from the point of view of some particular person. In the long, varied history of popular movies about minorities, underdogs, and subcultures, that is to say, movies about "them," it is typical to have one of "us" play the part of protagonist. The movie is from "our" point of view. "We" are the dominant group members from whose ranks come the movie makers and the hero characters in stories about outsiders. That is the mass culture's way of dealing with multicultural situations.

So the hero of *Broken Arrow,* a 1950s movie about the Apache chief Cochise, is the white scout who befriends the Apaches, played by Jimmy Stewart. The heroes of several movies of recent years about the struggle against Apartheid in South Africa have been sympathetic white liberals. In the popular, award-winning movie about the civil rights movement, *Mississippi Burning,* the hero is a white FBI agent. There is a familiar variant of this pattern which has noble members of out-groups serving as idealized adjuncts to the development of the main characters who belong to dominant groups. Decades of European popular culture have employed the stock figures of saintly black folks and wise Jews to catalyze the stories of white main characters. In a similar way, this year's movie *Quiz Show,* based on the television scandals of the 1950s, deals with the struggles of the Jewish contestant Herbert Stempel to bring respectability for his people through success on the quiz show of the title. But the central figure of the movie is Charles Van Doren, the WASP.

In *Schindler's List,* the Jewish workers being saved from destruction are not the protagonists; the movie is not made from their point of view. Instead, it is the tall Aryan Schindler, even though he is no Viking hero, whose perspective is presented. The sympathetic figure of the Jew played by Ben Kingsley is the familiar out-group sidekick. However, this is a movie made by a Jew about one of the most important defining moments of Jewish history. Why has this Schindler-centered story been chosen to explore the Holocaust?

Oddly enough, Schindler, as he is constructed by Spielberg, is very much like a familiar, stock Jewish character of popular culture—the clever, inventive, ingratiating merchant who survives by wit rather than power, rather like the Jewish title character of Franz Werfel's play,

Jacobowski and the Colonel (brought to the screen as *Me and the Colonel*, with Danny Kaye). The Aryan performing a Jewish role is a mirror image of the modern figure of the "non-Jewish Jew," the emancipated apostate who plays a pivotal role in the history of Western thought. Although the usual distinguished examples include Spinoza, Marx, Einstein, and Freud, Spielberg himself may be considered a candidate for this designation. This turnabout may remind us that there are some approaches to defining group-based individual identity that emphasize cosmopolitan universalism and that see it as a positive result of living in Diaspora.

Conclusion

At first sight, *Schindler's List* appears to be a peculiar kind of Holocaust movie for a Jewish filmmaker to produce and to gather so much honor, notwithstanding its obvious technical competence. In spite of the facile elements available to the director, the peculiar choice of a central character leads to a cheerful tone and a distance from the victims portrayed.

Perhaps the laughter of students, whose real lives are full of daily peril, at a story of how people who are weak and threatened survive anyway will bring us an unexpected insight. This movie shows the unlikely circumstances that saved the lives of hundreds when powerful forces tried to destroy them; it might really be a comedy.

New Colors

Mixed-race families still find a mixed reception

Melissa Steel

Melissa Steel is a senior at Williams College and is planning a career in education. She interned at Teaching Tolerance during the summer of 1994.

In late February 1994, the principal of Randolph County High School in eastern Alabama held an assembly of all juniors and seniors to talk about the upcoming prom. Among the students in the auditorium that day was Revonda Bowen, president of the junior class and the prom committee. She had worked hard planning and raising money for the prom, unaware that Principal Hulond Humphries had plans of his own for the big event.

At the assembly, Humphries asked how many of the students were planning to bring a date of another race to the dance. When more than a dozen students raised their hands, Hemphries threatened to cancel the event. Revonda, whose mother is black and father is white, felt that Humphries' stance against interracial dating put her in a particularly difficult situation. "Who am I supposed to go with?" she asked the principal.

"That's the problem," he reportedly replied. "Your mom and dad made a mistake." What he was trying to do, he supposedly added, was to prevent others from making the same "mistake."

What started as a casual remark in an obscure Alabama high school quickly became national news. Humphries announced the day after the assembly that the prom would go on after all, but the damage was already done. Revonda and her parents decided to bring a lawsuit against the principal and the school board charging Humphries with "willful derogation of (Revonda's] civil rights." The Randolph County School Board quickly agreed to settle Bowen's lawsuit for $25,000, although it found itself embroiled in a costly, high-profile dispute with the U.S. Justice Department over other possible civil rights violations in the school system.

The Revonda Bowen case illuminated more than the troubling racial divisions in our country's schools. It also brought to national attention the kind of struggles that many children of multiracial families face in their daily lives.

As the child of a black Ghanaian mother and a white American father, I felt keenly the irony of Revonda's question, "Who am I supposed to go with?" It was another variation of the kind of question I—like many other Americans of mixed heritage—have struggled with for years. And as the numbers of families like mine and Revonda Bowen's increase, the question of where we multiracial kids fit in becomes more urgent.

The number of interracial couples in America has increased by 78 percent since 1980. One in every 50 marriages is now between people of different races. In addition to interracial marriages, there were over 8,000 foreign and transracial adoptions in 1992 alone, according to estimates from the National Council on Adoption.

Yet, despite their increasing significance, multiracial families are often made to feel unwelcome or abnormal. All too often, families that cross racial boundaries are alienated from their disapproving relatives or suffer abuse from intolerant strangers. "Think about the poor children!" is the warning given to interracial couples—a warning that reflects the common assumption that transracial relationships are inherently problematic. The near invisibility of multiracial families in the media only reinforces such negative attitudes. In my experience, however, it's not the children of multiracial families who are the source of the problem; the problem stems from society's thinking that they should be pitied.

Revonda Bowen's experience, while extreme, is not uncommon. School is one of the main arenas in which multiracial children must deal with other people's assumptions about their families. Lauren, a 10th grader from Atlanta, Ga., remembers other kids in her predominantly black elementary school asking her questions about what it was like to have a white father. "They have stereotypes of what a white person's like, so they'd ask [things like], 'How does he talk?' and 'What kind of clothes does he wear?'"

Zorah, an 8-year-old from the same area, was once told by another girl who saw her family that black daddies weren't allowed to be with white mommies. Reactions like these from other kids can make many multiracial children feel different and alone.

Their feeling of social isolation is often reinforced in junior high school, a time when students begin exploring their own identities by singling out those they perceive as different. Jesse, the adopted Asian American son of a white family, remembers his experience in a predominantly black Washington, D.C., school. "In middle school . . . every kid has problems with identity. And mine were compounded by the fact that not only was I a minority, but I didn't fit into the Asian community, [because] my entire family was white. I knew I wasn't white either, and I didn't have any direction to go. . . . I was a misfit."

The number of interracial families in America has increased by 78 percent since 1980.

My own experiences at this age were just as confusing. When I was in elementary school, my family lived in the Ivory Coast, in West Africa. At the international school I attended, the students came from all over the world. Everybody's family was different, so I never felt that my own family was special or unique.

Moving to Washington, D.C., in 5th grade changed that comfortable feeling. Suddenly, I found that I was expected to be just like all the other African American girls in my predominantly white class. But, having been raised by a white man and a West African woman, largely outside of the U.S., I actually had very little exposure to African American culture, and I didn't fit in very well with the girls who had. I was an outsider to them in all the little ways that matter in 5th grade: I'd never heard of Double Dutch, I couldn't play Spades or jacks, and I didn't even know the difference between "break-dancing" and "popping." I was African and I was American, but I was not African American.

I found that I had more in common with some of the white girls in my class, but here, too, I wasn't totally at home. We may have talked more alike and dressed more alike, but my hair was a mystery to them, as was my life in Africa and the issues I was dealing with growing up black in America.

Throughout middle school and high school, I got used to being unable to identify completely with my white friends, while feeling somehow guilty because I wasn't what my black classmates expected me to be. I gradually realized that my problems were more the result of divisions in American society than of deficiencies in my biracial upbringing, but that didn't help much as the time. I felt stuck in the middle.

For some people, the messages they receive from others during this time can lead to years of painful self-doubt. Jesse, now a 24-year-old graduate student in secondary education, remembers an incident in 8th grade when a math teacher humiliated him in front of the class, insinuating that he should be doing better in algebra because he was Asian.

"I think that incident shaped a lot of how I saw myself in a racial context in this society," Jesse says, explaining that the teacher's statement confirmed his feeling that no matter how hard he tried to fit in, he would always fail. His self-confidence was so deeply undermined that he actually failed three classes in 8th grade, setting a self-defeating trend that would last throughout high school. After years of working through the negative messages he'd received about his identity, Jesse wishes that teachers had been more sensitive to the issues he was struggling with and had helped him address them earlier.

Marisa, a biracial college student, also found that other people's perceptions of her deeply affected her sense of identity as she was growing up. The daughter of a Japanese woman and a Mexican man, she went to school in an almost completely white Southern California environment where people were constantly trying to pigeonhole her. If she got good grades or played an instrument, it was because she was Asian. But when she told classmates that she was part Mexican, they were surprised that she was "so smart."

This constant sterotyping made Marisa unhappy with her non-white identity. It was only when she left home for college that Marisa discovered that not only did she not have to try to be "white," but she could embrace both of her heritages by identifying as a multiracial person of color. Now she realizes that "it would have been great to have had people be interested in my two cultures . . . instead of [my] having to change everything I was to try to fit in."

Some children from multiracial families have an easier time, especially if they find a group they can identify with. Lauren, whose mother is black and father is white, explains that she doesn't have any problem being interracial in her school. Most of her close friends are black, and her interracial identity is basically accepted by them. She does note that there is pressure to choose one side or the other, which can sometimes be a little isolating. "There's not a big group of mixed kids, so it's not like you can hang with people who are like you. But," she adds, "I don't really mind being different."

Although I was raised to be proud of both my heritages, a it wasn't until pivotal trip to Ghana with my mother that I came to terms with not always being able to fit in. It was the summer after my sophomore year in high school, and I looked forward to more than simply seeing my Ghanaian family again after a four-year absence. In America, I had learned that no matter how I chose to identify myself, I was inevitably perceived as black. So I expected that with my black family and other Ghanaians, I would finally find my niche—at least in terms of my appearance.

But instead, as I walked the streets of the capital city and smaller villages with my mother, I was stared at openly. And I kept hearing the word "Oburoni"—murmured by strangers as I passed by, yelled by excited children as they trailed behind me down a village road, or playfully tossed at me in conversation with a family member or acquaintance. When I asked my mother what it meant, I was amazed to learn that in Twi, her language, "Oburoni" meant, literally, "white person." Ghanaians saw me as more white than black!

6. SPECIAL TOPICS IN MULTICULTURAL EDUCATION

Shades of Gray: The Conundrum of Color Categories

Please choose one: American Indian or Alaskan Native, Asian or Pacific Islander, black, white. Of Hispanic Origin or Not of Hispanic Origin. Like a game of musical chairs, traditional racial categories always seem to leave someone out.

Today, the government requires racial categorization for statistical purposes — to monitor and enforce civil rights legislation, and to ensure that businesses and public programs comply with equal opportunity provisions in housing, employment and education. But with a population that is constantly changing, statistics regarding race can be arbitrary and imprecise.

The game of fitting people into categories has been played throughout history. The country's first census, in 1790, divided the population into four groups: free white males, free white females, slaves, and other persons (including free blacks and Indians). By the early 19th century, the census specified that slaves were to be identified with a "B" if they were black and an "M" if they were mulatto.

In 1815, Thomas Jefferson tried to nail down the science of racial categorization. He devised an intricate algebraic equation (see below) to show that "one fourth Negro blood, mixed with any portion of white, constitutes the mulatto."

To guarantee that mixed-race children of slaveholders would be included in the slave population, the "one-drop rule" was promoted in the antebellum South. The one-drop rule evolved out of the premise that each race had its own blood type and that a single drop of "Negro blood" was sufficient to define a person as black. It was, scientifically speaking, nonsense — but it got the slaveholders out of having to recognize that many of their enslaved progeny were basically white. Today it is estimated that between 75 percent and 95 percent of blacks could define themselves as something other than black because of their mixed heritage.

In the 19th century, the rise of Darwinian theory gave impetus to a new trend — "scientific racism." Some scientists devoted their entire careers to measuring skull sizes and shapes, seeking physical evidence of a racial ranking that would validate their prejudices. Other scientists measured body parts — from calf muscles to jaws to lips to noses — in an attempt to prove that "inferior" races resembled apes. But no matter what they measured or how many numbers they crunched, the scientists weren't able to come up with the evidence they were seeking. So, quite often, they made it up. The "science" of 19th-century racialists is shot full of wishful thinking, spurious reasoning and outright fraud.

The one-drop rule endures to some extent today. Many people of mixed black-and-white ancestry encounter more acceptance in the black community and therefore define themselves as black. But others of mixed heritage are no longer willing to adhere to this rule because they are determined to acknowledge the diversity of their heritage. Many times, how they identify themselves depends on how they feel at the moment. As one biracial student admitted: "If my mom yelled at me in Spanish this morning, I feel Hispanic; if I went out last night and listened to rap, I feel black." Or as another said: "What category I check depends on my mood."

One proposed solution is the addition of a "multiracial" category to the census and other forms. Opponents to the proposal argue that a new category is just a continuation of the divisions and categorizations that have bedeviled us for so long. They contend such a category would deprive the government of its ability to fight racial discrimination. Some even contend that the multiracial category would constitute an extension of the one-drop rule because nearly anyone could say "I've got one drop of something — I must be multiracial."

Advocates of the multiracial category view such objections as relatively unimportant. As one college professor explained, the addition of a multiracial category "has the potential for undermining the very basis of racism, which is its categories."

The debate over racial categories is bewildering because it is based on ever-changing social standards rather than scientific evidence. In fact, anthropologists tell us that we are nearly all multiracial. If we were to be perfectly accurate, we would all check the box marked "Other."

— *Glenda Valentine*

WHAT CONSTITUTES A MULATTO?
by Thomas Jefferson

Let the first crossing be of 'a,' pure Negro, with 'A,' pure white. The unit of blood of the issue being composed of the half of that of each parent, will be $a/2 + A/2$. Call it, for abbreviation, h (half blood).

Let the second crossing be of h and B, the blood of the issue will be $h/2 + B/2$, or substituting for $h/2$ its equivalent, it will be $a/4 + A/4 + B/2$ call it q (quarteroon) being 1/4 Negro blood.

Let the third crossing be of q and C, their offspring will be $q/2 + C/2 = a/8 + A/8 + B/4 + C/2$, call this e (eighth), who having less than 1/4 of a, or of pure Negro blood, to wit 1/8 only, is no longer a mulatto, so that a third cross clears the blood.

From these elements let us examine their compounds. For example, let h and q cohabit, their issue will be $h/2 + q/2 = a/4 + A/4 + a/8 + A/8 + B/4 = 3a/8 + 3A/8 + B/4$ wherein we find 3/8 of a, or Negro blood ...

That revelation opened my eyes to the irony of my situation. I was exactly as much white as I was black, but—depending on what side of the Atlantic Ocean I was on—people only saw one of those two colors in me. I realized that there was nothing arbitrary about my personal identity. I knew who I was, and that knowledge remained constant. What was arbitrary was other people's constructions of race and how they perceived me. Figuring this out didn't clear up all my problems overnight, but it did make me feel more secure. I was proud to have the ability to differ from the expected.

And that may be the key for many children of mixed heritage: to be proud of being different. We represent the kind of difference that defies people's prejudices. After all, each multiracial child is the product of a small act of one race reaching out to another—something that we seem to have so much difficulty doing on a national scale.

Peggy Gillespie, a Massachusetts woman who co-designed a photographic exhibit featuring multiracial families, agrees. Herself the white mother of an adopted biracial child, she explains the value of her exhibit as an educational tool: "With so much racial conflict in society, this exhibit provides examples of individuals who have created lives together where race is not a barrier to love."

Another School's Reality

The authors describe mainstreaming at the Dowling Urban Environment Learning Center in Minneapolis — a fully inclusive, racially mixed, general education magnet school for grades K-6 that is not cheap to operate but that is well worth the cost.

Jeffrey Raison, Lee Anna Hanson, Cheryl Hall, and Maynard C. Reynolds

JEFFREY RAISON is the principal of Dowling Urban Environment Learning Center, Minneapolis, where LEE ANNA HANSON is a special education teacher and CHERYL HALL is an integration specialist. MAYNARD C. REYNOLDS is a senior research associate at the National Center on Education in Inner Cities at Temple University, Philadelphia, and professor emeritus of educational psychology, University of Minnesota, Minneapolis. The research reported in this article was supported by a grant from the Office of Educational Research and Improvement of the U.S. Department of Education, through the National Center on Education in Inner Cities. However, the opinions expressed are those of the authors.

IN THEIR article "Mainstreaming: One School's Reality," which appeared in the September 1994 *Kappan*, Lawrence Baines, Coleen Baines, and Carol Masterson reported on Coats Middle School, where "mainstreaming was achieved every day under . . . absurd conditions and worse." The situation they described was clearly the result of inadequate communication, misgovernance, and poor allocation of resources. The "reality" of mainstreaming at Coats Middle School was, according to the authors, dreadful.

Yet other mainstreamed schools have different and more positive realities. The Dowling Urban Environment Learning Center in Minneapolis is one example. A decade ago Dowling was changed from a special school for disabled students to a fully inclusive, racially mixed, general education, urban environment center for grades K-6. Although it is a magnet school for the south side of the city, some students are transported from the north side because parents have chosen to send them to Dowling. More than 95% of the student population is bused.

The 450 students who attend Dowling range in age from 4 to 13 and come from five different racial/ethnic backgrounds. The students, needless to say, are not separated by racial/ethnic categories in any school program. Twenty-one percent of the students receive special education. (Fifty of them have multiple physical or cognitive disabilities, and 13 lower-grade students have severe emotional and behavioral disabilities; some of the most medically fragile students in the state of Minnesota attend the school.) The number of learning-disabled students is probably below district averages, owing to early intervention and collaboration between regular and special education teachers.

Dowling is an inclusive school in which thoughtful planning, much hard work, and continuous improvement are in evidence. The school has a clear purpose, there are few signs of emotional exhaustion among its staff members, and depersonalization is kept to a minimum. The levels of satisfaction are high for everyone: staff, students, and parents. Such schools do not just happen. The principal supports a strong conceptual framework and maintains a clear vision of what the school is about and where it is headed. Leadership is shared by the principal and faculty members. Decisions are made by those who are closest to the individuals that the decisions affect.

Coats Middle School, by contrast, appears to be a school where few (if any) persons are in charge, where power seems to rest with someone "out there," and where the levels of satisfaction are very low. Baines and his co-authors report that, in response to a survey, every teacher except one at Coats Middle School indicated that "mainstreaming had . . . deleterious effects for most students" and "contended that mainstreaming had increased the amount of stress in their lives."

In a recent survey conducted by the Minneapolis Public Schools, 100% of the Dowling staff members indicated that they like working at the school. (Citywide, 92% of the teachers reported that they like working at their schools.) Furthermore, measurements of children's achievement show that mainstreaming at Dowling has had no deleterious effects. In fact, children who have attended the school continuously over several years (there is an annual student turnover of about 7%) make substantial progress.

In 1991 the services for mildly disabled and low-achieving children at Dowling were restructured to emphasize team teaching and integrated delivery of compensatory services within mainstream classes. A "collaborative teacher" is assigned to each grade level, and he or she provides services by academic need area rather than by label. At the same time, in order to extend the restructuring goal, the staff initiated "20/20 analysis," an assessment technique developed by the National Center on Education in Inner Cities at Temple University.[1] Data are reported for the 20th and 80th percentiles as well as for the median. This procedure permits the staff to focus on the margins of achievement.

In 1991 the CAT Total Reading test was given to all students at Dowling. For Dowling students the 20th percentile on national norms was 18, the median was 50, and the 80th percentile, 78. These figures indicate that, for the school as a whole, the distribution of reading scores was remarkably similar to that of the national norm group. From 1991 to 1993, all indicators of reading achievement showed definite improvement. The improvement in CAT Math Concept scores from 1990 to 1992 was even greater.

High achievers are not neglected in the school. They are regularly challenged by such offerings as advanced computer techniques, higher-order thinking skills (HOTS), drama and art, and accelerated versions of all subject matter included in urban education. Many low-achieving students follow individualized education programs that are planned carefully by teachers and parents and that are used systematically.

One of the most moving sections of the article on Coats Middle School was the story of "Sabrina," the seventh-grader with cerebral palsy who needs help to go the bathroom. At Dowling "Becky" also needs help with toileting. She has been diagnosed with Rubinstein-Taybi Syndrome (congenital skeletal and organic defects), facial and hand disfigurements, and moderate mental disabilities. Although her physical needs differ from Sabrina's, we tell Becky's story here because it demonstrates how a problem similar to the one at Coats was handled at Dowling.

Becky started at Dowling as a 4-year-old, left for a couple of years, and returned as a first-grader. She was placed in a general education class with an educational assistant who provided supports for her as well as for another student. Becky also received services from a special education resource teacher and from speech, occupational, and physical therapists. This staffing arrangement was maintained through grade 3. At that time it became clear to the members of the team managing Becky's case that they were having difficulty meeting her needs. She was not yet toilet trained (despite several earlier attempts) and had become disruptive in class (speaking out, behaving inappropriately, and wandering around the room). The resource teacher consulted with a special class teacher to provide a more meaningful curriculum for Becky and to help toilet train her. With the participation of an educational assistant and the cooperation of her parents, Becky was toilet trained within two weeks.

35. Another School's Reality

WHY IS THE Dowling experience with mainstreaming so different from that observed at Coats Middle School? The Dowling community knows that inclusive schools need much focused work, a strong staff, and strong leadership. Indeed, the banner at the entrance to the building proclaims the school motto: "I Am the Solution!" — and everyone means it. Leadership and problem solving are shared. Everyone has a piece of the action. The principal has many functions: teacher, coach, cheerleader, strategic planner, facilitator, listener, customer service representative, and member of the team. All staff members are assumed to be creative and are expected to put forth new ideas and practices. Research is considered an important resource. The school is well-staffed. High-quality education leading to healthy, strong patterns of learning is the goal. Inclusive education is a part of that process.

Dowling is not cheap. In fact, it is quite expensive to operate. The leadership team seeks grants from local foundations and the U.S. Department of Education for new and extraordinary needs when appropriations are insufficient. The worth of the school, however, is reflected in the achievements of the students, the satisfaction of the parents, and the long-term benefits to the community.

1. Maynard Reynolds, Andrea Zetlin, and Margaret Wang, "20/20 Analysis: Taking a Close Look at the Margins," *Exceptional Children*, February 1993, pp. 294-300.

For Vision and Voice: A Call to Conscience

We look forward to the near-term future of multicultural education with a degree of optimism, yet aware that there are serious challenges before us. Concern in the American public regarding immigration is at a high level. The global economy and automation are putting pressure on both workers' salaries and government budgets, so that important social causes tend to lose their high priorities on the public agenda. Increasing poverty and urban violence exacerbate the ever-present problems of racial, cultural, and gender bias.

UNIT 7

Nevertheless, we need a vision for the future of our schools that includes a belief in the worth and dignity of all persons. We need to clarify that vision to take into account the ever more culturally pluralistic nation that the United States is becoming. As part of this effort, I offer the French revolutionary concept of fraternity. Fraternity and sorority refer to brotherhood and sisterhood, suggesting that people bond together as brothers and sisters who care for and are committed to one another's well-being. We need to communicate that sense of caring to the young people who attend our schools, and the teaching profession needs a good dose of fraternity and sorority as well. Teachers need to work together in solving problems and supporting each other's respective professional efforts, sharing their experience, knowledge bases, and expertise. We need to learn to team together and teach together more than we have in the past, and we need the professional autonomy to be able to do so at our own discretion and not because someone told us to. The future of teaching and learning from a multicultural perspective should include more emphasis on cooperative learning strategies that encourage students to develop a sense of community and fraternity, which will transcend competition.

The future will also see less dependence on standardized, system-wide, behavioral objectives and more emphasis on permitting teachers at the local school level to develop models for assessing whether or not their students are achieving their educational goals. There will be more informal, teacher-customized approaches to evaluation of student learning and less reliance on rigid statewide standardized learning objectives. Individual school faculties will be permitted to modify their schools' learning objectives for their students, and students will receive more individualized assessment and feedback on their progress in school.

Finally, a multicultural vision of the future of education will include a strong commitment to develop a powerful, critical sense of social consciousness and social responsibility between teachers and students. The educational settings of society are important terrain in the struggle to reconstruct public life along more egalitarian, just social policy lines. A multicultural vision of our educational future will encourage teachers to adopt a pedagogy of liberation that champions the development of critical social awareness among students and that empowers them to evaluate critically all that they may experience.

Looking Ahead: Challenge Questions

What might be the benefits if schools were to permit teachers more autonomy in how they assess their students?

Why would it help teachers and students to develop a "language of possibility" as part of the development of their critical reasoning skills?

What are some of the things that "transformative intellectuals" or "teacher prophets" do in their elementary and secondary classrooms?

How can teachers help students develop their talents and develop a vision of hope for themselves? How can teachers help students develop a sense of public service?

What are the most important challenges confronting multicultural educators as we enter the new century before us?

—F.S.

Multicultural Education and Technology: Promise and Pitfalls

Jim Cummins & Dennis Sayers

Jim Cummins is at the Ontario Institute for Studies in Education; Dennis Sayers is at the University of California, Davis.

It is common to observe that "change is the only constant" to highlight the rapidity of technological change that characterizes the Information Age in which we are now immersed. The implications of these technological changes for education are hotly debated in many countries. In this paper we wish to address one aspect of this debate: the implications of technology for multicultural education.

We will draw from the analysis in our book *Brave New Schools: Challenging Cultural Illiteracy through Global Learning Networks* (Cummins & Sayers, 1995) in which we examine the potential of global learning networks, operating for example through the Internet, to promote intercultural literacy and critical thinking. We suggest that E.D. Hirsch's (1987) call for schools to develop students' **cultural literacy** represents a regression to monocultural myopia that is part of the renewed discourse of intellectualized xenophobia that has escalated in the United States and elsewhere during the past decade. In order to prepare students for the changing cultural, economic/scientific, and existential realities of the 21st century, schools must adopt a pedagogy of **collaborative critical inquiry** that draws on the linguistic and cultural resources that students bring to school to analyze critically the social conditions and power structures that affect their lives and the world around them. We argue that technology can contribute significantly to this form of pedagogy through its power to link distant classrooms for purposes of collaborative projects focused on issues of mutual concern.

In order to contextualize the issues, we will briefly review the ongoing debates in the United States context on (a) cultural diversity and multiculturalism and (b) technology and education. Then we will outline the cultural, economic/scientific, and existential changes that will determine the nature of the society that our students will graduate into and presumably should define the directions for current educational reforms. Finally, we will examine the potential role of computer-mediated learning networks to promote the kind of multicultural awareness and critical literacy and that our society desperately needs if democracy is to survive as anything more than a meaningless ritual.

The Culture Wars

During the past decade, the alleged dangers of cultural diversity have been highlighted by academics concerned that the rapid growth of diversity endangers the coherence and unity of the United States. These authors have articulated a form of intellectualized xenophobia intended to alert the general public to the infiltration of the "other" into the heart and soul of American institutions. Cultural diversity has become the enemy within, far more potent and insidious in its threat than any external enemy. Most influential was E.D. Hirsch's (1987) *Cultural Literacy: What Every American Needs to Know* which argued that the fabric of nationhood depended on a set of common knowledge, understandings, and values shared by the populace. Multilingualism and multiculturalism represented a threat to cultural literacy and, by extension, nationhood:

> In America, the reality is that we have not yet properly achieved **mono** literacy, much less multiliteracy....Linguistic pluralism would make sense for us only on the questionable assumption that our civil peace and national effectiveness could survive multilingualism. But, in fact, multilingualism enormously increases cultural fragmentation, civil antagonism, illiteracy, and economic-technological ineffectualness. (1987, p. 92)

Hirsch's "cultural literacy" represented a call to strengthen the national immune system so that it could successfully resist the debilitating influence of cultural diversity. Only when the national identity has been fortified and secured through "cultural literacy" should contact with the "other" be contemplated, and even then educators should keep diversity at a distance, always vigilant against its potent destructive power.

All artwork and student writing is from Orilleros, the De Orilla a Orillas newsletter.

It is in this context that we can understand statements such as the following from Arthur Schlesinger Jr. (1991) in his book *The Disuniting of America*:

> In recent years the combination of the ethnicity cult with a flood of immigration from Spanish-speaking countries has given bilingualism new impetus....Alas, bilingualism has not worked out as planned: rather the contrary. Testimony is mixed, but indications are that bilingual education retards rather than expedites the movement of Hispanic children into the English-speaking world and that it promotes segregation rather than it does integration. Bilingualism shuts doors. It nourishes self-ghettoization, and ghettoization nourishes racial antagonism.... Using some language other than English dooms people to second-class citizenship in American society....Monolingual education opens doors to the larger world.... institutionalized bilingualism remains another source of the fragmentation of America, another threat to the dream of 'one people.' (1991, pp. 108-109)

The claims that "bilingualism shuts doors" and "monolingual education opens doors to the wider world," are laughable if viewed in isolation, particularly in the context of current global interdependence and the frequently expressed needs of American business for multilingual "human resources." Schlesinger's comments become interpretable only in the context of a societal discourse that is profoundly disquieted by the fact that the sounds of the "other" have now become audible and the hues of the American social landscape have darkened noticibly.

This discourse of diversity as "the enemy within" has fueled the anti-immigrant sentiment of California's Proposition 187 and the movement to make English the official language of the United States. It is also broadcast into classrooms in ways that affect (and are intended to affect) the interactions between educators and culturally diverse students. With xenophobic rhetoric swirling all around the classroom, educators are required to challenge this discourse and the power structure it represents if they are to create a climate of respect, trust, and belonging in their interactions with culturally diverse students.

Perspectives that promote multicultural awareness (*e.g.*, Darder, 1991; Delpit, 1992; Gates, 1992; Gay, 1995; Nieto, 1996; among many others) tend to occupy the much more limited public space of educational textbooks and periodicals, leaving the newspaper editorials and syndicated columns largely unopposed in preaching to the general public about the dangers of diversity. The media rarely, if ever, bring their readers' attention to the contradiction between the fear of diversity at home and the documented need of American business negotiating in the international marketplace for greater cultural awareness and linguistic competence.

The Promise and Threat of Technology

Business leaders and politicians tend to see the effective use of technology as one of the major means for improving education. Some go further in suggesting that the private sector is better positioned than the public school system to use technology effectively. They argue for the privatization of education as a means of boosting student outcomes while simultaneously generating profits for private investors. Technologically based instructional delivery will require fewer expensive humans, thereby realizing profits based on the same per-pupil expenditure as conventional schooling. In Douglas Noble's words: "Corporate leaders view schools as the last major labor-intensive industry ripe for colonization and modernization. Public schools, finally, represent for them an expensive public monopoly overcome by bureaucratic inefficiency and abysmal productivity" (1994, p. 65).

By contrast, progressive educators (*e.g.*, Apple, 1993; Olson, 1987, and many others) have tended to be highly suspicious of computers and technology in general. Canadian educators, Maud Barlow and Heather-Jane Robertson, for example, express their concerns about what they term the "disinformation highway" as follows:

> To reach young people, as consumers, as future workers, as the social architects of tomorrow, business is looking to the powerful medium-of-choice for kids, high technology. Information is increasingly delivered not by books and teacher lectures but by computers and telecommunications (which are less easily regulated to reflect the consensus standards set by boards, parents, and governments). Technology is becoming the way to bypass the system and go directly to students with a message. While this is as true for environmentalists, labor groups, and others trying to persuade young people to their view, no other sector will have as much financial access as corporations to ride the highway into the schools. (1994, pp. 89–90)

Student illustrations from the Orillas Proverbs and Tolerance Project: A comparative Oral History and Folklore Study. **Above:** People who live in glass houses should not throw stones. *El que vine en una casa de vidrio dehe abstenuse de tirar piedras.*—By Rubén Dávila. 5th grade. Truman School, New Haven, CT.

We share the concerns of many critics of the regime of technology. However, the dismissal of technology in general, and of the "information superhighway" in particular by many progressive educators ignores the fact that it is here to stay and will play a determining role in the life of every student who graduates in the next millennium. The same critics who dismiss the educational potential of technology as a "corporate plot" have no hesitation using the print medium (books, journals, etc.) to publicize their views and theories despite the fact that the publishing industry is likewise controlled by and largely serves the interests of the corporate sector. Rather than abandoning the field to narrow corporate interests, it seems imperative to us to articulate how powerful a teaching and

7. FOR VISION AND VOICE: A CALL TO CONSCIENCE

learning medium the information highway can be when aligned with a pedagogy of collaborative critical inquiry.

The Changing Realities of the 21st Century

In *Brave New Schools* we argue that the changing cultural, economic/scientific, and existential realities that we are currently experiencing highlight the importance of promoting students' capacity for collaborative critical inquiry into social issues of immediate relevance to their lives. Briefly stated, the **cultural** changes are reflected in dramatically increased population mobility brought about by both economic crises and political conflicts in many parts of the world. To illustrate, in the United States the Asian American population is expected to quadruple by 2038 (to 32 million) while Latinos will account for more than 40 percent of population growth over the next 60 years and become the nation's largest minority group by 2013. African Americans will double in number by the year 2050.

These changing cultural realities have immense relevance to educational restructuring. Increased diversity at home and globalization internationally highlight the importance of promoting intercultural understanding and additional language competence in schools. Bilingual and multilingual individuals are essential to maintaining cohesion within our societies and cooperation between social groups and nations. They are also likely to be more attractive to employers faced with providing service to a culturally and linguistically diverse clientele in societal institutions (hospitals, seniors' homes, airports, schools, etc.) as well as to those engaged in international trade. As Australian historian Robert Hughes (1992) has expressed it: "In the world that is coming, if you can't navigate difference, you've had it" (p. 100).

The **economic and scientific changes** are reflected in the explosion of information that individuals, communities, governments and business are dealing with on a daily basis. Both within the workplace and in our daily lives, we are increasingly required to get access to information and reduce it to manageable proportions through critical analysis of what is relevant and what is not. We must then be able to use the information for problem-solving in collaboration with others in the domestic and international arenas who will likely be from different cultural, racial, religious, and linguistic backgrounds.

The clear implication for any school that aspires to prepare students for anything beyond low-level service employment is that students must be given the opportunity for collaborative critical inquiry within the classroom. Unfortunately, large-scale classroom data from the United States (*e.g.*, Goodlad, 1984; Ramirez, 1992) suggest that most schools are still locked into traditional schooling patterns that emphasize transmission of information and skills rather than the generation of knowledge through critical inquiry.

By **existential realities**, we are referring to the increasing sense of fragility that characterizes our relationship to both our physical and social environment. A perusal of virtually any North American newspaper will quickly show the prominence of issues related to poverty, crime, racism, diversity of all kinds, environmental deterioration, global conflict, famine, etc.

Despite these changed existential realities, many schools appear dedicated to insulating students from awareness of social issues in domestic and global arenas rather than communicating a sense of urgency in regard to understanding and acting on them. In most schools across the continent, the curriculum has been sanitized such that students rarely have the opportunity to discuss critically, write about, or act upon issues that directly affect the society they will form. Issues such as racism, environmental

These are pages from the "New Places" report published by third grade Mexican and Zapotec students who arrived at their California Schools not knowing English. "New Places" is an international research project sponsored by *Project Orillas* on making schools better places for newcomers.

Left: Front Cover—"How boys and girls feel when they don't speak English."
Right: Recommendations—"Treat all children equally. Speak in the child's language so that the children don't feel inferior."

pollution, genetic engineering, and the causes of poverty are regarded as too sensitive for fragile and impressionable young minds. Still less do students have the opportunity to cooperate with others from different cultural and/or linguistic groups in exploring resolutions to these issues.

A major reason why schools try to maintain a facade of innocence in relation to social and environmental issues is that such issues invariably implicate power relations in the domestic and international arenas. Promoting a critical awareness of how power is wielded at home and abroad is not a task that society expects educators to undertake. In fact, renewed demands for a core curriculum and for imposition of "cultural literacy" can be interpreted as a way of controlling the information that students can access so as to minimize the possibility of deviant thoughts.

It is hardly surprising that issues related to how power is wielded and consent is manufactured in our society are on the taboo list of what is appropriate to explore in schools. However, there are major financial and social costs associated with this attempt to limit critical literacy. Students whose communities have been marginalized will increasingly perceive the omission of these fundamental issues as dishonest and hypocritical, and this will reinforce their resistance to achievement under the current rules of the game. The continued exclusion of culturally diverse students from the learning process at school is pushing us toward a society where everyone loses because every dropout carries an expensive price tag for the entire society. By contrast, a focus on critical inquiry, in a collaborative and supportive context, will encourage students to engage in learning in ways that promote future productive engagement in their societies. The research, critical thinking, and creative problem-solving skills that this form of education entails will position students well for full participation in the economic and social realities of their global community.

In summary, an analysis of the changing cultural, economic/scientific, and existential realities highlights the importance of collaborative critical inquiry as the core pedagogical orientation required for schools to prepare students for both economic and democratic participation. Why is this form of pedagogy so rare in our schools in comparison to traditional transmission-oriented pedagogy?

Despite its obvious relevance to the economic and democratic health of our societies, collaborative critical inquiry is not encouraged in most educational systems for the simple reason that critical literacy reduces the effectiveness of indoctrination and disinformation. James Moffett (1989) has expressed clearly our ambivalence in regard to critical literacy and multicultural education, both of which permit alternative cultural and social perspectives to be considered:

> Literacy is dangerous and has always been so regarded. It naturally breaks down barriers of time, space, and culture. It threatens one's original identity by broadening it through vicarious experiencing and the incorporation of somebody **else's** hearth and ethos. So we feel profoundly ambiguous about literacy. Looking at it as a means of transmitting our culture to our children, we give it priority in education, but recognizing the threat of its backfiring we make it so tiresome and personally unrewarding that youngsters won't want to do it on their own, which is of course when it becomes dangerous.... The net effect of this ambivalence is to give literacy with one hand and take it back with the other, in keeping with our contradictory wish for youngsters to learn to think but only about what we already have in mind for them. (1989, p. 85)

How can participation in computer-mediated learning networks contribute to the promotion of critical literacy and multicultural awareness?

Promoting Critical Literacy and Multicultural Awareness through Global Learning Networks

Sister class exchanges through global learning networks are by no means a new phenomenon. The French educator Célestine Freinet originated interscholastic exchanges in 1924 using the printing press to "publish" students' writings and exchange them and "cultural packages" with distant classes. By the time of Freinet's death in 1966, the Modern School Movement, which he founded, involved 10,000 schools in 33 countries. These schools carried out collaborative projects using the regular postal service to exchange materials and maintain contact.

Although computer and telecommunications technology dramatically facilitate interscholastic exchanges, the basic pedagogical underpinnings of global learning networks are no different than those implemented by Freinet many years ago using much less sophisticated technology. Students involved in both historical and current learning networks engage in collaborative critical inquiry and creative problem-solving. The issues they focus on have social as well as curricular relevance. Learning takes place in the context of shared projects jointly elaborated by participants in the network rather than from textbooks. Students at the present time also have access to the enormous range of informational resources available through the Internet and World Wide Web.

There are currently a significant number of national and international networks that promote student exchange and inquiry into issues of both social and academic relevance (Cummins & Sayers, 1995). As one example, the multilingual *Orillas* project links students in the United States, Puerto Rico, Mexico, Canada, and Argentina on a regular basis (Sayers, 1994; Sayers & Brown, 1987). Within this network, sister classes engage in two kinds of exchanges: (a) monthly culture packages of maps, photos, audio and videotapes, schoolwork and local memorabilia; and (b) collaborative projects planned jointly by teachers in different sites that involve interdependent, cooperative activity in small groups at both sites. These collaborative projects fall into several categories: (1) shared student publications (*e.g.*, newsletters); (2) comparative/contrastive investigations (*e.g.*, surveys of each community regarding topical social issues such as pollution); (3) folklore compendiums and oral histories (*e.g.*, collections of proverbs, children's rhymes and riddles, songs, etc); (4) cultural explorations (*e.g.*, students in the sister classes alternately playing the roles of anthropologist and cultural informant in order to explore each other's culture).

The common element of all networking projects that focus on social and cultural inquiry is the emergence of a community of learning that thrives on incorporating alternative perspectives in its search for understanding. Such networks potentially challenge the "cultural literacy" of socially approved interpretations of historical and current events by virtue of their incorporation of alternative perspectives on these events. These alternative perspectives derive from both the sister classes and the use of a much wider range of sources for research inquiry than just the traditional textbook. Critical literacy rather than cultural literacy is the goal. For example, the *Kids from Kanata* project links urban and rural First Nations (Native) students (and teachers) with non-

7. FOR VISION AND VOICE: A CALL TO CONSCIENCE

Native students (and teachers) across Canada to explore and share the experience of living in Canada from very different geographic and cultural backgrounds. Students and teachers participating in this network undoubtedly have far greater opportunity to develop an understanding of the roots of First Nations protests in recent years than students who are not involved in this kind of exchange.

At the heart of *Brave New Schools* are eight portraits that we present in Chapter 2 of teachers, parents, and students who are engaged in various global learning networks. These projects address a variety of issues that have immediate social relevance; for example:

- the impact of war and ethnic conflict on children and adults who have become refugees;
- understanding the different cultural realities experienced by deaf and hearing children from different countries;
- confronting inter-ethnic conflict between Latino and African American students;
- promoting intergenerational learning among children, adults, and extended families;
- exploration and critical analysis of proverbs from different cultures;
- researching the Holocaust and other genocides as a way of furthering an end to intolerance;
- promotion of global awareness through collaboration in raising money to build village wells in Nicaragua;
- publication of an international students' magazine, *The Contemporary,* that focuses on controversial issues of global importance.

In the third portrait, we describe a long-distance collaboration initiated by a Spanish-speaking bilingual teacher from San Francisco and her African-American colleague. The two teachers together sought ways to confront the growing inter-ethnic prejudice in their school between newly-arrived Latino children of Mexican heritage and the African-American students. To do so, they established a "distance team-teaching" partnership with a bilingual teacher in New York City who worked with Spanish-speaking students from the Caribbean. Their rationale, according to Kristin Brown of *Orillas*, who helped locate a suitable partner class to work with in confronting intergroup prejudice, was straightforward:

Since the partner classes in New York would include Spanish-speaking Latino students of African descent, we would be linking San Francisco's Latino students with faraway colleagues who in many ways were like them—students who spoke the same mother tongue and shared the experience of learning English as a second language—but whose physical attributes and pride in their African heritage more closely resembled their African-American schoolmates. In this way we hoped to provide a bridge between the African Americans and the Latinos who saw one another everyday at school but whose interactions were distorted by fears and deep-seated prejudice. (Cummins & Sayers, 1995, p. 36)

The two classes in San Francisco and their New York colleagues shared videos and other projects for a year, including an exchange of folkgames from Mexican, Caribbean, and African-American cultures.

How do these interchanges work to reduce prejudice among these children? Research suggests these attitudes change through a process similar to the way in

---

Student Report from the Orillas "New Places Project: An International Research Project on Making Schools Better Places for Newcomers

We are an ESL Classroom at Channel Islands High, in Oxnard, California—Mexican and Filipino immigrant students that live in this new place from 2-3 years. We're all struggling to learn the English language.

What We Hoped and Dreamed

Easy life style, freedom, the quality of life better than our own country, opportunity for work, college, and university; equal rights for all the people...

What our New Place was Really Like

Violent, racist, discrimination, low paying jobs for our parents, very expensive to live, crime and drugs, gangs that kill, difficult to survive in school, my people don't have equal rights, Prop. 187 is frightening, we Mexican women are pressured to move on and get married because our parents can't afford to support us...

What Helped Make our New Place Better

Students for Cultural and Linguistic Democracy, a student activist group, and Mr. Terrazas took many risks to establish the following historical events to make our new place better and more just and equal for all immigrants and oppressed students and parents.

Bilingual and Migrant Program: We did not develop this program, but it sure supports and teaches us English and academics in our native Language. Our bilingual program teachers are excellent with lots of love and sensitivity related to a bicultural existence.

Bilingual and Migrant Open House: This is ours! This is totally student centered and directed. We Voice with power, dance, sing, role play problem posing issues, educate our parents, and rise the political, social, and economics consciousness of our people and community. This is really our welcome place and we are proud of it. Our 9th year!

Students Voicing at Teacher and Communib Conferences: Students for Cultural and Linguistic Democracy have been going to and planning conferences since 1992. We've just worked hard to organize our district's first *Educatating Our Raza Awareness Conference,* which will involve over 350 students and parents.

Students and Teachers Co-authoring a Book: Our students and our teacher have just co-authored a book called *Reclaiming Our Voices: Bilingual Education and Critical Pedagogy & Praxis.* This books tells about real struggles and experiences immigrant students go through in new places.

Project Orillas: Sharing and caring with students from other places has made us understand that we are not alone in our struggles. We have learned a lot by just listening to each other over telephone voice box, computer modem, and telephone video. Orillas has introduced us to communication technology at it's highest form.

We hope our research will make better, just, and safe NEW PLACES for all students.
—Guillermo Terrazas and English 103 ESL 1st and 2nd period.

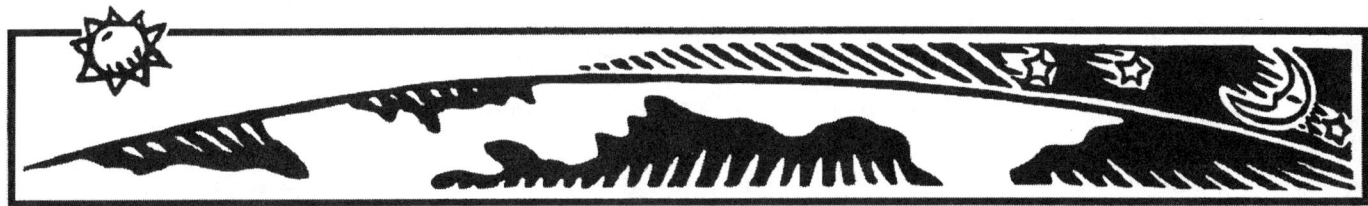

which cooperative learning works to reduce prejudice (Sayers, 1994). As Gordon Allport (1954) first proposed in his classic *The Nature of Prejudice*, dramatic reductions in prejudice can occur when children from different ethnic and racial backgrounds work interdependently in small groups. At a local level, cooperative learning helps break down barriers between "ingroups" and "outgroups" as a result of positive interdependence in achieving a common goal. In the same way, global learning networks can promote significant changes in attitude when two distant classes work cooperatively.

Was prejudice reduced as the San Francisco teachers hoped? There were definite signs it was. The parents of two African-American students in San Francisco **demanded** that their children be allowed to learn Spanish by studying with the children in the bilingual education class. Also, for the first time ever, Latina girls have joined the Girl Scout troop, originally organized by African-American and European-American mothers at the school. Who were the new recruits? Every single girl in the bilingual class that worked on the global learning project.

As a context for dialogue, intercultural learning networks provide an opportunity to find a voice, to have a say and to be heard in terms of learning goals shared with another distant group whose voices are equally valued. Above all, it is a dialogue about finding common ground for working with distant partners, about negotiating a joint site for meaning construction and the definition of identity. It is about jointly posing a significant problem of mutual interest to be investigated locally; about deciding on a basis for comparison of what is being learned; about discovering and refining comparable tools of study; and about sharing and comparing the outcomes of parallel locally-based studies and helping one another transform learning into action. It is about developing a working knowledge of what it means to "think globally and act locally."

Conclusion

We have argued that computer and telecommunictions technology has the potential to act as a catalyst for the development of both intercultural understanding and critical literacy. The emergence of electronic communities of learning potentially threatens the hegemony of "official knowledge," as encapsulated in textbooks, because it is much more difficult to pre-script and neutralize the content of communication across cultural and national boundaries. Only issues that relate directly to students' lives and to the world around them are likely to sustain long-term meaningful collaborative projects. In short, global learning networks represent a powerful tool to deconstruct the sanitized curriculum that most students still experience within the classroom and to prepare students to function within the cultural, economic/scientific, and existential realities of the 21st century.

References

Allport, G. (1954). *The nature of prejudice*. Reading, MA: Addison-Wesley Publishing Company.
Apple, M. (1993). *Official knowledge: Democratic education in a conservative age*. New York: Routledge.
Barlow, M. & Robertson, H. (1994). *Class warfare: The assault on Canada's schools*. Toronto: Key Porter Books.
Cummins, J. & Sayers, D. (1995). *Brave new schools: Challenging cultural illiteracy through global learning networks*. New York: St. Martin's Press.
Darder, A. (1991). *Culture and power in the classroom: A critical foundation for bicultural education*. New York: Bergin & Garvey.
Delpit, L. D. (1992). Education in a multicultural society: Our future's greatest challenge. *Journal of Negro Education*, 61, 237-249.
Gates, H.L., Jr. (1992). *Loose canons: Notes on the culture wars*. New York: Oxford University Press.
Gay, G. (1995). Bridging multicultural theory and practice. *Multicultural Education*, 3 (1), 4-9.
Goodlad, J.I. (1984). *A place called school: Prospects for the future*. New York: McGraw Hill.
Hirsch, E.D., Jr. (1987). *Cultural literacy: What every American needs to know*. Boston, MA: Houghton Mifflin Co.
Hughes, R. (1993). *Culture of complaint: A passionate look into the ailing heart of America*. New York: Warner Books.
Moffett, J. (1989). Censorship and spiritual education. *English Education*, 21, 70-87.
Nieto, S. (1996). *Affirming diversity: The sociopolitical context of multicultural education*. 2nd ed. New York: Longman.
Noble, D. (1994). The regime of technology in education. *Our Schools, Our Selves*, 5 (3), 49-72.
Olsen, P. (1987). Who computes? In D.W. Livingstone (Ed.), *Critical pedagogy & cultural power* (pp. 179-204). South Hadley, MA: Bergin & Garvey.
Ramirez, J.D. (1992). Executive summary. *Bilingual Research Journal*, 16, 1-62.
Sayers, D. (1994). Bilingual team teaching partnerships over long distances: A technology-mediated context for intra-group language attitude change. In C. Faltis, R. DeVillar, & J. Cummins (Eds.), *Cultural diversity in schools: From rhetoric to practice*. (pp. 299-331). Albany, NY: State University of New York Press.
Sayers, D., & Brown, K. (1987). Bilingual education and telecommunications: A perfect fit. *The Computing Teacher*, 17, 23-24.
Schlesinger, A. Jr. (1991). *The disuniting of America*. New York: W.W. Norton.

7. FOR VISION AND VOICE: A CALL TO CONSCIENCE

What is Orillas?

By Kristin Brown, Enid Figueroa, & Dennis Sayers

De Orilla a Orilla (Spanish for "from shore to shore") is an international teacher-researcher project that has focused on documenting promising classroom practices for intercultural learning over global learning networks. Since 1985, *Orillas* has employed modern telecommunications to promote and extend an educational networking model first developed by the French educators Célestin and Elise Freinet in 1924.

Following the Freinet model, *Orillas* is **not** a student-to-student penpal project but rather **clusters** of class-to-class collaborations designed by two or more partner teachers who have been matched according to common teaching interests and their students' grade level. *Orillas* has been an international clearinghouse for establishing long-distance team-teaching partnerships between pairs or groups of teachers separated by distance, forming "sister" or "partner" classes with a focus that is both multinational and multilingual (including primarily Spanish, English, French, Portuguese, Haitian, and American and French-Canadian Sign Languages).

The collaborating teachers make use of electronic mail and computer-based conferencing to plan and implement comparative learning projects between their distant partner classes. Such parallel projects include dual community surveys, joint math and science investigations, twinned geography projects, and comparative oral history and folklore studies. Often teachers in *Orillas* electronically publish their students' work over the Internet.

Research on *Orillas* has focused on those networking activities which effect social change, validate community traditions in the schools, and promote anti-racist education and linguistic human rights, while allowing teachers to explore the classroom practicalities of teaching based on collaborative critical inquiry. Robert DeVillar and Chris Faltis in *Computers and Cultural Diversity* judged *Orillas* "certainly one of the more, if not the most, innovative and pedagogically complete computer-supported writing projects involving students across distances" (SUNY Press, 1991, p. 116). In their recent book *Brave New Schools*, Jim Cummins and Dennis Sayers write that "*Orillas* remains-after more than a decade-the leading global learning network project working to explore and expand the theoretical and practical boundaries of multilingual, intercultural learning" (St. Martin's Press, 1995 p. 23).

How to Participate

Parents or teachers should contact *Orillas* if they are interested in participating in learning projects over global learning networks that:

1. Promote bilingualism and learning another language.
2. Validate traditional forms of knowledge, such as the oral traditions associated with folklore, folk games, proverbs, and learning from elders through oral history.
3. Advance anti-racist multicultural education.
4. Develop new approaches to teaching and learning that encourage students, parents, and communities to take action for social justice and environmental improvement.

This year, *Orillas* established a new relationship with I*EARN (the International Education and Resource Network), a non-profit organization with the goal of "youth empowerment to make a difference to the planet and its people." As a result of the *Orillas*-I*EARN collaboration, students and teachers in both networks now have extended opportunities to participate in partnerships and project work in Latin America and globally.

Orillas operates over various networks; thus, cost for participation ranges from no-cost to low and moderate cost, depending on the type of service provider available to a parent or teacher. For more information, or an annotated list of articles and research reports on Orillas, contact Kristin Brown, Enid Figueroa or Dennis Sayers.

Kristin Brown—<krbrown@iearn.org> 5594 Colestine Road, Hornbrook, CA 96044

Enid Figueroa—<efigueroa@igc.apc.org> Box 23304 University Station, San Juan, PR 00931

Dennis Sayers—<dmsayers@ucdavis.edu> 351 East Barstow Avenue, Fresno, CA 93710

---

*Kristin Brown is the co-founder and co-director of Project Orillas. Currently, she is ith International Program Director for I*EARN.*

Enid Figueroa is the co-founder and co-director of De Orilla a Orilla. She coordinates the project form the Department of Education at the Rio Piedras Campus of the University of Puerto Rico.

Invisibility: The Language Bias of Political Control and Power

Marta I. Cruz-Janzen

Marta I. Cruz-Janzen is presently at the University of Denver completing her dissertation toward a Ph.D. in Curriculum Leadership with a focus on equity and diversity. She is co-author of Educating Young Children in a Diverse Society *(Allyn and Bacon, 1994).*

Often people say, "We don't see color, we only see children." For quite some time I didn't understand what was so disturbing about this statement until one day when I asked a White woman in Atlanta for bus directions. Although I asked her repeatedly she acted as though I was invisible. I knew she heard and understood me, and I remember the bewildered look of both Blacks and Whites. An African-American woman finally pulled me aside, and told me that "Black folks don't ask White folks for help in public."

I felt naked, violated, stripped of all dignity as a member of humanity, vulnerable and helpless, wanting to run away in shame. I still vividly recall withdrawing deeply within myself for answers and protection. If you really want to hurt people, treat them as if they are invisible, and thus, excluded and rejected.

We have learned the power of invisibility, which clearly conveys the message that one is not worthy of membership within a group. We use invisibility when we punish children by banishing them to a "time-out area" or ignoring them for unacceptable behaviors. Fear of exclusion and rejection is strong within us all and leads to the adoption of behaviors deemed desirable for group acceptance and membership. Long-term invisibility has deep consequences for it violates the human integrity of those excluded.

If we don't see people of color, regardless of age, we are denying their rich and unique experiences. We are essentially denying their humanity and telling them that they do not exist. We are attempting to convince ourselves that we are not uncomfortable with their physical differences and that perhaps ignoring these differences will make them disappear.

This discomfort with racial diversity stems from internalized stereotypic images of "typical" Americans that have been sustained throughout our history and which ignore anyone not of White European ancestry. People of color cannot melt into America's mythical "melting pot" but we sometimes do attempt psychological assimilation.

Unfortunately, children of color often get the message that something is indeed wrong with their physical appearance. We, too, lead them to believe that ignoring their own unique differences will somehow make the differences all go away. The tragic outcome of this is that ultimately we betray children of color for they soon learn that their physical differences stay with them, that others around them do notice and are really uncomfortable with them. We betray they if we do not prepare them for the real world by instilling in them a sense that they too have a unique richness worth sharing.

Invisibility can be experienced in various ways besides blatant acts of discrimination and racism. People of color and women have been invisible from textbooks, curricula, decision making, positions of authority and respect, and economic and political power. As equity advocates, we discuss the six **"Forms of Bias in Curricular Materials and Classrooms"** (Grayson, 1990): Invisibility, Stereotyping, Imbalance/Selectivity, Unreality, Fragmentation/Isolation, and Linguistic.

As teachers and equity advocates, we rarely address "The Language Bias of Political Control and Power" inherent in our everyday vernacular. The opening statement above has less to do with the children's skin color than with their lower status as humans—their invisibility and worthlessness—and the politics of control and power that perpetuate their condition. Acknowledgement of people of color is tantamount to acknowledgement of their lesser status and the need for their inclusion as valued members of humanity. Doing so would represent a direct threat to the established dominant White structure.

Knowledge is power and those who control the knowledge also control the power. American education is very political and designed to maintain the status quo of White male power and White supremacy. It teaches what is valued and not valued in our

7. FOR VISION AND VOICE: A CALL TO CONSCIENCE

society. We need to understand how knowledge reflects the social, economic and political context of those in power along with their self-preservation interests. We also need to understand how this becomes reflected through our vernacular and knowledge gaps.

> *For female students and students of color it is not just what they are taught, but what they are not taught, that hurts them.*

For female students and students of color it is not just what they are taught but what they are not taught that hurts them. A school dropout once told me that "Education is for White people. It is about what White people have done and can do. It is about what we haven't done and can't do. It is about what Whites have done to us and for us. I am tired of hearing that we were slaves, field and laundry workers, or servants; that we had to sit on the back of the bus and drink from separate fountains. I am tired of seeing us as lazy, criminals and drunks."

Here are some examples of invisibility. Children learn:

1) Commander Perry, a White man, was the first person to reach the North Pole. They do not learn that Matthew Henson, an African-American man who was a skilled sleigh driver and Perry's ground breaker, reached Camp Jessup first.

2) Thomas Edison, a White man, invented the lightbulb, but they do not learn that Lewis Lattimer, an African-American man, invented the carbon filament that made the lightbulb possible.

3) Eli Whitney, a White man, invented the cotton gin, but they do not learn that the idea came from Catherine Littlefield Green, a Southern White woman who could not patent her invention and invited Whitney to help her develop and promote it.

4) Lewis and Clark explored the Northwest Territory, but they do not learn that Sacajewea, a 17-year-old Shoshoni woman with a newborn baby on her back, led Lewis and Clark across the Rockies to the Pacific and back.

5) Children learn about the human sacrifices of the "heathen" Aztecs in religious ceremonies, but they do not learn about the extermination of the Aztecs at the hands of Europeans in the name of Christianity. Nor do we teach them about the wasteful slaughter of buffaloes on the Western Plains as a systematic plan to starve and exterminate American Indians. We do not discuss the symbolic eating of the "Body of God" and the drinking of "His Blood" in some ancient religious ceremonies that prevail today.

Examples of such knowledge gaps are almost unlimited, representing not only invisibility, but also the relegation of women and people of color to positions of powerlessness and feelings of worthlessness. Invisibility is a clear statement of political control and power for it teaches that only White males have done anything worth mentioning and that all others are not as good. American education teaches people of color and women that they are sub-beings less deserving of human respect or consideration. That they are forced to learn schools' curricula about others and not themselves further reinforces their feelings of hopelessness and powerlessness to control their own lives and destinies.

Powerlessness creates feelings of vulnerability in a hostile and threatening environment. When individuals feel threatened they withdraw from the situation in search of a safe haven. It is an instinctual human survival mechanism. The safe haven could be physical, as when students drop out of school, but most often it is buried deep within students' subconscious, as when they withdraw emotionally and psychologically from the learning experience.

Female students and students of color internalize these messages of hopelessness and worthlessness. Gloria Ladson-Billings (1995) calls it "self-condemnation" and writes that "members of minority groups internalize the stereotypic images that certain elements of society have constructed in order to maintain their power" (p. 57).

America's language of control and power recognizes only five racial/ethnic categories: White, Black, American Indian, Hispanic and Asian. Of these, only Hispanic is considered an ethnic category because it purports to encompass persons of all racial groups. Yet, we are very cognizant of the fact that American society is comprised of more groups than those five, and that there is much diversity within each.

The census categories group all European Americans, with the exception of White Hispanics, together as Whites with everyone else in distinct and isolated subgroups. White Americans have excluded White Hispanics, who are also EuropeanAmericans, from American history and institutions because of a historical dislike for Spaniards. American history is written by the same English, German, Dutch and French people who were enemies of Spain for centuries (Cerio, 1991; Duncan, 1991).

The politics of race and racism have long been part of America's historical heritage. In light of this, it should be no surprise that White America extends its racist ideologies to its definitions of other groups. The term "Hispanic," from Hispania or Spain, was created by the U.S. government supposedly to identify speakers of the Spanish language or persons who, regardless of race, could trace their ancestry back to a Spanish-speaking country, and thus, to Spain. Yet, it does a lot more than that. For one, it claims to represent all Latinos including Brazilians and other Latin Americans who neither speak Spanish nor trace their ancestry to Spain. So why isn't the more accurate term "Latino" used?

Moreover, the term "Hispanic" creates a contradiction for Latinos of color, relegating them to invisibility through subliminal denial of the Black and Indian mestizos or mestizaje that also comprise one of the most salient characteristics of Latino culture and history.

The term "Hispanic" represents outright exclusion of White Hispanics from the White-European American culture and power structure. It is punishment for the "mestizaje" that took place over centuries of Moorish domination of Spain. It is a denial of the mestizaje that also took place over centuries of intermarriage in America.

Miscegenation has occurred between White EuropeanAmericans and American Indians, AfricanAmericans, and others since the beginning days of our nation, yet it is strongly denied and overlooked. One drop of "Black blood" has always meant being identified as 100% Black in America. The opposite axiom has never even been considered.

It is estimated that between 75 and 90 percent of all AfricanAmericans can claim White/European ancestry due to miscegenation (Hodgkinson, 1995; Steel, 1995). It is further estimated that one percent, or millions, of White Americans have some Black ancestry (Funderburg, 1994). Yet, the popular assumption has been that you are Black even if you have White blood but you cannot be White and have Black blood. Clearly the hidden message is that somehow the blood types of Whites and Blacks are different, with Black blood being inferior. This is related to White EuropeanAmericans' (Western Civilization) need to maintain their superiority, survival and growth through the maintenance of racial purity and prevention of racial mixture (Banks, 1995).

Most White Americans think of Americans as being White, relegating everyone else including American Indians, to invisibility and foreign status within their own country. "People come in all colors" is a popular American expression, yet it is most often used to define Latinos in reference to their mestizaje and implied lack of White racial purity. White Hispanics are not considered racially pure enough to be included as White Americans. "It is no accident and no mistake that immigrant populations... understood their 'Americanness' as an opposition to the resident Black population. Race, in fact, now functions as a metaphor so necessary to the construction of Americanness that it rivals the old pseudo-scientific and class-informed racisms whose dynamics we are more used to deciphering... Deep within the word 'American' is its association with race" (Morrison, 1992, p. 47). As a Black Latina I have often traveled outside this country and have been told that I "do not look American."

The power of the "majority" versus the "minority" or "minorities" is all encompassing. For one, it signifies that there is only one majority and many minorities in America. Even when combined, American minorities remain the minority. Our language of select control and power lets minorities know that they are small, isolated and therefore powerless. The thought of uniting all minorities within one inclusive category, such a "People of Color," is unthinkable and recent attempts to use this term have been met with criticism. Conceptually it represents a threat to the "Divide and Conquer" principles of White European-American dominance.

> *White Europeans continue coming to the U.S. as immigrants; yet Latino and immigrants of color are more often referred to as "aliens."*

We really do not need to search too far for examples. There are many persistent power-laden expressions in common usage that are unequivocally designed and allowed to stand which reinforce the invisibility and inferior status of women and people of color.

• The lack of a "Biracial/Multiracial" category in the U.S. census reflects the need of America's power elite to define Americans as White and perpetuate the isolated racial/ethnic categories that subjugate all others to inferior minority status. This exclusiveness denies persons of color entry into the power elite and further denies America's mestizaje for fear that significant numbers of Americans, including Whites, may claim biracial/multiracial ancestry.

• White Europeans continue coming to the U.S. as immigrants, yet Latino and immigrants of color are more often referred to as "aliens." We do not often hear of German, English or Dutch aliens. Alien not only means foreign and still lacking citizenship, it also means not belonging to the same government. Thus the word "alien" implies a threatening, unsympathetic outsider. We don't have to deal with the plight of fellow Puerto Ricans if we think of them as foreigners. The connotation is prevalent that Puerto Ricans, with

7. FOR VISION AND VOICE: A CALL TO CONSCIENCE

Spanish as a national language and a diverse culture, are foreigners to the U.S.

• Puerto Ricans did not come to America—America came to them with forced citizenship in 1917 and military service during World War I. Puerto Ricans asked for a plebiscite to determine how many wanted U.S. citizenship but the U.S. Congress ignored their request (U.S. Commission on Civil Rights, 1976).

• Puerto Ricans living in the continental U.S. are referred to as immigrants but they really are migrants. Puerto Ricans, as U.S. citizens, migrate within their own country without the need for passports or any other legal documents.

• We focus on Indian cultures of the Southwest to the exclusion of Native American Indians from other areas (Harvey, 1994). Clear in our minds remain the manufactured Hollywood images of the "drunken, ignorant and savage" Southwest Indians who were repeatedly defeated, decimated and forced from their lands by U.S. settlers and troops. We do not have to deal with the needs of today's Native American Indians if we make them invisible and turn them into sub-beings existing only in the past.

• We focus on the "romantic," friendly, and spiritual Indians still living in tepees, migrating after buffaloes, worshipping the land and spirits, attired in ceremonial clothes and feathers, while ignoring that they too have moved on to the 20th century. In reality, American Indians attend schools, live in urban areas off the reservation, hold jobs and are leaders today.

• We continue allowing the dehumanization of American Indians through sports team names such as "Braves," "Redskins," etc. We would not make reference to "White Skins," "Black Skins," etc.

• "Squaw" is one of the most debasing referents for American Indian females. Many books, state roads and counties still use the term officially. The equivalent of this word within other American cultures is much too inappropriate for use even in this essay; yet, it is considered acceptable for American Indian females.

• To "discover" something clearly means that no one else knew about it. To claim European discovery of America makes American Indians nonexistent.

• European Americans claim to have "colonized" the Americas. Although by definitional standards it was an invasion, and our curricula continue to ignore the American Indian perspective.

• It is erroneous to assume that all American Indians and Asian/Pacific Americans are the same. Each category represents many diverse groups with unique cultures, languages, religions, physical attributes, etc. Yet, the language makes those differences invisible and forces conformity within one of the categories defined by the dominant group.

• Continued reference to Asian/Pacific Americans as "Orientals" reflects the days when Europe ruled and considered itself the center of the world. Orient means to the east of Europe and includes many countries. Use of this term continues to set White Europeans apart and to insist on their control and superiority.

• We say that Asians have "slanted" eyes with the connotation that they are abnormal, mysterious and not fully trustworthy. We do not need to bother ourselves with the diversity of Asian/Pacific Americans if we define them as the same and assume that they all act, look, speak and think alike.

America's dominant White European culture defines everything from families and matrimony, education and success, to the concepts of time and ownership. It defines human classifications and relationships between people. These definitions are validated within their own cultural context with very little concern for whether they are harmonious with those of other cultural groups in our society. In essence, they become the standards of achievement and compliance by which everyone else will be measured—standards that often lead to the failure, dehumanization, and continued exclusion of women and people of color. American's dominant White European elite clearly conveys and exerts its power and control over the rest of society through language that excludes, rejects and relegates all others to an invisible and subhuman status.

References

Banks, J.A. (1995). The Historical Reconstruction of Knowledge About Race: Implications for Transforming Teaching. *Educational Researcher.* March 1995, pp. 15–25.

Cerio, G. (1991). The Black Legend: Were the Spaniards That Cruel? *Newsweek.* Special Issue, 1991.

Duncan, D. E. (1991). Spain: The Black Legend. *The Atlantic.* Vol. 268, No. 2, August 1, 1991.

Funderburg, L. (1994). *Black, White, Other.* NY: William Morrow and Co.

Grayson D. (1990). The Forms of Bias in Curricular Materials and the Classroom. Adapted from D. Sadker & M. Sadker, *Sex Equity Handbook for Schools.* (2nd Ed.) 1982. NY: Longman.

Harvey, K. D. (1994). Native Americans: The Next 500 Years. University of Denver.

Hodgkinson, H. (1995). What Should We Call People? *Phi Delta Kappan.* October 1995.

Knopp, S. L. (1995). Critical Thinking and Columbus: Secondary Social Studies. 3440 State Street Road, Eau Claire, WI 54701.

Ladson-Billings, G. (1995). Toward a Critical Race Theory of Education. *Teachers College Record.* Vol. 97, No. 1, Fall 1995.

Morrison, T. (1992). Playing in the Dark: Whiteness and the Literary Imagination. Cambridge, MA: Harvard University Press. In J. A. Banks, The Historical Reconstruction of Knowledge About Race: Implications for Transformative Teaching. *Educational Researcher.* March 1995.

Steel, M. (1995). New Colors. *Teaching Tolerance.* Spring 1995.

U.S. Commission on Civil Rights. (1976). *Puerto Ricans in the Continental United States: An Uncertain Future.* A report. October 1976.

Home Was A Horse Stall

Jim Carnes

Yumi Ishimaru was used to picking up and moving on. In 1905, at the age of 20, she left Yamaguchi, Japan, for San Francisco to marry a man she had only seen in a picture. After being detained with other "picture brides" for medical tests at Angel Island, Yumi reached the mainland, met Masajiro Kataoka, and found him shorter than she had expected.

Masajiro, also from Yamaguchi, operated a restaurant off Fillmore Street. After they were married, Yumi went to work as a housekeeper for an American family. Before long, she was expecting her first child. The Kataokas' prospects looked good.

But the great earthquake of April 1906 destroyed Masajiro's restaurant and left the young couple homeless. They lived for a while in a tent in Sacramento Park, then later in a succession of small apartments. Yumi gave birth to a daughter that summer.

Masajiro decided not to rebuild his restaurant. He was tired of city life, of the mobsters who pressured honest businessmen to pay for "protection." He and Yumi and their new baby left San Francisco, and Masajiro made a fresh start as a tenant farmer. He saw a bright future in strawberry farming and hoped one day to own some land.

In 1913, the state of California dashed Masajiro's hope of ever owning his own farm. A new law denied the right of land ownership to anyone who was not eligible to become a U.S. citizen. And, according to the federal Naturalization Law of 1790, only white immigrants were permitted to become naturalized citizens. Although the California alien land law didn't mention the Japanese or any other group by name, its intent was obvious. Ever since the Gold Rush of 1849, white workers in the Western states had seen Asians arrive in increasing numbers to find a place in the American economy. During hard times, competition for jobs brought racial tensions to the surface.

Only white immigrants were permitted to become naturalized citizens.

In 1906, the San Francisco school board segregated all Japanese, Chinese and Korean children into an "Oriental" school. When the Japanese government protested, Pres. Theodore Roosevelt offered a deal: He would reverse the school policy if Japan agreed to let only professionals of certain categories emigrate to the United States. The so-called Gentlemen's Agreement prevented an international confrontation, but bias against the Japanese in California increased. The 1913 alien land law was designed to make people like Yumi and Masajiro Kataoka permanent outsiders.

Farm life was hard work for the Kataokas. Yumi and Masajiro eventually had six children, and all of them had chores to do before and after school. Tsuyako, the youngest daughter, was born in 1918. She got her nickname, "Sox," from white friends who couldn't pronounce her real name. The nickname made her feel more American. Sox remembers that there was no Saturday or Sunday or Monday in the strawberry business, only Workday. And she remembers that no matter how difficult and tiring the labor, her mother was usually singing.

In 1932 Masajiro began renting farmland from a Mrs. Perkins, a strong-willed pioneer rancher whose family owned one of the largest rose nurseries in the world. Mrs. Perkins didn't make Masajiro sign a contract for the land. She even let him build his own house on it. She hired Sox's older sister, Nobuko, to work in her big ranch house. Nobuko got her nickname, "Nee," from the Perkins children, who were tall for their ages and considered her tiny. Nee cooked and cleaned and performed many more tasks than were expected of her, such as chopping firewood. In fact, she was such a vigorous worker that after she married and moved away, everyone else Mrs. Perkins hired seemed lazy by comparison.

Masajiro Kataoka died in late 1940. In keeping with Buddhist tradition, Yumi had his body cremated. Since he had always wanted to see Japan again, Yumi and Nee decided to take his ashes back for burial in Yamaguchi. They went in the late fall of 1941. At that time, World War II was raging in Europe, and many feared that conflict would soon erupt between the U.S. and Japan. Nee and her mother got back to California just before that fear came true.

On Sunday morning, December 7, 1941, Sox, her sister Lillian and their mother were riding in the car. A special bulletin on the radio announced that the Japanese had mounted a surprise air attack on the U.S. Naval base at Pearl Harbor, Hawaii. The girls translated the news for Yumi. "This is

7. FOR VISION AND VOICE: A CALL TO CONSCIENCE

terrible," Yumi said to them in Japanese. Because she was an Issei ("first generation" Japanese immigrant), she was not a U.S. citizen. Her native country was now the enemy.

Sox and Lillian knew that their lives were about to change. They were Americans, born on American soil. They listened to the same music, followed the same fashions, pledged allegiance to the same flag as everyone else. But now they wondered how other Americans would treat them. They wondered if the storekeepers would still sell them food. Over the next few weeks, shops in towns around the area began posting signs telling Japanese customers to stay away. Old hostilities found new expression in the name of patriotism. There were scattered incidents of violence against Japanese Americans and their property.

The Kataokas had a mailbox at the post office in Centerville. Every morning, Sox went in to pick up the mail. After the Pearl Harbor attack, the postmaster began holding the family's mail at the window instead of putting it in the box, so that Sox had to come and ask him for it. This way, he could ask her questions, such as "How do you feel about the bombing?" or "What do you think is going to happen to you people?" Sox hated this daily confrontation. She kept her answers short and left as quickly as possible.

The question about what was going to happen was partially answered on February 19, 1942. Pres. Franklin D. Roosevelt on that day issued Executive Order 9066, establishing "military areas" along the West Coast and limiting the activities of "any or all persons" within them. Two months later, Civilian Exclusion Order No. 27 narrowed the focus of the restrictions by announcing that "all persons of Japanese ancestry, both alien and non-alien," would be "excluded" from the West Coast. Even Nisei ("second generation"), or those born in America to Japanese parents, were now unwelcome. The order disrupted the lives of 112,000 people, two-thirds of them U.S. citizens.

Evacuation orders posted on telephone poles and public buildings declared that Japanese Americans had one week to prepare to leave their homes. In the meantime, they had to abide by an 8 p.m. curfew and get permits to travel.

The instructions didn't tell people where they would be going, but they did tell them what to bring: only the bare necessities, like clothing and linens and soap. When someone said they could take what they could carry in two hands, the Kataokas took this literally. They had never owned suitcases, so they got a permit to go to a nearby town and buy two each—flimsy cardboard ones, outrageously priced.

Deciding what to pack was easy; getting rid of the rest was not. Anything obviously Japanese could be interpreted as a sign of collaboration with the enemy. Yumi Kataoka burned her family's Japanese books and letters, advertising calendars from Japanese businesses, even her certificates from a Japanese bank. Many people burned family keepsakes such as photographs and antique kimonos.

As for their other possessions, the evacuees had two choices: either leave them to be stolen or sell them at the going rate. One of Yumi's sons sold two cars, a long-bed truck and a Caterpillar tractor for a fraction of their worth. The Kataokas got $15 for their piano, and Sox was so happy to see it going home with someone that she gave the buyer all her sheet music and even threw her tennis racket into the bargain. Some people in the valley refused to trade their brand new stoves or refrigerators for pocket change, so they stored them in the Japanese school building, in hopes of retrieving them when the war was over.

May 9, 1942, was leaving day. A few days beforehand, Mrs. Perkins got in touch with Nee and told her to bring her whole family to the ranch house for a farewell breakfast. The invitation meant a lot to the Kataokas because most of the other white people they knew had shunned them. That morning, Mrs. Perkins ushered them into her beautiful formal dining room. The long table was set with her best china and crystal and silver. She usually had someone to cook and serve meals for her, but this time she did everything herself. When Nee and Sox offered to help her bring the food out, she told them that now it was her turn to serve.

After breakfast, Mrs. Perkins drove the Kataokas in her Oldsmobile to the grounds of the Japanese school, where buses were waiting. The fellow who ran the local hamburger stand was the only other white person who came to say goodbye. It hurt Sox's feelings that her close friends didn't show up, but she decided the reason was that they were afraid.

Yumi Kataoka had moved her family many times, but never like this. The bus let them out at Tanforan Racetrack in San Bruno, Calif. No one knew what to expect. None of the Kataokas had even been to a racetrack before. Inside, military policemen searched each person. All suitcases were opened and ransacked. A nurse peered into every eye and down every throat.

On the infield of the track stood new, army-style barracks. Sox said that she wanted to stay in those, but the officer said they were for mothers with infants. He led the Kataokas around back to the stables: Their new home was a horse stall.

The building contained two back-to-back rows of 10 stalls each. Five adults—Sox and her three brothers and their mother—had a 9- by 20-foot enclosure to share. Manure littered the dirt floor. The walls had been recently whitewashed, but carelessly, so that horsehair and dirt were smeared in. And the walls reached only halfway to the roof—there were no ceilings. The nearest bathroom was a long walk away.

Sox worried about how her mother would take such humiliation. She was proud of Yumi for keeping the hurt hidden, for acting as if this were just another move. She knew that keeping the family together was Yumi's biggest concern.

The officers passed out cloth sacks for everyone to fill with hay for mattresses. In the dark stall that night, listening to the noises of all the other

38. Home Was a Horse Stall

people, Sox couldn't fall asleep. She couldn't stop wondering what any of them had done to deserve being penned up like animals. She couldn't believe this was happening in America.

It didn't take Sox long to learn the local routine, including how early she had to get up to find an empty tub in the laundry shed. Her brothers washed dishes in the mess hall. There were long lines everywhere—for the toilets, for the laundry, for food. As clothing wore out, people shopped by mail from the Sears Roebuck catalog.

Occasionally, Mrs. Perkins came to visit. When she saw the damp dirt floor of the drafty stall, she went home and ripped up the linoleum from the Kataokas' kitchen and brought it to them. She didn't want Yumi's rheumatism to get worse. Another time, she took Sox's broken wristwatch to have it repaired.

For four long months, daydreams and small acts of kindness made their internment bearable. Every night, Sox wondered what the next day would bring. There was very little official news about the government's plans, so rumors were the main source of information. Late in the summer a rumor went around that the Japanese were going to be moved inland, to a concentration camp in the desert. Everyone started ordering high-top boots from the catalog—there were scorpions and snakes out there. According to some people, once they got to the new location, the government was going to drop a bomb on them.

Some of the rumors turned out to be true. At the end of the summer, Sox, Yumi and the other Japanese were packed into buses and driven east into the desert. Sox had never seen a place as dry and dusty and lifeless as Topaz, Utah. It looked like the surface of the moon. But when she saw the rows and rows of new barracks, some of them still unfinished, she could have kissed the ground. She reasoned that if the government was spending the time and money to build housing for her people, then it must not be planning to kill them.

The Kataokas' new quarters measured 20 by 24 feet—a little roomier than the horse stall and a lot cleaner. A single naked light bulb hung from the ceiling. In the corner stood a pot-bellied stove. By stringing up a few sheets, family members could carve out the illusion of privacy. The communal bathroom had six toilets and no doors.

There were no chairs or tables. People scoured the construction site for materials. In just a short time, many families skillfully fashioned whole sets of furniture from orange crates and scrap lumber. Later, some residents laid out beautiful rock gardens on the barren ground.

Even in this strange new environment, much about camp life was familiar—the crowded living space, the boredom, the long lines for every necessity. But Sox began to notice changes in the people around her. In the dining hall, children made friends quickly and sat together in groups. The family meal—a central part of Japanese life—was losing its importance. A deeper toll resulted from unemployment: Fathers, no longer breadwinners, began to lose their self-respect and, sometimes, the respect of their families. Everyone was aimless now. Everyone was a small step from stir-crazy.

Camp residents had to pull together to avert despair. They formed social clubs and choirs and sports teams. They started newsletters to share information and ideas.

Sox had the good fortune to get a job as assistant block manager. She was responsible for looking after about 200 people in 72 rooms. The managers met every morning to discuss the needs of their residents. Extremes of climate caused many problems, since temperatures often reached well below zero in the winter and over 100 in the summer months. Food was another source of complaint. The animal innards such as liver, gizzard, tongue, brains and chitterlings that made up much of the meat ration were foreign to the Japanese diet. Sox found them sickening. When the quality of meat improved after a while, Sox decided

DOCUMENT

CONFIDENTIAL

After some Japanese Americans attempted to challenge the internment policy in the courts, the War Relocation Authority included the following statements in a confidential internal memo on August 12, 1942.

The action taken with respect to Japanese in this country is justifiable on the grounds of military necessity for several reasons.

1. All Japanese look very much alike to a white person — it is hard for us to distinguish between them. It would be hard to tell a Japanese soldier in disguise from a resident Japanese. The danger of infiltration by Japanese parachutists, soldiers, etc. is, therefore, reduced and the chances of detecting any attempt at infiltration are increased.

2. The Japanese Government has always tried to maintain close ties with and control over Japanese people in this country with the result that many of them have never really been absorbed into American life and culture. Many Japanese-Americans have been educated in Japan. Many, believers in Shintoism, worship the Emperor and regard his orders as superior to any loyalty they may owe the United States. Therefore, the action has reduced the danger of successful invasion by removing an element of the population which had never been assimilated and which might not successfully withstand the strong emotional impulse to change loyalties or give way to their true feelings in the event that Japanese troops should land on our shores.

7. FOR VISION AND VOICE: A CALL TO CONSCIENCE

DOCUMENT

"A GRAVE INJUSTICE"

On August 10, 1988, Congress enacted a law granting restitution payments for civilians interned during World War II.

SECTION. 2. Statement of the Congress

(a) With Regard to Individuals of Japanese Ancestry. — The Congress recognizes that, as described by the Commission on Wartime Relocation and Internment of Civilians, a grave injustice was done to both citizens and permanent resident aliens of Japanese ancestry by the evacuation, relocation, and internment of civilians during World War II. As the Commission documents, these actions were carried out without adequate security reasons and without any acts of espionage or sabotage documented by the Commission, and were motivated largely by racial prejudice, wartime hysteria, and a failure of political leadership. The excluded individuals of Japanese ancestry suffered enormous damages, both material and intangible, and there were incalculable losses in education and job training, all of which resulted in significant human suffering for which appropriate compensation has not been made. For these fundamental violations of the basic civil liberties and constitutional rights of these individuals of Japanese ancestry, the Congress apologizes on behalf of the Nation.

that the project director must have figured out that her people were human.

The block manager meetings gave Sox and the others some sense of value. But everywhere they looked, barbed wire and police patrols and curfews and watchtowers with armed guards constantly reminded them of their status.

"Americanism is not, and never was, a matter of race or ancestry."

The word around camp was "Don't go near the fence." Most of the military policemen were fresh out of combat duty, and they did not hesitate to use their weapons. At Topaz one day, a man was picking some wildflowers along the barbed wire. A guard yelled "Halt!" but the man was hard of hearing. He kept on picking and was shot. And once, a grandfather playing catch with his grandson went to retrieve the ball from just beyond the fence. The guard who killed him told authorities that the old man had tried to escape.

As the war in Europe and the Pacific intensified, the government realized that many potentially able soldiers were sitting idle in the camps. In early 1943 Pres. Roosevelt wrote to the Secretary of War and contradicted his earlier Executive Order: "Americanism is not, and never was, a matter of race or ancestry. Every loyal American citizen should be given the opportunity to serve this country . . . in the ranks of our armed forces."

By means of a "loyalty questionnaire," Uncle Sam began recruiting Nisei. In all, more than 30,000 Japanese Americans joined the service during the war. Others protested that they wouldn't serve until their families were allowed to return to the West Coast. About 300 so-called "no-no boys" refused to pledge their loyalty and were jailed for draft resistance. The questionnaire was also used as a means of releasing internees into the work force. In the camps, this process—however objectionable—stirred the first hopes of freedom.

On November 11, 1944, Pres. Roosevelt lifted the Civilian Exclusion Order. A month later, the government announced that the internment camps would be closed within a year.

Sox married a young man named Tom Kitashima in August 1945, just as the bombing of Hiroshima and Nagasaki brought the war to its conclusion. The camp supervisor offered her a job helping to process the closure of the camp. But since he didn't have a job for Tom, Sox said she couldn't stay. Even so, the supervisor found her a good position in San Francisco.

A few nights before Sox and Tom were set to leave Topaz, the supervisor and his wife invited them out for dinner and a cowboy movie in the town of Delta, 16 miles from the camp. There were rules against this kind of socializing, but the white couple didn't seem to care. The supervisor also gave them a blanket for the cold train ride to San Francisco—the government was using old dilapidated railroad cars to relocate the internees. On an October morning in 1945, Sox repacked the suitcase she had been living out of for three years and four months.

Yumi Kataoka, now 60 years old, prepared to move one more time. People were heading in all directions—there was nothing left to go back to. Yumi joined a large group headed for a housing center at Richmond, Calif. In time, Yumi and her scattered children heard reports from the valley that used to be their home. The Japanese school building had been emptied of all the stored appliances. The house that Masajiro had built on Mrs. Perkins' place was gone now, along with all the little things the family had left behind.

Turning the Tide:

A Call for Radical Voices of Affirmation

Bakari Chavanu

Bakari Chavanu is a teacher at Florin High School in Sacramento, California.

Reading essays by the Black feminist thinker, writer, and teacher, bell hooks, in which she speaks of the "awareness of the need to speak, to give voice to the varied dimensions of our lives..." (1989. p. 13) reminds me of my younger days in high school when I fortunately became aware of a distinctive existence of the Black voice in literature and consequently in my own life.

Bused, but not necessarily integrated, into a traditional white high school during the mid 1970s, I reflect now—as I didn't realize then—how this forced integrated school was unprepared for a different culture of students who came loaded with our own distinctive experiences and ignorance to the purpose of attending a predominantly white institution. But as far as I could tell, the first year of integration was not met with physically violent resistance on the part of White students or their parents. I even doubt that myself or the other Black students attending the school at the time were aware of Little Rock or what blood had been shed for us to attend. We were simply indifferent to attending because we could not go to one of the predominantly Black schools on the northeast side.

As I look back on it, high school was a kind of senseless four years of my life. The image of fellow students sleeping at their desks during class constantly comes to mind. So many of my Black peers in my graduating class made conscious and unconscious decisions to not take school seriously. We participated in forms of reckless indifference—skipping classes, refusing to do course assignments or homework, talking back to instructors, and laughing off three-day suspensions which to us meant a vacation. We came to school with little or no missions to fulfill.

I don't wish to make blanket generalization about every Black student at this forcibly integrated school. Some Black students, depending largely on their family background or where they grew up, actually made good grades and wound up, like myself, attending college (albeit through much trial and error and certainly not by design). One year, the school even elected a Black male as student body president; however, many of us didn't make much of it because we knew his light skin and growing up in the white community surrounding the school gained him quite a few votes.

There were also a handfull of Black teachers and a Black vice-principle. We brought with us our amateur Michael Jacksons, Stevie Wonders, Roberta Flacks, all-pro ball players, and theatrical jazz dancers. But when I say the physical resistance to our presence at John Marshall was not met with violent resistance, I don't mean such was true in the curriculum of the classroom.

As a literature and writing teacher today, I am keenly aware of the cultural silence that exists in most classrooms. When I look back on my high school years, I am painfully aware of how important voice is to culture. Fundamentally, little has changed since I sat behind a classroom desk over ten years ago. The literature curriculum back then rarely spoke powerfully or meaningfully to any students, especially us Black students. Many of us just didn't know that we existed in books which again served to remove us from any sense of purpose in attending an integrated school. In fact, as with the vast majority of Black and other minority students today, the literature and school curriculum was downright insulting and harmful in ways many teachers and society will never understand.

But it was in my junior year that I stumbled across the voice of a writer who helped change forever my sense of Blackness and how much larger life was than the bus ride to John Marshall. It was probably on a Sunday afternoon listening to the Black radio station that I heard an album recording of Nikki Giovanni reading one of her poems set to jazz music—no better way to capture the mind of a teenager.

For the first time, I really heard poetry and felt the presence of a Black voice which was not singing, even though Black singing voices were also important to me. (Even today, Black music remains unconsidered as an important form of communication worth studying.) I grasped hold of Giovanni's words as something valuable, new, bold, and culturally me. The next day I went out and purchased her album. Later, reading a book of her poems and her "extended autobiographical statement on my first 20 years of being a Black poet," titled *Gemini* (1971), lead me to other Black literary voices and, above all to an appreciation of reading.

Unfortunately, my experience is something not easily brought to students. Teachers who care about wanting their students to love reading and writing relish moments when a student takes hold of a book without being motivated by grades or the promise of a diploma. I value deeply the importance of my students discovering the power the written word and the power of their own individual and cultural voices. As bell hooks points out, however, so much in the American hegemony serves to silence voices of women, the working class, and non-European people. "Silence," she understands and clarifies, "is the condition of one who has been dominated, made an object; talk is the mark of freeing, of making one subject" (1979).

Black students who are met with literary core works like *Huckleberry Finn*, *To Kill a Mockingbird*, or even *Of Mice and Men* don't hear powerful Black voices. They hear passive, stuttering voices dominated by a white power structure. It is no wonder that so many Black students are captivated by Malcolm X. For them, he is subject, speaking his mind—boldly, intelligently, and with conviction. Rarely, if ever,

7. FOR VISION AND VOICE: A CALL TO CONSCIENCE

do students hear radical voices in the classroom—voices that speak to the joys, frustrations, and aspirations of the Black community.

Today, with the conservative control of education, students hear what I call politically passive voices in and outside the classroom. Teachers and the curriculum they are compelled to teach are either silent in their ignorance of the cultures in their classroom, or they are too passive or reluctant, for fear of reprisal, to share voices that may not belong to the dominate mainstream America—the white elite.

Today, for sure, a well developed and complex tradition of literature by people of African, Native American, and Asian descent is grounded and growing so much so that you have to step over it to avoid it. These post-colonial voices must be heard by all students if we are going to challenge them to see American society and the world as it really is. Far too many institutions—including education—exist to confuse and make students complacent about the issues and systems of the domination historically maintaining hundreds of years of race, class, and gender oppression.

I witnessed with dismay, for instance, how easily my students, taking their perspectives from the media, espoused the propaganda that the "riot" in Los Angeles was nothing more than hoodlums gone out of control. Only when I read to them a quote by Malcolm X (1991, p 29) about the motivations and tactics behind urban rebellions did they stop to rethink the message they received from the television.

The work of Malcolm X, Giovanni, and other Black writers and cultural workers I now realize were for me when I was growing up voices that constructively challenged the status quo and how the world, especially the Black world, is traditionally viewed. Theirs was and continues to be a voice of affirmation. As June Jordan has pointed out, "affirmation of Black values and lifestyle within the American context is, indeed, an act of protest" (1974).

How can students witness or hear about the racism and other forms of injustices they see acted out and are so often impacted by and not feel a sense of rage, indifference, or an innate feeling of protest? If and when they are silent about what they see around them, it is only because they are never led to constructively confront, dialogue, study, and reflect on the various forms of resistance struggles to dismantle oppressive infrastructures of racism, poverty, sexism—road blocks in so many people's lives. What they confront day after day are silent voices—passive, indifferent, and many times hostile.

In her essay on "coming to voice," hooks concludes by saying:

> To understand that finding a voice is an essential part of liberation struggle—for the oppressed, the exploited a necessary starting place—a move in the direction of freedom, is important for those who stand in solidarity with us. That talk which identifies us as uncommitted, as lacking critical consciousness, which signifies a condition of oppression and exploitation is utterly transformed as we engage in critical reflection and as we act to resist domination. (1979, p 17)

More teachers must become role models who "engage in critical reflection," even when it means often teaching against the grain. During the last presidential election, I was asked by my students the inevitable question of who I would vote for. I had avoided the question more than a few times when it was previously asked, until I thought I had the time to explain my response. I told them I didn't plan on voting. Many of them appeared shocked. How could I be a role model, one of them retorted, if I, myself, did not vote? I emphatically said that voting was not the only way to voice your opinion; that in fact not voting made a statement.

What they were getting from me was an oppositional view that for some of them was new and to others demonstrated outright contempt for the "democratic" process in America. But I understood before answering the question that the dominate ideology under which they were being taught did not put an emphasis on the radical tradition that had brought about various reforms in this country (very few fundamental changes in this country have been initiated in the voting booth). Nor had they been made aware of alternative political parties and their agendas. Again they were simply co-opted by the mainstream elite. I informed them that I was not advocating that voting is a waste of time, but that they should be as knowledgeable as they can of the various ways change comes about, and thus not to automatically, at such a young age, resign themselves to just one option.

As the struggle increases to expose, clarify, and dismantle forms of domination in this country and throughout the world, I think students growing up in oppressive/exploitive cultures will increasingly feel alienated and indifferent toward public education. They will, as many of my minority students have done in my classroom, speak out and make interrogations about the absence or silence concerning the cultural experiences that have shaped their lives and the people of their communities. Lecturing them about meeting the challenges of the "real world" in which they must learn to fit into rather than change will motivate only a minority of Black students—and perhaps that is by design in a system that has maintained itself on the back of fundamental inequalities.

I believe students really want to learn. But they must be heard. They must be exposed to various voices, especially literary and critically conscious voices speaking to the world they see falling apart around them. Frederick Douglas must be read along side Mark Twain. The voices of the civil rights, Black power, and African liberation movements must be understood and made just as important as the American revolution, the death of John F Kennedy, and the concept of America as the leader of the free world. Contemporary Black feminist or womanist writers—indeed female writers and cultural workers in general—must be equally a part of a core curriculum as the works of Jane Austin. Radical voices worldwide must play a part in making education truly multicultural and meaningful for all students.

References

Giovanni, Nikki. 1971. *Gemini*. Indianapolis, IN: Bobbs-Merrill Co.

hooks, bell. 1989. *Talking back: thinking feminist / thinking black*. Boston, MA: South End Press

Jordan, June. March, 1974. On Richard Wright or Zora Neale Hurston: Notes toward a balancing of love and hatred. *Black World*. p. 5.

X, Malcolm. 1991. *Malcolm X talks to young people*. New York: Path Finder Press.

KNOCKING ON HEAVEN'S DOOR

Surrounded by death and dying, the children of the South Bronx speak with painful clarity about the poverty that has wounded but not hardened them.

Jonathan Kozol

Jonathan Kozol is the author of many books, including Savage Inequalities *and* Rachel and Her Children. *His first book,* Death at an Early Age, *won the National Book Award.*

Over the course of a year, beginning in the summer of 1993, Jonathan Kozol made regular visits to a neighborhood in the South Bronx known as Mott Haven, one of the nation's poorest. Two-thirds of the local residents are Hispanic, one-third black. Thirty-five percent are children. Drug abuse, AIDS, murder, life-consuming fire are part of every day life. In this new book, Amazing Grace: The Lives of Children and the Conscience of a Nation, *Kozol, with sparing eloquence, lets the people themselves—the children, parents, teachers, and pastors—tell their own stories. Here, in an excerpt, he visits a local elementary school, P.S. 65, where only seven of 800 children do not qualify for free lunches. "Five of those seven," the principal tells Kozol, "get reduced-price lunches because they are classified as only 'poor,' not destitute."*

"What are these holes in our window?" asks a 4th grade teacher at P.S. 65 in a rapid drill that, I imagine, few of those who read this will recall from their own days in school.

"Bullet shots!" the children chant in unison.

"How do police patrol our neighborhood?" the teacher asks.

"By helicopter!" say the children.

"What do we do when we hear shooting?"

"Lie down on the floor!"

In the lunchroom, I talk with a serious-looking boy in the 6th grade, named Damian, who tells me he does not live with his parents. I ask him who takes care of him.

"My grandma," he replies.

"Where does your mother live?"

"She lives in Harlem."

"Why don't you live with her?"

"She gave me to my father."

"Why don't you live with your father then?"

"My father is in prison."

A teacher has told me that Damian is considered the top student in his class. I ask him if he knows what he would like to do when he grows up.

"X-ray technician," he replies without conviction.

After lunch, I ask the children in his 6th grade class to tell me what they hate or fear the most in life.

Several children answer, "Dying." One boy says, "The rats that have red eyes." A small girl with curly hair and large round plastic glasses says she is most afraid "of growing up," but when I ask her why, she says, "I don't know why." The only white boy in the class and in the school, an immigrant from Russia, says, "What I hate most is the unfairness on this earth."

I ask the children to tell me something they consider beautiful.

Virtually every child answers, "Heaven."

"What," I ask, "is heaven like?"

"A peaceful place with only the innocent," one child says.

"Where is heaven?"

Rolling her eyes and pointing above her at the ceiling, a child with a ponytail, named Anabelle, replies, "Upstairs."

"How far upstairs?"

"Oh, very far!" she answers.

"Where is the other place?"

"Downstairs," she replies, pointing with her finger at the floor.

I ask again, "How far downstairs?"

"All the way down!" she says, like someone giving orders to an elevator operator.

Before I leave the class, I ask the children if they'd speak of something wonderful or beautiful, not in the after-

7. FOR VISION AND VOICE: A CALL TO CONSCIENCE

life but here on earth. Several girls say, "Flowers." One of them says, "My mother," and another says, "My baby brother." One child says, "Myself." Anabelle, one of the smallest children in the 6th grade, answers, "My pet mouse." The boy from Russia answers, "Life itself. Being alive is wonderful."

The affirmation heard in certain of these voices, and the merriment in others, are, however, anything but universal in this school, which serves 800 of the poorest children in the South Bronx—many of whom are also known to be lead-poisoned—and which ranks 627th out of 628 New York City elementary schools in reading scores.

"So many of our children," says one teacher, "walk with their fists clenched and with scowls on their faces. I see a boy come in. I say, 'Good morning,' but he walks right by. I think, 'What can we teach this boy today?'

"One boy named Alexander looks down at the floor and mutters when his father's name is mentioned. He seems ashamed of him. There's so much bitterness within his eyes."

At the same time, the teacher says, despite this bitterness or shame, many of the children also seem to love their fathers. "There was gunfire last week during recess. When it stopped, we saw the man who had been shot. He was facedown across the street, covered with blood. Several of the children said, 'Oh God! It's my daddy! Is it my daddy?' It wasn't anybody's father that I know of, but you can see from this why children you've been meeting speak so frequently of heaven."

The notion of "trauma" as an individual event, he and other teachers say, does not really get at what they feel is taking place because these things are happening so often. "'Traumatization' as an ordinary state of mind is closer to the fact of things for some, though not for all, the children," says another teacher. "They lead the life most people only read about. A little one speaks to me, and I have tears in my eyes."

I ask if she makes referrals to a clinic or a hospital in cases where a child's state of mind particularly alarms her. She sighs and says, "We do. But every place is overbooked. You make the referral. Then you wait for months....

"A 13-year-old boy," she says, "came in one day during the winter in a despondent state of mind. I've never come across a child more depressed. He sat here and he said, 'I want to die.' We reached his mother. She took him to Lincoln hospital. They did a brief assessment, then turned him right around."

I ask, "What does that mean?"

"It means that they did nothing for him," says the principal, who is sitting with us in the teacher's room.

"A week later," says the school psychologist, "the mother took him back. This time, he got a blood test, whatever that was for, and was released again. They told the mother she would hear. But she heard nothing.

"Eight weeks after we referred him, he had still received no medication and no treatment. I told the hospital, 'This boy has suicidal ideation. He's in crisis.' But this is the way it is. They say, 'We'll see him in four weeks or so.' Then—nothing."

I mention Damian, the boy who said he wanted to be an X-ray technician when he grows up, although he had said it with a shrug. I tell the psychologist that I had wondered why, if he's one of the best students, he would not have had in mind at least the possibility that he'd become a doctor.

"Many of the ambitions of the children," she replies, "are locked in at a level that suburban kids would scorn. It's as if the very possibilities of life have been scaled back. Boys who are doing well in school will tell me, 'I would like to be a sanitation man.' I have to guard my words and not say anything to indicate my sense of disappointment. In this neighborhood, a sanitation job is something to be longed for."

At 2 p.m., a terrific, rhythmic sound of clapping fills the gym of P.S. 65, as 18 girls in 4th, 5th, and 6th grade go through a cheerleading routine. A few of the girls are fairly tall and look grown-up. Others, like Anabelle, who spoke of her pet mouse during the class discussion, still look like little kids. Small and skinny, full of pep, her big white T-shirt hanging down over her jeans, she snaps her fingers, stamps her feet, swings her ponytail back and forth, then claps her hands with a live-wire frenzy and a big, bright smile in her eyes. "If all this energy could be stored up somehow," a teacher says, "and used in just exactly the right way, I bet these little girls could lick the world."

The same energy is still there later in the schoolyard as the girls do double Dutch and other jump-rope games.

Grandma, grandma
Sick in bed
Called the doctor
And the doctor said:
Get the rhythm in the hands!
Get the rhythm in the head!

A number of teachers and some parent volunteers are standing by the side to supervise the children as they swing the ropes and chant the rhymes, some of them passed down for six or seven generations from grandmothers to their children and grandchildren.

Shake it to the east!
Shake it to the west!
Shake it to the one
that you love best!

The rhymes, combining mischief, challenge, and flirtation, fill the pleasant air of afternoon with innocence and fun.

I can do the hoochie coochie
I can do the split
Bet you five dollars
You can't do this!

Ten or 12 boys in the schoolyard, attracted by my tape recorder, seem overly eager to tell me of some recent murders they have seen.

"A man over there in front of the church shot another man," a 9-year-old announces. "The man he shot was a teenager. I guess he knew him, so he shot him."

"How many times did he shoot him?"

"Seven times," he answers.

40. Knocking on Heaven's Door

"How close were you when this happened?"

"He did it to him right in front of my face," the boy replies.

"My friend's mother was killed," reports another boy. "She uses cocaine. She overdosed and died. It happened in his house."

"Where is his house?"

"On St. Ann's Avenue," he says.

"His father died of a shot in the heart," he adds.

"Where did his father die?"

"On Cypress Avenue."

There isn't much emotion in their voices. They speak of these events the way that people speak of things they've seen on television. I ask the boys to lift their hands if any of them have asthma. Three of their hands go up.

"Do you have someone in your family who has asthma?"

Half the hands go up.

"What do they do," I ask, "when they can't breathe?"

"Go to the hospital, get some shots," one boy replies.

A small boy eyes me mysteriously and says in a half-whisper, "I got three quarters in my pocket." He squeezes his hand into his pocket and brings out the coins to show me. His mother, he says, gives him a quarter every morning. "When I get another quarter, I will have a dollar."

"What are you going to do with the dollar?"

"I'm going to buy a hot dog."

A blaring voice from a police car, which is moving slowly past the school, temporarily drowns out the voices of the children. "We are trying to locate a 4-month-old infant who is missing from her home," the magnified voice from the patrol car says. "If you have any information on this child, please telephone the following number...." The patrol car moves on toward a modern-looking homeless shelter, one of two shelters in the blocks behind the school.

As class lets out at 3 p.m., the sidewalk in front of P.S. 65 is filled with mothers and grandmothers waiting to escort their children and grandchildren to their homes. Some of the older children slip loose from the other kids and enter a bodega on the corner of the street. A toddler with a canvas backpack that looks almost as big as he is says goodbye to another toddler, hugs her awkwardly, then reaches up to take his grandmother's hand.

As long as I have visited in inner-city schools like P.S. 65, I have always found the sight of children coming out at 3 o'clock, their mothers and grandmothers waiting to collect them, tremendously exciting and upsetting at the same time. The sheer numbers of the children, the determination of the older women to protect them, and the knowledge that they cannot really be protected in the face of all the dangers that surround them fill a visitor with foreboding. You wish that while they were in class, someone with magic powers had appeared and waved a wand and turned the world outside the building into fields of flowers.

Sympathy for these children, though movingly expressed in some news stories, is not of the magnitude one would expect within a richly cultivated city. One of the most popular radio talk-show hosts in New York City, who refers to African blacks as "savages" and advocates eugenics in America, recently wondered aloud, during a monologue about black people, "how they multiply like that," then answered, "It's like maggots on a hot day. You look one minute and there are so many there.... You look again and wow! they've tripled." These are not unusual statements these days on the radio in New York City. It often seems as if the hatred for black women in particular is so intense

---

I ask the children to tell me what they hate or fear the most in life. Several children answer, 'Dying.' One boy says, 'The rats that have red eyes.' A small girl says she is most afraid of 'growing up,' but when I ask her why, she says, 'I don't know why.'

---

that there is no longer any sense of prohibition about venting the same hatred on their children.

"I didn't breed them. I don't want to feed them," says a woman cited in the *The New York Times*. The woman, who lives in Arizona, is speaking of Mexican children who enter border towns illegally; but the sentiment is not unlike the one you hear repeatedly in New York City from a number of the talk-show hosts whose scorn for children of black and Hispanic people, frequently conveyed with searing humor, seems to stir the deepest, most responsive chords among white listeners.

The sparklingly happy little girl, named Anabelle, who had explained to me where heaven is ("upstairs"), sees me opposite the school and walks right up and tells me, "Hi! Do you remember me?"

I ask her where she lives, and when she says, "Two blocks away," I ask if I can walk her home, so we can talk a little more. As we walk, I ask her to tell me more about her images of heaven. "Tell me everything. Who gets to go there? What's it like? What happens to the ones who don't get in?"

She seems more than willing to comply.

"People who are good go up to heaven," she begins in a singsong voice, as if this part is obvious. "People who are bad go down to where the Devil lives. They have to wear red suits, which look like red pajamas. People who go to heaven wear a nightgown, white, because they're angels. All little children who die when they are young will go to heaven. Dogs and kittens go to animal heaven. But, if you loved an animal who died, you can go and visit with each other on the weekend. In heaven you don't pay for things with money. You pay for things you need with smiles."

I ask her, "Can a pet mouse go to heaven too?"

7. FOR VISION AND VOICE: A CALL TO CONSCIENCE

"I don't know about a mouse," she answers. "He's quite small."

She tells me that she also has a dog and cat and parakeet. "If I had my own house, I would have nine animals. Cats in one room. Dogs in another. I would have a room for every animal, and I'd put pillows for them on the floor. My mother will not let me do it."

I tell her I'm not surprised by that.

"If I had my own house I would do it."

I ask the names and ages of her animals. When she gets to her parakeet, she says, "He's 59."

"How old are you?"

"I'm only 11," she replies.

She adds that she had another bird before she got the parakeet but that he died the year before. "When he died," she says, cupping her hands and looking into them, "he died in my hands." She smiles, however, as she says this, and does not look sad.

I ask if she says prayers at night.

"I do."

"Who do you pray for?"

"I pray for my dog and cat."

"What do you pray?"

"I pray for them to stay right next to me all night and wake me up if I have a bad dream."

"Do you have many bad dreams?"

"Many!" she replies.

"How do you know when you are in heaven?" I ask her, finally.

"You'll see an archway made of gold," she answers.

I meet Anabelle again a few days later. She has two quarters in her hand to buy a pineapple *coquito*. I go to the corner with her, and I get a pineapple *coquito* too. It's a beautiful day. She stands with me eating her icie and chatters about nothing of importance for a while.

Being treated as a friend this way by children always feels like a great privilege. It seems like something you just wouldn't have the right to hope for. Why should this child trust a stranger who can come into her world at will and leave it any time he likes? Why should she be so generous and open? In the drabness of the neighborhood, her friendliness seems like the sunshine that has not been seen in New York City during many months of snow and storm and meanness.

Anabelle's images of heaven give me a delightful feeling that I rarely have in New York City. I speak of these kinds of things as often as I can, and of the feelings children voice for animals they love, because I think they show us something very different from the customary picture we are given of a generation of young thugs and future whores. There is a golden moment here that our society has chosen not to seize. We have not nourished this part of the hearts of children, not in New York, not really anywhere.

Anabelle is, by any odds, one of the most joyful children I have ever met. There is seldom any hint of sorrow in her voice. Only once, when she told me of children at her school whose mothers or fathers or older sisters had died recently of AIDS, did she become quite solemn. I asked her how the children who are orphaned seem to handle what they have gone through.

"They cry. They suffer. People die. They pray," she answered softly.

A block from P.S. 65, I run into Cliffie, the little boy who was concerned about the "burning bodies" in the medical waste incinerator built on Locust Avenue. He's sitting on a high brick wall as I come up the street.

As I approach, he shows no particular surprise at seeing me again after eight months but asks me, "Do you see that wall back there, behind this yard?"

I say I do.

"This man I saw, he buried another man back there. The man he buried was alive."

"Is that true?"

'Many of the ambitions of the children,' one psychologist explains, 'are locked in at a level that suburban kids would scorn. Boys who are doing well in school will tell me, "I would like to be a sanitation man." I have to guard my words. In this neighborhood, a sanitation job is something to be longed for.'

"The man was alive! And then, when I went back in there, I saw a dead dog and I saw this little, little bottle with a purple top. The man was moving. I saw his fingers sticking out. There was a crucifix, and it was moving too."

I ask him, "Did you try to dig him out?"

"No!" he says. "It was too gross! I put more dirt on top of him so he would not get out. I asked him, 'Are you still alive?' But he said no."

He says this in a cheerful voice, adding, "People pee in there and bring their dogs to doodle on his grave."

"I think you're making this up," I say.

He doesn't contest my statement but slips down adeptly from the wall and reaches up and takes my hand and walks with me in the direction I was heading.

"Long ago," his mother tells me later, "one of the hospitals used to use that plot of land to bury people who had nobody to claim their bodies. There used to be markers on the graves, but they've been gone for years." She wonders if he may have heard this story and inflated it into his fable of the moving hand.

If it is true that children often make up fables to explain the things that trouble them or things they fear, then there is certainly sufficient reason for the many legends that

40. Knocking on Heaven's Door

some of the children have created in Mott Haven. Month after month, they witness shootings and police raids, hear of bodies found in trash chutes, other bodies found in elevator shafts, and always, and predictably, they see the consequences of life-taking fires.

The fires sometimes come so close together that the names and ages of the victims soon dissolve into a vague scenario of sadness that can seem uncomfortably abstract. "FIERY TOMB FOR TWO BRONX KIDS," reads a headline in the *Daily News*. "NO ESCAPE," reads a second headline. "TRAPPED TOT KILLED IN APARTMENT BLAZE," reads a headline one day later. "APARTMENT FIRE KILLS BRONX BOY," reads a headline on the next day. "BRONX APARTMENT BLAZE KILLS MOM AND SON," reads a fourth headline for another fire in Mott Haven.

The last of these fires, in which a mother and her child died together, took place in a building I have often passed in walking from the train to St. Ann's Church. The building is across an airshaft from another building where the child's uncle and grandmother lived. The grandmother and uncle, awakened by the fire, watched the flames consume the mother and the boy. The mother was last seen standing with the child in her third-floor window, screaming, "Mami! Mami! I can't get out!"

"The fire got bigger," says the uncle of the boy. Then "they became quiet," and then "we couldn't see them anymore." A photograph taken while the fire blazed shows a thin Hispanic man standing in the street outside the building, cradling a beagle puppy in his arms and looking upward with dark, shadowed eyes.

The boy who died, a 10-year-old, was, like his mother, believed to be somewhat retarded. A woman who works in a hardware store one block from where he lived tells me he used to come into her store to say hello. "He had a round face, like a Mexican boy," she says. "He'd pick up a key chain or some other little thing that didn't cost a lot, and he might ask me, 'Can I have it?' I would tell him, 'Take it!' His mother watched him like a hawk. She'd stand outside the door and wait 'til he came out.

"On the day before the fire, he came in and handed me a dollar bill. He asked me, 'Would you change it for five dollars?' I told him, 'I can't do that, Papi!' He looked up at me as if he was confused. 'Why can't you do it?' I explained, 'One dollar and five dollars aren't the same.' He gave me a look that made me laugh, as if he thought that I was fooling him. I asked him, 'Papi, what do you need five dollars for?' He said he wanted to buy a baseball at the store across the street.

"The store got crowded then. I couldn't talk. He gave me another look and went back out the door. Later, I learned that he went up the line of all the other stores and asked them all the same thing: Would they change one dollar for five dollars? That's when I knew that there was something wrong. Two days later, when I learned that he was dead, I wished that I had gone and bought the baseball for him. I wish that I could go and buy him 20 baseballs. A baseball's not a big thing for a boy who has so little."

"The boy who burned to death," a 3rd grade teacher at P.S. 65 recalls, "was sitting right there, right in that chair, the afternoon before he died."

I ask if it's true that the boy and his mother were retarded.

"No," she says. "That was the 138th Street fire. This is the boy who died on 140th Street. This boy was a little one. That boy there was older."

In order to keep these different children clear in my own mind, I finally had to make a map of the South Bronx and put it on the wall over my desk, placing a marker on each block in which a child died, using one symbol for death by fire, one for death by accident, and one for death by gunshot.

"This little boy was in a special class because he had a learning disability," the teacher says. "His regular teacher had to go to a meeting after lunch that afternoon, so I was asked to keep him here until the end of school.

"One of the things that makes me sad is that I didn't spend as much time with him as I would have liked. It was one of those hectic afternoons. I never had a chance to stop and just sit down with him and chat. The only thing that I recall is that this boy right here"—she gestures at a fat boy sitting near the door—"kept teasing him, and I finally had to interfere.

"One of the other boys, a sensitive child named Domingo, had befriended him. He made a date to visit him and play with him that afternoon. But Domingo had to stay late for some reason. By the time he got there to the house, he saw the child's body carried out."

"How old was this boy?" I ask.

"Eight years old," the teacher says.

"Was he the only victim?"

"No," she says. "His mother's in a coma at Jacobi Hospital. Another child, a 5-year-old, is dead. Two of the other children are in critical care." She then lifts one hand over her face and starts to cry.

Leaving the school, I walk three blocks to see the apartment building where this child died. A garbage bag is billowing from one of the upper windows, charred and open. It isn't apparent if the family has moved out. With the mother and two children in the hospital, however, that does not seem likely.

A few doors away, my attention is arrested by one of the most unusual memorials that I have seen in the South Bronx. In bright white paint against a soft beige background is a painting of a large and friendly looking dog, his tail erect, his ears alert for danger. Above, in yellow letters, I read "MOONDOG," which appears to be the nickname of the person who has died. "Gone is the face.... Silent is the voice.... In our hearts we'll remember," reads the epitaph.

As I am standing on the sidewalk copying these words, a plump Hispanic woman rises from the stoop nearby and comes up to my side.

"Is this where he died?" I ask.

"Yes," she answers. "He was shot right there, inside the door."

"Why was he killed?"

"He was protecting a woman who was pregnant."

"Did the woman live?"

"The woman lived. She's fine."

"Did the baby live?"

"The baby's doing fine."

"How old was the man who died?"

"He was almost 21," she replies.

I ask her how he got his nickname.

"He loved dogs. He used to bring them home." Her voice is jovial and pleasant.

7. FOR VISION AND VOICE: A CALL TO CONSCIENCE

"Did you know him well?"

"He was my son," she says.

Nearby, in the afternoon sun, dozens of children are playing in a playground flecked with broken glass. Puerto Rican music with a pounding salsa rhythm fills the air. In the distance is the jingling music from an ice cream truck, parked at the corner of Brook Avenue. Under a basketball hoop without a net, a number of teenage boys are warming up before a game.

At 5 p.m., I stand at the corner of East 139th Street and St. Ann's Avenue. Tall iron bars have been installed around the space where Children's Park once stood. There is no one enjoying the space inside the bars, which will remain an antiseptic fortress for a year to come, but it is, for now at least, defensible against drug dealers. At some of the local bodegas, store owners are installing stronger, more protective barriers to fend off bullets; bulletproof vests are also becoming part of their work uniforms. So the bodegas soon will be a little more defensible as well.

All the strategies and agencies and institutions needed to contain, control, and normalize a social plague—some of them severe, others exploitative, and some benign—are, it seems, being assembled: defensible stores, defensible parks, defensible entrances to housing projects, defensible schools where weapons-detectors are installed at the front doors and guards are posted, "drug-free zones" in front of the schools, "safety corridors" between the schools and nearby subway stations, "grieving rooms" in some of the schools where students have a place to mourn the friends who do not make it safely through the "safety corridors," a large and crowded criminal court and the enormous new court complex now under construction, an old reform school (Spofford) and the new, much larger juvenile prison being built on St. Ann's Avenue, an adult prison, a prison barge, a projected kitchen to prepackage prison meals, a projected high school to train kids to work in prisons and in other crime-related areas, the two symmetrical prostitute strolls, one to the east, one to the west, and counselling and condom distribution to protect the prostitutes from spreading or contracting AIDS, services for grown-ups who already have contracted AIDS, services for children who have AIDS, services for children who have seen their mothers die of AIDS, services for men and women coming out of prison, services for children of the men and women who are still in prison, a welfare office to determine who is eligible for checks and check-cashing stores where residents can cash the checks, food stamp distribution and bodegas that accept the stamps at discount to enable mothers to buy cigarettes or diapers, 13 shelters, 12 soup kitchens, 11 free food pantries, perhaps someday an "empowerment zone," or "enterprise zone," or some other kind of business zone to generate some jobs for a small fraction of the people who reside here: all the pieces of the perfectible ghetto, the modernized and sometimes even well-served urban lazaretto, with civic-minded CEOs who come up from Manhattan maybe once a week to serve as mentors or "role models" to the children in the schools while some of their spouses organize benefit balls to pay for dinners in the shelters.

All these strategies and services are needed—all these and hundreds more—if our society intends to keep on placing those it sees as unclean in the unclean places. "In reality, it *is* a form of quarantine," says Ana Oliveira, who directs an agency that serves ex-prison inmates who have AIDS, "not just of people who have AIDS but of people who have everything we fear, sickness, color, destitution—but it has been carried out in ways that seem compatible with humane principles.

"We don't have 'pass cards' in New York. Black women who have AIDS don't have to clip a photo ID to their dress. You don't need a permit to cross over at the magic line of 96th Street. We just tell you the apartment that's available is in Mott Haven, or East Tremont, or Hunts Point. 'That's where we can serve you best. Here's a referral number. Call this agency. They'll help you to get settled....' That's what I mean by 'humane principles.' For those who work within these agencies, as I do, it appears benevolent. And, of course, once you accept the preconditions, all these things are absolutely critical."

One of the humane principles of which she speaks is present, it appears, here at the former site of Children's Park. The city has apparently tried hard to make this into a "good" corner. By smashing the benches and the shelter where drug needles once were given out, and flushing out the last remaining symbols of a local drug lord, it has created something clean and modern-looking, metal, geometric, which will someday be transformed into a pleasant place for children. The part of the drug trade that once flourished here has moved both up and down the street, a number of blocks in each direction. The needle exchange is now in a new location, just four doors from P.S. 65.

A few of the people who once frequented the park, however, are standing on the sidewalk looking through the bars. A woman I have seen here several times and who, I am told, is HIV-infected holds a pack of Winstons in one hand, a single cigarette in the other. In a voice that is a bit peremptory and gruff, she asks me for a match.

Lighting the match and holding it for her as she cups her hands, I ask her something that, I realize, even as I say it, must strike her as somewhat strange. "What do you call this place?"

She looks perplexed. "What do I call *what* place?" she asks.

"This place here—what do you call it?"

"This place here?" she shrugs. "This here is the ghetto."

When she sees me taking out my pen, she says it louder, "GHETTO," and then spells it.

I ask, "Why do you live here?"

She looks around her at the street and shrugs again. "This is where poor peoples *lives*," she says. "Where else you think poor peoples goin' to be? You a professor? You wants to meet poor peoples, you come to the ghetto."

She seems frustrated by my question, no doubt with good reason. She walks away, repeating my words in a sarcastic voice and heads for St. Benedict the Moor, a residence for people in drug treatment, with a soup kitchen on its ground floor, which is just next door.

After she leaves, I leave the corner also and walk to St. Ann's, where vespers have begun. The pastor's clear and calming voice fills the chapel of the church, in which six people from the neighborhood have come to pray. It isn't my religion, but it lends a sense of blessed peace and sanity to my evening.

Index

academic knowledge: mainstream, 97; transformative, 98, 99
accountability, school reform and, 9–10
achievement attributions, 17–18
achievement, ethnic differences in school, 12–23
action research, 201–202
action response, to deconstruction, 113
adolescence: dangers of early, 27–31; ethnicity and achievement in, 12–23
advocacy, 120
aesthetic experiences, in multicultural education, 180
African Americans. *See* blacks
Afrocentric education, 36–37, 61, 97
allochthon, 87
Allport, Gordon, 139, 141, 143, 223
American Citizens for Justice, 123
American Negro Slave Revolts (Aptheker), 101
American Negro Slavery (Phillips), 101
Americanization: influence of, on school achievement, 19–21; of Mexican Americans, 186
Asian Americans, 46, 107, 234; adolescent achievement of, 12–23; Individual Family Service Plan for, 144–147; pan-ethnicity and, 122–123; during World War II, 229–232
assimilation, 86, 158, 195
attributional styles, 17–18
Attucks, Crispus, 168
autochthon, 87
autonomy, school reform and, 10
awareness, development of framework for multicultural learning and, 117–118
Aztecs, 101

"banking" approach, to education, 81
Banks, James A., 65, 106, 110
Barlow, Maud, 219
Bell Curve, The (Herrnstein and Murray), 101–102
biases, in textbooks, 68–73, 162
bicultural competence approach, to multicultural education, 88–89
bilingual education, 38–40, 41, 42, 44–45, 175, 219
blacks, 42, 106, 107, 206, 207; adolescent achievement of, 12–23; education of, 98–99; literature of, 232–233; scholars, 99–100, 101; school integration and, 32–37; self-determination of, 99in South Bronx, NY, 235–240; in U.S. history, 168–169; use of slavery to teach history of, in U.S., 165–174
Bloom, Alan, 60
Bracero Program, 186
Brown, John, 70
Brown v. Board of Education of Topeka, KS, 33, 35
Bullivant, Brian M., 105, 106
Burger, Warren, 33
busing, 33

California: ethnic nationalism in, 184, 185–188, 191–192; History-Social Science Framework of, 64, 164, 166, 170, 172; immigration to, 46–49

Canada, 87
Carnegie Corporation, studies of, on child and adolescent development, 24–31
carpetbaggers, 69
central school administrations, 11
"Charter Groups," 87
charter schools, 7
child care, 27
child development: changes in family and, 25–27; cultural models of, 53–54
Cichy, Stacy, 201, 202–205
citizenship education, social studies and, 155–160
civil rights movement, 72–73, 159
Civil War, teaching history and slavery in, 165–174
Civilian Exclusion Order No. 27, 230, 232
classroom displays, 119
classroom management, in homeless schools, 204
Clinton, Bill, 43
cognitive approaches, to counseling, 126
cognitive flexibility, 127–128, 129
cognitive styles, 126–127, 129
collective equality approach, to multicultural education, 89
Collier, Virginia, 39
communities of learners, classrooms as, 178–179
conceptual webbing, multicultural education and, 110
conformity, 116, 117
content integration, of multicultural education, 95, 96
contracting-out arrangements, school reform and, 8
cooperative learning, multicultural education and, 178
counseling, for dropout prevention, 125–131
"cowboy" culture, influence of Mexican Americans on, 185
critical literacy, 221–222
critical pedagogy, 61
Csikszentmihalyi, M., 116, 118
Cuban Americans, 38, 123
cultural flexibility, 127–128, 129
cultural groups, definition of, 106
cultural literacy, 61, 218, 221
Cultural Literacy: What Every American Needs to Know (Hirsh), 218
cultural pluralism, 86
cultural psychiatry, 132–137
cultural self-disclosure, 107–108
cultural stereotypes, 116–117
cultural styles, 126–127
culture, 150, 152; accommodating commonalities and differences in, 52–55
curriculum: multicultural, 156, 161–163; transformation, 93–103

Dargan, John J. 68, 69
deconstruction, multicultural education and, 112, 113
decontexualization, of multicultural education, 111
dependence cycle, of homeless women, 203–204
desegregation, school, 32–37

developmentally appropriate curriculum, multicultural education and, 112
disadvantage approach, to multicultural education, 88
"disinformation highway," 219
"distance team-teaching," 222
Dole, Robert, 38
Douglass, Frederick, 171–172
Dowling Urban Environment Learning Center, 214–215
dropout prevention, counseling for, 125–131

early adolescence, dangers of, 27–31
early intervention, 214; cultural issues and, 144–147
ecological model, for multicultural education, 150–154
Edison Project, 8
Educational Alternatives, Inc. (EAI), 8
Educational Priority Policy, of Netherlands, 90
Ellis Island, NYC, 46, 47
empowerment, of school culture and social structure, 96
English, as official language for U.S., 41–43
enrichment approach, to multicultural education, 88
equity pedagogy, multicultural education and, 96
ESEA (Elementary and Secondary Education Act), 44
Espiritu, Yen Le, 122
ethnic boundaries, 52–53
ethnic groups: achievement in adolescence and, 12–23; pan-ethnicity and, 121–124
ethnic nationalism, in California and Germany, 184–192
ethnic self-disclosure, 107–108
Eurocentric curriculum, 36–37, 156
existential realities, 220–221
experimentation, multicultural learning environments and, 118
exploration, multicultural learning environments and, 118
external locus of control/internal locus of responsibility (EC-IR), 126
eye contact, in Asian cultures, 145

families, 152–153; changes in, and child development, 25–27; schools and, 116–120
family literacy, 179–180
feminism, 159
field experience, for teacher education candidates among homeless children, 201–205
Fordham, Signithia, 22
Freinet, Célestine, 221, 224
Freire, Paolo, 81, 179
functional contexualization, of multicultural education, 111

genetic differences, in race, 101
genocide, 206–209
Gentleman's Agreement, 229
German Romanticism, 189
Germany, ethnic nationalism in, 184, 188–192
Giovanni, Nikki, 233, 234

glass-ceiling hypothesis, ethnic differences in school achievement and, 16
Gould, Stephen J., 101
Grant, Carl, 110
Great Transitions: Preparing Adolescents for a New Century (Carnegie Corporation), 24, 27–31
Greene, Maxine, 57–58
Guatemala, 122
Guba, Egon, 58
guest workers, 87, 188

Hampton, Wade, 71
Hansen, Chris, 32
harmony, as value in Asian culture, 145
health promotion, in early adolescence, 29–30
hidden curriculum, 81
Hilliard, A., 118
Hirsch, E. D., 60–61, 218
Hispanics. *See* Latinos
history: failures of multicultural education in teaching, 164–174; portrayals of race in South Carolina's textbooks, 68–73; recognizing diversity in, 60–67. *See also* social studies
History of South Carolina in the Building of the Nation (Huff), 68, 69–73
History-Social Science Framework (California State Board of Education), 64, 164, 166, 170, 172
Holocaust, 206–209
homeless children, 201–205
hooks, bell, 233, 234
HOTS (higher-order thinking skills), 215
Huff, Vernon, Jr., 68, 69–73

IFSP (Individualized Family Service Plan), 144–147
Illinois Bell, 122
immigration, 41, 43, 44, 46–49, 86, 87, 89, 195
inclusion, 112, 175, 208; magnet schools and, 214–215
Individualized Family Service Plan. *See* IFSP
infusion, 110–111, 112, 113
integration, school, 32–37
interdependence, as value in Asian culture, 145
intermarriage, 210–213
interrogation, multicultural education and, 113
inverse growth patterns, of multicultural education, 109–111
invisibility, power of, 225–228
isolation, social, 117
issues-centered education, 81

Japan, adolescent suicide rate in, vs. U.S., 18–19
Japanese Americans, 98
Jensen, Arthur, 101
Jews, *Schindler's List* and, 206–209
Jim Crow, 69, 71–72
Jones, Lewis P., 68, 69–73
Journal of Negro Education, 98, 99

knowledge reconstruction, in multicultural education, 96, 97–98, 113
Ku Klux Klan (KKK), 69

"land of the Golden Mountain," 97
Latinos, 43, 45, 107, 179; adolescent achievement and, 12–23; child development and, 53–54; immigration of, to California, 46–49; pan-ethnicity and, 122, 123; in South Bronx, NY, 235–240; in upstate New York, 193–200
Lemon Grove Incident, The, 186
LEP (limited English proficiency), 44–45
life sciences, developmentally appropriate education in early adolescence and, 29
life skills training, in early adolescence, 29
Light in the Forest, The (Richter), 62–63, 64–65
Lincoln, Yvonna, 58
literacy, family, 179–180
literature: black, 233–234; children's multicultural, 82–83
Lowell, Susan, 57

magnet schools, 36, 214–215
mainstreaming, 214–215
Manifest Destiny, 185
Margins and Mainstreams: Asians in American History and Culture (Okhiro), 98
"media literacy," 29–30
Melting Pot, The (Zangwill), 157, 158
mental health professionals, multicultural populations and, 132–137
Mexican Americans, ethnic nationalism in California and, 184, 185–188, 191–192
Mexico, 97
Milliken v. Bradley, 33, 34
miscegenation, 227
Missouri v. Jenkins, 35, 36
mixed-race families, 210–213
Modern School Movement, 221
Mohawk Indians, 62
More Perfect Union, A, 166, 168, 170, 172
Mujica, Mauro, 41, 42
multicultural education: dimensions of, 95–96; school reform and, 93–103
multiple perspectives, 65; paradigms and, 56–59
multiracial families, 210–213
My Bondage and My Freedom (Douglass), 171, 172

NAACP (National Association for the Advancement of Colored People), 73
Narrative of the Life of Frederick Douglass (Douglass), 171, 172
nationalism, ethnic, in Germany and California, 184–192
Native Americans, 44–45, 62–63, 64–65, 107, 176, 207, 208, 234
Naturalistic Inquiry (Lincoln and Guba), 58
Naturalization Act of 1790, 230
Nature of Prejudice, The (Allport), 223
Nazi Germany, *Schindler's List* and, 206–209
Netherlands, 86, 89–92
New College of California, teacher education program at, 175–181
New York, storytelling by senior citizens in upstate, and ethnicity, 193–200
Nicaraguan Americans, 123
Nieto, Sonia, 110, 175
Noble, Douglas, 219

Ogbu, John, 22
Ohio, 8
O.K. Corral, multiple perspectives and, 56
Okhiro, Gary, 98
operational bridging, between multicultural education theory and practice, 110
Orchardtown, California, 187
Orfield, Gary, 36, 37

Orillas, 221, 222, 224
Oyster Bilingual Elementary School, Washington, D.C., 39–40

Padilla, Felix, 122
paradigms, educational, 56, 58
peace movement, 159
peers, influence of, on school achievement, 21–22
Philadelphia, PA, privatization of schools in, 6, 7, 8
Phillips, Layli, 22
Phylon, 99
physical fitness, in early adolescence, 29
placebo effect, 121
Plessy v. Ferguson, 32–33
pluralism, 86
"Point of View" exercises, 63, 65
prejudice reduction, multicultural education and, 96
"prejudiced teachers hypothesis," ethnic differences in school achievement and, 16
prenatal care, 27
prescriptive counseling, 128
Primary Education Act of 1985, of the Netherlands, 90, 91
principle of blood-kinship, in Germany, 189
private domain, 86–87
privatization: in Philadelphia, 6, 7, 8; of schools, 7–8
problem-posing education, 81
Proposition 187, of California, 46, 47, 184, 185, 188
psychiatrists, multicultural populations and, 132–137
public domain, 86–87

race, 152; homeless children and, 202–203; inderiority in, 99; school integration and, 32–37
Race and Ethnicity (Rex), 86
Reconstruction, 69, 71
reform, school, 94–95
remigration policy, of Germany, 188
researchers, teachers as, 180
Rex, John, 86
Robertson, Heather-Jane, 219
Romanticism, German, 189
Roosevelt, Franklin, 230, 232

Scalawags, 69
Schindler's List, 206–209
schizophrenia, 134
Schlesinger, Arthur, Jr., 219
scholarship: history of, 99; racist, 99; transformative, 98, 99
School History of South Carolina (Dargan), 68, 69
school uniforms, 32
schools: as complex social system, 96; integration of, 32–37; privatization of, 8, 9; reform, 94–95, 96; structural reform of, 6–11
Schwallie-Giddis, Pat, 140, 141
Scientific Council for Governmental Policy (WRR) 87, 89–90
scientific racism, 212
Scieszka, Jon, 57
self-identity, pan-ethnicity and, 121–124
Shaw, Ted, 35, 36
sister class exchanges, 221–223, 224
slavery, 69–71, 101, 207; teaching history of blacks and, 165–174
Sleeter, Christine, 110

Small, Robert, 71
Smith, Lamar, 43
social isolation, 117
social reform movements, revisionism and, 158–159
social studies, citizenship education and, 155–160. *See also* history
South Bronx, NY, poor children of, 235–240
South Carolina, portrayals of race in current history textbooks in, 68–73
South Carolina: One of the Fifty States (Jones), 68, 69–73
Spielberg, Steven, *Schindler's List* and, 206–209
"squaw," 228
Starting Points: Meeting the Needs of Our Youngest Children (Carnegie Corporation), 24, 25–27
Stempel, Herbert, 208
stereotypes, cultural, 116–117
storytelling, ethnicity in upstate New York and, 193–200
structural pluralism, 86
student teachers: correspondence of, and cooperating teachers regarding interpretations of classroom events, 74–79; field experience for, and homeless children, 201–205
suicide rate, adolescent, in U.S. vs. Japan, 18–19
Supreme Court, U.S.:on bilingual education, 38–39; on school integration, 32–33

systematic multicultural development, 118–119
Taino Indians, 100–101
Taylor, William, 37
teacher education, 80–83; field experience for, among homeless children, 201–205
teachers, 74–79, 104–108, 119, 153–154, 161–163, 175–181
"teachers-as-technicians," 157
teaching strategies, 95, 96
technology, multicultural education and, 218–224
textbooks: biases in, 68–73, 163; portrayal of race in South Carolina history, 68–73
Thomas, Clarence, 35, 36
Thomas theorem, 121
Thompson, Charles H., 98
"Three Little Pigs, The," multiple perspectives on, 56–57
Tillmanism, 71–72
Todorov, T., 100, 101
tokenism, 162
tolerance, multicultural education and, 138–143
"tourist" curriculum, 62, 151, 161, 162
transformation, multicultural education and, 112, 113, 180
transformative approach, to multicultural education, 65
transformative scholars, 98, 99, 100
"trouble threshold," in school achievement, 23

Turner, Frederick Jackson, 97

uniforms, school, 192

Van den Berghe, Pierre L., 86
Vintageland, California, 187
Vozar, David, 57

Washington, D.C., bilingual education in, 39–40
Werfel, Franz, 208
West paradigm, 97
Wetenschappelijke Rand voor het Regeringsbeleid. *See* Scientific Council for Governmental Policy
"White bias," 96
Wilson, Lucy, 35–36
Wilson, Pete, 43, 47
Wisconsin, 8–9
women, dependence cycle of homeless, 203–204
women's movement, 159
World War II: *Schindler's List* and, 206–209; treatment of Asian Americans during, 229–232

X, Malcolm, 233, 234

Zangwill, Israel, 157, 158

Credits/Acknowledgments

Cover design by Charles Vitelli

1. The Social Contexts of Multicultural Education
Facing overview—United Nations photo by Y. Nagata.

2. Teacher Education in Multicultural Perspective
Facing overview—Courtesy of Pamela Carley.

3. Multicultural Education as an Academic Discipline
Facing overview—Photo by Dzanne DeChillo/NYT Pictures.

4. Identity and Personal Development
Facing overview—Courtesy of Pamela Carley.

5. Curriculum and Instruction in Multicultural Perspective
Facing overview—Photo by Louie Psihoyos/Woodfin Camp.

6. Special Topics in Multicultural Education
Facing overview—Photo by Brian Brainerd/NYT Pictures.

7. For Vision and Voice
Facing overview—United Nations photo by Y. Nagata.

PHOTOCOPY THIS PAGE!!!*

ANNUAL EDITIONS ARTICLE REVIEW FORM

■ NAME: _____ DATE: _____

■ TITLE AND NUMBER OF ARTICLE: _____

■ BRIEFLY STATE THE MAIN IDEA OF THIS ARTICLE: _____

_____

■ LIST THREE IMPORTANT FACTS THAT THE AUTHOR USES TO SUPPORT THE MAIN IDEA:

_____
_____
_____
_____

■ WHAT INFORMATION OR IDEAS DISCUSSED IN THIS ARTICLE ARE ALSO DISCUSSED IN YOUR TEXTBOOK OR OTHER READINGS THAT YOU HAVE DONE? LIST THE TEXTBOOK CHAPTERS AND PAGE NUMBERS:

_____
_____
_____
_____

■ LIST ANY EXAMPLES OF BIAS OR FAULTY REASONING THAT YOU FOUND IN THE ARTICLE:

_____
_____
_____
_____

■ LIST ANY NEW TERMS/CONCEPTS THAT WERE DISCUSSED IN THE ARTICLE, AND WRITE A SHORT DEFINITION:

_____
_____
_____
_____

*Your instructor may require you to use this ANNUAL EDITIONS Article Review Form in any number of ways: for articles that are assigned, for extra credit, as a tool to assist in developing assigned papers, or simply for your own reference. Even if it is not required, we encourage you to photocopy and use this page; you will find that reflecting on the articles will greatly enhance the information from your text.

We Want Your Advice

ANNUAL EDITIONS revisions depend on two major opinion sources: one is our Advisory Board, listed in the front of this volume, which works with us in scanning the thousands of articles published in the public press each year; the other is you—the person actually using the book. Please help us and the users of the next edition by completing the prepaid article rating form on this page and returning it to us. Thank you for your help!

ANNUAL EDITIONS: MULTICULTURAL EDUCATION 97/98
Article Rating Form

Here is an opportunity for you to have direct input into the next revision of this volume. We would like you to rate each of the 40 articles listed below, using the following scale:

1. **Excellent: should definitely be retained**
2. **Above average: should probably be retained**
3. **Below average: should probably be deleted**
4. **Poor: should definitely be deleted**

Your ratings will play a vital part in the next revision. So please mail this prepaid form to us just as soon as you complete it.
Thanks for your help!

Rating	Article	Rating	Article
	1. A New Vision for City Schools		22. Problems Caused for Mental Health Professionals Worldwide by Increasing Multicultural Populations and Proposed Solutions
	2. Ethnicity and Adolescent Achievement		23. The Inside Story
	3. A Developmental Strategy to Prevent Lifelong Damage		24. Respect, Cultural Sensitivity, and Communication
	4. The End of Integration		25. Proposal: An Anti-Bias and Ecological Model for Multicultural Education
	5. Putting Tongues in Check		26. Beyond Socialization and Multiculturalism: Rethinking the Task of Citizenship Education in a Pluralistic Society
	6. One Nation, One Language?		
	7. Tongue-Tied in the Schools		27. Multiculturalism: Practical Considerations for Curricular Change
	8. Go North, Young Man		
	9. Accommodating Cultural Differences and Commonalities in Educational Practice		28. Who Needs Multicultural Education? White Students, U.S. History, and the Construction of a Usable Past
	10. Of Pigs and Wolves at the OK Corral: Or the Emerging Alternative Paradigm and the Construction of Knowledge		29. Teaching: The Challenge of Change; Reclaiming Democracy
			30. Resurgence of Ethnic Nationalism in California and Germany: The Impact on Recent Progress in Education
	11. Recognizing Diversity within a Common Historical Narrative		
	12. South Carolina Unrevised: Portrayals of Race in Current South Carolina History Textbooks		31. Telling Stories: On Ethnicity, Exclusion, and Education in Upstate New York
	13. Correspondence in Cooperating Teachers' and Student Teachers' Interpretations of Classroom Events		32. Teaching Homeless Children: Exemplary Field Experience for Teacher Education Candidates
			33. The Road to Auschwitz: What's So Funny about Schindler's List?
	14. Why Do We Need This Class? Multicultural Education for Teachers		
	15. Multiculturalism and Multicultural Education in an International Perspective		34. New Colors
			35. Another School's Reality
	16. Multicultural Education and Curriculum Transformation		36. Multicultural Education and Technology: Promise and Pitfalls
	17. Multicultural Education: A Movement in Search of Meaning and Positive Connections		37. Invisibility: The Language Bias of Political Control and Power
	18. Bridging Multicultural Theory and Practice		38. Home Was a Horse Stall
	19. Families and Schools: Building Multicultural Values Together		39. Turning the Tide: A Call for Radical Voices of Affirmation
	20. Self-Identification, Pan-Ethnicity, and the Boundaries of Group Identity		40. Knocking on Heaven's Door
	21. Counseling for Dropout Prevention: Applications from Multicultural Counseling		

(Continued on next page)

ABOUT YOU

Name _____ Date _____
Are you a teacher? ❑ Or a student? ❑
Your school name _____
Department _____
Address _____
City _____ State _____ Zip _____
School telephone # _____

YOUR COMMENTS ARE IMPORTANT TO US!

Please fill in the following information:
For which course did you use this book? _____
Did you use a text with this ANNUAL EDITION? ❑ yes ❑ no
What was the title of the text? _____
What are your general reactions to the Annual Editions concept?

Have you read any particular articles recently that you think should be included in the next edition?

Are there any articles you feel should be replaced in the next edition? Why?

Are there other areas of study that you feel would utilize an ANNUAL EDITION?

May we contact you for editorial input?

May we quote your comments?

ANNUAL EDITIONS: MULTICULTURAL EDUCATION 97/98

BUSINESS REPLY MAIL
First Class   Permit No. 84   Guilford, CT

Postage will be paid by addressee

Dushkin/McGraw·Hill
Sluice Dock
Guilford, Connecticut 06437

No Postage
Necessary
if Mailed
in the
United States